PANATI'S
EXTRAORDINARY
ENDINGS OF
PRACTICALLY
EVERYTHING AND
EVERYBODY

BOOKS BY CHARLES PANATI

Supersenses, 1974

The Geller Papers (editor), 1976

Links (a novel), 1978

Death Encounters, 1979

Breakthroughs, 1980

The Silent Intruder (with Michael Hudson), 1981

The Pleasuring of Rory Malone (a novel), 1982

The Browser's Book of Beginnings, 1984

Panati's Extraordinary Origins of Everyday Things,
1987

Panati's Extraordinary Endings of
Practically Everything and Everybody, 1989

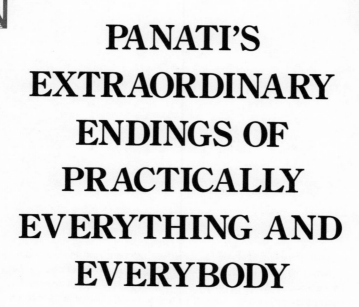

PANATI'S EXTRAORDINARY ENDINGS OF PRACTICALLY EVERYTHING AND EVERYBODY

Charles Panati

PERENNIAL LIBRARY

HARPER & ROW, PUBLISHERS, New York

Grand Rapids, Philadelphia, St. Louis, San Francisco
London, Singapore, Sydney, Tokyo, Toronto

FIRST EDITION

Designed by Alma Orenstein

Library of Congress Cataloging-in-Publication Data

Panati, Charles, 1943–
    Panati's extraordinary endings of practically everything and
everybody/by Charles Panati. — 1st ed.
        p.   cm.
    Includes index.
    ISBN 0-06-055181-X   ISBN 0-06-096279-8 (pbk.)

    1. Handbooks, vade-mecums, etc. 2. Curiosities and wonders.
I. Title. II. Title: Extraordinary endings of practically
everything and everybody. III. Title: Endings of practically
everything and everybody.
AG105.P118   1989
031'.02—dc 19   89-45111

89 90 91 92 93 CC/RRD 10 9 8 7 6 5 4 3 2 1
89 90 91 92 93 CC/RRD 10 9 8 7 6 5 4 3 2 1 (pbk.)

In memory of Ron and Marty

Contents

PART I

Last Things First

CHAPTER 1

Death,
the Ultimate Ending

Inhumation to Cremation

IN A BOOK DEVOTED TO ENDINGS, it seems fitting to begin with death, life's ultimate ending—from a personal standpoint the most important ending of all.

Death is, psychologists remind us, nothing less than the mainspring of our motivations, endeavors, and accomplishments. "It is because men know they will die that they have created the arts and sciences, the philosophies and religions," wrote Alan Watts. "For nothing is more thought-provoking than the thought which seems to put an end to thought." Freud and Jung plunged deeper into the matter: There is no moment day or night, the mind frenetic or quiescent, when the subconscious is not mulling the inevitability of the body's demise. The lamentation surfaces, no matter how hard we fight to suppress it.

Animals respond to a death threat, but they cannot contemplate their own ending. Our awareness of personal death may be the single most significant factor separating humans from all other life forms.

You first think of death not long after birth. Children become aware of the concept around age five, when the mind delineates "self" from "other" and the environment. In short: Once the "I" emerges as a separate entity, asserting its independence and importance, it begins to ponder the possibility of obliteration. As we age, the mulling over becomes an obsession. Death haunts all of life—and drives it. From the building of permanent shelters, to the invention of means of transportation, to the conception and execution of the highest expressions in the arts, the human reach extends out from our knowledge of life's inexorable ending.

If we did not know our tomorrows were limited, the only conceivable struggle would be for immediate bodily comforts, as witnessed on the animal level. At times we may act like animals and chase the comforts, but a brush with death soberingly sets values straight. How, though, did death originate?

Origin of Death: Pre–1 Billion Years Ago

Why, after about seven-plus decades, does the life force depart, leaving behind a corpse? The reason, believe it or not, is sex.

Life on earth did not always end in death. There was not always a corpse discarded. From a biological standpoint, death, as we view it, is a relatively upper rung on the evolutionary ladder. And the single activity that mandated bodily extinction for each and every one of us was the advent of sexual reproduction. To state it bluntly: Bodily death is the price we pay (and a high price it is) for the distinction and advantage of sexual mating.

To backtrack four billion years.

In the beginning, not all living creatures died. Few did. Some still don't. An amoeba, for example, need never die; it need not even, like the proverbial general, fade away. An "aged" amoeba late in life divides to become two "young" amoebas. Not much fun, perhaps, but there is no death, no corpse. Just offspring, a single parent living *as* its progeny. This is, of course, asexual reproduction. The amoeba has no sex life to speak of, but as compensation it is granted a long, long life indeed.

Whereas the amoeba produces daughters by the asexual process of fission, the more complex paramecium can propagate by conjugation, which also leaves no corpse. Two "elder" organisms cozy side by side and merge. They swap genetic material, then separate into new, "young" entities. (Later each one might divide by fission.) Again, no death of a parent, no discarded body.

That was the case for life on earth for billions of years. We trudge far through the evolutionary battlefield before encountering the first authentic corpse, the unmistakable evidence of bodily death.

When does death first appear?

If we take the estimate that life began on earth about 4 billion years ago—that genes emerged 3.9 billion years ago, bacteria 3.8 billion years ago, viruses 1.3 billion years ago—then death—and sex—arrived on the scene as companions as recently as 1 billion years ago. It is around this time that "parents," in the form of "mother" and "father," came together in the activity of sexual reproduction. They produced offspring, and having served their function died off, each leaving behind a telltale corpse, evidence of a sex life. We might justifiably ask: If sexual reproduction leads inevitably to the perishing of parents, why did nature introduce sex?

Attraction of Opposites.   Sex is a process of complementarity (as well as complimentary), a close-up commingling of opposites for the enhancement of a species. It evolved because it is more advantageous than asexual reproduction, producing a greater variety of offspring with a higher chance of survival.

In the beginning: A tiny and vulnerable cell sought to mate with a larger and heartier one; a cell with little food in its body preferred a mate that had a nutritional bonanza; a cell lacking locomotion chose a mate with whiplike flagella so their offspring could propel themselves through the primordial seas. As evolution advanced, cells increased in complexity and the all-important differences between them became more pronounced.

To size, motility, and food surplus were added countless other survival attributes. Finally the polarization of opposites resulted in cells that were "male" and "female," culminating in the development of the sperm and the egg. The precious hereditary material, or germ line, was sheltered in a disposable body, or soma, called "father" and "mother," which, after mating and nurturing the young, became useless. Sex was born. And so was death. (To say nothing of the funeral industry.)

Death was—and is—merely the discarding of the soma as a corpse while the germ line breezes on generation after generation. "Death," writes the eminent biologist and Nobel laureate Dr. George Wald in *The End of Life,* "is the casting aside of the body after it has done its work." That work is to carry the hereditary material of the race: "to feed it, to protect it, to warm it in a warm-blooded organism," says Wald, "and finally to mingle it with the germ plasm of the opposite sex"—all to enhance the survival of the species.

That may sound harsh, even repugnant—and it certainly skirts spiritual considerations—but it is a biological truth. It is also a readily evident reality for numerous creatures: For salmon, the act of sexual reproduction is precisely the last act of life; they mate, then die. Indeed, for salmon, sex trumpets death.

We humans, of course, are more fortunate. There is life after mating. We get to keep our soma for several decades after reproductive prime.

Other creatures, though, are even less fortunate than the salmon, which at least completes the mating act before the final curtain falls. During copulation between praying mantises, the female swings her head around on its conve-

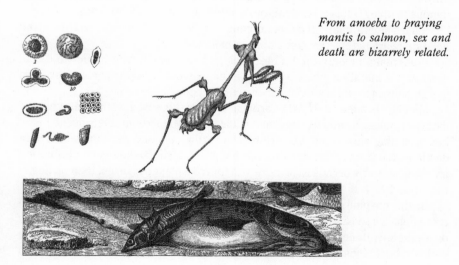

From amoeba to praying mantis to salmon, sex and death are bizarrely related.

niently long neck and begins voraciously to devour the male. She starts with his head, then chomps along the neck and torso. Dutifully he continues to copulate until she consumes his last abdominal segment, which contains an independent nerve center that controls copulating motion. In fact, it is by devouring the male's head, which houses a copulation inhibitor, that the female initiates his sexual gyrations. In a sense, the male's head cautions him, "Don't mate," and when he loses his head to sex, death is but bites away.

I set out in this section to investigate the origin of death. In summary: For the amoeba, there is no sex and no death; for the praying mantis, sex *is* death; for the salmon, sex is imminent preparation for the ultimate ending. For higher animals, including ourselves, the period of reproductive fertility is separated from death by the span required to nurture offspring. But in the end there is always The End: bodily extinction, the wages of sexual reproduction. Expressed another way: Any organism that reproduces sexually leaves a corpse. Sex and death are strange bedfellows.

To be rigorously complete, there is another avenue of argument. In one sense, we possess immortality, but not where we want it. We have it in our generational genes. We'd prefer it in our body, in the form we cherish, in the face that gazes reassuringly back from the mirror. "As for that potentially immortal germ plasm," concludes Wald, "where that is one hundred years, one thousand years, ten thousand years hence, hardly interests us." Hardly at all.

Whereas the origin of bodily death is definable, it is significantly harder, as we'll see, to determine the moment when life's ultimate ending comes to an individual.

Moment of Death: A Western Concept

A predominant fear among ancient peoples, extending into modern times, was of premature burial, a dread of being hastily pronounced dead, inadvertently buried alive, only to wake six feet under. The last wills and testaments of many famous people (George Washington, Frédéric Chopin, Eleanor Roosevelt) stipulate such death guarantees as draining the body of blood or removing the head or heart before the coffin's lid is nailed shut.

If anything, modern medical technology has made it even harder to define death, the time after which a person is unequivocally, irretrievably lost from life. A true case dramatically illustrates the point.

Michael Braden of North Carolina thought he saw his thirteen-year-old daughter, Julia, an auto accident victim, die in a hospital room. Bedside, he heard her breathing slow, then stop. Her hands grew cold and her pupils dilated in death's fixed stare. After Julia was pronounced dead, Braden gave permission for his daughter's organs to be removed for transplant purposes, then he began the painful task of making funeral arrangements.

In the hospital's operating room, Dr. Thomas Rusk was preparing to remove Julia's eyes and kidneys. He had scrubbed; surgical equipment lay neatly on a green cloth near his elbow. Leaning over the corpse, Rusk positioned the scalpel above Julia's right eye, pried open with a clamp. Poised to make an

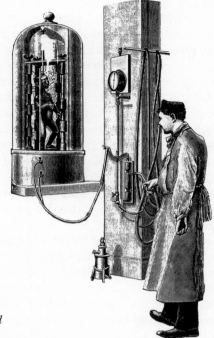

Technology has made determining the moment of death a medical, legal, and family nightmare.

incision to remove the cornea, he heard a faint sigh of air being sucked into Julia's nostrils. Glancing downward, he glimpsed her chest expand in a breath.

Julia Braden would not have been buried alive, just dissected before she was dead. Rusk was startled. Julia's father, accepting condolences when he received the news, was overjoyed. Then angry. How could his daughter have been officially pronounced dead?

The case is not unique in a technological age when accident victims displaying no vital signs are routinely resuscitated from clinical death.

Ancient peoples identified death by holding a mirror under a victim's nostrils or squirting citrus juice into the eyes. A mist or a flinch meant life. Later, physicians felt for a pulse and listened for a heartbeat, since death meant the cessation of heart and lung activity.

More recently, the definition of death was extended to include a flat brain-wave response. But, as we will see in the next section, even this seemingly reasonable criterion can in many instances be frighteningly unsatisfactory. Many doctors believe that the "moment of death," traditionally a Western concept, may not exist. That there is no magical instant when the sum of a body's life forces abruptly surrenders. That death is no more a single, delimited, momentary phenomenon than is life: When is the embryo first alive? When is the body finally dead?

Death (as is life) is coming to be viewed as a process, an extended happening. The spirit, or personality, may not flee because the heart and lungs have temporarily stopped, because the brainwave is briefly flat.

Consider, for instance, a victim of a drowning in icy waters. He shows no vital signs and is pronounced clinically dead. Years ago (and certainly centuries ago) no resuscitation would have been attempted. Today the body is gradually warmed, internally and externally, and after a spell of "death" he returns to life. Where, though, during the resuscitation was the victim's spirit? His personality? Had it started to move on to the "other side," then done an about-face? Had it hung around, hoping for resuscitation? And if resuscitation had not been initiated would the life force eventually—after fifteen minutes? an hour?—have abandoned hope and permanently departed? Thorny questions, ones spotlighted by modern lifesaving technology. The End is looking more and more like The Ending.

Still, though, we like to cling to the concept of a "moment of death." It is comforting. And it is also part of Western tradition, deeply embedded in our literature, art, and law.

But it is not a universal notion. Among many peoples, particularly in primitive cultures, a period of waiting is observed between death and burial. The interval—ranging from several days to the longest span still practiced, twenty years for a Malaysian tribe—represents a belief that death is not instantaneous. Rather, that dying involves a gradual passage from the visible society of the living to the invisible one of the dead, and that the deceased needs assistance, encouragement, and guidance in navigating the journey.

The Dayaks of Borneo delayed burial for months, offering a corpse food, drink, and conversation.

During the intervening period the corpse, often kept at home, is treated as if it were alive—offered daily food and drink, surrounded by company, proffered conversation. This was the practice of the Dayak people of Borneo until Western influence persuaded them for sanitary reasons to keep corpses in a specially built house until time for burial.

For groups of Indonesians the waiting period has mystical significance. They collect bodily liquids produced by decomposition of the corpse and drip them over rice, which is then eaten by members of the deceased's family. In this way the living believe they share in death, while the deceased is thought to exist in the living.

In Bali, the soul is believed to leave the body on a well-defined timetable, completing departure exactly forty-two days after death. Only then can a corpse be cremated.

In the West, we prefer to view death and departure of the spirit as instantaneous and simultaneous, then struggle to define what we mean by "clinically dead," "legally dead," "brain dead."

Brain Death: 1968, United States

The concept of a brain-dead individual, a modern attempt to pin down life's ultimate ending, was officially posited by a group of Harvard physicians in 1968. Under their criteria, a person must display a flat EEG, or brainwave response, for twenty-four hours. Then, after a lapse of time, he or she must be checked again; if the readout lacks the ripples of life the person is pronounced dead. This assumes that the individual has suffered an irreversible coma, that if resuscitated from the state, he or she would lead only a vegetative existence.

The issue seemed settled. For a while.

In the early 1970s, a California neurologist developed an auditory device one thousand times more sensitive than the EEG—a probe that monitored electrical activity deep within the center of the brain, instead of at the surface, where the EEG records. In one test twenty-six people pronounced dead by the flat EEG standard were redefined as living using the auditory criterion. Several people were revived, and without brain damage.

Might these "dead" have been buried? Of course, embalming would have killed them; but embalming aside, technology had, in a sobering sense, given a bizarre twist to the ancient fear of being buried alive.

By the mid-1970s, the issue of brain death was even more beclouded. In a dramatic experiment (conducted as something of a serious joke), an Ontario neurologist made an EEG analysis of a brain-size mold of Jell-O (lime flavored). He obtained readings that could easily be interpreted as evidence of life. The experiment was conducted in a hospital's intensive care unit, and the squiggly "lifelines" from the sugary aspic reflected stray electrical signals from respirators, sundry monitors, and even nursing hustle and bustle. The neurologist made his point: In the debate over how to determine brain death, physicians must consider electrical artifacts that can give the appearance of life, causing the dead to be artificially kept alive. Conversely, in eliminating such artifacts, can a doctor be certain he or she has not also eliminated a valid flag for life?

The more sophisticated life-detection and resuscitation technology becomes, the murkier will be the boundary between lingering life and demonstrable death.

This was not entirely unexpected in 1968. Dr. Henry Beacher, the physician who headed the Harvard group that proposed the irreversible-coma definition of death, stated: "whatever level [of brainwave activity] we choose, it is an arbitrary decision."

Arbitrariness soon showed up nationwide. A decade after the Harvard brain death definition, twelve states had enacted legislation on how death should be determined—only the criteria differed from state to state, which meant death differed as one traveled across America. Kansas and Maryland required the cessation of spontaneous respiratory and cardiac functions *or* the cessation of spontaneous brain function. Alaska and Michigan listed the cessation of respiratory and circulatory functions and considered irreversible coma a secondary criterion. Illinois made brain function the sole measure of life and death.

The ambiguity became broader still.

Whether you were alive or dead varied even more depending on the country in which you died. France's National Academy of Medicine considered a person dead if the EEG showed no activity for forty-eight hours, twice that of many American states. The Soviet Union, taking the prize for expediency, used a flat EEG criterion for as little as five minutes. In a nutshell, this meant that a victim of an accident or heart attack might be dead and buried in Russia, comatose but not yet legally dead in Maryland, or clinging to life and resuscitated in France. To this day there is no universally accepted set of death-determining criteria.

The arbitrariness of the brain dead definition of death is stunningly pronounced in cases of hypothermia, when the body's temperature drops below ninety degrees Fahrenheit. As stated earlier, a hypothermic victim can show a flat EEG for a considerable time and still be capable of full recovery. The patient appears dead by conventional standards when he or she is actually in a torporific state of artificially induced hibernation, all animation suspended. Each year more and more children fall into icy ponds and are thawed out and brought "back to life," children who only a decade ago would have been embalmed, buried, and mourned.

Today defining death clinically and legally—knowing when to pull the plug to satisfy the rights of the patient, the conscience of the doctor, the concern of the family, and the authority of the state—is a conundrum, and in many cases a nightmare for the family of the "living dead." One thing can be stated unarguably: Determining the end of life is not always a straightforward task. Death will continue to be defined and redefined. The biblical phrase "O death, where is thy sting?" has become in our technological age "O death, when is thy sting?"

However, once there is a corpse, it must be disposed of, and from prehistoric times man has devised techniques that boggle the mind and strain the purse strings.

Inhumation: 50,000 Years Ago, Africa and Asia

Life's ending has been surrounded by ceremony, if not pomp, for at least fifty thousand years. The first burials of which we have record were conducted by Neanderthals, who camped on the doorstep of modernity.

Neanderthal man lived throughout Europe and western Asia. With a brain capacity equivalent to our own, he possessed tool-making skills that enabled him to fashion the first flint knives. Of equal importance, Neanderthals mark the dawning of spirituality in the hominid lineage. This is graphically revealed by the Neanderthals' practice of burying their dead with ritual funerals rather than abandoning corpses as their ancestors did. They interred the deceased's body, along with food, hunting weapons, and fire charcoals, and strewed the corpse with an assortment of flowers. A Neanderthal grave discovered in Shanidar, Iraq, contained the pollen of eight different flowers.

This primal ritual revealed man's first inclination toward a belief in an afterlife and the subsequent nicety of a ceremonial good-bye. In fact, most of our knowledge of ancient cultures, from Neanderthal times until the dawn of writing about fifty-five hundred years ago, derives from funerary artifacts. Prehistory *is* the history of funerals.

In many ancient cultures, as diverse as Egyptian and Peruvian, the preoccupation with mortuary matters was nothing less than an obsession. A major portion of the social resources—capital and labor, as well as artistic, scientific, and technological skill—was devoted to building tombs. The Great Pyramids of Egypt, the world's only extant Wonders, owe their existence to man's fascination with and fear of the end of earthly life.

Inhumation is not only the oldest means of burial but also the most universal method of disposing of a corpse. (Indeed, many animals employ it.) The interment can be simple—such as among Eskimos, who cover a corpse with a conical pile of stones, a cairn—or elaborate—such as the huge barrows built by ancient Norse people.

The ancient Hebrews preferred natural caves and hewed oblong recesses lengthwise into the walls to accommodate the dead, a custom that led to the building of mausoleums. The chambers, initially regarded as sacred, by Christ's time were feared as repositories of disease and coated with lime so they could be recognized and avoided—the literal origin of the metaphoric "whited sepulcher."

To ancient peoples, even the positioning of a corpse acquired mystical significance. Whereas some cultures forced the dead into a fetal curve to symbolize rebirth in an afterlife, others extended the body, arms crossing the chest, in the posture of sleep, also implying a later awakening. In Babylon and Sumer, the sleeping position was reserved for rulers, while servants (killed and buried with a ruler) were placed in a crouching posture so they could spring forth and serve on command. To this day, bodies of Muslims are laid with the right side facing Mecca, while those of Buddhists are laid with the head to the north, directions with mystical meaning for both religions.

One's role in life often determined his or her position in the grave. In several African cultures a husband is laid on his right side facing east so the rising sun will wake him to hunt and farm. His wife is buried facing west so the setting sun will remind her to prepare the evening meal. In death, duty is thought to dictate with reassuring familiarity.

Upright burial was favored by other peoples. The postmortem stand was reserved particularly for warriors, signifying vigilance. In Vienna, as late as 1970, a male club for the "Vertically Buried Loved Ones" enjoyed a large, if faddish, popularity. The standing burial was achieved by means of a tight-fitting plastic tube around the corpse, which was inserted upright into a deep hole. Members of the Vertical Club touted their technique as space-saving—a practical, modern funerary concern.

The purpose of a funeral has changed radically. Centuries ago, when theological considerations predominated, funeral rites were primarily for the benefit of the dead, to ensure safe and smooth passage into the afterlife. In our more skeptical age, when immortality is less persuasive and pop psychology all-invasive, funerals exist to assuage the grief of the living, to ensure *them* smooth passage through life's shoals. A decade ago Americans spent more money annually on funerals and death accessories than on all hospital costs. Today, we spend more than two billion dollars a year on funerals.

Water Burial: Pre–7th Century, England and Iceland

We think of water burial in one of two ways: The body of a naval officer, sealed in a coffin, draped with a flag, is ceremoniously slipped into the sea; or, as is more frequently the case, the ashes of a cremated corpse are sprinkled over a body of water. Both customs are ancient, rooted in myth, which we have modified and shorn of their original meaning.

The idea of water burial originated in the ancient association between water and immortality, which is reflected in the myths of many cultures. Diverse as the myths are, they usually center around a human hero, possessed of divinity, who sails away from his people in death with the promise to return in an altered form. Bodies of Norse chiefs and heroes were set adrift on rivers and oceans in specially built death ships. And the custom reached peak popularity in the seventh and eighth centuries among seafarers in England and Iceland.

The most famous of such ship burials to be excavated was at Sutton Hoo in Suffolk, England. In one mound, archaeologists found the remains of a wooden boat, eighty-five feet long, built for thirty-eight rowers, which had been dragged a half-mile from the river and lowered into the ground. Another excavation, in Oseberg, Norway, of an impressive Viking ship, revealed that women of distinction also merited water burial. The Viking vessel served as a floating grave for two high-ranking females.

Not all water burials, ancient or modern, involve a ship or raft. In the Solomon Islands, bodies are simply laid on a reef to be eaten by sharks. In other island cultures, corpses are wrapped in cloth and weighted with stones to anchor them to the ocean floor. In Tibet, the bodies of the poor, as well as those of beggars, lepers, and babies, are often thrown into rivers and streams for inexpensive, expedient burial.

In Western cultures, water burial is still employed on occasions when death occurs during a sea voyage and there is no means to preserve the body. In one sense, water burial is experiencing a resurgence: With the cost of funerals and land interment rising, and the popularity of cremation increasing, more people than ever are turning to the practice of scattering the ashes of the dead on bodies of water.

Exposure: 6th Century, B.C., Iran

Hominids predating Neanderthal man abandoned their dead aboveground, but that is not what is meant by burial by exposure, a custom still practiced in many parts of the world. Exposure is the practice of deliberately displaying a corpse, often on a platform, so it can be devoured by carnivorous animals. The site is chosen to maximize the chance of consumption and its completeness.

Exposure developed out of the belief that the dead are so unclean that to inter or incinerate them would sully the "pure elements" of earth, air, fire, and water. Scavenger animals, viewed as equally unclean, became the logical choice to rid a tribe of its dead.

The most widely known practitioners of this type of burial were—and still are—the Zoroastrians, followers of Zoroaster, the sixth-century B.C. Iranian religious reformer. Zoroastrianism is the ancient pre-Islamic religion that survives in Iran in isolated pockets; it is more widely practiced in India, where it is known as Parsiism, and its followers are Parsis. The monotheistic religion—

Vultures awaited burial by exposure, cleaning a corpse in an hour.

which scholars believe influenced Judaism, Christianity, and Islam—prescribed burial by exposure to vultures. Buzzards of the zoological family Accipitridae are the birds of choice, since they dine exclusively on carrion, picking bones immaculately clean. It is the custom of Zoroastrians to expose their naked dead on elevated platforms at a "safe" distance from the community.

After a person dies, a "four-eyed" dog is brought in to guard the corpse from possession by evil spirits. A painted black dot above each eye qualifies any canine as four-eyed, and its stare is believed to be magical. On the third day, the corpse is transported to the Tower of Silence, one of three circular elevated platforms used for men, women, or children respectively. Vultures, which over the centuries have come to frequent the towers and know them as sites for a regular meal, strip flesh off the bones in one hour, two at most. The skeleton is then sun-dried and the bones swept into a pit.

Whereas the Zoroastrians of Iran and the Parsis of India practice exposure for religious purposes, in Tibet the dead are often unceremoniously abandoned on a mountainside to serve the first passing carnivore. Tibetan sects believe that a body devoid of its soul has no significance, and consumption by any animal is an expedient and inexpensive means of disposal.

One form of burial by exposure still practiced is, by Western standards, unimaginably heartless. Mongolian nomads, who consider death "on the plain" honorable, engage in live exposure. Those terminally sick and infirm, young and old, male and female, are carried from their tent homes as close to the time of death as can be determined. They are abandoned on the plain with a small supply of food and water—a token kindness that is usually ignored to hasten death. Even though scavengers may lurk on the sidelines waiting to partake, live exposure is not viewed as harsh, merely as a necessity for a people continually on the move. Needless to say, estimating the time of death is a critical decision, arrived at by the dying person's family, the tribal medicine man, as well as the individual who is to be exposed.

Cremation: Pre–1000 B.C., Northern Europe

The practice of reducing a corpse to its essential inorganic elements by fire was popularized in the Western world by the Greeks around 1000 B.C. The Romans later adopted and commercialized the ritual, and our word "cremation" comes from the Latin *cremare,* meaning "to burn up."

The Greeks, though, did not originate the practice. Anthropologists trace it back to early tribes that inhabited northern Europe. For them, as for the early Greeks, the ritual carried no religious overtones; it was done for a highly practical purpose: In times of war, cremation enabled heroes slain on alien terrain to be returned home weeks or months after death and there receive a national funeral attended by family and fellow citizens. Corpses were incinerated on the battlefield; the ashes were gathered up and transported by a fleet-footed messenger or retained in individual urns and brought back with the troops. Without means to preserve a body, cremation was the only way to save and ship the dead.

Frequent and protracted battles in the ancient classical world made cremation first a commonplace, then a preferred, means of burial. Although ground burials were held for most Greek and Roman citizens, cremation became so closely associated with valor, manly virtue, patriotism, and military glory that in time it was regarded as the only fitting end to an epic life.

The greater the hero, the higher the conflagration. The *Iliad* records how elaborate and elegiac cremation became for Greek heroes. Zeus, the supreme deity, compels the victorious Achilles to turn over the corpse of Hector so that the slain hero's father, King Priam of Troy, can cremate it in royal style. Achilles earlier had ordered a pyre built one hundred square feet to render to ashes the body of his slain friend Patroclus. And after an arrow pierced Achilles's all-too-vulnerable heel, the leader of the Trojan War was himself afforded the most spectacular incineration yet—a classical case of one-upmanship.

The Romans turned cremation into profit. Virgil, in the *Aeneid,* lambasts the tasteless, crude etiquette of cremation conducted without religious ritual and ceremonial fanfare, done merely for expediency. On the other hand, he praises a conflagration in which the correct kinds of dried leaves, twigs, and dead cypresses are set ablaze to the prayerful cries of mourners circling the pyre. The elaborateness of Roman cremations made them life's last status symbol. Whereas indigent dead went up in flickering flames, the wealthy departed in towering infernos.

Profit entered the picture in terms of selling bereaved families expensive urns for ashes, as well as renting space to store urns in a columbarium, a vault

The elaborateness of Roman cremations made them life's last status symbol.

with tiers of niches. As a sideline, morticians hawked ornate, bejeweled la-
chrymatories, vases to catch the tears of lachrymose mourners, which were
entombed along with the dead.

Then, around A.D. 100, the fires of cremation were slaked. The cutoff is
historically abrupt and only suggestively understood. The spread of Christianity
undoubtedly played a role. The early church did not explicitly forbid cremation
(as the later church would), but it sternly frowned on burning a body for two
reasons: Pagans had done it, therefore Christians should not; and rendering a
corpse to ash seemed to flout the promise of bodily resurrection on the Day
of Judgment.

Historians also offer a practical possibility for the end of cremations: Around
A.D. 100, the Roman Empire experienced a severe shortage of wood, specifically
because so many trees had been felled for pyres. With wood a principal building
material for ships and fortresses, a priority was placed on the use of timber and
citizens adhered to the bar. Outdoor cremation is, after all, not an activity to
be pulled off clandestinely.

Modern Cremation: 19th Century, England

Today the cremation conflagration is generated by bottled gas, synthetic and
natural, the kinds that fire a kitchen oven. Because of the intense temperatures
inside the furnace, and because a special draft control prevents the cremains
(an unavoidable neologism) from escaping into the air, a 180-pound man is
rendered in an hour and a half, in toto, into a few pounds of white powdery ash
and fragments of bone. With the older open-air fires, convection currents
carried away a good portion of the deceased on thermals.

As decomposition in the earth is a process of oxidation, so too is cremation—only the destruction of body tissue and loss of water is extremely rapid.
With organic components decomposed, what remains are inorganic minerals
and trace metals like calcium, potassium, zinc, and lead. Thus we preserve in
an urn all that during life was never itself alive, the inorganic you. Today's
crematories, which number more than five hundred in the United States, are
so expertly engineered that not even much of a corpse's gases escape into the
environment; the vapors are recirculated through the oven.

The modern revival in cremation in the United States and Europe began in
1874, when Queen Victoria's surgeon, Sir Henry Thompson, published an
influential book titled *Cremation: The Treatment of the Body After Death.*

Thompson extolled the sanitary virtues of the ancient practice and he
organized the Cremation Society of England. Overcrowding in cemeteries had
reached appalling proportions, and physicians and sanitation engineers had so
thoroughly terrified the public of the health threat of visiting a grave site that
the dead were never brought flowers. (See "Cemeteries," page 21.)

America's first crematory was constructed in 1876 in Washington, Pennsylvania; five years later the New York Cremation Society was organized. But
public acceptance of the practice, because of religious and social attitudes, was
slow. By 1970 only about eight percent of America's dead were cremated. By

contrast, in England, West Germany, and Denmark, the figure stood at more than fifty percent. And on the relatively small, densely populated island of Japan, cremation, illegal until 1875, is now the commonplace practice.

The rest of the world may eventually be forced to follow Japan's lead. The shortage of cemetery space in urban areas is becoming increasingly acute. At the same time, many Protestant churches actively champion cremation, and the Roman Catholic Church no longer prohibits it; Orthodox Judaism continues to forbid the practice.

In America, where you live gives a good indication of whether you'll be buried or burned. The highest number of cremations occur on the West Coast. Of the total cremations in the early 1980s, more than forty percent were in Alaska, California, Hawaii, Oregon, and Washington. On the other hand, in Alabama, Kentucky, Mississippi, and Tennessee just about everyone who dies is buried; less than one percent of the population is cremated. In Arkansas, Louisiana, Oklahoma, and Texas cremations account for about two percent of funerals. In between are the Middle Atlantic and South Atlantic states, which account for about one-third of U.S. cremations.

There is one problem with cremation that none of its advocates anticipated. Cremains of family members often go unclaimed, leaving funeral homes with heaps of cinders. The situation is severe; hundreds of cremators across the country claim they are running out of storage space. Legally, if they dump the ash at their own discretion, they risk lawsuits by disgruntled families. The dilemma is so critical in Florida that a recent law requires any person arranging a cremation to state in writing how the cremains should be disposed of. If they go unclaimed for 120 days, the law allows the cremator to use his or her imagination. Still unclear is whether the "ash law" will be retroactive. If not, it leaves Florida funeral directors holding a rather large bag.

Why do the cremains of a loved one go unclaimed? The possibilities are many: The person was not all that loved. Or, as is frequently the case, family members bicker over how the ashes of this aunt or that grandmother are to be disposed of; the debate drags on, fizzles out, and in time the family forgets— an oversight less likely to occur with a corpse.

The longer you live, the greater the chance that your permanent address will not be six feet under but an urn, as ash. The figures show why: More than two million acres of choice real estate in the United States are already given over to graveyards—and eyed greedily by developers. In many urban areas, the sprawling verdant slopes of cemeteries are the last open spaces. In congested New York City, it is estimated that the four thousand acres of cemetery land—much of it with excellent views—could accommodate housing for more than two hundred thousand families.

Across America, one person dies every sixteen seconds, a total of fifty-four hundred bodies each day. If we continue to die at the current rate of about two million deaths a year, in the next decade alone we will somehow have to dispose of twenty million new corpses. And that's a conservative estimate. The traditional burial plot for the dead is a species endangered, being driven toward extinction by the relentless encroachment of the living.

Embalming: 3000 B.C., Egypt

This last major act performed on a body originated with the ancient Egyptians, who preserved a corpse with aromatic resins from trees and plants of the genus *Commiphora;* the chief gum was balm, hence the term "embalming."

The earliest method, dating to about 3000 B.C., called for wrapping a corpse in cloth and burying it in charcoal and sand in the dry regions beyond the humidity of the Nile. By the dawn of the New Kingdom, around 1570 B.C., embalming was a challenging art, morticians competing to paint on the dead the most realistic visage from life.

The most extensive method of embalming royalty included major surgery. The heart, lungs, and intestines were excised, washed in palm wine, and sealed in urns filled with alcohol and herbs. (The brain, thought to be a functionless mass, was the one organ discarded.) Myrrh and other fragrant gums and oils, as well as specially prepared perfumes, were poured into the eviscerated cavity and the incision stitched closed. The body was packed in niter (saltpeter), an astringent, for two months, removed, soaked in wine, swathed snugly in cotton bandages, dipped in a porridgelike paste (which may have had antibacterial properties), placed in an ornate coffin, and lowered into a sepulcher.

Ancient embalming was a lost art by the dawn of the Christian Era.

Techniques remained so crude throughout the Middle Ages that burial was quick, even for kings who required homage and pageantry. In July of 1189, when England's Henry II died at Chinon, his offending corpse could be peregrinated only ten miles before the fetor forced a burial at the nearby Abbey of Fontevrault.

Egyptians eviscerated a corpse. Pope Boniface VIII mandated a Christian's body be interred with all its parts.

In the thirteenth century, the process of evisceration came into vogue as a means of prolonging funeral rites and for transporting the corpse of a war hero from a battlefield to his homeland.

The Catholic Church opposed evisceration on the grounds that a body should be intact for its glorious resurrection. A corpse missing organs could not be brought into a house of worship. In 1299, Pope Boniface VIII, who knew something about worship (he commissioned so many statues of himself he was charged with reviving idolatry), formally prohibited evisceration in his bull *Detestande feritatis*. But the ban proved moot after countless dispensations were granted for Europe's wealthy families.

Evisceration made possible one of the most macabre funerals in history, that accorded Inés de Castro, mistress to Portugal's Pedro I prior to his accession. The beautiful Inés was murdered in 1355 in her royal apartment and magnificently entombed by Pedro in the abbey church at Alcobaça. Upon his father's death Pedro assumed the crown, and, wishing his deceased mistress to receive the honor of queen, had her exhumed. Dead more than two years, she was propped up on a lavish throne, securely tied, and attired in robes befitting her new station.

Portugal's clergy, nobility, and commoners paid homage to the corpse, many kissing the bones of its wizened hand. A skeleton of her former self, Inés held a scepter in one hand, and her dry, yellowed hair was draped like a shroud about her ghostly form. She sat stiffly through a dinner feast, and after dark, in a chariot drawn by six black mules and lighted with five hundred candles, the propped-up monarch led a procession of Portuguese, extending for several miles, from the site of her joyous coronation back to the dreariness of her tomb. None of this would have been possible without evisceration.

Modern Embalming: 17th Century, England

Modern embalming, in which the arteries are injected with a preservative, was initiated in the 1600s by the English physiologist and discoverer of the circulatory system, William Harvey. Once Harvey proved that a network of veins and arteries channels blood throughout the body, he imagined replacing that blood with a preservative. Though the concept was conceived quickly, the practice, with its ghoulish overtones of draining off blood, did not become widespread for a hundred years.

In America, the modern embalming method, which involves the replacement of body fluids with a variety of chemicals, was patented in 1856 by a Washington, D.C., entrepreneur named J. Anthony Gaussardia. Ten rival patents soon followed, most of them issued to other Washingtonians, and the nation's capital became the center of the American embalming industry.

The timing could not have been more propitious. The Civil War was raging and Union soldiers were expiring by the thousands, and far from home. The new process allowed corpses to be preserved for the slow train rides and wagon trips north. The government's original policy was to bury dead soldiers on the battlefield, but an escalating civilian outcry made the decision politically foolhardy. Families wanted their sons returned home. Embalming made that possible. The nascent American funeral industry moved quickly to master the process; preserving the dead became a broad new avenue for profit. And America's morticians became the first to reap the benefits of giving the face of a corpse a countenance it never quite had in life. "Lifelike" corpses became vogue, and before the close of the war open-coffin viewings were commonplace.

One funeral more than any other sold Americans on the benefits of embalming: The preserved corpse of Abraham Lincoln was viewed by millions of mourners, first in Washington, then at depots along the solemn train ride to his home in Springfield, Illinois.

Today embalming is the cornerstone of the mortuary business. Without it there would be little actual business. A standard embalming textbook, *The Principles and Practice of Embalming,* acknowledges as much: Embalming "forms the foundation for the entire funeral-service structure. It is the basis for the sale of profitable merchandise, the guardian of public health, the reason for much of our professional education and our protective legislation." A Canadian mortuary publication states the case with little tact: "Throughout the industry there is an accepted axiom that closed caskets result in the sale of lower-priced goods. This, then, is the reason for embalming; there is no other."

Is embalming done for reasons of public health? The issue is hotly debated. Mortician Edward Martin, in his book, *Psychology of Funeral Service,* wrote: "Today's embalmer has done more to prevent the spread of disease in his community than most people realize."

But the vast majority of public health authorities disagree. And legal requirements concerning embalming vary greatly from state to state, with a few states having no requirements at all—a fact seldom told to grieving relatives. Embalming is usually required if a body is to be transported interstate, and it is mandatory in cases of death by communicable disease. Many religious groups, including Orthodox Jews, do not allow embalming and have for decades interred their dead without menace to the public health. Such a burial must be prompt, and is therefore seldom profitable and not likely to catch on.

CHAPTER 2

Cemeteries,
Our Last Address

Graveyard to Memorial Park

GRAVEYARD. GARDEN CEMETERY. MEMORIAL PARK.

All are sites where we inter our dead, but each name conjures a different time and place—a vastly different place. Death in the desolate graveyard is brutalized, in the landscaped garden cemetery romanticized, and in the often lampooned modern memorial park commercialized. How people in a certain era bury their dead says much about the people, their historical time, and the prevailing attitudes toward death and dying. In the last 150 years, we have seen the body's last earthly address undergo a radical transformation unlike any in previous history.

To look briefly at the change. The inhospitable graveyard of the early nineteenth century was situated within a town, by a communal square or in a churchyard, overgrown with weeds, crammed with coffins, shunned by town-folk. By way of much-needed reform, the garden cemetery of the late 1800s sprang up on the outskirts of a town, was painstakingly planned, meticulously landscaped, and visited and enjoyed as a park by the living—even by strollers who, as yet, had no deceased on the grounds.

Still more deliberately planned was the twentieth century's memorial park. Boasting of gushing fountains, Italianate statuary, and reproductions of art, it offered tours and seminars and touted its panoramic view of the environs. It was meant to entertain, enlighten, and reassure the living that death could be, with the right ambience, not that different from life—the good life. Jessica Mitford, in *The American Way of Death,* critically summed up this incarnation of the burial ground as "a nightmare" in which "the trappings of Gracious Living are transformed into the trappings of Gracious Dying." And one of the earliest memorial parks, California's Forest Lawn, was satirized by British novelist Evelyn Waugh in *The Loved Ones.*

It is an edifying story (at times a horror story) how that essential burial site, our last address, evolved from an austere rock cave, to a Christian catacomb—part church, part meeting hall—to a quaggy churchyard plot, to a verdant garden cemetery, and finally to something of an amusement park.

Graveyard: Antiquity to Pre–19th Century, Europe and America

In early times, a family had its own private graveyard. This stemmed from two beliefs: that a family (and not the state) bore an obligation to bury its dead and that ties of kinship endured beyond death. In the Bible, the land Abraham buys from the sons of Heth features a cave in which generations of his dead could be interred.

We still believe a family should bury its own dead. And though we no longer hold that kinship survives death, a family will spend enormous sums to transport a body back home—by air, rail, or ship—so kin can be buried with kin. The family plot and the private mausoleum are actually cultural hangovers from the ancient belief of kinship in death.

In the ancient world, a family also jealously protected its private graveyard. A clan would never permit the body of a stranger to lie beside relatives. Even in later times, when the family relinquished burial obligations to the community, interment in a communal graveyard was a rigorously guarded privilege. Strangers could visit a town; they might even dwell there temporarily. But in death they could not rest alongside permanent community members. The infamous thirty pieces of silver returned by Judas were spent to provide a grave specifically for strangers. Still today, cost considerations aside, no family would appreciate a stranger buried in its plot. We continue to regard the bodies of dead relatives as family, and hold that the family that prays together, and pays for the plot together, stays together.

Ancient peoples also segregated by standards of "desirable" and "undesirable." Special cemeteries were set up for Jews, Christians, the wealthy, the indigent, and especially the criminal. Throughout Europe, from the Middle Ages into the late nineteenth century, convicted witches and murderers, as well as suicides, were excluded from the best graveyards. Today, when a notorious mass murderer is buried in a public or private cemetery, management attempts to keep the site unpublicized—not merely to avoid vandalism or defacement, but also objections from families whose loved ones lie in adjacent plots. The attitude (though unspoken) is: Yes, a Wayne Gacey or David Berkowitz will eventually be buried, but not near my relatives.

Where we bury our dead, in town or out of town, has been strongly influenced by sanitation considerations. Romans and Jews regarded cemeteries as disease hazards and established graveyards outside the walls of Rome and

Jerusalem. So too did the ancient Egyptians and the Chinese.

A notable exception were the early Christians. Officially forbidden to practice their religion, they used catacombs as combined mass graves, meeting places, and houses of worship. Even when free to worship publicly, they continued to bury the dead not far from the living: in vaults inside churches and in adjoining churchyards—unheard of practices up until that time. It was also early Christians who first named the grave site a cemetery, borrowing from the Greek *koimētērion,* meaning "sleeping place."

Horror upon Horror.   Though most of us think of cemetery overcrowding as a contemporary phenomenon brought on by high population density and sprawling suburbs, this is not the case.

By the sixth century, Christians were so numerous that their preference for church and churchyard burials presented severe problems of space and sanitation. Burial vaults inside churches were crammed with cracked and rotted wooden coffins, the air polluted in summer by stench and flies. Most churches were a direct source of disease to worshipers.

Outside the stained-glass windows, in the adjoining churchyard, the situation was worse. Corpses were no longer six feet under; coffins had been stacked tier upon tier until the uppermost bodies were within inches of the ground's surface. In many churchyards, coffins rose above the natural earth line and the ground was regularly raised and recontoured until soil reached the sills of the church's lower windows.

Secular authorities attempted to enforce the ancient Roman custom of

Christians began the practice of interment in vaults inside a church.

permitting burials only outside a town. But church land was exempt from secular sanitary laws.

During the Middle Ages and Renaissance the horrors of overcrowding became nightmarish. To make room for fresh interments, church sextons surreptitiously snatched skeletons and partially decayed corpses, transferring the remains at night to secret pits; valuable coffin plates, handles, and nails were sold as waste metal. The churchyard cemetery was invariably unsightly, frequently unhealthy, and by the early nineteenth century the living shunned the dead like the plague they were.

In America the situation became intolerable. In 1820 the Scottish travel writer Basil Hall visited a New England graveyard and reported: "A soppy churchyard, where the mourners sink ankle deep in a rank and offensive mould, mixed with broken bones and fragments of coffins."

Reform, arriving on the heels of crisis, would come in the form of the picturesque "garden cemetery." It would be built not by a church, but by private or public funds; it would be managed by city and state government, or by individuals and cooperatives as a nonprofit organization—which would, nevertheless, show a scandalous profit. This "secularization of the cemetery" occurred throughout the Western world on a mass scale and transformed the image of our final resting place.

Garden Cemetery Movement: 19th Century, England and America

It was a series of virulent epidemics that struck the Northeastern United States in the early 1800s that forced cemetery reform.

Church graveyards were, as we've seen, stinking quagmires, chronically offensive and occasionally serious public health hazards. New York City's graveyards were deplorably overcrowded and rank. Early in the nineteenth century, the city's Board of Health surveyed the burial sites and recommended no more dead be interred within city limits. The dead, it stated, were injurious to the living. The board suggested that city graveyards be dug up, decontaminated, and converted into public parks, "instead of remaining receptacles of putrefying matter and hot-beds of miasma." "Miasma" was then a most dreaded word, characterizing the invisible but lethal vapors rising from decomposing organic matter, thought to cause all kinds of epidemics.

Despite dire warnings of miasma wafting about the city, no graveyard became a park. None was even dug up. Or closed.

City graveyards continued to pack in the dead until the steamy summer of 1822, when a killer epidemic of yellow fever took the lives of sixteen thousand New Yorkers in less than a month. Manhattan urgently needed sixteen thousand new grave sites and virtually no space was available. Frustrated officials glanced across the East River to rural Brooklyn, viewing it as a possible site for a commodious new kind of cemetery. Brooklyn would house America's second garden cemetery, Green-Wood (page 32).

An 1822 epidemic left New York City with thousands of corpses and no space for burial.

Meanwhile, in Boston and Philadelphia more egregious graveyard over-crowding existed. Philadelphia, hit by several epidemics in the early 1800s, turned to vacant city-owned lots to bury its dead. Sites where carefree children frolicked one day sprouted tombstones and crucifixes the next. Newspapers chronicled the macabre transformation of playgrounds into burial grounds. Boston fared no better. Its City Council called for the immediate termination of intercity burials as well as the exhumation of all crammed or shallow-buried corpses—many buried only inches deep. Philadelphia would solve its problem by constructing America's third garden cemetery, Laurel Hill (page 31); Massachusetts would pioneer the entire reform movement by turning a Harvard student picnic ground into Mount Auburn cemetery (page 27).

Romanticism and the Grateful Dead. Cemetery reform was also speeded along by a nineteenth-century cultural phenomenon and perverse sentimentality: the romanticization of death, a concept unimaginable to America's founding fathers.

For the early settlers, who experienced hardships and high infant and childhood mortality, death was the Grim Reaper, the Pale Horseman, the Avenging Angel. Graveyards were unadorned, forlorn tracts of land, overgrown with vines, unvisited by the living who needed no reminder of life's cruel end.

A breed of poet had arisen—the "graveyard school"—who dwelt on death in all its gloom: "The Grave, dread thing!/Men shiver when thou'rt named."

But with the dawning of the nineteenth century the gloom was recast as glory.

In Europe and America the emergence of Romanticism and the age of the common man made life's end sweetly melancholy. Poetry and popular literature spread the message that death was life's ultimate desideratum, a thing to be "hoped for with all one's heart." Death meant, according to a book of the period, "deliverance from this mundane world, a glorious reunion with loved ones in the palace of heaven." A popular author of the time, John Pierpont, in *The Garden of Graves* explained that God found it necessary to implant in man a "natural apprehension of death" in order to "keep his children from rushing uncalled into his presence, leaving undone the work which he has given them to do." Suicide was frowned upon, but its appeal sympathetically understood.

Perhaps nowhere was life's end more romantically portrayed than in death by tuberculosis.

The contagion was *the* plague of the era, lightly coughed off in prose, poetry, and plays as consumption. No disease in history generated more art, more sentimentality, more kitsch. Many of the pre-Romantics of the late eighteenth century were tuberculous—Rousseau, Goethe, Sterne, Schiller, Weber. With tuberculosis so prevalent for so long a time, it became fashionable to write dolorous meditations on the death of a youth or maiden. To speak of autumn in life as in nature. To envision tombs as abandoned ruins, willows as frankly weeping.

The sentiment was everywhere. Shelley, whose friend Keats died of tuberculosis, romanticized the disease in verse. Dickens, in *David Copperfield,* found

In the Romantic Age, death went from a dread to a desideratum; the Grim Reaper passé, sentimentality vogue.

it poetical to let Little Blossom wither gracefully of consumption. Emily Brontë, who lost three sisters and a brother to the "White Death"—so named because of its victims' ghostly pallor—allowed many characters in *Wuthering Heights* to waste lissomly, languorously away with the only symptoms a cough and an ashen complexion.

Artists everywhere stooped the stratagem. Alexandre Dumas let his lady of the camellias expire by a cough, a cough Puccini set lushly to music in *La Traviata;* and in *La Bohème* the composer sacrificed another heroine to the plaintive malady. Indeed, the gradual decline of life and vigor brought on by tuberculosis, along with its minor symptom of coughing and the sudden, dramatic appearance of crimson blood on a white handkerchief, made it the most popular way to kill off a character, especially a delicate young woman. A writer had only to let a character cough in chapter one, and the reader knew that that life would flicker out by the story's end. (See "Tuberculosis," page 247.)

The attitude of perverted sentimentalism toward tuberculosis would change in the last third of the nineteenth century, the disease going from the muse of literature to the symbol of all that was villainous in the industrial world. But before that happened, the romanticization of death, coupled with the pernicious health threat from overcrowded graveyards, ushered in what sociologists have called the Garden Cemetery Movement. With death now being desirable, the burial site could hardly be shabby. Thus the cemetery was transformed into a cultural institution, or as one author called it, "a charming dormitory for the deceased."

Mount Auburn Cemetery: 1831, Cambridge, Massachusetts

The first major cemetery in the United States not connected to a church or parish was Mount Auburn. Expectedly, it became the model for the Garden Cemetery Movement. Surprisingly, it also became the paradigm for the concept of the municipal park.

In a rural setting at Cambridge, Massachusetts, Mount Auburn was founded during the administration of Andrew Jackson and it was fortunate in having as the genius behind its conception New England's foremost botanist, Dr. Jacob Bigelow, also a physician and a poet. As a physician, Bigelow assessed the public health threat of Boston's church graveyards; as a botanist, he proposed a plan for a new kind of burial ground, recruiting nature, in its seasonal panoply, as a backdrop.

In 1825, Bigelow, backed by several prominent Bostonians, searched the countryside for a suitable location. A parcel stretching for 72 acres along the Charles River near Harvard College caught his botanist's eye. The wooded forest offered immensely variegated vegetation and topography: gentle hills, shallow valleys, labyrinthine paths, serpentine streams. The land's summit towered 125 feet above the Charles, with majestic views of Cambridge, Harvard, and Boston's spires. The pristine tract was known locally as Stone's

The Garden Cemetery Movement turned the miry graveyard into a sylvan verdure.

Woods after its original owner, but Harvard students who picnicked there dubbed it Sweet Auburn, an allusion to Oliver Goldsmith's idyllic poem, "The Deserted Village."

To promote his bold scheme, Bigelow ingeniously combined his cemetery-reform backers with members of the Massachusetts Horticultural Society. It was a marriage made for everyone heavenbound; graveyards would never again be the same. Horticulturalists were intoxicated with the idea of creatively landscaping seventy-two acres of verdure; it would be their playground. Cemetery reformers sighed with relief at the vastness of land and its potential for subdivision into countless family plots. Both groups could freely indulge in their interests—to the benefit of themselves, the living, and the dead.

By August 1831 the reformers and the botanists had rounded up a hundred wealthy Bostonians concerned about where they themselves would one day be buried. With contributions of six thousand dollars, Stone's Woods became Mount Auburn.

Everyone, particularly Bigelow, delighted in naming every hill, pond, brook, bosk, and bracken. There was, predictably, a Primrose Path, as well as walks christened after botanical plants like the Bellwort, Laurel, and Viburnum. The dead would be visited via Swan Avenue, Hummingbird Lane, or Meadowlark Path. The cloying of the environs melded perfectly with the century's romanticization of death.

This image of a sylvan cemetery—sprawling, manicured, and immaculately maintained by a permanent staff—appealed immediately to the public, the alternative being the local quagmire. Also inviting was the guarantee the grounds would be fenced off from vandals, grave robbers, and medical students in pursuit of cadavers, all familiar horrors of the period. And though founded by affluent Bostonians, Mount Auburn would break ground for anyone who cared where he or she would be buried.

The rush for plots was unprecedented. It gave a new twist to the quip "people are dying to get in." The rich paid cash for plots. The poor were permitted to barter goods and services. Farmers tilled paths in return for family graves. Blacksmiths cast ornate wrought-iron gates for entranceways in exchange for postmortem parcels. Small-businessmen swapped their administrative skills for a bit of turf, and housewives volunteered to plant the grounds if later they and their children could lie under them. Money for plots went to maintain the landscape, since Mount Auburn was to be a nonprofit organization.

America's first garden cemetery officially broke ground in September of 1831, though not to put a deceased into the ground. All those who had rushed to reserve plots were still alive. For nine months Mount Auburn remained a cemetery without a grave. Then the child of a Boston family died and her burial opened the cemetery to public review. The press heaped praise on the new graveyard as a "place of succor," a tract of land that taught the living a lesson in "natural theology."

One writer, capturing a newly emerging Western conceit, commented on Mount Auburn's abundance of untouched natural beauty: "It is difficult to persuade oneself that man had no agency in forming it." Dawning was the modern attitude that held nature's handiwork second fiddle to man's accomplishments.

The *New England Magazine*'s review emphasized that Mount Auburn enabled people to view death as the natural and fitting end to life: "In the mighty system of the universe not a single step of the destroyer, Time, but is made subservient to some ulterior purpose of reproduction." More straightforwardly it concluded: "The circle of creation and destruction is eternal."

The public, impressed with the grounds and the reviews, ordered deceased relatives exhumed from miry churchyards and reinterred in the garden setting, generating an unexpected monetary windfall. The minimum size communal plot, accommodating a family of four, measured fifteen by twenty feet and sold for a modest sixty dollars.

Education in a Graveyard. There was more to Mount Auburn than its natural beauty. Cemeteries, for the first time in history, were now intended to instruct the public with a crash course in eschatology.

The educational tone of the Garden Cemetery Movement was struck on opening day in the dedication speech of Justice Joseph Story. "Our cemeteries," he declared, "may be made subservient to some of the highest purposes of religion and human duty. They may preach lessons, to which none may refuse to listen, and which all that live must hear." Thus was born the cultural concept of the cemetery as an instructional institution for the living, an inculcator of morality. In Boston—and soon across America—the garden cemetery became "a school of both religion and philosophy." Amassing steadily were the pretensions Waugh would satirize, Mitford would scorn.

Art historians claim that the Garden Cemetery Movement, with its hallmark monuments of marble and bronze, supplied impetus to the development of sculpture in America. The *Boston Evening Transcript* urged Mount Auburn to employ America's best sculptors so the grounds would be "as remarkable for the treasures of art collected there, as it now is for its scenery." Management did just that. The results were eclectic. Mount Auburn had a Gothic chapel, a baroque tower, and an Egyptian entranceway.

Egyptian flourishes soon came to predominate in the garden cemeteries that copied Mount Auburn. The obelisk and the sphinx were gravestones people most frequently requested. And Egyptian symbols of death—the winged globe, banded cylinder, reversed torch, lotus flowers, and serpent devouring its tail—could not be easily overlooked on a stroll through the cemetery.

Why Egyptian? As a social commentator of the time explained: "It is the architecture of the grave. Imposing. Mysterious. Particularly adapted to the abode of the dead."

Whereas the quaggy, weed-strewn church graveyard was open round the clock and no one visited, the Egyptianate gates of Mount Auburn were open only from sunrise to sunset and welcomed throngs of spectators, many more spectators than mourners. The grounds' rules included countless *don'ts:* Horse-drawn carriages could go no faster than a solemn walk; food and drink were prohibited beyond the entranceway; no picking of flowers; no indecorous behavior. Today we find it hard to imagine going to a cemetery on lunch hour for relaxation or taking the family there on weekend outings, but that is precisely what thousands of people did at Mount Auburn and at later garden cemeteries.

Even a future president: Franklin Pierce, America's fourteenth president,

Franklin Pierce was enjoying Mt. Auburn's Egyptianate sepulchers when he learned of his presidential nomination.

did not attend the Democratic nominating convention in Boston in 1852. He went instead for a stroll through Mount Auburn. When there was a deadlock among the three presidential candidates—James Buchanan, Lewis Cass, and Stephen A. Douglas—Pierce was selected as the compromise choice. Efforts to locate him throughout Boston proved futile until a messenger, on a tip, found the next president seated under a shade tree beside an Egyptianate sepulcher. That was the kind of cemetery Mount Auburn was.

By that time, Mount Auburn ranked as *the* major point of interest in the Boston area, ahead of Harvard, a tourist's must-see for foreigners and Americans alike. People *were* dying to get in; on most days there were lines.

Mount Auburn has been termed the Westminster Abbey of America because of the notables buried there. Among the poets are James Russell Lowell (d. 1891), Oliver Wendell Holmes (1894), Henry Wadsworth Longfellow (1882), and Amy Lowell (1925). There, too, are John Bartlett (1905), editor of the reference work *Familiar Quotations,* as well as publishers George Houghton Mifflin (1921), Charles Little (1869), and James Brown (1855), whose names still grace Boston publishing firms. And no Christian Science member should pass up the grave of Mary Baker Eddy (1910). The list is long and illustrious.

Mount Auburn's success quickly spawned America's second garden cemetery: Philadelphia's Laurel Hill, which offered the dying a way out of burial in a city-owned vacant lot.

Laurel Hill Cemetery: 1836, Philadelphia, Pennsylvania

Like Mount Auburn, Laurel Hill, three miles up the Schuylkill River from the Philadelphia city limits, was advertised as a "sylvan eminence." And like the Boston cemetery, Laurel Hill was used more as a park by the living than as a burial site for the dead.

This fact concerning America's first two garden cemeteries should pose a question: Was America in need of parks?

The answer is yes.

The great success of early garden cemeteries in drawing strollers, sun worshipers, and picnickers (sans food) was the impetus for the establishment of America's municipal parks. People had demonstrated that their desire for a rural setting near a bustling city was so strong (if not desperate) that they would gladly walk among the dead for a breath of fresh air and glimpse of greenery. It was an offshoot of the Garden Cemetery Movement that graveyard reformers had never anticipated. Caught by surprise were the developers of Laurel Hill. Within a few months of its opening in 1836, the cemetery was Philadelphia's most popular tourist attraction, outdrawing Independence Hall and the Liberty Bell.

It offered outstanding natural features that today we associate with national parks: expansive flatlands, sinuous footpaths, gurgling brooks, spectacular stands of beech and oak—all overlooking a swift-flowing river. There was a lover's lane, where couples ambled hand in hand past tombstones and sepulchers—as nonchalantly as parents and children sunned on lawns, enjoying obelisks and winged globes as glorious "ruins" rather than the grave markers that they were. Granted it was the age of romanticism and death was being billed as life's glorious finale, but the real draw of a cemetery as a garden was that people viewed it as a park.

Americans wanted parks.

This was realized by a renowned landscape architect of the era, Andrew J. Downing. He took a head count of the crowds at Mount Auburn and Laurel Hill, closely studied the layout of America's third garden cemetery, Brooklyn's Green-Wood, and wrote: "Judging from the people in carriages, and on foot, which I find constantly thronging Green-Wood and Mount Auburn, I think it is plain enough how much our citizens, of all classes, would enjoy public parks on a similar scale." Downing complained to city governments that their new cemeteries were being sacrilegiously misused: "Too many citizens go simply to enjoy themselves."

The experience acquired in constructing America's first three garden cemeteries prepared the way for the development of New York City's Central Park. It opened in 1856 as the country's first's modern municipal park, and ogling spectators and reviewers commented on its resemblance to a garden cemetery, except for the lack of crypts and tombstones.

Green-Wood Cemetery: 1838, Brooklyn, New York

The sixteen thousand New Yorkers who died from the yellow fever epidemic of 1822 never made it into Brooklyn's Green-Wood, which was only a seedling of an idea at that time. Instead they were crammed into the filled-to-capacity graveyards throughout Manhattan. But the epidemic left little doubt in anyone's mind that New York needed a vast garden cemetery.

In 1832, a year after Mount Auburn opened, New York City businessman Henry E. Pierrepont strolled through the grounds and came home mightily impressed. Three years later Pierrepont was commissioned to lay out the streets of the newly incorporated City of Brooklyn and he remembered Mount Auburn. In addition to a street plan, he and his architects reserved a tract of picturesque, hilly farmland overlooking the Gowanus Canal for a garden cemetery. The site provided an unparalleled view of Brooklyn and Manhattan. At the time, no one worried that Brooklyn and Manhattan were separated by a strong-current river, that the dead—an entire cortege—would have to be ferried across. (The Brooklyn Bridge would not open until 1883.)

The farmland Pierrepont wanted for his cemetery belonged to four families that had settled the region—the Bennets, Bergens, Schermerhorns, and Wyckoffs. Their descendants conceded to part with the real estate for up to $650 an acre, a hefty sum at that time. The cemetery was planned to the smallest detail, laying out walks and carriage paths, recontouring hills, deepening valleys, and dredging six lakes. Existing docks on each side of the East River would be used to ferry funeral parties. Again, no one imagined the treacherous river as an affront to solemnity.

The cemetery officially opened on April 11, 1838, named Green-Wood because, said Pierrepont, "it should always remain a scene of rural quiet, and beauty, and leafiness, and verdure." The country's third garden cemetery eventually would sprawl over 474 acres (four times the size of Mount Auburn) and contain 22 miles of roads and more than 30 miles of meandering paths, which for more than 60 years would make it the largest landscaped cemetery in the world.

From almost the first funeral the turbulent river showed its orneriness, creating hazard and embarrassment. Funeral carts were horse drawn, and loading horses, carriage, and grief stricken mourners onto a flat barge in stormy weather invited catastrophe. Coffins slipped into the river, giving the deceased an unexpected water burial. Solemnity gave way to shrieks of horror. Mourners blessed themselves and left the scene. Others, mustering dignity, attempted to have loved ones retrieved from the murky depths, dried, and reloaded for a second try. There is no accurate city record of the number of unintentional water burials between the years 1838 and 1883, when the Brooklyn Bridge finally offered a longer, though safer, route.

Woodlawn Cemetery. The site in Brooklyn had been chosen specifically to move burials across the East River from metropolitan Manhattan. But the river was not the only obstacle to a dignified funeral; there was Manhattan's traffic. Even in 1838 city traffic was a nightmare, a gridlock of neighing and bucking horses, dodging carriages, and darting and shouting pedestrians. There were of course no traffic lights, just self-indulgent anarchy. Reports from the period paint a scene of mayhem and irascibility (as well as of stench from horse wastes) far worse than today's. Impatient carriage drivers cursed and cracked their horse whips on each other and on freewheeling pedestrians.

How was a funeral procession to proceed, even without decorum?

City planners argued that New York needed a second garden cemetery, north of bustling downtown Manhattan. They looked toward 313 acres of farmland in the Broncks (the original Dutch spelling of Bronx). It became Woodlawn Cemetery in 1863, and its popularity was immediate. Plots were purchased by composer Victor Herbert, producer George M. Cohan, and actress Laurette Taylor. Herman Melville, author of *Moby-Dick,* bought grave sites for himself and his wife, as well as adjacent land for his children, two of whom made unexpectedly early use of the ground: Stanwix died at the age of 35; Malcolm shot himself at age 18. Today Woodlawn is also the permanent address of such monied American families as the Vanderbilts, Whitneys, Belmonts, Macys, Goulds, and Woolworths.

The Garden Cemetery Movement had taken root. By the end of the 1850s one commentator declared, "There is hardly a city or town of any size in the union which does not possess its rural [garden] cemetery."

When the Brooklyn Bridge opened in 1883, a popular adventure for Manhattan residents and tourists was a trolley ride across the bridge's vast span followed by a leisurely stroll through Green-Wood Cemetery. Admirers of the grave site could choose from over one thousand stereopticon views of tombstones and the environs.

Bird lovers flocked to Green-Wood to glimpse species imported from England: forty-eight skylarks, twenty-four wood larks, forty-eight goldfinches, twenty-four English robins, twelve thrushes, and twelve blackbirds. Unfortunately that extrafunerary attraction lasted only a few seasons: None of the imported birds could survive New York's harsh winters.

But the cemetery as a garden was here to stay—for a while at least. Americans had unanimously accepted the idea of interment in a garden, and a social observer boasted: "The rural cemetery may be considered now to be one of our cherished American institutions."

Forest Lawn Memorial Park: 1917, Glendale, California

"Nature, under all circumstances was meant to be improved by human care. It is unnatural to leave it to itself."

This sentiment, penned by a turn-of-the-century landscape architect, sums up the philosophy that made possible Forest Lawn, the world's first memorial park, one of the best-known burial grounds in the United States.

The garden cemetery interred the dead in a largely natural landscape, assaulted with occasional man-made artifacts. But the memorial park was intended to rest the dead in an environment of pure fantasy. Nature was to be the subtlest of backdrops to art reproductions of taste and quality—only larger, bolder, brighter than the originals.

This was made evident early on at Forest Lawn. The reproduction of Michelangelo's *David* was touted as "taller than the original." The Venetian glass replica of the Sistine Chapel ceiling was more brightly colored than the Rome frescoes, with hues unavailable to Michelangelo. The copy of Ghiberti's doors on the Baptistry at Florence were heavier, busier. Forest Lawn appeared to take its larger-than-life philosophy from neighboring Hollywood.

As conceived in 1916 by cemetery reformer Dr. Hubert Eaton, Forest Lawn was to be a "permanent resting place for the departed" as well as "a place for the sacred enjoyment of the living." Eaton—dubbed the Master Builder by some, the Master of Kitsch by others—saw to it that no aspect of the park was left to chance, or to nature.

There had been a small, simple cemetery on the Glendale, California, site since 1906. But when Eaton opened Forest Lawn eleven years later, the site encompassed fifty acres; it expanded to three hundred acres by 1941, and later into an aggregate of twelve hundred acres spread over four separate parks, as it stands today. Such was—and is—the appeal of this new breed of burial ground.

In the 1940s there were four thousand burials a year in Forest Lawn. Today there are eight thousand (one out of every ten California burials) at Hubert Eaton's fantasy cemetery.

Memorial parks like Forest Lawn are, in every sense of the term, theme parks. Children are laid to rest in Forest Lawn's Lullaby-Land, which features a fairy-tale castle. Adults can opt for interment in crypts in the New World Westminster Abbey. The architecture at the Glendale site is Old World eclectic. By contrast, the theme at the sister cemetery, Forest Lawn–Hollywood Hills, is American colonial, with the country's past evoked by such things as the panoramic mosaic *The Birth of Liberty,* which re-creates twenty-five scenes of American history with ten million pieces of multihued Venetian glass.

At the still newer Forest Lawn–Cypress in Orange County the architecture is Virginia colonial. At Forest Lawn–Covina Hills it is Georgia colonial. The aggregate memorial park boasts in its literature that it contains more reproductions of Michelangelo's works than any other institution in the world, a statistic that would have delighted Eaton—and perhaps Michelangelo.

Expanding on the garden cemetery philosophy, Eaton envisioned a burial ground that would "remove man's fear of oblivion" and "bolster his faith in immortality," a place where "happiness is recalled and sorrow forgotten." Admirable goals, which Forest Lawn's developers attempted to achieve through lack of restraint.

The cemetery, a monument to imitation, is the last address of many cinema stars: Humphrey Bogart (d. 1957), Lon Chaney (1930), Errol Flynn (1959), Ernie Kovacs (1962), Charles Laughton (1962), Stan Laurel (1965), Spencer Tracy (1967), Clark Gable (1960), Carole Lombard (1942), and Jean Harlow (1937).

Comedian W. C. Fields, buried at Forest Lawn in 1946, was once asked for his choice of an epitaph and replied, "Here Lies W. C. Fields. I would rather be in Philadelphia." Perhaps at Laurel Hill.

CHAPTER 3

Wills,
Our Last Wishes
Plato to W. C. Fields

WHAT YOU CANNOT TAKE WITH YOU, you leave behind. But to whom? And under what conditions? For what reasons? To be remembered lovingly? To get even posthumously?

Wills fascinate because they are our last wishes; in effect, they are requests from the grave. They can (and often do) reveal emotions concealed in life: of love and gratitude, of spite and hate. People have used their last requests to redress wrongs committed by them in life, to gain revenge, and, most manipulative, to control events after they're gone but not forgotten: Charles Atlas bequeathed part of his bodybuilding fortune to his son with the stipulation he be baptized a Roman Catholic.

On the other hand, people accomplish in a will a goal elusive in life.

A business executive endowed acting scholarships stating a secret desire: "All my life I wanted to be on the stage. Lack of talent prevented me from realizing that wish." The money went to a theater, with one proviso: that his corpse be decapitated, his head shorn of flesh, and his bleached cranium used as the skull of the jester Yorick in Shakespeare's *Hamlet*. It was.

A wealthy banker cut two family members from his will with a stinging codicil: "To my wife and her lover, I leave the knowledge I wasn't the fool she thought I was. To my son, I leave the pleasure of earning a living; for twenty-five years he thought the pleasure was mine."

Not surprisingly, most vengeful clauses are handwritten by the "wronged" individual, without benefit of a lawyer. They invariably appear as startling addenda to an otherwise jargonistic, professionally prepared document. Such as the strident coda to one husband's will: "To my unfaithful wife I leave only

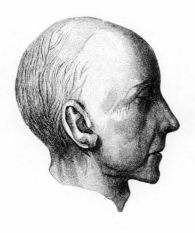
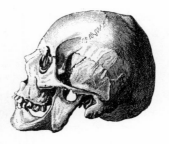

A frustrated actor bequeathed his skull to be used in Hamlet.

pocket change, the sum not to exceed that received by Judas when he betrayed Christ."

Wills can be terse. To date, the shortest valid will in the world is the plea of Karl Tausch of Germany, dated January 19, 1967: "All to wife."

Wills can be breathlessly long-winded. The record in the verbiage category is still held by a chatty American housewife, Mrs. Frederica Evelyn Stilwell Cook, written on November 2, 1925. Mrs. Cook was not a material girl, having few possessions, but her voluble good-byes, admonitions, best wishes, and incriminations—to family, friend, and foe—filled 4 bound volumes, running on for 95,940 words, the length of a James Michener novel. The will was not read at probate.

For largess of spirit, the will of a New York woman, Mrs. Robert Hayes, scores high marks. Deeply concerned for the security and happiness of her to-be-widowed husband and to-be-motherless stepdaughter from a previous marriage, she requested that the two marry within a week of her funeral. Mrs. Hayes was buried on a Wednesday, and the following Monday the grieving Robert Hayes, age thirty-five, married his twenty-one-year-old nonconsanguineous stepdaughter, Anna Mae—who, conveniently, did not have to change her surname.

Wills can be bizarre. Singer Dorothy Dandridge scribbled: "In case of death, don't remove anything I have on—scarf, gown or anything. Cremate right away!" And a bequest can be rebuffed: Actress Vivien Leigh willed her azure eyes to an organ bank only to have them rejected because she suffered from tuberculosis.

Pets as Beneficiaries.   It will perhaps come as no surprise that the largest group of will makers who leave unusual bequests are pet lovers. Dogs and cats are the most frequent legatees, but estates have been left to guppies, cockatoos, marmosets, ferrets, and pythons. Research has turned up nothing of a lion's share.

The largest canine bequest on record was that of Eleanor Ritchey, heiress to the Quaker State Refining Corporation. She died in Fort Lauderdale, Florida, in 1968, willing her entire fortune of $4.5 million to her 150 beloved dogs. The family contested. A court battle raged for 5 years, the dogs represented by a prestigious Southern law firm. By the time an agreement was reached in September 1973, Eleanor Ritchey's escrow estate had mushroomed to $14 million and 77 of the dogs had died (natural deaths). This meant the surviving dogs were even richer. As were their lawyers.

In the final settlement, the dogs were awarded $9 million, each receiving $123,287.67, to go for food, grooming, and housing. Two million dollars was divided among Eleanor Ritchey's brothers and sisters. The rest of the estate went as fees to the dogs' lawyers. But this was not the end of the issue. The Florida court, under Circuit Judge Leroy Moe, posed a thorny issue: What if two of the dogs mated and sired a pup? Upon the parents' deaths, was the pup entitled to the balance of their canine estate?

The legal answer: yes. To avoid dog trials in perpetuity, it was decided that the animals be tattooed to prove indelibly their identity as inheritors, then segregated by sex to prevent parenting. From their inheritances, the dogs "contributed" seventeen thousand dollars each year for their food and housing, and another twelve thousand dollars annually for weekly grooming and periodic medical checkups. Upon a dog's death, its estate passed on to Auburn University in Alabama for research into canine diseases.

Last Lark.   Eleanor Ritchey's will, though unusual, was serious in intent. But a person's final wishes can also serve as his or her last caprice. Collectors of strange and curious wills frame the document of wealthy Canadian attorney Charles Millar as a choice example in this category.

Millar died in 1928 at the age of seventy-three, leaving a testament that is a parade of practical jokes, ones revealing how far the living will go for the dead's money. To a judge and a preacher, fiery foes of gambling, Millar bequeathed lucrative shares in a racetrack, which would make the men, if they accepted the gift, automatic members of a horse racing club. They accepted.

To an outspoken group of ministers opposed to drinking, Millar left more than fifty thousand dollars' worth of shares in a brewery. All but one of the teetotalers took the gift. To three acquaintances whose abiding dislike for one another kept them from associating under the same roof, Millar willed his vacation home in Jamaica, which they were to share. And did, with acrimony.

But the most highly publicized aspect of Charles Millar's will, and the part most bitterly contested, was billed by the press as the "Baby Derby." The wealthy attorney bequeathed a fortune to the Toronto woman who "has given birth to the greatest number of children at the expiration of ten years from my death."

With the courts upholding the document, the derby was on. Within nine months Toronto hospital maternity wards were filled to capacity and the city's newspapers ran box scores of the women in the lead, highlighting mothers fortunate enough to bear twins and triplets. Millar's relatives—and Toronto's religious community—were outraged, claiming that the will "encouraged immorality" and degraded the "sanctity of birth." But Charles Millar was as good an attorney as he was a prankster, and the courts repeatedly upheld the document.

Exactly 10 years after Millar's death, on May 30, 1938, Judge MacDonnell of Toronto's Surrogate Court awarded the cash estate, worth $568,106. One mother of 10 offspring was disqualified because not all of her children were fathered by the same man; so was another mother who had 5 of 9 children stillborn. For their effort, though, each woman received a "consolation prize" of $12,500. The bulk of the money was split equally among 4 fertile mothers, each with 9 children born during the allotted period. On accepting the money, each woman vowed to practice birth control. Charles Millar, a straitlaced, stolid man in life, turned out in death to be one devilish joker.

In this chapter, I examine the origin of the last will and testament, then pry into the private documents of some of history's most colorful deceased.

Last Will and Testament: 2500 B.C., Egypt

The concept of a will is ancient. Originally the word "will" applied only to bequests of real estate, while "testament" was reserved for bequests from one's personal effects. Today "will" covers both categories.

The oldest document that can be interpreted as a will was discovered by archaeologist Sir Flinders Petrie while excavating an Egyptian tomb dating to 2500 B.C. Wills are alluded to in the Bible, as when the prophet Isaiah advises King Hezekiah: "Thus saith the Lord, Set thine house in order." But it was the Romans, in the first century, who originated the will as a binding legal document.

The Romans recognized that the inheritance of property or goods cannot occur unless such items are regarded as belonging to an individual rather than to a group or the state. They also stipulated that bequeathed goods must possess a permanence such that they continue to exist beyond their owner's death.

Roman lawyers established the notion of a "living will," with a novel twist on the function of the executor, called a middleman, or *familiae emptor,* literally "purchaser of the family property." In life, a husband would transact a fictitious sale of his estate to a middleman who would promise to let the husband keep his property for the duration of his life. Upon the husband's death, the middleman "owned" the estate and had to distribute it in accordance with the deceased's wishes.

The technique circumvented the direct transfer of goods from a dead person to a living person, a transaction Roman lawmakers felt posed legal and religious hurdles, since the dead no longer have rights and their corpses—and perhaps possessions—are the property of the gods. Thus the "sold" goods always remained in the hands of a living person. Eventually the Romans did away with the need for a middleman and simply recognized a dead man's testament as we do today.

Wills and the Christian Church share a long and infamous association.

The early church needed money and it played a prominent role in broaden-

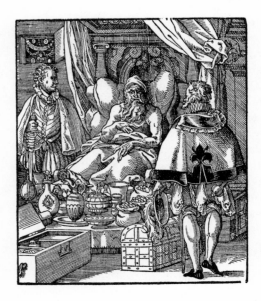

Leaving a fortune to the church, a man assured himself a place in heaven.

ing freedom of testation, that is, precisely who can benefit from a dead person's document other than family and friends, the only beneficiaries recognized by the Romans. In order to acquire funds for its own expansion, charitable works, and broadening secular activities, church fathers made it legal for a man or woman to bequeath the bulk of his or her estate to the pope. No longer were people forced to leave possessions to relatives or friends. In fact, the church ruled that only one-third of a person's wealth had to be left to family. In time, even that tithe would no longer be mandatory. Bequeathed cash and goods could also go to purchase indulgences, thus diminishing the wages of sin; a large enough estate willed to the church could entirely spare a sinner the flames of hell. It was just such abuses that troubled Martin Luther and touched off the Protestant Reformation.

From Roman times into the present, freedom of testation has never been absolutely unlimited—you cannot do with your money whatever you like. In various periods, a man was compelled to leave a portion of his estate to his wife and children to prevent them from becoming a burden on the state. (This is no longer the case.)

In other centuries, a father could disinherit an "able" son, but not a handicapped one (a kindness we no longer legally recognize). In republican Rome, a man could disinherit his wife only if he expressly stated so in his will; the mere omission of her name in the document was not viewed as disinheritance and entitled her to a hefty portion of his wealth. In the period of the Roman principate, from 27 B.C. to A.D. 284, a man wishing to disinherit his wife or children had also to state explicitly the reasons. And they had to be good ones. In the late Roman Empire, a man's descendants (biological children) and ascendants (biological parents) were entitled to demand some portion of his possessions.

"Make Sure I'm Dead" Clause. One aspect of a will was never challenged in the past: the deceased's wish that family make unequivocally certain he or she was dead. In fact it was a clause that appeared in most wills.

In the centuries prior to the advent of modern embalming, the fear of being mistakenly buried alive was so pervasive—because the possibility was so real—that testators often asked that a finger be amputated before the lid of the coffin was sealed. In the absence of a scream, the person was considered dead. Many wills stipulated the surefire extremes of decapitation or excision of the heart. Today we recognize that a comatose state can be temporary; all too often in the past a torpor or stupor was interpreted as death. For many centuries Europeans joined the Society for the Prevention of Premature Burial, incorporating into their wills gruesome demands: piercing the heart with a stake, clubbing the skull silly, even cremation—the fear of being burned alive being dreaded less than that of waking six feet under.

Wills often reflect the character of the writer and reveal his or her relationship with family, friends, and the world at large. A will also says something about the deceased's prejudices, interests, eccentricities, and, perhaps most interesting of all, *how much* he left.

Karl Marx (d. 1883), the founder of communism, left an estate of $500; co-founder Friedrich Engels (1895) left $50,530.

The estate of Poet Laureate Alfred Lord Tennyson (1892) was valued at $114,414; that of poet Rupert Brooke (1915) $1,846.

Joseph Lister (1912) founded antiseptic surgery, leaving a fortune of $134,-992; a woman in the medical profession, Florence Nightingale (1910), did almost as well, amassing a deathbed sum of $72,256.

Political economist John Stuart Mill (1873) left a measly estate of $28,000; the bequests of John Maynard Keynes (1946), an expert on the consequences of prolonged unemployment, totaled $979,728.

Supreme Court Justice Oliver Wendell Holmes (1935) willed virtually all of his $350,000 fortune to Uncle Sam. Patriot Patrick Henry (1799), who proclaimed "Give me liberty or give me death!," left his estate to his wife on the condition she never remarry. Mrs. Henry felt so strongly about liberty herself that she remarried, then fought the will in court. She won.

Plato: d. 348 B.C., Athens

Last wish: That he would die without debt.

The second of the great trio of ancient Greek philosophers—between Socrates and Aristotle—Plato laid the ethical foundations of Western culture; he preached there was no place for men of conscience in politics. As befitting a philosopher, he was concerned with death, not least his own. In *Phaedo* he argues there exists a "personal immortality" because the body's soul is divine, hence eternal. The soul is frustratingly tempted in life by "appetites," foremost passion, but in death is free to pursue wisdom and goodness. Plato got a chance to test his theory at the age of seventy-six, dying at a "marriage feast" or while

Plato, concerned with the fate of the soul and personal finances.

"writing a dialogue" (historians are divided). He was buried in the Athenian Academy, which he had founded as an institute for the pursuit of philosophical and scientific research.

Not a wealthy man by the standards of his day, Plato left his real estate—two farms outside of Athens—to his son Adimantes. His personal effects also went to Adimantes: one silver vase; a silver household drinking cup; jewelry consisting of a gold pendant on a chain and a gold finger ring; plus a cash bequest of three hundred drachmas, or silver coins.

The son also was bequeathed an additional three hundred drachmas, plus interest, which Plato had loaned to a friend, an Athenian jeweler, when the jeweler was in a position to repay the money. Of the chattel of four slaves he owned, Plato freed Diana, his favorite, passing on the others to his son. (As we will see in this chapter and the next, particularly in the wills of American presidents, slaves were a commonplace bequest that troubled just about every testator's conscience.) The great philosopher, who spent a lifetime mulling lofty issues, ends his will with a mundane pride: that though never a wealthy man, he departs the world having no creditors.

Aristotle: d. 322 B.C., Chalcis, Greece

Last wish: That his wife remarry—though not below her social station.

This Greek philosopher and logician whose scientific theories dominated Western thought for fifteen hundred years died at age sixty-two, financially better off than his mentor Plato. But, then, Aristotle had married a king's daughter and tutored another king's son, the future Alexander the Great.

Born in 384 B.C. to a physician in the court of Amyntas III, king of Macedonia and grandfather to Alexander, Aristotle learned Greek medicine and biology from his father. Following his father's death, the seventeen-year-old youth was

sent to school at Plato's Academy, where for the next twenty years he engaged
in vigorous dialogues. He married twice, his first wife, Pythias, being the
wealthy adopted daughter of the Macedonian king. Financially secure, he resided for many years at Pella, the capital of Macedonia, tutoring the then
thirteen-year-old Alexander; the two friends would eventually split over politics
and ideology. Upon Alexander's death in 323 B.C., civil anarchy erupted in
Macedonia, and Aristotle, then sixty-one, was falsely accused of impiety and,
like Socrates, he would probably have gone the way of hemlock. He escaped
to Chalcis (now Khalkis), north of Athens, where he died the following year due
to an unspecified but virulent stomach illness.

His will assigned three friends as executors of the estate until his much-
admired pupil, Nicanor, came of age and would oversee matters. He instructed
that Nicanor marry his daughter, Pythias (named after her mother), when the
girl was eighteen (Aristotle's "ideal age" for a woman to marry). And he
requested the couple take over the education of his son, Nicomachus, by his
second wife, Herpyllis, who was still alive at the time of his death.

Deeply in love with Herpyllis, Aristotle provided for her generously, "in
recognition of the steady affection she has shown me." To spare her a lonely,
insecure old age, the will allowed her to remarry, though the executors were
to make certain she did not disgrace Aristotle's name by marrying below her
class. He wished she'd choose a man of his own financial and intellectual caliber.
She received one hundred silver coins and the service of three slaves for life,
in addition to being allowed to retain the slave she already owned, a youth
named Pyrrhaeus.

Herpyllis—with or without a new husband—could, if she desired, reside in
their home at Calchis. There, she was entitled to a suite of rooms adjoining a
garden of herbs and flowers. Or she could retire to Aristotle's ancestral home
in Stagirus, Macedonia, in which he was born, and which he inherited from his
father. Whichever house she chose, the executors of the estate were to furnish
it exactly to her demands.

Aristotle's will reveals his generosity and thoughtfulness. He freed his
female slave, Ambaracia, and to make certain the liberation was not a descent
into poverty, he bequeathed her cash totaling five hundred silver coins plus a
slave of her own. A sizable portion of the will concerns the issue of slavery.
In Aristotle's lifetime the military attitude had shifted from slaughtering conquered prisoners of war to selling them into slavery—a small step for mankind,
a giant step for captives. This somewhat mitigated ownership of slaves in a
Greek democracy. In his will Aristotle ordered that the first-generation offspring of his slaves faithfully serve his own heirs; they, in turn, could free a
slave whose worthy service merited liberation.

The great philosopher's will concluded with two concerns. First, he asked
that several statues of animals he had recently ordered cast in bronze be
dedicated to Athena, goddess of wisdom, and Zeus, god of all gods. Then,
thinking of his first wife, who died early in their blissful marriage, he ordered:
"Wherever they bury me, there the bones of Pythias shall be laid, in accordance
of her own instructions."

Virgil: d. 10 B.C., Brindisi, Italy

Last wish: Burn the *Aeneid.*

Born Publius Vergilius Maro, on October 15, 70 B.C., near Mantua, Italy, this greatest of Roman poets, son of a prosperous farmer and best known for his national epic the *Aeneid,* died a month before his fifty-first birthday from a fever contracted on a trip to Greece.

At the time of his death, Virgil had completed only twelve books of the *Aeneid.* The work celebrates the human and divine birth of Rome and expresses the belief that the empire was divinely appointed to rule the world, spreading its civilization, law, and arts. Virgil requested that his executors, friends Varius and Tucca, destroy the unfinished masterpiece after his death. However, to the chagrin of generations of students, the friends persuaded the dying poet to delete the clause from his will. Virgil died, the epic was published, it enthralled literate Romans, and younger poets, like Ovid, began to imitate and echo the opus.

As a youth, Virgil never enjoyed robust health. Though the armies of Julius Caesar were engaged in a series of civil wars, the shy, soft-spoken poet avoided military service and became a virtual recluse, never marrying. Gradually his poetry of the Roman countryside and its colorful people won him fame, as well as the friendship of influential Romans. In the year 31 B.C., when Virgil was thirty-eight, Emperor Augustus Caesar brought the internecine strife to an end with the victory at Actium against the forces of Antony and Cleopatra. Virgil, like many Romans, felt a great sense of relief and embarked on an epic that would expand into the *Aeneid,* which reflects his admiration of Augustus and joy in the rebirth of Rome. It was the poem, in fact, that brought about his death.

Preoccupied with the work for eleven years, in 19 B.C., the fifty-year-old Virgil set out on a sea tour of Greece. He planned to spend an additional three

The birth of Rome in Virgil's Aeneid. *Romulus and Remus suckling the she-wolf.*

years revising and polishing the epic, and the journey to Greece was specifically to obtain firsthand local color for revisions of those parts of the poem set in Greek waters. In rough and inclement weather, he got drenched, caught a chill, and returned to his home in Brundisium (now Brindisi), Italy, where he died.

Whether or not it is true, legend has it that Virgil's executors were not alone in dissuading the poet from torching his masterpiece. Supposedly, Augustus, an admirer of Virgil, was informed of the poet's intentions and issued an edict that none of his writings be destroyed, especially the *Aeneid,* which was, after all, a celebration of the empire.

William Shakespeare: d. 1616, Stratford-on-Avon

> **Most controversial bequest:** That his wife receive his "second best bed."

William Shakespeare, widely regarded as the greatest writer of all time, drafted his will on March 25, 1616, when, as the document reads, he was "in perfect health and memory, God be praised."

That was just weeks before his unexpected death on April 23, his fifty-second birthday. Though little is known about the playwright's final days, John Ward, vicar of Stratford's Holy Trinity Church, where Shakespeare was buried, later recorded that the bard, accompanied by fellow writer Ben Jonson and Warwickshire poet Michael Drayton, had been on an outing. Shakespeare apparently "drank too hard," took ill, and died of "a fever." His priceless three-page last will and testament, discovered in 1747, is preserved in an airtight glass and oak box in Somerset House, London, and is probably the most famous will in existence.

At age eighteen, the unknown Shakespeare had married Anne Hathaway, a local Stratford girl. She bore him a daughter, Susanna, and twins: Judith, who married a vintner, Thomas Quiney, two months before her father's death; and Hamnet, the playwright's only son, who died at the age of eleven. Shakespeare bequeathed the bulk of his estate to the male heirs of his elder daughter, Susanna, "witty above her sex"; this included a large double bed belonging to him and Anne Hathaway. Within the formal, legalistic jargon of the will, one provocative line has caught many a reader's eye and sparked endless speculation: "Item: I give unto my wife my second best bed."

Is that notorious legacy confirmation of an unhappy married life?

Many Shakespearean scholars argue that the second best bed was actually the one most used by the couple, and so, rather than the bequest being a churlish slight, it was a sentimental act motivated by love.

Others are not so sure. They point out that it was custom in Shakespeare's time for men to mention wives in wills with high praise and florid terms of endearment. Not only is this effusion missing in the document of a fluid word-smith, but the scant bequest of the second best bed was, technically, an inter-

Shakespeare set tongues wagging, bequeathing his "second best bed" to his wife.

lineation, that is, an afterthought tacked on as an "Item."

Other historians argue that Anne Hathaway was in no way disparaged by the will. That she was automatically provided for by her widow's dower, which amounted to one-third of the income generated by Shakespeare's estate. And that the poet knew she would live out her days with Susanna and her husband, John Hall, a physician who, as a married man, could make better use of Shakespeare's "best" bed.

However strange the bequest of a bed sounds today, it was the practice centuries ago. A carved bed with a soft, comfortable mattress—free of fleas and vermin—was expensive and prized. In the fourteenth-century will of Edward, the Black Prince, after fastidious instructions on how his vault was to be prepared in Canterbury Cathedral, the prince settles in to disposing of four beds. The first goes to his son Richard, heir to the throne; it was the grand bed Edward had inherited from his father. The second bed, draped in silk, was bequeathed to Sir Roger de Clarendon, thought to be another of the prince's sons. The third bed, bearing the prince's arms embroidered on each silk corner, was left to Sir Robert de Walsham, Edward's confessor. And the fourth bed, "of camora embroidered with blue eagles," went to his friend Aleyne Cleyne. It was not uncommon for men to leave beds to men.

It is unknown how Shakespeare came to draft his will only weeks before his death. Coincidence? Or was he already ill?

Three signatures of the bard appear at various locations on the document, each in uncharacteristically shaky script (when compared with the six extant signatures of the poet). Many scholars view this as evidence of existing illness.

But in an essay in *Tenements of Clay,* biohistorian Dr. Ralph Leftwich ventures that Shakespeare's only "infirmity" was a spastic form of scrivener's palsy, or writer's cramp, prevalent among prolific authors before the invention of the typewriter. Indeed, a close analysis of other late samples of the bard's handwriting reveals typical signs of the palsy: fitful starts and stops; sudden lurches above or below a line; places where the pen point, out of the writer's control, digs into the parchment.

Shakespeare was familiar with the manipulative potential of wills; they play pivotal parts in several of his plays. In *Julius Caesar,* Mark Antony rouses the Romans against Caesar's assassins by suddenly producing his will, which bequeaths silver to the people: "Here is the will, and under Caesar's seal. To every Roman citizen he gives . . . seventy-five drachmas." The citizens, eager for their inheritance, shout, "Most noble Caesar! We'll revenge his death."

Another famous will appears in *The Merchant of Venice,* that of Portia's father. The document ordains that Portia must marry a suitor from a lottery her father devised. "So is the will of a living daughter," she laments, "curbed by the will of a dead father. Is it not hard . . . that I cannot choose one, nor refuse none?"

Cognizant of his own will's importance, Shakespeare summoned to his Stratford home not the legally required two witnesses, but five, thus hoping to thwart any challenge to the distribution of his literary estate.

Among his last wishes was that a particular verse be chiseled into his tombstone. It is a hex in the form of a doggerel, which reads in part: "Blest be the man that spares these stones,/And curst be he that moves my bones." It is believed that Shakespeare intended the threat to deter grave robbers, but the authority of his request also prevented the plot from being opened to accept the body of Anne Hathaway, who died seven years after her husband. To this day the body of William Shakespeare lies not in the famous Poets' Corner in Westminster Abbey, the resting place of many lesser talents, but where he was first interred, in the yard of Holy Trinity Church. The hex has served its function.

Henry VIII: d. 1547, London

> **Last wish:** To be interred beside Jane Seymour, one wife who
> retained her head.

The last will and testament of England's second Tudor king and one of its strongest monarchs was written on December 30, 1546, less than a month before his death at age fifty-five. At the time, Henry reeked from painful and putrifying leg ulcers, perhaps syphilitic, that had to be dressed several times a day. From chronic dropsy (now called edema), his legs were elephantine, his body obese at more than four hundred pounds. Irascible, bedridden, suffocatingly breathless, he realized the end was near and dictated a prolix will—almost seven thousand words.

Though Henry broke with the church in Rome, he had remained in most beliefs a Roman Catholic. His will opened with a pious preamble, declaring himself an exemplary Christian, and just in case his spirit was slated for a layover in purgatory (hell, he felt, was unmerited), he ordered a pageant of requiem masses in his memory to shorten the stay. Monstrously egotistical, he exempted himself from culpability in the executions of the country's leading humanists and intellectuals and saw nothing sinful in having caused two of his six wives to join the long march of statesmen to lay their heads on the block for trumped-up charges of treason.

Near the end, he was a pathetic, shattered man, lamenting that life cursed a benevolent soul such as himself with countless misfortunes—mainly chronic ailments and miscarrying wives. Typically, he never viewed his wives' disastrous pregnancies as resulting from his alleged syphilis.

The evidence for venereal disease is circumstantially incriminating.

1. His first wife, Catherine of Aragon, bore him a stillborn daughter and a plump son who lived only seven weeks. Then she presented him with four pregnancies that failed to reach full-term; mocked him with a second son stillborn; and in the end gifted him with only one surviving heir, a daughter Mary, who would eventually rule England as Mary Tudor, or Bloody Mary.

2. Henry's second wife, Anne Boleyn, miscarried at four months but did produce an illegitimate daughter, Elizabeth (born before their marriage), who would rule England for forty-five years.

3. After ordering Anne's beheading on dubious charges of adultery, Henry married Jane Seymour, who presented him with a male heir, Edward, but died herself nine days later, presumably of childbed, or puerperal, fever. Though Edward lived to rule England for six years, he was sickly, suffering chronic skin inflammations and a mysterious ailment that caused the tips of his fingers and toes to fall off.

4. Three years a widower, Henry then agreed to a politically arranged wedding, but without first seeing the bride—not unlike accepting a blind date. When he laid eyes on his betrothed, Anne of Cleves, he had the statesman

Henry VIII and Anne of Cleves.

responsible, Thomas Cromwell, beheaded. The marriage, unconsummated, was dissolved after a few months. She at least had been spared miscarriages and sickly offspring.

5. His fifth wife, the young and promiscuous Catherine Howard, was beheaded for infidelity before she had a chance to bear heirs.

6. By the time he married his sixth wife, Catherine Parr, in 1543, the fifty-one-year-old monarch was ailing and obese. By sparing her intercourse, he may have kept her from a syphilitic conception.

Biohistorians believe Henry may have contracted syphilis as a young man and that the disease was chronically active, infecting at least some of his wives, especially Catherine of Aragon. Mary Tudor, Catherine's only child to survive, is described in P. M. Dale's *Medical Biographies* as "a puny child who, even in girlhood, looked old, had defective vision, and a cranial conformation rather typical of congenital syphilis."

Henry makes arrangements in his will for the burial of his "cadaver" with stately pomp at "our college of Windsor." And he requests that the bones "of our true and loving wife Queen Jane be put also." Historians interpret the wish to be joined in death with Jane Seymour as evidence that she was his favorite wife.

After bequeathing much of his enormous fortune to charity, he turns to the issue of succession, complicated by his numerous marriages. He ordered that his successors be the sickly Edward, son of Jane Seymour, and Edward's children; then Mary Tudor and her heirs; and last the bastard Elizabeth, daughter of Anne Boleyn. Through illness, death, and machinations, Edward, Mary, and Elizabeth all ruled England.

As for Henry's alleged syphilis, Danish physician Ove Brinch, in *Tenements of Clay*, lists thirteen medical reasons to back his belief that Henry was chronically contagious. In addition to the miscarriage evidence, Brinch lists: a skin disease the king suffered at age twenty-two; a series of severe headaches beginning at age thirty-seven; unhealing leg ulcerations appearing at age forty-four; an acquired deformity of the right side of the nose at age forty-five, which could have been syphilitic gummata, a rubbery tumor; plus paroxysms of fits and violent rages.

Actually, a conclusive diagnosis is possible today through antibody tests and microscopic bone analysis. All that is needed is a splinter of bone from Henry's skeleton, which lies in the royal vault beneath St. George's Chapel, Windsor. It has proved easier to get papal permission to test the Shroud of Turin.

John Donne: d. 1631, London

Last act: Draped in a death shroud, he posed for his tomb's effigy.

Poet and prose writer John Donne influenced writers from his own time to the present. Adroit, poetic, and as playful with words as Shakespeare, Donne was an Anglican preacher at St. Paul's Cathedral, where the zeal and fervor of his sermons drew standing-room-only congregations. The final three months of his life, in which he orchestrated the details for his death and burial, are decidedly macabre by today's standards, but not uncharacteristic for his era—especially for the British, ravaged by a blight of health scourges.

People viewed life as a preparation for death, and the surest way to meet and calmly greet the end was to rehearse for it. Christian manuals instructed adults on how to die. The scholar and the clergyman propped a skull on his desk as something of a mnemonic, the way one might tie a string around the finger to aid recall. Most folk carried a pocket-size memento mori to keep death on the mind and, correspondingly, temptation at bay. As Sir Walter Raleigh expressed it: "Of death and judgment, heaven and hell/Who oft does think, must needs die well." Donne, nearing death at age fifty-nine, had witnessed his wife die in childbirth and six of his twelve children precede him into the grave—potent mementi.

On December 13, 1630, an ailing John Donne began preparations for death by handwriting his will, employing legal training he received before turning to poetry and preaching. His final days are chronicled in *Life,* a trustworthy biography published in 1640 by his contemporary, Izaak Walton. The exact cause of Donne's illness is unknown; Walton lists chronic tonsilitis, "growing weakness of the limbs," "infirmity of the spleen," and, most prominently, "fever." His body may well have been vulnerable to a host of infections due to a lifelong battle with tonsilitis.

Deeply religious, Donne bequeathed his household painting of Adam and Eve to the Earl of Dorset, his picture of Christ's entombment to the earl of Kent, and his Virgin Mary to the earl of Carlisle, now in the British royal collection. He specified preference for burial in his beloved St. Paul's Cathedral, in the south aisle, behind the choir—where one can find him today.

Wishing to have a life-size monument above his grave, Donne commissioned an artist to his deathbed. Stripped of his clothes, the poet dressed in the very death shroud that would soon drape his corpse, knotting the head and foot.

John Donne posed for his tomb's effigy.

With only his face revealed, he turned toward the east to symbolize dawning resurrection, then closed his eyes and stiffened his jaw to simulate rigor mortis. On a six-foot plank of wood provided by Donne, the artist sketched an image to be later sculpted into a realistic monument. Donne kept this verist memento mori by his sickbed, "his hourly object until his death," wrote Walton. A few days after the session, Donne bid farewell to family and friends and asked his executor to conclude legal transactions before "Saturday next, for after that day he would not mix his thoughts with any thing that concerned the world."

Donne miscalculated; he lay mentally alert, gazing at his death sketch for several days beyond Saturday, "happy to have nothing to do but die. . . . In the last hour of his last day, as his body melted away and vapoured into spirit," reported Walton, Donne believed he received a beatific vision and uttered his final words: *"I were miserable if I might not die. Thy Kingdom come, Thy Will be done."*

He died on March 31 and his will was read on April 5, two days after the funeral. His cash estate totaled eight thousand dollars. Each of his six surviving children received about one thousand dollars, with the balance divided equally among his manservant, coachman, houseboy, and kitchen and parlor maids. He bequeathed valuable books, such as his "great French Bible with prints," but made no provisions concerning his own voluminous literary works.

This caused considerable family squabbling. His eldest son, John Donne, Jr., felt he had rightful claim to his father's unpublished poems, sermons, and prose writings, and had the materials printed, pocketing the profits. Literary historians have forever been indebted to the son's prompt action and greed. For had the papers remained with the will's executor, Henry King, they likely would have vanished when, several years after Donne's death, King's residence was ransacked and most of his property destroyed or stolen.

Donne had written a poem entitled "The Will," which begins, "Before I sigh my last gasp, let me breathe,/Great Love, some legacies." Thanks to his son, he left many.

Peter I, Czar of Russia: d. 1725, Leningrad

Last wish: That Russia would "fertilize the impoverished lands of Europe."

One of Russia's greatest statesmen and reformers, Czar Peter I was six foot two, handsome and powerfully built, a man who as a boy suffered the embarrassments of epilepsy and as an aging autocrat was plagued by bronchitis, kidney stones, alcoholism, and syphilis. When he died on February 8, 1725, age fifty-two, he was so weakened by pain, infection, and a distended bladder that had to be surgically drained, that his trembling hand could not complete a will. He dictated a brief document, one chauvinistically ambitious.

By many standards of measure, Peter was indeed Great with a capital *G*. When he actively came to the throne, Russia, compared to European countries, was an insignificant, backward state with no effective army or navy. When he died, the professional army totaled 210,000 men and the navy sailed an impressive fleet of stalwart vessels.

Peter, however, was less than great from the viewpoint of the average Russian peasant. The common worker forfeited freedom for serfdom, a farm for forced labor in a shipyard or ironworks, and the burden of taxation guaranteed poverty. He came to be hated for his brutal dictatorship and terrifying rages in which he flogged anyone present, prince and pauper alike. News of his death was greeted in the streets without celebration, but with a sigh.

The proximate cause of Peter's death is traceable to an incident in November of 1724. Touring the frozen marshes on the Gulf of Finland to evaluate canal construction, the czar spotted a boat aground, its crew in peril. With characteristic rashness and valor, Peter plunged into the icy water and helped rescue the sailors. Days later his already infirm body was racked by chills and high fever. Just prior to the incident, he had passed an enormous bladder stone that left his urinary function impaired, with toxic waste poisoning his system. The uremic poisoning was compounded by scarring and blockage of the urethra from earlier gonorrhea. He experienced a constant urge to urinate. Despite precarious health, he celebrated the arrival of the New Year with a bout of drinking that in itself nearly killed him.

On January 9, his bladder was so distended with unpassed fluid that he lay in agony, exclaiming, "What a wretched animal is man!" For relief, a surgeon tapped the organ by forcing a hollow needle through the abdominal wall. The respite from pain was brief, for the bladder quickly reinflated. Bedridden, on January 22, he made his last confession and requested Holy Eucharist. After his trembling hand failed again and again to compose a will, he dictated his jingoistic wishes, a blueprint for Russian domination.

> God, from whom we derive our existence allows me to look on the Russian people as called upon hereafter to hold sway over Europe!
> My reason for thus thinking is that the European nations have mostly reached a state of old age, bordering on imbecility, or they are rapidly approaching it; naturally, then, they will be easily and indubitably conquered by a people strong in youth and vigor. I look on the future invasion of the eastern and western countries by the north as a periodical movement, ordained by Providence.

After lying semiconscious for several hours, he attempted to articulate a thought but managed only a fragment: *"Give back all to . . ."* His second wife, soon to become Catherine I, had surrounded the Royal Palace in St. Petersburg (now Leningrad) to guarantee her accession, so the lack of a successor's name in his will was moot. The document ends with a sententious summation of Peter's life work and hope: "I found Russia a *rivulet:* I leave it a *river:* my successors will make a *large sea,* destined to fertilize the impoverished lands of Europe."

Charles Dickens: d. 1870, Kent, England

Last wish: That mourners "who attend my funeral wear no scarf, cloak, black bow, long hatband or other such revolting absurdity."

Widely regarded as the greatest English novelist, Charles John Huffam Dickens died suddenly of a cerebral stroke at age 58. He left an estate worth $180,000, half from the sales and serialization of his novels, half from his popular, strenuous, dramatic public readings in England and America—performances that hastened his death.

Just months before his fatal stroke, Dickens, who as a youth considered becoming an actor, experienced seizures. During public readings, he displayed ministroke symptoms of limb lameness, paralysis, and loss of speech. His vigorous acting out of the murder in *Oliver Twist* left him prostrate for hours after each performance. One evening Dickens's doctor sat on the stage, monitoring the author's pulse. It began at 72, shot up during the violent "Bill Sikes" scene to 112, and stood at 124 when Dickens finished—breathless, slumped in his chair, aphasic, his hands puffy with fluid.

Nonetheless, Dickens continued to give the readings, for the enjoyment they brought him as well as for the money. He was supporting a wife, a secret mistress, and a large household. "My wife," his will reads, "since our separation . . . has been in the receipt from me of an annual income of six hundred pounds, while all the great charges of a numerous and expensive family have developed wholly upon myself."

Dickens's problems with his wife, Catherine, date from about fifteen years before his death, around the time he confided to a friend: "I find the skeleton in my domestic closet is becoming a pretty big one." The skeleton was his shapely mistress, Ellen Ternan, an actress twenty-seven years his junior.

However, Dickens had always been critical of the woman he married, finding her "amiable and complying," but more often a "whiny woman" given to "peculiarities of temperament," which included "a mental disorder" and the stress that "she felt herself unfit for the life she had to lead as my wife." He

The young Charles Dickens wanted to be an actor.

complained they were intellectually mismatched. The extramarital affair had been conducted so discreetly that at the reading of his will friends were shocked that the first bequest was one thousand pounds to Ellen Ternan. It amounted to a posthumous unveiling of the long-hidden skeleton.

The night of Dickens's fatal stroke—June 8, 1870—he was sitting across the dinner table from his devoted sister-in-law, Georgina Hogarth, who had taken over running the household after his wife's departure. He had worked energetically all day on his new book, *The Mystery of Edwin Drood,* but in the last hour had felt strangely ill and discombobulated. Abruptly he stood, announced he must go immediately to London, then clutched at his temples in pain, sinking to the floor. Georgina attempted to lift him to the sofa, but Dickens murmured, *"On the ground,"* his last words. He slipped into a coma and died the next day, after visits by both his wife and mistress.

His will reflected his gratitude to Georgina Hogarth for years of service. He bequeathed her eight thousand pounds in cash, most of his jewelry, all of his priceless private papers, and the enjoined thanks of his children for her role as surrogate mother. One son, Charley, inherited Dickens's vast library, and all his children split a large cash bequest. Catherine received a modest income for the duration of her life.

Dickens had been a man accustomed to getting his way, and his last wishes underscore that temperament. Of his interment: "I emphatically direct that I be buried in an inexpensive, unostentatious and strictly private manner." He demanded, "No public announcement be made of the time or place of my burial" and ordered "not more than three plain mourning coaches be employed." He was hardest on mourners: "who attend my funeral wear no scarf, cloak, black bow, long hatband or other such revolting absurdity."

All these requests were ignored, on a grandiose scale. He was honored ostentatiously, publicly, with a long cortege, and by spectators attired in the full paraphernalia of mourning. His funeral was a national event.

As a writer popular with the masses, Dickens had always been at odds with the British literary establishment, who viewed him as "an entertainer," a term more than a little illogically derogatory. But as Charles Dickens was being mourned throughout the English-speaking world, *The Times* of London, which had consistently panned most of his novels, declared that he was important enough to be buried in Westminster Abbey, along the south transept in the hallowed Poets' Corner, beside such greats as Tennyson. He was. His crypt remained open for several days while tens of thousands of people filed past. For months thereafter fans heaped mounds of fresh flowers around his tombstone. As Auden said of Yeats, "he became his admirers."

The moving quotation that appeared on his funeral card had been spoken by Dickens at his last public appearance in London. Reading from *The Pickwick Papers,* the ailing author repeatedly mispronounced words and slurred his speech; at the end, exhausted, he had to be carried from the stage. An audience of over two thousand admirers in St. James's Hall gave a standing ovation, and Dickens felt compelled to return to the stage for a final good-bye. "From these garish lights," he said, "I now vanish for ever more, with a heartfelt, grateful, respectful, affectionate farewell."

George Bernard Shaw: d. 1950, Hertfordshire, England

> **Last wish:** He ordered no religious service and that his tombstone not "take the form of a cross or any other instrument of torture or symbol of blood sacrifice."

The most significant British playwright since the seventeenth century, George Bernard Shaw died at age ninety-four, leaving a fortune of over three-quarters of a million dollars, at the time one of the largest ever left by a writer.

A literary giant whose witty and amusing plays are permeated with his passion for social reform, Shaw composed a fascinating will in which he attempted major educational reform from the grave. He bequeathed a sizable portion of his estate for the establishment throughout the English-speaking world of the so-called Proposed British Alphabet consisting of forty letters, one of his lifelong pet projects.

In 1898, at age forty-two, Shaw married a nurse and Irish heiress, Charlotte Payne-Townshend. The marriage, notoriously chaste, lasted thirty-five years, with Shaw satisfying his sexual needs through affairs with actresses in his plays. When Charlotte died in 1943, the playwright—whose wiry figure, bristling beard, and dandyish cane were as well known throughout the world as his plays—became reclusive. He had triumphed with *Man and Superman, Major Barbara,* and *Saint Joan,* won the 1925 Nobel Prize for literature, was rich after early years of adversity, and all he now wanted was death.

He lived, however, to celebrate his ninety-fourth birthday on July 26, 1950, at his home near Welwyn, Hertfordshire. A short time later he fell in his garden while pruning shrubs, fracturing a thighbone. His recovery was complicated by a necessary operation for kidney stones, and the playwright sensed his decline. "You won't be famous if I recover," he told his physician. "Surgeons only become famous when their patients die."

George Bernard Shaw's bequest to found a new alphabet went unfulfilled.

Shaw expressed his desire for death frequently to his Scottish housekeeper, Alice Laden. And he joked, only halfheartedly, with his nurse: "Sister, you're trying to keep me alive as an old curiosity, but I'm done, I'm finished, I'm going to die." The last words he wrote reflected his understandably fatalistic frame of mind, but a sardonic, lucid mind, still: "The will to live is wholly unexplicable. Rationally I ought to blow my brains out but I don't . . . and won't."

While waiting for a "natural death, as I mean to," Shaw read over his will: "I desire that my dead body should be cremated and its ashes inseparately mixed with those of my late wife." He wanted the joint remains scattered in the garden of the home where they had lived for thirty-five years.

In his will, Shaw was hard on religion. Never fearing he'd offend a God whose existence he questioned, he included a statement to the effect that he championed Darwin's millennial saga of creation over the Bible's six-day synopsis. He demanded there be no religious services that might imply to the world he "accepted the tenets peculiar to any established church." And always outspoken, near death he was blasphemous, instructing executors that no tombstone on his grave "take the form of a cross or any other instrument of torture or symbol of blood sacrifice."

The end came on November 2, when his fever soared to 108 degrees. The impudent, irreverent showman whose buoyant wit kept him in the public eye for more than half a century said wryly to a bedside visitor: *"Well, it will be a new experience anyway,"* then lapsed into a coma and was dead an hour later. Those present said Shaw died with a whimsical smile on his face, "as if he had the last laugh."

The endowment of his hobby, the Proposed British Alphabet, brought out cries from many who believed the money could be better spent. The phonetically based forty letters were to make spelling easier and less arbitrary and had fascinated Shaw since his boyhood in Dublin. His will requested that a phonetics expert prepare the text of his play *Androcles and the Lion* in the new alphabet, and that was done. But the British Probate Court ruled that the provisions of Shaw's will concerning the alphabet, which was to reform Western writing, were impossible to carry out. Instead, the money was distributed to three organizations.

Shaw, anticipating problems, had hand-selected the organizations as his second choice to receive the estate. Each was special to him: Ireland's National Gallery, where the young Shaw spent many hours learning about art; the British Museum, which, in his decade of poverty, served as his library and club; and the Royal Academy of Dramatic Art, in gratitude to the scores of actors who kept his plays alive. The will's last words are addressed to the "artists cooperating with me in the performance of my plays," who "not only made my career possible but hallowed it with kindly human relations."

Benjamin Franklin: d. 1790, Philadelphia

Last wish: That in a democracy his daughter not engage in "the expensive, vain and useless pastime of wearing jewels."

The tenth son of seventeen children of a Boston soap- and candlemaker, Benjamin Franklin was a printer, publisher, author, inventor, scientist, and diplomat—one of the most admired men in the Western world in the late eighteenth century. By the time of his death from a lung abscess at age eighty-four, he had invented the Franklin stove, bifocal spectacles, and the lightning rod and had showed the scientific world that electricity flows with positive and negative charge.

In January of 1788, the eighty-two-year-old Franklin suffered a fall on the steps of the garden of his Philadelphia home, badly injuring his right wrist and arm. While convalescing, he was forced to take opium to kill the pain from a recurrent kidney stone ailment. Scarcely able to move, he was carried from room to room in a sedan chair. By summer, sensing the end was near, he wrote his will.

The fortune from his *Poor Richard's Almanack* and inventions enabled him to provide handsomely for his children—except for maverick son William, "late Governor of the Jerseys." The will displays the bitter break between father and son over politics: "The part he acted against me in the late war . . . will account for my leaving him no more of an estate he endeavored to deprive me of."

As former ambassador to France, Franklin had received a portrait of Louis XVI, set in a gold frame studded with 408 diamonds. The expensive gift went to his daughter, Sarah Bache, with a proviso typifying Franklin's democratic bent: "that she would not form any of those diamonds into ornaments . . . and thereby countenance the expensive, vain and useless pastime of wearing jewels in this country."

At the time he composed his will, Franklin had no premonition of the explosive events that almost exactly a year later would drive French mobs into the Bastille and so many tumbrils to the guillotine.

On April 10, 1790, a fatal symptom of pleurisy appeared. His physician, Dr. John Jones, later wrote that an abscess in Franklin's lungs "suddenly burst, and

Grave of Benjamin Franklin.

discharged a quantity of matter, which he continued to throw up while he had power." Emaciated and in constant pain, he lay suffocating, and when a daughter expressed the wish that he would recover, he answered, "I hope not." Asked for his views on Christianity a month earlier, he had written: "As to Jesus of Nazareth . . . I think his system of morals and his religion the best the world ever saw and is like to see." But Franklin expressed "doubts as to his Divinity," wryly adding, "I think it needless to busy myself with that now, when I expect soon an opportunity of knowing the truth."

That opportunity came on April 17. Ten months had passed from the outbreak of the French Revolution, and a bedside visit by Thomas Jefferson, then secretary of state, brought Franklin up to date on the bloodshed in his beloved France. As the former ambassador listened to Jefferson, his breathing grew labored and "the organs of respiration became gradually oppressed," recorded Jones. When advised to shift positions to facilitate breathing, Franklin murmured his last aphorism: *"A dying man can do nothing easy."* Then he slipped into a "calm, lethargic state," dying at 11:00 P.M. that night.

Franklin's death sparked a disagreement between Jefferson and George Washington, then president. Franklin bequeathed his "fine crabtree walking stick" with a gold head "wrought in the form of the cap of liberty" to "my friend, and the friend of mankind, General George Washington." Washington cherished the cane, but strenuously declined Jefferson's suggestion that the executive branch of government mourn Franklin for an entire month by dressing in black. As Jefferson later explained, Washington declined "because he said he should not know where to draw the line, if he once began the ceremony." In France, though, the National Assembly wore black for three days.

Franklin was laid to rest in Christ Church Burial Ground, with a funeral attended by twenty thousand, the largest ever in Philadelphia.

In his will Franklin displayed his love for Philadelphia and Boston and a desire to assist them even in death. Each city received a bequest of "1,000 pounds sterling in trust" to be invested, the interest to be used for public works. A century after his death, each city skimmed off $500,000 for improvement of streets, bridges, and sanitation. Today the trust runs into the millions of dollars, and when the will terminates the bequest in 1991, both cities will be able to apply the balance to the cost of running municipal government. Franklin composed a will with foresight.

Earlier in life, he had jokingly penned his own epitaph: "The body of B. Franklin, printer, like the cover of an old book, its contents torn out, and stript of its lettering and gilding, lies here, food for worms. But the work shall not be wholly lost: For it will, as he believ'd, appear once more, in a new & more perfect edition, corrected and amended by The Author."

Napoleon: d. 1821, St. Helena, South Atlantic

> **Last wish:** That his body be cremated after his head was shaved and his hair divided among friends.

Once the most towering figure in Europe, Napoleon Bonaparte, crowned emperor of France, died at age fifty-one in exile, stripped of power, possessions, and wealth. Nonetheless, he wrote the will of a magnanimous emperor, bequeathing six million francs to family and friends, though the money was nonexistent.

Specifically, Napoleon left ten thousand francs to the French officer, Cantillon. Cantillon had made a valiant attempt to assassinate the duke of Wellington, who had engineered Napoleon's defeat at Waterloo and his subsequent confinement on St. Helena. "Cantillon," wrote the bitter emperor, "had as much right to assassinate that oligarchist, as the latter had to send me to perish upon the rock of St. Helena."

Disembarking on St. Helena on October 15, 1815, the forty-six-year-old exile appeared to be in vigorous health and settled into a life of routine. He woke at nine, breakfasted at ten, seldom ventured from his assigned house, dictating to his secretary, Las Cases, his former chamberlain; he supped at seven, read classics aloud till eleven, then retired. The monotony of that existence for a once active man, a man who attempted to conquer all of Europe, contributed to Napoleon's deteriorating health.

What killed Napoleon?

Despite persisting hypotheses that he was surreptitiously poisoned—with arsenic, antimony, or lead; all were found in modern analyses of his hair—the former emperor was already dying of a malignant stomach ulcer that also invaded his liver (what recently killed Salvadoran president José Napoleon Duarte). Napoleon feared stomach cancer, which ran in his family. It had killed several relatives, including his father at age thirty-eight.

The exiled emperor experienced the first fateful signs in 1817, and within three years was vomiting what looked like coffee grounds—his own dark, digested blood. Confined to bed in 1821, in March Napoleon dictated his will,

Hairs embedded in Naopleon's death mask and bequeathed to friends contain poison.

opening with a line once familiar to every French schoolboy: "I wish my ashes to rest on the banks of the Seine, in the midst of the French people, whom I have loved so well." However, it would not be until 1840, during the reign of Louis Philippe, that Napoleon's ashes would be brought to Paris. Though, by then, he was far too famous to be scattered; his urn was interred beneath the dome of Les Invalides.

On St. Helena, Napoleon also suffered the mental anguish of receiving no communications from his wife, Marie-Louise, and his son. It is uncertain whether he learned of her liaison with the Austrian officer appointed as her guardian, Graf Adam von Neipperg, whom she secretly married without waiting for Napoleon's death. His will is without rancor: "I have always had reason to be pleased with my dearest wife Marie-Louise. I retain for her to my last moment the most tender sentiments."

Nor did Napoleon probably know that his son, the former king of Rome, was living safely in Vienna as duke of Reichstadt. "I recommend to my son," his will states, "never forget that he was born a French Prince, and never to allow himself to become an instrument in the hands of the Triumvirs who oppose the nations of Europe." He requested that his son "ought never to fight against France, or to injure her in any manner," and concluded with the suggestion that his son accept "my motto—'Everything for the French people.'"

Euthanasia.   There is no question that Napoleon's doctors hastened his death. Beginning in the spring of 1821, Napoleon was in agonizing stomach and liver pain. His vomiting—combined with acute diarrhea from amoebic dysentery picked up on the island—severely dehydrated him. His physician at the time, Francisco Antommarchi, sent by the former emperor's relatives in Corsica, began feeding him a harsh tartar emetic, a poisonous antimony compound, masked in lemonade. It was a standard medical purgative. The drink made Napoleon writhe on the floor in agony, but the dosings continued. A second physician, military doctor Archibald Arnott, suggested that the emperor would be helped by even more purging.

Today their judgment seems appalling; in fact, purging the stomach of a patient with stomach cancer seems downright malicious. And murderous. But in that day doctors routinely subjected weak, dying patients to copious purging, bleeding, blistering, and enemas. (See Chapter 11.)

When Napoleon's suffering intensified, Dr. Arnott mercifully administered ten grains of the toxic mercurial laxative calomel, more than three times the recommended maximum dose. Within hours, the former emperor was unconscious. He died at 5:49 P.M. that day, May 5. Advanced stomach and liver cancer remain incurable today. His final words, murmured in fits, were, *"God! . . . France! . . . My son! . . . Josephine!"*

Less noble but equally emphatic were the closing words of his will: "I die before my time, killed by the English oligarchy and its hired assassins."

That claim has been the grounds for speculation over whether the emperor was being gradually poisoned by his British captors. Napoleon requested that before cremation his head be shaved and locks of his hair divided among his

St. Helena retinue. Two valets saved their hirsute bequests, which have become the forensic relics for modern chemical sleuthing. The results of a technique called neutron activation analysis found thirteen times the normal amount of arsenic in Napoleon's hair. However, arsenic has also been detected in the soil of St. Helena and even in the paste of the wallpaper in Napoleon's room, suggesting instead environmental poisoning. It's possible that the British were poisoning Napoleon, and the environment, at the same time his own doctor mixed the coup de grace quaff.

Alfred Nobel: d. 1896, San Remo, Italy

Last wish: The capital shall be invested . . . the interest shall be annually distributed in the form of prizes to those who, during the preceding year, shall have conferred the greatest benefit on mankind.

Of philanthropic wills, the most famous is that of Alfred Bernhard Nobel, born in Stockholm on December 10, 1833. The Swedish chemist, industrialist, and inventor of dynamite amassed a fortune of almost nine million dollars, bequeathing the bulk of it to endow the prizes that bear his name.

Nobel's will specified only five prizes—for physics, chemistry, physiology or medicine, literature, and world peace. A sixth award, in economics, was instituted in 1968 by the National Bank of Sweden. Over the years cash gifts have ranged from about thirty thousand dollars to well over one hundred thousand dollars. It's believed that Nobel's distress over the military destructiveness of explosives motivated his creation of the award for peace.

Contrary to popular opinion, Nobel demonstrated the practical application of nitroglycerin (in 1860) but did not invent it; that was achieved in 1846 by Italian chemist Ascanio Sobrero. The temperamental oil—syrupy, flammable, canary yellow, and detonated by the slightest jar—is so risky to manufacture on a commercial scale that for a decade and a half it remained a laboratory curiosity—maiming many a curious chemist. Nobel discovered a way gently to introduce glycerol, a harmless starchlike liquid, to volatile nitric and sulfuric acids to safely handle the resulting explosive. Though not without tragedy: His first nitroglycerin factory exploded, killing four workers and his youngest brother, Emil. His next factory was built on a barge moored in the middle of a calm lake.

Nobel wrote his will in Paris on November 27, 1895, a year before his death, concluding that "in awarding the prizes no consideration whatever shall be given to nationality of the candidate." Generous in many humanitarian and scientific philanthropies, he was, paradoxically, pessimistic, bitterly satirical, and convinced his discoveries, rather than deterring war, would make conflict inevitable and more lethal. He died at age sixty-three, never seeing World War I, which turned his worst fear into devastating reality.

The first prize from his bequest was awarded in 1901, to the German physicist Wilhelm Roentgen for his discovery of X rays. Later, in the three-year period 1940–42, as the world waged an even fiercer battle, the Nobel prizes were suspended—not because travel to Stockholm was hazardous, but because the heads of factories supplying ammunition to the warring forces were all descendants of Alfred Nobel, an irony that fits with Nobel's pessimistic view of human nature.

Harry Houdini: d. 1926, Detroit

Last wish: To be buried beside his dead mother, with her letters to him beneath his head.

A single line in the will of a dying man can say much about his nature. This is the case with a short clause in the testament of master escape artist Houdini, who thoughtfully bequeathed the rabbits featured in his disappearing acts to the children of friends.

Born Ehrich Weiss in Budapest, Hungary, on March 24, 1874, Houdini adopted his stage name (later his legal name) from the famed French conjuror Jean Eugène Robert Houdin. At age twenty, he married Wihelmina Rahner, who as "Beatrice Houdini" served as his trusted stage assistant in death-defying escapes—and as his "spiritual contact" when, as he promised, he attempted to communicate with her from beyond the grave. She outlived him by seventeen years, declaring before her own death that the postmortem "trick" was the only one in which Houdini failed.

To his wife, Houdini left a home, jewelry, paintings, income from investments, and his library—except for books on the black art of magic, which were willed to the Library of Congress.

To his brother, Theodore, Houdini made a monetary bequest, but with a proviso concerning grandchildren. Son of a rabbi, who throughout life maintained close ties with his faith, he allowed the money to pass on to Theodore's children only if they were reared in the Jewish religion.

Countless stage escapes from shackles, the "water torture cell," and sealed coffins continually forced Houdini to confront death. He became obsessed and fascinated with the subject, to the point that he experienced many premonitions of his own ending. None, though, was as unsuspectedly simple, accidental, and tragic as the actual event.

Prior to a matinee performance in Montreal on October 22, 1926, Houdini was reclining on a sofa in his dressing room, reading his mail. A student from McGill University, who earlier had sketched the magician, was invited backstage to meet Houdini, and brought along two friends; one, J. Gordon Whitehead, was an amateur boxer. Whitehead asked if Houdini could, as the press claimed, withstand punches to the midriff. Mistaking Houdini's casual nod as permission, the boxer delivered one—possibly three—violent blows to the magician's relaxed abdomen. Houdini gasped, jumped to his feet, and, breathless, explained that first it was necessary to tense his muscles, which he then did, inviting Whitehead, by some accounts, to deliver several additional punches.

The following night, on board a train to a Detroit engagement, the fifty-two-year-old Houdini developed abdominal cramping and fever. He began his performance, but collapsed during the act, suffering from what doctors diagnosed as a ruptured appendix and spreading streptococcal peritonitis, which before the advent of antibiotics was fatal. He was given twelve hours to live.

Ironically, Houdini's wife was at that time in the same Detroit hospital, recovering from a case of food poisoning. The magician decided there and then that whoever died first, that person would attempt to contact the survivor.

Houdini fought death for several days, undergoing two futile operations and expiring peacefully at 1:26 A.M. on October 31, Halloween. His last words were to his brother, Dash: *"I'm tired of fighting. I guess this thing is going to get me."* Because his appendix was accidentally ruptured, his insurance policy paid double indemnity to Beatrice of fifty thousand dollars.

Houdini had specified the details of his burial. He had worshiped his mother, and after her death in 1913 he visited the grave daily, usually at quarter past midnight, the time she died. Unable to accept the loss, he began attending seances, a situation as poignant as it was paradoxical: The world's greatest master of deception was challenging deception in the vain hope that spiritualism would in this one instance prove genuine. In one darkly lit seance his Hungarian mother spoke—though in clipped, unaccented English, a language she never learned. When Houdini could no longer suspend disbelief, he conceded seances were a sham and unleashed the vehemence of a pogrom against spiritualists and their kind that railed lifelong.

He requested that he be interred beside his mother's grave in Brooklyn and

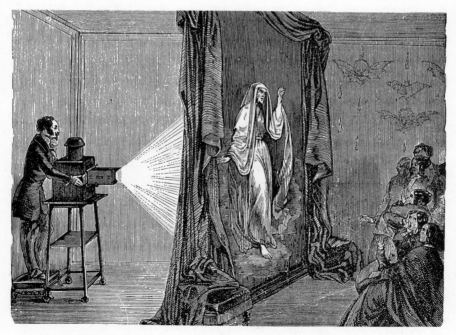

Houdini, deceptionist supreme, turned in grief to spiritualism and exposing the sham of seances.

that her letters to him, which he had saved, be placed on a pillow beneath his head. This was done—and more. His body was laid to rest in the famous "buried alive" stunt coffin, a bronze casket that toured with him from city to city, drawing immense crowds. He liked the familiarity of the box, the irony of the symbolism, and the chance, however remote, to perform the trick once more.

Attached to Houdini's will was a letter he had written to his wife just days before his death: "Sweetheart, When you read this I shall be dead. Dear Heart, do not grieve. I shall be at rest by the side of my beloved parents, and wait for you. . . . Yours in Life, Death and Ever After, Houdini."

Adolf Hitler: d. 1945, Berlin

> **Last wish:** "The establishment of a picture gallery in my home town of Linz."

The Austrian-born dictator of Nazi Germany composed his will while secluded in his Berlin bunker under the Chancellery on the afternoon of April 29, 1945, exactly one day before he and his new bride, Eva Braun, committed suicide. Shortly before dictating the "Political Testament," Hitler married his longtime mistress in a civil ceremony.

The highly personal document opens with Hitler's rationalization that given his priority of conquering Europe, "I could not undertake the responsibility of marriage." But with Russian troops practically knocking at the Chancellery door, he concedes: "before the end of my life, I have decided to take as my wife" Eva Braun, "who will go to her death with me at her own wish." Their brief, one-day marriage, reasoned the new groom, "will compensate us both for what we both lost through my work in the service of my people." What the artist-turned-dictator admired most about Eva Braun, a warmhearted woman who had been a shop clerk in Munich, was her "lack of intellectual ability" and "unquestioning loyalty."

In his final years, Hitler suffered from Parkinson's disease. Hand tremors, a shuffling gait, and a tendency to drool are symptoms recorded by the dictator's physician, Dr. Theodore Morrell. It was the inclination of Hitler's upper body to lurch forward faster than his festinating feet could support it that, said Morrell, caused him to order "benches spaced along the walls of the great bunker," the bunker in which he'd end his life.

Hitler's bequests were few; his executor, "my most faithful party comrade, Martin Bormann." "My possessions," the will instructs, "belong to the party, or, if this no longer exists, to the state." Then he addressed the possibility of defeat: "If the state, too, is destroyed, there is no need for any further instructions on my part." Of immense importance to him was his collection of paintings, left "solely for the establishment of a picture gallery in my home town of Linz on the Danube."

Though the will mentioned the intended joint suicides in three separate clauses—both opening and closing on that somber note—it did not describe how the planned deaths were to be carried out. Hitler did, however, request that their corpses be doused with gasoline and "cremated immediately" to avoid possible revilement by his enemies.

Their bodies were found by Hitler's valet, Heinz Linge, seated side by side on a sofa in the bunker. The führer had crushed a glass ampule of cyanide between his teeth, but was finished off by a bullet, either self-inflicted or—given the unreliability of his tremorous hands—fired by Eva Braun at her husband's behest. She, then, swallowed cyanide.

Their bodies were, as the will ordered, carried to the courtyard of "the place where I have performed the greater part of my daily work during twelve years of service to my people" and set ablaze. Due to a shortage of gasoline, however, the corpses were not rendered completely to ash, and the charred remains were discovered days later by occupying Russian forces.

Many Russian doctors performed autopsies, and a curious, if insignificant, fact emerged: Adolf Hitler had gone through life with only one testicle (the right, lower-hanging one), a congenital deficiency. The führer's friends denounced the medical find as blatant derision, though it was popularized in a ribald ditty sung to the tune of "The Bridge on the River Kwai": "Hitler has only got one ball,/Goering has two but very small,/Himmler has something similar,/But poor Goebbels has no balls at all."

"My wife and I chose to die," concluded the will, "in order to escape the shame of overthrow or capitulation." But the principal hate Hitler harbored most of his life could not go silently with him to the grave. The fifty-six-year-old dictator included a denouncement that reads in part: "Above all, I enjoin the government of the nation and the people to uphold the racial laws to the limit and to resist mercilessly the poisoner of all nations, International Jewry."

Hitler's will was witnessed by high-ranking Nazi doctor Josef Goebbels, whom Hitler unrealistically requested be made chancellor. But the devoted Goebbels quickly followed his führer into death. Hitler and Eva Braun committed suicide at 3:30 P.M., April 30. That morning, Goebbels, in the bunker with his entire family, poisoned his six children, then, mimicking his leader's dramatic ending, at 8:30 P.M. marched proudly into the Chancellery courtyard with his wife on his arm, where he was shot in the head by an obliging SS officer. His wife swallowed cyanide. Their bodies were doused with the little gasoline that remained and incompletely cremated.

Kahlil Gibran: d. 1931, New York City

> **Last wish:** That his book royalties go to charities in his home country of Lebanon.

Seldom does a will lead a city to political corruption, mob violence, and murder, but such was the effect of the last will and testament of the peace-loving Lebanese poet and mystic Kahlil Gibran. An alcoholic, dying of cirrhosis of the liver, Gibran composed the final draft of his will in his Greenwich Village, New

York, studio in March 1930, a little more than a year before his death on April 10, 1931, at age forty-eight.

Most of the document involved simple, straightforward bequests, but two sentences turned Gibran's generous last wish into a legal nightmare. Of funds in the local West Side Savings Bank, he wrote: "I wish that my sister take this money to my home town of Besharri, Republic of Lebanon, and spend it upon charities." Then the best-selling author of *The Prophet* made a similar request of all future monies from his several publications: "The royalties on my copyrights, which can be extended by my heirs for an additional period of twenty-eight years after my death, are to go to my home town."

The joint bequests would in time total in the millions of dollars, and in order to calm warring charities in Besharri the Lebanese government would eventually have to assume distribution of the estate.

Born on January 6, 1883, Gibran spent only his first twelve years in Besharri, emigrating with his parents to Boston in 1895. There he met Mary Haskell, the wealthy founder of a girls' school, who became his devotee and benefactor for life, providing him with a monthly stipend that enabled him to write and paint. When his will was read in April 1931, relatives refused to believe the largess to Besharri was Gibran's own intention. But Mary Haskell claimed that it had long been Gibran's secret desire, that he'd once told her, "If I had fifty thousand dollars to spend, I could get three or four hundred acres in Lebanon . . . and make a model agricultural station of it." Lebanon "needs one man with five or ten millions who will deliberately work for her growth and development and consciousness of herself."

Gibran's multimillion-dollar estate came mainly from his most famous book, *The Prophet,* which at the time of his death was not yet a worldwide phenomenon. The history of the book—a slender, one-hundred-page volume of sentimentality that touches on all aspects of life—is the key to understanding the upheaval generated by Gibran's copyright bequests.

In 1910 Gibran left Boston and moved to a studio at Fifty-one West Tenth Street in Manhattan. He became the high guru of a doting coterie of women, though he remained chaste and celibate. He had already written *The Prophet* in his native Arabic and translated aloud from it to his followers. At one Greenwich Village soiree in 1916, Gibran was introduced to Alfred Knopf, a twenty-three-year-old newcomer to the publishing world in search of new authors. Knopf had Gibran rewrite the book in English and he published it in 1923. "It is perhaps the best English I have written," assessed Giban, assuring Knopf that he had complied with a requested editorial alteration, changing "every *thou* in it to *you.*"

The public and the critics were not overwhelmed. Americans in the Roaring Twenties cared nothing for a prophet's pious pronouncements on love and sorrow, food and drink, clothes, housing, beauty, prayer, and crime and punishment. The volume sold only 1,159 copies its first year. A *New York Times* reviewer ripped into it: "Of all the limp, mucid hooey now being sold without prescription, *The Prophet* is the most blatant and outrageous."

But sales of the book rose steadily, reaching 240,000 in 1962 alone. By the late 1960s it had found its milieu and minions, becoming the all-time best-seller of the prestigious publishing house of Knopf. Gibran's bequest to Besharri, modest at the time of his death, now was in excess of 1 million dollars a year in royalties.

As the estate had mushroomed, Besharri charities materialized overnight to claim a share of the bounty. By the mid-1960s, most local politicians were corrupt, the sincerity of all charities suspect, the city a hotbed of feuds, intrigues, and physical violence—all to control the fortune. By 1967, when the Lebanese government assumed management of the estate, the annual magnitude of Gibran's legacy was affecting the national economy.

Shockingly, auditors discovered that Gibran's hometown of Besharri had virtually nothing to show from the bequests except a meager two hundred thousand dollars worth of real estate investments, the tip of the royalties iceberg. The bulk of the monies had unaccountably disappeared, gone into the hands and pockets of an untold number of individuals and organizations, none of which kept records. A newspaper half jested: "Had alcohol not already killed Kahlil Gibran, this would surely drive him to drink." Gibran's books continue to sell, and in the last two decades royalties have gone to fund scholarships, grant interest-free loans, and found a music academy, two schools, and a medical clinic.

John B. Kelly: d. 1960, Philadelphia

> **Last wish:** That the clothing bills of his daughter, Princess Grace, not bankrupt the principality of Monaco.

Bricklayer turned millionaire contractor, John ("Jack") Kelly of Philadelphia was already a well-known public figure in Democratic politics when his movie-star daughter Grace married Prince Rainier of Monaco. Two months before his death from intestinal cancer, a weakened, suffering Jack Kelly, who had once headed Franklin D. Roosevelt's physical fitness program, composed a will—unorthodox, but legal—that displayed his indefatigable spirit and puckish Irish wit. He signed it in Kelly green ink, and it immediately became a classic among collectors of wills. The opening paragraph sets the tone:

> For years I have been reading Last Wills and Testaments, and I have never been able to clearly understand any of them at one reading. Therefore, I will attempt to write my own Will with the hope that it will be understandable and legal. Kids will be called "kids" and not "issue," and it will not be cluttered up with "parties of the first" and a lot of other terms that I am sure are only used to confuse those for whose benefit it is written.

A devoted family man, Kelly made his fortune in construction and the bulk of his bequests were to his widow, Margaret, three daughters, and son—though always with a jocular aside. After leaving real estate to Margaret, he instructs her to pass on to son John Brendan Kelly "all my personal belongings, such

as trophies, rings, jewelry, watches, clothing and athletic equipment, except the
ties, shirts, sweaters and socks, as it seems unnecessary to give him something
of which he has already taken possession." Of his unorthodox testament he
wrote: "I believe I am of sound mind. Some lawyers will question this when
they read my Will, however, I have my opinion of some of them."

Known throughout life as a ladies' man, the dying Kelly lightly broaches the
chauvinism of male marital infidelity in a bequest to his manservant of forty-five
years. After leaving the servant cash and bonds, he added: "I want him to be
kept in employment as long as he behaves himself well, making due allowances
for minor errors of the flesh, if being slightly on the Casanova side is an error."

Following financial bequests "in equal shares" to his son, John, and his
daughters, Kelly addresses to the issue of sons-in-law, including Prince Rainier.
He leaves them nothing, saying, "I don't want to give the impression that I am
against sons-in-law. If they are the right type, they will provide for themselves
and their families, and what I am able to give my daughters will help pay the
dress shop bills, which, if they continue as they started out, under the able
tutelage of their mother, will be quite considerable."

Jack Kelly knew when he wrote his will on April 14 that he had only weeks
to live and he confronted his impending end: "So just remember, when I shove
off for greener pastures, or whatever it is on the other side, that I do it unafraid
and, if you must know, a little curious." He died at his Philadelphia home on
June 20, 1960, and the final words in his will are to his four children:

> In this document I can only give you things, but if I had the choice to give you
> worldly goods or character, I would give you character. The reason I say that,
> is with character you will get worldly goods because character is loyalty,
> honesty, ability, sportsmanship and, I hope, a sense of humor.

W. C. Fields: d. 1946, Pasadena, California

Last wish: That he receive "no religious service."

Born Claude William Dukenfield on January 29, 1880, in Philadelphia, W. C.
Fields ran away from home at age eleven and soon became a popular vaudeville
juggler. His pretension-pricking humor, deadpan expression, and flawlessly
timed lift of an eyebrow or flick of a cigar made him one of America's greatest
comedians.

But beneath that jovial facade Fields struggled with a dread that he would
one day return to the poverty of his boyhood. He developed the secretive quirk
of opening bank accounts in every city he toured, usually under assumed
names. Once he confided to a friend that he held more than seven hundred
accounts throughout the world. This made the disposition of his estate difficult,
to say the least. When he died at age sixty-five of a stomach hemorrhage and
cirrhosis of the liver, he left a *known* fortune of three-quarters of a million
dollars; there may still be bank accounts in fictitious names that have never
been discovered.

A heavy drinker, Fields recuperated in several sanatoriums. The woman who stood by him for the final fifteen years of his life, and figured prominently in his will, was his great love, Carlotta Monti. She was at his bedside on Christmas Eve, 1946 as he fought a losing battle to retain consciousness. Soothing his hand, she spoke continuously to him, and when at one point she begged his stilled body to respond, Fields opened his eyes and winked. As Christmas Day dawned, blood began to bubble from his lips as he struggled to breathe. Following his death, Fields's estranged wife, Harriet, and son, Claude, overrode many of the comedian's last wishes.

Fields's will stipulated that his body be quickly cremated and there be no religious service or public funeral, rituals he had often lampooned. Harriet, a devout Catholic, forbade cremation (as did the Catholic Church in 1946). Fields's friends held a simple nonsectarian service, then Harriet staged a Catholic funeral. Finally Fields's mistress, Carlotta, arranged a spiritual reading of her own. He had wanted no observance and got three, and as for cremation, his corpse was interred in toto in a crypt at Forest Lawn Memorial Park, a cemetery whose grandiloquent trappings Fields had satirized in life. Carlotta Monti was prevented from entering the crypt until after the burial service.

The squabbling over funeral arrangements lasted only a week; the battle over Fields's money was fought in the courts for four years. Fields's will bequeathed his wife "Hattie" and son Claude the sum of twenty thousand dollars, to be divided equally. More generously (and protractedly) provided for was Carlotta Monti, who received twenty-five thousand dollars in weekly installments of twenty-five dollars for one thousand weeks—or for about nineteen years, two months, and two weeks.

Carlotta Monti was also willed Fields's Cadillac, two bottles of Shalimar perfume, books, recording equipment, and various household items. Under California's community-property laws, Fields's estranged wife claimed half of everything. She also charged that the comedian had, over the years of their marriage, given gifts to friends without her consent, totaling a half-million dollars; she wanted reimbursement from the estate for half of that amount. In the end she settled for sixty-five thousand dollars.

Another of Fields's last wishes was ignored. The comedian, who joked that he loathed children, requested in his will the establishment of a "W. C. Fields College for orphan white boys and girls" and stipulated that "no religion of any sort is to be preached." Between the court squabbles and lawyers' fees, nothing ever came of the nondenominational, if racist, orphanage.

CHAPTER 4

Bequests & Behests
of Dying Presidents

Washington to Hayes

George Washington: d. December 14, 1799, age 67

Will signed: July 9, 1790

Estate value: $530,000

Place of rest: Mount Vernon, Virginia

Presidential salary: $25,000

A fervent desire expressed in the will of George Washington, the only president to be elected unanimously by the electoral college, was that his many slaves be freed—not, though, upon his death, but upon his wife's.

"To emancipate them during her life, would," lamented Washington, "though earnestly wished by me, be attended with ... *insufferable* difficulties." Not only did Martha Curtis Washington rely on the family's slaves, but the constitution of Virginia recognized many of them as a rightful part of her dower. Freed slaves too old, too infirm, or too young to support themselves were to be housed, clothed, and fed by Washington's heirs. As we saw in wills of the last chapter, the inhumanity and servility of slavery pricked the conscience of dying men from the time of Plato.

Washington had other regrets. In his time children of wealthy families went abroad for their education, "often before their minds were formed or they had imbibed any adequate ideas of the happiness of their own." His will is emphatic

Washington's birthplace and residence, Mount Vernon. His medicine chest.

that a European education leads to "habits of dissipation and extravagance" and that in studying abroad many young men and women acquire "principles unfriendly to Republican Government and to the true and genuine liberties of mankind." To upgrade the quality of home-shore higher learning, he bequeathed funds to endow a college in the District of Columbia, giving birth to George Washington University.

Washington was a fanatically exacting man, and his handwritten will—composed without legal assistance—underscores the trait with its almost maddening neatness and precision. Penned on fifteen sheets of personal watermarked parchment, he used both sides, numbered and signed each, and with a nod to aesthetic appeal engineered every line of precisely the same length, dashes extending short lines, hyphens breaking a long line's last word irrespective of proper syllabication. The document looks computer-set, with justified margins.

There were no witnesses, but in the 1790s a handwritten testament was legally binding.

When he died, Washington was one of the nation's wealthiest men, with an estate of $530,000. He owned a distillery, gristmill, several fisheries, and livestock worth $15,653. And giving new meaning to "father" of the country, he held 33,000 acres in more than 6 states: 5,000 in Kentucky, 3,051 in the Northwest Territory, 1,119 in Maryland, 1,000 in New York, and 234 in Philadelphia. Though Martha Washington received a hefty portion of the wealth, Washington willed his 8,000-acre Mount Vernon estate—which grew *Cannabis sativa,* or marijuana—to his nephew, Bushrod, a recent appointee to the Supreme Court.

Final Days.   Washington's agonizing death illustrates the horrifying ineptness of medicine in the early nineteenth century.

True, he was never really healthy, and was, with valid gripe, a hypochondriac. Tuberculosis had hollowed his chest, smallpox cratered his complexion, and a full set of ill-fitting dentures of hippopotamus ivory distorted his bite causing chronic dyspepsia. In addition he endured a tumor hacked without anesthesia from his left hip and suffered recurring bouts of malaria fever and chills. But worse was to come at the hands of his doctors.

Two days before his death, the sixty-seven-year-old former president, two years out of office, went horseback riding at his Mount Vernon estate in a blustery winter snow. The next day he suffered laryngitis and called his doctors. They copiously bled him four times, then smeared his raw, inflamed throat with a poultice of dried cantharide beetles, or Spanish flies, to induce "curative" blisters. To soothe the fire, they concocted a gargle of molasses, vinegar, and butter, which nearly choked the life out of Washington.

To "cleanse" his system, he was given the toxic laxative calomel (which had killed Napoleon), and this induced dehydrating diarrhea. When his breathing became labored, one physician, Elisha Dick, proposed cutting into the windpipe for a tracheostomy, a new and unproved operation that was vetoed by Washington's other doctors. Instead, to shock his lungs to fuller inhalation, they applied blistering mustard poltices to his chest. This was the nineteenth-century equivalent of keeping a patient alive by "extraordinary means."

In the ebbing afternoon of his last day, Washington said graciously to his physicians: "I thank you for your attention. You'd better not take any more trouble about me, but let me go off quietly. I cannot last long." He lasted until ten o'clock that night. His final words were funeral instructions, and they reveal Washington's well-known fear of premature burial: *"Have me decently buried, but do not let my body be put into a vault in less than two days after I am dead. . . . Tis well."*

Today biohistorians claim that George Washington died of an acute streptococcal infection of the larynx, which caused painful swelling on the interior of the windpipe, resulting in suffocation. A tracheostomy might actually have prolonged his life. Before his burial on December 18 at Mount Vernon, with full Masonic rites, a lock of the president's hair was cut and given to his wife.

John Adams: d. July 4, 1826, age 90

> **Will signed:** September 27, 1819
>
> **Estate value:** $30,000
>
> **Place of rest:** First Unitarian Church, Quincy, Massachusetts
>
> **Presidential salary:** $25,000

By coincidence, John Adams, the country's second president, and Thomas Jefferson, its third, died on the same day and in the same year. By further coincidence, the day was July 4, Independence Day, and the year, 1826, marked the nation's fiftieth anniversary of the signing of the Declaration of Independence. As irony would have it, Adams's final utterance was about Jefferson.

A short, plump man—and one of the healthiest presidents; the only one to reach the age of 90 years, 274 days—Adams helped the American colonies obtain independence from Great Britain. At age 28 he married the witty and attractive Abigail Smith, who would win historical footnotes as the first first lady to be criticized for running her husband's affairs and dubbed Mrs. President, and for stringing clotheslines throughout the East Room of the White House to dry the family wash.

Adams served two terms as vice president under Washington at an annual salary of five thousand dollars, far too little to live on, he complained. To meet official expenses, he dipped repeatedly into his own modest fortune, a practice he followed even during his presidency from 1797 to 1801, and it drained his estate. After serving a single term, he passed his last twenty-five years in restful seclusion at his Quincy estate, composing his will at age eighty-four. By then, most of his preferred beneficiaries—his wife, two daughters, and one son—were dead. Two sons were living—Thomas Boylston and John Quincy, who would become the country's sixth president. They, as well as a phalanx of grandchildren and in-laws, shared the estate.

It was not much. Adams had lived so long off his fortune that its worth had dwindled to thirty thousand dollars. The older son, John Quincy, favored in the will, inherited the presidential library, private papers, and a most cherished gift: an album of family pictures, a treasure in the early days of photography.

Adams's death, though sudden, was not unexpected; he was almost ninety-one. His eyesight was poor, rheumatism pained every joint, and his heart pumped under the strain of worsening arteriosclerosis that left him winded and bedridden. On the morning of July 4, he asked to be dressed and propped up at his bedroom window. He did not glimpse any Independence Day celebration but lapsed into a coma, dying late that afternoon. His last words were about

John Adams. His wife strung clotheslines in the White House.

his former opponent for the presidency: *"Thomas Jefferson still survives."* Unbeknown to him, Jefferson had died at 9:50 that morning.

The confluence of two presidents dying on the same day, and on July 4, and on the fiftieth anniversary of the Declaration of Independence created a public sensation. Too much was read into the coincidences. Doomsayers predicted impending apocalypse, or if not the end of the world, then at least the destruction of the young nation. Optimistic astrologers cast charts on the country's future, establishing a tradition between the White House and the starry art that lasted well into the Reagan presidency.

Thomas Jefferson: d. July 4, 1826, age 83

> **Will signed:** March 16, 1826
>
> **Estate value:** $200,000
>
> **Place of rest:** Monticello Memorial Park, Charlottesville, Virginia
>
> **Presidential salary:** $25,000

The "democratic" custom of shaking hands instead of bowing at White House receptions was initiated in the Blue Room by Thomas Jefferson early in his first term. Though well bred, Jefferson eschewed "aristocratic" manners and in his will debated the economics versus the inhumanity of slavery in a democracy.

"I give to my good servants John Hemings and Joe Fosset, their freedom at the end of one year after my death," he wrote, "and to each of them respectively, all the tools of their respective shops or callings." He asked that "a comfortable loghouse be built" on his land for each of three freed slaves and their wives, and that "the legislature of Virginia [confirm] the bequest of freedom to these servants." He had inherited 30 slaves from his father and 135 from the father of his wife, Martha Wayles Skelton.

Egalitarian as he could be, Jefferson savored gourmet food. During his eight years in the White House, his grocery bill often topped fifty dollars a day

Where Thomas Jefferson signed the Declaration of Independence.

(mostly for European imports), and the cost of wine alone came to more than eleven thousand dollars. His expensive tastes repeatedly brought him to the brink of bankruptcy.

In the spring of 1790, when he left his Monticello home for New York to become secretary of state, his annual salary was thirty-five hundred dollars, woefully inadequate for his needs and wants. Six years later he complained of his annual five-thousand-dollar vice presidential pay, then found that the twenty-thousand-dollar raise that came with the top office also never stretched to cover expenses. Part of the problem was that Jefferson was generous to a fault, unable to turn away the many friends who dropped in at Monticello for lodging and fancy meals.

Following his second term, age 64, he returned to private life and to more debt—in excess of $40,000. To his mortification he had temporarily to refuse guests accommodation at Monticello. In 1814 he was forced to sell his impressive library to Congress for $23,950, and in 1826, the year he'd die, he petitioned the Virginia legislature to hold a lottery to dispose of all his property, including Monticello and its furnishings—not unlike the modern-day insolvency auction of former Texas governor John Connally. For extra money, Jefferson rented out his slaves for $2,000 a year.

Final Days. The last year in life of the president who drafted the Declaration of Independence and doubled the nation's territory with the Louisiana Purchase was plagued with the threat of bankruptcy. Physically weakened by financial worries, the eighty-three-year-old Jefferson suffered recurrent bouts of amoebic dysentery and rheumatism. Though his health steadily declined, he forbade doctors to bleed him and refused their harsh purgatives. The dysentery was dehydrating him and on July 2, 1826, he drifted from beclouded consciousness into a stupor.

The next evening, he woke briefly, asking in a soft, husky voice, *"Is it yet the Fourth?"* Perhaps by dint of desire, he clung to life a few hours longer, dying at sunrise on Independence Day.

His wife had died some forty years earlier, at age thirty-three, and Jefferson had kept his promise to her that he would never remarry, though this did not deter him from a relationship with one of his teenage black slaves, Sally Hemings, who bore him five children.

On paper, Jefferson's estate was valued at two hundred thousand dollars. But his lands were poorly farmed, his mill and copper factory unprofitable. In short, he died broke. His surviving legitimate daughter, Martha, and her children had lost the magnificent Monticello as well as their means of support. In gratitude for Jefferson's services to the country, the states of Virginia and South Carolina each voted Martha ten thousand dollars.

Jefferson's material bequests were few. He left a friend "my gold-mounted walking staff," his grandson "my silver watch," and he wrote: "I subject all my other property to the payment of my debts." For many years Monticello went unoccupied, the grounds choked by weeds, the mansion's paint peeling, the plaster cracking. Not until the 1920s was it restored as a national monument.

In accordance with his last request, Jefferson was buried in the graveyard he laid out at Monticello, under a favorite oak tree. He had designed his own tomb and composed his own epitaph, which mentions several accomplishments but not the most prestigious: "Here was buried Thomas Jefferson, author of the Declaration of Independence, of the Statute of Virginia for Religious Freedom, and the Father of the University of Virginia."

James Madison: d. June 28, 1836, age 85

Will signed: April 15, 1835

Estate value: Less than $100,000

Place of rest: Montpelier Station, Virginia

Presidential salary: $25,000

The only president to engage in military combat while in office (the War of 1812), James Madison, secretary of state under Jefferson, succeeded Jefferson in the White House. His attractive wife, Dolley Payne Todd, seventeen years his junior and addicted to snuff, brought new social sparkle to the executive mansion. The couple had no children of their own, but Madison enjoyed such close ties to nieces and nephews that his will divides the estate among them, his stepson, and his wife—what little wealth the latter two spendthrifts left him.

Like Washington and Jefferson, Madison, a wealthy planter, married a widow—who had a son, Payne Todd. Dolley and Payne were notoriously extravagant. They quickly exhausted the sizable inheritance from her first husband, a Philadelphia lawyer, then greatly diminished Madison's fortune. Even after British troops burned the executive mansion in 1814, Dolley, temporarily residing at the nearby Octagon House, continued to entertain lavishly. Chronicler Washington Irving described the free-spending Dolley as a "fine, portly, buxom dame," and her husband as "Jemmy, ah, poor Jemmy."

Departing Washington in 1817, the Madisons returned to their estate in Montpelier, Virginia, residing there for the next twenty years. During that time the former president laid out forty thousand dollars of his savings to cover debts of his profligate stepson, an action that eventually forced Dolley, a year after Madison's death, to sell her bequest of the Montpelier mansion in order to survive. Friends like Daniel Webster regularly brought the former first lady baskets of groceries; finally Congress, to assist Dolley, purchased her husband's papers for fifty thousand dollars.

Madison had foreseen his wife's financial woes. A major portion of the will deals with the publication of his detailed record of the proceedings of the Constitutional Convention. One of the first decisions of that body was that it conduct deliberations secretly, presenting the country with the final opinions of delegates without revealing who voted for what and why. Madison, a leader of the convention, took daily notes of the heated, historic debates.

Years later, whenever questions arose over the intentions of the Founding Fathers, Madison was urged to publish his journal. But he would not allow publication until every Founding Father was beyond the reach of earthly criticism. As it turned out, Madison was the last survivor. His will revealed that he had withheld publication of *Notes of Debates in the Federal Convention of 1787* specifically because he viewed the historic document as a source of income for his widow. As it was. A year after Madison's death, Congress paid Dolley thirty thousand dollars for *Notes,* which her son rapidly spent.

Concerning Madison's final days: At Montpelier, the aging ex-president grew progressively weaker. By 1836 he had to be carried from room to room. In June he developed a swallowing problem that cut severely into his nutrition. On the 28th, bedridden, he stared fixedly across the room and when a niece asked, "What's the matter, Uncle James?" Madison answered, *"Nothing more than a change of mind, my dear,"* then died. Dolley survived her husband by thirteen years.

James Monroe: d. July 4, 1831, age 73

Will signed: June 17, 1831

Estate value: Near bankruptcy

Place of rest: Hollywood Cemetery, Richmond, Virginia

Presidential salary: $25,000

The first heavy drinker in the White House, as well as the first presidential college dropout (though to fight in the Revolution), James Monroe—like John Adams and Thomas Jefferson—died on Independence Day, the last president to bear that trivia distinction. Somewhat more significantly, Monroe, born on April 28, 1758, in Westmoreland County, Virginia, was the last of the so-called Virginia dynasty, which included four of the country's first five presidents: Washington, Jefferson, Madison, and Monroe.

Monroe's two years as U.S. minister to France enabled him later to play a key role in the negotiation of the Louisiana Purchase; it also marked the start of his slide into financial ruin. Enamored with French opulence, Monroe, and his wife Elizabeth Kortright, a New York debutante, entertained lavishly, vastly exceeding his salary of nine thousand dollars. When he was elected president in 1816, further debts quickly mounted from the great "furniture scandal," which makes Nancy Reagan's china purchases pale in comparison.

The first residents of the White House after its renovation after the British burning in 1814, the Monroes were in need of furniture. Congress appropriated twenty thousand dollars. The Monroes used this to purchase French antiques. Then, removing chairs, tables, sofas, and beds from their two Virginia estates, Ash Lawn and Oak Hill, they sold the items to the U.S. government for White House use. With still too much empty space for the Monroes' liking, the next year Congress appropriated an additional eighteen thousand dollars for furniture. However, the Monroes sat and slept on their worn estate pieces and diverted at least a third of the congressional allotment for private entertainment.

The ensuing scandal, and Congress's demand for repayment, damaged the president's popularity and compounded his indebtedness. Still the Monroes continued to entertain extravagantly, spending as much as one hundred dollars a night on candles for the drawing room alone. Their daughter Maria became the first presidential offspring to be married in the White House, and with a wedding whose lavishness did nothing to help her parents' finances.

At the end of his presidency in 1825, his popularity at an all-time low, Monroe and his wife left Washington broke. They retired to their Oak Hill estate, which, due to a panic decline in real estate prices, was seventy-five thousand dollars in debt. Congress, hounding Monroe for reimbursement, withheld fifty-three thousand dollars that the former president claimed was his due. (It eventually paid Monroe thirty thousand dollars, without interest.) A year after his wife died in 1830, the seventy-two-year-old Monroe was forced to sell Oak Hill and live out his remaining months with his daughter in New York City.

Following a cold, it's believed he came down with tuberculosis. He died on Independence Day, 1831. His will, written about two weeks before his death, is brief, with few bequests, reflecting his destitution.

Like all presidents before him, Monroe wrestled with the issue of slavery. He supported the efforts of the American Colonization Society to set up a homeland for freed American slaves in the West African nation of Liberia. The society never achieved its goal, but due to Monroe's backing the capital city of Liberia was named Monrovia—and remains the only foreign capital named for an American president.

John Quincy Adams: d. February 23, 1848, age 80

> **Will signed:** January 18, 1847
>
> **Estate value:** $60,000
>
> **Place of rest:** First Unitarian Church, Quincy, Massachusetts
>
> **Presidential salary:** $25,000

The only American chief executive who was also a published poet, John Quincy Adams is also the only president descended from a president, his father. This despite his father's complaint of Virginians' near monopoly on the office: "My son will never get a chance at the Presidency until the last Virginian is in his grave." Slightly more than a year before his death at age eighty, John Quincy Adams wrote a long and complex will with thirty-three clauses of bequests.

In 1797, age thirty, Adams was U.S. minister to the Netherlands. That year he married Louise Catherine Johnson, daughter of the American consul in London, whom he had first met when she was four and he twelve. When he returned from foreign service to become secretary of state, Adams found that his finances, wisely managed in his absence by his brother, Thomas, had mushroomed to over one hundred thousand dollars. This was fortunate, Adams found, since his yearly salary of thirty-five hundred dollars met only about half of Washington expenses. Thus he began the all-too-necessary practice of his time, supporting public life with private funds.

The president's salary had not increased since Washington's day, though the cost of living in the capital had soared. Consequently, during his four years in the White House, from 1825 to 1829, he further depleted his personal bank account to run the country. Nearly broke on returning to private life, he worked hard to rebuild his wealth. He never did completely. At age sixty-four, the appeal of public life again beckoned, and Adams returned to Washington—and to the financial drain of public life—to serve in the House of Representatives, becoming the first ex-president to serve in Congress. Public officials then did not have the avenues they do today for earning extra income.

While debating in the House on February 21, 1848, the eighty-year-old Adams became dizzy. The resolution up for vote concerned the presentation of swords to officers who had fought in the Mexican-American War. Adams considered the war unrighteous, and when a count was called he stood and shouted vigorously above a chorus of "Ayes" his booming "No!" He suddenly became flushed, unable to speak, and clutching his chair fell into the arms of a fellow House member, suffering a stroke.

As it happened, four House members were doctors. They examined Adams and determined he needed "more air," so he was carried to the Rotunda for the obvious benefit of its vaulted ceiling. The dome seemed to work: Adams, paralyzed on the right side, rallied enough to thank his doctors. Then he lapsed into a coma.

To "awaken" the ex-president, doctors applied hot mustard plasters to his flesh. When the stinging failed, they bled him by two accepted methods of the day: the application of leeches and cupping, in which an extinguished fire in a glass cup pressed tightly to the skin forms a vacuum to draw up blood. At nightfall, semiconscious, he murmured, *"This is the last of earth. I am content,"* and drifted into a coma. He died two days later.

The principal beneficiaries of Adams's sixty-thousand-dollar estate were his widow, his sole surviving son, Charles Francis Adams, and the widow and daughter of his deceased son, John. The many remaining clauses of the will bequeath personal mementos: an "ivory cane," now in the Smithsonian Institution, "to the People of the United States"; a "gold headed cane cut from the timbers of the frigate Constitution"; "a cane made of olive from Mount Olivet in Jerusalem." Reading the will one is reminded that quality walking canes were once fashionable and were favorite bequests.

Andrew Jackson: d. June 8, 1845, age 78

Will signed: June 7, 1843

Estate value: $150,000

Place of rest: The Hermitage, Old Hickory, Tennessee

Presidential salary: $25,000

America's seventh president was the first to enter that high office from a background of abject poverty in a backwoods log cabin. In the appearance-conscious world of today, Jackson for numerous reasons might never have been elected to any office.

Born a drooler, throughout life he continually dribbled, spit, and wiped saliva from his lips. From a chronic case of urticarial hives, his body regularly itched from head to toe and was covered with unsightly red weals. He was forever scratching. As a young man, he had nearly died from smallpox, which marred his complexion, and a near-lethal bout of dysentery left him a lifelong legacy of abdominal cramps and rectal bleeding. Later in life, a bullet from a duel lodged in his left lung, causing him to cough up blood and pus until, at age seventy-eight, he succumbed to dropsy (edema) and tuberculosis.

Jackson never tried to keep his medical problems secret. It would have been futile: His unhealing bullet wound alone, chronically infected, smelled as vile as it looked. If anything, the infirmities became an asset to his presidential ambitions: Voters saw him as indestructible. So poor was his health that at age fifty-seven he accepted the nomination for the presidency only if, for medical reasons, he could be exempted from campaigning. He was. And he won.

Despite adversity—including in 1835 the first assassination attempt on a president (committed by an insane house painter who believed himself the rightful heir to the British throne)—Jackson lived a vigorous life, greatly expanding the power and prestige of the presidency and carrying it through an unprecedented program of domestic, economic, and social reforms.

Adversity can be said to have plagued Jackson from before birth. His father, a linen weaver from Ireland, died months before Andrew was born on March 15, 1767. At age thirteen, he saw his mother die of yellow fever contracted when nursing wounded Revolutionary War soldiers. And with his two brothers both war fatalities, the young Andrew Jackson was suddenly alone. Through his

Andrew Jackson survived an assassination attempt, the first on a president.

own diligence he acquired an education and in 1787 was admitted to the North Carolina bar. In 1791, he married Rachel Donnelson, but the happy event was marred by the fact that a divorce from her first husband was not yet final. This earned Jackson the sobriquet "the first bigamist president" and forced him to fight duels in defense of his wife's honor, for political enemies often hurled the slur to impugn his integrity. One such duel left him with the bullet in his lung. The strain of the scandal eventually drove Rachel to a nervous breakdown, dying shortly before her husband reached the White House.

Final Days.   Jackson served two terms in office. Throughout his presidency, the regular draining of the bullet wound became so painful that he consented to have the slug cut out—in the White House without anesthetic. The wound still refused to heal, and in his final year as president his lung hemorrhaged. Physicians bled him of two quarts of blood and he survived—for seven years, reinforcing voters' confidence that he was indestructible.

Retirement was spent at the Hermitage, his estate near Nashville, Tennessee, where he composed his will at age seventy-six, almost exactly two years before his death. By that time his body had ballooned enormously from dropsy. He suffered tubercular hemorrhages, coughing up blood, and one lung gave out entirely. Near the end, mental faculties impaired, he incessantly sang "Auld Lang Syne," his coarse, frail baritone echoing throughout the Hermitage. Visitors to his sickbed invariably found Jackson smoking his silver pipe, fanned by a black servant.

On June 8, 1845, his breathing painfully labored, Jackson died, his farewell addressed to bedside relatives: *"Please don't cry. Be good children, and we'll all meet in heaven."*

His will, one of the most personal of presidential wills, brims with religious avowal, patriotic sentiment, and warm farewells. Though his estate was valued at $150,000, Jackson died land poor, that is, with little cash. He left his mansion, "with the negros and all else on it," to a nephew he had adopted as his only son, Andrew Jr. The young man's extravagant ways had cost Jackson a fortune in his lifetime, and a decade after inheriting the property, Andrew Jr. forfeited it through debt. Bequests of pistols, canes, watches, and swords are on display today in the museum at the Hermitage, which was eventually purchased by a philanthropic organization.

Andrew Jackson's final request was that his funeral be as simple as possible, and it was, attended largely by neighbors from surrounding farms. Three months before his death Jackson was offered as his casket a sarcophagus alleged to have once contained the bones of Roman emperor Alexander Severus. His refusal embodied his lifelong beliefs: "My republican feelings and principles forbid it. The simplicity of our system of government forbids it." His tombstone does not mention that he served as president.

Martin Van Buren: d. July 24, 1862, age 79

Will signed: January, 18, 1860

Estate value: $250,000

Place of rest: Kinderhook, New York

Presidential salary: $25,000

The first president born after the American Revolution and one of the healthiest—he did not experience a major illness until after age seventy—Martin Van Buren was the son of a Dutch tavern keeper and farmer from Kinderhook, New York. After practicing law, at age twenty-five he married his cousin, Hannah Hoes, who bore him four sons before her early death in 1819. He was a widower for eighteen years before he entered the White House in 1837.

By then, despite a humble background, Van Buren had acquired luxurious tastes and cultural pretensions. One of his first acts as president was to squeeze from Congress twenty-seven thousand dollars to renovate the executive mansion. Then, believing that the country's chief executive should have a private estate—as had his predecessors—Van Buren sank a fortune into a mansion, Lindenwalk, on two thousand acres along the Hudson River. At both homes he entertained lavishly.

The extravagances might have gone overlooked if the country had not been in the grips of high unemployment, economic depression, and a crush of bank failures. Public criticism was harsh. His term became known as the "gold and silver administration." For four years Van Buren did not collect his annual presidential salary of twenty-five thousand dollars, taking it instead in a lump sum when he left office.

With his youngest son he retired to Lindenwalk, and about two years before his death at age seventy-nine he composed his will. Van Buren was a have while many of his relatives were have-nots who had frequently borrowed from him. Thus much of the document concerns the wisdom or folly of expunging or extracting unpaid loans. He tackled each case, concluding, "Some advances are to be forgotten, others taken strictly into account," which he then deducted from the bequest each debtor would otherwise have received.

Aware that all three sons coveted Lindenwalk and would fight over it, he adopted a Solomonic solution: sell off the property, house, and furnishings and equally split the profits. No son was pleased, but they remained a family.

By the year of his death, the seventy-nine-year-old ex-president suffered debilitating attacks of asthma. The ailment became suffocating with the arrival of spring, straining his heart. By June he was confined to bed on the second floor of Lindenwalk. His breathing grew more labored, and at nine in the morning of July 24 he suffered a fatal asthmatic attack. His last words, almost inaudible, concerned religion and the certainty of death: *"There is but one reliance."*

For a president, he received an austere funeral. He lay in state at his home for three days, in an unadorned coffin of rosewood. And observing his final request, no church bells tolled; only a hymn was sung at a local Kinderhook church. His casket, draped with the Stars and Stripes, was carried by firemen to the town cemetery.

William Henry Harrison: d. April 14, 1841, age 68

Will signed: Undated and not witnessed

Estate value: Near bankruptcy

Place of rest: Pioneer Cemetery, North Bend, Ohio

Presidential salary: Uncollected in life

About to have the shortest presidency in history (thirty-one days), William Henry Harrison delivered his two-hour inaugural address in a freezing Washington downpour. Refusing to wear hat, scarf, or coat, he caught a cold. Though chilled, feverish, and achy, he danced and drank at three inaugural balls, and quickly his cold dropped to his chest and developed into pneumonia. The nation had a new president; it would soon have another.

Ill throughout his one-month term and bedridden near the end, Harrison had no time to make significant national decisions and became the first chief executive to die in office.

Understandably, Washington physicians fought valiantly to save the new president, which meant sundry forms of torture. He was purged at the mouth with emetics, at the rectum with physics; his skin was blistered with hot irritating plasters and he was bled until he could no longer tolerate treatment. As his fever soared, doctors attempted to bolster his spirits with the lie that they expected full recovery. But Harrison, who had studied medicine and as governor of Indiana introduced smallpox inoculation, could not be duped.

"I am ill," he insisted to a friend, "very ill, much more so than they think me." For years he had suffered from duodenal ulcers; most foods caused burning, and sleep was elusive. He had acquired the visage in his day known as "ulcer face"—gaunt, sunken cheeks and darkly circled, pained eyes. The treacles physicians now forced him to swallow—ipecac, calomel, and Virginia snakeweed (a Seneca Indian remedy)—only further inflamed his stomach.

In the final moments of life, his spirits suddenly roused to admonish an imaginary adversary: *"Sir, I wish you to understand the true principles of government. I wish them carried out. I ask nothing more."* The first president to lie in state in the White House left behind a large family and the crudest of all presidential wills.

By the age of thirty, Harrison, and his wife, Anna Tuthill Symmes, daughter of a judge, had a family of ten children, one of whom died in infancy. Though he owned a profitable farm in Ohio, family expenses as well as a burgeoning political career mired him in constant debt. One visitor to the Harrison home gave the decor a tongue-lashing: "The furniture of the parlor could not have drawn very largely on anyone's resources. The walls were ornamented with a few portraits, some in frames, some disembodied from a frame. The drawing room was fitted in more modern style; but the whole furniture and ornaments in these rooms might have cost $200 to $250."

Finances never got much better. Harrison died in debt, his estate passing to his widow, who lived to the age of eighty-eight. To assist her and the children, Congress agreed to pay Mrs. Harrison the full twenty-five-thousand-dollar presidential salary that her husband had never collected.

At some point in his life Harrison wrote a will, and clearly without legal assistance. It was not witnessed, not dated, not signed (except for a signature in the opening line), and according to Ohio State law should never have been admitted to probate. Worse still, Harrison delineated the boundaries of his property by ambiguous and impermanent landmarks: running along the "Walnut grove pasture," reaching to the "cold spring field," terminating "upon the hill which has been for some years cultivated." Had Harrison lived through his presidency, his will most certainly would have been professionally redrafted.

Though briefly president, Harrison was mourned extensively. In Washington cannons boomed as a military parade marched solemnly down Pennsylvania Avenue. The funeral carriage was drawn by six pairs of white horses, while Harrison's favorite horse, Old Whitey, walked riderless behind his master's body. After a viewing in the East Room of the White House, through a glass-topped coffin, the president's body traveled by train to burial at North Bend, Ohio.

William Henry Harrison would go down in history as having delivered the longest inaugural address, and its cost was the shortest stay in the White House.

John Tyler: d. January 18, 1862, age 71

> **Will signed:** October 10, 1859
>
> **Estate value:** More than $100,000
>
> **Place of rest:** Hollywood Cemetery, Richmond, Virginia
>
> **Presidential salary:** $25,000

With the unexpected passing of William Henry Harrison, John Tyler, a graduate of William and Mary College, became the first vice president to attain the office of chief executive through a death. He would also become the first president to remarry while in office, and the first to face a serious threat of impeachment.

John Tyler was born in Charles City County, Virginia, on March 29, 1790. At twenty-three, he married Letitia Christian, daughter of a wealthy Virginia planter. His political rise was rapid: four years in the House of Representatives, two terms as governor of Virginia, and in 1827 election to the Senate. In 1840 he was chosen as Harrison's running mate under the often-debated slogan "Tippecanoe and Tyler too!" Tippecanoe is a river where Harrison as a general won a battle against Indians. Presumably, searching for a catchy campaign phrase, Harrison thought association through alliteration would tip Tyler toward victory too.

And it did. After assuming the presidency, Tyler succeeded in bringing about the annexation of Texas as a state of the Union.

Tyler's personal life was saddened by his wife's poor health. The bedridden first lady was confined to the executive mansion until her death in 1842, becoming the first presidential wife to die during her husband's term. The president, now a widower with 8 children, found his second first lady in Julia Gardiner, the 24-year-old daughter of a wealthy New York senator. They married in 1844 and the president fathered 7 more children, earning the trivia title "most prolific president." (For collectors of such statistics: The time span from the birth of first child in 1816 to the death of last in 1947 is 131 years.)

Not surprisingly, a good deal of Tyler's will is devoted to the politics of family harmony and the determination of how a dying man provides for a wife and fifteen children. His solution in a nutshell: Bequest priority went first and foremost to his widow, then to his youngest children, and last, with a plea for kindness and understanding, the smallest amounts to his grown children.

As president, Tyler lived frugally. His largest purchase was a run-down twelve-hundred-acre estate in Virginia bought for twelve thousand dollars and christened Sherwood Forest. After his failed bid to hold the presidency, he spent most of the last seventeen years of his life on the estate, dying at age seventy-one from a respiratory ailment. His last words: *"Doctor, I'm going. Perhaps it is best."*

Tyler's last wish, expressed in his will, could not be carried out. He chose burial on his Sherwood Forest Plantation, but had died while on a stay in Richmond, Virginia. With the Civil War escalating, his body could not be transported and was interred in Richmond's Hollywood Cemetery, beside the tomb of President James Monroe. Washington, preoccupied with war, took no official

John Tyler, with fifteen children, wrote a will devoted to the politics of family harmony.

notice of Tyler's death, nor was he honored with the customary thirty-day mourning period for presidents.

His body lay for years in an unmarked grave until Congress (which never liked Tyler) appropriated ten thousand dollars to erect a monument, but not to relocate him to Sherwood Forest, a trip deemed "pointless." Congress extended one kindness to Tyler's forty-one-year-old widow. Recognizing that she was faced with raising a brood of children—one an infant—while running Sherwood Forest with its seventy slaves, and during a war, it voted her an annual pension of five thousand dollars.

James K. Polk: d. June 15, 1849, age 53

Will signed: February 28, 1849

Estate value: $125,000

Place of rest: State Capitol, Nashville, Tennessee

Presidential salary: $25,000

The eleventh president, a devout Methodist, was the first to ban drinking and dancing at the White House; even his inaugural reception was dry and less a ball than a stand-around.

The pressures of office took an extraordinary toll on Polk, who had had a sickly boyhood and adolescence. When he left Washington in 1849 for his home, Polk Place, in Nashville, Tennessee—visibly aged and in frail health—he would live only months. His will, composed during that period, displays its author's tenacity and xenophobia.

Born in Mecklenburg County, North Carolina, on November 2, 1795, the son of an Irish farmer, Polk studied law in Tennessee. At age twenty-eight and a member of the state legislature, he married Sarah Childress in a union that would be childless. When a deadlock arose among presidential contenders in 1844, Polk became the country's first dark-horse candidate for the office. Whereas his campaign stands on the annexation of Texas and the acquisition of Oregon won him the election, once in the White House his ban on the "sinful" pleasures of drinking and dancing made him many Washington enemies.

That the couple had no children presented a problem in terms of bequests, particularly of his home. Polk's will made it clear that he and his "beloved wife Sarah" must be "interred on the premises of Polk Place." Then he expressed a wish not quite legal: "It is also our desire that the said house, lot, and premises should never pass into the hands of strangers who are not related to us by consanguinity."

Forever is a long time. Since the Roman era property could be tied up for only a limited number of years after a person's death. The law in Polk's time imposed strict restrictions on how long the wishes of the dead could prevail over the desires of the living. As a lawyer Polk knew this. He was, however, hardheaded and hated strangers. Perhaps he felt that the power of his presidency could bend the law. In the end, he would get his wish, though in a perverse way.

Shortly after retiring to Nashville, Polk was seized with intestinal cramps and severe diarrhea. An epidemic of cholera had hit Nashville, felling victims at all levels of society, and the bug found an easy host in the exhausted ex-president. With doctors helpless to reduce his fever or counter nutritional loss and dehydration from diarrhea, he grew weaker by the day. Assuring his wife that one day they would lie together on the estate, he expired saying haltingly, *"I love you Sarah. I . . . love . . . you."*

Sarah Polk survived her husband by 42 years, living for a time off an inheritance of $125,000 (a good portion saved from Polk's presidential salary). In 1882, 33 years after her husband's death, Congress granted her an annual widow's pension of $5,000. According to her husband's wishes, she resided at Polk Place and she was buried beside him on the grounds. No stranger ever did move into the mansion. With the city limits expanding, property was needed for roads and commercial development, and shortly after Sarah Polk's death the city bought the estate, demolished the house, and relocated the graves to the grounds of the state capitol.

The only extant Polk home, which serves as a museum of the president's memorabilia, is in Columbia, Tennessee, once occupied by Jane Knox Polk, the president's mother. It was owned by Polk, and he would undoubtedly be happy that it is not lived in by strangers, since his will also requested that that house, "at present occupied by my aged mother Jane Polk," pass on to "my brother William H. Polk and his heirs *forever."*

Zachary Taylor: d. July 9, 1850, age 65

> **Will signed:** July 20, 1846
>
> **Estate value:** $142,000
>
> **Place of rest:** Zachary Taylor National Cemetery, Louisville, Kentucky
>
> **Presidential salary:** $25,000

The only president to die of sunstroke, Zachary Taylor never once voted in a presidential election, not even his own. A hero of the Mexican War, he became president having never held a political office, and he was the first president to state publicly that he despised politics. As fate would have it, he was not in politics long—less than eighteen months in the White House.

Sunstroke, or heatstroke, is an ailment familiar to runners. When the body's temperature soars, the lungs, liver, kidneys, and blood-clotting mechanism begin to fail. If overheating continues, the damage is irreversible. Statistically, ninety-eight percent of all acute sunstroke cases are fatal.

The nation's capital on Independence Day of 1850 was oppressively hot and humid. Taylor, dressed in a high-neck collar and black suit, participated in ceremonies at the laying of the cornerstone of the Washington Monument.

Throughout the ordeal, he was flushed and perspired profusely. When he became faint and dizzy, he downed a large quantity of water from a pitcher that had been sitting in the sun for hours. (Some biohistorians feel the water itself may have been contaminated with cholera or typhoid microorganisms.)

On returning to the White House, he broke out in chills, sweats, and claimed to be "very hungry." An hour after eating several large bowls of strawberries and cherries, he doubled over with stomach cramps and collapsed to the floor. His mysterious symptoms persisted for several days, as his fever climbed.

Doctors were puzzled. Had it been the unwashed fruit? The water? By July 9, the president was bedridden, feeble, and only intermittently conscious. He was aware enough of the gravity of the situation, for he said to his physician, "I should not be surprised if this were to terminate in my death."

Rumors that Taylor was dying—and that he had already died—drew enormous crowds outside the White House. At 3:30 P.M. a bulletin was released announcing that the president was "out of immediate danger." The crowds cheered and dispersed. Church bells tolled throughout Washington, though the ringing was perversely fitting for in truth his condition had been gravely worsening. His family kept a bedside vigil while doctors consulted to determine why the president's vital functions were slowly shutting down. They implicated the water, the strawberries, the cherries, and even a glass of iced milk Taylor had enjoyed.

Weak though lucid, Taylor knew he would not recover. *"I am prepared to die,"* were his final words to his family. *"My only regret is in leaving behind me the friends I love."* Within less than twelve hours, the city's bells were again tolling. White House physicians, unable to announce the death of a president without offering a cause, agreed that Zachary Taylor died of "remittent bilious

Water and fruits, contaminated with typhoid organisms, were once thought to have killed Zachary Taylor, who died of sunstroke.

fever" following an attack of "cholera morbus." The contemporary belief is that Taylor suffered acute sunstroke and possibly picked up intestinal organisms from contaminated water or fruit, which hastened his decline. He became the second president to die in office.

Taylor had hastily written a will in July 1846, when he was a military officer fighting in the Mexican War. Its temporary nature is apparent in the opening sentence: "Life being at all times uncertain; and, more especially, as regards one in my situation, therefore in the event of my being cut off by the hand of the enemy . . ." After the war, and during his brief tenure in the White House, he never revised the document. Thus the battlefield jottings became valid by default.

At age 26 he had married Margaret Smith, daughter of a Maryland planter, who accompanied him to the many frontier posts he held while fighting in the War of 1812, the Black Hawk War, the Seminole War, and the Mexican War. With $60,000 in cash and $30,000 in bank notes, the couple had bought a four-room home, the Spanish Cottage, in Baton Rouge, Louisiana, and a 1,923-acre cotton plantation, Cypress Grove, with 81 slaves. It was on this plantation that Taylor planned to become a farmer before war rerouted him to the presidency.

The Spanish Cottage and cotton plantation were bequeathed to his wife, who would die two years after her husband. The estate, valued at $142,000, also consisted of stocks and cash, which Taylor divided among his wife and their children, Richard, Mary, and Ann. The battlefield will was simple and the bequests few, all to immediate family. Maybe it was the best will Taylor could have written.

Millard Fillmore: d. March 8, 1874, age 74

> **Will signed:** December 8, 1865
>
> **Estate value:** More than $300,000
>
> **Place of rest:** Forest Lawn Cemetery, Buffalo, New York
>
> **Presidential salary:** $25,000

Abigail Adams, wife of the second president, complained that the newly built "White House" (not yet white) had "not the least convenience," but it was Abigail Fillmore, wife of the thirteenth president, who went farther by refusing to live in the executive mansion unless it had a bathtub and a Bible. Her protest prompted Congress to fund the executive quarters' first library and first fully equipped system of indoor plumbing.

As the bright, red-haired Abigail Powers of Stillwater, New York, she was the schoolteacher of teenager Millard Fillmore of Cayuga County, New York, and two years his senior. Fillmore himself had been a slave, indentured by his parents to a cloth maker, faithfully serving his master for seven years before buying his freedom for thirty dollars. After studying law, he became comptroller of New York, then vice president to Zachary Taylor. Upon Taylor's untimely death from sunstroke, Fillmore became the country's chief executive in a ceremony without parade or fanfare.

Fillmore was the nation's first presidential health addict. He neither smoked nor drank, and was fastidious about diet and exercise, believing both could prolong physical well-being. The new president and first lady—with their daughter, Mary Abigail, and son, Millard Powers—took quickly to the executive mansion. But they would not have many years to enjoy the technological amenities provided by Congress. Millard Fillmore lost the election in 1853 (to Franklin Pierce); four weeks later his wife fell ill and died. She had caught a cold at Pierce's inaugural ceremony, which turned into pneumonia. The fifty-three-year-old president and his children retired to their simple home in Buffalo, New York. Within less than a year, illness claimed the life of his daughter. Had Millard Fillmore himself died then, his estate would have been unimpressive.

While still mourning his wife's death, he met and married a wealthy forty-four-year-old widow, Caroline Carmichael McIntosh. By terms of the marriage contract, he gained complete control of her sizable fortune. He bought a large mansion in Buffalo, lived splendidly, became a philanthropist, and entertained two later presidents: Abraham Lincoln and Andrew Johnson. He was active, healthy, and not thinking of death when he wrote his will at age sixty-five, thoughtfully bequeathing the bulk of his money back to his wife. Unfortunately, he left his presidential papers, "to be preserved," to his son, who in his own will (for reasons unknown) directed that the materials be destroyed, as they were. (A few hidden papers escaped destruction and are now at the Buffalo Historical Society.)

Millard Fillmore was still not thinking of death when in the winter of 1874 he declared, "My health is perfect. I eat, drink and sleep as well as ever." But while shaving one morning in February, his left hand suddenly lost sensation

Millard Fillmore's inaguration day parade, Washington, D.C.

and function. Within a short time the paralysis had traveled up the left side of his body and to his face. Two weeks later he suffered a more devastating stroke and further paralysis. On March 8 he was being fed breakfast when he commented, *"The nourishment is palatable,"* then experienced a fatal brain hemorrhage.

Franklin Pierce: d. October 8, 1869, age 64

Will signed: January 22, 1868

Estate value: $70,000

Place of rest: Old North Cemetery, Concord, New Hampshire

Presidential salary: $25,000

Though the presidencies of Millard Fillmore and his successor Franklin Pierce are remembered for substantive things such as Fillmore's treaty negotiations with Japan and Pierce's push to develop transcontinental railroads, other events took place in the White House that are trivia to an outsider but significant to inhabitants of the mansion. Whereas, for instance, the Fillmores installed indoor plumbing, the Pierces added central heating.

America's fourteenth president, an acknowledged alcoholic, literally drank himself to death. Back then a fondness for drink was not something to hide, even in a president. Nor was tuberculosis of the lungs, which plagued both the president and first lady, causing them chronically to cough up sputum stained with blood.

Pierce began his term unconventionally—the only president who refused to take the oath of office's opening line, "I do solemnly swear," substituting the word "affirm." And he ended it as had none of his successors, a tragic, lonely figure, shunned for his opposition to the Civil War, depressed over the death of his three sons and his wife's slide toward insanity and her fight against the tuberculosis that finally claimed her life. By the time he wrote his will at age sixty-two, less than two years from his death, he was, by his own admission, ready to die.

Birthplace of Franklin Pierce, Hillsborough, New Hampshire—a president hated at the time of his death.

From boyhood he'd been bibulous; his family's home in Hillsborough, New Hampshire, doubled as the local tavern. At age sixteen he entered Bowdoin College, where two of his classmates were Henry Wadsworth Longfellow and Nathaniel Hawthorne. The latter became a lifelong friend, and Hawthorne's death, seven years after Pierce left office, drove the grief-stricken ex-president to even heavier drinking.

As a junior member of Congress, Pierce met and married Jane Means Appleton. The death in infancy of two of the couple's three sons began his wife's lifelong fight with depression. For a while, Pierce abandoned politics to resume his hometown law practice, "never again to be voluntarily separated from my family," he vowed, "except at the call of my country in time of war."

Then came the Mexican War. As a brigadier general commissioned by President Polk, Pierce became a hero (for his role in the capture of Mexico City), then the Democratic presidential candidate—which the Pierces did not want. His wife implored him to decline. His only surviving son, eleven-year-old Benjamin, prayed his father would lose. Pierce himself accepted only because he was certain he'd lose. No one in his family took his landslide win as a victory.

Then, while the family was on a train ride, the axle of their car broke and Benjamin was killed. So hysterically distraught was Mrs. Pierce that she could not attend her husband's inauguration; he took the oath of office in a tearful daze. No president ever entered office in the wake of such personal tragedy.

Throughout the four-year term, Mrs. Pierce wore black. White House social activities were greatly curtailed, and those that did take place were guardedly festive. In 1857, unpopular for the failure of his foreign and domestic policies, as well as for his inability to resolve the issue of slavery, Pierce gladly left office. To assuage his wife's grief, he took her on tour of Europe, but the travel only hastened her consumptive decline and death.

Embittered by events, Pierce composed a will that is, if anything, upbeat. "I, Franklin Pierce . . . with profound thankfulness to God for prolonged life and many mercies," begins the document, which divides his estate of seventy thousand dollars among nieces, nephews, other relatives, and friends—fifty-one in all. Franklin Pierce did not have much money, but he seems to have given something to everyone he knew—if not "a hundred dollars," then a "case of pistols," a "cane made from the flag staff of the Castle of Chepultepec," his "neatly mounted hickory cane" with "My name in Roman letters on the Knots of the stick," or his favorite picture of "the destruction of Sodom." There is not a line of pathos in the final testament of a tragic president who came out of private life to serve his country and who at the time of his death was shunned by its leaders and forgotten by its people.

James Buchanan: d. June 1, 1868, age 77

Will signed: January 27, 1866

Estate value: $310,000

Place of rest: Woodward Hill Cemetery, Lancaster, Pennsylvania

Presidential salary: $25,000

America's only bachelor president (and perhaps only homosexual president: Washington gossip of the day linked him with Pierce's vice president, William Rufus Devane King, nicknamed "Miss Nancy"), James Buchanan sought the office of chief executive with a Richard Nixon–like doggedness, losing three times (in 1844, 1848, and 1852) before clinching it in 1856.

Born near Mercersburg, Pennsylvania, on April 23, 1791, Buchanan enrolled in Dickinson College at the age of sixteen but was expelled a year later for "misconduct" (though eventually he returned and graduated). When his youthful interest in Ann Coleman, daughter of a millionaire industrialist, was thwarted by her father and then preempted by her early death, Buchanan swore never to marry. His "first lady" and hostess in the White House was his niece and ward, Harriet Lane, who had been orphaned at nine.

Historians rate her second only to Dolley Madison in poise, charm, elegance, and frequency of stylish entertainments in the executive mansion. What marred Buchanan's term (1857–61) was an issue festering since Washington's time: slavery. It was about to become the centerpiece of a civil tragedy and Buchanan felt helpless to do anything about it. Departing the White House the ex-president said to his successor, Lincoln, "If you are as happy, my dear sir, on entering this house as I am on leaving it and returning home, you are the happiest man in the country."

Age seventy, Buchanan retired to his estate, Wheatland, outside Lancaster, Pennsylvania, where he lived his final seven years in contentment, excellent health, and cherished obscurity. He had been a wealthy lawyer, senator, and minister to England and Russia before assuming the presidency, and when it came time to compose a will he had much to leave to many: $310,000 in stocks, bonds, and real estate, plus presidential papers and memorabilia. "I James Buchanan," he wrote, "in the humble hope of Salvation through the merits and atonement of my Lord and Saviour, Jesus Christ . . ." Then, lacking dependents, he listed bequests to his Irish relatives, friends, "the Presbyterian Church of the City of Lancaster, of which I am a member," his servants, and mainly to his faithful niece (then married) Harriet Lane Johnston.

In the last month of his life, May 1868, the seventy-seven-year-old Buchanan caught a cold that settled in his lungs. As his health deteriorated, he made arrangements for his funeral. He asked that the service be "plain and simple," the trip to the burial site be "without parade," that he be interred "in the Woodward Cemetery," and that his headstone be made of the most durable of marbles. Leaving nothing to others, he composed the tombstone's inscription, providing blank spaces to be filled in "with the day of my death, now so near." The entire epitaph is laid out precisely as he wanted it chiseled. At eight-thirty in the evening of June 1, struggling against fluid-filled lungs, he whispered, *"Oh Lord God Almighty, as Thou wilt!"*

Abraham Lincoln: d. April 15, 1865, age 56

Will signed: No will

Estate value: $83,343

Place of rest: Oak Ridge Cemetery, Springfield, Illinois

Presidential salary: $25,000

Just seconds before Abraham Lincoln's death by assassination his wife, Mary Todd, asked coyly what guests in their presidential box at Ford's Theatre would think if the couple held hands. Lincoln replied, *"They won't think anything about it."* Then came Booth's bullet.

Much has been written about the first presidential assassination. The president's bodyguard, John F. Parker, was not on duty, so that John Wilkes Booth, who made no secret of his Southern sympathies, was easily able to enter the box. Parker later told authorities that the play, *Our American Cousin,* bored him, so he went for a drink at the nearby Taltavul's Tavern. He was never prosecuted, dismissed, or officially reprimanded. Speculation arose that the twenty-six-year-old Booth, who had been drinking heavily that night, was at the same saloon minutes before the president's bodyguard arrived.

Born in a one-room dirt-floor log cabin on the Nolin River, three miles south of Hodgenville, Kentucky, Lincoln was a strong, healthy man most of his life, despite his Marfan syndrome: a skeletal anomaly characterized by a tall, willowy stature, long spidery fingers and toes, and dislocation of the lenses of the eyes. His major health problem was mental, his self-admitted tendency toward periods of intense, almost suicidal, depression, which, by dint of will, he was able to override.

He met Mary Todd at a ball and awkwardly approached her, saying, "Miss Todd, I want to dance with you the worst way," doing precisely that—again by his own admission. They married when Lincoln was thirty-three and pur-

Lincoln's New York City funeral, April 25, 1865, up Broadway.

chased what would be their only home (other than the White House) in Springfield, Illinois. Bought at a cost of fifteen hundred dollars from the minister who
married them, it was several steps down from the estates of prior presidents.

Following a fiery speech—"A house divided against itself cannot stand. I
believe this government cannot endure permanently half slave and half free"—
he was nominated for the Senate but lost. In a later speech, in his bid for the
presidency, he said: "I am not ashamed to confess that twenty-five years ago
I was a hired laborer, hauling rails, at work on a flatboat—just what might
happen to any poor man's son. I want every man to have a chance." That year,
1860, he got a chance. Selling their furnishings and renting their home, he and
his wife moved to Washington to begin one of the most eventful administrations
in American history.

Lincoln is the first president to leave no will.

Never a wealthy man, by the time of his death, though, he had accumulated
a little more than $83,000. The estate, belonging to his immediate family, was
turned over to Supreme Court Justice David Davis whose wise management
soon increased it to over $110,000. Cash settlements of $36,765.60 went to
Lincoln's wife and to each of two sons, Thomas ("Tad") and Robert Todd, who
later became secretary of war. Stunned by the president's death and mindful
of his contributions to the country, Congress voted Mary Todd Lincoln a lump
sum of $25,000 plus an annual pension, first of $3,000, then increased to $5,000.

Lincoln's autopsy was conducted at noon on Saturday, April 15, about four
hours after his death. Army physician J. J. Woodward determined that the bullet
entered the skull from behind the left ear and tore a path through the left
hemisphere of the brain. As he lay in state in the East Room, in a mahogany
coffin lined with lead and draped with black broadcloth, some twenty-five thousand mourners passed to view the body.

The president traveled by rail to his hometown of Springfield, and the train's
engineer commented, "History has no parallel to the outpouring of sorrow
which followed the funeral cortege." At depots in Baltimore, Harrisburg, Philadelphia, New York City, Albany, Buffalo, Cleveland, Columbus, Indianapolis,
Chicago, and finally Springfield, throngs of people crowded the platforms to
glimpse the somberly draped seven-car caravan. Seventy-five thousand mourners crammed into the Capitol to view the coffin, and even larger crowds, silently
praying, lined the procession to Oak Ridge Cemetery, his burial site. Not until
the assassination of John F. Kennedy would the country experience such
profound and profuse mourning.

Eleven years after Lincoln's burial, grave robbers broke into the tomb and
dragged the casket partially out before they were caught. With no law then
against body snatching, the men were convicted merely of breaking and entering and served a year in prison. In 1901, Lincoln's remains, as well as those
of his wife, were cemented into a new, marble tomb. But Robert Todd Lincoln
felt his parents' bodies were still not safe, so the coffins of the president and
first lady were reinterred thirteen feet underground and embedded in six feet
of solid concrete.

Booth's Ending.   After Booth shot Lincoln, he leaped from the presidential box to the stage, fracturing his left fibula. *"Sic semper tyrannis!"* he shouted ("Thus always to tyrants," the motto of Virginia) as he limped quickly across the stage to make his escape on horseback.

He was the only member of his family who had sided with the defeated Confederacy, and he lived just long enough to regret his last act in support of the Southern cause. Twelve days later he was trapped in a Virginia barn, surrounded by federal troops, and shot.

Exactly how the presidential assassin met his own end is still debated. Several people present claimed he committed suicide. Others pointed to a Union soldier, Sergeant Boston Corbett (himself a strange case, a religious monomaniac who castrated himself at age thirty-six to better "resist sin" after a prostitute solicited his attentions; he was committed to a mental institution, but escaped, never to surface again). The fatally wounded assassin was carried out of the barn, laid on the grass, and uttered his final regret: *"Tell my mother I died for my country. . . . I thought I did what was best. . . . Kill me! Useless! Useless!"*

John Wilkes Booth, an actor who belonged to one of the most distinguished theatrical families of the nineteenth century, is buried in an unmarked grave at Green Mount Cemetery, Baltimore, Maryland.

Andrew Johnson: d. July 31, 1875, age 66

> **Will signed:** No will
>
> **Estate value:** Less than $75,000
>
> **Place of rest:** Andrew Johnson National Historic Site, Greenville, Tennessee
>
> **Presidential salary:** $25,000

America's first president never to attend school, Andrew Johnson was born in Raleigh, North Carolina, on December 29, 1808. A tailor by trade, he was still illiterate at age eighteen when he married Eliza McCardle, an educated woman who taught the future president to read and write.

Once Johnson entered politics, he rose quickly—House representative, governor of Tennessee, senator, vice president, and, upon Lincoln's sudden death, president. His unilateral attempt to remove his disloyal secretary of war, Edwin Stanton, resulted in him being the first president impeached by the House and tried by the Senate for misconduct; he was acquitted by a single vote.

The frugal president, applying his tailoring skills, made his own clothes and some of the first lady's; he even boasted of his sewing and showed off his handiwork. Mrs. Johnson, though, did not need many formal frocks: Due to chronically poor health, she attended only three official functions, delegating the role of hostess to their daughter, Martha.

Johnson had no trouble living on his $25,000 annual salary. In fact, the parsimonious president saved a good portion of it over his 4-year term. When he left the office in 1869 to return to his home in Greenville, Tennessee, he was comfortably well off, worth $150,000. But that was not to be his final estate.

Two years before his death, the country experienced a financial panic. Banks collapsed, and one of them was First National Bank of Washington, where Johnson had his money. There was no FDIC then, and overnight the ex-president saw his worth plummet to seventy-seven thousand dollars. He took the loss badly. In need of money, and missing political life, at age sixty-six he regained his Senate seat, the only president ever subsequently to become a senator.

That same year, on a visit back to Tennessee to see his daughter, he suffered two strokes. The first occurred after a family lunch, while playing with his granddaughter. Lifted into bed, Johnson refused to be examined by a doctor, and on the afternoon of July 31, he suffered a second stroke, never regaining consciousness.

He left no will, but a last wish: "When I die, I desire no better winding sheet than the Stars and Stripes, and no softer pillow than the Constitution." His body, wrapped in the American flag, was placed in a coffin with a folded copy of the Constitution beneath his head. His tomb, decorated with the Stars and Strips, an eagle, and a hand resting on the Constitution, bears the inscription: "His faith never wavered." He had not had time to rebuild his fortune, and his estate of less than seventy-five thousand dollars passed on to his family. Today, Johnson's Greenville home and its original furnishings, as well as the tailor shop he ran as a young man, are historic sites.

Ulysses S. Grant: d. July 23, 1885, age 63

Will signed: No will

Estate value: Complete bankruptcy

Place of rest: Grant's Tomb, New York City

Presidential salary: $25,000 first term; $50,000 second term

The only president known to have played the role of Desdemona in Shakespeare's *Othello* (in an 1845 all-soldier production during the Mexican War), Hiram Ulysses Grant was born in Point Pleasant, Ohio, on April 27, 1822. A heavy smoker who puffed on at least twenty cigars a day, he died an agonizing death from throat cancer, his last word a plea: *"Water!"*

Grant acquired the name "Ulysses S." when at age seventeen he was appointed to the West Point Military Academy by a congressman who erroneously submitted his name as Ulysses Simpson, Simpson being his mother's maiden name. A lackadaisical youth, Grant never bothered to correct the mistake, studied infrequently (graduating twenty-first in a class of thirty-nine), and amassed a slew of demerits for sloppiness and tardiness.

In 1854, at age thirty-two, he married Julia Dent, the daughter of a military man. Resigning from the army after numerous admonitions from commanding officers about his heavy drinking, Grant foundered through a series of undistinguished jobs until the Civil War became his vehicle to success, fame, and the presidency.

The Grants had little money when they moved into the White House in 1869. The annual salary of twenty-five thousand dollars, untaxed, seemed a windfall. During his second term, Congress doubled the presidential salary (which had not changed since Washington's term), and for the first time the money was taxed. The Grants and their children—three sons and a daughter—reveled in their newfound wealth; when their daughter, Nellie, married in the White House, her gown cost five thousand dollars. On leaving office in 1877, the family toured the world for three years, living to the hilt.

Then financial ruin struck.

Settling in New York City—at 3 East Sixty-sixth Street—the ex-president entrusted his finances to a banking firm that was being secretly and systematically looted by one of its owners, Ferdinand Ward. When in 1884 it became clear that the bank was on the verge of collapse, Grant borrowed $150,000 from friend William Vanderbilt to keep the firm solvent and protect his assets. Unwittingly he turned the money over to Ward, who in his desperation absconded. The next day the bank failed.

The sixty-two-year-old Grant was penniless, and at the time he was recovering from pleurisy. Friends contributed money so the family could buy food and other necessities. Vanderbilt generously offered to cancel the debt, but the proud former president would not hear of it. Instead, he transferred to Vanderbilt the deeds to real estate he held in three states, plus ownership to all of the family's furnishings. From a personal fortune of two hundred thousand dollars, with annual income from trusts of fifteen thousand dollars, the Grants were down to pocket change of eighty dollars.

Under the financial stress, Grant's health steadily deteriorated. And things were to get even worse.

Dying, Ulysses S. Grant finished his memoirs, which swelled his bankrupt estate to a half-million dollars.

In October of that year, 1884, while eating dinner, he felt a sharp pain at the base of his tongue. When the sensation spread downward, he passed it off as a sore throat. Forced by his family to consult a doctor, Grant learned he had inoperable cancer, and no more than a year to live. In a race against time to provide for his wife and children, he moved into a cottage in upstate New York, loaned by a friend, and wrote round-the-clock to complete his memoirs. Mark Twain, whose company promised to publish the book, had convinced Grant that the royalties would help support his family. Unable to swallow solid food or to sit up for extended periods of time, he nonetheless finished the manuscript four days before his death on July 23, 1885. The formerly robust war hero weighed less than a hundred pounds.

Grant died without a will and without estate. He owned nothing and had not a penny. But Mark Twain had been right: He sold 300,000 copies of Grant's autobiography, turning over to the former first lady $480,000.

Shortly before his death, unable to speak, Grant wrote out his last wish: to be buried in New York City because "the people of that city befriended me in my need." When he lay in state in New York's City Hall, more than three hundred policemen fought to control a crowd of three hundred thousand mourners who came to see the Civil War hero and president. He was interred in Riverside Park, in a red brick vault, which twelve years later was replaced by the imposing Doric monument that now is a New York landmark.

Rutherford B. Hayes: d. January 17, 1893, age 70

> **Will signed:** April 12, 1890
>
> **Estate value:** More than $100,000
>
> **Place of rest:** Oakwood Cemetery, Fremont, Ohio
>
> **Presidential salary:** $50,000

When Congress complained that the annual Easter egg rolling festivities staged on the Capitol's lawn were gouging the grass, the wife of the nineteenth president, Lucy Webb Hayes, who loved children (and had eight), moved the event to the White House, starting a tradition. That action won her public favor. But her unswerving ban on liquor and wine at state functions gained her applause only from the Woman's Christian Temperance Union, which paid to have her portrait painted. A disgruntled public, though, began calling the first lady Lemonade Lucy.

Lucy Webb married Harvard Law School graduate Rutherford Hayes when he was twenty-nine years old, a decade before he would be wounded four times in the Civil War, then rise to the rank of major general and be elected to Congress while still on the battlefield. After a heated debate, Hayes won the presidency by one electoral vote, the only man to reach the office by such a narrow margin.

Rutherford Hayes banned liquor in the
White House and his wife became known
as Lemonade Lucy.

With their children (then numbering five), the comfortably well-off Hayeses moved to Washington from their twenty-five-acre estate, Spiegel Grove, in Fremont, Ohio. As he'd promised, Hayes pursued a conciliatory policy toward the South, withdrawing troops from the Southern states.

Serving only one term, he retired to Spiegel Grove where he spent the remaining twelve years of his life engaging in many philanthropic projects. By the time he wrote his will, in April of 1890, his wife had been dead a year. The document is brief. It opens on a religious note, "In the name of the Benevolent Father of all," and it bequeaths all of the ex-president's wordly possessions to his children. Spiegel Grove was to be owned jointly by them and sold only when "all parties of the survivors of them agree," at which time the profits were "to belong equally to my said children or their heirs." The will makes no mention of the high office Hayes held.

Hayes lived three years after signing his will. In the winter of 1893, completing a visit to a son in Cleveland, Ohio, the seventy-year-old ex-president suffered a heart attack at the railroad depot. Conscious, he spurned medical help, refused to remain in Cleveland, and insisted he be lifted onto the next train back to his hometown, saying, "I would rather die at Spiegel Grove." Waiting at the unheated depot, he was wrapped in blankets, given brandy to palliate his chest pain, and he did indeed manage to cling to life until he arrived back home. He died that evening, in his own bed, his last words about his wife: *"I know that I am going where Lucy is."*

CHAPTER 5

Bequests & Behests
of Dying Presidents

Garfield to L.B.J.

James A. Garfield: d. September 19, 1881, age 49

Will signed: No will

Estate value: $61,733.06

Place of rest: Lake View Cemetery, Cleveland, Ohio

Presidential salary: $50,000

James Garfield was shot by a would-be assassin but killed by his doctors. His ending is a case of monumental malpractice. At his trial, Charles Guiteau, who fired the probably nonfatal gunshot, shouted, "Your honor, I admit to the shooting of the president, but not the killing."

Guiteau was crazed, but that courtroom utterance was rational and accurate. "Garfield's death," states the 1987 book *Medical Cover-Ups in the White House,* "included all of the worst elements that could be found in a presidential medical crisis: faulty diagnosis, grossly improper treatment, prideful bickering among doctors and a massive cover-up of the truth before and after death. In short, Garfield never had a chance."

The second president to be assassinated, once a professor of Greek and Latin, Garfield served a brief term of office: only two hundred days. On July 2, 1881, he arrived at the Washington railroad depot to depart for a reunion at his alma mater, Williams College in Massachusetts, where he had also taught

An assassin shot Garfield at the Washington depot, but medical malpractice killed the president.

and served as its president. Guiteau, a lawyer, incensed by the rejection of his application for U.S. ambassador to France, had vowed to murder the president, whom he imagined had denied him the foreign post. After stalking Garfield for several days (passing up one opportunity to shoot the president because Mrs. Garfield was present and he considered her "a dear soul"), Guiteau hid in the station, racing from cover when Garfield entered the room. He fired two shots and was apprehended.

The wounded president exclaimed, "My God, what is this?" and collapsed to the floor.

Garfield remained fully conscious, though in traumatic shock. His pulse alternately raced and grew feeble, and his breathing became shallow. He was rushed to the White House, where doctors discovered that one bullet had grazed his arm but the other had lodged internally. Though the president complained of numbness of the legs and feet, which would suggest damage to the spinal cord, several of the physicians believed the troubling bullet rested in the abdomen.

As the doctors argued over the bullet's location and what to do about it, Garfield lingered for eighty days, conducting state business from his bed.

But the lodged bullet was rapidly poisoning his blood. Within a month the once robust, 210-pound president was down to an emaciated 130 pounds, with new infections throughout his lungs. With Washington's summer heat soaring to almost a hundred degrees, Garfield was kept relatively comfortable by a primitive "air cooling" system: rows of cotton towels dampened by ice water that was evaporated by fans. The blood poisoning and related infections finally claimed his life on September 19.

At the autopsy, the bickering doctors discovered they had blundered gravely: Guiteau's bullet had settled about four inches to the right of the spinal cord, resting harmlessly in a bed of tissue. The first doctor to examine the president, Willard Bliss, had first stuck an unwashed finger, then a nonsterile metal instrument, deep into the wound probing for the bullet. Not only had he likely infected the president, but he dug a false passage in tissue that later confused other physicians of the bullet's actual trajectory. Having mistakenly concluded that the bullet penetrated the liver, Bliss projected the president would die quickly from hemorrhage and that an operation on the liver would only exacerbate the bleeding and hasten death.

In all, sixteen doctors consulted on Garfield's condition; several worsened that condition.

The army surgeon general stuck his unwashed finger into the wound and dug as deep as the president's ribs. The navy surgeon general probed so extensively with his unwashed finger that he actually punctured the liver, destroying its protective outer covering. He agreed with Bliss that the liver was violated (as it now was) and that the president would be dead within twenty-four hours from internal bleeding.

Days passed and Garfield did not die. His fever climbed (from multiple infections) and he was put on a diet of only brandy-spiked milk. His doctors puzzled that he had "not improved in strength." Worse, they persisted, with unclean fingers and instruments, to poke inside the wound for the lost bullet. The gross damage: They turned a three-inch-deep, harmless hole into a twenty-inch-long contaminated canal stretching from the president's ribs to his groin and oozing more pus each day. The doctors themselves had produced most of the infection and all of the hemorrhaging that disrupted the president's bowels, bladder, and eventually beclouded his mind. Their ineptness, combined with the bullet's poisoning, fatally weakened Garfield's heart.

Even a massive heart attack was a botched diagnosis: Clawing at his chest Garfield moaned, *"This pain, this pain."* But his doctors claimed it was only a blood vessel rupturing in the stomach. Minutes later Bliss said to the first lady, "It's all over. He's dead."

The Washington Post was the first of several papers to accuse the doctors of malpractice. When the treating physicians submitted their bill of eighty-five thousand dollars, the Senate authorized payment of only ten thousand dollars, privately denounced the doctors as quacks, and pointed to them as the real assassins. Bliss was forced to admit publicly that he had erred.

Only 49 when he died, Garfield left no will. He had collected only a portion of his $50,000 salary, and his estate, passing on to his family, was valued at $61,733.06. Just weeks before taking office, he had providentially taken out a life insurance policy for $25,000 with his wife as beneficiary. And Congress, a year after the president's death, awarded his widow an annual pension of $5,000 plus a lump sum of $50,000.

Guiteau's Ending. Charles Julius Guiteau was hanged for assassinating the president about one year after the shooting.

Bizarrely, the day of the incident, Guiteau had a hansom cab waiting at the depot to take him directly to jail, terrified an angry mob might lynch him. As Washington police dragged him from the station, he even pleaded, "I *wish* to go to jail." Stranger yet, only days before the assassination he had visited the Washington jail to evaluate its amenities and liked what he saw: "An excellent jail." He was crazed, but also savvy.

Both states of mind were on display at his trial. Given his legal training, he acted in part as his own defense attorney, aided by his brother-in-law, George Scoville, a Chicago lawyer. Scoville's defense was insanity, for which there was ample evidence: Guiteau had a long history of erratic, violent behavior as well as a family tree of institutionalized relatives. Guiteau, however, used the then uncommon defense of medical malpractice. Alternately ranting irrationally and reasoning brilliantly, he concluded that the president's doctors were the murderers, abetted in their deed by the will of God.

To support the claim that he had only harmlessly wounded the president, he introduced newspaper accounts and doctors' journals. "According to the physicians' statements," he said, "the president was not fatally shot on the 25th of July, at the time they made the official examination, and said he would recover." He cursed the judge, the jury, and at one point lambasted the prosecutor as "a low-livered whelp." But he calmly summed up his claim: "If he was not fatally shot . . . we say that his death was caused by malpractice. My defense here is that it is the Deity's act and not mine."

After five minutes of deliberation, he was found guilty of murdering the president. Shaking a finger at the jury he snarled, "You are all low, consummate jackasses!" He was sentenced to the death he feared most—hanging, to be carried out at Washington's Old Capitol Prison on June 30, 1882.

Guiteau's sister, aware of her brother's dread of the hangman's noose, visited him in prison carrying a bouquet of flowers that concealed a vial of arsenic; but his suicide was prevented. Jailers claimed that he even slept in terror of hanging, blankets clutched protectively over his neck, and that he awoke screaming from nightmares of dangling at the end of a rope. On the actual scaffold, the forty-one-year-old political malcontent recited a poem he composed for the occasion—"I am going to the Lordy . . ."—then shouted his farewell: *"Glory, hallelujah! Glory!"*

Government officials refused to turn Guiteau's body over to his family or to bury it. They had other plans. Army physicians stripped the corpse of all tissue, tendons, and organs with the intention of slaking the public's anger over the assassination by publicly displaying his skeleton. Admission was to be free. Sensibly, this was never done. Doctors did, however, progress as far as producing a cleanly bleached skeleton. The surgeon general, C. H. Crane, took custody of the dismantled bones and is supposed to have secretly disposed of them. However, historians believe that the bones, divided among several metal trays, are in the huge storage vaults of the Army Medical Museum.

Mourners in Washington, deprived of a glimpse of the assassin's mounted frame, satisfied themselves by choosing among the souvenirs that went on sale throughout the capital. There were pictures of Guiteau dangling from the scaffold, facsimiles of the murder bullet, and many snippets of the hanging rope—too many to be authentic.

Chester A. Arthur: d. November 18, 1886, age 56

Will signed: March 8, 1886

Estate value: $161,000

Place of rest: Albany Rural Cemetery, Albany, New York

Presidential salary: $50,000

Upon the assassination of James Garfield, the presidency passed to Chester Alan Arthur, long believed to have been born in Fairfield, Vermont, on October 5, 1830. But recent evidence favors the charge, leveled in Arthur's own lifetime by his opponents, that he was really Canadian-born and therefore ineligible under the Constitution to be an American president.

At age twenty-eight, a successful New York City lawyer, he married Ellen Lewis Herndon, daughter of a Virginia naval officer. His well-documented problems with money and corruption date from this period in his life. The Customs House of the Port of New York was already notorious for financial wrongdoing when Arthur took over the agency at a salary of forty-six thousand dollars, almost what he'd soon make as president. Though not himself corrupt, Arthur did not rock the boat of patronage abuses among New York politicians and even condoned many questionable activities—things he would work to rectify on a national level as president.

When he assumed the presidency in 1881, his wife had been dead a year from pneumonia. His widowed sister became the White House hostess as well as surrogate mother to his son and daughter.

Though the executive mansion had been restored and redecorated after the fire of 1814, Arthur, with a penchant for heavy Victorian clutter, insisted on a

Chester Arthur auctioned off White House antiques to fill the mansion with Victorian clutter.

total revamping. He hired the pricey Louis Tiffany to refurbish rooms and add stained glass wherever possible. The "old" furniture, twenty-four carts of historically irreplaceable items dating back to Washington's presidency, Arthur auctioned off—all for three thousand dollars. He installed the White House's first elevator and modernized the bathrooms with tiles and the latest plumbing and toilet fixtures. And to ensure elegant dining, he employed a French chef and a steward from one of New York's best restaurants. Living well, he saved not a dollar from his presidential salary.

Nine months before he died, the fifty-six-year-old ex-president, who had returned to New York City, wrote his will. Most of his worth of $161,000 dated from the days before and after his presidency. "To my faithful and devoted servant Bridget Smith," his family's cook who had accompanied him to Washington and then back to New York, he bequeathed $500. Most of the balance of the fortune went to his son, Chester Alan, and daughter, Ellen Herndon.

At 8:00 A.M. on November 17, 1886, Bridget Smith entered Arthur's bedroom with his breakfast. He was conscious, eyes opened, but could not respond to her questions. A doctor informed the family that the ex-president had suffered a stroke and might not recover. Throughout the night his breathing grew erratic and alarmingly shallow. His children sat by the bed and they later claimed that their father had fixated on the ticking of a large mantel clock and used its rhythm to will his breathing. At sunrise the next morning, he lost the battle. A funeral service was held at the Church of the Heavenly Rest on Fifth Avenue, and one of the pallbearers was Robert Todd Lincoln, son of Abraham Lincoln.

Grover Cleveland: d. June 24, 1908, age 71

> **Will signed:** February 21, 1906
>
> **Estate value:** $250,000
>
> **Place of rest:** Princeton Cemetery, Princeton, New Jersey
>
> **Presidential salary:** $50,000

Hangman Grover Cleveland, age thirty-three and sheriff of Erie County, New York—and no opponent to capital punishment—personally placed the rope, tightened the knot, blindfolded the eyes, and sprang the trapdoor for two convicted criminals. Later, the man born Stephen Grover Cleveland (he dropped Stephen early in life) would be both the twenty-second and twenty-fourth presidents, the only chief executive to serve two nonconsecutive terms.

From New York sheriff to mayor to governor to president, the ascent was meteoric for Cleveland, a climb so rapid he had no chance to marry. For a time, his sister Rose served as official hostess, but there was a real first lady waiting in the wings. Frances Folsom, age twenty-one, was the attractive daughter of one of Cleveland's business partners who had died when the girl was eleven, naming Cleveland her ward. They wed fifteen months after his inauguration, Cleveland explaining, "I was waiting for my wife to grow up." He became the first president married in the White House (he promised to love, honor, and comfort, he'd not say "obey"). She was the youngest first lady, as well as the first to give birth in the executive mansion, to Ester; in all, the couple would have five children.

In 1888, Cleveland was defeated by Benjamin Harrison. But on leaving the White House the young—and either confident or prophetic—first lady turned to the servants and instructed them to leave "everything as it is," since they would be returning in four years.

When the sixty-nine-year-old ex-president wrote his will, the couple was living at their thirty-thousand-dollar home, Westland, in Princeton, New Jersey. One child had died, and Cleveland bequeathed each of the surviving four, ranging in age from two to twelve, ten thousand dollars. The bulk of his quarter-million-dollar estate he left to his wife.

Cleveland had not been well for some time. During the first year of his second term, 1893, the president developed a sore on the roof of his mouth. A heavy cigar smoker, he feared the worst and for weeks avoided a medical examination. By the time a dentist studied the mark, it was "an ulcerative surface nearly as large as a quarter with cauliflower granulations and crater edges." It resembled a syphilitic lesion, and one physician questioned the president about his alleged promiscuity as a young man (he had fathered an illegitimate child). Under a microscope, though, the tissue appeared to be malignant.

White House Cover-Up. The grim diagnosis (and it may not have been correct) came at a time when the nation was in the throes of a severe economic crisis. Thus the ailment and planned surgery were kept secret. (White House secrets could still be kept in those days.) It was decided that the operation should take place under the guise of a pleasure cruise.

On July 1, the private yacht *Oneida* sailed up Manhattan's East River with the anesthetized fifty-six-year-old president aboard, propped up in a chair lashed to the mast. Two surgeons, W. W. Keen and J. D. Bryant, and dentist F. Hasbrouch, first extracted two left upper bicuspids, then worked rapidly to remove most of Cleveland's upper jaw, since the disease had metastasized. One out of seven patients died from the procedure, usually from hemorrhaging. "If the president dies during the surgery," said Keen, unaware of the identity of his patient until Cleveland boarded the boat, "I hope the yacht sinks and we all drown."

Remarkably, the president strolled unaided off the yacht at his summer retreat in Buzzard's Bay, Massachusetts.

When a second "pleasure cruise" was scheduled to remove further tissue, newspapermen became suspicious. None fell for the press-release excuse of a simple tooth extraction; one coaxed Hasbrouch to indiscretion. (He had already told several dentist colleagues.) By the time the real story broke in the *Philadelphia Press,* Cleveland, wearing a horribly uncomfortable rubber prosthesis that at least restored his appearance, was addressing Congress, if not in his old voice, in an equally vigorous one. Not until 1917, when Dr. Keen donated the

Grover Cleveland, who observed that "Public office is a public trust," engaged in a White House medical cover-up.

president's excised jaw to Philadelphia's Mutter Museum and published a detailed account of the surgeries, was the story officially acknowledged.

It was not the cancer that killed Grover Cleveland.

Today there is strong evidence that what the president actually had was a verrucous carcinoma, a rather harmless tumor that resembles a wart and is not uncommon among heavy tobacco chewers. If this modern diagnosis is correct, the radical surgery Cleveland received was unwarranted; a simple and completely safe surgery would have sufficed. Considering the medical knowledge of the time, the doctors probably proceeded wisely in an attempt to save the life of a president who was just beginning an ambitious second term.

Cleveland actually died from either a heart attack, an intestinal obstruction, or a stroke, depending on which doctor's report one reads. It is clear that the ex-president was sick much of the last year of his life, though his family continually denied press reports. The day before his death, he drifted in and out of consciousness, intermittently coherent when he spoke, though there was nothing ambiguous in his final phrase: *"I have tried so hard to do right."*

After his death, the family finally admitted he had been sick, in a typewritten notice that also announced that the funeral would be "strictly private." And it was. After a Princeton sculptor cast a death mask, there was a simple service at the Presbyterian Church where no hymns or eulogies were heard. Only the immediate family, a few friends, and President Theodore Roosevelt accompanied the casket to Princeton Cemetery.

Benjamin Harrison: d. March 13, 1901, age 67

Will signed: April 20, 1899

Estate value: $375,000

Place of rest: Crown Hill Cemetery, Indianapolis, Indiana

Presidential salary: $50,000

Benjamin Harrison, born in North Bend, Ohio, on August 20, 1833, was the only grandson of a chief executive to also hold that office. He was also the president responsible for having the White House wired for electricity, though there were times the first couple questioned the wisdom of that innovation.

In the early 1890s, during Harrison's term, Thomas Edison's incandescent bulb was an impressive and intimidating invention. Much of the country was not yet "electrified," and the marvel of electricity so delighted and frightened Harrison and his wife, Caroline Lavinia Scott, they were afraid to flick off a switch for fear of electrocution—at that time, the newest form of capital punishment. Newspapers were filled with the latest experiments in electrocuting animals in an attempt to perfect an electric chair for humans. And just prior to the White House being wired, that goal had been achieved: On August 6, 1890, ax murderer William Kemmler was electrocuted with horrifying first-time ineptness. (See "First Electrocution," page 156) Little wonder that people feared an electric wire, a socket, a switch. So terrified was the first lady to turn off White House lights, or to allow her husband to do so, that bulbs often blazed throughout the night, even in the couple's bedroom as they slept.

In the last months of Harrison's administration, his wife died. His profound mourning cut into his campaigning for reelection and he lost to Grover Cleveland.

Benjamin Harrison had the White House wired for electricity but the first lady, fearing electrocution, would not touch a switch.

Age 60, the ex-president and his two children retreated to their home in Indianapolis. In less than 3 years, Harrison shocked his children when he married his wife's niece, Mary Scott Lord, who had served as a White House secretary. Neither child attended the wedding, and the action estranged Harrison from the family. In his will, however, Harrison bequeathed a large portion of his $375,000 estate to his two children by his first wife. The one child Mary Scott Lord bore him received $125,000.

His life was ended by a cold caught in March 1901 that turned quickly into pneumonia. Death was "quite sudden and unexpected," read a statement released by the family, who until the end expected him to recover. "Statesman," reads the epitaph on his tombstone at Crown Hill Cemetery, "yet friend to truth of soul sincere. In action faithful, and in honour clear."

William McKinley: d. September 14, 1901, age 58

Will signed: October 22, 1897

Estate value: $215,000

Place of rest: McKinley Tomb, Canton, Ohio

Presidential salary: $50,000

The twenty-fifth president, a devoted husband who kept his frail, depressive, and epileptic wife continually by his side, was only six months into his second term when he was assassinated, the third American president to meet his end through violence.

At the Pan-American Exposition in Buffalo, New York, at noon on September 6, 1901, McKinley was shaking hands with fairgoers excited about meeting a president face-to-face. A short dark-haired man, age twenty-eight, who had suffered a nervous breakdown three years earlier and was known to police as a dangerous anarchist, waited patiently in line. His head was bent downward and his bogusly bandaged hand concealed a gun.

Secret Service men gently nudged the crowd up to the president, known for his fifty-people-a-minute handshake. One bodyguard stared at the man with the bandaged hand, but when the man glanced back calmly, the guard ushered him up to the president. In three minutes the reception was due to end. As McKinley, smiling, reached for the man's "good" left hand, the right hand quickly produced a gun. The first shot hit a button and richocheted away from the president, the second penetrated his abdomen.

McKinley, conscious, stiffened and held himself erect as police wrestled with the attacker. "I done my duty," shouted Leon Czolgosz, which prompted one officer to drive a punch into Czolgosz's face. "Be easy with him, boys," the president said weakly.

The injured president was rushed to an ill-lighted, inadequately equipped exposition emergency tent set up to treat fainting fairgoers and nauseated children. The only doctor around, a local gynecologist, Matthew Mann, did the best he could to clean and suture McKinley's internal and external wounds. The bullet, though, which had pierced completely through the stomach, could not be retrieved.

The president asked to see his wife and was taken to the home of the exposition's director, where she was staying, too ill to attend the fair. Chronically ill—from phlebitis, deep depression, and epilepsy—the first lady was grieving the death in infancy of two daughters and was confined to a wheelchair. The shock of her husband's arrival on a stretcher brought her to her feet, and over the next seven days she found the strength to help nurse him.

Nursing alone, though, could not save the president. Doctors never inserted a drainage tube into his abdomen, and McKinley developed a rabidly gangrenous infection. Nor did they test his urine for abnormal levels of sugar, which would have revealed that the insulin-secreting pancreas was nearly destroyed and threatened to kill him faster than the gangrene. As his fever soared and consciousness flickered, he was unable to take nourishment except rectally through enemas.

He rallied briefly on September 13 and said to his doctors, "It is useless, gentlemen. I think we ought to have prayer." On the following day, profusely sweating and quivering with chills, he murmured his last words: *"We are all going. . . . We are all going. . . . Oh, dear."*

McKinley left a will, written four years before his death, bequeathing everything to his wife, Ida Saxton, daughter of a wealthy banker. His devotion to her had been extraordinary by any measure. Instead of hiding a wife who frequently experienced embarrassing facial spasms and seizures, McKinley took the first lady to state functions and dinners, and when her head jerked and muscles twitched, he held a handkerchief over her face until the spell passed.

Though wealthy when he died, with an estate valued at $215,000, he had been bankrupt when he and his wife moved into the White House in 1897. He had lost his own savings and his wife's inheritance of $100,000, by loaning money to a boyhood friend, Robert Walker, who went bankrupt, taking the soon to be first couple with him. From wisely investing a large portion of his $50,000-a-year presidential salary, he had during his first term in office rebuilt his fortune. Ida McKinley survived her husband by only 6 years.

Czolgosz's Ending. At New York's Auburn Prison the recently perfected electric chair waited for McKinley's assassin. Born in Detroit and reared in northern Michigan, Czolgosz had been living in Buffalo for several weeks before the president's arrival at the exposition. The police knew he was dangerous, and *Free Society,* an anarchist publication that Czolgosz praised, publicly urged its readers to avoid him as a hotheaded crank and possible spy.

Czolgosz went on trial nine days after McKinley's death. With a vacant face and inert body, he appeared to take no interest in the proceedings. Refusing to speak with his court-appointed lawyers, he also declined to take the stand and he revealed no expression when one day later the court pronounced him guilty and sentenced him to death by electrocution.

Early on the morning of October 29, 1901, Czolgosz was strapped into Auburn's electric chair. For the first time he had something to say: *"I killed the President because he was the enemy of the good people—the good working people. I am not sorry for my crime."* His corpse was autopsied primarily to study his brain, the suspicion in those days being that gross criminality could be read in the cranium. His normal cranium seemed to refute the theory.

Czolgosz's brother demanded the body, but prison authorities would not release it. Afraid that enraged citizens might attempt to snatch Czolgosz's corpse from the grave, authorities—after the open coffin was lowered into an unmarked site—poured sulfuric acid over the body, predicting that it would decompose within twelve hours. His clothes and personal possessions were incinerated. Only later was it learned that the assassin's brother's insistence on being given the corpse had nothing to do with family loyalty and everything to do with profit: A New York crime museum had offered the brother five thousand dollars for permission to display the body.

Theodore Roosevelt: d. January 6, 1919, age 60

> **Will signed:** December 13, 1912
>
> **Estate value:** $811,000
>
> **Place of rest:** Young's Memorial Cemetery, Oyster Bay, New York
>
> **Presidential salary:** $50,000

Following the assassination of McKinley, his successor, Theodore Roosevelt, took to carrying a gun in public so he would, as he liked to say, "have some chance of shooting the assassin before he could shoot me"—not at all surprising behavior for America's first cowboy president.

In his twenties Roosevelt had sought work as a cowboy on a ranch in the Dakota Territory, rounding up cattle, hiking, hunting, and fishing in the wilderness. He had gone west at age twenty-six to assuage his grief over the death—on the same day in 1884—of both his wife, Alice Hathaway Lee, and his mother, Martha Bullock Roosevelt. For two years he lived the arduous, outdoors life of a cowboy, acquiring a love for nature that as president would lead him to create the country's first national park, Yellowstone. While ranching, he ventured into a cattle deal that lost him fifty thousand dollars, but even then Teddy Roosevelt was rich enough easily to take the loss.

Born in New York City, into the wealthiest family circumstances of any American president up to his time, the young Roosevelt was privately tutored, dividing his summers between his parents' retreat in the Adirondacks and their estate in Oyster Bay, Long Island. While at Harvard his father died, and Roosevelt inherited $125,000. He used the money to purchase (for $30,000) 155 acres of scenic hilltop land in Oyster Bay, on which he built a magnificent 23-room home (for $17,000) named Sagamore Hill for himself and his wife, who would die in less than 4 years.

The reputation he acquired as head of the Rough Riders fighting in the Spanish-American War led to his election as governor of New York in 1898. Two years later he was McKinley's vice president. Only forty-two when McKinley was assassinated, Roosevelt became the youngest man at that time to hold the executive office. Already remarried—to his wealthy childhood friend, Edith Kermit Carow—Roosevelt populated the White House with four boys and one girl from his second marriage and a daughter, Alice, from his first. Entertainment under the first lady was more frequent, if not more lavish, than under Dolley Madison. None of her predecessors had thrown more White House parties.

The president who expressed his foreign policy with the aphorism "Speak softly and carry a big stick" and won a Nobel peace prize for ending the war between Russia and Japan met his end abruptly and unexpectedly, though he had had several prior brushes with death: As a Rough Rider he was injured in battle; as president a carriage he was riding in collided with a trolley car and he was thrown forty feet through the air; as ex-president he was shot in the chest, his life saved by the metal spectacle case in his breast pocket (the bullet, which penetrated three inches, was never removed). These he survived.

But while exploring in South America five years after leaving office, Roosevelt suffered a leg abscess that left him lame and drained his health. In addition, he experienced inflammatory rheumatism and acute mastoiditis, which left him deaf. Yet the single event that struck the aged ex-president the hardest was news in July 1918 that one of his sons had died in a plane crash.

A half-year later, on January 5, 1919, Roosevelt—ill, depressed, but not ostensibly near death—climbed into bed at his Sagamore Hill home. To his butler, James Amos, he made the usual nightly request: *"Please put out the light."* During the night, Amos noticed that Roosevelt's breathing slowed and was shallow, and he summoned a nurse. By the time help arrived, Roosevelt had stopped breathing altogether. No autopsy was performed, but the cause of death was officially stated to be coronary embolism.

A Modern Last Testament.   Seven years earlier, Roosevelt had written his will. In the interim his worth had grown to $811,000, making his estate the largest of any president up to that time. He bequeathed all his silver to his children. The former first lady was made chief beneficiary, and upon her death the property was to pass to his descendants. But for the colorful, adventurous man Roosevelt was, he left an extraordinarily bland will—that is, the first truly "modern" presidential will.

The wills of earlier presidents, many composed by the men themselves, reveal each man's voice, penchants, prejudices, personal indebtedness to his Creator, and affections for those he himself created. They abound with personal niceties: "to my beloved wife," "for my ever obedient children," "in thanks to my humble and faithful servant."

By contrast, the modern will reveals nothing personal about the to-be-deceased. Written in legalese, it reflects the convoluted machinations of legal minds attempting to protect the deceased's last wishes from lawsuits. George Washington, for instance, bequeathed in a simple paragraph thirty-three thousand acres of land in six states. Today it would takes pages of jargon to protect so valuable an inheritance. Starting with the will of Roosevelt, presidential testaments become unrelentingly dull and complex, obsessed with tax shelters, trust funds, stocks, securities, annuities, corporate contributions, pork bellies, and insurance policies.

In Roosevelt's will children become "issues" and the man behind the document is known only as the "Testator"—a valid enough word, though it sounds more like the title of an Arnold Schwarzenegger movie. And, too, starting with Roosevelt, a president's will is no longer "signed"; it is "Subscribed, sealed, published, acknowledged, and declared by [of course] the Testator."

One final note of interest: It is perhaps reassuring to know that every one of America's chief executives takes every legal means allowed to slap the taxing hand of Uncle Sam.

William H. Taft: d. March 8, 1930, age 72

Will signed: April 27, 1927

Estate value: $475,000

Place of rest: Arlington National Cemetery, Arlington, Virginia

Presidential salary: $75,000 plus $25,000 travel allowance

William Taft entered the White House at age 51, the fattest president ever, weighing 325 at his inauguration, and he installed the famous "luxury-size" bathtub. Though he distinguished himself with a thoroughly honest (if unspectacular) administration, he's also known for starting two executive office traditions: He was the first president to play golf and the first to toss the ball to open the baseball season.

He came to the White House by way of a ten-thousand-dollar-a-year job as tax collector for the IRS, handpicked by his successor, Theodore Roosevelt—though his real ambition was to serve on the Supreme Court. The first president to keep a car at the executive mansion (actually four: a Baker Electric, a White Steamer, and two Pierce Arrows), Taft benefited from Congress's increase of the presidential salary from fifty thousand to seventy-five thousand dollars and the addition of a twenty-five-thousand-dollar travel allowance. Taft, though, was no big spender. With the help of his frugal wife, Helen Herron, he saved over one hundred thousand dollars from his four years of paychecks.

The first lady was an educated, well-traveled woman. On a trip to Tokyo, she was impressed with a profusion of flowering trees and became instrumental in the planting in 1912 of three thousand Japanese cherry blossoms along the Potomac.

In time Taft got his lifelong wish. Eight years after leaving office, he was appointed chief justice of the Supreme Court, the only person ever to hold the country's two most powerful offices. In his last year on the bench, 1930, he experienced the dizziness, breathlessness, and heart flutter of severe hardening

Taft (right) and Roosevelt fish for delegates. First lady plants three thousand Japanese cherry blossoms.

of the arteries and was hospitalized in February. There were no such treatments as a heart bypass or balloon angioplasty, and his health steadily deteriorated; he passed the time reading detective stories.

During the night of March 8, while sleeping, he suffered a heart attack and never woke.

Three years earlier he had composed a will. He bequeathed Yale University, where he had served as Kent Professor of Law, $10,000, noting it was to be "credited to the class anniversary fund of the Academic Class of 1878," his own undergraduate class. The All Souls Unitarian Church in Washington, where he and his wife had worshiped, received $2,500, and his three children received "All my papers, manuscripts, correspondence, addresses and copyrights." The bulk of his $475,000 estate went to his wife, who survived him by 13 years, dying on May 22, 1943. His last wish—that his funeral service contain no eulogy or sermon—was reluctantly observed, and he became the first president laid to rest at Arlington National Cemetery.

Woodrow Wilson: d. February 3, 1924, age 67

> **Will signed:** May 31, 1917
>
> **Estate value:** $600,000
>
> **Place of rest:** National Cathedral, Washington, D.C.
>
> **Presidential salary:** $75,000 plus $25,000 travel allowance

The only American president with a doctorate (in political science from Johns Hopkins University, with a thesis "Congressional Government, a Study in American Politics"), Thomas Woodrow Wilson, son of a Presbyterian minister, married Ellen Axson, daughter of a Presbyterian minister, a woman of great common sense and sound political judgment who, only months after moving into the White House, died of Bright's disease, leaving Wilson with three daughters.

The fifty-eight-year-old president, while mourning the wife he dearly loved, met and married the widow of a Washington jeweler, Edith Bolling Galt. Criticism from the public, press, and especially Wilson's political opponents—all felt the president had not grieved long enough—was relentless and harsh. The new first lady was unfairly disliked, though soon she would be widely despised, charged with usurping the presidency during Wilson's debilitating illness. "Mrs. President" became her label, with her reign referred to as "Mrs. Wilson's Regency."

At the close of World War I, when Wilson traveled to Paris for the peace conference, he became the first American president to visit Europe while in office. Crowds in Britain and France greeted him with unprecedented honors, and he used his prestige to promote his concept of the League of Nations. But back home, refusal of the Senate to ratify the Versailles Treaty launched Wilson on a national speaking tour, despite doctors' advice. This marked the start of his decline in health.

First Lady's Ascendancy.   The tour was exhausting and the president returned to the White House for a brief rest. On the morning of October 2, 1919, Mrs. Wilson found her husband unconscious on the bathroom floor. His head had struck the sink and was bleeding. Bypassing the White House switchboard because operators might leak information, the first lady used a private phone to call Dr. Cary Grayson, the president's physician. Thus began one of the most celebrated medical cover-ups in the history of the American presidency.

Wilson had suffered a massive stroke, which paralyzed the left side of his body, impaired his vision, and would produce bizarre changes in his personality and judgment. The strong-willed first lady decided that the country should learn of the president's "ailment" only in sugared bits and easy-to-swallow pieces. A string of press releases contained phrases like: "nervous exhaustion," "not alarming," "the President had a fairly good night," "his condition is less favorable today," "absolute rest is essential for some time."

No one besides the first lady and the medical team had the slightest idea that the president of the United States had suffered a debilitating stroke. During this initial crisis state, America's newspapers headlined the mystifying losses in the World Series by the heavily favored Chicago White Sox to the Cincinnati Reds. It would be a year before the country learned that the Sox had thrown the games and the series, even longer before the truth about the president would be published.

For seventeen months the office of chief executive was filled by a frail, incapacitated, hallucinating man on the brink of death, too weak to sign his name.

First Lady Edith Wilson later described this period as her "stewardship."

With the complicity of Dr. Grayson, she shielded her husband from contact with virtually everyone, playing the roles of nurse, executive secretary, and, by many accounts, chief executive. All matters of state were submitted to the president in writing through the first lady. Then she would pass into the president's sickroom, close the door, and emerge later with "his wishes" written in her hand.

The unsteady signature "Woodrow Wilson" on official documents was said by the first lady to be a result of the president's weakness; but even Cabinet members suspected they were the first lady's forgeries. On virtually every policy decision for a year and a half, as well as on official appointments to government offices, the Cabinet had to take Mrs. Wilson's word as the expressed wish of the president.

"The consensus among historians and political scientists," write the authors of *Medical Cover-Ups in the White House,* "is that the republic underwent a dangerous and unconstitutional transference of power."

Eventually Congress would pass the Twenty-fifth Amendment to the Constitution: "Presidential Disability and Succession." But there was no such provision at the time, and the president's disability critically influenced national policy and possibly even the prospects of future world peace. "A strong argument can—and has—been made," says *Medical Cover-Ups,* "that had Wilson not been impaired he could have won Senate approval for American membership in the League [of Nations], a step that many historians contend conceivably could have prevented World War II."

Wilson had already dictated his will when he left office in 1919 for his townhouse in Washington, D.C., where he would live out his last three years. The $150,000 townhouse was purchased with the help of contributions of $10,000 from each of 10 friends who wished to assist the disabled president. One contributor, business tycoon Bernard Baruch, also bought the lot adjacent to the house so the first couple could have extra privacy.

Several smaller strokes had taken their toll on Wilson's vision, speech, and coordination as well as interfered with bowel and renal functions. Near the end, on February 3, 1924, the sixty-seven-year-old ex-president shook his head at one of the doctors about to minister to him, saying, *"The machinery is just worn out. I'm ready."* He died that night, peacefully in his sleep.

His will is brief—five short paragraphs—and unlike most modern wills of contemporary presidents, it displays some affection: His widow is mentioned three times as "my beloved wife Edith," no child is an "issue," nor is Wilson himself anywhere the "testator." Edith Wilson received the bulk of the six-hundred-thousand-dollar estate, with his children sharing in handsome portions. He requested a small, private funeral, which he received at Washington's National Cathedral.

When asked about where he would like to be buried, Wilson had shaken his head and said that in a cemetery as large and significant as Arlington he would find it hard to "rest easily." His body was entombed in a vault at the National Cathedral, the only president buried there.

Warren G. Harding: d. August 2, 1923, age 57

Will signed: June 20, 1923

Estate value: $930,444.54

Place of rest: Marion Cemetery, Marion, Ohio

Presidential salary: $75,000 plus $25,000 travel expenses

The only president rumored to have black blood in his ancestry, Warren Harding, and his wife, Florence Kling De Wolfe, a divorcee five years his senior, were the first presidential couple to die during a president's administration—in this case, one of the most corrupt administrations in American politics. Though Prohibition outlawed wine and liquor from White House parties, Harding kept his own stock for a circle of intimates, which included tire magnate Harvey Firestone, Henry Ford, and Thomas Edison.

Born on November 2, 1865, on a farm outside of Blooming Grove, Ohio (where rumors of his black ancestry originated and persisted), Warren Gamaliel Harding married into money at age twenty-five. Florence Kling De Wolfe, a stern, authoritative, cold woman, was the daughter of a wealthy banker, and it was her money, as well as her insistent prodding that Harding achieve success, that helped him forge a political career. One noted historian described Harding as a "semieducated political hack," with a "large taste for women, liquor and poker," possessing "an utterly empty mind," and "probably the least qualified candidate ever nominated by a major party."

Their marriage was stormy, though not passionate; Harding sought sympathetic female companionship elsewhere, fathering an illegitimate daughter and secretly supporting the child and her mother.

He had become enamored with the mother, Nan Britton, when she was a girl of twelve and he was forty-two and soon to be a senator. Their romance intensified, with clandestine rendezvous in Washington and sexual relations in the Senate office building, and it eventually led to the birth of a daughter in October 1919. The next year Harding became president, and to conceal the child's parentage, she was secretly adopted by Nan Britton's married sister. All this Harding was able to keep hidden for years—from his wife and the press. "I'm glad you're a boy," his father once told him, "because if you were a girl, you'd always be in a family way."

Florence Harding occupied herself by throwing huge garden parties at the White House. Meanwhile, Harding surrounded himself with public officials all of whom were mediocre, and some of them corrupt. Soon he was troubled by impending revelations of gross misconduct involving improper actions by several Cabinet members, other high government officials, the Interior Department, and the Veterans Administration. It was the beginning of the Teapot Dome scandal, which would disgrace his administration, and Harding, like several later presidents, was besieged with questions: What did the president know? When did he know it?

As the vortex of scandal expanded, public misdeeds regularly leaked to the press. At the same time, Harding feared his passionate affair with Nan Britton would also become public. For the fifty-seven-year-old president, less than two years in office and with a history of heart trouble, the combined pressures were too great. In the glare of disgrace and under the looming cloud of impeachment, Harding eagerly left Washington in the summer of 1923 to tour Alaska.

Final Days. He was in Alaska only weeks when he received a ciphered message from Washington. The contents caused him to collapse on the spot. Corruption in his administration was far worse than anyone had imagined. Feeling betrayed by the people he had entrusted with the country's survival, he began the train trip home, reaching only San Francisco before falling gravely ill.

The chest pains had not let up since Seattle, the abdominal cramps were more acute, his fever higher. The diagnosis shifted from "gastric upset" (brought on, as one Seattle physician diagnosed, "from eating rotten crabs") to "mild cardiac seizure." Though his heart was rapidly failing, in his weakened state pneumonia took hold of his lungs. (Later, after his somewhat mysterious death, when all possible causative agents were under scrutiny, it would be learned that he had never eaten crab.)

On August 2, the day he would die, Harding was feeling considerably improved. He sat up in bed, ate breakfast and lunch, then following dinner his wife Florence read to him from the *Saturday Evening Post.* The article, "A Calm View of a Calm Man," suggested that the public, and especially Harding's political foes, withhold a character assassination of the president until the full details of the scandal were revealed. He liked what he heard and at one point said, *"That's good. Go on. Read some more."* But he heard no more, expiring suddenly, said his wife, in a convulsion.

The first lady phoned for Harding's two personal physicians. They found him dead and pronounced the cause of death a stroke. Other physicians claimed that a more likely diagnosis was a massive heart attack and internal hemorrhaging. His wife would not permit an autopsy. That, combined with the hostilities in their marriage, led to inside Washington rumors that the first lady, fed up with her husband's extramarital affairs, had poisoned him.

Today it is thought that Warren Harding experienced a massive heart attack following years of suffering from cardiac asthma. It is characterized by a heart too weak to pump blood from the lungs, causing puddling there. The fluid-clogged lungs result in labored breathing, bluish lips, and a gurgling noise, the so-called death rattle. Harding exhibited all of the symptoms.

It was while the Teapot Dome scandal was brewing that Harding wrote his will, in June 1923, the same month he fled Washington for Alaska. It opens in an anachronistic fashion: "IN THE NAME OF THE BENEVOLENT FATHER OF ALL: I, Warren G. Harding . . ." The will lists many beneficiaries—a church, a park, friends, family, his father—but most of the nearly one-million-dollar estate went to the first lady who, unfortunately, died a little more than a year after her husband, before his term would have expired. In life Harding had provided amply for his mistress and illegitimate daughter (whom he never once saw), but they are not mentioned in his will.

Calvin Coolidge: d. January 5, 1933, age 60

Will signed: December 20, 1926

Estate value: $500,000

Place of rest: Notch Cemetery, Plymouth, Vermont

Presidential salary: $75,000 plus $25,000 travel allowance

Whereas it was rumored that Warren Harding had black blood in his ancestry, it is fact that John Calvin Coolidge descended from Indians on one side of his family, the only American president with Indian blood.

Born on the Fourth of July, 1872, in Plymouth, Vermont, Coolidge attended Amherst College and remained a bachelor until age thirty-three when he married Grace Anna Goodhue, daughter of an engineer. Not until ten years later did he run for his first major public office, and within five years he was Warren Harding's vice president. In August of 1923, Coolidge was vacationing at his father's home in Plymouth when he received news of Harding's sudden death. His father, a notary public, administered the oath of office in the family living room. "Keep Cool and Keep Coolidge" was the slogan under which he was later elected president in his own right.

At age fifty-four and midway through his presidency, Coolidge wrote his one-sentence will—the shortest, most straightforward testament of any president: "Not unmindful of my son John, I give all my estate both real and personal to my wife Grace Coolidge." A lawyer by training, Coolidge explicitly mentioned John so that the son could not contest the will on the grounds of inadvertent oversight, as is otherwise possible. Coolidge would live another six years as the estate grew to half a million dollars.

Much of Coolidge's wealth came after leaving office. His annual salary went from seventy-five thousand dollars as president to two hundred thousand dollars as a syndicated newspaper columnist. At the time, he was living at his secluded estate, the Beeches, and the country was in the throes of the Great Depression, brought on in no small measure by Coolidge's favorable policies toward business, which sparked stock market speculation and the crash. The ex-president devoted many of his columns to exonerating himself of blame.

His main physical complaint was indigestion, but when the discomfort expanded to his chest he was examined for heart disease. Pronounced fit, a few days later, on January 5, his wife returned home from shopping to discover Coolidge's body on the bedroom floor. The last person to see him alive was a carpenter working on the house. Coolidge had passed the man on the stairs hours earlier on his way to the bathroom to shave, saying, *"Good morning, Robert,"* his last known words.

The cause of death was coronary thrombosis: a clot of blood lodged in an artery, which blocks the flow to the heart. At his request, he was buried in a simple grave in Notch Cemetery, Plymouth, Vermont, because, as he had said, he did not want his grave to upstage those of the townspeople he had known all his life. His wife outlived him by twenty-four years, dying on July 8, 1957.

Herbert Clark Hoover: d. October 20, 1964, age 90

Will signed: August 31, 1964

Estate value: More than $8 million

Place of rest: Herbert Hoover Historic Site, West Branch, Iowa

Presidential salary: $75,000 plus $25,000 travel allowance

The first self-made millionaire elected to the presidency, Herbert Clark Hoover was born in West Branch, Iowa, on August 10, 1874, making him also the first president born west of the Mississippi. From mining engineer to business tycoon, Hoover, one of only two Quaker presidents (the other was Richard Nixon), amassed a fortune of four million dollars by the time of his inauguration at age fifty-four. Blessed with excellent health, he would live to age ninety, more than thirty-one years after leaving office—longer than any other president. (Only John Adams was older when he died.)

Graduating from Stanford University in 1895, Hoover worked as a mining engineer and then as a consultant. Residing in China around the turn of the century with his wife, Lou Henry, Hoover was chief engineer of the Chinese Imperial Bureau of Mines at a salary of twenty thousand dollars. By the time he was forty, he had a worldwide chain of offices. It was his humanitarian efforts during World War I, organizing the American Relief Committee to relieve starvation in Belgium, that won him national recognition. And he won the presidential election in 1928 with one of the greatest landslide victories in history, carrying forty of the forty-eight states. Political opponents quickly made him a scapegoat for the Depression.

He signed his final will at the age of ninety, two months before his death; earlier wills had to be repeatedly altered since he kept outliving beneficiaries. His wife had been dead for twenty years, and he was living in a suite at Manhattan's Waldorf Towers. To sons Herbert Jr. and Allan, he left a sizable portion of the multimillion-dollar estate, plus all "paintings hanging in my apartment at the Waldorf-Astoria Hotel." His last wish: "I direct that I be buried in the grounds of my birthplace at West Branch, Iowa, and I wish the remains of my wife to be moved there."

Hoover had served under five presidents in thirty-five posts and had published almost fifty books and articles on government and politics. It was a full life and it ended abruptly. On the afternoon of October 17, 1964, the ex-president, in his Waldorf suite, was stricken by a massive internal hemorrhage. He received several blood transfusions, but his advanced age worked against recovery. By October 19 he was only semiconscious of his sons' presence at his bedside. That night he sank into a deep coma, dying peacefully at 11:30 the next morning.

His body first lay in state in New York City, then traveled by train for services in Washington, where he lay on the same catafalque that had held the bodies of presidents Lincoln and recently deceased John F. Kennedy.

Franklin D. Roosevelt: d. April 12, 1945, age 63

Will signed: November 12, 1941

Estate value: $1,940,999

Place of rest: The Roosevelt Home, Hyde Park, New York

Presidential salary: $75,000 plus $25,000 travel allowance

The scion of an aristocratic Dutch family that came to America around 1636, Franklin Delano Roosevelt, the only president to serve more than two terms, was an inspiration to the handicapped and to feminists. At age twenty-nine he contracted polio and spent the rest of his life dependent on crutches and a wheelchair, displaying a courage and preseverance that helped him win the presidency.

Then as president he did something none of his successors had done. He appointed women to high government posts—Frances Perkins as secretary of labor and Ruth Bryan Owens as minister to Denmark. Fittingly, his wife, Anna Eleanor Roosevelt, a sixth cousin, became the first first lady ever to vote in a presidential election—presumably for her husband who was on the ballot in 1920 for vice president.

ROOSEVELT INAUGURATED, ACTS TO END THE NATIONAL BANKING CRISIS QUICKLY; WILL ASK WAR-TIME POWERS IF NEEDED

F.D.R., first president to appoint women to high government posts.

The presidency was, in a way, in Franklin Roosevelt's blood. Not only was he the fifth cousin of Theodore Roosevelt (who became president when Franklin was nineteen), but genealogists trace blood or marriage relationships to eleven first families: Washington, Adams, Madison, John Quincy Adams, Van Buren, William Henry Harrison, Taylor, Grant, Benjamin Harrison, and Taft. In 1940, the gathering crisis that was World War II prompted Roosevelt to run for an unprecedented third term, and four years later he was elected to a fourth term, which he would not complete.

His inaugural speech, on January 20, 1945, presaged his death four months later. "You will understand and, I believe, agree with my wish," said the ailing president, assisted to the lectern, "that the form of this inauguration be simple and its words brief." Suffering the pain of angina, Roosevelt delivered the shortest inaugural address in American history, twenty-three concise sentences. As he was assisted back to his wheelchair, the widow of Woodrow Wilson astutely observed, "He looks exactly as my husband did when he went into his decline." At the inaugural luncheon, to dull the chest pain Roosevelt asked for bourbon—"Better make it straight"—and he discussed his will with his son James.

Roosevelt had written the document one month before the bombing of Pearl Harbor and America's entry into the war. "If my wife, ANNA ELEANOR ROOSEVELT, shall survive me" (which she did by eighteen years, dying from a rare tuberculosis of the bone marrow), she was to receive a large portion of his two-million-dollar estate, including "jewelry, books, paintings, pictures, works of art, statuary, silver, plate, china, glass, ornaments, rugs, tapestry, automobiles and boats. . . ." Wishing to be buried at neither Arlington National Cemetery nor the Washington National Cathedral, Roosevelt requested the Rose Garden of his Hyde Park home.

Final Days. At the time the will was composed, Roosevelt already suffered from hypertension and accompanying heart problems, compounded by his inactivity from polio and heavy smoking. But the war contributed immensely to his physical decline, inwardly and outwardly; his appearance at the historic Yalta Conference—the grayish skin, halting speech, vapid stare—was greeted by "an audible gasp of dismay." Joseph Stalin saw death in the president's face, and Winston Churchill's doctor, without examining Roosevelt, confided to the British prime minister, "He has all the symptoms of hardening of the arteries of the brain and in an advanced stage. I give him only a few months to live." The prognosis could not have been more accurate.

Three months later, on April 12, 1945, Roosevelt was relaxing at the "Little White House," his cottage retreat in Georgia. He had awakened with a headache and stiff neck, but those symptoms passed, replaced by an eerie sensation that rippled throughout his body. He was talking with two cousins, his intimate female companion Lucy Mercer Rutherfurd and Elizabeth Shoumatoff, a New York artist who was in Georgia to paint the president's portrait. For a moment his expression went blank, then, hands raised to his skull, he said in a soft, distinct voice, *"I have a terrific pain in the back of my head."* He collapsed back into his chair.

His physician, Dr. Howard Bruenn, later wrote: "It was apparent that the President had suffered a massive cerebral hemorrhage." For three hours that afternoon Roosevelt lingered, semiconscious, his blood pressure and pulse steadily weakening. The stimulant papaverine and the inhalant amyl nitrite were administered to no avail, and when his body temperature began to fall hot-water bottles were pressed to his skin.

But his major bodily functions were irreversibly shutting down. He had suffered the stroke at 1:00 P.M. and was dead by 3:30.

News of the death of the four-term president spread quickly around the world. Phone calls from American officials woke Churchill and Stalin from sleep, and in Berlin an exultant Joseph Goebbels, Nazi minister of propaganda, contacted Hitler in his bunker under the Chancellery: "My Fuehrer, I congratulate you, Roosevelt is dead! . . . It is the turning point." (Not quite, for in less than three weeks both Hitler and Goebbels would write their own wills and commit suicide. See page 65.)

Although the use of copper was restricted in wartime, a special copper-lined coffin was prepared for Roosevelt's body, with craftsmen working free of charge to complete the task before the day of the funeral. "A cloud of grief descended on the country and the world," wrote one commentator. "Citizens saw the headlines and burst into tears on the street." After a funeral procession in Washington, Roosevelt's body traveled to his Hyde Park home for burial.

Later, in going through the president's papers, his wife found an envelope containing two handwritten final requests: Roosevelt had not wanted to be embalmed and he had not wanted a Washington procession.

Interestingly, Eleanor Roosevelt's last request when she died on July 25, 1962, was that her body not be embalmed, and *hers* wasn't. However, fearing the centuries-old dread of being buried alive, she stipulated that her major veins be severed so there could be no chance of her waking in the grave.

Harry S Truman: d. December 26, 1972, age 88

> **Will signed:** January 14, 1959
>
> **Estate value:** $610,000
>
> **Place of rest:** Harry S Truman Memorial Library, Independence, Missouri
>
> **Presidential salary:** $100,000 plus $40,000 travel and entertainment and $50,000 expense account

Inheriting a world war on Roosevelt's death, Harry S Truman became the first, and it is hoped the last, president to authorize the use of atomic weapons in warfare: The bombs dropped three days apart on Hiroshima and Nagasaki.

Interestingly, as vice president, Truman was not privy to the secret Manhattan Project to develop the A-bomb. With astonishment he learned of the weapon's existence shortly after taking the oath of office—in something of the atmosphere, We've got this new bomb, do you want to use it? It's been suggested that Truman's inability to ruminate on the horrific power and destruction of the atomic bomb eased his decision to drop it.

Considering the unambitious first third of Truman's life, no one could have predicted he would become president.

He was born in Lamar, Missouri, on May 8, 1884, to a poor mule trader who could not decide whether his son's middle name should be Solomon or Shippe, the names of the boy's grandfathers; the compromise was to give him a dual-purpose *S.* Rejected by West Point for poor vision, Truman became a farmer, foregoing a college education—the last chief executive to do so. For twelve years he worked his family's six-hundred-acre farm in Grandview, Missouri, then at age thirty-three married his childhood sweetheart, Elizabeth (Bess) Wallace, and opened a haberdashery. The business quickly failed, leaving the couple in debt, but Truman refused to declare bankruptcy, swearing one day to pay off his creditors.

It was a turning point in his life. He became a lawyer (though with no college credits) and rose quickly in politics. By the time he entered the White House, he was accustomed to hard work and frugal living, a pattern that characterized the simple life and austere entertaining in Harry and Bess's Washington. He benefited from a jump in the presidential salary from seventy-five thousand to one hundred thousand dollars, as well as special allotments of forty thousand dollars for travel and entertainment and fifty thousand dollars as part of a taxable expense account—much of which he saved.

Against the first couple's personal wishes, Congress undertook an extensive renovation of the executive mansion, costing $5,761,000 and lasting 3 years, during which time the Trumans lived, even more frugally, across the

Under Truman, warfare changed from tanks to nuclear bombs.

street in Blair House. Other presidents and first ladies had begged for renovations and salary increases and not got them; the Trumans got more than they ever wanted.

Truman wrote his will six years after leaving office, while in retirement at his home in Independence, Missouri. It is an extremely long document in which the ex-president, who for so many years owned nothing, makes bequests of virtually every item he has to just about every person he ever cared for. There are gifts to friends of one thousand dollars; others of five hundred dollars; and grandnephew John Ross Truman received a token five dollars because he was then a seminarian with a vow of poverty. Truman could leave no one out.

As thorough are Truman's instructions for the words to be written on "the slabs over the graves, *which will lie flat,*" for himself and Bess. He omits nothing, highlighting not only the dates of his birth and death, but also the birth date of his daughter Mary Margaret; his various public offices, listing them (and the dates of term) chronologically from "County Judge Eastern District Jackson County," to "Presiding Judge," to "United States Senator," on through the presidency. It is the only résumé of a president to appear on a tombstone. Reading Truman's will, it becomes clear how frankly proud he was of each and every hard-earned achievement. And though Bess's tombstone résumé is shorter, nothing she accomplished in life is left out either.

While in retirement he helped plan the Truman Library, where he would be buried.

In December 1972, following a cold that settled in his lungs, the eighty-eight-year-old Truman entered the Medical Center in Kansas City, Missouri. His lungs continued to fill with fluid and his heart weaken so that by midmonth he was on the critical list and only intermittently conscious. Whenever possible he took telephone calls from Lyndon Johnson, Hubert Humphrey, Edward Kennedy, and the shah of Iran. On several occasions Richard and Pat Nixon sent flowers. But given his age, the doctors were not surprised as one organ after another failed. He died the day after Christmas, 1972.

As requested, he received a simple funeral service in the Truman Library, attended by hometown friends instead of Washington dignitaries, and he was one of the few presidents not returned to the nation's capital to lie in state. The largest portion of his $610,000 estate was split almost equally between his wife, Bess, and his daughter, Margaret.

Dwight D. Eisenhower: d. March 28, 1969, age 78

Will signed: May 25, 1965

Estate value: $2,870,000

Place of rest: Eisenhower Center, Abilene, Kansas

Presidential salary: $100,000 plus $40,000 travel and expenses and $50,000 expense account

The president who ushered in the age of television politics—being the first to appear on national public television, the first to hold a televised press conference, and the first to campaign (for reelection) on television—Dwight David Eisenhower was born of Swiss-German stock on October 14, 1890, in a poor section of Fenison, Texas. Though christened David Dwight, to avoid confusion at home with his father, named David, the family called him Dwight.

A West Point graduate, at age twenty-six he married Mamie Geneva Doud, daughter of a Denver meat packer. It was his distinguished military career during World War II that brought him to national prominence and in 1953 the presidency, being the first chief executive limited by statute to two terms.

Eisenhower wrote his will at age 75, while living in retirement at his 189-acre farm near Gettysburg, Pennsylvania. The century-old brick house, originally with only 9 rooms, was renovated and enlarged with an addition of 14 rooms, at a cost of more than $100,000 during Eisenhower's final years there. His worth of almost $3 million came mainly from the farm, wise investments made with his presidential salary, a half-million dollars in royalties on his book *Crusade in Europe,* and a presidential pension of $25,000.

Eisenhower was already in guarded health during his presidency. Two years in office, he suffered chest pains, which his wife attributed to the raw onion he'd had on a hamburger; she forced the president to take milk of magnesia. Ike's doctor correctly diagnosed the worsening symptoms—pallor, perspiration, a quickening pulse—as a heart attack. To allay public concern the ailment was initially billed as a "digestive dysfunction," a plausible lie since Eisenhower had a history of abdominal problems. But with almost unprecedented White House candor, within twenty-four hours the public was told the president had suffered a "mild" heart attack. Seven weeks later, Ike left the hospital and returned to the Oval Office.

Less than a year later, Mamie was again giving Ike milk of magnesia, this time on doctors' orders. His abdominal pain came from ileitis, an inflammation of the intestines caused by blockage. During a risky operation (due to Ike's weak heart), surgeons at Walter Reed Army Hospital discovered the president had ten inches of blocked, diseased colon. Rather than entirely remove the colon (a more complicated procedure), they performed an ileium bypass from which the president quickly recovered.

Out of office, Eisenhower continued to have health problems. His gallbladder, which contained sixteen stones, was removed, then another section of infected bowel had to be cut away. Throughout all of his illnesses, it was clear to doctors that his weak heart and coronary blood clots were imminently life threatening.

The most traumatic thrombosis occurred on April 29, 1968, when Eisenhower was relaxing at his home in Palm Desert, California. It was his fourth attack, and from that point onward his heart would often have to be electrically shocked into normal rhythm. He remained at Walter Reed, alternating between states of semiconsciousness and full lucidity. A necessary intestinal operation in February of 1969 posed a dilemma: Doctors knew that surgery could induce a fatal heart attack, but if they did not unblock the bowel the patient would die

of self-poisoning. Ike survived the surgery for a month, weak, frequently unconscious, his life sustained by extraordinary medical means—which after his death
would be fiercely criticized for delaying his inevitable end.

The day he died, March 28, he had several hours of consciousness, with his
wife at his bedside. His last words were clear and totally in character: *"I've loved
my wife, I've loved my children, I've loved my grandchildren, and I've always loved
my country."* Dressed in full army regalia, he was given a military funeral and
eulogized by President Nixon as a man "who spoke with moral authority seldom
equaled in American public life."

John F. Kennedy: d. November 22, 1963, age 46

Will signed: June 18, 1954

Estate value: $10 million

Place of rest: Arlington National Cemetery, Arlington, Virginia

Presidential salary: $100,000 plus $40,000 travel and
entertainment and $50,000 expense account

John F. Kennedy died the wealthiest of American presidents up to his time, with
an estate valued at ten million dollars. For his twenty-first birthday he had
received from his father a million-dollar trust fund. His final wealth would be
equaled by that of his vice president, Lyndon Johnson, money being one of the
few things the two men had in common. Kennedy once said, trying to compose
a kind birthday telegram for Johnson, "This is worse than drafting a state
document."

At 12:30 P.M. on November 22, 1963, America's first Roman Catholic president, the first born in the twentieth century, and the only one to win a Pulitzer
prize (for *Profiles in Courage*) was shot to death in Dallas, Texas. The weapon
was a mail-order rifle belonging to a 24-year-old stock boy who was employed
for $1.25 an hour at the Texas School Book Depository Building, the sixth floor
of which afforded a sniper's dream vantage of the presidential motorcade.

Evidence to date suggests that Lee Harvey Oswald fired three times, killing
Kennedy and wounding Texas governor John B. Connally, who was seated in
the executive limousine in front of the president. Whether Oswald acted alone,
was part of a foreign conspiracy, or was a scapegoat for the Mafia who wanted
to thwart and intimidate the administration's war on organized crime has, for
many Americans, never been satisfactorily answered.

The wounded president, struck in the head and at the base of the neck, was
rushed to Parkland Hospital, where he was pronounced dead at 1:00 P.M. He
was forty-six years old, in office only a thousand days, and he left behind
Jacqueline Lee Bouvier, whom he had married ten years earlier, and two
surviving children, Caroline, and John Fitzgerald Jr. Ten months after his
marriage, Kennedy, then a first-term senator, wrote his last will and testament.

Kennedy opened his will with the phrase "mindful of the uncertainty of life." His rocker was the first piece of furniture Johnson had removed from the White House.

His sudden death prevented him from updating the document; thus, unlike the wills of other presidents, Kennedy's makes no mention of presidential papers or what should be done with other historically valuable presidential possessions. His family eventually turned such items over to the government, to be housed in a Kennedy Library and Museum.

Kennedy also had no children when he wrote his will, a legally complex but highly readable document that begins, "I, JOHN F. KENNEDY, married, and residing in the City of Boston . . . and mindful of the uncertainty of life," retrospectively a poignant phrase.

Nor was Kennedy then worth the ten million dollars he would be when he died (though he was far from poor, already a millionaire in his own right). "I give and bequeath unto my wife, JACQUELINE B. KENNEDY, if she survives me, the sum of Twenty-Five Thousand Dollars." Not much, but she was also to receive "all of my personal effects, furniture, furnishings, silverware, dishes, china, glassware, and linens, which I may own at the time of my death." Still not much for a woman whose spending would one day threaten the fortunes of the world's richest man.

However, farther into the will, Kennedy establishes a trust fund to be administered throughout his wife's lifetime in annual amounts that are, as Kennedy writes, "necessary to ensure her health, welfare, or comfort, or to enable her to maintain the standard of living to which she is accustomed." Nonetheless, Kennedy puts a ceiling on his wife's standard of living as supported by the trust: annually no "more than ten percent of the principal." If she remarries, any number of times, she remains entitled to the trust. Kennedy also makes provisions through trusts for any children he and his wife might have. The will ends by naming as executors his wife and his brothers Robert and Edward.

Kennedy's body was flown back to Washington on board Air Force One and lay in state in the Capitol Rotunda. Not only was he mourned by a nation, but also by his parents, being the only American president whose mother and father survived him.

His funeral was an international event, attended by royalty, prime ministers, and dignitaries from ninety-two nations and the papacy, while it was watched by more than a million people in the streets of Washington and millions more on television. He became the second president to be buried at Arlington National Cemetery (after Taft), and received full military honors for his bravery while skippering a PT boat that was sunk by a Japanese destroyer during World War II. Although given up for lost, Kennedy swam to safety, towing an injured enlisted man.

The man who ended Kennedy's life had his own life ended soon thereafter.

Oswald's Ending.   Following the assassination, Oswald, who had served in the U.S. Marine Corps and was rated as a sharpshooter and became a Marxist about that time, calmly went for food into the Book Depository Building's lunchroom, four floors below where he had fired on the presidential motorcade. As police searched the building, Oswald returned to his home, changed jackets, and hid a pistol in his pocket. Stopped on the street for suspicious behavior by officer J. D. Tippit, Oswald shot Tippit dead with four bullets and then entered the Texas Theater to watch a movie, where he was arrested.

On November 24, two days after Kennedy's death, Oswald was being transferred by Dallas police from the city jail to the county jail, when, in front of television cameras broadcasting the event, a fifty-two-year-old Dallas nightclub operator who called himself Jack Ruby (his real name was Jacob Rubenstein) stepped from the crowd of newsmen and fired a single shot into Oswald's left side.

In a bizarre irony, Oswald was taken to Parkland Hospital, where Kennedy had been rushed, and some of the same doctors who had worked to save the president's life found themselves attempting to save the life of his assassin. With the murder of Oswald, many people believed that the true motives behind Kennedy's assassination were lost forever.

Whereas Kennedy's funeral is unforgettable, Oswald's is less clearly remembered—except by his family. On November 25, under heavy police protection, his body was taken to Rose Hill Cemetery in Forth Worth, Texas. The simple funeral service was attended only by his wife, Marina Prusakova (a Russian he married in the Soviet Union in 1961), his brother, and his mother, who years earlier had purchased four grave plots at Rose Hill for her family. The cemetery's management felt that the assassin's body would be bad for business, but Texas law forced them to accept the corpse. When the family's clergyman did not show up, a local minister was called to the scene. "We are not here to judge," he said. "We are here to lay him away before an understanding God." So few people were present that two reporters had to help lower the coffin into the grave.

Years later, to quell claims that the body interred at Rose Hill was not Oswald's but that of a Soviet agent who had assumed Oswald's identity, the corpse was exhumed. A team of pathologists at Baylor University Medical Center compared the teeth with Oswald's marine corps dental records and matched a body scar from a childhood mastoid operation. Although the official conclusion was that the Rose Hill corpse was indeed Lee Harvey Oswald, to this day efforts are underway to prove that the real Oswald was killed in Russia and that the man who married Marina Prusakova was a Soviet agent hand-selected and surgically tailored to carry out the most shattering murder of the century.

Ruby's Ending.   Jack Ruby, convicted of Oswald's murder, died on January 3, 1967, also at Parkland Memorial Hospital, from a blood clot that lodged in his lungs. At the time he was also suffering from lung cancer. The day he died, Ruby reiterated to his brother, Earl, in a tape-recorded conversation, that he had acted alone as a distraught, ardent admirer of the president. Perhaps not even Earl believed that story.

Lyndon B. Johnson: d. January 22, 1973, age 64

Will signed: July 25, 1972

Estate value: More than $10 million

Place of rest: LBJ Ranch, Stonewall, Texas

Presidential salary: $100,000 plus $40,000 travel and
entertainment and $50,000 expense account

Lyndon Johnson, who following Kennedy's assassination took the oath of office on board Air Force One on a Dallas runway, amassed a multimillion-dollar fortune in Texas real estate and television stations. But a straightforward reading of his will, signed less than six months before his death, makes the wealthy Texan appear stingy near the end of his life, particularly in providing for his wife, Claudia Alta ("Lady Bird") Taylor.

First Johnson bequeaths generously to his daughters, Lynda Bird and Lucy Baines; then to his brother, Sam Houston, and his sisters, Lucia Alexander and Rebekah Bobbitt. More gifts follow to dozens of friends. Then one's eye catches the name of his wife and follows along the bequests: ". . . kitchen furniture, personal automobiles, musical instruments, books, pictures, jewelry," and the like. A string of nifty but niggardly items.

But the unique aspect of Johnson's will, unlike that of any other president, is that it was written in the "community-state" of Texas. That is, Lyndon Johnson was the first president whose permanent residence was in a state that recognized a wife as fifty-percent owner of a couple's entire community property. Thus Johnson could not will his wife what by law was already hers. She owned about half of his more than ten-million-dollar estate.

The first Southern president since Andrew Johnson (interestingly, both Johnsons succeeded assassinated chief executives), Lyndon Johnson was born in Stonewall, Texas, on August 27, 1908. Successful in fighting for far-reaching civil rights legislation and a Medicare program for the aged, Johnson decided not to run for reelection because of his unpopularity over the war in Vietnam. "I'm going to be known as the President who lost Southeast Asia," he's quoted as saying in *Remembering America,* a 1988 book by former Johnson speechwriter Richard Goodwin. Near the end of his term, Johnson was, according to Goodwin's critical analysis, "a textbook case of paranoid disintegration," stalking the White House at night, convinced that Communists "control the three major [television] networks," plunging "into unreason" that "infected the entire presidential institution."

Johnson retired to the LBJ Ranch in Stonewall, where he devoted his full time and energy to the planning and building of the library and museum that bear his name. His death at age sixty-four was sudden.

On January 22, 1973, Johnson was in the bedroom when he picked up the telephone to call one of the Secret Service agents assigned to him. In an alarmed voice he gasped, *"Send Mike immediately!"* Another agent rushed into the bedroom, but Johnson already lay unconscious on the floor, having suffered a massive heart attack. He died while being flown to a hospital in San Antonio. His home and the two hundred adjoining acres that made up the LBJ Ranch were donated to the National Park Service, with the provision that Mrs. Johnson could continue to live there, and, as the former president had requested, that he be buried on the grounds—in a service that included two of his favorite hymns: "Onward, Christian Soldiers" and "In Christ There Is No East or West."

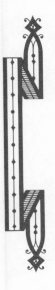

PART II

Ways to Go

CHAPTER 6

Capital Endings
Crucifixion to Lethal Injection

STONING, PRESSING, DRAWING AND QUARTERING, burning, hanging, and crucifixion (not to mention for the moment the modern sophistications of the gas chamber and electric chair). These are the tried-and-true, black-and-blue punishments devised by man (and exclusively by the male of the species) to end the life of his fellow human beings.

They may not be endings to be proud of, but they display in their own way an ingenuity unknown in the animal kingdom for inflicting a cruel and lingering death. And that's the point: These modes of capital punishment were devised specifically to make death sheer torture for the victim, stunning spectacle for onlookers.

Animals kill swiftly—and not as a form of reprimand. Even predators that toy with prey are usually teaching their young the fine points of carnivorous foraging. Only man kills protractedly, and the public staging of an execution is not done only as a deterrent to crime: For centuries it has also had what we call today "entertainment value." A contemporary text on criminology makes it clear that, "It is only within the last hundred years that the least attempt has been made to make capital punishment swift and humane." Though, as we'll see, miscalculations in the use of the first electric chair produced deaths that would have delighted Torquemada.

This chapter is not about the rights or wrongs of capital punishment. Rather, given its existence as a centuries-old reality and spectator sport, the chapter is devoted to various kinds of endings ingeniously devised, judiciously or vindictively ordained, planned to the minute, staged for maximum effect, then (excuse the pun) executed.

Capital Punishment: Pre–1500 B.C., Egypt

Today the penalty of death is reserved for "serious" crimes such as murder, treason, espionage, and rape. And when it is actually carried out (as it is in only one of every thirty death sentencings in the United States), the means of execution in Western countries are by firing squad, hanging, gas chamber, electric chair, and lethal injection—all relatively fast ways to go.

In ancient and medieval times, death was meted out for many more offenses, some trivial by modern standards. In India, you could have been sentenced to death for spreading falsehoods, killing a cow, or stealing a royal elephant. In Egypt, during the peak of feline idolatry, death was the punishment for injuring a cat (even if it recovered). Judeans imposed the death penalty for cursing. The Babylonians for selling bad beer. The Assyrians for giving a bad haircut, since stylish coiffeurs were cachets of class.

In parts of the Middle East, a perjurer in a trial was himself executed, intravenously embalmed while alive. The embalming solution, replacing blood, quickly caused cardiac arrest, and in that regard the mode of execution was a forerunner of the modern lethal injection.

For many centuries the Christian Church burned heretics alive, and it kept the definition of heresy flexible enough to net foes, friends, or anyone with a truly creative idea. Later, in colonial America, eccentric old women were drowned for possessing a "crazed" stare, companioning a black cat, or because they were alleged to own a lighter-than-air broom. Attractive young women met the same fate for sexual indiscretion.

The oldest extant death sentence is contained in the Amherst papyri, dating to 1500 B.C., which list official state trials in Egypt. The criminal was a teenage male, his crime was recorded simply as "magic," the mode of death was left to his choosing (poisoning or stabbing), and the executioner was to be himself.

When punishment was seldom swift and humane.

His corpse was to be turned over to his family for burial. This is quite a sophisticated sentence when contrasted to the first record of capital punishment in Europe: In fifth-century B.C. England, anyone convicted of a crime was tossed into a quagmire; an inextricable position that dispensed with the cost of burial.

In Rome during the same period, a citizen could be executed for many serious offenses, but also for trivial matters, as detailed in the legal Twelve Tables: for "publishing libels," for singing "insulting songs" about high-ranking officials, for "cheating by a patron of his client," and for "making disturbances in the city at night"—all enjoyments today.

From the earliest times, cruelly and publicly ending a criminal's life was viewed as a deterrent to crime. A torturous death was the ultimate means of instilling terror among people for whom the harsh struggle for daily existence was acute; an official quick death could be counterproductive: homicide as a form of suicide. "When criminals are executed," wrote the first-century Roman rhetorician Quintillian, "the most public places are chosen, where there will be the greatest number of spectators, and so the most fear of punishment will work upon them." In the same period, Seneca, the Roman philosopher and statesman, argued that, "The more public the punishments are, the greater the effect they will produce upon the reformation of others."

Unfortunately, history has repeatedly shown that public executions never decreased the incidence of crime. In England the gallows became a scene of merrymaking, drunkenness, and weekly family entertainment—while pickpockets worked the revelers.

Unlike today, in ancient times a punishment had to fit the crime, often in a bizarre parallel. In Babylonia, if a poorly erected home collapsed on the owner, the architect was executed. If the home fell in on the owner's son, the architect's son was put to death. (If the homeowner's wife or daughters were killed, the architect was only fined.) In ancient India, a man who damaged a dam, causing a serious leak, was drowned near the site of the damage. Theft of a

Public executions and roadside hangings never deterred crime; an 1800s woodcut depicts police pursuing a pickpocket at a hanging.

military sword or lance was punishable by death with the stolen weapon. A condemned man of high social standing was often allowed to select his ending, either by choosing his executioner (as did Anne Boleyn, sending to Calais for the swiftest axman) or by drinking poison in the presence of family and friends (as did Socrates).

For more than a thousand years, hanging was considered a lowly way to pay for one's crime. On the other hand, beheading was the most honorable way a felon could make atonement. Thus, the sentence of how a person was to die became more significant to society than the death itself. Not surprisingly, hanging has been the most frequently meted out form of execution in history: During just the reign of England's Henry VIII (1509–47) more than sixty-five thousand hangings were staged, all public spectacles and private humiliations.

Stoning: Pre–Christian Era, Near East

Although the fear of pain—especially protracted pain—is common to all people, a coveted Christian goal during the formative years of the church was to die a martyr's death, which was seldom expedient. Indeed, martyrdom was believed to ensure the faithful's place in heaven by "baptism of fire," and the more agonizing the death, the greater the eternal reward.

The first official Christian martyr was St. Stephen, a Hellenized Jew with a reputation as a fiery, zealous preacher, who met his end by stoning, a mode of punishment dating back at least to the time of Moses. Ancient Mosaic law itemized a long list of offenses punishable by stoning. A woman could be stoned for adultery, a man for stealing or, as in the case of St. Stephen, for heresy. With sentence passed, the culprit, hands bound behind his back, was led outside the town to an open site reserved for the lapidation, one easily recognizable to locals and travelers by telltale mounds of stones.

Death was not haphazard; protocol was followed.

First a crowd circled the condemned, each member holding a single heavy stone that he had brought with him. Through a gap in the ranks advanced a person who today would be called the plaintiff, the citizen who lodged the criminal accusation. He wore a white robe symbolizing his righteousness (or self-righteousness), and by law he was to "cast the first stone." There followed a shower of rocks, *though not to the head,* for the goal was to inflict injury and suffering, not a quick and kind unconsciousness. Ideally the stones continued to rain until their accumulated weight literally crushed the breath from the condemned. Thus the instrument of torture became the deceased's burial cairn. Depending on a crime's severity, the punishment did not always end with the victim's death; his property could be confiscated and both his livestock and close relatives could be stoned to death as well.

Our knowledge of the stoning of St. Stephen, which took place in Jerusalem in A.D. 35, comes mainly from the Acts of the Apostles. According to the tale, Stephen, one of the church's early deacons blessed by the apostles, was a "man full of faith and power" who performed "great wonders and miracles." At a lengthy trial for blasphemy, where he eloquently defended himself, he denounced the Jewish council in Jerusalem as the murderers of Christ, calling them "stiffnecked and uncircumcised in heart and ears." Gazing upward, he concluded his summation with an apparition: "Behold, I see the heavens opened, and the Son of man standing on the right hand of God."

He was condemned, dragged outside the city walls, and when the first stone was thrown, Stephen cried, *"Lord Jesus, receive my spirit."* Falling to his knees under the barrage of rocks he prayed, *"Lord, lay not this sin to their charge!"* Standing approvingly by was a young man from Tarsus named Saul, who later, as the convert Paul, was to become the apostle of the Gentiles. The stoning is regarded as a historical fact because of Paul's eyewitness account.

Stoning, prior to St. Stephen's death, had been merely one of many forms of capital punishment. His martyrdom and veneration, however, elevated stoning to a status way to die. For early Christians it became a noble, even desirable, ending of earthly life, which was then viewed as an unimportant existence in the face of the ever-imminent apocalypse.

Crucifixion: Pre–Christian Era, Phoenicia

The Romans who crucified Jesus Christ did not originate that cruel form of capital punishment. They copied it from the Phoenicians, the ancient people who occupied the region that today is Lebanon and parts of modern Syria and Israel—the same people who gave the Western world the alphabet.

By the second millennium, the Phoenicians were well known to their contemporaries as seafarers and traders, exporting rare cedar and pine, fine linen and embroideries, wine, metalwork, and a prized cloth dyed a passion purple with the body fluid of the *Murex* snail. Their city of Byblos (modern Jubayl) was the port from which papyrus traveled to Egypt and Greece, and the city's name is immortalized in many Western words: "bible," "bibliography," and "bibliophile." In addition to their many cultural accomplishments, the Phoenicians honed death by crucifixion, which they also exported—to the Assyrians, Egyptians, Persians, and Carthaginians.

In Carthage, crucifixion became a form not only of punishment but also of ritual sacrifice. The Carthaginian general, Malcus, wishing for a military victory, dressed his son Cartalo in royal robes, placed a crown on his head, then had him crucified to the god Baal.

But by the time of Christ's death, crucifixion, under the Romans, had become the most degrading form of capital punishment, as well as the most painful. It was reserved for slaves and the worst of criminals, who, if they could prove Roman citizenship, might be allowed a different manner of death.

The earliest "cross" was actually just a vertical stake to which the condemned was tied and left to expire from thirst and starvation. Later, Roman ingenuity conceived three varieties of crosses: The *crux commissa,* shaped like a *Y;* the *crux decussata,* or St. Andrew's cross, in the form of an *X;* and the one used for Christ's crucifixion, the *crux immissa,* with four arms in the shape of a *T.* The Romans dreamed up a fourth cross, infrequently used, which took the form of a modern football goalpost, to which the victim was hanged by one arm and one leg.

Whatever a cross's configuration, events leading up to the crucifixion were

*Romans perfected crucifixion
and staged multiple deaths
as spectacle.*

ordained by law. The accused was first scourged with a whip, then small pieces
of bone were usually inserted under the skin to increase suffering. Finally he
was forced to transport his cross in whole or in part (depending on his strength)
to the site of the execution. He was called the crucifer, from the Latin *crux*
("cross") and *ferre* ("to bear"). Stripped naked, except for decency's loincloth,
he was tied to one of the crosses.

Convicted of a more serious crime, he was nailed to the cross. The "hand"
nails were never hammered through the palms, which have thin bones and could
easily rip loose, but through the sturdier wrist joint between two major bones.
The feet were then nailed to a block of wood called the suppedanum, or support,
to prevent the weight of the body from pulling free. Contemporary chroniclers
recorded that a sufferer could remain alive for two to three days, unless,
mercifully, his limbs were broken to hasten death or he was speared by a lance
or arrow. Deed done, both the cross and the victim were burned.

Capital punishment by means of crucifixion was never a popular death
sentence in courts in the city of Rome itself. However, it was commonplace
throughout the provinces and conquered states. And Christ's death, between
the crucifixions of two other victims, illustrates that the practice was seldom
done to one individual alone; rather, Roman authorities waited until several
such sentences were passed and then staged the deaths in tandem as spectacle.
Occasionally, as with the death of St. Peter, the accused was crucified upside
down. The inverted position was something of a kindness since it hastened
unconsciousness; socially, though, inverted crucifixion was deemed a more
ignoble means of death.

In the Roman Empire, death by crucifixion was abolished by the Emperor
Constantine in A.D. 315. However it reemerged in several countries. In France,
as late as 1127, Louis VI (also known as Louis le Gros, the Fat), ordered the
assassin of Charles the Good, count of Flanders, publicly crucified. And in
France this punishment was also reserved at various times for Jews and here-

tics. In Japan, into the early nineteenth century, a variation of classical crucifixion was used on certain criminals: The condemned was tied by ropes to a cross,
then the executioner, by way of sadistic sport, strategically shot arrows to
wound the victim to slow death.

Pressing: Middle Ages, England

Peine forte et dure, literally "pain hard and long," was a form of capital punishment by pressing the life out of the accused. It arose in the Middle Ages, a
period in which the number of crimes punishable by death soared while the
mode of inflicting penalty became diabolically cruel. Torture was incorporated
as an essential part of even the simplest form of execution, and every nobleman
had in his castle a drowning pit, stretching rack, waterwheel, gallows, and a
device for pressing.

During this dark period in history, the number of executions increased
steadily each year, for human life was considered of less value than that of
livestock, which could be made to work for less than a fair share of food. Under
the writ *de heretic comburendo,* in effect in England from 1382 until 1677, the
rubric "heretic" was so widely cast (particularly with regard to Jews) as to net
a man who "lived with a Jewess," prescribing death by pressing for committing
"an unnatural offence." And any accused who stood doggedly mute, dared plead
innocence, or with some equivalent contumacy bucked authority could be
pressed until he shouted out what the law wanted to hear.

A victim, naked except for the standard-issue loincloth, lay on his back on
the ground, arms and legs tied spreadeagle to stakes. Across his chest rested
a flat board. The torturer applied weights, one at a time, making breathing
difficult, but taking measured care not to extinguish life too soon. Fed bread
and water, the condemned was kept alive from day to day to endure further

*Henry IV devised weights for
pressing.*

pressings. Large stones served as weights until the reign of Henry IV when special iron disks (resembling modern bodybuilding plates) were cast in various thicknesses, a creative brainstorm of the monarch that Shakespeare omitted from his otherwise encompassing *King Henry IV.*

An early victim to suffer the new weights was a woman, Juliana Quick, whose only crime was that she spoke contemptuously of the king. Another woman, Margaret Clitheron, underwent *peine forte et dure* in 1586 for her constancy to the Catholic faith, becoming the martyr of York. The practice was ended in 1741, when a shoemaker from Stratford, Henry Cook, was pressed to death for robbery.

Boiling Alive.   A later Henry, the VIII, not only favored death by pressing, but created a record for capital punishment, executing an estimated seventy-two thousand of his subjects. He also made legal death by boiling, with an act passed in 1531.

As an ironic footnote to history, the first victim to be immersed in a caldron and boiled alive was a cook. He was one Richard Roose, chef of the bishop of Rochester, accused of attempting to poison the bishop's household with a meat sauce seasoned with hemlock and deadly nightshade. Six people became gravely ill; two died. The cook was convicted, dragged to the town square in Smithfield where a pot hung from an iron tripod over a pile of logs, and was himself cooked. He sweated, simmered, and suffered for two hours as the water's temperature rose gradually to a roiling boil.

The punishment of death by boiling lasted for exactly sixteen years. With the death of Henry VIII in 1547, his successor, Edward VI, repealed the act, substituting public hanging, a far more humane execution. With, however, one glaring exception: A woman convicted of a capital crime was not to be hanged but burned alived, fully clothed and out of public view. Why the sex discrimination?

The answer is found in the fittingly titled "The Apology for Burning Women," a tract by the eighteenth-century English jurist Sir William Blackstone, the first professor of law at Oxford. Blackstone, of course, used the word "apology" to mean a formal written defense of an idea, but its other sense, as an expression of regret, certainly seems called for. His four-volume legal textbook, *Commentaries on the Laws of England,* a standard for over a century, explains: "As decency due to the sex forbids the exposing and publicly mangling of their bodies, their sentence is to be drawn to the gallows, and there to be burnt alive." Thus in the name of decency women endured a far more torturous death than did men.

Drawing and Quartering: Pre-1283, Europe and Asia

Drawing and quartering a criminal, the official penalty for treason in parts of Europe and Asia, is one of the most gruesome forms of capital punishment conceived by man. It was done in either of two ways, both ghastly.

In the more ancient form, practiced in Russia, the arms and legs of the condemned were tied by ropes to four horses. Struck with whips, the horses galloped away in four directions. Limbs that weren't ripped off before the ropes snapped were wrenched so forcefully that joints dislocated. This constituted both the drawing and quartering, after which the victim was usually decapitated.

But an even more grisly version of the punishment arose in England in the thirteenth century, one closer to the literal meanings of the words "drawing" and "quartering."

A man condemned for treason was dragged along the ground by horse from jail to the site of his execution. The favored route was through the center of a town to accumulate as large a procession of spectators as possible. At the site, the victim was gently hanged, but never permitted to die, for he still had to endure disembowelment, the "drawing" out of his intestines, which he then was forced to watch tossed into a fire. When the crowd's lust for entertainment was sated—or, more important, the fear of similar treatment adequately instilled; for determent was the supposed purpose of such public and gory executions—the victim was mercifully decapitated. And, strictly for the theatrics of further terrifying the crowd (for the victim was already dead), the corpse was cut into quarters—the "quartering."

That witnessing such a spectacle (or merely being told of it) did not put an end to treason must say something about the significance of public execution as a deterrent. And say something equally significant about the murky divide between horror and entertainment.

The first unfortunate victim of this extreme form of capital punishment was David III, the last native prince of Wales. His crime was that in 1282 he and his followers attacked an English garrison in a final desperate effort to establish Welsh independence. Captured and convicted of treason in the summer of the following year, he was publicly drawn and quartered at Shrewsbury in the fall. The same fate befell the Scottish patriot Sir William Wallace in 1305.

Drawing and quartering remained a legal form of punishment into the early years of the nineteenth century.

In December of 1802, an Irish patriot, Edward Marcus Despard, and six of his companions were charged with plotting to assassinate King George III. Newspaper accounts of the crowd turnout leave little doubt that the death spectacle—in this case in seven acts—had not lost its drawing power (so to speak). The tandem executions, having been much publicized for eight weeks, were staged on a frigidly cold day, February 21, 1803, in London's Horsemonger Lane. By six o'clock that morning, two hours before the condemned men were brought to the scaffolds, every inch of spectator space with a view of the platforms was thronged with humanity, including men, women, and children. Two regiments of cavalry were called out to tame the crowds.

The first victim, ringleader Edward Despard, age fifty-one, once a colonel in the British Army, took his fate with wry nonchalance. To one of his terrified companions who said, "I'm afraid, Colonel, we have got ourselves into a bad situation," Despard answered, "There are some better, some worse." Then as his ordeal was about to begin he glanced out over the thousands of spectators and commented, "What an amazing crowd!" As the executioner placed the rope around his neck for the partial hanging, he observed, " 'Tis very cold. I think we shall have some rain." His convicted companions, who were forced to watch Despard's agony, were not given to such understatement when their times came.

Drawing and quartering was ended by an act of Parliament in 1870. Three years earlier, two members of the Irish revolutionary group known as the Fenian Brotherhood, William O'Brien and Richard Burke, were convicted of conspiracy and sentenced to be publicly drawn and quartered. The savage inhumanity of the punishment was fiercely argued in the press, and the sentences were never carried out. Hanging became the acceptable penalty for treason.

Hanging: Antiquity, Worldwide

One of the earliest forms of deliberately ending life, hanging has been practiced by all societies throughout recorded history. With the exception of the United States and a few other Western countries, it is still the most common method of capital punishment worldwide. Hanging is sanctioned in the Bible, in Deuteronomy, with the mention that "he that is hanged is accursed of God" and with the proviso that "His body shall not remain all night upon the tree, but thou shalt . . . bury him that day."

The most primitive gallows was nature's own tree branch. And in fact the word "gallows" is from the ancient Indo-European root *ghalgh,* meaning "pliant branch," since Indo-European peoples used a sturdy pulled down branch that lifted the victim with it when it was allowed to spring upward. In Old English, the perfect tree for a hanging, sturdy and pliant, was a *galgtrēow,* or gallows tree.

The history of hanging is a long trial-and-error experiment in the quest for a "clean" hang, that is, a fast, efficient execution. And, it should be pointed out, hanging is an art, many would say a science, as opposed to lynching, which by comparison is impromptu and seldom "clean."

Anglo-Saxon gallows.
A "clean hang" draws
spectators.

In early rope hangings, a group of men, tugging on a cord tossed over a tree branch, would, hand over fist, hoist up the victim. Suffocation was torturously slow. The first improvement, considered a humane breakthrough and introduced throughout Europe during the Middle Ages, was the ladder, which the condemned climbed himself then leaped off or had pulled out from under him. His upper spinal cord might snap, making unconsciousness instantaneous: a "clean" hang.

This kind of hang, though, was not considered clean enough by humanitarians of the seventeenth century. Thus was introduced the hanging cart, which served two functions. The victim rode in the horse-drawn cart from jail to the gallows; then, with the noose secured, the cart was abruptly trotted away, supposedly guaranteeing a more consistently clean hang. Executioners of the era, who actually timed deaths, praised the expediency of the technique (though they were known to cheat by tugging on the dangling victim's legs), and essays on capital punishment claimed that the hanging cart lessened the condemned's suffering.

Coincidently a new publishing phenomenon arose throughout Europe in conjunction with the hanging cart. It began with the custom of the condemned man or woman using the elevated cart as a platform to address the assembled spectators. The appropriate speech for salvation of one's soul was a lamentation of the misdeeds that led to a life ruined. The pious sentiments, often penned by the condemned's priest, were meant to instruct listeners. So inspirational were these last dying confessions that printers began collecting and issuing them in bound volumes complete with artists' sketches of execution scenes—often romanticized: a tearful mother blowing kisses to her brood; a man so repentant that his hanging is attended by the Holy Ghost; and one Mary Blandy shown about to be hanged at England's infamous Gallows Tree at Tyburn (in what is now Hyde Park), when in fact she was hanged from a beam in a prison yard.

These decidedly religious tracts never mentioned the unsavory side of a hanging: the stench from the victim reflexively urinating, defecating, and, in the case of a man, getting an erection and actually ejaculating—the last a titillation well known to regular spectators of hangings. These immensely popular early publications—which also gave the "appalling curses that rent the air and rendered the last moments of the unfortunate sinner more odious"—eventually broadened their scope to include trial transcripts, essays on criminal law, and statistics on crime, becoming the forerunners of modern criminal magazines and journals.

Quest for the Clean Hang.   The experimentation from ladder to hanging cart in search of a clean hang was minor compared to the research efforts of seventeenth-century physicians. They argued over such fine points as the best knot, the best placement of the knot (behind the ear? beneath the Adam's apple? at the nape of the neck?), as well as the length of the rope and the height of the drop. The debates were fierce, serious, and raged on for two centuries.

British doctors championed placing the noose's knot securely behind the victim's left ear (also the modern recommendation). This cut off blood to the brain and produced unconsciousness before death by stangulation—or as one seventeenth-century physician explained: It quickly caused "effusion and concentration of tumours in the brain." In the next century, Irish physicians introduced the "long drop," anywhere from ten to seventeen feet. Centuries earlier criminals dropped no more than twelve inches, and often as little as six, the acceleration due to gravity not yet appreciated.

But even the Irish long drop was distressingly unpredictable. A Dublin prison journal records two cases in which the criminals each weighed 160 pounds and were dropped a distance of 14 feet. In one man, the second vertebra snapped, producing instantaneous unconsciousness; the other man lost his head, severed by the rope.

These two "experiments" drew most of Ireland's leading surgeons of the day into the clean hang debate. From animal experiments and actual human hangings, they calculated "scientific tables," factoring in a man's weight, the girth of his neck, an estimate of the strength of his neck muscles, the thickness of the rope, and, of course, the length of the drop. One conclusion: A lightweight man could not withstand a long drop without risk of decapitation. Another: Italian hemp, three-quarter inch in diameter and consisting of five strands, each capable of supporting a ton, made the safest rope.

Every rope had to be stretched overnight under the stress of a bag of cement, since a taut rope made for a more expeditious death. For more than a century in England and Ireland a professional hangman provided his own highly prized ropes for an execution, and he could make a sizable profit by selling a rope that had choked a famous neck. The most highly sought ropes were cut up and sold by the inch. Many intact ropes that strangled monarchs are on exhibition in crime museums around the world.

Despite the considerable science that went into a clean hang, mistakes still occurred, one of the most famous being the attempt to end the life of coachman John Lee, convicted of the 1884 murder of his employer, Emma Anna Keyse, of Babbacome, England. At the public execution on February 23, 1885, hangman James Berry placed a bag over Lee's head, adjusted the noose, stepped back, and pulled the bolt that should have released the trapdoor. But it didn't. Berry stamped on the door, as did prison officials, then helpful spectators. Lee was moved aside and the trapdoor tested: It worked. He was put back in position, and the door again jammed.

Lee was returned to his cell while the executioner and a crew of assistants oiled and adjusted the release mechanism until it worked perfectly. Understandably distraught, John Lee was brought back, again prepared, and again the trapdoor would not make way for its victim. After a half hour of additional stamping, cursing, and tampering, in which the trapdoor refused to cooperate, Lee's sentence was commuted to life in prison. He was paroled in 1907, and four years later died of natural causes.

Lynching: 18th Century, United States

Defined as the unlawful killing of a person by a mob, generally by hanging and usually associated with vigilante justice and racial violence, lynching—the word and the practice—is said to have originated with a man named Lynch. One possible candidate was an eighteenth-century Virginia judge, Charles Lynch, a founder of Lynchburg and known for dispensing injustice, particularly by flogging those accused, without a trial, of loyalty to the Crown.

More likely, however, the first lyncher was another Virginian, Captain William Lynch, renowned for his acts of violence against the British and their sympathizers during the Revolutionary War. The accusatory finger was first pointed at William Lynch in 1836, sixteen years after his death, by a man who dealt in horror himself, but of a harmless kind: Edgar Allan Poe. Researching the practice of hanging for his stories, Poe discovered a dated execution pact signed by Lynch and his followers founding the first lynching organization on September 22, 1780, when Lynch would have been fifty-six. One of Lynch's men described the practice: "The person . . . was placed on a horse with his hands tied behind him and a rope about his neck which was fastened to the limb of a tree. . . . When the horse in pursuit of food or any other cause moved from his position the unfortunate person was left suspended by the neck—this was called *aiding the civil authority*."

Although the South popularly holds the title of "Lynching Capital of the U.S.," it is not the only section of the country where life was ended by lynching. In fact, there are only four states in which no lynchings have ever been recorded: Massachusetts, New Hampshire, Rhode Island, and Vermont. Five states in the South account for most lynchings: Alabama, Georgia, Louisiana, Mississippi, and Texas. And population figures reveal that the fewer residents who live in a county, the greater the number of lynchings there; shared sentiments, similar mind-sets, less opposition, and greater approbation are among the offered reasons.

Contrary to popular belief, blacks were not the only people to suffer this unlawful execution. More whites were lynched than blacks in nine states: Indiana, Iowa, Kansas, Montana, Nebraska, New Mexico, Oklahoma, South

Only four states never had a lynching: Massachusetts, New Hampshire, Rhode Island, and Vermont.

Dakota, and Wyoming (though the small population of blacks in some of these states in the eighteenth and nineteenth centuries skews the statistic toward insignificance).

San Francisco used lynching to rid the city of crooked politicians. Western towns found that lynching was the only way to drive away bands of outlaws. And the various Ku Klux Klans, which were established starting in 1866 with the aim of keeping the South under the control of white Protestants, lynched not only blacks, but Jews, Catholics, "Bolshevists," "suspicious foreigners," believers in Darwinian evolution, and pacifists, in addition to people who actually committed crimes.

Blacks, though, suffered the worst. The N.A.A.C.P. lists the total number of lynchings of blacks since 1882 (almost a century after the practice began; no earlier figures are available) at around five thousand. Of those, about a hundred were women.

Lynching, by and large, has ended. The decline began in the 1890s as the frontier was tamed with law replacing vigilante justice. It died most slowly in the South where white men argued that lynchings of black men were necessary to protect the virtue of white womanhood. No one wished to entertain the possibility that some of white womanhood might have sexually preferred blacks and have been, if not the aggressor, then the enticer, or at the very least a willing participant.

From 1930 to 1937 Southern states accounted for ninety-five percent of all American lynchings. And less than thirty percent of the black men lynched were ever proved guilty of rape or even attempted rape. The three-year period from 1952 to 1954 marked the first time in almost two centuries that there were no known lynchings in America.

Since then, if lynchings have occurred, they have not been publicized, as was long the practice. The last public lynching in the United States occurred in Walton County, Georgia, in 1946, when four blacks—two men and two women—were hanged. The last suspected nonpublic lynching was the "suicide" death by hanging of a black serviceman in 1982, also in Walton County, Georgia. Whether the unfortunate man placed the rope around his own neck or had unsolicited help has never been clearly established.

Beheading: Antiquity, Greece and Rome

The swiftness of death by the sword or ax is what made beheading an honorable way to meet one's end. On the other hand, the indecorousness of kicking, gasping, flailing, to say nothing of the choking body's reflexive voiding of wastes, is what made hanging an ignoble end.

The distinction is ancient and appreciated by all Western societies.

The ancient Greeks and Romans regarded beheading by sword as the single most honorable form of mandatory death. The fifth-century B.C. Greek historian Xenophon, in his military history *Anabasis,* even distinguishes between the niceties of a sword over an ax, the former guaranteeing a faster cleaner cut and thus a more dignified ending. The Roman statesman and orator Cicero, sen-

Swift death by the ax was preferred to hanging; Sir Walter Raleigh about to lose his head (inset).

tenced to death in 43 B.C. for opposing the alliance between Mark Antony and Octavian (later the emperor Augustus), chose the sword to meet his death.

Roman emperor Caligula, according the historian Suetonius, kept his chief headsmen's skills honed for public executions by having them secretly practice decapitation of prisoners chosen at random from city jails. Though the Romans occupied Britain, they did not pass on the practice of beheading, which they called *decollatio* and *capitis amputatio*.

Beheading arrived in England late: in the eleventh century, introduced by William the Conqueror. And once it arrived, it flourished, beginning with England's first beheading, that of Waltheof, earl of Northumberland, in 1076. Thus began the tradition that condemned commonfolk hanged, whereas the ax or sword was reserved for the necks of those of high rank.

Because those beheaded had wealth and social position—from archbishop to queen—scaffold etiquette was drawn up and rigorously followed. If, for instance, two or more peers were to be beheaded, they were brought to the block in order of rank, highest to lowest. If addressing the spectators, the accused male had to remove his hat. When in 1746 two friends and Scottish noblemen were sentenced for conspiracy, Lord Kilmarnock and Lord Balmerino, the former offered the latter the honor and kindness of going first. Balmerino accepted, saying, "My Lord Kilmarnock, I am only sorry I cannot pay this reckoning alone." But the execution was halted when a British nobleman pointed out that Kilmarnock's family pedigree was longer and more distinguished, and therefore Kilmarnock had to be beheaded first. The weightiness of noblesse oblige.

From the fifteenth century onward, the blade fell on many of the highest personages in England and France. A French physician writing in the 1600s observed: "In this country you will not meet with any great nobles whose relations have not had their heads cut off." Then he suggested that a visitor look around, "For you will see these great lords in grand pomp and magnificence for a time. Turn your head and you will see them in the hands of the executioner." Here are several of history's notables who met their end by decapitation and what they had to say about it.

Thomas More: d. 1535.   For refusing to recognize the marriage of Henry VIII to his second wife, Anne Boleyn, the English statesman and author spent fifteen months in the Tower of London before his beheading on the charge of treason. Ascending the shaky ladder to the scaffold, More addressed the executioner, "I pray you see me up safe," and once positioned at the block, requested, "Let me shift for myself."

The assembled crowd was immense. More beseeched them to pray for his soul and to remember that he "died the King's good servant, but God's first," a last dig at Henry's limited sovereignty. As was scaffold etiquette, with a commoner mortally touching a nobleman, the executioner begged Sir Thomas More's forgiveness for what he was about to do, and More, head on the block, spoke his last words: *"Pluck up thy spirit, man, and be not afraid to do thy office. My neck is very short; take heed therefore thou strike not awry."* Then to spare his beard, he lifted it out of the ax's way, murmuring, *"It has never committed any treason."*

The head of a traitor was usually staked on a pole and displayed at London Bridge. The head of Sir Thomas More drew such a crowd that the bridge was impassable to horse and coach traffic for two entire days.

Anne Boleyn: d. 1536.   Less than a year after Thomas More lost his head for condemning the marriage of Henry VIII to Anne Boleyn, she was to go to the scaffold for failing to present the king with a male heir (though she was already the mother of the future Elizabeth I). Since her shortcoming was not grounds for a beheading, evidence was manufactured through bribery and threats of torture that Anne was an adulteress. At her trial in King's Hall on

Thomas More's publicly displayed head caused traffic jams for two days.

May 15, 1536, she was charged with sleeping with four men, one of them her brother, Viscount Rocheford. For safe measure, she was also charged with plotting to assassinate the king, which clinched the death sentence.

Henry, already enamored with Anne's lady-in-waiting, Jane Seymour, allowed his queen to select as her executioner a master swordsman from Calais. At twenty she had been Henry's mistress, at twenty-six his queen, and now at twenty-nine she was to be his victim. Shortly before noon on May 19, Anne went to the scaffold wearing a gown trimmed in fur over a crimson petticoat, her hair tightly plaited and tucked into a pearl-embroidered cap.

In a scaffold speech, she refused to condemn her false accusers or to criticize the king, saying, "I pray to God to save the King, and send him long to reign over you—for a gentler nor a more merciful prince was there never." The "merciful prince" was a reference to the fact that she had been condemned to death by beheading *or* burning and Henry had kindly spared her the agony of the flames. (Her brother, Rocheford, was drawn and quartered.)

Some accounts refer to the queen's "gaiety" in her last hour—her vivaciousness, talkativeness, giddiness; others say her mood was more one of hysteria. There is little question that she was frightened. The lieutenant of the Tower of London, Sir William Kingston, assured her that with a good executioner there "should be no pain, it is so subtle." She answered, "The executioner is very good, I have a little neck."

The sword was a long, heavy, two-handed one of the kind employed for centuries for beheadings in Germany, and no block was used that would stop the sword's downward momentum. The queen merely knelt and extended her neck. Her final utterance—a soft, rapid palilalia: *"O God have pity on my soul. O God have pity on my soul. O God . . ."*—was at some point abruptly severed with the sword's single swift stroke.

Catherine Howard: d. 1542. Six years after Anne Boleyn's death, Henry's fifth wife, Catherine Howard, age twenty-two, was also convicted of adultery (probably justly so) and sentenced to death.

For the first fourteen months of their marriage, Henry was enamored with his latest young queen. But in November of 1541, he learned that before their marriage Catherine had had numerous affairs: with her music teacher; with one man who claimed they were married; and with her cousin, Thomas Culpepper, to whom she had been engaged and in all likelihood was still seeing clandestinely. On February 11, 1542, Parliament obliged Henry and passed a bill making it treason for an unchaste woman to marry the king. Two days later, in the Tower of London, Catherine was beheaded, her final words a brazen slap at Henry: *"I die a Queen, but I would rather die the wife of Culpepper. God have mercy on my soul. Good People, I beg you pray for me."*

Lady Jane Grey: d. 1554. Queen of England for only nine days, the sixteen-year-old Lady Jane was beheaded for treason against a Roman Catholic rival for the crown, Mary I. Herself innocent, a victim of political machinations that forced her to accept the crown (she had fainted when told she was to be queen), Lady Jane—as well as her nineteen-year-old husband, Lord Guilford Dudley—was sentenced to die on February 12, 1554.

By grisly chance, on her way to the scaffold she glanced up from a prayer book to spot palace guards carrying the body and detached head of her husband, just executed. With the sympathy of the populace and the executioner, she tearfully professed her innocence, then blindfolded herself, beseeching the hooded headsman, "I pray you dispatch me quickly." Afraid that he might swing the sword before she fixed her neck on the block, she asked, "Will you take it off before I lay me down?" and he promised, "No, madam." But blindfolded, frightened, and disoriented, she was unable to locate the block and pleaded, "Where is it? What shall I do? Where is it?" He led her to the block, helped position her neck, and she cried out: *"I die in peace with all people. God save the Queen!"*

Mary, Queen of Scots: d. 1587.   After her forced abdication for marrying the murderer of her husband, Mary, Queen of Scots (Mary Stuart), spent eighteen ailing years in prison at the hands of the new queen, Elizabeth I. When a conspiracy to return the Roman Catholic queen to the throne failed, Mary, then forty-five and badly crippled with rheumatoid arthritis, was convicted of treason and declared she was glad to shed blood as a martyr for her faith. "Today, thou seest the end of Mary Stuart's miseries," she said. "I die a true woman of my religion, like a true Queen of Scotland and France. But God forgive them that have long desired my end and thirsted for my blood."

She went stoically to the block, dressed in a black cape that she removed to reveal a red petticoat. Refusing the prayers of a Protestant clergyman, she spoke her own Catholic verse in Latin, then, with almost defiant bravery, blindfolded herself, knelt, felt for the block, and positioned her head. Her last words were in Latin: *"In te, Domine, confido spiritum meum,"* but when the first blow of the sword missed her neck and cleaved open the back of her skull, she cried, *"Sweet Jesus!"*

After the second blow did the job, the executioner lifted her head by its bright auburn hair and yelled, "God Save the Queen." To the horror of three hundred spectators, the hair was actually a red wig that was left in the executioner's hand as the head plummeted to the floor with a thud. When her body was lifted, hiding beneath her red petticoat, trembling, was her miniature pet terrier. To deprive Mary's Catholic sympathizers of relics of the martyr, every item connected with the execution was burned, and her body, sealed in a lead coffin, was walled up within the castle. It was later moved to Westminster Abbey where it became the center of a Catholic shrine. Her terrier is said to have pined for his mistress and died.

The list of sword and ax beheadings goes on and on—the earl of Essex (1601), Sir Walter Raleigh (1618), Charles I (1649)—in effect ending in the year 1792, not because beheading was outlawed as a form of capital punishment, but because that year the sword and ax were replaced with a more "scientific" instrument to carry out the same sentence of death: the guillotine.

Guillotine: April 25, 1792, France

The guillotine, that "terrible swift sword" of the French Revolution, was in many ways itself a revolution. Technologically innovative, it was also meant to be a democratic device, making the privilege of a "painless" execution by decapitation no longer the exclusive death sentence of the upper classes but something available to common folk, too.

Contrary to popular belief, the instrument was not invented by French physician Dr. Joseph Ignace Guillotin; he merely was a central figure in persuading the French National Assembly in 1789 to pass a law requiring all capital punishment to be carried out by "means of a machine."

The actual machine was the collaborative effort of a French surgeon and a German harpsichord maker, Dr. Antoine Louis and Tobias Schmidt, each contributing his own special expertise. Louis knew how a neck should split; Schmidt knew how to hone a sharp edge.

Their prototype machine consisted of two upright posts topped by a crossbeam and grooved to guide an oblique-shaped, heavily weighted knife downward. With precise intent. The first tests were carried out on human cadavers at Bicetre Hospital, then Schmidt advanced to beheading live sheep in the alley behind his harpsichord shop. When the proto-machine proved satisfactory, a full-scale model was erected in the Place de Grève (today the Place de l'Hôtel-de-Ville) to receive its first human victim: a lawless highwayman named Nicolas Jacques Pelletier.

At 3:30 P.M. on April 25, 1792, more than three thousand curious citizens jammed the square. The "executioner of high works," Charles-Henri Sanson, announced proudly that he would do his duty "with the skill and love of an artist." Pelletier's head plopped into a bucket, and the following morning *La Chronique de Paris* editorialized that the new machine had "in no way stained any man's hand with the murder of his kind" and that "the speed with which it struck is more in accordance with the spirit of the law—which may often be severe but which should never be cruel."

Dr. Guillotin, present at the execution, was pleased with the effectiveness and humaneness of the device. "The victim does not suffer at all," he had told the assembled spectators. "He is conscious of nothing more than a slight chill on his neck." Not from the steel, presumably, but from the advancing draft of the descending blade.

Within a week of the execution tiny models of the machine were selling in Paris streets as toys, souvenirs, and earrings. Pelletier was "guillotined," and the world had a new word—if not a truly new invention.

Louis and Schmidt had actually adapted and bettered a design that had been used on and off for at least two centuries. Never perfected, these older machines frequently jammed, with the blade stopping above the condemned's neck, on it, or in it. One such instrument, known in Scotland as the maiden, had occasionally been used since the Middle Ages, most notably in 1581, when it functioned perfectly, decapitating James Douglas, 4th earl of Morton, convicted of complicity in the murder of Mary, Queen of Scots's first husband, Lord Darnley. A different maiden is today on exhibit at the National Museum of

Antiquities in Edinburgh. A similar device, equally unreliable, was sometimes used in England under the name the "Halifax gibbet," *gibet* being Middle English for "gallows."

England and Scotland were not the only countries to attempt to mechanize death. In Germany, an automatic beheading machine went through at least three incarnations without achieving perfection. The imperfect devices were named, respectively, the *diele,* the *hobel,* and the *dolabra.*

The most steadily reliable version existed in Italy, under the name *mannaia,* meaning "axlike knife." It was this device that came to the attention of Dr. Guillotin, prompting him to suggest research into a French model. Guillotin got his "infallible instrument" as well as his wish that it be used nondiscriminately on "all persons regardless of rank." In fact, he was to see it democratized beyond his wildest dreams: During the French Revolution alone 2,498 heads rolled away from the swishing of the steel blade, including, of course, those of France's king and queen.

Louis XVI.   Nine months after the guillotine debuted, Louis XVI, the last monarch in the line of kings preceding the French Revolution, ascended the scaffold on the Monday morning of January 21, 1793. Charged with conspiring with foreign powers against the Revolutionary government, he had been held as a prisoner since his unsuccessful attempt to escape the country almost two years earlier. Above drumrolls the king made his final speech: *"I die innocent of all the crimes of which I am charged. I forgive those who are guilty of my death, and I pray God that the blood which you are about to shed may never be required of France."*

Louis apparently had more to say, but the impatient general overseeing the execution ordered the drums to drown out the king's voice. His neck was fitted into the concavity that would snugly receive the knife, and above the deafening drums he was heard to shout, *"May my blood cement the happiness of France!"*

Forerunners of the guillotine: Scottish maiden; a medieval model.

Marie Antoinette.   That same year, on October 16, Louis's wife, no friend of the masses, arrived at the scaffold in a white chemise, her hair cropped close to her scalp. She cocked her head haughtily at the jeering spectators, but glancing up at the blade, composure failed her and she began to cry. To deprive the crowd of the pleasure of her fear and discomfort, she moved so quickly to the guillotine that she stepped on the executioner's foot, which prompted her only final utterance: *"Monsieur, I beg your pardon. It was an accident."*

To be accurate, when Louis and Marie Antoinette stepped up to France's new machine to be beheaded, it was not yet called a "guillotine" but a "Louisette," in honor of its inventor, anatomist and surgeon Antoine Louis. But soon the French people began calling the dreaded instrument *la guillotine,* and Dr. Guillotin was not flattered. To his dying day he argued that it is was inappropriately named. And after his death in 1814, his family spent years in the French courts attempting unsuccessfully to have the machine called anything except their surname.

Despite Guillotin's assurances that the victim felt only a "slight chill" and that the device introduced "speed and mercy" to the ending of lives, other medical men of the day had their doubts. One wrote that "the severed head still retains the faculty of feeling and thinking during several seconds." Another claimed he had made a pact with a condemned man, who promised to blink three times immediately after his beheading; he blinked twice.

Such tales, and they were numerous, prompted ghastly experimentation. French doctors and medical students stood on the scaffold beside the condemned, awaiting a fresh head, then snatched it up, stuck pins in the lips, ammonia under the nostrils, and to the bared eyeballs applied stinging silver nitrate and searing candle flames.

Their findings were as varied as their tortures. Faces grimaced, twitched, blinked; lips pleaded silently for mercy. Or they seemed to. On November 13, 1879, three doctors, driven by the inconclusive evidence to date, subjected the freshly severed head of a twenty-three-year-old man, Theotime Prunier, to a rapidfire series of punishments within seconds of the beheading. But their only conclusion was: "The face bore a look of astonishment."

Today we know that following a decapitation facial muscles are still alive and can contract in response to inflicted stimuli. Also, brain neurons do not die instantaneously, though unconsciousness can come that quickly. But does it always? As late as 1956 two French doctors wrote that "death is *not* immediate. Every vital element survives decapitation. It is a savage vivisection followed by a premature burial."

Some would say that Dr. Guillotin took the answer with him to the grave, for a widely believed anecdote has it that he met his own end under the "terrible swift sword." Understandably appealing as irony, the tale has been traced back to a single line in the work of Victorian novelist William Makepeace Thackeray, author of *Vanity Fair* and *Barry Lyndon. The Adventures of Philip on His Way Through the World* is one of Thackeray's lesser works, but it contains the line that launched the legend: "Was not good Dr. Guillotin executed by his own neat invention?"

The answer to that rhetorical question is no. Age seventy-six, Joseph Ignace Guillotin died in his own bed at Rue St.-Honoré from an infected carbuncle of the shoulder. When Thackeray wrote *Philip* in 1861, Guillotin had been dead forty-seven years.

Another story about Dr. Guillotin may or may not be true. It was spread by his family. His birth at Saintes on May 28, 1738, was supposedly "accompanied by an augury almost unbearably apropos." His mother, in her ninth month of pregnancy, was strolling along a promenade when she passed a lake where a criminal was being tortured on a waterwheel. Horrified, she went into labor on the spot, giving birth to the man who would make capital punishment painless. It seems that Guillotin's life both opened and closed with anecdotes.

For a century the guillotine would reign as the condemned's chosen means to meet his or her end. No one imagined death could be swifter, surer, more painless. Then came electricity.

Electric Chair: August 6, 1890, United States

Considering the number of scientists accidentally shocked, and shocked to death, in the early days of electric current experimentation, it is not surprising that the electric chair was the invention that followed the light bulb. Or that Thomas Edison played a key role in the development and promotion of each device.

In September of 1882, the world's first electric bills were sent out to about three hundred fortunate New Yorkers who had the privilege of paying for illumination from history's first incandescent bulbs. Less than five years later the New York legislature empaneled a commission to investigate "electrical alternatives" to hanging as a means of execution.

It did not have to look far. Inventor Harold Brown had already applied for a patent in New York State for "An improved device for executing criminals condemned to death," the improvement being current. At the time, Brown was working with the chief researcher at Edison's laboratory in Menlo Park, New Jersey, Dr. A. E. Kennelly. They produced a prototype chair and tested it more than fifty times on cats and dogs rounded up at night from New Jersey suburbs. The animals were alleged to be strays, not pets.

(The animals experimentally electrocuted by Brown were not the first to die by electricity. In 1773, Benjamin Franklin wrote to a friend that he had used six Leyden jars for the successful electrocution of a ten-pound turkey, a heavier lamb, and an unspecified number of chickens.)

The New York commission pored over the Menlo Park results and concluded that simply because the chair could electrocute small animals was no guarantee it could kill a human adult. So before panel members' eyes, Brown electrocuted a cow. The men were impressed. Then Brown electrocuted a horse, and the commission reported to New York Governor David B. Hill that their task was completed. They had the chair. On June 4, 1888, the governor signed a bill making electrocution a legal means of capital punishment. To convince state officials and the public of the benefits of death by electrocution, Brown was encouraged to take his animal act on the road, and he did, though animals did not travel with him; they were recruited in the city he visited. In Albany, at the request of the commission, he electrocuted an orangutan and its hair caught fire.

Even before the first criminal was electrocuted nascent electric companies in the Northeast vigorously opposed the electric chair. Not for humanitarian reasons. They feared that showing the public that electricity could kill, and instantaneously, would prevent them from having their homes wired for current. If the electric chair could fry a criminal, might a lamp's frayed cord do the same to a housewife?

Enter Thomas Edison.

For some time Edison had been touting the advantages of his own direct current, or DC, system. Rival businessman George Westinghouse was attempting to interest the power industry in his more efficient, reliable, and easier to transmit alternating current, or AC, system. The two men engaged in a bitter press dispute. Since the electric chair worked with alternating current, Edison saw an opportunity to defeat Westinghouse through a campaign of negative association. To this end, Edison had offered Harold Brown the use of his Menlo Park laboratory to carry out experiments on cats and dogs. But the stratagem eventually backfired. Westinghouse's AC system won out, the electric chair became a reality, and citizens by the thousands attended Brown's public electrocutions of animals, then went home and fearlessly turned on their lights.

First Electrocution. The first, and unfortunate, criminal to be electrocuted in the new chair was William Kemmler of Buffalo, New York, who had killed his mistress, Tillie Zeigler, with a hatchet in a fit of jealous rage. In effect, Kemmler became a pawn in the economic battle between two power industry giants: Edison pushed for Kemmler's electrocution by Westinghouse's system, and Westinghouse hired New York's best legal talent and spent over one hundred thousand dollars in a failed campaign to save Kemmler's skin—and his own, he believed.

The botched electrocution, carried out in New York's Auburn Prison on August 6, 1890, nearly caused the new means of capital punishment to be abolished.

The event drew a host of curious doctors who positioned themselves in a circle around the chair as Kemmler was strapped into the device. The first jolt of current (for seventeen seconds) failed to kill him; the doctors found that he was still breathing after the current had been off for several minutes. Embarrassed prison officials sent a second dose of current coursing through his body—thirteen hundred volts for seventy seconds. Kemmler thrashed, convulsed, and the drying of the electrodes in contact with his head and arms seared the flesh and filled the room with a pungent scent. Several witnesses fainted. Others, nauseated, bolted from the room. The whole death took eight minutes.

Reports in the New York papers the following morning were sensational and not always accurate. A reporter for the *World* who observed the execution firsthand wrote that after the first burst of current, "There was a straining at

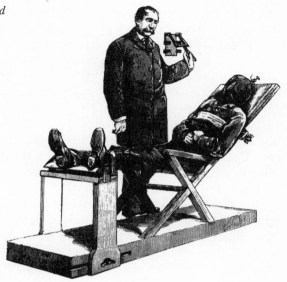

the straps which bound him. . . . The man was alive!" Alive, yes, and breathing, but unconscious. The initial blast of current had instantaneously knocked Kemmler out. However, violent reflexive muscle spasms of the body had fooled many reporters and horrified even the doctors. The *World*'s reporter concluded: "Warden, physicians, everybody, lost their wits."

In informing the public on the appearance of the chair, one paper made the pointless observation that "it was not at all uncomfortable to sit in."

The bungled first electrocution was the cause of editorial diatribes from the press condemning electrocution, torture, crime, and a society that could produce all three. The *Buffalo Express* predicted that "Kemmler will be the last man executed in such a manner." Reports of his autopsy stunned the public: The muscles were carbonized, soft tissue resembled well-cooked beef. When the press asked a beleaguered George Westinghouse for his opinion of the execution that employed his AC system, he exclaimed, "They could have done better with an ax."

The *New York Times* was a holdout, commenting, "It would be absurd to talk of abandoning the law and going back to the barbarism of hanging."

Two succeeding electrocutions passed without technical error and with minor press criticism. Then on July 27, 1893, the horrific execution of William Taylor, also at Auburn Prison, once again caused an outcry against the electric chair.

Taylor was condemned for the cold-blooded murder of a fellow inmate. With the first burst of current, his legs stiffened so forcefully that they tore loose from the chair's ankle straps. He was still alive, and the switch was quickly thrown for a second charge, but nothing happened. The generator in the powerhouse had blown. In front of stunned physicians and members of the press, a partially electrocuted Taylor, severely burned, barely clinging to life, was lifted from the chair and placed on a cot. Prison officials rushed to get chloroform and morphine, and the former was held under his nostrils while the latter was injected into his veins—not to kill him, but to keep him alive and unconscious until the generator was fixed.

It was one hour and nine minutes before he was returned to the chair, then given a blast of current that could have cooked a small animal. The warden announced to all present, "Gentlemen, justice has been done." (By comparison, today it takes two to three seconds to electrocute a person, and unconsciousness comes in less than $\frac{1}{240}$ of a second.)

As crowds in earlier centuries had flocked to witness stonings, drawings and quarterings, and hangings, there was no shortage of volunteers to witness electrocutions. The press seemed to hope that the bungling would continue; botched jobs made better copy. Four electrocutions at Sing Sing in 1891 went off smoothly. But in a 1903 disaster, which received enormous press coverage, the criminal, Fred Van Wormer, was electrocuted, pronounced dead, and taken to the autopsy room. When he started to breathe and move about, doctors frantically phoned the home of the executioner, Robert Elliott, ordering that he return to the prison immediately and electrocute Van Wormer again. By the time Elliott arrived, though, Van Wormer was dead. Nonetheless, his corpse was hauled back to the electric chair and given seventeen hundred volts for thirty seconds. The press noted that Van Wormer became the first dead man to be electrocuted.

Gas Chamber: February 8, 1924, United States

The several bungled attempts at death by electrocution renewed the search for a swifter and more humane form of capital punishment. One immediately presented itself: poisonous gas, which had been so effective a decade earlier in World War I. If chlorine, phosgene, or mustard gas could injure or kill hundreds of men out in the open air, several whiffs in a sealed chamber, the reasoning went, should be quickly lethal.

Much evidence was already in. The Germans had introduced chemical warfare in 1915 against Allied forces. In January of that year they released pungent chlorine gas against Russian troops in Poland, then they scored a major tactical victory in April gassing the French and British at Flanders. When the Allies developed gas masks and their own chlorine gas, the Germans switched to phosgene, a more injurious type of choking gas that was delivered in projectiles by artillery.

In a tit-for-tat tactic, the Allies improved their gas masks, introduced phosgene, and the Germans, in 1917, came up with mustard gas, a fiercely stinging agent (called a vesicant) that blisters the skin and lungs. A year later, both sides were abundantly raining the latest poison on their opponents. The universal revulsion against poisonous gas put an end to its use—in war, that is; by the 1920s several people thought it would be ideal for capital punishment.

One man was Major D. A. Turner of the U.S. Army Medical Corps, who developed the prototype of the modern gas chamber. Within the sealed chamber was a chair and beneath it a shallow pan. Through tubes various mixtures of water, sulfuric acid, or cyanide pellets could be combined to produce rapidly rising fumes. The condemned was to be strapped into the chair and his death was supposed to be quick and painless. Nevada was the first state to adopt the new form of capital punishment, and its first victim was Gee Jon, a Chinese convicted of a gang-style killing.

On February 8, 1924, Jon was taken to the chamber, strapped into the chair, and told that once he smelled "rotten eggs" he should hold his breath, count to ten, then take several deep inhalations. If he followed instructions, he was assured, he would pass out quickly and die painlessly. The gas was cyanide, and, distressingly, it took Jon six minutes to expire.

The problem with the instructions was that despite the condemned's best intentions to breathe deeply, the body instinctively resists inhaling something that stings the lungs and is lethal. Subsequent gas chamber deaths revealed that many victims gasped, wheezed, and struggled for oxygen like beached fish. Physiologically, death is by asphyxiation since the poisonous fumes make oxygen unavailable to the lungs; thus, as opponents of the new form of capital punishment pointed out, in the gas chamber the victim was being asked to suffocate himself. Was this more humane than suffocation by hanging? Or faster than death by electrocution?

Following Nevada's lead, eight other states adopted the gas chamber, California introducing in 1938 the most famous chair at San Quentin. The question many physicians and prison officials attempted to answer was whether a gassing death was painless. And as earlier doctors had examined the eyes of beheaded men for signs that the brain still functioned, modern doctors established prearranged eye signals with victims about to be gassed (for with air depleted from their lungs they could not verbally tell if they were in pain).

One of the most famous of such experiments was conducted in 1960 with convicted murderer Caryl Chessman. Chessman agreed to inhale the lethal fumes rapidly and blink and nod his head to indicate varying degrees of pain. To the horror of doctors and news reporters observing the execution, Chessman signaled vigorously, indicating that the gassing death was agonizing. The next morning a reporter wrote: "I thought he must be dead but no, there was another agonizing period during which he choked on the gas. And again. And then again. There was a long period, another deep gasp. At the fourth such straining, Chessman's head lolled in a half circle, coming forward so that he faced downward with his chin almost touching his chest. This must be the end. But the dying went on."

Some victims have died relatively quickly, after two or three minutes. But the average death process from gassing takes eight or nine minutes, and the longest on record, in North Carolina, took eleven minutes. Most eyewitnesses to this form of execution that was intended to be more humane than electrocution (which, in itself, was supposed to be preferable to beheading, which was deemed better than hanging, etc.) claimed that it did not live up to its early billing. The quest was on again for the perfectly painless ending.

Lethal Injection: December 6, 1982, United States

At 11:30 P.M. on December 6, 1982, forty-year-old Charles Brooks, convicted of the 1976 murder of an auto mechanic, lay himself on a hospital gurney at the Department of Corrections in Huntsville, Texas. His body was secured by five leather straps, and at 11:35 prison medical technicians inserted two intravenous needles, one in each arm. A harmless saline solution began to flow into Brooks's bloodstream, then an unseen executioner, behind a wall, opened valves that released a mix of three chemicals into the IV tubes.

The chemicals had different purposes. The two grams of sodium thiopental Brooks received was a lethal dose of a barbiturate, or sleeping drug, given in much smaller dosage to render a hospital patient unconscious before surgery. The drug acts directly on the brain to shut off sensory awareness. The second drug, pancuronium bromide, is a muscle relaxant that in large enough dosage paralyzes the diaphragm muscles and prevents breathing. The third drug in the chemical concoction, potassium chloride, a salt, in high concentration acts directly on the heart to cause cardiac arrest.

How did Charles Brooks, the world's first victim of capital punishment by lethal injection, actually die? From which of the three drugs?

The overdose of the barbiturate, which acted within ten to thirty seconds, killed him, rendering his brain permanently unconscious. The other two drugs were insurance, to make death unequivocal by stopping the lungs and heart. After centuries of searching for a painless form of execution, was the lethal injection capital punishment's Holy Grail?

Most doctors, especially anesthesiologists, contend that Brooks (as well as others who have died by injection) could not possibly have been aware of his death. That under the effect of the tranquilizer his brain fell asleep before his body stopped functioning. Opponents of capital punishment in any form argue that no physician who swears under the Hippocratic oath to save life should end life. The American Medical Association is equally concerned that doctors not be drawn so actively into the centuries-old debate on capital punishment. Chances are the debate will continue, and, if anything, accelerate as more and more states adopt the lethal injection as a legal means of ending life.

Although the first lethal injection death occurred in Texas in 1982, three states (Idaho, New Mexico, and Oklahoma) had legalized the method in 1977 but not carried out executions. Since Brooks's death, several criminals have died by injection. But a glance at the methods of execution in just a few states reveals the disagreement about ending a life and how that should be done: Alabama, electrocution; Arizona, gas chamber: Illinois, lethal injection; New Hampshire, hanging; New York, no death penalty; Utah, lethal injection or firing squad. And so on. On the positive side, at least there are no more beheadings, drawings and quarterings, stonings, burnings, or pressings, that is, not in the continental United States.

CHAPTER 7

Engineered Endings

Life-Span to Obsolescence

THERE IS A BUILT-IN ENDING to everything in existence, engineered by nature or man. A 100-watt light bulb is designed to end its illumination after 750 hours, and the glow from the sun will end in about 5 billion years. More immediately, your car's muffler has a life-span of 2.5 years, its water pump 3.5 years; and an unopened can of water-based paint will lose its usefulness in 7 years, 50 if it's oil-based.

Who cares? Insurance companies, for one. Their actuarial tables on which your premiums are based are in themselves long lists of endings in the form of maximum life-span, average usefulness, and factory built-in obsolescence.

All of us care about endings. Or we should. In purchasing a pet, it's helpful to know that a guppy can live at most six years, a goldfish fourteen. A small dog will outlive a larger one, and they both will live longer than a cat. And most important of all, nature has designed you, an "average" American, to meet your end twenty-eight thousand days after your birth. Statistically this means that there is a specific year, day, and time to the minute when your life will end. Excluding unexpected accidents, which can put an abrupt end to anything, this chapter is about endings that are designed, by manufacturers or by nature, to extinguish the life and usefulness of the very things they brought into existence.

Human Life-Span: 115 Years

In Sumerian legend king Karke lived to be 28,800 years old. In the Bible are records of lesser longevity: Methuselah lived to be 969, Noah 950. More recently, and with only somewhat more authenticity, the oldest living man, Russian Shirali Mislimove, died at 165, while his female counterpart, Ashura Omarova, also a Russian, died at 195.

Gerontologists believe, though, that the truest record for longevity is shared by about a half-dozen people who lived to age 113, including a French-Canadian bootmaker named Pierre Joubert, and an American, John Sailing, who died in 1959. (The age of 137 of a former Southern slave, Charlie Smith, who died on October 7, 1979, is still open to debate.)

The figure of 113 years is interesting because it correlates closely with the best scientific estimate, 115 years, for the time that a human being could live if he or she were spared all life-shortening diseases and infections. Presumably, at age 115, your undiseased body parts would be just too worn down to continue functioning. It's believed that 115 years is the genetically planned obsolescence for the species *Homo sapiens*.

Few people, of course, live out the maximum number of years genes theoretically allot them. Many will reach 71.3, the life expectancy of a baby born in 1989 in the United States. This average ending is, however, influenced by several factors. If the baby is white, its life will end at age 72.7; if black, at 67. The life-span for a female white baby jumps to 77.3 years, whereas for a white male it's down to 69.7 years—less than the 72.6-year life-span for a black female baby. (It's 64.1 for a black male baby.) Females, as we'll see in more detail, regardless of race or species, live longer than their male counterparts.

Life's end also comes at different times based on nationality, occupation, and marital status. A Swede, for instance, can expect to live twice as long as a Nigerian and nearly three times as long as a male from Guinea, whose life expectancy is only twenty-six years; a low standard of living is a major life-shortening factor.

In terms of jobs, professionals such as doctors and lawyers have the longest life-spans, followed by administrators and managers, then farmers and skilled

Shifting sands of time: Life expectancy in Neanderthal times, thirty years; ancient Greece, thirty-six; Renaissance, thirty-eight; today, seventy-plus.

laborers, and, at the bottom of the list, unskilled laborers. Whereas it's true that excessive on-the-job stress can hasten life's end, a lifetime of unhappiness with one's work is even more life-threatening.

The happiness factor is paramount in determining how marital status affects longevity. From a list of the twenty most traumatizing life events that can hurtle a man or woman toward an unexpectedly early ending are death of a spouse, divorce, and marital separation. Divorced women, for example, die of cervical cancer almost twice as often as married women, and in many potentially fatal diseases, the strain of being divorced or widowed is one of the strongest predictors of death.

Even being single is comparatively unhealthy. The death rate from heart disease is markedly higher for singles than for those who are married; and from suicide and stroke it is nearly twice as high; while from cirrhosis of the liver the difference is three-fold. People need people—it's part of the engineered program for a longer life.

Life's ending has been pushed substantially back in our own century, due largely to medical advances and decreased infant mortality. Had you lived in Neanderthal times, fifty thousand years ago, you might have reached twenty-nine, a figure suggested by skeletal remains. Had you been part of the Golden Age of Greece, about 500 B.C., you could expect to live to thirty-eight. During the arduous period that was the Dark Ages life expectancy dropped to thirty, though by the first glimmer of the Renaissance in Europe it was up to thirty-eight—midlife by today's measure.

True strides began in the 1600s with the birth of modern medicine, which lifted the figure to 51 by the close of the century. It's been climbing steadily since, with predictions that the average life expectancy in Western countries by the year 2020 will be 110. The end, though inevitable, can be delayed, even if only up to age 115.

That upper limit, which some people might find annoyingly low, apparently is very real and explained by various theories of aging. Aging is an ending that is happening all the time, from the moment of conception. Even if we escape the ravages of war, accident, and deadly disease, the body's decline proceeds at a surprisingly steady and clearly programmed pace. The truth is that virtually no human being dies *of* old age (just those few people who reach the maximum of 115). Just about every one of us alive today will die from his or her body's decreasing ability to ward off disease.

It is the progressive weakening of the immune system by aging that eventually prevents us from conquering the challenges posed by colds, infections, cancer, and the like. In youth we met the invading enemies and won; in old age the enemies win almost every time. This is one of the great lessons that AIDS has taught the science of immunology: With the immune system weakened or down, life's end is not far off. As Alex Comfort noted in *Aging: The Biology of Senescence,* "If we kept throughout life the same resistance to stress, injury, and disease that we had at age two, about half of us here today might expect to survive another 700 years." Well, 115 represents current optimism.

Sensory Obsolescence: Taste to Touch

Life's ultimate ending is foretold in countless ways from childhood onward. This is particularly true in the subtle but real waning of our five senses, which peak surprisingly early in life. Much is written in magazines and the popular press about extending youthfulness and usefulness. And to some degree those goals can be modestly achieved as we monotonically and relentlessly age. But this book is about endings, and thus its perspective is the reverse of what you might find in an article on how to stay young. A note of caution: If you are more sensitive about aging than you are curious of physiological endings, skip this section and resume at page 172.

Taste. As a child, no one told you how lucky you were to be able to taste food that touched the roof of your mouth, the walls of your throat, and the entire central upper surface of your tongue. Too late now. For by age ten, all humans lose the tens of thousands of taste buds in these areas. Food must have tasted differently in childhood, but we have no memory of it.

After age ten, the remaining taste buds are concentrated at the tip and rear of the tongue and around its periphery. Even these deteriorate with age. This is why adults, not children, are more likely to sweeten their food artificially; a teenager can identify an experimentally prepared solution as sweet at a third the sugar concentration required by a person age sixty.

In terms of actual numbers: At age 30, each tiny ridge on your tongue, called a papilla, has 245 taste buds. By age 80, only about 88 are left. Once atrophied, taste buds do not regenerate. And, too, your mouth gets drier as the mucous membranes secrete less fluid to liquefy chewed food, also diminishing the sense of taste. When elderly people complain that they don't have much of an appetite, that food tastes bland, there is often a sound biological reason.

While our sense of taste is running down, something else in that area of the body is also signaling to us that life's end is nearing.

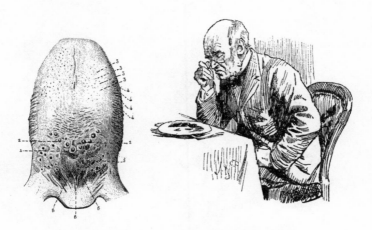

As taste buds die, food loses its appeal.

Voice.   With advancing years your voice, once definitive and clarion, begins to quaver as you lose control over your vocal cords. You end up talking more slowly. And as the vocal cords stiffen, they vibrate at a higher frequency like the tighter strings of a guitar. If in early-to-middle adulthood your voice was pitched at the C below middle C, by age seventy your conversation will be centered around E-flat. Voice is such a good barometer of aging that we can often guess a person's age by hearing the voice.

Vision.   Blues will be darker, yellows less brilliant, for as we age the lenses of the eyes thicken, discolor like aged paper, and thus refract light differently.

   With advancing years the eyes detect progressively less of the violet end of the spectrum. Several studies of the changing palettes of aging painters confirm they use less dark blue and violet on their canvases—the subtleties between the shades simply no longer exist for them. And though green and orange are less affected by thickening lenses, every older person requires more light, particularly at night, to activate the cells of the retina, which are losing sensitivity.

   Vision peaks at age seventeen. At that age our eyes are as close to 20/20 as they are ever going to be. That is because eye muscles are at their maximum flexibility, shifting rapidly to focus on an object near or far. And the pupil is largest, inviting in the maximum amount of light, day and night. The decline begins relatively early, in our twenties, levels off for about a decade, from thirty-five to forty-five, then resumes steadily, with near vision deteriorating faster for most people than far vision. The hardening of the lens can cause cataracts.

   By age seventy distance vision is sharply in decline. Night vision is markedly worse, and if you turn down the rheostat to dim the lights in a room, creating what was once a romantic ambience, you are for a time in almost total darkness until the sluggish pupils widen to let in more light. If you live long

*Near and far vision
deteriorate, as does
perception of colors,
brilliance dulling.*

enough, chances are you'll be blind. This is obsolescence every bit as planned as that in a light bulb or battery. Only we are not the planner but the planned.

Hearing. One of the oldest of the senses, hearing evolved to an acute level long before vision, when tiny four-legged creatures scurried through brush not in need of distance vision but dependent on sounds (as well as on smells). Its decline, when not artificially hastened by deafening rock music, clearly signals that life is winding down.

Our hearing peaks early in life, developed fully by age seven. Its deterioration with aging is measured by our increasing inability to perceive high frequencies. For example, as infants, we, like dogs, respond to sounds up to forty thousand vibrations per second (or hertz), far above the limit any adult hi-fi fan can appreciate. At age sixteen our sensitivity to audible high tones is down to twenty thousand hertz (while the dog's is not), and it continues to drop by about eighty vibrations per second every six months.

By age forty, we are deprived of hearing the rich multiple overtones in classical music. Women, though, because of thinner eardrums and lighter inner ear bones, are now hearing sounds about an octave higher than men. To express this decline more concretely: By forty we have trouble hearing above a cricket's chirp (fifteen thousand hertz); by sixty we can't hear above the top notes of a robin's song (ten thousand hertz).

Fortunately, up until age sixty we have had little trouble hearing the full range of human speech. But starting at sixty, this aural ability begins to narrow and we find ourselves craning for bits of conversation, or crankily asking, "What's that?" By seventy-five, we're missing full phrases of conversation and much of the upper beauty of fine music. So much that if a composer had to write a score strictly for the enjoyment of the elderly his creativity would be truly challenged. We are stone-deaf, for instance, to the high notes of even a pipe organ.

None of this saddening loss is biologically mysterious. The built-in end points in hearing result from the breakdown of cells deep within the ear that

When other sounds are muted, the ability to hear a scream for help remains strong into old age.

transform an outside vibration into an inner nerve impulse that registers in the brain as sound. Loud environmental noise greatly accelerates nature's programmed decline. A classic study was conducted on the Mabaans, a primitive tribe in the Sudan whose Stone Age culture remained essentially untouched by progress until discovery of the people in 1956.

The Mabaans were rare. They used neither drums nor guns, traditionally spoke in whispers, never shouted, and rarely were assaulted by a loud sound other than nature's roar of a lion or clap of thunder. Not only was their hearing better at all ages than Westerners', but better than any human hearing ever examined. All because their inner ear cells were spared trauma.

Today the generation of young Westerners addicted to headphones and deafening music will by age forty-five hear only half as well as their parents did at sixty-five. Thus the teenager who resents having to repeat himself for the benefit of grandpa will himself be barking grandpa's "What's that?" a full two decades earlier.

There is one amazing exception to the natural deterioration of hearing, a hangover from primitive times when survival was linked to aural acuity. We may miss the high notes of an aria or half of a spoken sentence, but we retain the ability to hear a human scream for help. A distress scream does not contain arbitrary frequencies; it exists between F-sharp and G in the fourth octave above middle C. To broadcast sound in that portion of the vocal spectrum requires the least amount of energy to activate the nerves of a human ear. No one talks in these rarefied frequencies; they are reserved, like a civilian radio band, for an emergency broadcast—which gets through even the deterioration in hearing brought on by old age. The hearer may be near the end of his own life, weak and feeble, but perceiving a human call for help he might be able take steps to save another life from ending. We may be genetically planned to self-destruct, but it's a fine plan while it lasts.

Smell.   Smell is the sense that holds up the best, and it is nature's oldest, existing in prehistoric deepwater fish that troll the black ocean depths without vision, without hearing, without touch, merely sniffing their way from meal to meal. Sniffing is still the way most advanced land and sea animals receive the bulk of their information about the environment; salmon and turtles smell their way through thousands of miles of ocean to return to the spawning ground where they were born.

The olfactory nerves in the nose are, of all the body's nerves, those wired most directly to the brain with fewest intermediate relay points. They are suspected of being a possible major route by which aluminum particles found in talcs, deodorants, and other sprays enter the brain producing a plaque that might be the cause of Alzheimer's disease.

But as vital as smell is evolutionarily, it, too, has a programmed ending. In tests using scents such as anise, coffee, gasoline, and peppermint, males and females from age ten to sixty showed little decline in their ability to distinguish slight concentrations of each. From about age sixty-five, though, the sense of smell begins to deteriorate—unless you are a smoker, in which case the acuity can wane decades earlier. Perhaps it is not surprising that nature's most important animal sense lasts the longest in all species.

Touch.   In the field of sensory research, relatively little work has been done on touch, a sense that is largely influenced by psychological factors. Most tactility studies have used pain as a barometer, inflicting it by pulling a hair on the arm or pricking a fingertip with a pin. Males, young and old alike, show great tolerance, but researchers wonder how much of the pain endurance is culturally based, especially since teenage boys, with a psychological need to feel stoical, often report feeling no pain in such studies, even when they are caught grimacing. In the same studies, women readily confess to feeling pain; yet in real-life situations, such as childbirth, they display extraordinary pain endurance.

To date, the evidence suggests that our sense of touch (as measured by pain tolerance) is programmed to diminish with age in order to protect us from the countless daily aches associated with aging body parts. In other words, nature kindly desensitizes us to the havoc it is wreaking in tearing down tissue and organs toward programmed demise.

Outward Obsolescence: Skin and Height

The decline of our five senses occurs internally, away from the gaze of friends and the image of ourselves in the mirror. Outwardly, though, there are two major indicators of life's calculated ending. Skin, the body's largest single organ, is the most obvious, to ourselves and others. Even if you never laughed, never frowned, never sunned, you'd still wrinkle, and badly if you lived long enough, since the skin is programmed to lose moisture, fat, and elasticity—all under the inescapable tug of gravity.

On the average, here is how the program progresses: At thirty, horizontal forehead creases appear. By forty, there are crow's feet from squinting, and from smiling we display the downward "umbrella" arc stretching from the nostrils to the corners of the mouth.

At fifty, we experience substantial water loss and drying in the skin. At the same time, subcutaneous fat has migrated away from the once-firm face to infiltrate internal body organs. Skin on the cheeks and along the jawline is sagging. Around sixty, the fat beneath the eyes that once produced a flattering firmness bunches downward into bags. By seventy, because of the loss of fat and water, the skin has lost its uniform color and reflects light in the yellow range of the spectrum, shifted away from rosy red, its broadcast hue in youth.

Unkindest of all, these changes can occur a full decade or two earlier in women than in men because of estrogen depletion after menopause. Nature, whose honesty knows no tact, is callously saying to the female, "You're past reproductive prime, you no longer need to attract a mate."

But the man has it no easier. His skin may be a bit firmer, but he's growing hair in his ears and on his back while at the same time losing it on his head; these unwanted features are almost exclusively part of aging's Y-chromosome program. In addition, from age thirty onward cartilage has been accumulating in his face, making his nose, by age seventy, wider and longer, his earlobes fatter, and the ears droopier by a good quarter-inch. Nature may be telling the elder male, "I've made you less attractive to the opposite sex so you won't attempt to mate and rear more offspring." But with humans, enticements such as money, power, and social position can cloud the message.

As we are growing less attractive, we are also getting shorter, which works to the same effect. In fact, you've been shrinking since your twenties.

Height.	You were tallest in your twenties—and in the mornings.

Most people are unaware that they shrink by day and stretch during the night. Erect stature decreases almost an inch in adults between rising in the morning and retiring at night, because while we are erect our intervertebral discs become compressed. As we age, these same discs of cartilage down the spinal column get permanently thinner, so that by age forty, even if you were to measure your height first thing upon waking, you'd be shorter than you were twenty years earlier. Factor in too that the arches of your feet flatten and that nature has programmed your bones to slow down their uptake of calcium. By age eighty, you will probably be as much as six inches shorter and thirty pounds lighter than you were in your prime.

The human skeleton is a major indicator of the timed fate nature has in store for us. The body has some two hundred distinct bones, which grow for a number of years and then stop. Our collarbones, for instance, terminate their outward reach between the ages of eighteen and twenty-five. The skull bones fuse, ending enlargement of the head, between fifteen and twenty-five. Bones in the palm and fingers end their growth around age fifteen. The ribs at twenty-three. The foot and toes stop growing around age sixteen. And the long bones in the legs end their stretch between thirteen and twenty, whereas the arm bones are finished around age eighteen. In fact, by age twenty-five you have ceased all bone growth, and now that you're standing tall, you commence to shrink.

And not just shrink, but creak. With loss of calcium the bones eventually become brittle and the lubricated joints start to dry out. The rubbing of bone against bone causes the erosion known as osteoarthritis. The net effect is that you are shorter, slower, and stiffer. Nature is saying in its inimitable directness, "So what if you can't escape a lion, you've already reared a family and made a contribution to your species. Good luck."

Memory Decline: Long-Term to Short-Term

As it turns out, cerebral function is consistently our most dependable servant up until the end of life. You can think even when you can do very little else. And, to a point, there is a seemingly fair tradeoff between the mental sharpness of youth and mature wisdom of old age.

The average person is at his or her IQ peak from age eighteen to twenty-five—if "smartness" is measured by the scores on standard intelligence tests. Schoolbook knowledge is, so to speak, still on the tip of your tongue, even if you don't have the experience to apply it wisely in real-life situations.

As we age beyond late childhood, the brain actually gets smaller, lighter, and wetter, pulling away from its sheath, but the deterioration has scant effect on cognitive ability, especially memory. Neural reserves are so plentiful that for many years we barely notice a decline. This turns out to be doubly true for extroverted people; introverts suffer a more rapid memory loss with age.

In general, everyone's memory begins to wane around age thirty, but the effects are observable only when tested for. If, for instance, an old man and a young man both try to memorize a list of words and are then given clues to each word, the older man recalls them as well as the younger man. But without clues, the older man has a harder time of it. With a list consisting of twenty-four words, a twenty-year-old typically recalls fourteen; a forty-year-old recalls eleven; at age sixty only nine words are remembered; and at seventy only seven words.

Recalling items from lists, though, is a function of short-term memory. And although short-term memory is in decline, the aging brain provides its user with compensations. Vocabulary, for example, is three times as great at age forty-five as when you graduated from college. And by sixty, your brain possesses almost four times as much information as it did at age twenty-one, making judgments based on complex correlations from decades of experience. At this age, standard IQ tests are irrelevant; you'd most certainly score poorly even though you are the wisest you have ever been. Psychologists are seriously proposing that elderly people, applying for jobs, be given MQ, or Maturity Quotient, tests, which give a more accurate picture of a sixty-year-old's mental acuity.

As consistent—and compensating—as cerebral function is, it does, however, reach an end point. For though the brain itself may be a highly dependable organ, it depends on the body to keep it fit, and major body systems are in decline. By age seventy, the lung's oxygen-transfer capacity has been halved; the immune defenses are down twenty-five percent from their peak; the kidneys can filter waste from the blood only half as fast as when you were thirty; and hardened arteries that supply oxygenated blood to the brain can induce strangulation, which brings on senility. Though there is every indication that a lifetime of information remains stored in the brain right up until death, retrieval of that information with advancing age and bodily decline becomes increasingly difficult and unreliable. You instinctively feel you know a fact, but you can't recall the information in detail. The fault is the body's, not the brain's.

As if all of the above declines do not proclaim convincingly enough that the end of life is extensively programmed, sound and restful sleep, a luxury we enjoyed throughout childhood, has been steadily in retreat. As a two-week-old infant you slept twenty hours a day. At age one sleep time was down to thirteen hours, then down to nine hours at age sixteen, seven hours at age forty, six hours at age fifty, and five hours or less after age sixty-five. It's as if nature is saying, "No need to sleep now, you'll soon be getting an eternity's worth."

Cruel? Only in the sense that we alone among all lifeforms can comprehend cruelty, can comprehend our own decline and demise. But as we're about to see, human beings already live longer than any other mammal on the planet.

Mammalian Endings: Shrew to *Homo Sapiens*

In the entire kingdom of mammals, we rank highest in terms of a maximum life-span of 115 years and an average life expectancy of 71.3 years. The closest contender, though far behind, is the Indian elephant, *Elephas maximus,* which has been known to live 77 years in the wild but a disheartening 24 years in captivity. The elephant is followed by the horse, *Equus caballus,* which can live 62 years, though due to disease and environmental hardships usually dies at about half that age, 30 years.

Descending the life-span ladder to our closest mammalian relative, the chimpanzee, there is the African elephant (fifty-seven years maximum, forty years average), the donkey (fifty, forty), the hippopotamus (forty-nine, forty), the Indian rhinoceros (forty-five, thirty-nine), and then the chimp. Although recent genetic studies reveal that human and chimpanzee DNA and blood types are more than ninety-five percent similar, and that the chimpanzee is more closely related to humans than it is to the gorilla, the chimp meets its end considerably sooner than humans, with a maximum life-span of thirty-nine years and an average life expectancy in captivity of fifteen years. Such are the payoffs for humans of medical science, pharmacology, sanitary engineering, and proper nutrition. It is only in terms of life-spans that the chimp is more closely related to the gorilla: thirty-six years maximum and on the average twenty-six years in captivity.

In "Our Allotted Lifetimes," Harvard's Stephen Jay Gould points out that the lifetimes of all mammals are scaled to their "biological pace." That is, all mammals—from the tiny shrew to the towering elephant—endure for approximately the same amount of "biological time." How is this so?

A small mammal, like the frenetic shrew, "ticks" fast internally, burns energy rapidly, and consequently burns itself out in the short lifetime of one to two years.

Sharing a long mammalian life-span with humans are the elephant (fifty-seven years), donkey (fifty), hippopotamus (forty-nine), and monkey (forty-five).

On the other hand, a large mammal, like the majestic grizzly bear, functions at a sedate and stately pace. It ticks slower, digests sluggishly, and enjoys a longer maximum life-span of thirty-one years (twenty-five average).

But remarkably, if you multiply the pace of each mammal's internal ticking by each mammal's life-span, the resulting number is virtually a constant. With one exception: Human beings live longer, says Gould, than the "allotted mammalian lifetime." Our ultimate ending has, for some reason, been delayed.

"We are prevented from grasping this important and comforting concept," Gould continues, "by a deeply ingrained habit of Western thought." Namely, we are taught from childhood to regard absolute Newtonian time—that is, the steady, observable ticking of our kitchen clock—as the single valid measuring stick for all things in the world. The shrew is quick, we say, whereas the grizzly bear is ponderous. However, each of those animals is living at the appropriate pace of its own biological clock—and the result, living quickly for two years or ponderously for thirty-one years, is in the end the same. To express it another way, each animal marches to its own internal drummer, but each enjoys essentially the same parade.

Getting down to numbers: Gould calculated the ratio of an animal's breath rate to heartbeat rate versus its body weight. The result is that all mammals, whatever their size, from shrew to blue whale, breathe once for every four heartbeats. Small mammals just breathe and beat their hearts faster and die sooner. For larger and larger animals, both breath and heart slow down at the same relative rate and the creatures live, respectively, longer and longer. Therefore, measured not by the absolute time of our kitchen clock, but by relative biological time, all mammals on the planet live for the same duration. Except humans.

If you are over age thirty and count your breaths and clock your pulse, you can calculate that your life should have ended years ago. You are living on borrowed mammalian time. "We live," Gould estimates, "about three times as long as mammals of our body size should." Why the threefold gift?

No one is certain of the answer. Gould offers a partial theory: "I regard this excess of living as a happy consequence of neoteny—the preservation in adults of shapes and growth rates that characterize juvenile stages of ancestral primates." That is, humans experience a delayed maturity; we arrive at all stages of life later than other mammals arrive at those same stages. We have a long gestation, an extended and dependent infancy, a protracted childhood, a stalled

Based on "biological time" the gigantic whale, lumbering bear, and swift shrew all live the same duration.

sexual awakening, and, in like fashion, death itself is delayed, arriving years
later than it should. About forty-eight years later!

Gould's calculations tie in nicely with current life-extension research. Studies with mice show that if their rapid metabolic furnace is slowed by reducing
caloric intake (eating less) they live three times longer than normal. In effect,
eating less food (while still getting proper nutrition) requires the body to do
less internal work, and this slowing down of internal biological time, or "ticking," prolongs life. Conversely, taking in large quantities of food forces the body
to burn faster and more quickly to burn itself out. Many researchers are
investigating if the end of human life can be pushed back by carefully restricting
calories.

We have looked at the longevity of several animals in the wild. What follows
are life's endings for two of our favorite pets.

Cat: 27 Years Maximum, 15 Years Average

Although the evolutionary line for cats began seven million years ago, producing both jungle felines and domestic kittens, the direct ancestor of the modern
cat was the Kaffir cat of ancient Egypt, tamed, bred, and used to protect
granaries from rodents. The oldest two cats on record (both rare exceptions)
were two tabbies. One, owned by a Mrs. Thomas Holway of Devon, England,
died in 1939 at the advanced age of thirty-six. The other, also from Devon and
owned by a Mrs. Alice St. George Moore, lived to thirty-four, dying in 1957.
Few cats exceed the species maximum life-span of twenty-seven years.

There are, however, two factors that extend the life of a cat. A study at the
University of Pennsylvania School of Veterinary Medicine found that neutering
a cat, particularly if it is a male, can prolong life by two years; the extension
is less for a female. The reason may be that female hormones help activate the
immune system while male hormones work to deactivate it slightly. Thus, by
castrating a male early in life, its immune defenses are reinforced and it lives
longer.

The second life-extending factor for a cat has to do with purity of breed:
A pure genetic line is at a disadvantage in terms of longevity. Mixed breeds live
about three months to one year longer than the less hardy pure breeds, which
are more susceptible to infection.

Conventional wisdom has it that the rule of thumb in calculating the "human
equivalent" of a cat's age is to multiply by seven. But that's wrong. Cats (and
dogs) sexually mature faster than humans, and by the time a cat is one year
old it's already far more advanced than a seven-year-old child. Researchers at
the University of Pennsylvania suggest that pet owners follow conversion
guidelines developed by French veterinarian Dr. A. LeBeau. The LeBeau
schedule is based on feline stages such as sexual maturity and tooth growth.

Dog: 34 Years Maximum, 15 Years Average

The LeBeau table also applies to dogs with only the slightest modifications
since their average life-spans are not that dissimilar from those of cats.

Time Since Birth	*Animal's Analogous Age to Humans*
3 months	5 years
6 months	10 years
12 months	15 years
2 years	24 years
4 years	32 years
6 years	40 years
8 years	48 years
10 years	56 years
14 years	72 years
18 years	91 years
21 years	106 years

Contrary to the general rule that large animals live longer than smaller ones, a large breed of dog usually dies sooner than a smaller breed. The Great Dane, for instance, seldom exceeds ten years of age, whereas it is not uncommon for a poodle to live beyond fifteen years. And a tiny Pekinese outlives a lumbering St. Bernard by about six years. But then statistics on dogs are full of contradictions; the two longest living dogs on record, both approaching the maximum life-span of thirty-four years, were large breeds: a sheepdog and a black Labrador retriever.

Though the domestic dog descended from the wolf, the health and nutritional benefits of being out of the wild have conferred on it added longevity. The wild wolf lives a maximum of only sixteen years and an average of nine, about half the dog's life-span. Spaying a dog, particularly a male, will, as with a cat, extend its life by about two years.

Man-Made Obsolescence: Technologic to Aesthetic

So far, everything in this chapter has concerned genetically engineered endings, nature's own kind of obsolescence. But there are other kinds of endings, arbitrary ones, that are calculated by organizations such as the American Society of Appraisers and the National Association of Independent Insurance Adjusters. They tell us, for instance, that the real, usable lifetime of neckties, aprons, work shoes, panties, and housecoats is one year; whereas garments the average American household considers obsolete after two years are bathing suits, negligees, scarves, sheets and pillowcases, and towels.

Such lists are long and tedious to read, and figures on the lifetime of a particular garment or appliance may not correspond remotely to the number of years some individuals get out of the product. Nonetheless, such lists are used every day to determine the "replacement value" of property that is damaged, destroyed, or stolen. The lifetime of some of the longer-lived household items are: steam iron, seven years; home freezer, nine years; air conditioner, ten years; heating pad, fifteen years; home's electrical wiring, twenty years; grand piano, forty years.

If you hold on to an item longer than its average lifetime—or replace it before it's supposedly worn out—you may be the victim of several other kinds of obsolescence dreamed up by manufacturers and Madison Avenue. These are clever endings that within manufacturing industries go by specific names that can be helpful to know.

Planned Obsolescence, for instance, is where the designer and manufacturer collaborate in devising a product that will meet its useful end in a given time-span. The most costly of such items is the multimillion-dollar nuclear power plant that is deliberately constructed to last only thirty years. On a smaller scale, planned obsolescence's philosophy is simple: Why build a widget to last ten years when a "better" widget can be available to the consumer in five years?

Technologic Obsolescence is unique to our century. A typical case is audio reproduction, or the phonograph record, two words that are themselves dinosaurs of an earlier day. The industry's 78 RPM records were driven to extinction by 33⅓ discs, which in turn were endangered by tape formats such as reel-to-reel, eight-track, and cassette. And of course, one tape format quickly replaced in usefulness and popularity its predecessor, the way stereo killed off monophonic sound. Records are now dying off to be replaced by the CD or compact disc, though in the wings stands the DAT or digital audio tape, which may in time end the life of CDs. And the record is only one example of technological obsolescence.

At no previous time in history has humankind experienced such rapidfire and costly turnover. Rapid obsolescence may have other consequences. Psychologists believe that the fast turnover of products can breed a mentality of short-term reasoning, philosophy, and expectations that infiltrates all aspects of life. In our relationships, will we replace each other long before our actual usefulness and lifetime are up? Are we doing it already?

Size Obsolescence is another phenomenon unique to our time, a direct result of the technology of micro-miniaturization. Take, for instance, the various incarnations of the personalized electronic calculator. In the 1950s, for about five hundred dollars you could buy a two-hand-held calculator that could add, subtract, multiply, and divide. Some machines did square roots. They were marvels in their time, bulky, slow dinosaurs that children today probably can't imagine—not when for less than five dollars they can own a credit card–size calculator, operated not by thick batteries, not even by disc-thin batteries, but by light, a calculator that performs higher mathematics and is a gift with a trial subscription to *Newsweek* or *Time.*

Smaller, of course, does not necessarily mean better, but today it does spell the end for many larger products. In the past, items—whether for the person, the home, or the military—lasted for decades. Today their replacement is predicted before their peak popularity is achieved. The phenomenon has generated a perplexity: Do I buy this year's VCR or wait twelve months for the more compact model that can do more?

Powered Obsolescence is a consequence of the electronic age. Put simply: Is the electric can opener really that much of an improvement over the manual kind? On the other hand, is not the hand-operated carpenter's saw a tool that justifiably met its virtual end by the buzz of the power saw? But what about the electronically operated garage door? The powered venetian blinds on an electronic timer? The problem with electrifying everything is that during a power failure nothing works.

Powered items are seductive and they often render obsolete their manual predecessors. But the kind of obsolescence for which most of us are easiest prey is:

Aesthetic Obsolescence. Here we fall for exteriors. Detroit, for instance, deliberately changes the outward appearance of cars every year, though even spokespeople for the automotive industry would be hard put to explain how one year's model is a substantial improvement over the last. We are well aware of this kind of aesthetic obsolescence and willingly pay the price. And of course the fashion industry exists solely on the concept of aesthetic obsolescence, applying it not yearly, but seasonally.

Is the modern phenomenon of rapid obsolescence dangerous? Sociologists say it is. Next to watching television, America's favorite pastime is shopping, and a large part of that activity involves buying a "new," "improved," "miniaturized," "faster" item to replace an earlier version that still functions perfectly. Or at least adequately. Psychologists are treating more and more "spendaholics" whose addiction is "binge buying" and who use words like "high," "rush," and "turn-on" to describe the feeling of acquiring new goods.

Psychiatrists treat compulsive buying as an anxiety disorder in which the act of shopping becomes a "dysfunction of impulse control." The dizzying obsession to buy initially produces in the shopper a mental high, which is followed by a letdown—the classic addiction cycle of pleasure then pain. And, too, shopping, unlike other disorders, is not perceived as antisocial behavior. Quite the contrary. It is, in a real sense, American, part of a capitalist way of life. Spending is encouraged and encountered at every turn—from the staggering federal budget to the T-shirt that proclaims "Born to Shop." In addition, the old goods we are discarding in staggering quantities create their own problem: what to do with millions of tons of trash a year?

This book is about endings, and the modern phenomenon of rapid, planned, advertised obsolescence—as well as the spending frenzy that is its desired goal—may be leading America into a financial strait that is an ending of a most dangerous kind. It is the theme of this book that everything under the sun (and including the sun) must end; it is the theme of many other books that through uncontrolled spending America's days as a great world power may well be nearing their end.

CHAPTER 8

Ancient
Extinctions

Trilobite to Mastodon

EXTINCTION IS FOREVER, an ending from which there is no return. It is the harshest reality of the history of life.

Consider one statistic: At least ninety-nine percent of all species that ever lived are now extinct. Thousands of extraordinary animals no longer walk the land, swim the ocean, or glide on the air, though at one time the earth was exclusively theirs. Although the disappearance of any species is unarguably sad, the loss of some, we'll see, is sadder than others. This chapter and the next are about permanent endings on a massive scale.

Worrisomely, mass extinctions are periodic. They occur about every thirty million years, wiping out fifty to ninety-five percent of the species living at that time. Sandwiched in between are smaller extinctions, but these are dwarfed by the gigantic regulars.

Scientists believe mass extinctions are, have always been, *and will continue to be* a routine fact of life on earth, caused probably by cataclysmic changes on the planet and in the cosmos. Mass global warmings and coolings, devastating meteorite showers, deadly supernovae radiation are but a few of the possibilities that snuffed out most of earth's fauna and flora. One concern is unavoidable: Are the current depletion of the ozone layer, greenhouse warming, tropical deforestation, radioactive and toxic pollution of earth's soil and water a set of woes that will bring about the next mass extinction? Which will, if geologic history faithfully repeats itself, wipe out up to ninety-five percent of all creatures now alive? Individually each one of us must die, but that is quite different from the species collectively becoming fossils trapped in a stratum that might henceforth be known to someone or something as the Sapiens epoch.

Darwin helped legitimize fossils and popularize natural history museums.

The word "fossil" comes from the Latin *fodere,* meaning "to dig," and originally applied to almost anything of interest that was dug out of the ground, not just the telltale remains of living organisms. Today we know that for an animal or plant to become a fossil it must be buried quickly after death, natural or catastrophic, so that scavengers or bacteria cannot ravage it. Through the science of paleontology we can look back about six hundred million years, the time when well-skeletonized organisms first appear in abundance in the fossil record.

Fossils as Evidence: 1st Century B.C., Rome

A child touring a natural history museum today would recognize a fossil for what it is—a relic, evidence of a creature that has passed on. But correct recognition was far from always the case, even among scientists.

Throughout the Middle Ages and well past the Renaissance, no one, layman or scientist, knew quite what to make of the bones and skeletally etched rocks that were routinely unearthed in Europe and Asia. In addition, the idea of the extinction of a species—an unarguable given today when animals are vanishing yearly under our encroachment—was abhorrent and condemned as heresy. It contradicted the religious axiom that each of God's creations would survive unchanged until Judgment Day. Until recently, both scientist and preacher envisioned only one great ending, with no intermittent extinctions, and certainly with no creature altering its shape to become a new creation.

But this dogmatic view has not always held sway.

The first-century B.C. Roman poet and philosopher Lucretius wrote about the continual flux of living organisms. In *De Rerum Natura* ("On the Nature of Things") he brilliantly summed up much of the fossil knowledge of his time: "Nothing remains forever what it was. Everything is on the move. Everything is transformed by nature and forced into new paths. One thing, withered by time, decays and dwindles. Another emerges from ignominy, and waxes strong." A highly accurate, modern assessment.

Lucretius was of course no Darwin; he held many fanciful ideas about man and nature. But his insight into the process of extinction was shrewd: "Many species must have died out altogether and failed to reproduce their kind."

Though Lucretius never saw the giant thighbone of a dinosaur, let alone an assembled dinosaur skeleton, to learn such a creature once existed and vanished could not have shocked him as it did later scientists, scandalizing Christians and Protestants alike.

By the fourth century A.D., Christianity had condemned Lucretius's view of fossils (while embracing many of his most improbable notions). The word of the Bible became literal truth, and nowhere did it hint that new animals might appear or established ones vanish.

Even in the sixteenth century, when various Protestant groups began to split away from the original church, they took with them the impossibility of evolution as well as the ongoing mystery of fossils; thousands more had been found, many full skeletons, but their meaning remained baffling. "I hold that the animals took their being at once upon the word of God," wrote Martin Luther, "as did also the fishes in the sea." An individual bird dies, said Luther, but its species could not.

A century later, in 1650, Archbishop James Ussher of the Irish city of Armagh added up the ages of all the men and women mentioned in the Bible and came to his famously precise dictum: God created the earth on Sunday, October 21, at nine o'clock in the morning, in the year 4004 B.C. That did not leave much time for the emergence and extinction of new creatures, to say nothing of the civilizations of Egypt, Sumer, and Babylon. But having a precise date was comforting, and for many it became dogma.

To explain away the bones being unearthed by miners, scientists and clergy resorted to a mélange of conflicting arguments. The bones, went one theory, though shaped like thighs, fingers, and clavicles, were in fact stones; resemblances were coincidental. Another theory maintained that the mysterious bones were truly bones, but "models of God's rejected works," creatures He test-created then discarded, littering the landscape. Still other people believed that the bones were "outlines of future creatures," on the Lord's drawingboard. The cleverness of two concepts captured many people's fancies.

The Deluge Theory: Not Everyone Made It to the Ark.   Of all the arguments devised to explain away fossils, the most popular for a time, put forth by clergy, was also the shrewdest. It conceded that fossils represented evidence of creatures that had become extinct, but extinct only because they had dilly-dallied on the way to Noah's ark. As punishment, God allowed all the tardy to drown in the deluge. Thus the strange-looking unearthed fossils, which matched the skeletons of no existing animals, were bones of antediluvian, or before the deluge, stragglers.

This idea in itself was a strong compromise with strict biblical teaching. For the Bible is explicit that God ordered Noah to bring into the ark "every living thing of all flesh." However, so overwhelming was the rapidly accumulating fossil record that compromise was needed to save face, and faith.

Credulity soon had to be stretched even farther. Hundreds of new living species of birds, reptiles, and mammals were being discovered by explorers in the Americas and Australia—like the kangaroo. Being shipped back kicking to

Europe, kangaroos had obviously made it to the safety of the ark. But how did they get from Noah's disembarkment to Australia? Even more perplexing, faraway places were yielding thousands of never-before-seen fossil skeletons. Clearly the ark had not been large enough to save two of every kind. Such troublesome issues soon sank the deluge theory, that is, the single deluge theory.

The leading nineteenth-century French naturalist, Baron Georges Cuvier, suggested there had been several deluges, each wiping out most of the creatures alive at that time, leaving behind their bones and skeletal imprints. Following each depletion, God created replacement life-forms, always different. Cuvier's idea of catastrophe-extinction-replenishment was in essence correct, and though it would take Darwin to clarify the replenishment process in terms of evolution, Cuvier, in abandoning the notion of the fixity of species and by charting geological catastrophes, became the founder of both comparative anatomy and paleontology.

Why Adam Had a Navel, When the First Man Had No Mother.
One of the last scientists to deny the true nature of fossils before publication of Darwin's 1859 *Origin of Species* was English naturalist Philip Gosse. A renowned marine biologist, Gosse is credited with inventing the public aquarium; he was the first scientist to successfully build and house a variety of marine animals that lived long enough to be enjoyed by the public. (Previous attempts at filtering and oxygenating aquarium water had failed.)

But three years after Gosse described that success in his 1854 book *The Aquarium,* he had the misfortune to have published his *Omphalos.* The title is Greek for "navel," and the book addressed the centuries-old conundrum of Adam having a navel when he had neither parents nor a natural birth.

Clergy of the day taught that Adam did indeed have a navel. Gosse, a member of the highly conservative Plymouth Brethren, reasoned that just as Adam's navel was the relic of a birth that never occurred, so too were fossils relics of animals that never existed—except in the mind of God, who created the earth replete with buried bones and skeletally etched rocks. And he went farther, claiming that *all* the supposed signs of a vast antiquity—not merely fossils, but geological strata, the scratches from one ancient glacier sliding past another—were simply appearances. God, for His own reasons, had created the world with an illusion of a former existence.

Wasn't that divine deception?

Gosse answered the question rhetorically: "It may be objected that to assume the world to have been created with fossil skeletons in its crust— skeletons of animals that never really existed—is to charge the Creator with forming objects whose sole purpose was to deceive us. The reply is obvious. Were the concentric timber-rings of a created tree formed merely to deceive? Were the growth lines of a created shell intended to deceive? Was the navel of the created Man intended to deceive him into the persuasion that he had a parent?"

Bringing added scientific scorn upon himself, Gosse advanced the idea that

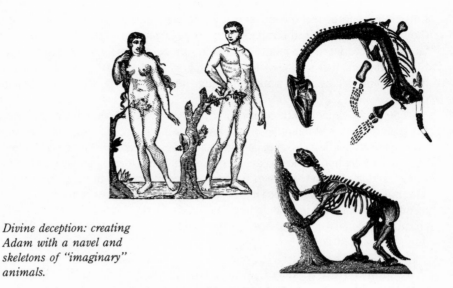

Divine deception: creating
Adam with a navel and
skeletons of "imaginary"
animals.

Adam was even created with urine already in his bladder and digested waste matter in his colon. *Everything* was created as if it had a past.

Gosse went into retirement at St. Mary's Church on the Devon coast (soon publishing his noncontroversial *A Year at the Shore*), and Darwin came out with his own views on fossils. In the earth's long history there had been repeated catastrophes and mass extinctions of species, and survivors, under environmental pressures, evolved to fill vacated niches.

Today scientists recognize at least fifteen major catastrophes or geological endings, each marked by the extinction of certain dominant animals. The great dying off of dinosaurs is one of the five largest wipeouts, though not the largest, as we'll see in examining ten of the most interesting ancient endings.

Cambrian Extinction: 500 Million Years Ago

> **Dominant life form:** *Trilobites,* marine animals distantly related to the modern horseshoe crab, which ranged in length from three inches to almost two feet.

The country of Wales, once known as Cambria, gives its name to the vast span of the earth's history known as the Cambrian period (600 million to 500 million years ago). It marked the opening of the age of ancient life, or Paleozoic era (*palaios,* "old"; *zoön,* "animal"). Near the end of Cambrian times, more than fifty percent of all animal species vanished, including numerous kinds of trilobites.

(Although microscopic life emerged on earth some 3.5 billion years ago, evolving into myriad soft-bodied, multicelled organisms of bacteria, green algae, viruses, and protozoa, there are relatively few fossils from this Precambrian time.)

Cambrian fossils were first discovered in northern Wales, in the area's sandstones and slates. In 1835, English geologist Adam Sedgwick named the animal relics Cambrian, because "Cambria"—a Latinization of the Welsh word *Cymry,* meaning "people"—was popular among English writers as an ancient name for Wales. But similar fossils also exist throughout Europe, Asia, and North America.

The fossils reveal that the era pullulated with the forerunners of modern sea sponges, jellyfish, starfish, worms, clams, scallops, nautiluses, and horseshoe crabs. Their relatives were the lucky creatures that survived predation and changes in the earth's oceans to evolve into the versions we collect, eat, and admire today. Existing in less-developed forms at the time of this first mass extinction were also prototypes of modern crabs, shrimp, lobsters, octopus, and squid—also survivors. Who died?

Thousands of sea animals that had also learned to protect themselves from predators by building hard shells using minerals dissolved in the oceans. The most numerous that would eventually reach extinction were the trilobites, whose name means "three lobes" and describes their body divisions. They were the first earth creature to develop well-defined eyes. A single eye might contain as many as fifteen thousand elements, each with its own lens precisely placed to catch ocean-depth light. The trilobites' eyes gave them a nearly hemispherical field of vision.

As the species evolved, the eye became even more complex, probably because trilobites lived in muddy ocean depths where sharp vision was crucial in collecting food. For visual acuity and sophistication, the trilobite's eye has never been rivaled by another animal that survived the great Cambrian ending. After reigning as the most common animal on earth for hundreds of millions of years, the trilobites would vanish. Today's oceans would be vastly different if the extinction had not occurred.

It would be wrong to imagine trilobites disappearing abruptly; their extinction happened over an extended period. It can't be entirely explained by the emergence of the earth's first fishes, for when that era began the trilobites were already on their way out. But certainly this new breed of fast-swimming, agile sea creatures made survival difficult for the trilobites, eating them and their eggs.

We do know from their fossil imprints that the last trilobites developed grotesque spiny protuberances and other strange and seemingly useless features. This is frequently a sign that a species is under enormous environmental stress, vigorously attempting to adapt to the new pressures with haphazard enlargements and excrescences. In the end, though, none of the trilobites' valiant efforts met with victory. Their useless appendages were a sign they were nearing extinction, and each year more trilobites died than were born, until finally no new ones would be born at all.

Ordovician Extinction: 440 Million Years Ago

Dominant life form: *Cephalopods,* or "head footed" mollusks,
related to modern squid, which inhabited multichambered shells
and swam rapidly backward by squirting water forward.
Tentacles at their heads (hence the name "head footed") enabled
them to seize prey and feed on it with beaklike jaws.

The fair-skinned, dark-haired Ordovices were an ancient Celtic tribe that lived
in the western part of Wales. They were undoubtedly unaware that they built
their homes and tilled their farms above fossil remains of prehistoric jawless
fishes and exotic sea lichen, moss, and fern—the first such remains from the
area to be studied by scientists. In 1879, geologist Charles Lapworth used the
name of the ancient Celts to characterize the period in the earth's history from
500 million to 440 million years ago.

In Ordovician times, the world's northern landmasses were drifting together. The southern continents had already formed into a single stretch of
land. The present South Pole region lay over North Africa, which was itself
beneath ice. The seas, shallow from ice formations, washed over large parts
of North America. Animals and plants still lived only in the sea; nothing had yet
come onto land.

Clams and oysters were developing a more modern appearance. Fish had
emerged as the earth's first creatures with backbones, ushering in the verte-
brate lineage that would lead to amphibians, reptiles, mammals, marsupials, and
man. The most primitive fish (really a proto-fish) was the jawless agnatha,
whose mouth was merely a sucking organ; one relative escaped the Ordovician
extinction to evolve into the present-day sea lamprey. These are all creatures
that evolved.

Dying off were animals with bizarre spines and knobs, many distantly
related to today's starfishes and sea urchins. Others were headless mollusks
with a hinged bivalve shell similar to that of modern clams. Extinction also came
to forms of soft and stony coral and countless sea mosses and ferns. Though
the Ordovician extinction was massive in scale, it was never emblazoned on
popular consciousness because it, like the Cambrian extinction, was confined
to the earth's oceans and mainly to small, exotic sea creatures.

Silurian Extinction: 395 Million Years Ago

Dominant life form: *Eurypterids,* water animals with a pair of
broad swimming appendages (hence their name: Greek *eurys,*
"broad"; *pteron,* "wing"), related to modern scorpions.

The Silurian period (440–395 million years ago) is named for the warring
Silures, a fierce, savage tribe that lived on the Welsh-English border during the
time of the Roman occupation. To the schooled, sophisticated Romans, the
unkempt Silures were barbarians. But to geologist Sir Roderick Impey Murchi-

son, who in 1835 catalogued fossils of ancient animal and plant life in the region, the warriors' name suggested a geological rubric.

During Silurian times, lichens and mosses adapted to life on land. The first land animals, segmented millipedes, emerged from the seas to stake a claim for themselves and their descendants. Despite their name, millipedes had not a thousand legs but at most two hundred, with some species possessing as few as eight. Certain species, now extinct, measured up to six feet long (some extinctions are not as missed as others). Three groups of these millipedes (all small) have survived into modern times: of them, the centipedes are the closest kin, segmented like the ancient millipedes; the scorpion shows divisions only along its tail; and spiders, except for a few species in Southeast Asia, have lost all traces of their segmented past.

By the end of Silurian times, the earth's colliding continents had pushed up mountains and forged two supercontinents: Laurasia in the north and Gondwanaland in the south. Though life had begun on land, it still thrived largely in the shallow seas that invaded much of swampy Laurasia. Jawed fishes emerged, and the shallowest seas supported a rich array of coral reefs, sea lilies, lampshells, and mollusks. Again, because the extinctions from this period include primitive fishes and millipedes (and these at the top end of the evolutionary ladder), they have not captured the popular imagination as did loss of the dinosaurs or the later loss of America's mastodons and saber-toothed cats.

Devonian Extinction: 345 Million Years Ago

Dominant life form: *Fishes,* among them sharks. On land, beginning to emerge, were wingless insects.

The name Devonian comes from Devon, England, the region in which fossils from this era were first studied. Devonian rock is rich in tin, zinc, and copper, first appreciated by Bronze Age peoples. Near the end of Devonian times, thirty percent of all animal life, including many species of primitive fishes, vanished.

During the Devonian period (395–345 million years ago) the two major north and south continents, Laurasia and Gondwanaland, drew closer together until they met at what is now North and South America to form a single supercontinent, Pangaea, meaning "all Earth." Mountain ranges thrust up and the climate throughout the world was warm and muggy. Many land plants had equipped themselves with tubes for sucking moisture from the soil, while giant horsetails and feathery tree ferns produced the world's first forests. Much of the land was swampy, populated by the amphibious forerunners of newts, salamanders, frogs, and toads. Spiders were everywhere.

One great extinction from this period was numerous kinds of sharks. Called chondrichthyes, or higher fishes, sharks developed skeletons of tough gristly cartilage *(chondros),* not bone, and swim bladders to adjust buoyancy. They evolved relatively quickly, but those that were not the most ferocious, streamlined killers with razor-sharp teeth died out even faster. The survivors also ate into extinction hundreds of kinds of primitive rays, skates, ratfish, and the

Life comes on land: comparison of a Devonian fish (left) with a later amphibian, reptile, mammallike reptile, and primitive mammal.

vulnerable jawless fish that already were on the way out. Had all of the great varieties of sharks lived, the novel *Jaws* might have been written sooner—or never at all.

Carboniferous Extinction: 280 Million Years Ago

> **Dominant life form:** Amphibians. As their name implies (*amphi*, "on both sides"; *bios*, "life"), these creatures lived a double life, beginning in the water, as, say, a tadpole, then developing lungs to live on land.

When the world's seas washed inland they drowned vast expanses of tropical forests causing plants to fossilize into carbon. These thick carbon bands in the earth's crust, our source of coal, give their Latin name (*carbo*, "coal"; *fero*, "to bear") to the Carboniferous period (345–280 million years ago), also known as the age of amphibians.

Sprawling amphibians, some as big as crocodiles, lurked on swampy mud-banks below surviving trees, ferns, and giant horsetails. Others hunted fishes in inland pools. Amphibians with sturdy limbs walked easily on land. Those with tiny limbs (or none at all) swam like eels or burrowed through leaf litter on the forest floor. Snails slithered through the humid undergrowth. Rotting logs sheltered centipedes, scorpions, and countless kinds of cockroaches—for this was also the time of beetles, weevils, and termites.

Other insects took to the skies on nature's first wings. And though some were the forerunners of bees, wasps, and mosquitoes, none yet had the ability to sting. The world belonged to creepers and crawlers and the amphibians that dined on them.

Meanwhile, vast ice sheets smothered much of the world's great southern landmass. The creatures dying off during this period still were not spectacular by popular standards, being the remainder of jawless fishes and many of the proto-animals that paved the way for heartier amphibians and stinging insects. The death toll during the Carboniferous extinction was enormous, but it would be the next wipeout, the Permian, that would captivate scientists like no previous one had.

Permian Extinction: 225 Million Years Ago

> **Dominant life form:** *Reptile,* particularly *Edaphosaurus,* or "soil lizard," a large herbivore with blunt teeth, some in the roof of its mouth. Up to eleven feet long, it had a high dorsal "sail" of skin running down its back.

Fossils unearthed near Perm in Russia explain the name given to the Permian period, where reign on land passed from the amphibians to the reptiles. Nineteenth-century British scholar Richard Owen coined the name "dinosaur" (*deinos,* "terrible"; *sauros,* "lizard") for these creatures, large and small, that lumbered everywhere during the Permian period (280–225 million years ago). One of the first was the primitive cotylosaurs (*cotyl,* "cavity" lizard), which was followed by more mammallike reptiles. They all lived on the supercontinent of Pangaea, which was drifting north, while glaciers retreated southward. Great earth movements threw up mountain ranges ancestral to the Appalachians, Rockies, Alps, and Urals. The land belonged to lizards, and the Permian period marks the end of the Paleozoic era, that is, the end of the age of ancient life.

The earth's first truly devastating extinction occurred at the end of Permian times. For some reason, seventy-five percent of amphibian families and more than eighty percent of reptilian families vanished (though these families had yet to become hugely populated).

The greatest havoc occurred in the sea. More than ninety percent of all shallow-water marine species died off. To express it another way: Fully half of the families of marine organisms vanished from the face of the earth—all during the relatively short span of a few million years, minutes to a geologist. The victims of this mass extermination included all surviving trilobites; all ancient corals; all but one lineage of coiled, hard-shelled mollusk known as ammonites; most hinged shellfish called brachiopods; most stalklike sea animals called crinoids; and virtually all of the minute, mosslike bryozoans. In sheer numbers, this great dying was the most profound of earth's many extinctions, more devastating than the later destruction of the dinosaurs.

Since the Permian extinction dwarfs all the others, it has been the focus of

"Terrible lizards" could be small and strange: Naosaurus *(left) and* Triceratops flabellatus.

much investigation. Understanding how it occurred might provide clues not only to earlier mass endings, but also to what may lie ahead for earth's present inhabitants.

One hint may come from the unique geology of the Permian period. All the continents we know today had coalesced into the single landmass Pangaea. The ocean floor topology changed drastically. Sea levels probably fell far enough to expose the entire continental shelf. Most of the world's shallow bodies of water disappeared, taking with them thousands of marine animals. As ocean water and fresh water mixed, salt concentrations were toxically altered, harming marine animals in both the sea and inland lakes.

But sea changes alone are not the whole story. Climatic changes were enormous and abrupt, many areas warming substantially as hot rocks were thrust up to become mountains. The patchwork of vegetation on the earth's surface was ripped apart, much of it burned. And, too, there may have been cosmic forces at play: the deadly influx of radiation from violent sunspot activity or the explosion of supernovae.

The great Permian extinction continues the pattern of mass catastrophes occurring about every thirty million years. To explain the periodicity, scientists have invoked, as mentioned, cyclic meteor showers, regular galactic rotation, and climatic change. Most recently they have theorized that periodic extinctions can actually occur through random catastrophes.

How is that possible?

Paleontologists at Johns Hopkins University devised a computer model to simulate the diversity of species throughout time. Into the model they incorporated a random series of environmental upheavals—such things as comet impacts, rises in sea levels, and massive volcanic eruptions. They found that a single event drastically reduces the number of different species, but that following this first event the biosystem is temporarily immune to further random cataclysms; the species that survive are hardy and resistant to subsequent upheavals. Moreover, after an extinction, there are simply fewer species left to die out. Therefore, the scientists say, until many new species have evolved, including extinction-prone types, intervening catastrophes have little effect. In summary: After each extinction, the biological community requires a distinct recovery period before it is again ready to go out with a bang.

Scientists are still uncertain what caused the massive Permian dying. But the monumental rubout of species created a niche that favored the already numerous reptiles. In fact, it ushered in the age of the reptiles.

Triassic Extinction: 193 Million Years Ago

Dominant life form: *Reptiles,* particularly *Cynognathus,* a wolf-size (*cyno,* "wolf") mammallike scavenger with fierce teeth and limbs directly beneath the body that made for fast running.

With the end of the age of ancient life (Paleozoic era) began the age of middle life (Mesozoic era) more popularly known as the age of dinosaurs. Though, given our current fascination with the giants of the species, the age opened with disappointingly small representatives, hardly "terrible lizards."

The Triassic period (225–193 million years ago) gets its name from the Latin *trias,* meaning "three," after a fossil-rich three-layer sequence of strata first studied in central Germany. During Triassic times, the vast supercontinent Pangaea was still intact. Thus animals could colonize the world by simply walking overland, though hostile deserts made many routes deadly traps. Reptiles of many shapes and sizes flourished, sharing the land with tortoises. Gradually dinosaurs got larger and some, like the pterosaurs (*ptero,* "wing"), took to the air.

Other saurians inhabited the world's warm, shallow seas. These were chiefly the "fish lizards," ichthyosaurs, which had fins, flippers, a long narrow jaw, and a superbly streamlined body. The largest individuals measured about twenty-five feet but some species were no larger than a man (a comparison that could not yet be made). The saurians—masters on land, in fresh water, and in the air—were members of one group: the archosaurs, or "ruling lizards." These beasts, large and small, bulky and streamlined, plated and thin-skinned, dominated life throughout the remainder of Mesozoic times. They would not die off for many millions of years.

But as the Triassic period drew to a close, large families of nonsaurian animals—amphibians, birds, proto-mammals—started dying off in record numbers, forever changing the character of life on earth and paving the way for the unchallenged reign of the truly gigantic dinosaurs.

Scientists previously had thought that Triassic extinctions occurred gradually over the course of fifteen million to twenty million years. However, a late-1980s analysis of fossil finds in Nova Scotia suggests that they happened quite suddenly—and may have resulted from the impact of a large meteor. Paleontologists at the Lamont-Doherty Geological Observatory in Palisades, New York, concluded that "the disappearance of dominant Triassic forms was abrupt, occurring in less than 850,000 years. And that is an absolute maximum. Our gut feeling is that it was a lot less."

Scientists are now attempting to determine whether the sudden mass extinctions at the end of the Triassic are related to the roughly contemporaneous impact of a meteorite that punched a forty-four-mile-wide hole in the ground nearby Quebec. The meteorite-impact theory is also advanced as one mechanism that ended the reign of the dinosaurs, though that extinction was still a long time in the future.

Jurassic Extinction: 136 Million Years Ago

> **Dominant life form:** Dinosaurs, particularly *Brontosaurus,*
> "thunder lizard," a huge (up to thirty tons and seventy-five feet
> long) plant-eating American dinosaur with a long slender neck
> and a thick tapering tail.

The Jura Mountains run through France and Switzerland and contain a sequence of chalky rock deposits rich in fossils dating from 193–136 million years ago. Around 1800 scientists first unearthed such fossils and named the geological period after the mountain range.

In Jurassic times the single supercontinent was beginning to break up and shallow seas were stretching inland. Land animals could still walk freely to almost anywhere, in a climate that was warm and moist, with abundant vegetation to satisfy the appetites of the plant-eating dinosaurs. Short armored dinosaurs munched on the low-growing ferns and fungi. Agile bird-footed ornithopods, which walked upright on hind legs, feasted on knee-high leaves. While the stegosaurs, "plated lizards" with a small head and heavy bony plates and sharp spikes down the backbone, stood on hind limbs to browse on low tree branches.

But the king of the forests was the gigantic brontosaur. It chomped off treetop leaves beyond the reach of other creatures, and with its monstrous body beat paths through forests—making gaps where smaller dinosaurs could follow and find food. The daily droppings of a single brontosaur were like a ton of fertilizer, enriching the soil and nourishing seedlings into full-grown trees. Tiny shrewlike mammals, which would evolve to rats, mice, squirrels, rabbits, and hares, ate seeds in the dinosaurs' droppings. Meanwhile, in the seas, the "fish lizards" were eating the ammonite mollusks to near extinction. When the mysterious catastrophe came that ended the Jurassic, it was in the sea where most deaths occurred. But on land the stage was populated with a full cast of characters for one of the most spectacular swan songs of all times: the exit of every single dinosaur.

Iquanadon, *a bulky, "bird-hipped" dinosaur, early Cretaceous, with a toothless beak and hoofed nails. Skeleton of* Camptosaurus, *late Jurassic in Wyoming.*

Cretaceous Extinction: 65 Million Years Ago

Dominant life form: Dinosaurs, particularly the three-horned
Triceratops, a massive four-legged, plant-eating browser with a
large, bony crest over its neck, a long horn above each eye,
and a short horn on its nose.

Something disastrous happened at the end of the Cretaceous period (136–65
million years ago), a geological time span that derives its name from the vast
thicknesses of fossil-rich chalk (Latin *creta*) laid down around the world. Rather
quickly by geological measure, nearly half of all living organisms—animal,
vegetable, marine, and terrestrial—disappeared. The Cretaceous debacle
stands as history's second-largest extinction, after the Permian, and it is best
known because of the complete dying off of the dinosaurs. Recent measurements indicate that no land creature weighing more than fifty-five pounds
survived. Among those tiny survivors was, of course, a mammal that would lead
to man.

Before searching for the cause (or causes) of the Cretaceous extinction, it
is important to know what those times were like.

By late Cretaceous, as the great dying neared, the breakup of the supercontinents Gondwanaland and Laurasia was well advanced; landmasses were taking
on their modern outlines and locations. Southern continents became vast islands. Seas split the northern landmass Laurasia in two: Asiamerica (East Asia
with western North America) and Euramerica (Europe with eastern North
America). Mountain building began pushing up the mighty Rockies and Andes.
There can be no doubt that these changes isolated many groups of dinosaurs:
Creatures that evolved in Asiamerica could no longer easily reach other continents, and vice versa. But such a geological argument alone cannot explain the
massive extinction that was about to happen.

Experts still dispute the causes of the catastrophe that brought on the
massive Mesozoic murder. Humorist Will Cuppy wrote in the 1940s, "The Age
of Reptiles ended because it had gone on long enough." There is considerable
truth in that wisecrack; no species lasts forever, and the dinosaurs had reigned
for more than fifty million years (by contrast, *Homo sapiens* has been around
for about one hundred thousand years). In a sense, their time was up. But
glibness explains nothing. And extinction of the dinosaurs comprises only a
minor ending in comparison to all other life forms that perished along with
them. Something spectacularly cataclysmic had to have happened.

Paleontologists continue to dream up explanations, some whimsical, all
incredible. Britain's A. Hallam observed that climatic changes killed off many
of earth's "naked seed" plants, or gymnosperms, a number of which contained
purgative oils that kept the dinosaurs regular. In other words, dinosaurs experienced a terminal case of constipation.

German paleontologists, studying dinosaur eggshells embedded in rock,
concluded that over time the shells became dangerously thin due to dietary

changes, and eventually broken eggs took a deadly toll on future generations.

But two hypotheses entertained most seriously by scientists may explain
not only what killed the dinosaurs, but also what may lie in our own future.

Depletion of Earth's Ozone Layer.   It's happening now, due largely to
man-made pollutants, but there may have been a forerunner to today's phenomenon.

The end of Cretaceous times saw widespread volcanic activity as the supercontinents broke up and drifted apart. Volcanic gases contain hydrochloric acid,
which in turn releases chlorine into the atmosphere. It's been suggested that
chlorine, acting like today's industrial chlorofluorocarbons, ate gaping holes in
the atmosphere's protective ozone mantle.

We know that this protective region acts as a shield against the most
damaging ultraviolet radiation from the sun—not just the cancer-causing ultraviolet B (burning) rays, but also the far more deadly ultraviolet C rays, which,
generated in laboratories by special bulbs, are used to sterilize equipment from
bacteria, viruses, and fungi. Had the dangerous portions of the sun's spectrum
showered earth, bare-skinned creatures such as dinosaurs, with no place to
hide, would have been particularly vulnerable. On the other hand, small furry
mammals, feathered birds, and deep-sea creatures—animals that did survive
the extinction—might have had enough natural protection from the deadly rays,
as well as places to hide. It does not take the savvy of a Sherlock Holmes to
juggle the ideas of bare-skinned humans, increased skin-cancer deaths, and
ozone depletion to come up with a scenario for extinction.

Carbon Dioxide Buildup and the Greenhouse Effect.   Scientists are
certain that automobile exhausts, the burning of fossil fuels for energy, and the
destruction of rain forests (where trees take in carbon dioxide and give off
oxygen) have already produced a greenhouse warming. The suffocating layer
of carbon dioxide accumulating in the atmosphere serves to trap heat near the
earth's surface, preventing it from escaping harmlessly into space.

During Cretaceous times, volcanoes are thought to have set the stage for
a massive greenhouse warming by spewing out enormous quantities of carbon
dioxide. The earth's temperature rose sharply. Ice floes melted. We know from
deep-sea drilling that ocean levels climbed, flooding coastal regions. The rising
temperatures parched inlands. The net effect was to disrupt the food chain,
starving many animals and those that preyed on them. It is also possible that
higher ambient temperatures triggered infertility in larger animals by diminishing their ability to generate viable sperm (as a man attempting to father a child
is cautioned against taking a hot bath before intercourse).

It's possible that greenhouse warming killed off the dinosaurs. It's also
possible that ozone depletion was the culprit. Perhaps it's even more likely—
and discomforting—that both phenomena, growing realities today, were responsible for the Cretaceous extinction.

Meteorite Impact and Nuclear Winter.   Another leading hypothesis for
the sudden dying off of so many species sixty-five million years ago has to do
with dense dust and stinging rain. In this scenario, a shower of meteorites
blasting through the earth's atmosphere burns up partially, releasing noxious
gases that produce acidic rain. The unburned meteorites collide with the planet,
lifting skyward clouds of dust that block sunlight, reducing global temperatures.
Under dark, reddish-brown, acidic skies animals suffocate and vegetation shriv-
els. It happened on a small scale when Vesuvius smothered Pompeii and
Herculaneum. And it could be the aftermath of all-out nuclear war—blackened
skies and barren, frozen landscapes; a nuclear winter.

Did meteorites, asteroids, or comets hit earth sixty-five million years ago?

There is compelling evidence for this in radioactive elements found in
earth's soil, which are the scars of extraterrestrial pelting. In addition, there
is a famous crater in Iowa, the Manson structure, measuring twenty miles wide;
scientists believe it was dug out by an asteroid impact almost exactly sixty-five
million years ago. A similar crater of the correct age exists in the Soviet Union.
It may be that over a period of time, a shower of asteroids hit the earth or a
major one split up on entering the atmosphere and its giant fragments crashed
at locations around the globe, some pummeling land that today is under the
seas.

In February of 1988, atmospheric scientists at the Massachusetts Institute
of Technology made new calculations for the asteroid-collision model. They
concluded that if an asteroid or asteroid shower struck, the environmental
"conditions at that time were not just bad. They were ghastly"—far worse than
earlier scientists had imagined. "The aftermath of such an impact could have
included a year of darkness under a smog of nitrogen oxides; waters were
poisoned by trace metals leached from soil and rock; the global rains were as
corrosive as battery acid."

Whereas other scientists had concentrated on the aftereffects of dust and
smoke, the M.I.T. experts zeroed in on the impact of toxic chemicals. So
poisoned would the atmosphere be that, "The problem isn't how to kill species
off," but "to think of safe havens where *anything* could have survived."

With the asteroid-impact theory currently the most popular possibility
among scientists, two questions arise: How likely is the chance for another
impact? Do asteroids collide with earth about every thirty million years, the
periodicity of mass extinctions?

There is a growing body of evidence that the earth has indeed been hit
frequently by asteroids and comets. That we are, quite simply, a sitting duck
for disasters. Perhaps this should not be surprising considering the debris in
space.

Millions of asteroids orbit the sun in a belt between Mars and Jupiter. They
can be swept out of orbit and head earthward due to perturbations in Jupiter's
gravitational field. In addition, comets course through space far beyond the
outer planets of our solar system, and there are gravitational mechanisms by
which they too could be reaimed at earth.

Whatever the driving mechanism, earth is truly a target for comets and asteroids. For example, the cratering rates on earth and on Ceres—the largest asteroid in the asteroid belt—are not radically different. When comparing moderate-size impacts—those that produce craters about six miles across—Ceres is hit only about four times more often than earth. This figure has prompted many scientists to argue that earth is actually embedded in the asteroid swarm.

Returning to the second question—Do asteroids or comets hit the earth every thirty million years?—geologists are still collecting evidence. At present the data for a match between an asteroid impact and an extinction are not overwhelming. But some scientists argue that at least one impact of a celestial body accompanied four of the five major extinctions over the past one hundred million years. And so far, based on calculations made in 1988, the best match between an impact and an extinction is at the end of Cretaceous times.

Whatever caused the Cretaceous ending, we know clearly what the survivors were: small snakes, crocodiles, turtles, lizards, and tiny mammals, who, with the stomping dinosaurs gone, emerged from hiding and flourished, filling the niche to become the next lords of the planet. It is certainly no exaggeration to say that the death of the dinosaurs and the close of the age of reptiles made possible the dawn of mammals and the age of ape-man, then man.

Dinosaur Obituary

Diplodocus: The Longest Dinosaur. *Diplo* means "double," and this double-beamed herbivore that munched off treetops was named because sixteen of its tail vertebrae (numbers twelve through twenty-seven behind its hips) were paired flanges that protectively enclosed a major artery that ran along the underside of the tail. Topside there was another protective channel that ran to its head. In terms of balance and maneuverability, it was a gigantic mechanical crane that roamed terrain that today is western North America, particularly Colorado, Utah, and Wyoming.

A composite skeleton of three double-beamed dinosaurs excavated near Split Mountain, Utah, between 1909 and 1922 is on display at the Carnegie Museum of Natural Science in Pittsburgh, Pennsylvania. It is called *Diplodocus carnegii* and measures eighty-seven feet six inches in length (longer than two city buses) and eleven feet nine inches in height at its pelvis, double-beam's highest point. It weighed about eleven tons.

Brachiosaurus: The Heaviest Dinosaur. *Brachio,* meaning "arm to arm," gives the gigantic "shoulder lizard" its name. It lived in what is now Rhodesia and Tanzania, but also had a large family of relatives in Colorado, Utah, and Oklahoma (earth's landmasses were then connected). Weighing as much as one hundred tons, it measured only a few feet shorter than *Diplodocus,* with a thirty-nine-foot neck stretching up into the trees.

At one time scientists believed that the shoulder lizard had to be largely aquatic to carry around its enormous weight, buoyed up by water. And in fact

Brachiosaurus, *the heaviest dinosaur and most popular with children after* Tyrannosaurus rex.

its nostrils and ears exist high up on the head like those of a hippopotamus. But the aquatic theory has been challenged, since in crossing a swamp to solid land the weighty creature would have become hopelessly mired and starved. A composite skeleton exists at the Museum for Nature in East Berlin, Germany.

Tyrannosaurus Rex: The Fiercest Dinosaur. "King tyrant lizard," which seems to have favored Montana and Wyoming over Oklahoma (all states where remains have been unearthed), measured up to forty-seven feet long, had a bipedal (standing) height of nineteen feet, and a stride of about thirteen feet. Relatively lightweight at seven tons, it had a four-foot-long skull with sharp serrated teeth, each about seven inches long—all the better to rip apart flesh with. A carnosaur, it dined on fellow saurians—and viciously. No complete skeleton has ever been found of nature's largest flesh-eater, but what composite remains have been assembled pose an impressive picture. Children partial to dinosaur coloring books and stuffed toys rate *Tyrannosaurus rex* their favorite. If one is going for horror, there is no better selection than the planet's largest land predator.

Stegosaurus: The Most Brainless Dinosaur. This plated lizard was a fairly large, heavily built herbivore that roamed across the Northern Hemisphere. For its body size, it had an extremely tiny head, and, by inference, a walnut-size brain. Calculating from skeletal remains, the brain weighed only 2.5 ounces, which represents .004 percent of its body weight (compared with .074 percent for an elephant and 1.88 percent for an adult human).

Perhaps plated lizard was not all that dumb. It did have greatly enlarged ganglia in its lower neck and hips. Ganglia are masses of nerve cells that serve as centers from which nerve impulses are transmitted, sort of satellite mini-brains. Its neck and hip ganglia were twenty times larger than its brain. The large nerve centers controlled the functions of its huge legs and tail.

Pleistocene Extinction: 10,000 Years Ago

Dominant life form: *Homo sapiens,* literally "sapient man."

The Pleistocene epoch stretches from two million to ten thousand years ago and is popularly known as the period of the last great ice age. Its name derives from the Greek *pleistos kainos,* meaning "most new," for it is by geological standards the newest of times.

Well, almost. Still newer, of course, is the time in which we are living, the Holocene, or "recent new," which began when the Pleistocene ended and which will end—and it *will* end at some point—with the next great mass extinction. By that time, deteriorating environmental conditions or threat of an extraterrestrial collision may have forced humans to colonize space.

It would be wrong to think there were no mass extinctions from the dying of the dinosaurs up until the Pleistocene ending. There were several species wipeouts: at the end of the Paleocene ("old new") epoch fifty-four million years ago, at the end of the Eocene ("dawn new") thirty-eight million years ago, of the Oligocene ("few new") twenty-six million years ago, of the Miocene ("less new") seven million years ago, and last, at the close of the Pliocene ("more new") two million years ago. (Paleontologists had long since run out of clever names for geological times.) But the number of small rodents, mammals, birds, and fishes lost in these extinctions is slight compared to those that disappeared rather suddenly ten thousand years ago.

Worldwide, fully fifty percent of large mammals became extinct. In the Americas, about sixty-seven percent vanished.

The Pleistocene extinction is a vanishing trick that falls under the heading, "Now you see them, now you don't," for at the time human beings were numerous all over the earth. Many peoples must have witnessed the great dying—if not been a large part of the cause. What died that otherwise might be roaming the world today?

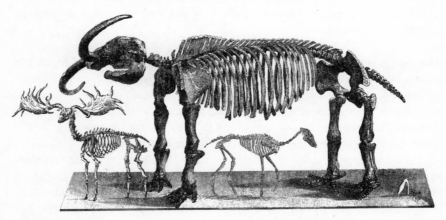

Mastodon and giant mountain deer. In the Americas, sixty-seven percent of the large animals vanished.

The massive mastodon, the shaggy-haired mammoth, and the fierce saber-toothed cat are among the most familiar. But vanishing at the same time were the woolly rhinoceros, a truly giant breed of dog, the cave lion, and the cave bear. Our North American continent lost its native horses (horses were not reintroduced until the 1500s by the Spanish conquistadors), plus ground sloths, native camels, giant peccaries, species of mountain deer, extremely large beavers, four-pronged antelopes, the dire ("terrorizing") wolf, and our own native lions. A rich and diverse menagerie.

There are clues as to who (or what) brought about the Pleistocene murder.

Scientists, who have been grappling with the issue for nearly two centuries, agree that the extinction occurred between eleven thousand and ten thousand years ago. They attribute the disappearing act either to a substantial change in climate that came with the end of the Ice Age or to early nomadic hunters who had not yet settled down to become farmers, agriculture being the event that kicks off the beginning of civilization. Here is the circumstantial evidence for each suspicion.

Human Overkill.   What is called the pleistocene overkill hypothesis was first posited in 1967. It holds that prehistoric inhabitants of the Americas, having arrived from Asia over the landlocked Bering Strait, simply hunted the animals to extinction. Not only for food, but also for the wonderfully warm and woolly capes and blankets and tents that the hide of a hairy beast could provide.

Scientists who back the overkill hypothesis point out that extinction came primarily to large plant-eating mammals whose adult weight exceeded one hundred pounds. Unlike earlier episodes of mass extinction during the previous sixty-five million years, this one did not significantly affect small mammals, amphibians, reptiles, or invertebrates.

In parts of North America, archaeologists have unearthed man-made stone knives and fluted spearpoints among the skeletal remains of mammoths, mastodons, horses, tapirs, and camels. These hunting ground locations belonged to a people called the Clovis, named after a site near Clovis, New Mexico.

Evidence suggests that the Clovis, hunters of big game, crossed the Bering land bridge and traveled through an ice-free corridor just east of the Canadian Rockies about 11,500 years ago. Wandering southward, in a climate already warming, they entered a hunter's paradise: forests and plains teeming with 50 million to 100 million large mammals—not strange beasts, but mammals similar to prey they had hunted in Europe and Asia. But the American mammals were unfamiliar with human predation. Spears and arrows felled them by surprise and in staggering numbers.

With food plentiful, climate warming, and diseases few, human population soared. Families spread out in all directions and within several hundred years the large mammals of North America were extinct.

There is, however, another angle to consider. When the necessities of life are abundant, people direct their free time to sport. It's been suggested that the Clovis and other early Americans found the great beasts excellent game; the extinction of species was not merely a result of man putting meat on the table, but also trophies in the den, so to speak. From everything we know about primitive peoples, hunting was a primary act to test and reaffirm manhood; many hunters today feel it still is. If we, civilized as we like to think we are, hunt animals to near extinction (held back only by mandated limits), it is quite likely that fathers and sons of eleven thousand years ago found stalking the woolly mammoth, lithe horse, and saber-toothed cat excellent sport. This is not a condemnation of the prehistoric peoples; if anything, it makes them even more like us.

End of the Last Ice Age.   Climate may also have played a significant role in the Pleistocene extinctions. The end of the last Ice Age saw a rise in sea levels as ice floes melted and inland temperatures evaporated lakes and streams by many feet. Large mammals were forced to congregate at the few remaining springs, becoming easier victims for man's spears.

Also, as areas warmed, species once confined to particular areas were able to migrate to new locations where they encountered unfamiliar predators and easily fell prey. In all likelihood, herds were stressed and diminished by environmental change, and it is possible that man, the superpredator, through hunting and sport applied the coup de grace to scores of species. With the extinction of numerous herding species, many predators that fed on them—the dire wolf, saber-toothed cat, and American lion—were doomed through a domino death.

The final word on the Pleistocene extinction is not yet in. If it is eventually proved that the first Americans caused the last great mass extinction, that would fit smoothly with the fact that the killing of species goes on and on, and at accelerating rates. As we'll see in the next chapter, we are extinguishing more species today than our ancestors ever did.

CHAPTER 9

Modern
Extinctions

Dodo to Heath Hen

SINCE THE TIME OF CHRIST, humans have exterminated about two percent of the known species of the world's mammals: warm-blooded, partially hairy vertebrates that nurse their young—members of our own class.

Astonishingly, more than half of these losses have occurred since the year 1900. And the rate at which man is exterminating mammals—and just mammals—has increased fifty-five-fold in the last century and a half. The kill-off rates for other animals, like birds and reptiles, are drastically higher, climbing inexpiably.

What causes modern-day extinctions?

About ten percent are due to natural causes, animals meeting their own end.

The rest is divided almost entirely between two factors: human overkill (for food, furs, feathers, ivory, and skins) and human encroachment of animal habitats. As the first Americans spread out across the continent more than eleven thousand years ago exterminating mammoths and mastodons, modern man is spreading faster, farther, and doing far more damage.

A major threat comes from the rate at which we are destroying tropical rain forests, the earth's greatest haven for most of the planet's wildlife. The forecast is dire: Within the next two decades approximately twenty percent of all nonhuman species on earth could be wiped out. Not since the Cretaceous extinction, which took the dinosaurs, has the world experienced loss of life on such a scale.

Tropical forests, which blanket only seven percent of the earth's surface, have been dwindling rapidly since World War II, particularly those in Latin America, Africa, and Asia. These forests, which support half of all earth's species, are cleared to graze cattle for cheap beef and to log trees for inexpensive lumber. The lumber is exported worldwide; the beef goes to make patties for fast-food outlets in the United States and western Europe.

A third of the world's rain forests are already gone. Ecuador has lost half its forests. In Madagascar, which has a quarter of a million species, two-thirds of which occur nowhere else on earth, ninety percent of the forests have been cleared flat. This is the case in country after country. If current trends continue, two million animal species will be extinct by the year 2050. That equals the wipeout of Permian times five hundred million years ago, the largest known single loss of life in the planet's history.

One Ending Breeds Another.   The problem is not merely the loss of many unique forms of animal and plant life. Mass extinctions of species threaten the ecological equilibrium of the planet.

With countless fauna and flora gone, there would be a fundamental shift in evolution itself—and in what direction no one can predict. Evolutionary processes would simply go to work on the vastly reduced pool of species, and several new species would rush in to fill the niche. Assuming humans survived (and there are no hard data to back the assumption, just hubris and desire), we might inhabit a world without birds or blossoming plants, but teeming with stinging insects and slimy fungi. In the last chapter, we saw this kind of replacement scenario happen again and again at the end of each geological period. Frighteningly, hardy insects could well predominate and fragile birds could easily perish.

It's already happening.

Birds have been particularly hard hit by human overkill and encroachment. From the year 1600 (when good records were first kept) until 1800, only twenty-five known birds of the world were lost. But from 1800 to 1950, a briefer span, seventy-eight species became extinct. The loss has accelerated to the point that every three years we now lose two kinds of birds. At that rate, by the end of the century every new year will mark the disappearance of one more bird species. To put the entire modern-day extinction picture in perspective: We are killing off wildlife today fifty times faster than nature destroyed the dinosaurs.

As we're about to see, the disappearance of some animals is particularly tragic. It may be hard for the nonconservationist to lament the loss of a pesty beetle or a tiny coral reef fish, but anyone who opens Lewis Carroll's *Alice's Adventures In Wonderland* to the sketch of the dodo can appreciate how sad its loss was. And a needless loss it was.

Dodo: Year of Extinction, 1681

The Dutch called it "disgusting bird," and to the Portuguese it was *doudo,* meaning "simpleton." Either way, the dodo—the name a British corruption of the Portuguese—was a bird that could get no respect. Of all the animals to disappear from the face of the earth, nine out of ten have been birds, and among these the most famous and lovable is surely the lumbering, befuddled-looking dodo.

A dove zoologically, it more closely resembled a bloated, misshapen pigeon, though at a height of three feet it was mistaken for a turkey, except that its hooked beak was similar to that of a cockatoo, only much larger. That was the dodo's problem: The first drawings of the southern Asian creature to reach Europe were greeted as fantastical composites, fakes produced by an artist's whimsy. People were told that the heavy-footed bird was so fat its belly scraped the ground when it waddled. And though it could not fly, it was said to be a true bird. Neither could it run, or climb trees. Perhaps the dodoes' days had always been numbered.

For centuries the dodo needed no defenses.

It lived on Mauritius, a volcanic upthrust between Madagascar and Australia. Mauritius, along with Réunion and Rodriguez, is part of the Mascarenes. These islands have virtually no neighbors, standing alone in a wilderness of water that stretches for thousands of miles. They had no human inhabitants and the defenseless dodo had no animal predators. Which was a good thing, since even in its heyday the dodo was not a prolific species; the female laid one egg a year. Within less than a hundred years after the rare birds were discovered by the Dutch in 1598 not a single dodo was alive.

It is possible that humans had seen dodoes as early as the High Middle Ages. In the twelfth and thirteenth centuries, Arab ships sailed the Indian Ocean, plying trade routes from the Near East to Africa, India, and China. The dodo's home island of Mauritius appears on all Arab maps of that time.

European explorers discovered the Mascarenes in 1507. It was mainly the Portuguese who investigated the islands' fauna and flora—though not too thoroughly, perhaps, because written accounts of their observations claim the islands were inhabited only by small animals. Nowhere is there mention of a peculiar potbellied, flightless bird.

The three landmasses still had no names.

Dodos were extensively sketched, painted, and lampooned. Lewis Carroll's version from Alice in Wonderland.

Then in 1598 a Dutch navigator, Admiral Jacob Corneliszoon van Neck, explored one of the islands for his patron, Prince Maurice of Nassau, ruler of the Netherlands. Van Neck named the island Mauritius in honor of the prince and reported that its forests of ebony trees were abundant with wildlife—doves, parrots, turtles, and a colony of queer birds unlike any seen before. The birds, having never known predators, were utterly fearless as van Neck poked through the low-lying nests for young. But the birds were instinctively good parents, for he recorded in his ship's log that disturbed mothers "peck mighty hard."

Van Neck took a pair of adults. One bird was presented to Prince Maurice and remained in the Netherlands; the other was purchased by Emperor Rudolf II, going to live in Germany. The totally tame creatures were a sensation, and van Neck was encouraged to publish the sea journal. He described the birds as "larger than our swans, with huge heads only half covered with skin, as if clothed with a hood." Not overly fond of the species himself, he named them *walghvogels* ("disgusting birds"), and explained that the creatures "lack wings, in the place of which three or four blackish feathers protrude. The tail consists of a few soft incurved feathers which are ash-colored."

The journal also revealed that van Neck and his crew killed several of the birds on Mauritius: "The more and the longer they were cooked, the less soft and more unpalatable their flesh becomes."

By this time, pictures of the birds were beginning to circulate throughout Europe. The Netherlands' specimen had been sketched numerous times, and Germany's bird had stood for its portrait in oils by Emperor Rudolf's court painter. "Disgusting birds" were in demand, and many, without batting a feather in protest, were picked up on Mauritius, carried to ships, and returned to Europe for sale to the wealthy or to naturalists.

The docile creatures were a particular favorite of artists. Before its death, the original Netherlands *walghvogel* posed for fourteen oils and watercolors. And the Dutch painter Roelandt Savery built his career on dodo renditions, doing the birds in charcoal and oils, and at times taking considerable anatomical license (as if nature hadn't already). He made their hooked beak more fearsome and turned their forked dovelike feet into the webbed toes of a duck. Today there is no shortage of extant dodo pictures, though not all of them can be trusted.

From all seventeenth-century artists' accounts, dodoes made excellent subjects. Once positioned in a favorable light against a flattering backdrop, the bird remained virtually motionless. Few sights or sounds seemed to distract it. The bird was thought to be either slavishly obedient or profoundly dumb. In a way, it is fitting the dodoes were painted extensively, for while the captive specimens posed, the free birds back on Mauritius were quickly decreasing in number.

Last Survivors.   Dutch colonists to the island, along with sailors and visitors, did not find the dodo as unpalatable as van Neck and his crew had. And, too, the bird was an easy capture. Within a short time, colonists consumed most of the adult dodo population, while the animals they introduced to the island—dogs, cats, and farm hogs—ate the fledglings as well as yolks from the rare dodo eggs. By 1638, just thirty-seven years after van Neck published his description of the bird, the dodoes on Mauritius were nearly extinct and every one of the birds imported to Europe as curiosities was dead.

Unfortunately, not a single naturalist had attempted to mate any of the captive dodoes; they left no descendants.

In England—where the bird had been called "dodar," "do do," and "dodo"—one specimen that had been the main attraction in a London sideshow was stuffed upon its death by English naturalist John Tradescant. "A Dodar from the island of Mauritius," Tradescant labeled the specimen, with a legend that read in part: "It is not able to fly being so big."

When Tradescant himself died in 1662, he bequeathed his natural history collection, thought to be the best in Europe at that time, to an acquaintance, Elias Ashmole, and the condition of the dodo deteriorated. In 1683, Ashmole donated the bird to Oxford University. That was two years after the last living dodo was seen on Mauritius—a single adult bird, observed by a part-time naturalist to the island, Englishman Benjamin Harry.

By 1755, the islanders of Mauritius could not even remember that there had been a bird such as the dodo. That year the Ashmolean Museum at Oxford assessed the condition of its mangy, moth-eaten specimen, the only one in existence, and discarded it. A museum curator did remove and save the dodo's head and right foot, all that remain today. The rest of the bird was burned as trash.

A unique creature, docile and trusting, had been allowed to perish virtually without a trace. Tradescant, in stuffing a captive, had immortalized the dodo (at least in pieces); later he himself was memorialized by the Swedish botanist Linnaeus, who named a newly discovered flowering plant *Tradescantia.*

Just how unique a bird the dodo was became apparent late in the eighteenth century.

Only a hundred years after the dodo was officially declared extinct, Europeans refused to believe such a fantastical creature had ever existed. It became a myth like the unicorn. By 1800, professional naturalists were casting doubt on written descriptions of the bird, as well as on extant drawings, many of which did display striking inconsistencies. It became scientific vogue to deny the bird's existence and to challenge the Oxford head and foot as fakes. Why, skeptics asked, had no one preserved a skeleton? Unless there had never been a dodo. Skepticism was so strong by 1850 that a group of zoologists journeyed to Mauritius in search of dodo bones.

No bones were found (because zoologists looked in the wrong places), and the dodo was denounced a scientific fraud.

Finally, in 1863, George Clark, a resident of Mauritius with an interest in natural history, undertook an extensive search of the island's vast marshes. He discovered numerous scattered bones that he painstakingly assembled into several complete dodo skeletons. Clark shipped his specimens to major museums where they were studied and pronounced authentic. Thanks to his efforts, we not only know with certainty that the dodo existed, but what it looked like. Anyone visiting Washington, D.C., or New York City can marvel over a dodo skeleton firsthand at the Smithsonian Institution and at the American Museum of Natural History.

But even George Clark was unable to answer one nagging issue: Was the strange-looking dodo related to any existing bird?

The answer came in the late 1800s—and by accident. At that time, explorers on the Pacific island of Samoa discovered a fairly large, powerful bird with a thick hooked beak like the dodo's. It appeared to be an exceptionally large dove, except for its beak. Darwin's theory of evolution was gaining supporters, and the large dove of Samoa was assigned an intermediary position between the familiar smaller doves of Europe and the flightless dodo of Mauritius.

Today we know that modern doves and pigeons once shared a common ancestor that had a stocky body, a prominent beak, and the capability of flight. Millions of years ago the family tree split into three branches: One evolved into the dove and pigeon; another into the large-beaked dove of Samoa; and the third yielded a bird that happened to settle on the isolated island of Mauritius, the dodo. Initially it could fly. But without predators, dodoes seldom took to the air, and in time they grew fat, earthbound, clumsy, only moderately fertile, and trusting to an extent that cost them their existence.

Aurochs: Year of Extinction, 1627

On the walls and ceilings of caves at Altamira, Spain, an area in the Pyrenees, are superb prehistoric paintings of reindeer, ibex, jungle cats, bulls, and aurochs—the last a relative of the European bison and an ancestor of our modern cattle.

The wall frescoes and ceiling murals are among the earliest works of art by human hands, painted in color and sketched in charcoal by hide-clad hunters about fifteen thousand years ago. The powerfully built aurochs stood six feet high at the shoulder, had large, forwardly curved horns, and shiny black fur and skin. Though its zoological name *Bos primigenius* means "ancestor of cattle," it more closely resembled the modern oxen of the tropics, such as the gaur of India, the gayal of Burma, and the banteng of Malaya.

Aurochs were once plentiful, roaming the forests of Europe.

Their native homeland was North Africa and Asia, but they migrated to Europe at least fifteen thousand years ago, most likely during a mini–ice age, in search of a warmer climate and grains and grasses, the staple of their diet. Though they were numerous in the forests of France, not a single aurochs is depicted on the older cave frescoes at Lascaux dating to thirty thousand years ago. If the huge animals had existed in the region, it is almost certain that the world's first artists would have worked them into their frescoes. It's the absence of aurochs in the Lascaux paintings (which are replete with reindeer, ibex, and bison) and their presence in the Altamira paintings that place their arrival in Europe between the two events.

Julius Caesar had no trouble distinguishing an aurochs from a bison, its

The aurochs resembled a cross between a wild ox (top) and bison.
Siegfried, in Nibelungenlied, *slays four of the beasts.*

smaller, shaggy-haired, humpbacked cousin. Bison were routinely captured in forests outside Rome and matched with gladiators for bloody spectacle. Little wonder that Caesar was impressed with the larger, fiercer aurochs. Around 58 B.C., when he launched a campaign to conquer Gaul, Caesar marched north into forests that border the Danube River and met head-on his first herd of aurochs. He became one of the first writers to describe the creature, but whether aurochs were ever enlisted to battle gladiators is uncertain.

For centuries aurochs were a common wild beast throughout Germany, appearing in art, literature, and on the dinner table. In the Middle High German epic, *Nibelungenlied,* written about 1200 by an unknown Austrian from the Danube region (and immortalized in Wagner's opera cycle of the same name), the hero, Siegfried, a prince from the Lower Rhine, slays "four strong aurochs." It was the killing of aurochs for food and sport that wiped out the species. By the sixteenth century, aurochs were so rare and unfamiliar to Europeans that they were mistaken for bison, even by naturalists.

Last Survivors. European nobility finished off the species. Hunting the giant aurochs had become the sport of aristocrats, with most of the surviving animals confined to forests that were private estates. The animals were also valued for their thick ornamental horns and tender meat. In 1563, Duke Albrecht of Prussia in Königsberg ordered one of his few estate animals killed to serve guests a "dinner of aurochs veal."

Naturalists realized the species was facing extinction. Several aurochs were captured and placed in private parks for their own protection. But trapped in their new homes, they became easy targets for peasant poachers who gazed at the lumbering beasts and saw steak. By the start of the 1600s, the only place

in the world where the aurochs existed was in the Jaktorowka Game Preserve
in Poland. Despite efforts to save the beasts, poachers continued to deplete the
herd, until in 1602 there were only four aurochs left. They would not breed,
and in 1620 a single aurochs remained, an elderly cow. Though Polish game-
keepers assiduously guarded her from poachers, they were helpless against the
advance of age. She died in 1627.

Is the aurochs really extinct?

In recent times, German breeders have repeatedly claimed to have re-
created the species by crossing Spanish fighting cattle with longhorns. The
hybrid animals do resemble aurochs, though they are smaller. But in terms of
genetics, the two creatures are not the same. Nature produced the aurochs
over tens of thousands of years of breeding and natural selection, and when the
elderly cow died in Poland the hereditary germ line vanished from the earth.
It remains to be seen if the new science of genetic engineering can tamper with
the present German hybrid to produce something closer to a true extinct
aurochs.

Steller's Sea Cow: Year of Extinction, 1768

Sightings at sea of plump pink-skinned bodies with pendulous breasts high up
on the chest made sailors, long away from home, think of mermaids. The fact
that the creature sported bristly whiskers from a square snout, stunted arms
with no fingers, a bald head, had no discernible neck, and measured up to eleven
feet long was overlooked in the frenzy of spotting a woman, naked.

The creature was a dugong, a marine mammal. Like all mammals, it nursed
its young from milk-filled breasts which, in this case, hung down over a fleshy
belly. Its long body, actually a grayish pink, tapered into a flipper, and its stubby
arms were in fact short rounded flippers. Floating dugongs, spotted by early
seafarers, are thought to be the source of mermaid legends as well as tales of
femme fatale sirens.

The mistake in identity is even more understandable in terms of the dugong's voluptuous cousin, the pinker, fleshier, more buxom Steller's sea cow.
It, too, perhaps because of its breasts, was mistaken for what seamen wanted
to see. These large sea cows, about twenty-five feet long, were not seen often
(undoubtedly adding to their appeal), for the entire world population in the early
1700s numbered about five thousand. Within a mere three decades after they
had first tricked the eyes of lustful sailors the species was extinct.

Steller's sea cows were discovered by accident, and almost not by a man
named Steller.

In 1689, Czar Peter the Great came to the throne of Russia. Among his
high-priority projects was the complete exploration of the vast mysterious
region of Siberia and its coastal waters. He commanded: "Everything shall be
discovered that has not yet been discovered." For decades expedition after
expedition discovered nothing but snow and more snow. Certainly no mermaids. Peter died, but the exploration of Siberia continued.

In June of 1741, a team of seventy-eight men were to set sail on the flagship

St. Peter under a Danish officer, Captain Vitus Bering—who soon would be navigating through the strait that divides Russia and Alaska and now bears his name. The crew's Russian physician fell ill days before the departure, and a German professor of medicine and botany volunteered for the job. He was thirty-two-year-old Georg Wilhelm Steller. Three weeks after leaving port, Bering knew that the two large continents were nowhere connected as had been suspected. The crew navigated around the snowy peaks of the Alaskan mainland, preparing maps, then, satisfied with their discovery, began the journey home.

Severe weather continually blew them off course. By September, with the supply of fruits and vegetables exhausted, many sailors suffered from scurvy; a dozen were dead, thirty-four incapacitated by severe diarrhea. With winter approaching, they anchored off a jagged landmass (later to be named Bering's Island). More men died, and in November a gale beached the *St. Peter,* demolishing it. Bering's spirits were also dashed. Himself feverishly ill, he died on December 8.

Only one of the original seventy-eight men was completely fit: Dr. Steller. He ministered to the survivors and explored the uninhabited island. It was rich in small mammals, seals, and a multitude of birds, and these were served up to the sick crew, who began to recover and explore on their own. Homesick, love-starved, and stimulated easily by fantasy, several crewmen reported seeing full-bodied women—always in the distance, basking on ice floes or floating leisurely along the rocky coastline. Steller ignored the tales until—unfortunately for fantasy—a group of crewmen approached a mermaid close up.

On May 21, 1742, Steller and the crew attempted to catch one of the remarkable Bering Island beasts, which Steller believed were giant dugongs. It is worth quoting his description of this extinct animal, for Georg Steller, it would turn out, would be the only scientist ever to see the rare mammal alive.

> It is 28 to 35 feet long, and 22 feet thick about the region of the navel, where they are thickest. To the navel this animal resembles the seal species; from there on to the tail, a fish. . . . In the mouth it has on each side in place of teeth two wide, longish, flat, loose bones, of which one is fastened above the palate, the other to the inside of the lower jaw. . . . The lips are provided with many strong bristles. . . . The eyes of this animal in spite of its size are not larger than sheeps' eyes [and are] without eyelids. . . . They are occupied with nothing else but their food.

As the sea cows were occupied with their food, the stranded sailors became preoccupied with the tasty cow as their own food. Not only were Steller and the crew tired of eating birds and small seals, but a single sea cow provided more than seven thousand pounds of red meat and rich fat. One kill lasted for months. Steller recorded in his journals that the deep red meat was indistinguishable from high-quality beef. The men boiled the fat, which melted to the consistency of olive oil, and drank it as avidly as wine.

By June the weather had improved enough for the men to construct a small boat and sail home. In many ways it had been a fruitful journey. Alaska was discovered and charted. Bering located a strait. Steller challenged mermaid chimera with his own sea cow, *Hydrodamalis Stelleri*. And, too, he wrote a book of his scientific discoveries: *De Bestis Marinis* ("On Marine Animals"). Published in 1751, it established Steller as one of the great naturalists of his time, a posthumous honor since he had died five years earlier at the age of thirty-seven, months after completing the manuscript.

Last Survivors.   In a way, Steller was inadvertently responsible for the extinction of his sea cow.

Steller and the crew of the *St. Peter* slaughtered only two cows during their months on Bering Island. They did not kill the first animal until late May and they were off the island by August. The fourteen thousand pounds of meat and fat from the two animals was more than enough to sustain them. But Steller's rave that sea cow tasted like prime beef piqued the appetites of Russians, who had few cows. Furthermore, the crew displayed sleek, handsome pelts of the island's sea otters, and Russians had a passion for furs; they were the world's leading fur traders. Reports of pelts and "beef" was news that launched a thousand ships for Bering Island.

Trappers found catching the unsuspecting otters too easy to be sport and irresistible in terms of profit. Skilled harpooners found it even easier to kill the harmless, slow-moving sea cow, especially during the long inactive periods it spent digesting. Every ship that departed Bering Island had on board thousands of lustrous pelts and tons of high-grade red meat.

Unfortunately, the animal that many sailors mistook for a woman had a curious maternal trait that accelerated its extinction: When one cow was harpooned and cried out in pain, females, instead of fleeing, flocked protectively around it, exposing themselves to danger. It was butchery. And the sailors boasted of exactly that.

Four years after Steller's book was published, a Russian geologist named Jakovlev visited the island in search of copper mines. Witnessing the slaughter firsthand, he realized the sea cow was doomed and petitioned Russian authori-

Reports that Steller's sea cow tasted like prime beef doomed the animal.

ties to put the animal under protection of law. But this was not done. A group of hunters searched the island's coastline in 1768, determined not to head home without sea cow meat. They found only one adult, harpooned it, and returned complaining of how long the search had taken.

Four years later a Russian zoologist explored the island from coast to snowy crest and recorded: "Of *stelleri;* none are to be found."

Sea cow skeletons became prized by many European museums. Georg Steller's detailed account of the animal, its behavior, and diet is a unique document, for it contains all the information we will ever have on the extinct species. The pink, plump sea cow is unique in that it remains the only animal to be observed by a single scientist.

Might a pair of sea cows have survived?

In the summer of 1962 a Russian whaling ship spotted a group of large marine animals. They measured about twenty feet long, were floating in shallow water not far from Bering Island, and were preoccupied with eating a dense pasture of seaweed. The ship's captain and several mates peered through binoculars. The animals were not whales. They were not seals. And no one mistook them for anything other than animals. The speculation was that they might be a few surviving sea cows. However, no specimens were captured, and, curiously, the creatures have never been spotted again. Unless proof of their existence is forthcoming, the official word is that the mermaidlike sea cow has gone the way of the dodo. And the aurochs. And, as we're about to see, the legendary moa.

Moa: Year of Extinction, 1670

According to the Maori of New Zealand, the flightless, ostrichlike moa was a swift runner that when cornered defended itself by kicking its attacker. The kick could discourage the most determined predator since the thirteen-foot-high moa had powerful, rapid-motion legs.

The otherwise gentle bird ate a diet of seeds, fruits, leaves, and grasses, which it ground internally with the help of about seven pounds of stones in the gizzard, a veritable mortar and pestle. Early Polynesian peoples hunted moas for food, crafted jewelry from their bones and feathers, and made water buckets from moa eggs, which measured seven inches in length by ten inches in diameter.

The giant moa was already a native of New Zealand when the Maori became the first inhabitants of the island, arriving by canoe about a thousand years ago. They found the area richly populated with birds and reptiles, but absent were all mammals except two inedible species of bats. Easily the best meal on the island was the flightless, unsuspecting moa, which with a weight of six hundred pounds went a long way in feeding a family. As for the moa's kick, the Maori had spears.

By 1769, when the first European, Captain James Cook, set foot on the continent, the giant moa was nowhere to be found; the bird had been extinct for about one hundred years. No living Maori had ever seen a moa. Thus an

The flightless moa (right) resembled a gigantic ostrich.

islander could fabricate any fancy about the bird, which is just what tribes had been doing. Tales of its size, ferocity, and particular hatred for humans had reached mythic proportions. Cook and the early European settlers of New Zealand listened with fascination to horrific legends of huge ostrichlike birds, grateful for their extinction.

In the summer of 1838, William Colenso, a printer by trade and naturalist by avocation, traveled throughout part of New Zealand collecting living specimens of plants and animals, picking up sundry bones as well as rumors of the giant killer that by now was said to have been half-bird half-man. Publishing the results of his observations in the *Tasmanian Journal of Natural Science,* he wrote: "I heard from the natives of a certain monstrous animal; while some said it was a bird, others a person, all agreed that it was called a *Moa.*" (Named understandably by, and for, the people who anthropomorphized it; it was their monster.)

Unable to defend its reputation, the gentle moa had become a terror. Not only had it kicked the Maoris' ancestors, but, as Colenso reported, a person who simply gazed on the bird "would be invariably trampled on and killed by it."

To his credit, Colenso disbelieved that the ostrichlike bird had "a face like a man," but he fell wishingly for the creature's mythic dimensions and consequently did not believe that the strange bones in his collection (large as they were) belonged to the legendary moa. The gullibility was to cause him much grief, for soon he would be arguing that he was the rightful discoverer of the extinct species *Dinornis maximus,* meaning "terrible giant," a derision the docile moa has never shed.

A year after Colenso published his observations, a battered thighbone of a large creature was unearthed in New Zealand. The discoverer was Sir Richard Owen, a leading British anatomist and paleontologist. Famous for his reconstruction of flightless birds, Owen immediately recognized the bone's uniqueness. It did not match the thighbone of an ox or horse—Owen's first guesses—but it correlated in shape if not size with that of an ostrich. In November of 1839 Owen announced to the Zoological Society of London that there had once existed in New Zealand a giant, flightless bird.

William Colenso was angered and embarrassed by his oversight.

Returning to New Zealand for a full moa skeleton, he came up with only five thighbones and a few ribs. As he continued to scavenge the outback, he wrote numerous articles to establish his claim as the bird's rightful discoverer. Meanwhile, Owen extrapolated from additional bones that there had been several kinds of moas, the smallest the size of a turkey. Eventually it became clear to scientists that there were about twenty-four species of moas, that they never all coexisted on New Zealand, and that the smallest had been extinct for millions of years. The biggest bones, though, were quite recent.

This last fact provoked speculation. Was the moa really extinct?

During the last half of the 1800s, many scientists questioned Maori tribes for evidence of sightings. The stories resemble modern-day claims for yeti, or abominable snowman. People had glimpsed moas trampling through forests, had muffled their ears against the bird's blood-curdling caterwauls, had heard tell of a neighbor kicked to death.

In 1939, excavations in the swampy Pyramid Valley region of New Zealand turned up virtually complete skeletons of 140 moas of 4 genera and 6 different species. Nearly a third were *Dinornis,* the tallest of the moas. Some moas were so well preserved by the peat bogs that the contents of their stomachs were intact. Seeds and twigs that had been the last meal of one giant *Dinornis* were subjected to carbon 14 dating: The bird had eaten 670 years ago. Thus the biggest of the moas had been in existence during the height of the Maori migrations to New Zealand. Scientists had to conclude that the Maori hunted the moas to extinction, then preserved them in legend, if distortedly.

Great Auk: Year of Extinction, 1844

The great auk, a diving bird and splendid member of the penguin family, met its end through the unwitting wishes of museum directors: Realizing the bird was near extinction, they put out a call and offered a price for stuffed specimens, which guaranteed that the few survivors would be hunted down, carefully slaughtered, and handsomely mounted. Today we have many attractive specimens, but no actual birds.

The extinct bird, *Pinguinus impennis,* was the largest of twenty-two species of auk (of which twenty-one survive). It stood about two feet tall, sporting a penguin's formal wear coloration. Its head was a bittersweet-chocolate brown and on its cheeks were patches of white rouge, which complemented the white grooves that striped its black beak. In the sea it was agile; on land clumsy, an easy catch. Since its meat was tasty, and its thick layer of fat made excellent fuel, the great auk was a frequent target of hunters.

Thousands of years ago the bird enjoyed a wide range of habitats.

The extinct great auk; the surviving little auk.

Unable to fly, it swam to numerous parts of the northern world, preferring the coasts of Russia, Scandinavia, and Canada. When the world's climate was colder, the great auk mated along the coast of Italy, United States beaches from Maine to Florida, and in the waters off Spain. They were well known to early artists who fifteen thousand years ago painted portraits of great auks on the cave walls in Altamira, Spain. And the birds were thoroughly enjoyed by American Indians in New England who ate their meat, waterproofed clothes with their fat, and dressed in their warm hides. Excavated Indian campsites attest to the enormous numbers of great auks processed there.

The great auk was being eaten and worn into extinction.

The birds were so trusting (or so lacking in memory) that even the bloody sight of one year's slaughter did not instill in them dread for the next year's massacre. There are numerous reports of hunters in the seventeenth and eighteenth centuries dropping a ship's gangplank to an "auk rock" (as the nesting sites were called), walking up to a bird, and clobbering it on the head. By the early 1800s the surviving auks seemed relatively safe, having been driven to the jagged coastline of Iceland's remote Geirfugl peninsula. Their colony was small, about fifty birds, but the outcropping of rocks they inhabited discouraged ships from approaching their nests. But this lonely colony was to know no haven, for in 1830, a mere two decades after the auk had settled in, a nearby underwater volcano erupted, sinking their "auk rock."

Homeless, they swam along Iceland's coastline.

Last Survivors.   Directors of natural history museums realized that the great auk, which once numbered in the millions, might be extinct in a few years. Their aviary collections lacked not only stuffed birds, but auk skeletons and eggs. Directors took a count and discovered that two stuffed birds did exist: one specimen in a Belgian museum, another in the Ashmolean Museum at Oxford, a bequest from English naturalist John Tradescant, who had also left the world's only stuffed dodo. The specimens were moth-eaten; besides, two was an inadequate number. Several museums offered high prices for stuffed great auks, auks' skins, full skeletons, and unbroken eggs.

The fifty surviving great auks had found a haven from the quake, though not from man, on Iceland's small, accessible, and inhabited Eldey island. Between 1830, when the first call for auks went out, and 1844, the year of their extinction, the birds, their young, and their eggs were hunted one by one. By the spring of that year, forty-eight great auks had been killed and sold to museums.

Two remained. That knowledge alone might seem a deterrent to killing the survivors, but instead it proved an invitation for Icelandic bird collector Carl Siemsen. Auks had never been rarer, more pricey.

On June 4, 1844, Siemsen, who wanted auks for his private collection, paid three local fishermen to find and kill with skillful finesse the two surviving great auks. They boated to Eldey and spent the day walking the coastline looking for the unmistakable silhouettes of the solitary giant penguins. The two turned out to be adults, still trusting of humans, and they were knocked unconscious and then eviscerated with minimum damage to their coats. One of the three fishermen returned empty-handed, for his companions had just completed the extinction of a species. Siemsen stuffed his birds, but the lure of big bucks persuaded him to sell them to museums. By that time, 1845, a bird lover could see any of fifty great auks in museums around the world. But none in the wild.

Not surprisingly, with notice of the great auk's extinction, the price of the stuffed birds and their eggs soared. And it continues to climb.

In 1934, at a London auction, six intact, empty auk eggs fetched $1,575 each. Two mounted birds went for $4,615 apiece. Two perfect eggs and two auk skins were purchased by pioneer aviator Vivian Hewitt, the first person to fly the Irish sea (in 1912), for a total of $7,245. Added to Hewitt's previous collectibles, this made him the world's greatest private collector of auk material.

More recently, in 1971 the director of the Natural History Museum of Iceland paid nine thousand dollars for a stuffed Greak Auk.

Today the birds and shells are priceless, since virtually all specimens are owned by museums that would not part with them. Perhaps the fifty last great auks would have become extinct on their own. Then again, had they not had a price put on their heads, they might have kept their heads and gone on to multiply, if not to fill the earth, at least to make it a richer, more diverse place for all.

Quagga: Year of Extinction, 1883

The extinct quagga, never a plentiful animal, was a distant relative of the zebra, which, by the way, is genetically a black animal with white stripes, not a white animal with black stripes.

The issue of stripe color for the zebra and quagga was long debated and only recently resolved. Geneticists have learned that the coloration cells in a zebra's skin are programmed to produce black pigmentation and it is only when a genetic switch is thrown "off," which occurs at spaced intervals along the animal's body, that stripes lacking pigmentation, that is, white bands, occur.

The quagga, *Equus quagga,* resembled an unfinished zebra, a zebra in which the black pigmentation switches were thrown "off" only in the animal's head, neck, and forequarters; the rest of the quagga was a solid chocolate brown. Except, that is, for its lower legs, where all the switches were "off," producing pure white coloration. Visually the quagga was a strikingly beautiful variant of the zebra, though zoologically it was a species in its own right.

The white-black animal would be driven into extinction chiefly by the white Dutch Boers who fed it as cheap meat to their black slaves.

For thousands of years, quaggas, in herds of about thirty animals, roamed the plains of South Africa from the Cape of Good Hope to as far north as the Vaal River. They shared the vast expanse with the Hottentots, nomadic bushmen with a way of life based on sheep and cattle herding. The Hottentots did not call themselves by that name; they were for centuries Khoikhoi. It would be the Dutch settlers of South Africa, the Boers (Dutch for "farmers") who coined the term in an attempt to capture in writing the tribe's click-sound pronunciation of Khoikhoi.

It's certain that the Dutch, before settling South Africa, had never seen a quagga. It is less certain whether the animal was known to the Romans. The third-century Roman historian Dio Cassius, who served as the proconsul in Africa, wrote in his eighty-volume history, *Romaika,* of "horses of the sun which resemble tigers"—a reference to zebra and/or quagga.

In 1652, the Dutch East India Company established a shipping station on the Cape of Good Hope, home of herds of quagga. The first published reference to the animal appeared thirty-three years later when a Boer incorrectly identified the quagga as a *wilde esel* ("wild ass"). As the staunchly Calvinist Boer colony grew, the whites saw themselves as God's children in the wilderness, ordained to rule the backward Hottentots, who were made field-workers and servants.

Whereas the Hottentots killed quaggas only in hard times for their meat, which was tough and sinewy, the Boers slayed the animals in large numbers. Not for themselves; they found the horselike flesh unpalatable. But quagga steak was an inexpensive meal to feed to their growing number of slaves. The Boers kept for themselves the animals' beautiful striped hides, turning them into shoes, tote bags, and storage sacks for grain, dried fruit, and salted meat (other than quagga meat).

The Boers made an industry of quagga skins. And in the middle of the eighteenth century they shipped two live quaggas, a male and a female, to London for study and public display. Only the female arrived alive. She was sketched and oil-painted, and a color plate of her appeared in a book, *Gleanings of Natural History* (1758) by George Edwards, a naturalist and librarian of the Royal College of Physicians. "This curious animal was brought alive . . . from the Cape of Good Hope," wrote Edwards. "She lived several years at a house of his Royal Highness the Prince of Wales, at Kew."

The quagga, probably lonely and frightened, was not well behaved. She was mistaken by leading naturalists of the day for a poorly striped example of a rather ferocious zebra. "The noise it made was much different from that of an ass, resembling more the confused barking of a mastiff-dog," Edwards noted. "It seemed to be of a savage and fierce nature: no one would venture to approach it, but a gardener in the Prince's service, who was used to feeding it, could mount on its back."

The mistaken notion that the London animal was a variant zebra was laid to rest by the Swedish naturalist Andrew Sparrman. He observed in his 1786 book, *A Voyage to the Cape of Good Hope,* that the quagga was stockier and more powerful than a zebra, and that it could easily be tamed. At close range he had examined the pet quagga belonging to a Hottentot youth, which was used by the family to protect sheep and horses against raids by hyenas and wild dogs. Sparrman was unaware that the quagga was being driven toward extinction by the Boers.

That realization came soberingly to naturalist William John Burchell on a visit to South Africa in 1811. He witnessed the horror of a Boers quagga hunt. Scores of herds of quaggas, about a thousand animals, were rounded up, circled by men on horseback, then killed by rifle fire.

Last Survivors. As a result of the Napoleonic Wars, the Cape of Good Hope Colony had become a British possession in 1806, and Boers, disgruntled with liberal British policies, especially in regard to the freeing of their Hottentot slaves, headed north for the relatively empty spaces of the high veld. About twelve thousand Boers resettled between 1835 and 1843, and whereas they had nearly wiped out the quaggas in the region of their Cape Colony, they did a more thorough job in their new surroundings.

The few quaggas the Boers missed the British shipped back to England to decorate the estates of nobility. Black-and-white quaggas on a lawn with peacocks made a full-spectrum feast for the eye. The estate of a Mr. Parkins boasted of a pair of animals that had been taught to pull a carriage. "Among the equipages [horse-drawn carriages] occasionally exhibited in the gay season at Hyde Park and other fashionable places of resort," wrote a social commentator, "may be seen a curricle [light, two-wheeled carriage with horses side by side] drawn by two Quaggas, which seem as subservient to the curb and whip as any well-trained horses." The heads of these two quaggas, removed after their natural deaths, are preserved today in a London equestrian museum.

By the mid-nineteenth century it was clear to naturalists that the quagga was almost extinct. A male-female pair was shipped to a London zoo with the hope of saving the species by rearing a herd in captivity. But they refused to mate. One attempt by zoo officials artificially to arouse the male resulted only in a fit of rage that caused fatal injuries. He died that year, 1864.

The female lived into the age of photography, the only quagga ever to be photographed. When she died of old age in 1872, her skeleton was purchased by Yale University's Peabody Museum of Natural History, where it is kept today.

Quaggas were no longer seen in the wild. Although the London female was not the last of the species, its fate was sealed.

Two quaggas remained in zoos: one in Berlin, one in Amsterdam. There was no attempt to get them together since both were females, though they probably would have enjoyed each other's company. The Berlin quagga died in 1875, and the world's last quagga expired on August 12, 1883. The species was pronounced extinct. The Hottentots are not extinct but their nomadic culture is. The Boers are not extinct but their name is, their descendants now called Afrikaners.

Passenger Pigeon: Year of Extinction, 1914

One of the most famous extinctions of modern times is that of the passenger pigeon in North America. Never have so many animals disappeared so fast. The story is replete with incredible figures and equally hard to believe eyewitness accounts. All are true, though.

The passenger pigeon was an attractive, graceful bird with slate-blue upper feathers and a deep pink breast. It didn't coo like its cousin the dove; it crowed and clucked like a cock. Its greatest claim to fame was the gigantic size of its populations; it may have been the most abundant bird ever to exist on the planet.

The numbers are mind-boggling. Scottish-American ornithologist Alexander Wilson watched steadily for *two days* as a flock passed over his home in Kentucky; he estimated its length at 250 miles. Naturalist John James Audubon described another barrage of birds as a "torrent of life" that took *three days* to pass, blotting out the sun. When they landed, their roost measured 40 miles long by 3 miles wide. Audubon estimated they had passed overhead at the rate of 300 million birds an hour. The incessant roar of wings, he wrote, was heard 6 miles away.

Wilson and Audubon, who founded American ornithology, calculated that another flock contained two billion birds and caused a local solar eclipse blacker than the moon could achieve.

Needless to say, bird droppings were a problem. When the pigeons alighted from a roost of several acres, all herbs, grasses, and low-lying shrubs were dead, with trees eventually succumbing to the acidified soil. From the air, their dropping splattered houses, barns, pastures, and roads into a Jackson Pollack–like canvas. And when they fed on the fruits of forest trees—preferring acorn and beechnut—they left nothing but bare branches.

It was said that a single rifle blast killed at least two hundred birds. In the 1700s passenger pigeons sold throughout New England at six birds for a penny, to be baked into pigeon pie, a "delicacy," though today we associate that word with a rare dish.

For centuries the passenger pigeon prospered and posed no problems to human populations. To the contrary; it was a major source of food. It was the passenger pigeon that in 1648 saved the New England Pilgrims from starvation when a severe winter destroyed their crops. And the bird, baked, roasted, or simmered in a stew, became a staple of the colonists' diet. Numerous recipes for passenger pigeon exist; the bird was consumed much like chicken is today. The taste was similar, if somewhat gamier.

Baked, roasted, or stewed, the passenger pigeon was the "chicken" of earlier times.

During the 1700s and early 1800s hunters devised clever ways of killing the greatest possible number of birds. In one method, men waited until a flock of pigeons roosted for the night in tree branches. With the arrival of darkness the birds became motionless, and the hunters, having prepared the ground with flammable dried grass and sulfur, ignited the mixture whose dense smoke suffocated the pigeons. Millions were felled in hours.

In another method, hunters soaked grain in alcohol and sprinkled it on the ground. The birds, drunk, soon were dead, clobbered with sticks, shot, or netted (after which their heads were crushed with pincers).

Perhaps the most ingenious trapping device was a live passenger pigeon that had been captured and had its eyes sewn shut. Set out on a perch called a "stool," the blinded bird, unable to fly, called loudly, reining in an enormous flock, which was then shot. Hence the term "stool pigeon" for one person who sets up another.

Last Survivors. The most remarkable aspect of the passenger pigeon's demise was its rapidity, influenced by a confluence of factors. As the human population expanded, oak and beech forests were cut down, reducing the pigeons' food supply. The extension of the railroad westward exposed isolated bird havens to depopulation; the railroad also provided a quick means of shipping slain birds back to the voracious East Coast market. Passenger pigeons, being plentiful and cheap, also became live targets in shooting galleries at city and county fairs.

By the mid-1860s, the flocks were gone from the skies over coastal states. Within the next twenty years their populations were dwindling everywhere.

The passenger pigeon's last stronghold was in the state of Michigan. And the last great pigeon hunt took place in 1878 in the vicinity of Petoskey. It conveys a clear picture of how the bird became extinct so quickly. In a twenty-five-mile-long forest the pigeons roosted in a compact flock about five miles long by a mile wide. The number of birds was estimated at one billion. Hundreds of local hunters with shotguns began shooting birds on the periphery of the forest, moving inward. Birds not killed took flight, but at dusk returned to the same trees, again easy targets. It took the hunters thirty days to fell the entire pigeon population, packing each day's kill into five railroad cars for shipment to Boston and New York. A total of three hundred tons of bird went to market.

But the passenger pigeon was not yet extinct.

On the morning of March 24, 1900, a teenager in Ohio sighted down the barrel of his rifle and extinguished the life of the last passenger pigeon in that state. Maine reported that its last bird was shot in Bar Harbor by a hunter in 1904. Arkansas recorded the extinction of the species in 1906, when a single bird was shot on the bank of the Black River. The Canadian hunter who shot a passenger pigeon in the woods of St. Vincent, Quebec, on September 23, 1907, merited a special distinction: No one after him would ever be able to kill a member of the species in the wild.

The bird that only a century earlier had represented about thirty-five percent of the entire avian population of the United States was now down to three, all in the Cincinnati Zoo. Audubon, who died in 1851, had never imagined that a species that "darken the noon-day light as if obscured by an eclipse" could become extinct, and only a half-century after his death. Two of the Cincinnati birds died, leaving behind the pigeon named Martha. She died on September 1, 1914, at the age of twenty-nine. Her body was frozen in a three-hundred-pound block of ice and shipped to Washington, D.C., where she was thawed, eviscerated, stuffed, and mounted. She can be viewed today in the Smithsonian's collection of rare birds.

Heath Hen: Year of Extinction, 1932

Of the heath hen, an extinct species of prairie chicken or North American grouse (two names for the same bird, as field mouse and vole are the simple and showy names of the same rodent), *The New York Times* editorialized in May 1900: "Scientific persons who ought to be more than a little ashamed of themselves are offering the natives of the island from $25 to $30 apiece for specimens of the doomed race."

Doomed was right, for the heath hen (*Tympanuchus cupido cupido,* to be extremely showy) had exactly thirty-three years to live.

Its obituary appeared not in *The Times,* but in the *Vineyard Gazette,* a Martha's Vineyard newspaper, on April 21, 1933: "All around us nature is full of casualties. . . . But to the heath hen something more than death has happened. . . . There is no survivor, there is no future. . . . There is a void in the April dawn, there is expectancy unanswered. . . . We are looking upon the uttermost finality . . . glimpsing the darkness which will not know another ray of light. We are in touch with the reality of extinction." The melodrama was intentional, one supposes, but the fact was that the grouse that had fed the Pilgrims was gone.

The buff-brown heath hen was commonplace throughout New England in the 1600s. It inhabited virtually every Northeastern forest, making its home in trees, preferably oak. It fed on acorns and berries, and occasionally wandered into open fields for clover and grain. During breeding season, it nested on the ground, reluctant to move even when confronted with a threat. Thus breeding season became the favorite time to shoot heath hens, and a bonus was provided by their eggs. The Puritans grew so tired of eating the bird that the dish was relegated to servants—who on one occasion went on strike to protest having to eat heath hen more than three times a week. The concept of opened and closed gaming seasons had yet to be appreciated, or needed, since the human population was relatively small.

The story of the extinction of the heath hen involves no horror tales of brutal slayings, no desire for hides that could be made into handbags; the heath hen's drab feathers weren't even that attractive on a hat. People simply ate the bird and its eggs at breeding time, killing two generations at once. It was particularly effective, dealing a double blow in geometrical progression.

By 1870, there were no heath hens in New York State. Throughout New England the bird was as good as gone. By 1880, the heath hen could be found in only one place—the wooded, sandy island of Martha's Vineyard, off the coast of Massachusetts.

Last Survivors. A hundred heath hens existed. A law was passed to protect them, and for a while they appeared to be making a comeback. Yet the number was insufficient to allow the bird to multiply beyond the casualties nature took each year. In 1912, with fewer than seventy-five hens surviving, the *Bulletin of the New York Zoological Society* reported: "The cycle of the lives of these few individuals are guarded and watched as carefully as is possible by wardens and scientific investigation."

Their population soared over the next few years, up to 2,000 birds. Then, in 1916, a brushfire raged across Martha's Vineyard during nesting season, burning chicks and mothers that refused to abandon their broods. Among the smoldering ash a game warden counted the survivors: 105, mostly males. The devastating fire was followed by several severe winters that claimed more birds, and when the weather warmed the island was invaded by hawks that swooped down on the hens and their young. The hawks left when the birds existed in too small a quantity to tempt them, but their departure was followed by a viral epidemic that ran through the survivors. On March 11, 1932, the last heath hen died.

The American Museum of Natural History in New York City has a realistic-looking display of a heath hen guarding her eggs. It's a poignant display, capturing the extinct species in the situation that helped contribute to its decline and demise.

CHAPTER 10

Decimating
Disease
Bubonic Plague to Spanish Flu

PLAGUES ARE ONE OF NATURE's most treacherous endings, taking more lives than all the wars in history. One plague alone, the Black Death of the Middle Ages, in less than four years exterminated a third of the population of Europe. Another scourge, smallpox, brought by the Spaniards to America, did more than gunpowder for the European conquest of the New World.

We do not have to reach far back into the past for such epic endings. In 1918 a pandemic of influenza (which may have originated at a United States military base) ended the lives of more than twenty million people in four *months*—a greater toll than four *years* of World War I.

Epidemics are endings of a tragic kind, and they are neither rare nor, lamentably, foreseeably eradicable. Viruses, bacilli, fungi, and parasites are as integral a part of the earth's ecosystem as the plants, animals, and people they destroy. And the microorganisms have seniority; their ancestors were the first forms of life on the planet. And their descendants may well be the last.

It is all too easy to imbue a scourge with motives insidious and moral, but virulent organisms are, of course, obediently carrying out nature's mandate to be fruitful and multiply—as quickly and efficiently as possible. The AIDS virus did not target four high-risk groups; it chose a hospitable blood cell and, by trial and error, found an expeditious route to the host. The bacterium responsible for the bubonic plague of the fourteenth century found a means of contagion so effective (via fleas and rats) that the high-risk group was humanity itself. It took its toll equally among clergy, landowners, and serfs, and it helped bring about the end to feudalism.

What we will see in this chapter, again and again, is the utter indiscriminacy of disease and the terrifying normalcy of plague.

People in the past attributed epidemics to retribution from the gods. Today, when technology is a god we created, we feel we should be able to end plagues for all times. That's a natural reaction if we imagine ourselves above nature and in control of the environment. But no species has ever won independence from the forces that created it. Frightening though it is to contemplate, disease in the form of plagues and scourges is a natural phenomenon, always part of human history. An entire new scientific discipline, paleopathology, now studies the evidence of plagues in shaping the evolution of life on earth, while another field, biohistory, examines the havoc wrought by disease in the decline and fall of rulers, dynasties, empires, and nations. We'll look at the conclusions drawn by both fields.

Epidemics: 9,000 Years Ago, Europe and Asia

Bacteria and viruses have been around for billions of years, but human epidemics and pandemics date from the dawn of civilization, about nine thousand years ago.

"Upon the people" is the meaning of epidemic *(epi dēmos),* and when a disease is upon all of the people it is a *pan*demic. Diseases "upon the people" and of "all the people" became major new phenomena once early man changed his style of living from small tribal families scattered throughout a region to communal city dwellers. When tribes were isolated by distance, the only diseases they knew were regional ones, or *en*demic, ailments that are "in the people."

When people began to emerge from primitive self-contained communities the chances of major health disasters rapidly multiplied. Although a greater

Indiscriminacy of disease: Scourge attacks bishop, peasant, physician, and musician.

degree of civilization brought benefits—a higher standard of living, a fuller, more intellectual life—it invited in grave hazards. The chance for contact with a regional disease once in a certain people rose until that disease was upon the newly heterogeneous community.

The invention of the wheel and the construction of roads meant easier and faster travel; but traveling just as swiftly was disease, coming and going now to all the people. Before resistance to new invading organisms could develop, the lives of entire unprotected populations came to an end.

What follows are history's greatest scourges. In every case the organisms that caused the plague are probably still with us. Some are as virulent as ever; others are temporarily in retreat, awaiting favorable conditions in which to be fruitful and multiply; one—and one of the worst—exists only as frozen samples in two laboratories in the world (in Atlanta and in Moscow), caught in a scientific debate over whether a germ that destroyed hundreds of millions of lives should itself be destroyed.

Bubonic Plague: 6th, 14th, and 17th Centuries

> **Agent:** *Pasteurella pestis,* a bacterium
>
> **Transmitted by:** Flea bites from infected rats
>
> **Symptoms:** Swollen lymph nodes (buboes), fever, prostration, delirium

From the fall of the Roman Empire until the great fire of London—a period of roughly 1,200 years—the world's population was devastated by 3 major pandemics of bubonic plague, or the Black Death, as the middle outbreak was called, though it was not the worst. The death toll from the 3 encounters is estimated at 137 million victims, and occurring in centuries far less populated than our own.

Today we cannot comprehend a disease—*any* disease—that can abruptly end the lives of so many people. The bubonic plague was extraordinarily contagious and deadly, with a mortality rate of ninety percent. You could experience the first symptoms on a Monday and be in your grave by Sunday.

One of the early and most dreaded symptoms was buboes (hence the disease's name), enlarged lymph glands in the groin, armpit, and neck. We now know that bubonic plague is primarily a bacterial disease of a rodent, the black rat *(Rattus rattus),* and named in Europe, where it existed in great numbers, as the Old English rat. This is not your rangy brown sewer rat. The Old English rat is a handsome beast with silky black fur that disdains the muck and mire of sewers and farmyards, preferring, tragically for humans, warm houses and dry ships.

An uninfected Old English rat is a mere pest. But a rat that has picked up the bacillus *Pasteurella pestis* can be the start of a pestilence. The plague is passed from rat to rat by fleas, which also like a warm dry environment and

choose to live in the silky black fur of *Rattus rattus.* A flea bites an infected
rat and ingurgitates plague bacilli, which can live in the flea's intestinal canal
for up to three weeks. If, during that time, the flea bites a person, regurgitating
the bacilli, the end of life was, for centuries, virtually certain.

As the causative organism multiplies rapidly in the person's bloodstream it
produces high temperature and death, perhaps from septicemia, or blood poisoning.

Or, worse, the person's lungs can become infected. This pneumonic form
of bubonic plague is far more dangerous because it spreads directly from person
to person, with symptoms like those of an exceptionally pernicious pneumonia.
The person's breath and sputum are literally swarming with bacilli; as he
speaks, coughs, or sneezes, he scatters the microorganisms far and wide. Any
bystander who has the misfortune to inhale them into his own lungs develops
the plague himself. In its pneumonic form bubonic plague spreads rapidly. A
single case can launch a pandemic. And did, at least three times: the plague of
Justinian in the sixth century; the Black Death in the fourteenth century; and
the great plague of London, which raged throughout Europe during the years
1665–66.

Bubonic Plague of Justinian: 540–90, Europe and Asia

Justinian I, known in his day as Flavius Petrus Sabbatius Justinianus, was the
great Byzantine emperor whose legal and architectural monuments have lasted
into our own century. In 525, at the age of forty-two, he received the title of
caesar, and his reign as emperor began two years later when he received the
rank of augustus. His wife, Theodora, a former actress, was crowned augusta.

It should have been a reign of imperial splendor, and it began that way.
Justinian erected magnificent buildings, fortified his territories with chains of
castles, recruited excellent armies of skilled pikemen and bowmen, and his code
of laws, which embodied those of ancient Rome, would be the basis of European
justice.

However, in 540, at the height of Justinian's political and military successes,
bubonic plague struck. It is probably the worst pandemic that has ever har-
rowed humankind. We know of its devastation mainly from the records kept
by Justinian's chief archivist and secretary, Procopius. No invasion of Goths or
Vandals could have more effectively demolished armies, cities, and governments. The plague began that year in Lower Egypt, in Pelusium, where the
region's black rats were never once suspected of being the culprits. Within a
month, traders and itinerant scholars had carried the epidemic to Alexandria and
Palestine.

At the time, Justinian was engaged in wars with both Italy and Persia. But
soon the plague was claiming the lives of more generals and soldiers than were
battles. He returned to Byzantium to find that the mortality rate in the city was
up to ten thousand a day.

*Corpses were stacked into fort
towers and set to sea on boats.
Emperor Justinian, Empress
Theodora. Rattus rattus.*

Individual graves had long been abandoned; even mass graves could not be
dug fast enough. To accommodate the corpses (which were themselves infectious), Justinian ordered that the roofs be removed from the towers on forts
and that the towers' high columns be stacked with bodies. When no more
corpses could be crammed in, lye was poured down the shaft and the roof
replaced. Once all fort towers were filled, ships were loaded with the mounting
dead, rowed out to sea, and abandoned or set ablaze.

Procopius also recorded the human dimension of the tragedy.

A typical victim was seized with sudden fever, often waking in a pool of
perspiration. The cavalcade of symptoms was rapid. The first day the person
could feel the hard nodules of buboes in the groin and armpit. By the second
or third day the fever produced violent delirium in which victims hallucinated,
seeing "phantoms of death and hearing its call." Procopius astutely observed
that a person who coughed and spit up phlegm died quickly, usually by the fifth
day (clearly a victim of the plague's pneumonic form).

In victims of the disease's blood poisoning, the buboes erupted into gangrenous sores that produced a protracted and more painful death. To live beyond
ten days was considered a miracle, spare time in which to offer additional
prayers for the inevitable end. Of course there was no cure.

Divine Punishment.   Everyone was at risk, but more men died than
women. It was common for entire families to be wiped out, their lineage ended,
their surnames and professions lost to history. During the half-century that the
plague raged, no town or village was spared. Many cities vanished from European maps. Agriculture largely ceased. Historians claim that entire regions of
the continent never regained their previous density of population. The total
death toll: one hundred million people.

Justinian and his actress wife were survivors. He withdrew from public affairs during the last years of his reign, devoting himself to theological problems, a fitting subject when everyone viewed the plague-in-progress as an act of God. Justinian believed that Christ was entirely divine (not of a dual human and divine nature, as Rome then taught) and responsible for the punishing plague. That kind of reasoning—plague as reprimand—was acceptable theology then, although Greek and Roman physicians sought earthly causative agents. But Justinian lapsed into heresy with his edict that the human body of Christ was incorruptible and only appeared to suffer on the cross, his death an illusion. Justinian's own death two years after the blasphemy was very real. As for the plague, it waxed and waned another thirty-five years, throwing the entire Roman Empire into chaos and confusion.

Historical Consequences. The plague of Justinian (so named because it began in his reign) was more than disease; it made history. It's been argued that there were three major historical ramifications to the pandemic: 1. the downfall of the Roman Empire, from which no recovery was possible; 2. the strengthening of the nascent religion of Christianity, to which people turned in extraordinary numbers in order to be spared further sickness and death; and 3. the virtual destruction of the learned field of Greek and Roman medicine, since its notions and nostrums proved useless at a time when they were most needed.

No small accomplishments these, brought on by a microscopic bacterium, a flea, and a handsome black rat. An epidemic is humbling. A pandemic underscores the insignificance of any one species in the scheme of things.

The effect of the plague of Justinian on the field of medicine is unarguable, and was unfortunate. The Christian Church rushed in to fill the medical void, becoming doctor to the soul *and* the body. Progressive Greek and Roman physicians had taught that disease was caused by pathogenic agents; they were slowly, but correctly, creating the discipline of medical science. The church, however, in its new role as healer, equated disease with vice and sin, the punishment for leading an errant life, that is, for not listening to Rome. The brilliant ideas of Galen and Hippocrates became heresies. This repressive attitude lasted until the fourteenth century and vastly altered what would have been a very different course of medicine had it not fallen under the domination of dogma and miracles.

When the plague of Justinian ended in 590, the causative bacillus did not vanish. The germ had simply wiped out so many people that it lost the critical mass of susceptible hosts needed to sustain catastrophe. It killed off too many people for its own good. And it had allowed the few survivors to develop immunity. There were occasional small regional eruptions during the Middle Ages, but the bubonic bacterium as a plague lay almost dormant until the middle of the 1300s, when it awoke with a vengeance.

Black Death: 1346 to 1361, Europe and Asia

The name Black Death arose to characterize the particularly virulent pneumonic form of bubonic plague that surfaced in Europe in the fourteenth century. It produced dark hemorrhages just beneath the skin of the body and around the eyes. The infection caused gangrene of the lungs, and it spread from person to person as easily as the flu or a cold. Only it was almost always fatal. From massive internal hemorrhaging, a person died discolored black, hence the disease's name.

Whereas the plague of Justinian lasted on and off for fifty years and killed one hundred million people, the Black Death disappeared after fifteen years, taking a toll of twenty-seven million lives. The ratio of duration to lives lost is about the same—two million victims per year—with the plague of Justinian the greater killer by a margin. The reason the Black Death is often called "the worst epidemic the world has ever known" is primarily because we know more about it from numerous extant eyewitness accounts.

If a deadly organism had intent, it would pick a bustling center of commerce to launch itself on the world, and that is what the Black Death did.

It began late in 1346 as an epidemic in the fortified trading port of Caffa (now Theodosia) on the Crimean shore of the Black Sea. From the start, the disease was a pestilence of inconceivable fury and severity. Like a tidal wave, it struck in England in the summer of 1347, prostrating the city of London. By the spring of the following year it had washed over Sweden, France, Spain, Italy, Russia, Ireland, the Netherlands, and Scandinavia, ravaging the populations of their large cities. "I buried with my own hands five of my children in a single grave," wrote Italian author Agnioli di Tura. "No bells. No tears. This is the end of the world."

That is how the scourge was viewed. Pits were hastily dug and as rapidly filled with corpses. As a commentator of the time graphically wrote: "The testator and his heirs and executors were hurled from the same cart into the same hole together."

It was quickly perceived by laymen and doctors alike that a cough or sneeze could spread the plague, and people responded with understandable panic and perhaps forgivable cruelty. Healthy parents abandoned a coughing child. Doctors, dying as quickly as their patients, refused to treat the sick. The clergy prayed over the dying for divine intervention, but when they too began to die in huge numbers, every man became his own confessor. And with the church's sanction. The British bishop of the diocese of Bath wrote to Rome: "No priests can be found who are willing, whether out of zeal and devotion or in exchange for a stipend, to take on the pastoral care of the sick. . . . Many people are dying without the Sacrament of Penance." Rome announced an emergency relaxation of canonical law, permitting the dying to confess aloud to God or to any person who would listen, "even to a woman"—a concession, given the church's attitude toward women, that surely underscored its desperation.

The plague hit England particularly hard. Of a population of four million, thirty-three percent died. The religious suffered even higher casualties because they continued to treat the sick long after doctors abandoned them. Among parish priests the death rate was forty-five percent. And when the Black Death entered behind the walls of secluded monasteries and nunneries, fifty-one percent of the pious succumbed.

Pope Clement VI, at wit's end to elicit divine intervention, conceived a plan that actually fanned the fires of the contagion. If individuals' prayer had not put an end to the scourge, he reasoned, perhaps mass devotion would. By edict he announced 1348 a Holy Year, encouraging all of Europe's and Asia's Christians to undertake a pilgrimage to Rome.

It was an invitation to genocide. In order to bribe a diseased and frightened laity, he offered advance absolution to anyone who might die en route to Rome. Their souls, he promised, would not be delayed in purgatory, but gain immediate entrance into heaven. By Easter of that year more than 1,250,000 pilgrims, most sick and ailing, had poured into the eternal city. Only 10 percent lived to return home. The rest, one hopes, went to heaven.

Mass devotion, and even mass death, did not appease God; clergy persisted in placing the blame for the scourge on a merciful Lord instructing a wayward world. As Italian author Giovanni Boccaccio wrote in the *Decameron:* "In the year of Our Lord 1348, there happened . . . a most terrible plague, which was sent from God as a just punishment for our sins."

Another Italian writer when asked "How do you explain the pestilence?" answered, "It is surely necessary that God should sometimes remind us of His existence." But when the reminder went on month after month, year after year, God was exonerated and a scapegoat substituted.

Jewish Persecution.   Jews (who were dying as fast as Christians) were accused of poisoning wells. Poison was suddenly blamed as the baneful agent of the plague. Their synagogues and ghettos were burned, and they went on trial throughout Europe. Under threats of torture many Jews "confessed" their

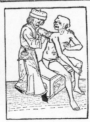

Pope Clement VI (left) exacerbated the plague by inviting pilgrims to Rome (top). Physician opens lymph nodes in armpit.

guilt, and officials in several towns found "proof" of poison in wells. Until new wells could be dug, people drank only rainwater.

The persecutions were worst in Germany. City gates were guarded, and any Jew found carrying an envelope or bottle of suspicious substance was tried and invariably convicted. In one city the "guilty" were "enclosed in a wooden building, constructed for the purpose, and burnt together with it."

To his credit, Pope Clement VI, himself looking for a scapegoat for the scourge, issued two bulls declaring the Jews innocent. He admonished all Christians, though without success, to cease from the groundless persecutions. And though the Emperor Charles IV shared the pope's views, he dared not interfere with the injustices, for "He found himself obliged to yield to the selfishness of the nobles, who were unwilling to forego so favorable an opportunity of releasing themselves from their Jewish creditors."

In time the plague burned itself out. It had taken the lives of writers and artists like Ghirlandaio, Titian, and Chaucer. Italian lyric poet and scholar Petrarch, who lost his daughter Laura to the plague, wrote that future generations would be "unable to imagine the empty houses, abandoned towns, the squalid countryside, fields littered with the dead, the dreadful silence and solitude that hung over the whole world." The plague years were thought to be the end of the world.

Last Scourges.   When the bubonic plague resurfaced in 1665–66 to be named the great plague of London, it was less severe—a true but thoroughly inadequate assessment. For at its peak, in London in the summer of 1665, each week 2,000 people died. Mercifully, within months it was gone. But not entirely: It has remained endemic on the southern and eastern shores of the Mediterranean, and in Asia, Africa, and South America. In the United States, it struck as recently as 1907, in San Francisco, with 160 cases and 77 deaths. One theory to account for its relative mildness today is that a less lethal strain of bacillus

Physician's protective costume during the pestilence of 1665. Curatives of tarragon, dill, chives, basil, and garlic were better fitted for a stew.

evolved, which means that fewer rats die from the infection and therefore there is no need for the transmitting fleas to abandon rats to bite humans for a meal of blood.

In 1971 the World Health Organization reported a total of 965 cases of bubonic plague and only 47 deaths, a mortality rate of about 5 percent—close to the *survival* rate during the plague of Justinian. In the late 1970s the death rate from bubonic plague was down to about 3 percent. Control of rat populations and antibiotic drugs have certainly helped diminish the microorganism's destructiveness. But though the bacillus is far less virulent, it is still on the planet, and no one can say that one day it might not mutate toward a more deadly strain.

Malaria: Pre–5th Century B.C., Africa

Agent: *Plasmodium vivax,* a protozoan

Transmitted by: The female *Anopheles* mosquito

Symptoms: Chills, fever, anemia, enlargement of the spleen

Mal aria could be a complaint for a poorly sung melody. But in its ancient medical usage "bad air" was thought to be the cause of a devastating disease, a disease that has nothing to do with air quality but is transmitted by the bite of the female *Anopheles* mosquito (male mosquitoes don't bite since they don't need human blood to nourish eggs).

Once, before modern eradication programs began, malaria had an enormous distribution: about three-quarters of the inhabitants of the world live in regions hospitable to the bug. The disease is characterized by a paroxysm of chills and sweating, anemia, enlargement of the spleen, and, for the young and elderly, often death. Until 1948 the disease struck about three hundred million people in a bad year, of which three million died. But that's only an average. In the worst hit countries, such as India, as many as thirteen million people were stricken annually, with up to four million killed.

In Indochina, one-fifth of the population always had malaria, and it was calculated that every native by the age of twenty-five had successfully fought off at least one bout of the disease.

It is impossible to measure how the vitality and capacity of a population must be diminished by such unrelenting stress. Or perhaps it is not: Many biohistorians believe that a chronic malaria epidemic weakened Roman citizens and soldiers and paved the way for the fall of the empire—which was never able to recover because it was then hit with the bubonic plague of Justinian.

Even more significant claims have been made for the "bad air" disease that is the oldest known to man.

Existing since prehistory, malaria is thought to be a primary stressor that forced early peoples to migrate in great numbers out of the warmer parts of Africa and Asia where the race originated—as did the disease—to cooler climates where the scourge could not easily track them down. Since human migrations, through adaptation, are believed to have produced various racial features—skin color, eye shape, hair texture—malaria could, if the disease-stressor theory is proved, be a significant indirect factor that led to race.

More factually, the disease was well known to the Greeks.

According to the *Iliad,* malaria is probably the epidemic that struck Greek forces at the siege of Troy. The far-reaching campaigns of Alexander the Great are thought to have helped spread the disease, which may have caused Alexander's early death. Not always fatal, the disease is, however, enervating, producing a general deterioration of physical and intellectual strength as well as a pessimistic view of life. Some historians argue that later generations of Greeks, battling in large numbers the chronic assaults of malarial debility, permitted a Golden Age to tarnish and crumble around them.

Greek and Roman physicians thought that malaria was caused by tiny airborne creatures. In his *De re rustica,* Columella, the first-century Roman agriculturist, wrote of "marshes where there live little animals which cannot be seen by the human eye, but which penetrate via the air into our bodies and cause severe sickness."

Malaria and the Fall of Rome.   What is the evidence that a female mosquito played a role in the decline of the Roman Empire, perhaps the most stupendous single event in history in both extent and longevity of its effect?

Ancient Rome, with its extensive aqueducts and magnificent public baths, was a paragon of cleanliness, not that different from a modern metropolitan city. Its sanitation standards were high, its water supply continually fresh.

But as the city became the hub of an ever-expanding empire—which at its height stretched from the Sahara to the border of Scotland, from the Persian Gulf to the western shore of Portugal—Rome opened itself to an invasion of outside microorganisms. The evidence for malaria, which physicians called the "Roman airs," is cogent; the disease's death toll, enormous.

In the first century B.C., during the years of Julius Caesar's civil wars, over sixty percent of the Roman population was chronically infected, with thousands of soldiers incapacitated. Caesar himself fell victim.

Columella, in his twelve-volume work on gardening, farming, and agriculture theory, wrote of how fatigue from the disease greatly curtailed efforts of farmers to produce enough food for the Roman population, itself continually growing through births and conquests. At one time, all of the Campagna, which supplied the city with fresh vegetables, ceased cultivation. Stricken farmers, seeking medical help, flooded into Rome, bringing with them the contagion. The infant mortality rate in the city soared; adult life expectancy sharply declined. Whereas an adult's immune system might successfully fight off an attack of the disease, a newborn's invariably lost the battle.

We know from numerous written accounts that Roman airs plagued the city for about five hundred years. Major epidemics are recorded in 79 A.D., the year Vesuvius erupted; in 125 A.D.; and in 165 when the outbreak was called the sickness of Galen, after the renowned physician who treated many patients and scrupulously recorded his efforts. That epidemic raged for fifteen years, taking as one of its last victims the author of *Meditations* and emperor of Rome,

Marcus Aurelius. He died on the seventh day of his illness, having refused to see his sixteen-year-old son, Commodus, whom he had made coemperor, for fear of infecting the boy.

By the fourth century A.D., most of the Roman army's men did not come from Rome or even from surrounding towns. They had to be recruited and conscripted from conquered Germanic lands, colder climates where malaria was not endemic. While there were periodic bouts of smallpox, as well as isolated occurrences of bubonic plague, malaria seems to be the disease most consistently associated with the empire's expansion. As a contemporary medical historian writes: "Probably malaria, rather than decadent luxury, accounted for the slackness of spirit which characterized the later years of Rome."

When a weakened Rome did fall late in the fifth century under invasions from the north, fleeing refugees carried the illness into France, England, and Germany. By the time of the Crusades at the close of the eleventh century, malaria had gradually conquered most of the continent.

Malaria in the New World.   The disease originated in Africa. How it reached the shores of America is uncertain.

We know that it began to flourish in the Virginia marshes shortly after the arrival of the colonists. As a conservative estimate, well over half of the population of New England probably suffered at one time or another from the disease, then commonly called the ague. Entire families, even communities, were laid low with malarial chills and fever, headaches, nausea, and exhaustion. The young and the elderly often died.

By the time of the American Revolution, malaria was a serious health problem in the colonies. General George Washington and his troops were chronically encumbered by it.

Under the belief that malaria was caused by bad air, millions of Americans flocked to breathe the good air of the great Western plains. "Malaria," writes a modern biohistorian, "may have had more direct influence on the western movement than any other single disease." In Indianapolis in 1822, then a city of 1,000 people, 900 were shaking with the ague. The next year, 90,000 of the 165,000 settlers in 17 counties around Columbus, Ohio, had malaria. A craftsman who fled the region warned a traveler to turn back: "The people die there like rotten sheep. They have filled one graveyard already and have begun upon another." When the traveler shrugged off the warning, the craftsman said, "Well, go on, but I can tell you, you will shake!"

Though quinine was now available, a truly effective treatment would not be developed for many years.

Indeed, probably the worst enemy American soldiers had to face in World War II was the female *Anopheles* mosquito. On Pacific islands they often had to build greater defenses against the insect than against their human foes. And on Sicily, malaria took more lives than military gunfire. Unlike diphtheria, typhus, cholera, and typhoid, the malaria bug has defied all attempts to produce a vaccine, though immunologists are currently testing several compounds that look promising.

Finding the Culprit.   Although malaria was the world's number-one disease for at least five thousand years, it was only toward the close of the nineteenth century that a French physician, Charles Alphonse Laveran, began to unravel its cause.

A medical officer stationed at Constantine, Algeria, where malaria was rife, Laveran detected waving, hairlike projections of a protozoan under his microscope. Convinced that the microorganism, now known as *Plasmodium vivax,* was the culprit, Laveran suspected that it might be transmitted by mosquitoes. The medical community still believed that foul air rising from swamps and decayed vegetable matter caused the illness and it would take seventeen years of dogged investigation to prove the mosquito theory.

On August 19, 1894, British physician Ronald Ross killed two mosquitoes that had been allowed to feed for four days on the blood of malarial patients. To his great delight, he found Laveran's protozoans in the insects' stomachs. It would take another scientist, Italian zoologist G. B. Grassi, to prove that only one species of mosquito was dangerous.

Grassi also detailed the habits of the female *Anopheles.* She requires mammalian blood every three days to nourish her egg-forming tissues. She'll fly up to two miles in search of blood, and unlike other insects, she does not return to a "home" after a meal; she roams, and over a large area, until it's time to feed again. Thus a single female mosquito can infect a large number of people— though only at night, for she remains quiescent in a dark corner during daylight hours. When she punctures a host's skin, a small amount of her saliva flows into the victim's blood. The saliva contains a toxin that prevents coagulation and causes the characteristic itching. The victim's blood is already swarming with malarial parasites when she begins to suck some of it into her alimentary canal.

Even today, while the AIDS epidemic continues to spread at an alarming rate, malaria remains the world-champion killer disease, infecting two hundred million new victims every year and killing millions of them. Control has become increasingly difficult because the mosquito quickly gains resistance to new insecticides, and the causative parasite itself becomes resistant to new drugs. A vaccine is the only hope of truly containing the disease that has plagued *Homo sapiens* since their emergence in the warm climate of Africa.

Smallpox: Pre–2nd Century B.C., Far East

> **Agent:** *Variola virus*
>
> **Transmitted by:** Contact, direct or indirect, with an infectious person
>
> **Symptoms:** Fever, scarring pustules, blindness

Historically, the *great* pox people dreaded was syphilis, with its characteristic skin eruptions. The lesser pox, with its own scarring pustules, or pockmarks, was called *small* pox. The great pox you could conceal for decades, until its fatal third stage erupted. But the suppurating facial lesions of smallpox could cause grotesque disfigurement and blindness; even a mild case could leave the victim scarred for life.

The two smallpox epidemics that struck Europe in the seventeenth century facially scarred more than half the population. They led to the vogue of artificial paste-on beauty patches as an attempt to conceal the ravages of the disease. The same scourge, brought to the New World by settlers, is a chief reason the white man was able to conquer and nearly annihilate the Native Americans, who had no resistance to the virus.

The virus, of the variola family, exists today, but only in sealed test tubes in two places in the world: in a high-security laboratory in Moscow and at the Centers for Disease Control in Atlanta. So scientists believe.

They are so confident of that belief that the disease is said to be eradicated, the last naturally transmitted case having occurred in Merca, Somalia, in October of 1977. (The next year, two cases occurred in England because the virus accidentally escaped from a research laboratory, but security controls were tightened and the samples centralized in Moscow and Atlanta.)

Today no scientist is working with the smallpox variola, and the unprecedented quandary facing virologists is what to do with the sealed samples, which are viable, frozen at minus ninety-four degrees Fahrenheit. Quite simply, the organisms are the most fearsome endangered species on earth.

It is also a species that over thousands of years has killed tens of millions of people and disfigured even more. Whereas some scientists opt for extinction (by heat or chemical poison), others argue that the microorganisms should not be erased altogether from the world, partly because unforeseen research uses might arise in the future. Philosophically, they question whether human beings have the right to bring about the deliberate extinction of a species—something that would be a first. (Though human beings have certainly wiped out more endearing species with a doggedness not far removed from deliberate intent. See "Modern Extinctions," page 199.)

While scientists ponder the quandary, the virus's wake of destruction is well documented.

An acutely infectious disease, smallpox began with a fever, progressed in two days to pus-filled skin lesions, and if a victim survived—as more than five out of ten did—the scarring was permanent. You caught it not from mosquitoes or fleas or rats, but from other people, specifically by inhaling flakes from the disease's scabs, which bore the virus. With the last cases now more than a decade behind us, it is hard to conceive of how horribly this flesh-eating plague was dreaded in earlier centuries—except for the fact that it struck primarily children, disfiguring the survivors for life. Acute cases led to blindness, the eye eaten by the virus.

In the eighteenth century alone, smallpox killed sixty million Europeans. Ninety-five percent of the people who survived to adulthood bore smallpox scars. Police "wanted" posters often identified a criminal by the pattern of pockmarks on his face. A betrothed woman who caught the disease and survived scarred abandoned all prospects of marriage. Indigent parents abandoned severely disfigured children; wealthy parents encouraged their scarred sons and daughters to enter religious orders. An advertisement from the period read: "Wanted, a footman and butler in a great family . . . must be of the Church of England and have had the pox in a natural way"—since a bout of the disease conferred immunity. Today we worry about the effects on our skin of sun, wind, and aging; not long ago the chief concern was pox.

From the Far East to Spain.   Smallpox was dreaded by ancient Hindu people, who had many names for the disease and who left the oldest description of its symptoms. In China, during the eleventh century B.C., it was known as "venom from the mother's breast," since it appeared so frequently in children.

Just when the pox traveled west is uncertain. The mummified head of the Egyptian pharaoh Ramses V suggests that he died (in 1160 B.C.) of the disease, but there is no clear mention of a smallpox epidemic in the west until the seventh century A.D., when the city of Alexandria, then the emporium of trade, was struck hard. Through trading, the disease was carried by Muslims in 647 to Tripoli, and by the end of the century it had spread the length of the African coast and the Mediterranean mainland.

Smallpox entered Spain in 710 as the indirect consequence of a rape. Roderick (also known as Don Rodrigo), Visigothic king of the country, sexually forced himself on the queen's lady-in-waiting, Cava. Cava's father, Count Julian, by way of revenge betrayed Spain to Islamic invaders from North Africa, who were themselves battling an epidemic of smallpox on their home turf. As the victorious Muslims settled in Spain, they brought with them the disease, triggering the first outbreak of smallpox in the country. It nearly decimated native Spaniards, who had no immunity. Thus Julian's revenge had a high price. Higher still, considering that the Spaniards would bring the disease to the New World in the 1500s, effectively wiping out the Aztec civilization.

Smallpox, brought from Europe, helped the Spaniards conquer the Aztecs.

From Spaniards to Aztecs.   The effect of smallpox on the Aztecs during the thirty or so years from 1519 to 1548 cannot be underplayed. It illustrates the devastation wrought upon a people who have no immunity to a virus rapidly introduced into their culture.

It was on February 19, 1519, that Hernando Cortez sailed from Cuba with a force of eight hundred Spaniards and Indians. Landing on the Yucatán coast, he made his way inland and received friendly greetings and gifts from the Mexican emperor, Montezuma. The friendly relations soured once Cortez demanded that the emperor submit to European rule. By that time, a new disease had visited the Indian population of Mexico, which they named "the great leprosy."

It was not leprosy, though, as the natives thought. Nor was it the great pox, syphilis, as historians long surmised. It could have been neither of those diseases because the mysterious new infection spread too rapidly throughout the population, hitting children particularly hard. Though we have no medical proof of what the disease was, we know that it had to be a highly infectious, nonsexually transmitted (since it struck children), and a contagion to which the majority of Spanish men had a natural immunity since they survived.

With little doubt, it was smallpox.

Aztec mortality was appallingly high. In the first wave of the epidemic, half the native inhabitants of infected Mexican cities died. A new contingent of Spanish ships arrived in 1531, and that year a second epidemic erupted. A third outbreak followed the arrival of Spanish ships in 1545. Further visitations of the disease—and visits by Spaniards—occurred in 1564, 1576, and 1595. By that time, the new diseases of mumps and measles had also been introduced to the region, and most of the native Indian population had died off.

The death toll: 18.5 million natives dead out of a population that 80 years earlier had numbered 25 million.

Medical historians feel certain that smallpox, mumps, and measles had not existed in new Spain before the coming of the conquistadors. Disease, especially smallpox, played no insignificant role in the Spanish conquests and the destruction of the Aztec race. And, too, smallpox played a similar role in Pizarro's astonishing conquest of the Inca empire in South America.

But there is more to an epidemic than its ravaging effects on the body. Mass disease and dying attack the psyche of the living. The native Indians of Central and South America were told that their conquerors were superior people who worshiped the one true God. Spaniards rode horses and fired guns—impressive beasts and intimidating weapons unknown to the natives. Although they may have initially disbelieved the Spaniards' claim to superiority, when they began to die by the tens of thousands from a mysterious pestilence from which their overlords were spared, they could only admit to their own inferiority and the ineffectiveness of their constellation of gods and goddesses, and accept their woeful fate. God, in the form of Christianity, had clearly shown Himself to be on the side of the Spaniards. Little wonder that the ancient religions of Mexico and Peru vanished abruptly and utterly, while conversion to Christianity was embraced earnestly and frantically.

The Americas were conquered by guns *and* disease, and it is only now that historians are turning to the true role of epidemics in the evolution and expansion of the races.

Vaccination.   The first successful counterattack on smallpox came in 1796, when the English country doctor Edward Jenner developed a vaccine and launched the modern practice of vaccination. Most people were terrified to be inoculated with Jenner's live serum, but one of the early brave guinea pigs was the sixty-seven-year-old empress of Russia, Catherine the Great. She submitted to the procedure as an example to her subjects, who had suffered through many smallpox outbreaks. The disease had killed Czar Peter II at age fourteen, on his wedding day.

Jenner's vaccine was highly effective. In America, George Washington—troubled that half of his ten-thousand-man Continental Army in the Northern states had come down with smallpox—asked Congress to approve inoculation of the healthy soldiers. Due to improved vaccines, the last case of smallpox in the United States occurred in 1949. In 1971 South America was finally rid of the disease that had changed the face of its country, peoples, and religions. And, as mentioned, in 1977 scientists reported the last case of smallpox in the world. The disease has met its end, as long as no organism is biding time in an animal host or the frozen samples in Moscow and Atlanta do not thaw and escape their confinement.

Syphilis: 11,500 Years Ago, Africa

Agent: *Treponema pallidum,* a spirochete bacterium

Transmitted by: Contact with an infectious lesion or active spirochete

Symptoms: Skin lesions, progressing to invasion of the heart, brain, eyes, and central nervous system

Smallpox scarred the body; syphilis, known as the great pox, also scarred the soul. Transmitted sexually, it carried with it the stigma of profound moral turpitude and an invitation to social ostracism. It was a disease made for bigots, the scantimoniously pious, and celibates who secretly resented their chastity. Not surprisingly, victims riddled with the disease's concealed genital sores and mouth lesions denied being infected.

In fact, denial was everywhere. The British called it the French disease, the French swore it was a German disease, the Germans blamed the Spanish, and the Spanish emphatically denied introducing it to the American Indians, from whom they said *they* caught it.

Historically, syphilis is a fascinating disease because of the tremendous influence it has had—and continues to have—on the general view of morality and hygiene. In more ways than one, it was the AIDS of past centuries.

It rapidly hit Europe in the sixteenth century, diminishing promiscuity, awakening a rebirth in monogamy, and instituting "safe sex" by way of condoms, euphemistically called "overcoats." They were of waxed linen, came in

Syphilitic sufferers herded into a "pox house." Dionysius (inset), the disease's patron saint.

only one length (an ambitious eight inches), and were held on by a ribbon threaded through the base which, to add romance, could be knotted into a bow. The syphilis pandemic of the sixteenth century helped establish the puritan mind-set of the Reformation and beyond; who can say what moral legacy AIDS will pass on to future generations? And, too, people's reactions in earlier times to victims of syphilis were not that different from the spectrum of modern reactions to AIDS sufferers.

Modern evidence suggests the syphilis spirochete originated in Africa (as the AIDS virus probably did). The corkscrew shaped organism is almost identical to the agent that causes African yaws, a common skin-lesion disease. The great unsolved mystery surrounding syphilis is how it appeared so suddenly in sixteenth-century Europe, its entrance into modern Western society. There are two schools of medical opinion, both reminiscent of the name-calling historically associated with the sexual scourge.

The European school (pointing an accusatory finger toward the New World) opines that the disease was endemic among the dark-skinned aboriginal inhabitants of the West Indies, who brought it with them from Africa. It was transmitted by West Indian women to Columbus's sailors, who, in turn, imported it into Spain, from which it spread throughout Europe.

On the other shore, the American school argues that the disease had already been slumbering unnoticed in Europe for centuries before it made its historic debut in Spain. That occasional random cases went undiagnosed or were misdiagnosed (as has happened in our own century with toxic shock syndrome and AIDS). And that it was Columbus's men who brought the disease to the New World.

Who is right?

There is some evidence that the disease had already traveled with traders and slaves out of Africa and into the ancient Roman Empire, where it was mistakenly called "sexual leprosy." But until 1987 there was about equal evidence to justify the accusations of both the European and American schools of thought.

In that year the scales tipped. The most recent medical clues support the European school. Examining fossilized bones of a bear that lived in Indiana 11,500 years ago, scientists have discovered tiny holes, and small spiky projections exactly like those found in syphilis victims. Moreover, when they applied an antibody test to the bones, they observed a typical spirochete-positive reaction. This evidence is reinforced by studies of human grave site remains from the American South and Latin America: New World natives had syphilis at least 5,000 years ago.

The "AIDS" of the Sixteenth Century.   What is unarguable, however, is that the disease, in a particularly noxious form, spread widely and swiftly after Columbus's return from his first voyage in March of 1493. Doctors were helpless in the face of a new pandemic that corresponded to nothing in their medical texts.

Within one year the disease had entered France. And when the young French king, Charles VIII, led his army of thirty thousand men against Naples in 1494–95, he unwittingly introduced the epidemic to all of Europe. For his army was composed of men from France, Spain, Germany, Switzerland, Britain, Hungary, Poland, and Italy. In addition, Naples was defended by Italian *and* Spanish soldiers. For many months tens of thousands of men lived a sexually loose camp life, away from girlfriends and spouses, comforted by Neapolitan prostitutes. Syphilis was rampant and no one knew what the strange disease was, who was giving it to whom, and how—though on the latter two issues victims must have had their suspicions. Because, toward the end of the campaign, we are told by a camp physician that the men "violently drove out their harlots, especially the most beautiful ones whom they knew to be suffering from the infectious disease."

The disease was poised to travel far and wide.

King Charles retreated from Italy and his thirty thousand soldiers disintegrated into lawless bands, many wandering the countryside homeless, others eventually returning to their native lands—thousands of young men with genital lesions. They were the high-risk group of their day, and not comprehending the long-term neurological effects of the disease—from blindness to senility to death—their lovemaking turned an epidemic into a pandemic. In 1498, at age twenty-eight, Charles VIII died from the virulent case of syphilis he had picked up in Naples three years earlier.

"Safe Sex" and the End of the Age of Amorous Adventures.   There was no cure. And the only assumed preventative aside from abstinence was use of a prophylactic, which was no guarantee of safety since early condoms variously cracked, were porous, slipped easily off, were awkward to use, and were routinely reused again and again until they fell apart. Often they weren't even washed. Of course, for the masses, there was not much education of any kind, and sex education was a concept as unthinkable as it was unavailable. Little wonder that the disease spread swiftly and made sex a fearsome undertaking.

At the height of the scourge, victims with severe lesions were shipped off to leper camps called leprosariums, though often, in tragic irony, the lepers refused to accept the new members. When syphilis victims were forceably placed into leper colonies, lepers refused to associate with them, judging the sexual disease a stigma worse than their own wasting. Many cities opened "pox houses," or *blatternhausen.* In the once insouciant city of Paris, where promiscuity was a way of life, it was estimated that a third of the population was infected.

The sick found they had nowhere to turn.

The clergy used the scourge to maximum advantage. It was, they argued, God's punishment for sins of the flesh. The era had been known as the age of amorous adventures and now God had directed that Cupid's arrows be tipped with poison. Priests suggested that victims pray to St. Dionysius (*not* Dionysus, the Greek god of debauchery; the similarity in names broaches farce), who was the chaste patron of France, a holy bishop beheaded in 258 at the place in Paris now called Montmartre, "Martyrs' Hill."

Physicians offered even less help. Because of the disease's implicit moral turpitude, its alleged high degree of casual contagion, and the reality that there was no cure, many doctors refused to have anything to do with patients. They handed the sick over to barbers, bath attendants, and charlatans, who welcomed the business. And unexpectedly it was these non–academically trained people who came up with the first cure. Trying every bogus nostrum and treacle in their arsenal, they discovered that the ancient remedy for scabies, an itching skin disorder caused by parasitic mites, worked for syphilis. It was a gray ointment made from mercury and it became known as the "quicksilver cure." Not that recovery was quick.

The treatment was gruesome. In one form, devised by bath attendants borrowing from the concept of the old-fashioned steam room, the patient was immersed in a barrel that contained cinnabar, a toxic sulphide of mercury. The barrel was then heated to the highest temperature the patient could endure, allowing the fluid to liquefy and seep into every body lesion and orifice. The sessions were long and repeated frequently until the toxic mercury killed the syphilitic agent. Cruelly, many patients recovered from syphilis only to die of mercury poisioning.

The Shepherd Syphilis.   For many years, the disease went by numerous names, most of them national slurs. The term "syphilis" arose not as a suggestion in a medical journal, but as the name of a romantic character in a poem. The first time the term appeared in print was in 1530 in the title of a Latin verse, *"Syphilis sive Morbus Gallicus"* ("Syphilis or the French Disease"). The author was Girolamo Fracastoro, a physician and astronomer from Verona, Italy, who told the story of a handsome, amorous young shepherd named Syphilis, an early victim of the disease.

Whatever it was called, though, the sixteenth-century pandemic altered the way a generation thought about sex. A carefree, indulgent era that worried little of extramarital affairs and less of prostitution came to an abrupt end. The Reformation only too gladly adopted a puritan attitude that was severe in matters of morals—a word fittingly chosen from the Latin *puritas,* meaning "purity." And spelled with a capital *P,* it characterized the Protestant peoples in England who founded the American colonies.

As for the fate of the virulent syphilis spirochete?

After its first century of destruction, the organism became less potent, but it did not disappear. There were many smaller epidemics, and they reached into all levels of society. The disease diminished the quality of life of numerous historical personalities, killing many of them. Among explorers infected: Columbus and Captain James Cook. Among composers: Donizetti, Schubert, and Beethoven. Among artists: Cellini, Gauguin, Goya, and Toulouse-Lautrec. Among writers: Keats, Sade, Goethe, Baudelaire, Dumas, Maupassant, Stendhal, Joyce, and Wilde (so many writers). Among philosophers: Schopenhauer and Nietzsche. Among royalty: Peter the Great, Henry VIII, Mary Tudor, and Napoleon. And last but not least, among clergy: Pope Julius II, Erasmus, Pope Alexander Borgia, and his majordomo the cardinal-bishop of Segovia. To mention a few.

Typhoid: Antiquity, Worldwide

> **Agent:** *Salmonella typhosa,* a bacillus found in human feces and urine
>
> **Transmitted by:** Contaminated food or water
>
> **Symptoms:** Fever, insomnia, malaise, diarrhea, peritonitis

It is very likely that many times—if not most times—you thought you had a twenty-four-hour case of the flu, you actually had a mild case of food poisoning, which is primarily a gut-and-bowel ailment caused by a salmonella bacillus, though not the one that causes typhoid.

There are over a thousand strains of salmonella, a rod-shaped bacillus that lives in humans and animals and is named after the early-twentieth-century American veterinarian D. E. Salmon. Salmonella poisoning does not usually produce a stuffed nose, sore throat, or respiratory congestion—symptoms that signal a cold or flu. But it does cause fever, listlessness, and its major hallmarks, intestinal rumbling and diarrhea. That's why if you experience only these symptoms, you may not have a viral flu.

All cases of salmonella contagion—from mild food poisoning to deadly typhoid fever—are labeled "diseases of filth" because they are transmitted by contact with human and animal waste and thrive in unsanitary conditions. Today two major sources of salmonella are uncooked or undercooked chicken and eggs, which is what probably gave you that "flu" that struck without chest and head symptoms.

But throughout history millions of people's lives have ended by eating food or drinking water contamined with the bacillus' virulent strain, *Salmonella typhosa.* The bug is not extinct. It thrives in poor, unsanitary communities and can even strike in the immaculately maintained homes of the rich, as it did in New York in the early decades of this century, because, as we'll see, a professional Irish-American cook named "Typhoid" Mary Mallon, a carrier of the bacillus, refused to abandon her profession.

"Bare-Bottomed Armies." Typhoid, and related dysentery, changed the course of history more directly than any other human ailment. That is because epidemics of typhoid most often struck soldiers in battle, easily tipping victory toward the healthier forces.

Though the image of tens of thousands of soldiers plagued with diarrhea, having no toilets, no toilet paper, and no privacy sounds like one of Monty Python's more tasteless skits, it was a common reality. Soldiers drank water from streams and creeks that communities miles away used to carry off their wastes. Military history is replete with references to "the campaign disease," to "bare-bottomed armies" waging "breechless battles."

The English soldiers at the Battle of Crécy in August of 1346 were so riddled with dysentery that the French learned to wait and cut them down while they were squatting, pants around their ankles, helpless. During one day, August 26, most of the British forces under Edward III—some four thousand men-at-arms and ten thousand archers—suffered acute diarrhea on the battlefield. Camped along the Seine, the men made the most of the picturesque river, enormously contaminating its downstream flow. The king's son, Edward the Black Prince, who led the cavalry and was one of the outstanding commanders during the Hundred Years War with France, succumbed to an acute case of dysentery, an event in itself that may well have affected the course of history.

The prince's early death at age forty-six, one year before his father passed away, meant that the British crown went to his insipient ten-year-old son, Richard II. Since he had not come of age, the government was run by special-interest nobles whose duplicity and bickering hastened the economic deterioration brought on by the Hundred Years War, as well as by the Black Death that already had Europe in its fierce grip. Whereas Edward might have guided England through one of the darkest and most difficult periods of development, the ineffectual Richard eventually was forced to abdicate, was imprisoned, and starved himself to death.

We do not have to travel far into history for examples of the ravaging effects of typhoid and dysentery. Highly reliable statistics give a grim picture of disease in nineteenth-century wars. Between 1861 and 1865, about one million American men took part in the Civil War. In the Northern armies 93,443 men were killed outright on the battlefield or died later of wounds. Almost exactly double that number of men—186,216—died from disease, with typhoid fever and dysentery accounting for 81,360 of those deaths. And figures for the South, though less accurate, indicate that epidemic infection, particularly typhoid, caused even more deaths. During those years, the husband of Queen Victoria, Albert, died of typhoid fever, and his son, the future Edward VII, nearly lost his life from the same disease ten years later.

Sanitation to the Rescue.   Military doctors understood the progression of the "disease of filth." After a ten- to fourteen-day incubation period, the early symptoms appear: headache, lassitude, generalized aching, fever, and restlessness that may interfere with sleep—all devastating for a soldier in battle. There may be a loss of appetite, nosebleeds, cough, and diarrhea. Persistent fever develops and climbs to 104 degrees Fahrenheit. The intestinal wall can become inflamed; it may ulcerate or perforate, causing hemorrhage or peritonitis.

By the twentieth century doctors realized that a causative micro-organism could produce complications, including acute inflammation of the gallbladder, heart failure, pneumonia, encephalitis, and meningitis. Since most of history's major epidemics of typhoid (and related bacterial or amoebic dysentery) have been caused by human pollution of public water supplies, the dawn of sanitation engineering in the late eighteenth century began to cut into the disease's death toll. Following the American Civil War the organisms causing typhoid and dysentery were discovered, which ushered in new preventive measures: from a simple precaution such as boiling water to antityphoid inoculations.

However, on the battlefield, precautions were often ignored.

This occurred with drastic consequences during the Boer War of 1899–1901. British soldiers in South Africa realized that streams carried wastes from native villages and most likely contained typhoid bacillus. Yet the time and trouble required to boil water and then let it cool in the tropic environment drove them straight to riverbanks for a drink. Military records show that from February 1900 until the end of 1901, battle wounds took the lives of 6,425 British soldiers, whereas 11,327 died from typhoid. The total number of men fighting off typhoid and not the enemy during that period was 42,741.

As we've seen in previous sections, disease has always taken more lives than has war. In fact, military historians claim that the first major war in which fatal field casualties outnumbered the death toll from sickness was in contemporary times: the Russo-Japanese War of 1904–05. And most of the disease-related deaths that did occur were from typhoid and dysentery—this, even though Russian and Japanese troops were ordered never to drink unboiled water.

The historical trend has apparently been turned around for all times. This is because of the humaneness of modern medicine and the inhumanity of modern warfare. In our century, guns, gas, and bombs end more lives than field diseases, which military doctors treat effectively. It would be interesting to calculate normalized averages battle-for-battle to see if we have not replaced nature's means of killing through disease with our own man-made devices. Are the gains in battlefield lives won by inoculation and emergency medical treatment eroded by modern weapons' mass destructiveness?

"Typhoid" Mary Mallon: d. 1938, age 68.   Once called "the most dangerous woman in America" and "the greatest microbe carrier in history," itinerant cook Mary Mallon, perhaps born in the United States around 1870, personally caused more than a dozen severe outbreaks of typhoid fever. She was a one-woman epidemic.

How many people Mary sent to their graves or infected with the salmonella that became a deadly accent to her dishes will never be known. She refused to cooperate with health authorities, withholding information about her past, and she continually used pseudonyms and changed jobs and cities.

Medically she was that immunological marvel: a person who carries a deadly agent without ever becoming sick but who can kill others with a kiss or a meringue pie.

Her trail of destruction began in 1900. She was a cook in a house in Mamaroneck, New York, for only ten days before residents came down with typhoid. She moved on to employment in a Manhattan townhouse the next year and members of that family quickly developed fevers and diarrhea; their laundress died from typhoid. Mary again changed jobs, cooking for a lawyer, until seven of his eight household members developed typhoid. No one thought to accuse the cook; in fact, she spent months caring for the people she made sick, many of them getting worse.

In 1904, she took a position with a wealthy family in Sands Point, Long Island. Two weeks after they had enjoyed her first meal, four out of ten family members were hospitalized with *Salmonella typhosa*. As Mary nonchalantly changed employment on Long Island, she infected three more households and their servants, mysteriously disappearing after each outbreak.

The cluster of New York cases piqued the suspicion of epidemiologist Dr. George Soper in 1906. A skilled investigator, he discovered that the element common to all the outbreaks was an unmarried, heavyset Irish cook, about forty years old, with thick graying hair, round steel-rimmed glasses, and a somber, sullen countenance. No one knew her whereabouts. In each instance she had vanished, leaving no forwarding address. Soper traced Mary from a waning typhoid outbreak at an estate in Tuxedo, New York, to an active case of the disease at a Park Avenue penthouse, in which two servants were hospitalized and the family's daughter died.

Soper interviewed Mary—fittingly, in the family's kitchen. He tactfully suggested there might be a link between the dishes she served and a string of deaths and infections of her diners. A surly, secretive woman, Mary cursed at the doctor, and when he requested a stool sample to test for bacilli, she

Mary Mallon, an asymptomatic carrier, refused to abandon her profession.

threatened him with a meat cleaver. With assistance from the New York health commissioner and the police, Soper had Mary arrested, though not without a fierce battle. She went kicking and screaming, claiming that she seldom washed her hands when she cooked and had no need to.

Daily cultures made of her urine and stools—each forcibly taken with the help of several prison hospital matrons—revealed that her gallbladder was teeming with typhoid salmonella. She emphatically vetoed the idea of removing her gallbladder, and she also refused to abandon her profession of cooking, stubbornly maintaining she did not carry any disease.

Authorities had no choice but to label her public health enemy number one and make her a "guest" of New York City. She was given a comfortable cottage on North Brother Island in the East River off the Bronx, where she lived and ate alone. She worked at the adjacent Riverside Hospital as its laundress, a rebellious "prisoner" who swore she was the victim of a medical conspiracy. Soper had already identified her as the most likely cause of the 1903 typhoid epidemic in Ithaca, New York, that resulted in fourteen hundred cases. In 1910, promising to remain a laundress and never return to cooking, Mary won her release.

Mary's Last Years.   Following her pattern, she changed her name to Mary Brown and found employment as a cook. For the next five years Mary Brown passed through a series of family kitchens spreading typhoid illness and death. She managed to keep one step ahead of a furious and frustrated Dr. Soper. Then in 1915 a serious typhoid epidemic erupted among the staff of New York's Sloan Hospital for Women, with twenty-five cases and two deaths. When city health authorities interviewed the kitchen help, they learned that a portly Irish-American woman with glasses had suddenly disappeared. The police finally tracked Mary to the kitchen of an estate on Long Island and this time she went without a fight.

She was quarantined for life on North Brother Island.

Mary Mallon met her own end on November 11, 1938. In the intervening years she had mellowed, suffered a stroke, and become a celebrity of dubious distinction, interviewed frequently by journalists. She entertained reporters in her comfortable cottage, but was forbidden to serve them as much as a glass of water. She died of pneumonia, and at autopsy her gallbladder was found to be as actively shedding typhoid bacilli as ever. Her funeral mass, at St. Luke's Roman Catholic Church in the Bronx, was attended by three men, three women, and three children, all of whom refused to identify themselves to reporters. She was buried that day, November 12, by the Department of Health at Saint Raymond's Cemetery, also in the Bronx.

Today, known typhoid carriers are kept under the surveillance of their state health departments and are prohibited from working in restaurants and other public places that serve food. At the time of Mary Mallon's death, the state of New York alone was carefully following over three hundred carriers.

Unfortunately, little can be done medically for a permanent carrier of any infectious disease—typhoid, diphtheria, hepatitis, AIDS. The responsibility rests with the individual to ensure that he or she does not pass the microbe on to another person, someone whose immune system might not be able to keep the antigen at bay.

Poliomyelitis: 4th Century B.C., Egypt

Agent: *Poliomyelitis virus*

Transmitted by: Contact with infected human body secretions

Symptoms: Fever, muscle pain, sore throat, paralysis

In abandoning the chamber pot for the modern flush toilet, a seemingly sage substitution, we unwittingly transformed the rather harmless, centuries-old polio virus into a paralyzing agent of epidemic proportions.

Polio is often called a "disease of modern living," for the higher a country's health standards, the less natural resistance its people have to the polio bug—which to this day is ubiquitous. During any summer, for instance, a microbiologist can isolate polio virus from the mucous or excretory secretions of a healthy population.

In the past, polio epidemics were rare and mild. Babies, under the less sanitary conditions of earlier centuries, were automatically exposed to human bodily secretions containing the virus. Most infants developed a very mild, passing infection, called an "inapparent infection" because its symptoms of a fever, aches, pains, and sore throat often went unnoticed or were not regarded with alarm. These babies recovered quickly and with antibodies that offered lifelong protection. A small percentage of unfortunate infants did develop paralysis, and that is why polio was at one time referred to as infantile paralysis, since it was seen only in the very young. A doctor seldom saw more than one or two cases in a town, and he or she usually diagnosed it as "teething paralysis" or the "summer complaint."

Then came modern sanitation and hygiene. Parents were encouraged to keep their babies antiseptically clean. Most of these infants passed into adolescence without natural immunity, and it is a characteristic of the virus that the later in life it strikes the more devastating the consequences. Thus, about a century ago, the sanitized Western world was hit with its first major polio epidemic—and not in infants, but in young children.

The first truly large American pandemic occurred in 1916. That summer polio killed six thousand young children and paralyzed twenty-seven thousand others. The first wave hit hardest in New York City. As thousands of children were stricken each week, panic erupted in the streets. Families fled Manhattan, seeking refuge on farms, in suburban towns, and in summer resorts. The Health Department attempted to quarantine the city by posting armed military troops at entrances to highways and bridges. Families in cars and carriages were forced to turn back.

By summer's end, the disease had taken the lives of two thousand Manhattan children and maimed nine thousand others. In terms of the total number of cases, America has had bigger years (fifty-eight thousand cases in 1952, the worst year), but in terms of death toll, no later polio epidemic surpassed that of 1916.

Poliomyelitis is a viral infection. The virus enters the body through the throat, travels to the stomach, and enters the bloodstream and lymphatic system. The commonest early symptoms are mild headache, fever, sore throat, nausea, vomiting, diarrhea, restlessness, and drowsiness. Most victims recover within about four days, and without paralysis.

But this is not the case in acute attacks in which the virus destroys the motor nerves of the spinal cord. Paralysis of limbs can occur, and if the virus injures the upper segments of the spinal cord, the person may need to be put into an iron lung to assist breathing mechanically. Because the virus causes an inflammation of the motor cells in the spine's gray marrow, the Greek words *pilios* ("gray"), *myel* ("marrow"), and *itis* ("inflammation") were combined to form its name.

Ancient Virus.   The misshapen bones of an Egyptian mummy of about 3700 B.C. identify the oldest known case of polio. The second piece of circumstantial evidence also comes from Egypt: The stone relief of an Egyptian priest who lived about 1500 B.C. depicts an atrophied shortened leg, indicating that the muscle was destroyed early in life, crippling bone growth.

In the fourth century B.C., Hippocrates, the Father of Medicine, mentions several cases of "infant paralysis," but the condition was rare. Later Roman and Celtic physicians described the disease as "the pestilence that is called lameness." But, importantly, in these past outbreaks victims seldom died.

For centuries polio remained such a mild, infrequent infant ailment that it was ignored (or misdiagnosed) by physicians. Medical documents from most European countries do not even show evidence the disease existed. When polio struck the Scottish poet and novelist Sir Walter Scott at the age of eighteen months, eighteenth-century doctors considered it a new affliction.

Scott was diagnosed as having "teething fever." As he later wrote: "I was discovered to be affected with the fever which often accompanies the cutting of large teeth. It held me three days. On the fourth, when they went to bathe me as usual they discovered that I had lost the power of my right leg."

His maternal grandfather, Dr. Rutherford, suggested that the boy be exposed to country air and given exercise as the best cure for his leg. Scott later recalled: "Among the odd remedies recurred to aid my lameness, some one had recommended that I should be stripped, and swathed up in the [sheep] skin, warm as it was flayed from the carcass of the animal. In this Tartar-like habiliment, I well remember lying upon the floor of the little parlour in the farmhouse, while my grandfather, a venerable old man with white hair, used every excitement to make me try to crawl."

Scott's muscle atrophied, his leg became stunted, and he was left lame. His case of polio is regarded as the first in modern medicine.

At that time, polio was not thought to be contagious. The first authoritative study of the disease was published in Stuttgart in 1840 by the German orthopedist and exponent of physical medicine, Jacob von Heine. He was the first to regard acute poliomyelitis as "an affection of the central nervous system, specifically the spinal cord." Later a virus was isolated and imaginatively named Brunhild (meaning "fighter in armor"), for a queen of Iceland in the German epic *Nibelungenlied*. Back then, during a warm summer, a child could be attacked by Brunhild; now the attacker is prosaically called Type I Polio Virus.

Though the dread of polio epidemics ended with the development of the Salk (1955) and Sabin (1961) vaccines, the virus still strikes in unprotected populations. And as sanitation conditions around the world have continually improved, polio has shifted from being a disease of children to one of adults.

Tuberculosis: 5000 B.C., Germany

Agent: *Mycobacterium tuberculosis*

Transmitted by: Inhalation of bacilli from the sputum of infectious persons

Symptoms: Cough, pallor, bloodied sputum

"My brother was an invalid, and the horrid word, which of all words was the most dreadful to us, had been pronounced."

The word was "consumption," the speaker, nineteenth-century British novelist Anthony Trollope. His brother succumbed at Christmastime 1834; two years later his sister died of tuberculosis at age eighteen; four of his own children passed away from the disease between the ages of twelve and thirty-three. It was *the* disease of Trollope's century.

His contemporary, Charles Dickens, appropriately named tuberculosis the disease that "medicine never cured, wealth never warded off." Though Napoleon ravaged Europe in the same century, a full quarter of the continent's graves were filled by tuberculosis victims.

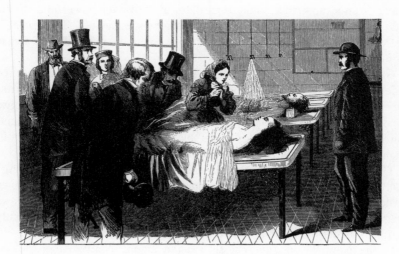

The "White Death," tuberculosis, filled morgues in the nineteenth century.

Across the Atlantic, in the crowded Eastern United States, the "White Death," as it was also called, ended the lives of five out of every thousand Americans. It was so highly contagious and invariably fatal that Quaker physician Thomas Young labeled it the first disease "to deter practitioners from attempting a cure."

Tuberculosis's vernacular names—consumption and the White Death—tell much about its effects on a victim. The infected person's skin becomes alabaster pale and translucently thin, revealing a network of milk-blue veins. The pallor prompted nineteenth-century Romantics to label the disease White Death, just as the victim's feverish reddening of the cheeks, swooning faints, and fragile demeanor caused them to view tubercular invalids—whose health and strength were *consumed* by the disease—as the ideal of feminine beauty.

The disease is ancient, older than the human species, which is only one of its victims. The culprit microbe, *Mycobacterium tuberculosis,* occurs in at least three types—*humanus* (in humans), *bovinus* (in cattle), and *avium* (in birds). Thus mammals and birds suffered from epidemics of TB before modern man populated the planet.

The first known human victim, determined from an analysis of skeletal remains, is taken to be a young male who lived near Heidelberg, Germany, about 5000 B.C. He suffered from a rare bone form of the disease, but it is impossible to determine if he also had the more common highly contagious pulmonary type, which accounts for more than ninety percent of tubercular cases.

Around the same time, there is evidence of tuberculosis of the bone in ancient Egypt. Statuettes and stone reliefs portray tubercular hunchbacks, and a mummy exists of a young priest whose spinal column is damaged by the disease.

In India lung tuberculosis was known by 1000 B.C. and described as a wasting away that usually attacked women and children. Laws were enacted to prevent contagion. A man from the higher castes was forbidden to marry a woman from a tubercular family regardless of "however powerful and rich in cattle, horses, sheep, corn and other possessions she may be." The law labeled her "unclean" and stated that "in the conjugal union, the man will be drawn into her uncleanliness."

Greek and Roman doctors believed (incorrectly) that a child inherited a tendency for the disease from his or her parents, though not the ailment itself. They also taught that high-risk individuals could be identified by four outward signs: excessive tallness, small chest, pale skin, and fair hair. Thus, among swarthy, short Greeks, a tall, slender blond was suspect; and if that blond coughed, he or she was to be avoided *as* the plague.

This physical characterization, lacking all credibility (and stigmatizing no small measure of the Scandinavian population), was posited by the revered physician Hippocrates. Consequently, belief in the hereditary tendency toward tuberculosis continued as a sacred axiom of medical science until the culprit microbe was discovered late in the nineteenth century.

In the New World, tuberculosis existed among Native Americans long before the arrival of Columbus. Analyses of skeletal remains reveal that particularly virulent epidemics flourished in the territories that today are the states of Ohio and California. And in Central and South America, both Peruvian pottery and Mexican art show the presence of tuberculous hunchbacks from pre-Columbian days.

Physicians in ancient times underestimated the deadliness of a tubercular cough. Today we know that the minute droplets discharged by a cough (or sneeze) contain tens of thousands of bacilli, which are so lightweight that once airborne they hover and waft on ambient currents for hours. Not surprisingly, the crowding that grew from the industrialization of European cities, beginning in Britain in the 1700s, contributed to chronic tuberculosis epidemics.

The Age of Consumption. Whereas the sexual revolution of the 1960s and 70s ushered in an era of sexually transmitted diseases, the Industrial Revolution created a change in life-style that favored the spread of tuberculosis. As society shifted away from hand-produced goods toward machine-made merchandise, the face of the countryside radically changed. The new machines were housed in large factories, and towns sprang up around these buildings to provide homes for the workers—who lived in cramped conditions, deprived of the gardens and farms that used to be the sources of their fresh food.

The rich grew richer, and the poor became sick, blighted by inadequate nutrition, sanitation, and shelter. Bacilli, relentlessly on the lookout for a hospitable home, found an ideal environment in which to prosper. Once tuberculosis took hold of indigent workers, their coughs and sneezes filled the air of industrial cities with deadly contagion, bringing down the rich and renowned as well. We don't know the names of the dead poor, but we have a long roster of the famous who succumbed.

Emily and Anne Brontë coughed over each other behind closed windows overlooking the windswept Yorkshire moors. Their sisters, Maria and Elizabeth, were already dead from the disease, which was about to take their only brother, Patrick. Emily, age thirty, expired before Anne, her last words too late: *"If you will send for a doctor, I will see him now."*

When Anne, a year younger, succumbed, her parting sentence was meant to strengthen her one surviving sibling: *"Take courage, Charlotte, take courage!"*

Charlotte soon needed courage. Her own end came from "a chill," which her death certificate recorded as phthisis (what doctors called tuberculosis before the discovery of its causative microbe). The most prolific of the writing sisters, Charlotte, age thirty-nine, lived only a year after her marriage, her final utterance addressed to her husband: *"Oh, I am not going to die, am I? He will not separate us, we have been so happy!"*

As entire families were almost wiped out by tuberculosis, so too were the cloistered religious. In fact, the "White Death" hit confined clergy and charity orders the hardest. **Saint Bernadette** (died age thirty-five), who as a child reported a series of visions of the Virgin Mary, was stricken with tuberculosis while working in the Hospice of the Sisters of Charity at Lourdes. *"Open my chest and let me breathe,"* she begged on her deathbed.

The disease caused extreme physical wasting. Illustrator **Aubrey Beardsley** (died age twenty-five), who once said of his already thin, spidery frame, "If I am not grotesque, I am nothing," became a skeleton in his final days. Propped up in bed, he abandoned his black-and-white drawings for religious reading, and in his final breath implored his publisher: *"Destroy all obscene drawings; all bad drawings, too."*

Henry David Thoreau's tuberculosis was particularly acute when he made his last journal entry on November 3, 1862. His wasted appearance horrified a relative who asked the famous author of *Walden* if he had made peace with the Lord. *"I did not know we had quarrelled,"* Thoreau answered in a whisper, then he uttered the words *"Moose . . . Indian . . . "* and expired. The words are thought to be a delirious reference to the "Maine Woods" essays he was working on.

There was a base social side to the chronic TB epidemics of the 1800s. The White Death was so universally dreaded that landlords mercilessly showed the door to any tenant suspected of having the disease. Equally ruthless were the landlords who took advantage of the sick and bedridden through exorbitant increases in rents. Too ill to relocate, or unable to find lodgings, dying victims were forced to part with savings to be spared eviction. Since doctors were helpless to cure the affliction, many hospitals turned away tuberculous patients. The few hospitals that accepted the invalids acquired reputations that drove away people suffering from other ailments.

Even a home in which a consumptive person died acquired a reputation that made it hard if not impossible to sell. No healthy person was willing to live in rooms where death stained the walls and lurked between the floorboards. In parts of the world the fate of consumptives was gruesome; like lepers, they were ostracized, forced to die in isolation.

Neither fame nor wealth mitigated harsh treatment.

Frédéric Chopin, one of the most famous victims of the 1800s' tuberculosis epidemics, was also the victim of public panic. In the winter of 1838, a feverish Chopin, accompanied by George Sand and her consumptive son, journeyed to Majorca for "a cure." When the composer's fits of coughing intensified, Sand sent for the best doctor on the island. This aroused suspicion among the populace, and the landlord evicted the pianist and his companions into the street.

They found asylum in the remote, gloomy, abandoned Carthusian monastery of Valdemosa. Although its dampness took a toll on Chopin's health, its haunting beauty ignited his creative genius to produce a series of unforgettable nocturnes and ballads. Longing for Paris, Chopin attempted to leave the island but could find no carriage driver willing to transport him and his party to the harbor. With a large sum of money, Sand finally bribed a local, who used his delapidated butcher's cart.

Once on board the ship, still at port, Chopin hemorrhaged from the lungs and his fellow passengers demanded he be put ashore. The renowned pianist, who had entertained in the smartest salons of Paris, found passage on board

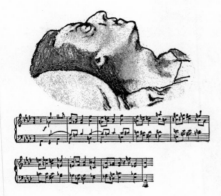

TB sufferer Frédéric Chopin on his deathbed, treated like a leper.

a cargo ship that was transporting a hundred pigs to Barcelona. At a harbor hotel in Barcelona, Chopin coughed up blood and the proprietor demanded that he move out. Again Sand resorted to bribery, but this time she also had to pay to have the room entirely refurnished once Chopin departed. The health code throughout most of Europe at the time demanded that the contents of a tuberculosis patient's room be burned.

The Romantic composer, suffering horribly from almost incessant violent coughing, made it to Paris. Bedridden in the Place Vendôme, Chopin, age thirty-nine, realized the end was near. To the physician who attempted to take his pulse he said, "It is not worth the trouble—soon you'll be rid of me." Then when he was weakened by paroxysms of coughing, he asked for paper and a pen and, in a shaky hand, wrote his last request: *"The earth is suffocating. . . . Swear to make them cut me open, so that I won't be buried alive."*

A Cause and a Cure.   Chopin died in 1849. In 1882, Robert Koch, a country doctor from Rhineland, Germany, discovered the cause of tuberculosis: a slender bacillus that grasps a crimson stain to reveal its presence under a microscope. Unfortunately, the theory of germs put forth by Louis Pasteur was still not widely accepted, and many physicians regarded Koch's crimson germs as fantasy. The prescribed treatment for tuberculosis at that time was a long stay in a sanatorium, and the sanatorium business was booming.

The sanatorium "cure" was prescribed for Prague-born writer **Franz Kafka.** In agony from hemorrhaging lungs, he begged the doctors of the Vienna sanatorium for a lethal dose of morphine: *"Kill me, or else you are a murderer."* Then he asked that his unpublished manuscripts (which were most of them, since he published little in his lifetime) be destroyed, saying finally, *"There will be no proof that I ever was a writer."*

The year Kafka died, 1924, over two hundred thousand Americans also died from tuberculosis. It was the nation's leading killer, claiming more lives than heart disease and cancer combined. As late as the 1940s, there were one hundred thousand new cases of TB each year, with about forty thousand deaths. It was in the 1950s that the antibiotic streptomycin drastically cut the death rate. And also knocked the bottom out of the sanatorium market. The large

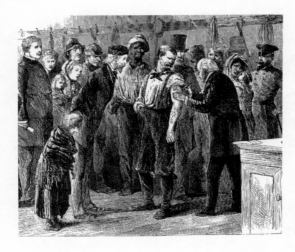

TB inoculation with Koch's new vaccine.

complexes with sweeping, wraparound porches and scenic views became hotels, promoting their sunny balconies to a new clientele.

Once nearly eradicated in the Western world, tuberculosis is, tragically, on
the rise again. Sharply so in America, due primarily to the problems of home-
lessness and drug addiction. Both lead to overcrowding, poor sanitation, and
improper nutrition—the very factors created by the Industrial Revolution that
ushered in the age of consumption. The spread of AIDS and the toll the disease
takes on the immune system have also made victims easy prey to the tuberculosis microbe. Health authorities predict that if the social problems of homeless-
ness and drug addiction are not quickly solved, the world might be revisited in
pandemic proportions by the White Death, a plague that in the era of modern
medicine should never happen.

Influenza, or the Spanish Flu: 1918–19, Worldwide

Agent: A virus, still unidentified

Transmitted by: Contact with mucous secretions from an
infectious person

Symptoms: Flulike fever and aches, virulent pneumonia

Imagine a flu that quickly infects half the world's population, killing a minimum
of twenty-five million people, most within days of becoming ill.

Though it sounds like a plague from the past, it was the particularly deadly
influenza that ravaged the world in 1918 and 1919. World War I had just ended,
claiming the lives of nine million men in four years; the influenza pandemic's
death toll was about three times that number of men, women, and children—
and in *eighteen months.* In the United States alone, where the flu is thought to
have started, twenty million cases were reported in one year, with nearly a
million deaths. The plague's high-risk group: everyone on the planet.

We tend to forget that history's worst plague—for the largest number of

The flu of 1918 took twenty-five million lives worldwide, forcing mass burials.

people dead in the shortest time—was not the Black Death of the fourteenth century. It was a pandemic of our own time, still remembered by survivors, and, most remarkably, caused by a usually mild flu bug that in the spring of 1918 went genetically berserk.

The story is chilling and riveting, not merely for the mind-boggling death toll, but because it could easily happen again.

All influenzas are caused by viruses, and they are usually seasonal, visiting us year after year in slightly altered genetic form. They owe their name to Italian astrologers who once blamed the flu's periodic appearances on the *influenza,* or "influence," of heavenly bodies. That remained almost as good an explanation as any other until 1918, when a bug that had previously killed only infants and the elderly teamed up with pneumonia to become one of the worst pestilences civilization has ever experienced. In the United States, insurance actuarialists expressed the pandemic's devastation in their own revealing way: In the year 1918, the average life expectancy of Americans dropped by twenty-five percent. In the medical literature, doctors refer to the influenza as "the last great plague," which is surely more a hope than a certainty.

Where did this flu come from? And what caused it suddenly to become a mass killer? Though there are still mysteries to be answered, this much is known.

On the morning of March 11, 1918, at Camp Funston, Kansas, a company cook named Albert Mitchell reported to the infirmary. His complaints were a low-grade fever, mild sore throat, slight headache throbbing at the temples and behind the eyes, and muscular aches and pains. The nurse on duty did not rush to assign Mitchell to a bed.

While he sat in the admitting room, reading and feeling generally miserable, another soldier, Corporal Lee Drake, arrived. His symptoms were similar, but his fever was higher: 103 degrees. The men were diagnosed as having an end-of-winter flu. Before either of them was put to bed, a third soldier entered the infirmary.

For the first hour of that morning, it appeared to doctors that a slight flu epidemic had broken out in one barrack on the base. But by noon doctors at the camp's hospital in Building 91 were treating 107 very sick soldiers. Within two days 522 beds were filled, many with men critically ill, suffering from severe pneumonia. Already doctors realized that there was something out of the ordinary with this flu, for reports had come in of similarly rapid outbreaks in army camps in California, Florida, Virginia, Alabama, South Carolina, and Georgia.

And more: Naval ships berthed along the entire length of the East Coast reported thousands of sick sailors, with new cases turning up hourly. By the end of that week, the influenza had struck places as isolated as the island prison of Alcatraz. Something was in the air, sweeping across the country like a tornado, only more deadly.

Sweeping across the Atlantic Ocean, too. For by early April French troops and civilians were ill by the tens of thousands. Later there would be conjecture that U.S. military forces carried the bug to France. And they may have. But that is not a completely satisfactory explanation, since by mid-April epidemics had gripped Japan and China; by May the bug had covered the continents of Africa and South America. No disease in history has moved more swiftly. In all likelihood, the virus had hitched a ride on troops, birds, exports of fruits and grain, as well as rain droplets in clouds and air currents. It was a determined strain with a worldwide agenda.

The flu was announced in the city of Boston that summer by a small, not at all alarming newspaper report that probably few people noticed. It read in part: "A sailor, on a transport being tied up to a Boston dock, has symptoms of influenza." Four months later fifteen thousand citizens of the state of Massachusetts were dead from the flu's accompanying pneumonia. Many sailors from that Boston-docked ship were routinely transferred to bases in Michigan and Illinois. And it's likely they were in part responsible for the waves of influenza that epidemiologists helplessly watched spreading from those states throughout the American Midwest. In all, it took the bug only seven days to entrench itself in every state in the Union.

Worldwide Death Toll. It is hard for us today, though we are in the middle of a deadly epidemic that has not yet peaked, to imagine the swiftness with which people died that summer and fall of 1918. You could wake up one morning with a sore throat and achy muscles and be dead by week's end. The actual killer was the pneumonia that ravaged the lungs of a person who came down with the flu. The two bugs traveled in tandem. At the height of the scourge the death toll in America's largest cities was staggering. In Philadelphia, out of every 1,000 residents 158 died. In Baltimore the number was 148 out of 1,000; in Washington, 109; in Boston, 100.

The disease followed the same pattern everywhere: It began quickly, took its maximum death toll in two to three weeks, then as quickly subsided, permitting those who survived the onslaught gradually to recover. Throughout the country, the problem of caring for so many sick was exacerbated by both a lack of medical supplies and reduced nursing personnel, since a large quantity of goods and staff were still overseas from the war effort.

America, however, with "only" 850,000 deaths was among the areas least devastated by the influenza. In the islands of the South Pacific, where a respiratory disease like pneumonia was uncommon if not unknown, 20 percent of the entire population died between June and August of 1918. An American newspaper reporter in the Fiji Islands wrote: "For a full week I was the only person moving about." The *Sydney Daily Telegraph* reported that on Samoa "80 to 90 percent of the people were lying helpless, many died from starvation, being too weak to prepare food." Within a period of two weeks, the article stated, "More than a thousand Samoan children were orphaned." A full two-thirds of the island's dead were adults.

The Pacific islands were not the worst hit. In Nome, Alaska, where respiratory disease was rare, influenza killed sixty percent of the Eskimo population.

And Spain was visited by a strain of the bug so deadly that the worldwide pandemic would be remembered in history as the Spanish flu, a misnomer since it appears to have begun in America. By the end of the summer of 1918, U.S. army camps were reporting an average death rate among recruits of three percent.

Luxury ocean liners from Europe docked at New York harbor with up to seven percent fewer passengers than had embarked. Donning masks, health authorities removed the dead before the living, virtually all of them ailing, were permitted to come down the gangplank. The confined environment on board a ship proved particularly conducive to the spread of the bug.

The world's 1918 pandemic can be aptly characterized by a quote from the fourteenth-century Italian author Giovanni Boccaccio who said of the Black Death: "How many valiant men, how many fair ladies, breakfasted with their kinsfolk and that same night supped with their ancestors in the other world."

The worldwide death toll of twenty-five million is a conservative estimate; the figure has been put as high as thirty-seven million. Though, really, once a tragedy reaches some numbing figure errors in estimates seem picayune at best. Suffice it to say that for sheer devastation, our grandparents lived through (or died in) the world's worst plague.

Then, mysteriously, in 1919 the flu bug vanished almost as quickly as it had appeared. And vanished so thoroughly from the face of the earth that no modern-day microbiologist has been able to find a specimen for study; and many have tried, looking among human survivors, birds, and swine.

Flu viruses are notorious for their rapid mutations and corresponding migrations into new populations. (The AIDS virus is mutating one thousand times faster than a mild flu bug.) This is probably the route taken by the bug that caused the 1918 pandemic. What genetic guise it assumed, or what host it invaded, is open to speculation, though current evidence suggests that it mellowed and might have moved into swine. Swine, in more ways than one, may pose a threat for future diseases.

The Next Pandemic. Before looking at the possible source of another pandemic like the 1918 flu, it's necessary to backtrack a bit.

Normally, changes in a flu virus are subtle ones, known among virologists as antigenic drifts. The drifts occur every couple of years and involve only minor changes in the virus's outer coat, changes that the immune systems of most people are able to recognize and combat fairly effectively.

But every ten to twenty years a major change, or antigenic drift, occurs, in which the virus's spiky protein coat changes so dramatically that most human immune systems cannot recognize the virus and fight it off. This is undoubtedly what happened *a fortiori* with the 1918 bug. And, to a lesser degree, it happened again with the 1957 Asian flu and the 1968 Hong Kong flu. It appears that antigenic drifts are now happening faster and faster. And that the culprit is farming practices in China and Southeast Asia that involve raising fowl, fish, and pigs in one integrated operation.

The farming procedure is economically sound. The feces and excess food from each kind of animal are used to feed another kind. In Thailand, for example, hens are kept in cages above pigpens, which are located above fishponds. Droppings from the hens fall into the pigpen; the runoff from the pigs fertilizes the fishpond.

But "integrated farming" encourages viruses from different species to intermingle, thereby increasing the risk of mutation—and raising the risk of producing a mutant that favors human hosts. And much of the world's diet consists of chicken, fish, and pork. Many scientists believe that if integrated farming practices continue, we are opening ourselves to perhaps a rapid series of pandemics whose combined virulence could actually threaten the human species.

Today, of course, we can prepare vaccines against an influenza. But that takes weeks or months, with immunization programs requiring even longer. Many medical authorities point out that had science been able to produce a vaccine against the 1918 flu, it would have done virtually no good at all because the bug moved through the population so swiftly. Most victims were dead in a shorter time than it takes a virologist to decode a virus and concoct a vaccine.

There is another immunological fact that cannot be overlooked: Any effective vaccine must be available in quantities sufficient to inoculate a population at risk (all of humanity for a flu) at least two or three weeks *ahead* of an outbreak; the body needs time to build antibodies.

The 1918 influenza pandemic frighteningly emphasizes that it is always nature that has the upper hand. And that despite our high level of medical sophistication, if nature wishes to strike hard, fast, and mean, we are, one and all, equally vulnerable, helplessly at its mercy. Integrated farming practices, though an economic blessing to Third World countries, could turn out to be a curse for humanity in general. Viruses are dangerous enough, as the AIDS epidemic makes tragically clear, without human intervention to speed up their rate of mutation. As a leading virologist recently wrote, when a virus decides to become virulent, "The puny character of our preventive efforts only emphasizes our present impotence."

PART III

Vanished Vogues

CHAPTER 11

Bygone Beliefs

Bloodletting to Cannibalism

THE STEADY ADVANCE OF MEDICINE in the twentieth century, often called the age of therapy, has left in its wake a shame of bygone beliefs—not the quack cures of a few mad eccentrics, but treatments, often horrendous, advocated by the medical establishment and undertaken by distinguished physicians with honorable intentions. Many of these practices were at best ineffective, at worst iatrogenic, resulting in physician-produced ailments: aches and infirmities that did not trouble the patient when he visited his doctor, but that after treatment plagued him for life, or took his life, as was not infrequently the case.

It has been estimated—and by physicians—that more patients were harmed by medical practices in past centuries than were healed. The famous Harvard biochemist and medical historian Lawrence Henderson concluded that not until the second decade of the present century did the average patient, consulting the average doctor, begin to have a better than fifty-fifty chance of actually being helped.

That's a dismal statistic. For fifty-fifty represents maximum uncertainty, a precise statement of perfect randomness. If, for instance, you were sixty percent certain a doctor might harm you, you could protect yourself by not visiting him. Odds of fifty-fifty leave you completely at the mercy of a medical practice or malpractice. And as we're about to see, most past treatments were by today's standards malpractice.

The problem lay of course in physicians' beliefs as to what caused disease.

If you believe, say, that insanity is caused by evil spirits possessing the mind of the deranged individual, then the cure you attempt may be darkly nightmarish.

This chapter is about vogues now vanquished, themselves victims of changing attitudes based largely on the modern notion that much disease is caused by pathogens, that diseases caused *by* the mind are the result of factors such as stress and negative cognition, and that diseases *of* the mind have nothing to do with spirit possession and much to do with endogenous chemical chaos.

The once legitimate "cures" of old constitute the dark side of the medical ledger. They were responsible for instilling mistrust and dread into anyone who needed medical help. It was such a roster of beliefs that kept alive the medical maxim of a renowned physician: "There are some patients whom we cannot help; there are none whom we cannot harm."

The Four Humors: Persisted Until the 18th Century

Today the phrase "black humor" might be found in the review of an uproariously funny dark farce. Not long ago it appeared in medical texts and there was nothing funny about it. If a doctor told you that you had too much black humor, he was as much as saying, "Prognosis negative."

The point is, *humor* is not what it used to be. The word is Latin for "moisture" (as in tears of laughter) and early physicians believed that the body was made up of four cardinal humors, or life juices. The theory of the four humors is the origin of medical science, and later, when the humors were linked to personality temperaments, the framework became the basis of psychology. For centuries life's juices were:

- The *red* humor of blood that flushed a person rosy, feverish, and sweaty
- The *yellow* humor of bile that jaundiced flesh a carrot orange
- The *white* humor of mucus that originated in the nose and lungs and was spit up in coughing
- The dreaded *black* humor that formed deep within the body and indicated that organs were rotting away

It was a colorful theory in more ways than one, and greatly useful; it housed a wealth of observable phenomena, a prerequisite for any workable hypothesis (even a wrong one). Disease was thought to result from imbalances or excesses of one or more of life's juices. And a physician, proffering a diagnosis, could blame your complaint on any imaginative combination of red, yellow, white, and black, much the way a painter achieves a spectrum of shades by blending primary hues.

Why four humors and not six or ten?

It had to do with philosophical beliefs of the ancient Greeks. They taught from the fifth century B.C. onward that all matter in the universe was composed

"Black bile" was a death warrant, in a later time the cause of a melancholic disposition.

of four ingredients: earth, air, fire, and water. The idea itself was a composite of the views of four sixth-century B.C. Greek thinkers.

Thales of Miletus, the first philosopher of Western civilization, maintained that life's primary ingredient was water, "which existed before all existing things came to be, out of which all things came and into which all things return." His contemporary, Anaximander, Father of Metaphysics, championed fire. Their compatriot Anaximenes opted for air: "Just as the air which is our soul surrounds us, so do the wind and air encompass the world." Heraclitus, known for his sullen disposition as the Weeping Philosopher, in effect combined the three theories and added the element earth.

The number four took on magical significance, becoming the ideal metaphysical quantity. Human and animal bone, for instance, consisted of two parts of earth, two of water, and four of fire. Interestingly, the theory of earth, air, fire, and water anticipated the modern law of the conservation of energy in that nothing is created or destroyed, only transformed. Then adding a twist to the theory the philosopher Empedocles associated colors with life's basic elements.

The four elements of the Greeks were reworked to become the basis of Roman medicine by the second-century physician Galen. He taught that human health required a certain equilibrium among the humors. This idea was to influence medicine for the next fifteen hundred years.

"Colorful" Personalities.   The theory was reworked again in the Middle Ages, when the humors were ascribed psychological dispositions. They were called *blood* (the red humor), *choler* (the yellow humor), *phlegm* (the white humor), and *melancholy* (the black humor). Various mixtures in a person determined his or her "complexions" or "temperaments." If you were happy, sanguine, and well adjusted, it was because you possessed an ideally proportioned blend of humors. But if you were cursed with an imbalance, you could be, depending on the skew, phlegmatic, choleric, or melancholic—that is, dull and apathetic, quick-tempered and foul, or sad and depressed.

Today, the four temperaments—sanguine, phlegmatic, choleric, and melancholic—have fallen from usage and the words have lost their impact. But for many centuries the labels stamped a person for life.

For instance: *Sanguis* is Latin for "blood" (the red humor), and a sagnuine woman had a cheery, optimistic outlook on life, was a warm and loving mother, a passionate wife, of sturdy health, and with a ruddy complexion to prove it. It would be her misfortune to marry a choleric man, for *cholera* (Latin for "jaundice" and the yellow humor) characterized not only his pasty, yellowish skin, but also his bilious temper, arrogance, and vaingloriousness; if crossed, the choleric man was shrewd and vengeful.

An equally unfortunate, but more closely matched, pair would be a phlegmatic man and a melancholic woman. *Phlegma* is Greek for "inflammation" and hence characterized the thick, mucous secretions (white humor) from a cold. Thus the phlegmatic man had a thick build, clammy palms and forehead, was sluggish, dull, and impossible to interest in any subject. *Melanos* is Greek for "black," and a melancholic woman shed an excess of black bile from her kidneys, spleen, and pancreas, which did not make her easy to live with. Relentlessly sad-spirited, she rose from gloominess only to express irritability, plunging back into depression. Fortunately, few people were entirely all red, yellow, white, or black; most were combinations of the temperaments.

(Not to stretch an analogy too thin, it is interesting to note that temperaments today are being diagnosed in terms of an abundance or deficiency of brain neurotransmitters such as serotonin, dopamine, norepinephrine, and acetylcholine. They don't have innate colors, but they can color a personality in shades of anxiety, tranquillity, or insanity. In a sense, brain chemicals and their combinings are our modern-day personality humors.)

Thus the theory of four essences was paramount in the development of much of Western intellectual thought. As earth-air-fire-water, the theory formed the basis of the natural philosophy that became the science of physics. As red-yellow-white-black, the theory represented the humors that became the foundation of human physiology. And as sanguine-phlegmatic-choleric-melancholic, the theory laid the groundwork for psychology. It was in these latter two incarnations that the notion of fundamental essences persisted into the nineteenth century, producing, as we'll see, horrific "cures" for diseases of the mind and body.

Bloodletting: Persisted Until the Mid-19th Century

We think of bloodletting as an archaic medical practice, but it began as an economical form of human sacrifice among cultures whose populations were too small to offer up the actual bodies of virgins, first sons, and infants. A little blood went a long way in appeasing a god and preserving the race. Only later did doctors turn this parsimonious form of sacrifice into a horrendous medical procedure.

However, whole body offerings were always preferred in ancient societies.

To give back to a god the "gift of life" was the supreme act a human could perform to gain the deity's ear and favor. But the harsh realities of life often necessitated compromise. A cup of blood could supplicate a deity when living bodies were needed for hunting, warfare, and foraging. This kind of common sense was also practiced by a cult of pious Phoenicians, who abandoned ritual castration as a form of worship to the god Moloch, substituting masturbation into fire, sacrificing replaceable semen instead of irreplaceable manhood at a time when their numbers were dwindling.

There was an added benefit to sacrifice by measured bloodletting. The victim, once abused, could be reused. Both the Egyptians and Babylonians slashed the vein of a virgin, offering up a quantity of blood that left her dizzy but not dead. The goal—not always achieved—was to produce as copious a blood flow as possible while sparing the victim's life.

The practice of ritual bloodletting was universal, with one exception: By pinpricks, the ancient Chinese took only drops of sacrificial blood from a victim. It's believed that Chinese priests accidentally discovered that pins stuck into certain parts of the anatomy relieved aches and pains and cured diseases, and that over centuries they organized the observations into the medical art of acupuncture.

Medical Bloodletting.   In the West, the link between sacrificial bloodletting and medicine is less clear.

According to the second-century Roman statesman Pliny the Younger, physicians copied the practice of bloodletting from the instinctive behavior of ailing animals. The hippopotamus, Pliny noted, when agitated, tore open a vein on a sharp reed and quickly calmed down. The Egyptians also recorded this observation, as well as the fact that a bull with infected testes dragged them across a jagged tree stump, inducing profuse bleeding followed by healing with no sign of prior infection. Bleeding, the ancients concluded, had beneficial properties.

It was Hippocrates, around 400 B.C., who incorporated bloodletting into the framework of the four humors. Abandoning the demonic possession theory of disease, he regarded medicine as a science based on bedside observations of patients. When a fever rose dangerously high and would not subside by the use of purgatives and diuretics, he prescribed bloodletting, used sparingly. One arm was tightly bound with a broad bandage until its principal vein engorged with blood. With a sharp knife, the doctor opened the vein, collected fluid in a bowl, then studied it in order to estimate the portion that was truly "red blood" and how much contained the contaminants of "black bile," "yellow bile," and "white phlegm." Knowing the ratio of humors, the doctor could hazard a diagnosis.

There are many extant accounts of this procedure, and their most interesting aspect comes from a medical aside: Greek physicians repeatedly observed that manics, at the sight of their own free-flowing blood, grew calm and remained "tranquilized" for hours or days after the procedure. How much of the effect was due to pain of a vein slashed, to lightheadedness at the sight of blood, or to dizziness from the loss of blood is not known. But it was this casual

observation that centuries later would be used to justify the ruthless bleeding
of mental patients to cure them of various insanities. If four pints of blood did
not produce tranquillity, the reasoning went, take four more. But this is getting
ahead of the story.

Sexual Bloodletting.   The medical nightmares of bleeding began in the
early Middle Ages, initiated not by doctors, but by Christian monks who viewed
the procedure not as a curative (as had Greek and Roman physicians) but as
a preventative against sexual arousal.

Cloistered in monasteries that dotted the dreary landscape of the Dark
Ages, monks were the only members of the Western community who could
read and write. They alone interpreted Latin medical texts, and they found in
the volumes one recommendation particularly salient to their isolated, all-male
form of society. Sworn to celibacy, they continually had to suppress natural
sexual urges, and ancient Roman physicians taught that "withholding the
semen" *(retentic semenis)* led to the poisoning of a man's blood through an
imbalance of the humors. Hence a truly chaste community of men should be
one riddled with disease. Unless, that is, men vented the toxic imbalances by
bleeding each other. Which is precisely what the monks did. Regularly. Bleeding among cloistered Christian monks became a preventative against disease
(if not something of a bizarre substitute for sex).

The practice was prescribed monthly. Senior monks bled junior ones, and
the runoff juices were examined for the decayed matter that should be present
if a man weren't illicitly copulating or masturbating. A monk who confessed to
great temptations of the flesh was forced to shed volumes of blood until his
desires abated. Such profuse bleeding surely must have taken the mind off sex,
for a while at least. Then there was the next bloodletting.

*To quell sexual passion,
older monks bled younger ones,
regularly and often.*

Monks promulgated their medical theory among the laity. Since premarital sex was among the most grievous of sins a man could commit, unmarried men (even male children) were bled to cleanse them of "evil juices" that caused disease. It was thought that menstruation in women was nature's own way to monthly detoxify the blood, thus for many centuries they were spared the procedure; though a postmenopausal woman was supposed to undergo periodic bleedings.

In this manner, bloodletting moved from a one-time medical cure-all to a prophylactic and then to an abuse of the bodies of both the healthy and the sick. For the physician of the Middle Ages, bleeding became his "take two aspirin and call me in the morning." Extant texts in the Christian and Islamic world detail the hazards of "withholding the blood" *(retentic sanguis),* and men, children, and the elderly were profusely bled. Bleeding hemorrhoids became an ailment to be desired.

Heyday of Abuse.   There was money to be made in bloodletting, and barber-surgeon guilds sprung up throughout Europe, advertising with their red-and-white barber poles the symbol of a bloodied, bandaged arm that had been well vented.

Astrologers, too, profited, since they determined the days favorable for an individual to be bled. Bloodletting calendars were published, recording when, say, the vein of a Pisces should be opened. On certain universally bad days no one could be bled, and barber-surgeons were forbidden to hang out their poles until the heavens favorably realigned.

"Bloodletting banishes melancholy and passion," began a ballad of the day. "It quenches the fires in the blood of the lovesick." From the sixth to the sixteenth century, there is actually a literature of odes and ballads on bloodletting. And by the sixteenth century, it was such a medical abuse that it was killing tens of thousands of patients annually, including many of Europe's leading monarchs.

The medical rule of thumb was: For *any* malady, regardless of the patient's degree of ill health, bleed him or her a minimum of three to five times, taking about two pints of blood on each occasion. That's a near lethal amount of bloodletting. But then doctors at that time believed the human body contained more than 10 quarts of "red humor" (the actual figure is closer to 6). Consequently, they often extracted as much as ten pounds, and when the ghost-white patient passed away, the physician blamed not the letting of blood, but lamented only that the procedure had not been begun earlier in the course of the disease and been done more aggressively. By this logic, bloodletting itself never killed, it only came too late.

Gross Malpractice.   One of the most notorious cases in the history of bloodletting involved the treatment in the seventeenth century of England's Charles II. Because the king had no fewer than fourteen royal physicians, all under great pressure to save his life, he endured excruciating agonies in the name of medicine before he finally expired (presumably of a brain hemorrhage).

The ordeal began at eight o'clock on the morning of February 2, 1685. Charles was about to have his daily shave when he suddenly uttered a cry of pain and erupted into thrashing fits (most likely from a stroke that produced a brain seizure). A physician by the name of Edmund King, then a guest at Whitehall Palace, was summoned and applied "emergency treatment," that is, he let sixteen ounces of blood from a vein in the king's left arm. While this was occurring, messengers galloped off to fetch the king's chief physician, Sir Charles Scarburgh.

"I flocked quickly to the King's assistance," Scarburgh recorded in his diary, in which he detailed Charles's treatment. After consulting with six colleagues, Scarburgh concluded that the king was no better because the first doctor had taken insufficient blood. Thus Scarburgh drew off an additional eight ounces by a method called cupping, in which the king's shoulder was cut in three places and three cylinders shaped like wineglasses were flamed to expel air then used as suction devices to draw out the blood.

Unfortunately for the king, he stirred, and this "auspicious sign" was taken to mean that he would benefit from more fluids being extracted from his body. This Scarburgh did with a "volumous Emetic" that induced retching vomiting; it consisted of poisonous antimony potassium tartrate (also used at the time as a caustic corrosive for permanently dyeing cloth).

Again His Royal Majesty stirred, and this time he was given an enema to extract still more ill humors.

The staff of physicians grew impatient with the king's lack of progress; he was unconscious. Charles was turned over and another enema administered, only two hours after the first; then he was flipped back and force-fed an oral purgative. When he still did not rally, the doctors shaved his head and smeared it with blistering camphor and mustard plasters. The plasters contained cantharis—Spanish fly, the timeless aphrodisiac—which is readily absorbed through the skin and irritates the urinary tract, encouraging frequent urination and the loss of more humors.

The patient, who thus far had felt no pain, spontaneously regained consciousness. The doctors were ecstatic. Their treatment had worked! Surely the king would benefit from more of it. This was Scarburgh's reasoning when he administered another emetic to "bring up" the yellow humor (bile), and then blew a powder of *Veratrum album,* the poisonous rhizome of the white hellebore lily, up the king's nostrils to initiate paroxysms of sneezing—to, of course, extract the phlegmatic (white) humor or mucus.

One would think that the king was by now humorless, but before he was permitted to go to sleep that night, he took the most massive purgative yet, to "keep the bowels open during the night." Which could not have given him much rest.

All of the therapy had been administered within a period of twelve hours. Charles was dehydrated.

The next morning, Tuesday, Charles was not only alive, but actually alert, though profoundly weak. "The blessing of God being approved by the application of proper and seasonable remedies," reasoned Scarburgh, who returned that day accompanied by eleven consulting physicians. After examining Charles, they decided he would benefit from more bleeding, so they opened both jugular veins in his neck for ten ounces of "ill humors." Then, to prevent another fit, they gave him a sweet julep of "black cherry, peony, lavender, crushed pearls, and white sugar," which he must have appreciated.

But on Wednesday the king suffered more fits. He was bled, then given a draft made from the pulverized skull of an "innocent man" who had met a violent death. The treatment smacked of homeopathy in that "forty drops of extract of human skull were administered to allay convulsions," as Scarburgh wrote, thus attempting to cure a symptom with a "like" substance. Charles had a fitful night's sleep, though no more fits.

On Thursday, exhausted, dehydrated, and in great pain, the king was rebled, repurged, flipped onto his stomach for another enema, then given the miraculous Jesuits' bark. This was a much-touted preparation of the day, laced heavily with quinine. Its main champion in the 1630s was the Society of Jesus, or Jesuits. With ministries throughout the world, the priests were called on to treat epidemics of malaria, and they had discovered that quinine palliated malarial fever, a remedy they encouraged the medical profession to make routine treatment. Its association with a religious order conferred upon it an aura of miracle, but it was inappropriate for Charles's condition, and on toxic quinine the king grew gravely worse. The phalanx of royal physicians were mystified.

On Friday Scarburgh wrote: "Alas! After an ill-fated night His Serene Majesty's strength seemed exhausted to such a degree that the whole assembly of physicians lost all hope and became despondent."

Though not defeated; they could not let a king die. Charles was bled almost bloodless, and, if that were not sufficient measure of the doctors' desperation, he was given an "antidote which contained extracts of all the herbs and animals of the kingdom." The known apothecary was exhausted. As was Charles, who could not hold up his head or swallow another draft, so one was, as Scarburgh recorded, "forced down the king's throat."

He grew breathless. Again he was bled. At eight-thirty Saturday morning his speech faltered and failed. At ten he was mercifully comatose. At noon he finally died, a testament to the stamina of the human body.

Today Scarburgh's account reads more like a novel by Sade than a medical treatise by a doctor. Yet the king's physicians were practicing accepted procedures and doing their best. In a sense, they were attempting to extend life by the "extraordinary means" of earlier centuries.

But medicine then killed more patients than it saved. And the risk of dying at a physician's hands was higher if you were among the nobility or royalty. That Charles was king and had a loyalty of doctors who felt they must not let him die cost him a painful and wretched end to his life. An indigent commoner, unable to afford a doctor's care, at least had a fighting chance.

One aspect of Charles's treatment brings us to the next bygone belief, which was once a high medical art.

Purging: Persisted Until the Mid-19th Century

Louis XIV, the Sun King, ruled France for seventy-three years, the longest reign in European history. Under his guidance, France attained the zenith of its military powers and the French court reached an unprecedented level of culture and refinement—in food, drink, manners, and administering enemas, as many as four a day.

For the enema, known as the clyster (from the Greek *klystēr,* "to wash out"), was the mode at the French court, touted to rid the body of wastes, freshen the complexion, and brighten the spirits. It is hard for us today to appreciate fully the heights the enema fad reached in society and medicine, unless perhaps we think of it in terms of the contemporary physical fitness craze or dieting obsession. It had elements of both.

The history of Louis's reign, often told, seldom recounts his court's clyster passion. Here is a typical morning in the mid-1600s, at court and on the estates of nobility.

Day began with the arrival of two or more pharmacists, known as the *limonadiers des posterieurs,* literally "lemonaders of the rear end." They worked out of fashionable chemists' boutiques and were armed with a dazzling array of clyster syringe tips and aromatic mixtures. The calibrated tips were straight or curved to varying degrees, short and thick or elegantly long and slender, and craftsmen vied to combine aesthetic shape, function, and convenience in handling. The dramatist Molière, then at the height of his fame, said the clyster tip was used "to converse with the *other* cheeks."

As the modern executive might boast of his or her personal exercise trainer, the seventeenth-century noble had a personal *limonadier.* He determined the syringe configuration that aligned best with the patient's bowels, though he or she chose from tortiseshell, mother-of-pearl, or gold construction. Depending on his or her mood, health complaint, state of complexion, or the day's goals to be achieved, he or she could receive a clyster mixture of extracts of orange blossom, angelica, thyme, rosemary, bergamot, and damask rose; each was said to possess certain curative or restorative properties.

Administering an enema was a high art. The *limonadiers* trained, practiced, and advertised their skills, and much literature of the day, prose and poetry, erotic and florid, details the preferred techniques. "At the moment of the operation," reads one of the more prosaic texts, "the patient must raise any obstructive veil. He should lie on his right side with knees drawn forward and do all that is demanded of him without shame or false modesty." The lemonader, "as a skilled tactician," was to be gentle and discreet and "not take the place by storm, but like a trained sharp-shooter prepares for action and fires as soon as he catches sight of the enemy."

Instructions employ terms of musical composition: The "pressure pump" is inserted *"amoroso"* and "set in motion *pianissimo."* The text is embellished with medical illustrations that were meant to teach and titillate.

The clyster was like a daily vitamin pill, facial, and high-fiber breakfast. It cleansed and rejuvenated, and during the reign of the Sun King, a day without an enema was a day without care to health and hygiene. Nobility and royalty typically took three or four clysters a day. Commoners administered their own. Even in French jails, prisoners from the better families were not deprived of their right to a daily clyster. Through advertisements and word of mouth, clysters acquired the reputation of increasing sexual potency and curing impotency, which heightened their appeal.

Costing more, and concocted by apothecaries from secret formulas, the sexual enemas were known as *restaurants,* the present participle of the French *restaurer* ("to restore"). They were indulged in regularly by the French cardinal and statesman Richelieu, and his successor, Jules Mazarin, chief minister to Louis XIV. When Richelieu married for the third time at age eighty-five, he announced that if the marriage with his young bride produced no children, it would not be his fault since he still took sexual clysters, as he did until his death at ninety-two.

Clyster Highs.   After receiving a *restaurant,* elderly women were said to turn skittish; men of all ages, fiery. There was probably a simple reason for the high: The most popular of the rejuvenating enemas was the tobacco clyster. Physicians claimed it purified the system and palliated cramps of the stomach and bowels. What they did not realize was that nicotine is absorbed directly through the bowels to produce a rush and an addiction, a fact that might explain in part clyster abuse.

Initially the enemas contained a solution of tobacco, but later craftsmen constructed a "clyster pipe" by which the lemonader, puffing mightily, blew tobacco smoke into his client's bowels. This was rectal smoking, and the heightened effect was said to be "superlative." The smoke clyster became standard fare for reviving a fainted woman or anyone who had drowned.

To the seventeenth-century physician, the clyster was an indispensable tool of his trade. He considered constipation a lethal condition, convinced that vapors emitted from accumulating wastes poisoned the body, producing black bile, the dreaded melancholic humor. A standard diagnosis of a profoundly sad or depressed person was constipation, and the clyster was the cure.

The German engraver Albrecht Dürer, in his famous picture *Melancholy,* included a clyster syringe as a symbol of the complaint and of the medical profession of his day. And Martin Luther, chronically constipated to a degree that alarmed his physicians, accepted clysters of all sorts and noted in his diaries: "In that act, reverence finds its culmination." He claimed that in the procedure "the doctors behave to their patients as the mother to her children."

Learning from the Ibis.   The clyster was not a new medical procedure; the seventeenth century had simply rediscovered it.

Its first mention is in the Ebers papyrus, an Egyptian text written around 1500 B.C. A constipated person was advised either to "chew with beer" the seeds of the ricinus plant (the source of castor oil) or to take an enema of the crushed seeds, assured that either "will expel the stool from the body."

The papyrus recommended hefty-size enemas, consisting of three pints of purgative, administered for three consecutive days. This was also the prescription to be followed once a month by anyone wishing to retain sound health. It is not surprising that the term "physic" was used both for purgatives and for the physician who administered them as his chief weapon against disease.

The Egyptians were almost as elaborate as the later French in their use and design of clyster tips and mixtures. The fifth-century B.C. historian Herodotus claimed that Egyptian physicians got the idea of the enema from their sacred bird, the ibis, which when constipated relieves itself with the aid of its long, slender beak attached to a longer, accommodating neck.

The Egyptians not only imitated the ibis, but, as hieroglyphics and stone reliefs attest, they sculptured their clyster tips in the shape of the bird's head, skull, and beak. The long, curved clyster was first rediscovered in the fifteenth century by a professor of anatomy in Pavia in northwestern Italy. It quickly became a rage in France, and for three hundred years was, along with bloodletting, a physician's cure-all.

When Louis XIII of France was ill, his chief minister, Richelieu, supervised the doctoring; within a period of 6 months, the ailing king was subjected to 47 bleedings, 215 oral purgatives, and 312 clysters—2 enemas every day except holidays. His son, the Sun King, in the long course of his reign, had to endure only 38 bloodlettings (for various health complaints), though he accepted several hundred clysters and countless thousands of oral purgatives to mitigate the effects of gluttony, which burdened the royal bowels.

Though physicians regarded clysters with utter seriousness, writers often lampooned the practice. It was, after all, a natural for low humor.

Molière, in *La Malade Imaginaire* ("The Imaginary Invalid"), mocked the "vain and foolish doctors" who purged and bled patients to death. In the biting comedy's opening scene, a doctor, in the foreground, earnestly prescribes "an insinuating laxative, a little enema to soften up the intestines of Your Highness, to make them more supple and to restore them," while in the background characters parade across stage brandishing gigantic, baleful-looking clyster syringes. The final act contains a burlesque ballet in which a candidate for his doctorate degree is questioned by a chorus of physicians and pharmacists, the exchange revealing the pretensions and pitiful shortcomings of a profession at a loss to do anything substantive to cure the sick.

Ironically, at the third performance of *La Malade,* Molière suffered a brain hemorrhage, becoming a helpless victim of the physicians he satirized and the practices of bloodletting and purgatives he portrayed as useless. And for him they proved to be just that.

In the next century, clysters remained popular through both the efforts of physicians and the boasts of Casanova, who hailed the erotic art of the sexual enema for its sensations and promise of extended potency. Though the practice continued to be ridiculed in print, now chiefly by Jonathan Swift, tens of thousands of upper- and lower-class Europeans submitted to regular clysters in the belief it guaranteed a long and healthy life.

Clysters were, of course, medically supported by the theory of the four humors. Disease was still thought to be caused by an excess of ill juices, and at the court of Versailles, in private boudoirs, and on the battlefield, healthy men, women, and children were purged (and bled) to keep them fit. Every spring Frederick the Great had his troops parade before a phalanx of doctors who administered oral purgatives, clysters, and took blood in order to keep the soldiers strong. Frederick himself, in the midst of a fierce battle, ordered his royal physician to cut open a vein and bleed him in order to restore his calm.

Excessive purging weakens and ruptures the bowel, and thousands of people were dying from peritonitis. (And, too, the wounds from bloodletting became infected and suppurated, so that patients often died of dermatitis.) Doctors either did not or refused to believe that they were killing the sick as well as the healthy. They must have had strong suspicions, because by the nineteenth century they were eager to herald the safety of a new means of bloodletting that did not necessitate a gashing wound. Merely a little bite.

Leeches: Persisted Until the Late 19th Century

A leech bites twice, with the small mouth and sucker at its front end and with the large mouth and sucker at its back end. To appreciate fully the bygone practice of leeching, it's helpful to understand the leech itself, a mysteriously ambisexual creature with a taste for human blood.

All leeches have thirty-four body segments; some are only a half-inch long while others measure eight inches. A leech has no nose and breathes through its skin, can have one to four pairs of eyes, and has functional reproductive organs of both sexes. Convenient as that may be, a leech cannot fertilize itself; the sperm of one individual must enter the body of another to fertilize her/his eggs. Who plays what role and when—and why—is still known only to leeches. They engage in group sex, and it's believed that a leech remembers its last sex role and the next time out (or in) enacts a reversal.

Infirmary with trays of leeches; doctor treating a headache with "neck" leeches.

In the nineteenth century, physicians preferred to bleed with the green and brown striped European leech, *Hirudo medicinalis.* Its jaws are set with sharp teeth that make a Y-shaped incision in the flesh, and doctors assured patients that a leech bite was painless—which it is, though they did not understand why. We now know that nature has built into the leech's saliva a compound that anesthetizes the wound area; another chemical dilates the host's blood vessels to hasten the meal; while a third ingredient, an anticoagulant (hirudin), keeps the meal flowing.

Leeches had always awaited their victims in damp vegetation until the early 1800s, when they were brought by the bucket load into European hospitals.

The idea to use leeches for "safe" bloodletting is credited to Broussais, the leading physician in France at the start of the nineteenth century. Whereas ancient medical books mention the leech and its convenience, Broussais was the first physician to use the swamp parasite as a cure-all. Mental illness, tumors, skin rashes, gout, and whooping cough are but a few of the ailments turned over to leeches between the years 1827 and 1836, when the hospitals of Paris alone employed six million bloodsuckers a year to treat patients.

The common treatment for a headache was to apply six Algerian dragon leeches *(Hirudo troctina)* to the forehead and temples and allow them to draw blood for several hours.

Broussais, an adherent to the theory of cardinal humors, taught that leeches were capable of sucking deleterious juices from the body. His fame was such that two years after he introduced the leech treatment, every pond and swamp in France had been scoured of the parasitic worms. The species *medicinalis* and *troctina* were then imported from Bohemia, Hungary, the Baltic countries, and Algeria at a cost of eight million francs a year, a staggering sum for medicine in the 1820s.

Whereas Paris hospitals took their share of six million leeches, the annual demand throughout France reached thirty-three million worms. They lay in readiness in rows of glass jars in every hospital ward. With a gloved hand, a doctor reached in, extracted a cluster of the critters, and applied them to a patient's skin. Descriptions of the day claim that a woman being treated for menstrual cramps had her bare belly plastered over so heavily with dark glittering leeches she appeared to be wearing a coat of mail. They fed until sated, then released their biting grip, which was taken as a sign that all of the ill humor causing the complaint had passed from the patient to the worms.

Vampirism.   Doctors praised the therapy. Patients feared it but submitted, trusting the wisdom of their physicians. Critics lambasted it. "Vampirism" was the main charge, with allegations that more French blood was taken by Broussais's therapy than had been shed during the Revolution and the Napoleonic wars combined.

But the estimates of critics were, by modern calculations, far below the real figures. A leech can drink up to 17 grams of blood, then after a digestive respite of three months, he/she is ready to eat again. The billions of leeches that Broussais and his colleagues fetched from the slimy depths of ponds sucked

1,680,000 liters of blood from the French people alone; and the technique was copied throughout Europe and introduced to America.

(Interestingly, in America, therapeutic leeches of the species *Hirudo medicinalis* were discarded as waste from hospitals into lakes and streams where they established themselves as wild parasites, the medical waste of an earlier time.)

Broussais was so highly regarded, and the theory of humors so ingrained, that leech therapy led to the death of Broussais's star pupil. The young student, to prove the effectiveness of his mentor's treatment, inoculated himself in the arm with fresh syphilitic pus containing the active organism. (This was done in front of an audience.) Within days he bore the unmistakable skin lesions that characterize the first stage of the disease. According to Broussais, the red sores were merely a "local" infection; the truly dangerous disease lay in the intestines and could be sucked out by leeches.

The trusting student submitted to copious bloodletting (by leeches and by opening veins), but the chancres refused to heal. As they grew larger and ruptured, lymph glands in his armpits, groin, and along the clavicle swelled. Within weeks of the experiment, the student was a mass of pustulating syphilitic lesions. With his belief in medicine shattered and his prognosis dire, he committed suicide.

By 1850, the public, too, had lost faith in bloodletting, as well as in purgatives and clysters. They had witnessed within their own families more deaths than cures, and among their doctors more blind advocacy of a treatment than genuine evidence of its effectiveness. In short, the public woke to the fact that doctors had no better idea of the underlying causes of diseases, or of how ailments should be treated, than they themselves had.

It is the great irony of medicine that this too-long-in-coming realization dawned just at the time a French chemist, Louis Pasteur, was about to posit the germ theory of disease, and when a British surgeon, Joseph Lister of Lyme Regis, was to introduce his breakthrough of antiseptic surgery. Genuine help and understanding were on the way.

Yet as the foundations of modern medicine were being laid, the masses were fleeing from doctors toward homeopaths, faith healers, spiritualists, and the large gaggle of quacks and bogus cures that characterized the health field in the last half of the 1800s. Doctors had driven away the patients they hadn't killed, and they would have to win them back through sheer competency. Nothing less would do.

Radical Colectomy: Persisted Until the 1930s

"Take it out, take it all out" was the cry of surgeons in the early decades of this century. They were talking about the colon. Not a diseased colon, not even the colon of a person with a disease, but the healthy last lap of the gut, the four-and-a-half-foot-long part of the large intestine extending from the cecum (near the appendix) to the rectum (at the anus).

They viewed the colon as it lay coiled in the abdomen like a snake in the grass, and just as deadly. It was the alleged cause of a host of ailments, and throughout the 1910s and 1920s thousands of Americans and Britons willingly underwent a colectomy in the belief that it guaranteed a long and healthy life. Shockingly, the useless and dangerous surgery did not entirely end in some hospitals until the 1930s, making it one of the outstanding nightmares of modern medicine.

In a way, the colectomy was the logical successor to purgative and clyster abuse, for it was the ultimate act toward self-purification of the system. Instead of flushing out the bowel's wastes with a fluid delivered through the mouth or rectum, as earlier physicians had done, why not, went the reasoning, simply remove the troublemaking organ.

Physicians in the past may have wished they could have operated to remove the colon, but it was, ironically, the modern advances of anesthesia and antiseptic surgery that made the operation possible with a reasonably low mortality rate. Surgeons, heady with the ability to operate for hours at a time (prior to anesthesia surgery progressed rapidly), dillydallied in an opened patient, searching for tissue diseased, discolored, or misshapen. The colon, they believed, like the appendix, was a primitive vestigial organ of no value and the source of much misery.

This belief was held by the famous Russian biologist and 1908 Nobel prize winner, Élie Metchnikoff. For him the winding organ was a static, seething sac of solid waste that built up over one day, and was not always, or completely, discharged the next day. The poisons backed up into the bloodstream, eventually spreading disease to all organs. A chronically constipated person, slipping daily toward death, was supposedly identifiable from his or her "nasty graveyard odor." Metchnikoff, who had done his prizewinning work in immunology, published a book explaining that the entire snaking colon was humankind's major source of trouble.

That argument spawned a major turn-of-the-century theory known as autointoxication, or self-poisoning. Though it was hailed as something new, it was in truth merely a revamping of the ill humor theory of disease, which had led to the abuses of purgatives and clysters. In its new guise, the misconception ushered in worse abuse.

The operative procedure that was to save healthy humans from poisoning themselves—the radical colectomy—was first advocated in the early 1900s by perhaps the most skillful, famous, and indefatigable surgeon of the day, Sir William Arbuthnot Lane, chief of surgery at the prestigious Guy's Hospital in London. Lane's versatility was such that he devised useful techniques for the treatment of fractures, harelip and cleft palate, acute intestinal obstruction, and infections of the mastoid. Surgeons came from Europe and North and South America to watch him operate. Sir Arthur Conan Doyle later admitted that Lane, because of his powers of observation and eccentricities of personality, was one of the models for the character of Sherlock Holmes. When Lane said, "Take it all out," colleagues listened.

Surgical Insanity.   In all fairness to Lane, it should be pointed out that he had first attempted to flush the colon clean in ingenious ways: He tried to drown the bowel's microbes in heavy cream, advising people to consume the thick, nutritious dairy fat as they might drink water. But the short-term corpulent side effects (to say nothing of the long-term clogging of the arteries) led Lane to reconsider; he substituted for heavy cream the even thicker, but nonabsorptive, liquid paraffin. It transformed the body's waste into a long wickless candle. But to Lane's surprise it did not prevent people from developing the broad spectrum of diseases then attributed to autointoxication: duodenal ulcer, bladder cancer, rheumatoid arthritis, tuberculosis, schizophrenia, high blood pressure, arteriosclerosis, and intestinal cancer. Thus, in the end, he advocated surgery.

At first Lane and his followers in England and America only short-circuited a major segment of the large colon. They connected the lower end of the small intestine to the far end of the large one, an ileosigmoidostomy. But patients still seemed to suffer self-poisoning from their body wastes; that is, they continued to come down with all of life's cruel but normal diseases. Then, with Metchnikoff's encouragement, Lane decided to bypass the colon entirely. In effect, the small intestine was connected to the rectum so that once the nutrients in food had been absorbed the waste was excreted. Nothing loitered overnight to putrify.

The operation was received enthusiastically. Lane staged demonstrations for fellow surgeons. The radical colectomy was soon viewed as something a sane person gladly submitted to. It prevented disease, delayed aging, and warded off depression. With consummate skill and a low mortality rate, Lane himself performed the procedure on more than a thousand patients.

However, virtually none of these patients needed to have their colons removed, and no one benefited from it. A patient who visited Lane with the complaint of a stomach ulcer could within a week's time find himself without a colon. A husband, to cure his wife's depression and nagging, turned her over to Lane. So routine was the procedure in Lane's operating theater that a boy, hospitalized for a tonsilectomy, was accidentally wheeled into Lane's OR and wheeled out an hour later missing a colon, but with tonsils intact.

In the United States, the colectomy was also a much performed operation in the 1910s and 1920s.

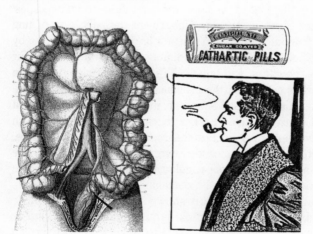

The insanity of a colectomy gave way to a profitable laxative market. Sherlock Holmes was molded on Dr. William Lane.

But it did have its critics, in medicine and in literature. It is thought that George Bernard Shaw used Lane as the model for his aggressive, authoritative surgeon Cutler Walpole in *Doctor's Dilemma.* Shaw has the cut-happy Walpole say: "Ninety-five per cent of the human race suffer from chronic blood-poisoning and die of it. It's as simple as A.B.C. Your nuciform sac is full of decaying matter—undigested food and waste products—rank ptomaines. Now you take my advice, Ridgeon. Let me cut it out for you. You'll be another man afterwards."

Certainly the operation had that effect on its victims. Many lived a life of great bowel inconvenience. Others developed infections and died. Some were permanently disabled by the surgery.

During this same period it also became vogue in establishment medicine to remove *any* organ that was deemed useless or a potential troublemaker: Countless men, women, and children gave up perfectly healthy appendixes, appendectomy being the most popular of the surgeries. Painless, antiseptic surgery was now possible, and surgeons, perhaps understandably, were eager to show off their skills.

How did Sir William Arbuthnot Lane himself keep regular?

Though he would remove a patient's colon as soon as shake his hand, he kept his own last lap of gut. To detoxify it, he consumed harsh cathartics, soothing laxative oils, and wore a tightly cinched abdominal belt that he believed squeezed out his waste (in fact it merely trimmed his waist). No healthier for all the discomforts he endured, he sported a youthful figure.

Laxative Market.   Due to Lane, his followers, and the radical colectomy, Americans during the first two decades of the 1900s were obsessed with regularity. It became a moral virtue. Internal cleanliness was every bit as close to godliness as its external manifestations. Parents gave colonic irrigations to their children—up to thirty pints of fluid over a two-hour period—then took the enemas themselves.

In fact the high colonic became the standard treatment for any health complaint. A child who complained of an earache got an enema. A woman with a headache curled up on the bathroom floor for one. And at luxury spas throughout Europe, every client, every day, underwent detoxification of the bowels under the French-sounding euphemism of a lavage.

Little wonder that the best-selling over-the-counter drugs in the 1910s were laxatives—in pills, fibers, powders, and liquids. When a Hungarian-American pharmacist named Max Kiss conceived the brilliant idea of combining American's two favorite obsessions—chocolates and laxatives—he created an empire. Kiss's "Excellent Laxative," called Ex-Lax, became an overnight sensation, a welcomed improvement over such standard foul-tasting cathartics as castor oil. The new market for "laxative candy" eventually rose to 530 million doses a year, making Americans the most regular race on the planet.

The theory of autointoxication suffered a damaging blow under the penetrating new science of radiology. X rays clearly showed that the colons of most people were not blocked, that normal waste did not accumulate in the intestines' nooks and crannies to produce putrifying obstructions. New blood tests revealed that even during a bout of constipation a person was not poisoning himself with a reflux of toxins. Chemical analysis of the colons excised from thousands of patients showed that the tissues were in no way infected or rotting.

And finally, careful observations on normal, healthy patients revealed that many people have only one bowel movement a day, others have only two a week, and on occasion a healthy individual can go for more than ten days without emptying his bowels and without health complications. All of this evidence had been amassed by the late 1920s, when one physician wrote: "Constipation should be defined as any condition that causes the patient to complain that his bowels are not moving often enough. . . . One man's constipation is another man's diarrhea."

But the misconception of autointoxication died slowly. And the abuses were even slower to disappear. In 1935, one of Lane's early critics, the eminent British gastroenterologist Sir Arthur Hurst, delivered a lecture at Harvard University titled "On the Unhappy Colon." He denounced "the vast army of hypochondriacs, who are never happy unless their stools conform to an ideal which they have invented for themselves." He advised Americans to cure themselves of their bowel obsession by following the example of the dog rather than the cat: "never look behind you."

The theory of autointoxication was finally condemned in the textbooks and medical schools in the 1930s.

By that time doctors were no longer removing healthy colons (though the excision of uninfected appendixes continued into the 1950s). Medical science had learned that the gut is indeed filled with microbes, but beneficial ones vital for the proper maintenance of health, and that a germ-free gut is an open invitation for pernicious organisms to set up house. Lane lived to witness most of this enlightenment, dying during World War II at eighty-six, outliving his operation by thirty years.

Today we have a better understanding of bowel function, but we are not without our own obsession for regularity: Laxatives and cathartics of all types still enjoy enormous sales, and in many ways the word "fiber" has the auspicious cachet once enjoyed by "clyster."

Spontaneous Generation: Persisted Until the 18th Century

To ancient peoples, who saw maggots mysteriously form on rotting meat and insects materialize under the dark dank of rocks, the origin of life could not have been more obvious: Mud, silt, sweat, excrement, and the decaying parts of dead animals were the raw materials of creation.

The Bible referred to the molding of man out of earth: "I also am formed out of the clay." And as late as the 1600s, Shakespeare, in *Antony and Cleopatra,* was hailing the same staff of life: "Your serpent of Egypt is bred now of your mud by the operation of your sun: so is your crocodile."

The major theory to account for the appearance of biological life, including human life, was spontaneous generation. Whereas cheese wrapped in a rag and left in a dark corner *generated* a mouse, a man's sperm deposited in the moist darkness of a woman's uterus spontaneously *generated* a fetus (she was thought to be nothing more than the "corner" in which the miracle occurred).

It was a fascinating, science-fiction-like theory that would produce much damage before it gave way to the science of microbiology.

The origin of life was the grandest question early philosophers pondered. Aristotle laid down the theory that persisted for two thousand years: Living things arise from inanimate matter, but the transformation is so gradual that the boundary between the two will remain forever clouded. The dictum discouraged investigations into the clouded region.

Aristotle also maintained that nature is not constrained to produce organisms that are mere duplicates of past creatures. Any day spontaneous generation might create beneath a rock a new kind of worm or beetle. But such surprises are not likely among humans since they are the ultimate of life forms. Aristotle's biology fit neatly with older Greek mythology which, for instance, viewed Aphrodite, goddess of love, born from the foam of the sea.

In his *History of Animals* we find Aristotle's exact words on the subject, which for centuries would be the last word:

> The hermit crab grows spontaneously out of soil and slime, and finds its way into untenanted shells. . . . Some insects are not derived from living parentage, but are generated spontaneously; some out of dew falling on leaves, ordinarily in springtime, but often in winter when there has been a stretch of fair weather and southerly winds; others grow in decaying mud or dung; others in timber, green or dry; some in the hair of animals; some in the flesh of animals; some from excrement after it has been voided, and some from excrement yet within the living animal.

God created man, but a child, with a bit of cheese and a damp cloth, could create a mouse.

Because Aristotle's teachings were held in blind-faith esteem, the theory was hard to dislodge, even when evidence seriously threatened it.

In the latter part of the eighteenth century, when Maria Sibylla Merian, the great investigator and painter of butterflies, observed that caterpillars came from eggs and that butterflies came from pupated caterpillars, her statements were ridiculed by many experts and labeled outright fraud by others. This despite the fact that a good deal was already known about the reproduction and metamorphoses of insects.

One of the strongest arguments offered in favor of spontaneous generation was the case of the eel. It had been Aristotle's own favorite. We do not know how many eels the great philosopher dissected, but he was emphatic that "no eel was ever found supplied with either milt or spawn, nor are they when cut open found to have within them passages for spawn or for eggs." Without sperm, eggs, or birth tubes, eels clearly couldn't reproduce themselves, argued the philosopher. They arose from mud.

Unfortunately, Aristotle took as his prime example the river eel. It reaches sexual maturity—and thus develops its "missing" parts—only after its spawning journey into the sea. "Eels are not the issue of pairing," he wrote, for he could not see them pairing off at sea. He concluded that "in some standing pools, after the water has been drained off and the mud has been dredged away, the eels appear again after the fall of rain." He did not see them swimming from the sea back to their home rivers. The eel misconception, as well as the entire theory of spontaneous generation, was not seriously challenged until the seventeenth century.

Microscopic Evidence.   One of the first challenges to the theory of spontaneous generation came from the Dane, Jan Swammerdam, regarded as the most accurate of classical microscopists. After years of staring down his magnifying cylinder, Swammerdam looked up to announce: "What folly it is to regard the larger animals as perfect while smaller creatures are seen as aberrations of chance products of putrefaction!"

Penniless by this time, Swammerdam entered a period of extreme privation and continual depression, unable to champion his hypothesis. He lost all scientific credibility when, suicidal, he sought help from a religious cult leader, Antoinette Bourignon, who believed herself the fulfillment of a prophecy in Revelation: the "woman clothed with the sun."

Swammerdam's view of the genesis of life was supported by Antonie van Leeuwenhoek, the first microscopist to observe bacteria: "Mites, intestinal worms, and infusoria can no more arise without reproduction than an elephant can spring from the dust!" But no one had yet conducted an experiment to demonstrate the facts.

That fell to the Italian physician and poet, Francesco Redi. Having com-

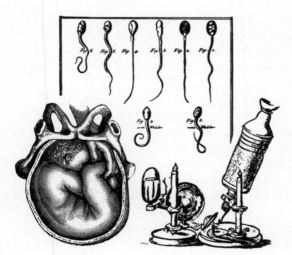

The microscope proved a fetus developed from more than just sperm and ended belief in spontaneous generation of animals.

pleted the chief poetical work for which he is remembered, *Bacco in Toscana* ("Bacchus in Tuscany"), Redi turned his attention to maggots. He had read in a book by William Harvey, the English physician and discoverer of the circulatory system, a speculation that vermin such as insects, worms, and frogs do not arise spontaneously, but from seeds or eggs too small to be seen.

In 1688, in one of the first examples of a biological experiment with proper controls, Redi set up a series of flasks containing different meats, half of the flasks sealed, half open. He then repeated the experiment, but instead of sealing the flasks, covered half of them with gauze so that air could enter.

Although the meat in all of the flasks putrefied, only in the open and uncovered flasks, which flies alighted on freely, did the meat contain maggots. Though he correctly concluded that maggots came from eggs laid on the meat by flies, Redi still believed Aristotle's spontaneous generation applied to other kinds of worms. He returned to poetry, confident he had cleared up a centuries-old controversy.

Gradually scholars began to believe that all life forms were begotten by parents who resembled them. But in 1745 the theory of spontaneous generation gained renewed support. In *An Account of Some New Microscopial Discoveries,* John Turberville Needham, an English Catholic priest, related his own controlled experiments. He boiled fruits and meats at high temperatures, let them cool, then sealed the samples in test tubes. The molds and fungi that grew, he argued, despite the heat treatment that should have killed insect eggs that had contaminated the food, proved the theory of spontaneous generation.

Of course the flaw in Needham's experiment is obvious to anyone who has ever canned fruits or vegetables. Boiling is not enough. Air must not be allowed to touch the foods after they are heated. Today, familiar with Pasteur's theory of airborne germs, we would say that the food must be kept sterile.

Pasteur's Proof.   One scientist who suspected that air itself could be a contaminating influence was the Italian biologist Lazzaro Spallanzani. This abbot and professor at Pavia filled nineteen bottles with mixtures of foods and water, waxed the necks of the bottles to seal them, then brought the contents to the boiling point. After this sterilization, the bottles showed no signs of microorganisms. Spallanzani published his findings in 1775, and they should have disposed of the theory of spontaneous generation. But people refused to believe him.

Death finally came to Aristotle's spontaneous generation on April Fool's Day, 1864. Louis Pasteur stood before an audience of noted scientists, philosophers, and writers in the amphitheater of the Sorbonne to announce the results of years of research. Pasteur, with the assistance of English physicist John Tyndall, had prepared, years earlier, sealed heated vessels containing hay and refuse. Now he was about to open them. In principle, of course, he had repeated Spallanzani's work, but Pasteur had developed his own highly effective method of pasteurization to exclude all possible airborne organisms.

In the presence of the assembled group, he opened the vessels one by one and examined their contents under a microscope. In none of the pasteurized test tubes was there a trace of protozoans, bacteria, or fungi. George Sand, Alexandre Dumas, and other notables heard the esteemed bacteriologist pronounce, with great assurance, the death knell of a twenty-two-hundred-year-old scientific theory: "There is no longer any reason whatsoever for us to believe that living organisms can arise except from germ cells, from parents that resemble them. The theory that maintains the opposite will never again recover from the fatal blow inflicted by this experiment."

Infanticide: Persisted Until the 19th Century

In an age when physicians labor valiantly to save the lives of newborns with the severest of handicaps, it is hard to image a time when infants (even healthy ones) were deliberately killed—by parents or high priests—as a method of birth control, to rid a tribe of the weak and deformed, or as ritual sacrifice.

But infanticide has a long history that only from a later vantage point seems ignoble—perhaps as today's legal abortions might be viewed by future generations as barbaric.

The killing of newborns was widely practiced in most cultures since prehistoric times. Religious sacrifice, especially of the firstborn, is described in Hebrew scripture as well as in the histories of Egypt, Greece, and Rome. This ritual infanticide—which continued in India until the nineteenth century—represented offering a deity the family's most valuable possession. Killing a child was not a sin, but a prayer. And the practice was by no means confined to less "civilized" tribes, but found equally among "cultured" peoples of the eastern Mediterranean region, particularly the Phoenicians and the Israelites.

Most frequently the sacrificial bodies of firstborns were burned alive. But in the famous biblical case of Abraham's intended sacrifice of his son, Isaac, the child was to be slain before the body traveled heavenward as smoke.

Infanticide began as a fertility sacrifice. Poison-tipped nipples gradually killed an unwanted newborn.

The first-century B.C. Greek historian Diodorus Siculus, in his voluminous *Bibliotheca historica,* recounts the Carthaginian custom of placing the infant in the huge, cradling arms of a stone idol from which the child slid downward into a raging fire.

The Carthaginians, despite their many cosmopolitan airs, practiced a religion that to a modern observer is brutally harsh. Infanticide was a main tenet.

Founded on the north coast of Africa by the Phoenicians in 841 B.C., Carthage (now a residential suburb of Tunis) is one of the best-known cities of antiquity. Masters of commerce, the Carthaginians manufactured beds, cushions, and mattresses that were regarded by the Mediterranean world as luxuries. The city was a favorite of Roman emperors, site of an amphitheater modeled on the Colosseum, numerous Romanesque baths, temples, and a circus, of which many remains are extant.

The Carthaginians were no barbarians, yet in an average year they sacrificed a hundred children to the chief gods, Baal and Tanit. The charred remains were placed in urns and buried in Tophet, a sacred site. In periods of economic hardship, when godly favors were much sought, Carthaginian families, noble and common alike, sacrificed as many as five hundred of their children in a single year.

Scholars have recently suggested that in addition to the religious motives the sacrifices served a social purpose: By reducing the number of heirs, families could better retain their wealth.

This practice flourished throughout the seventh century B.C., and though it was briefly suppressed by Josiah, king of Judah, it was revived by his son, Jehoiakim, and persisted until the Babylonian captivity. The Bible makes it clear that in Babylonia, too, infants were routinely sacrificed: "The Sepharvites burnt their children in fire to Adrammelech and Anammelech, the gods of Sepharvaim."

Archaeological excavations of the Canaanite levels of the region yielded scores of jars containing the bones of newborns. Many infants had been sacrificially burned, but others had been bled to death as an offering to "mother deities," the givers of children. By offering back the firstborn, families believed they would be blessed with an abundance of offspring. Sir James Frazer, in *The Golden Bough,* traced the origin of the Hebrew Passover directly to the sacrifice of firstborn infants, which he considered to have been an article of the ancient Semitic religion.

Female Infanticide as Population Control.

Is ancient infanticide in the name of god, or God, more justifiable than killing newborns because they are weak, deformed, the result of incest or rape, or conceived out of wedlock? These are some of the reasons for the practice that has persisted into our own time.

In many countries, the deliberate killing of an impaired, handicapped, or deformed baby—before the advent of modern medicine—was considered a humane act that spared the child a life of hardship or suffering. However, the Eskimos believed it was sinful to kill for any reason other than preservation of the tribe. In a year when the conditions of life were severe and food in short supply, all female infants were killed immediately after birth. In a time of relative plenty, no child was allowed to be destroyed.

Perhaps the hardest form of infanticide to reckon is the killing of newborns to limit population. Yet it was in this form that infanticide extended into modern times. Anthropologists claim that female infanticide was the primary means of population control in most parts of the world until the early decades of the twentieth century.

The first Christian missionaries to the South Sea Islands found that more than two-thirds of newborns were destroyed before they uttered their first cry. The technique for killing was called *tamari'i 'u'umi hia* ("children throttled") and it consisted of twisting a vine around the infant's neck as it emerged from the womb, strangling the child before it drew a breath. In years of extreme economic hardship, all newborns were throttled.

Missionaries were appalled; but they were even more disturbed to learn that food shortage was not the only factor that determined the number of children throttled. The rulers wished to keep the population of commoners and upper castes sufficiently in check to maintain a social abyss between the two.

Among Arioi tribes, the lowest caste of worker was tattooed above the knee for identification and their children were permitted to live only when an increase in the labor force was desired. Parents who saved a baby in a year when all infants were to be killed became social outcasts, shunned by family and friends. Control of conception was never attempted, only the control of population after birth.

In India, well into modern times, infanticide was also practiced mainly to limit population, especially in times of famine. But it also was used to maintain a caste system among the Hindu people, who disposed of children by throwing them into rivers under the guise of appeasing a crocodile god.

Other Indian groups practiced a less severe, though in a way more chilling, means of infanticide into this century. After childbirth, a mother anointed her nipples with a sweet-tasting poison, then allowed the newborn to nurse. A single application killed the child, usually an unwanted female, and the practice was considered by adherents as infinitely more civilized than the pretense of placating a crocodile.

India, though, was not the only country to sanction infanticide in this century. In China, the practice of killing infant girls was justified by the belief in reincarnation: A slain girl was given a chance to be reborn as a boy.

Multiple-Birth Superstitions. Infanticide has been commonplace in many parts of South America, and it has existed into modern times for the most superstitious of reasons. Cultures that lived along the Orinoco River in Venezuela regarded a woman who bore twins or triplets as being lower than a rat that bears a litter, and the mother herself, in order not to dishonor the family, secretly killed any co-sibling that issued after the first.

In such primitive societies, the possibility of twins or triplets was unknown before birth. A woman in labor, surrounded by midwives and family, was often caught unawares. Among the Salivas who inhabited the west bank of the Orinoco, if a woman bore a child and then sensed a second was on the way, she concealed the fact despite great pain and wandered into the bush where she would release the baby in secret, then bury it. This spared her ridicule from neighbors and scorn from her husband, who accepted no blame for a litter; a man produced only one child at a time. Multiple births suggested that a wife had cheated on her husband, the number of paramours evident by a count of the offspring.

Other South American peoples killed all multibirths, believing that twins or triplets were an ill omen. And an unmarried girl killed her newborn without hesitation, for the concept of an unwed mother was nothing less than an oxymoron. These practices and superstitions persisted long after the arrival of Christianity.

Christian missionaries were horrified by the cruel methods of infanticide. Some tribes broke an unwanted infant's neck; others pressed down on the breastbone, preventing a newborn from inhaling; many cut the umbilical cord so near the navel that the infant bled to death. The practice that was considered most humane by Orinoco tribes was to bury the newborn alive, and the local word for the custom translates as "death without pain at all."

Missionaries and medical authorities contend that in many poorer parts of the world (South America being only one example) infanticide is still practiced, though it has gone underground, done quietly by families to limit their size and to rid themselves of handicapped children. As many observers have noted, infants born hunchbacked, lame, dwarfed, crippled, or otherwise malformed often have a way of quietly disappearing from impoverished families.

Women in a No-Win Situation.   In classical times, infanticide was outlawed in Western cultures by the fourth-century Christian emperor, Constantine. He abandoned the Roman practice of exposing deformed newborns on a mountainside for the good of the state and invalidated the Roman law that strictly forbade parents to rear a deformed child.

Ironically, whereas Christianity brought an end to infanticide in Roman times, during the feudal period of the Middle Ages it was the same religion that caused more mothers to kill their unwanted babies than at any other time in Western history. For religion, along with what scholars call "the male feudal prerogative" (rape), worked against women. Thousands of peasant girls worked on the estates of the great feudal lords. It was expected that they submit to their masters' sexual demands, yet a tremendous religious and social stigma was associated with illegitimacy and bastard offspring—for the mother and for her bastards. The modern concept of an unwed mother was unthinkable. Thus countless unwanted pregnancies ended in secret infanticide.

This number was compounded by the fact that during the Middle Ages members of the military exercised the same sexual prerogative as feudal lords, leading to more secret infant killings.

Women were in a bind: They were to provide pleasure without becoming pregnant. For a period of more than a thousand years, women bore the sole

Being sewn into a sack with a snake and drowned was the punishment for a woman committing infanticide.

responsibility for unwanted pregnancies. Worse still, they had no choice but to kill bastard offspring, yet at the same time women alone could be executed for infanticide.

Secrecy was vital, and women banded together to protect each other. If caught and convicted of infanticide, a woman was usually sewn into a sack with a snake, then submerged in a river for six hours.

Thus for at least ten centuries peasant girls were supposed to submit quietly to sex outside of marriage, conceal a subsequent pregnancy, dispose of all offspring, and not get caught. The number of newborns that perished during those centuries (as well as the number of unfortunate mothers who were drowned) will never be known, but scholars of the period claim the figures are unique in the long history of infanticide.

There is of course a great irony to the end of the story of mass infanticide. The practice has been greatly reduced throughout the world, and eliminated in industrialized countries because of two modern customs: contraception and abortion. Abortion, though, can be viewed as infanticide within the womb, the result of medical advances that permit the fetus to be killed before birth with minimum risk to the mother. It certainly would have been practiced in earlier times if it were as safe as it is today, for what woman, aware that killing was her only option to an unwanted pregnancy, would endure the travails of going full term, then the trauma of murder? Has medical science simply shifted mass infanticide back a few months, from shortly after birth to shortly after conception?

Cannibalism: Persisted into the 20th Century

The Catholic Church has taught for centuries that the Holy Eucharist, in the form of bread and wine, is not a symbolic representation of Christ's body and blood, but the substances themselves, human flesh and human blood, miraculously transformed, altered only in their outward appearances to make them more palatable.

The doctrine is, by definition, an example of cannibalism, one of the most ancient forms of human ritual.

Since earliest times, one person ate the flesh of another to share in the victim's strength, goodness, wisdom—the list of attributes is long. Cannibalism, symbolically or in the flesh, existed in all cultures, over all times. Martin Luther, when he broke from the church in the sixteenth century, retained the cannibalistic interpretation of the Sacrament, unequivocally affirming the "Real Presence" of the body and blood of Christ "in, with, and under" the bread and wine.

Ritualistic cannibalism (as opposed to the eating of human flesh as a desperate act of survival) has, according to anthropologists, several fine points. Exocannibalism is eating the flesh of a person outside your own family or tribe. It was fairly common until recent times among Australian and Maori tribes, the Eskimos, and many Central African peoples. The preferred corpses were those of fallen warriors, medicine men, and virgins, to gain, respectively, bravery, wisdom, and purity.

Endo-cannibalism, on the other hand (no pun intended), is eating the flesh of a close relative or member of your immediate family or tribe. The preferred corpses are those of people most deeply cherished in life. Only parents were eaten by Slavonic peoples. All blood relatives (not in-laws) were enjoyed by the early settlers of Ireland.

The Mayorunas and Acumas along the Orinoco River in Venezuela made requests in life of whom they wanted to be eaten by in death—a last wish, and one that could not be denied the departed. In the funeral feasts of coastal tribes of north central Australia, relatives ate their loved ones to diminish the loss from death; it was custom until recently to carry a piece of the relative, nibbling on it when overcome by grief. The practice was ancient, widespread, and noble in intent. Anthropologists have named it "morbid affection."

Cannibalism Western Style.   The term "cannibalism" derives from the Spanish *canibal*, meaning "savage," and was applied by the Spaniards to the Caniba people, a flesh-eating tribe of the West Indies known to Columbus. Though documented centuries earlier in ancient Greece, the practice was long forgotten in Europe until the discovery of the New World, where ritualistic cannibalism was in full flower.

The Christian conquistadors (who symbolically ate the body and blood of Christ) were appalled to learn that the Aztecs of Mexico, in elaborate ceremonies at hundreds of temples, killed and consumed totally or partially a minimum of fifteen thousand sacrificial victims a year. The reasons behind ritualistic flesh eating on such an immense scale have yet to be fully explained. For, as we'll see, in earlier times in the Western world, people ate people in moderation.

Participants in ancient Greek mystery cults might sip the blood of a high priest or consume a token amount of flesh of a slain warrior. A nibble. The flesh eating was symbolic and, to express it bluntly, a little went a long way. In mainland Greece and on Crete, the human sacrifice, a priest, was eaten because he was an earthly representative of a god and so that the congregation might become "one with god."

Martin Luther affirmed the cannibalistic definition of the Eucharist. Aztecs "ate" fifteen thousand victims a year.

A person who received the body or blood of the priest supposedly became "enthused," that is, temporarily infused with divinity or grace. The ritual was often restaged to receive additional infusions. This custom that so closely prefigures the Christian sacrament of the Eucharist (from the Greek *eucharistia,* "gratitude") was enacted hundreds of years before Christ's birth.

Herodotus, the fifth-century B.C. Greek historian and Father of History, reported several reasons for ritual cannibalism. The aged were eaten after death by relatives in order to keep their souls within the clan. Warriors slain in battle were eaten by their own troops to prevent the remains from being desecrated by enemies who might use them for magical purposes. But whatever the reasons, in Western cultures the practice was never enthusiastically embraced, and substitutes for real blood and real flesh (wine and bread being the most common) were quick to surface.

The emotions that cannibalism arouses are powerful. Many remote cultures abandoned it (or transferred it underground) once they saw the horror-struck faces of visiting missionaries and anthropologists. Although the custom has virtually ended (often to be subsumed under eucharistic rituals), there remain a few tribes in the interior of New Guinea and in southern Australia that are suspected of still engaging in "morbid affection."

Cannibalistic Fairy Tales. Though ritualistic cannibalism has virtually ended, the custom lives on in many of the favorite bedtime stories we tell our children. The witch in the gingerbread house has every intention of eating Hansel and Gretel. The giant with a castle in the clouds earnestly hopes to devour Jack, who has scaled the beanstalk. The vain, wicked queen in the forest orders a huntsman to cut out the heart of Sleeping Beauty (which she plans to eat), then instructs her cook to prepare a stew from the bodies of the two illegitmate children born to Sleeping Beauty, fathered by the queen's own husband (details in the original fairy tale, which Walt Disney left out of the movie). The queen plans to serve the dish to her unfaithful husband, along with the zinger, "You're eating your own!"

One of the most cannibalistic of all popular fairy tales is the original version of "Little Red Riding Hood." The wolf eats Granny and tricks Red into drinking Granny's blood (and in a later rewrite devours Red herself)—details so gory that earlier artists refused to illustrate the story.

Cannibalism also lives on in popular phrases. Psychologists have written volumes on the "oral eroticism" in endearments between lovers such as, "You look good enough to eat," and our joking threat to children: "I'm going to eat you."

If the vast literature on cannibalism makes anything clear, it is that there is no hard evidence to support any single theory of why people eat people, in fact and in fiction, or why noncannibals like ourselves continue to utter blatantly cannibalistic endearments and threats. Anthropologists would like to conclude that cannibalism became a universal practice when, millions of years ago, hominids went from eating roots and berries to being omnivorous, but there is no more evidence for that assumption than for the reality, say, of Little Red Riding Hood.

The only form of cannibalism generally accepted today is flesh eating as a last, desperate act of survival. The most famous example was the well-publicized plight of the Uruguayan rugby team that was stranded in the Andes Mountains after a plane crash. The dead provided nourishment that kept the survivors alive until they were rescued.

Another celebrated cannibalism case involved one infamous Alfred Packer. Stranded in the Colorado Rockies in 1874, Packer ate five members of his traveling party. He achieved notoriety as much from the identity of his victims as from the act of devouring them. Parker was saved, only to be arrested and indicted for cannibalism. His five companions had comprised the majority of the Democrats in the local county. The judge who tried the case, himself a Democrat, condemned Parker, saying: "There was seven Democrats in Hinsdale County, and you've ate five of them, God damn you! I sentence you to be hanged by the neck for reducing the Democrat population of the state. I would sentence you to hell but the Statutes forbid it." Parker escaped execution on a legal technicality, and the Democrats have never made a strong comeback in the area.

CHAPTER 12

Past Sex Practices—His

Castration to Circumcision

MUCH OF THIS CHAPTER is about castration, an end in itself.

Why remove a male's testes? Historically, the reasons are as numerous as the benefits. Conquerors castrated the vanquished as a means of subduing them; without a daily dose of testosterone aggressive tendencies quickly wane. This punishment was carried to humiliating extremes among American Indians, where it was the women of the winning tribe who amputated the manhood of the defeated, who must have felt just that.

Certain Christian sects castrated themselves—testes and penis—as a means of rising above sexual temptation and eventually through the gates of heaven. Other men endured the briefer horror of testicular self-castration to make themselves the most desirable of lovers, the way a modern man might have a vasectomy, only from the former butchery there was no return.

Impresarios castrated choirboys so the youths as adults could sing as full-bodied sopranos in the best cathedrals of Europe. Though the church officially discouraged the operation, the Vatican's interest in emasculated men kept the castrati bel-cantoing into our own century: The last male soprano, Alessandro Moreschi, died in 1922, leaving behind the only gramophone recordings of that kind of unique, unnatural voice: high and flexible as a female's, robust and powerful as a male's.

Art aside, a vengeful husband could demand in court the castration of his wife's lover—and get it. A slothful Chinese might remove his own testes to obtain a pension and dispensation from work at a time when the government sought to limit population growth. The handsomest Roman men were testicularly castrated against their will to become the play doodads of wealthy matrons who could copulate at whim without worry of offspring. And by making the fateful incision an inch or so higher the penis was also removed to produce a eunuch, who, because he could not copulate at all, was in greatest demand in all spheres of society. Eunuchs served as "safe" cooks and bedchamber servants in stately homes, as transvestite "wives" of pleasure-loving Roman emperors, as close and constant companions to prominent church fathers, including many cardinals and several popes, and eunuchs served, of course, as the hands-off protectors of sultans' harems.

These are only a few of the reasons we'll examine in this chapter for removing a man's testes and/or penis, practices that flourished for centuries and have, reasonably, ended.

Castration: Antiquity, Europe and Asia

Castration is ancient, first performed on animals after an unidentified group of cavemen made an astute, accidental observation.

About ten thousand years ago, early man began domesticating animals for their meat, milk, and hides, then employing them as draft animals to supplement his own muscle power. More than once he observed that a diseased bull or buffalo that severed its testes on a jagged tree stump recovered to become a considerably more docile, tamable animal. Soon man was wielding a knife to do what the tree stump had done—to beasts of burden and to captured warriors from neighboring tribes. He had learned in effect to transform a proud, pugnacious cock into a useful, submissive capon. Centuries later the technique would be used to transform a violent criminal into a resentful citizen.

Castration became a favorite subject of psychiatrists. Sigmund Freud, and especially his follower Wilhelm Reich, maintained that castration is a phenomenon of a patriarchal era, which in the West began some five thousand years ago. That man used physical or psychic castration to control his fellowmen, making him sinless, submissive, and molding him into the precise opposite of that ideal of the democratic world: the self-determined, genitally uninhibited, free man,

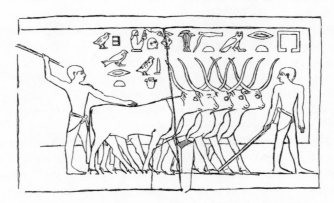

Astute observation: A castrated bull made a better worker.

enjoying the fruit of his own labor. Whereas physical castration removed the asserting organ, psychic castration implanted enough anxiety and guilt to render it flaccid.

How to Castrate. The ancient method of fully castrating a boy or adult male (that is, removing testes and penis) was no different from that practiced in the Middle East into this century.

To obtain a eunuch for a harem, or permanently to punish a rapist, the individual was strapped, arms and legs, to a table. A thin ligament or cord was knotted tightly around his genitals, and then, with a sharp razor, the organs were amputated. The wound was cauterized by the application of a searingly hot poker or molten tar. The mutilated youngster or adult was deprived of food and water for several days to prevent urination, which could infect the healing region.

If lucky enough to survive—and not that many did; the mortality rate was about eight in ten—the freshly made eunuch was fed a liquid diet until his bladder pressure was sufficiently high to force a stream of urine through the still soft scar tissue, providing him with an orifice.

At the turn of the century, this operation was still being performed in the Middle East on boys seven to ten years of age to produce not only harem eunuchs, but also a large supply of docile, sexually nonthreatening slaves.

On the other hand, to obtain a singing castrato, or an active but "safe" lover, the cord was tightened only around the testes, which were then cut off. Though the loss of testosterone rendered a man facially hairless, plump in the buttocks and hips, smooth-skinned, and capable of hitting a high C with ease, it did not prevent him from getting an erection and sustaining it—often longer than his intact male counterpart, since there was no ejaculatory orgasm to release sexual tension. Little wonder that the mythical Greek god Priapus, son of Dionysus and Aphrodite, who lent his name to the complaint (some might say boast) called priapism—persistent erection without sexual excitement—became the patron saint of castrati.

The Bible recognizes three types of eunuchs: an infant born without genitalia, a prisoner castrated by his captors, and the pious who mutilate themselves in an effort to fight temptation. Matthew (19:12) addresses such zealots who "have made themselves eunuchs for the kingdom of heaven's sake." Many biblical scholars believed that at one time the passage went so far as heartily to recommend castration as a means of spiritual salvation, but was later toned down to its present version: "He that is able to receive it [castration], let him receive it." Which is certainly no condemnation of the operation.

It is supposedly Matthew's once strongly worded, now missing reference that inspired early Christian cults to mutilate themselves such that fornication, then deemed the greatest of evils (even for married couples), was impossible in the face of the most flagrant temptation. Confronted with widespread castration in the name of Christ, the church eventually decreed that no male missing any body part, even so little as a pinkie, could be consecrated as a priest—a requirement that has only recently been relaxed.

Political Castration: 2000 B.C., Near East

In the ancient world, the Egyptians, Persians, Assyrians, Ethiopians, Medes, and Hebrews all practiced castration as a means of humiliating and subduing their vanquished enemies. So did the Chinese. In these cultures, men emasculated men.

Anthropologists believe that only among American Indians was it the women, as mentioned earlier, who castrated prisoners. Numerous explanations have been offered to account for this exception, but historically it seems that the practice had no intentional overtones of gender ridicule; castration of a prisoner was considered a minor bloody chore left to squaws, whereas major tortures that ran on for hours were reserved for the enjoyment of braves.

Genitalia were always trophies of war, with a peck of penises more impressive than a tally of testes. A German prisoner fully emasculated by his Roman captors was called a *castrato assoluto*, whereas one who relinquished only his gonads was a *spandone*. Many ancient monuments and stone reliefs depict conquerors brandishing the genitalia of their enemies. In the inventory of trophies taken by Egyptian troops that invaded Libya in the thirteenth century B.C. are a total of 13,230 penises, 6 belonging to generals (not that they are recognizable as such).

A stone relief in the ancient city of Thebes (modern Luxor and Karnak) shows a band of victorious Egyptian men amassing their trophies into a great pile with the inscription: "Prisoners brought before the king, 1000; phalli, 3000."

In the sixth century B.C., Nebuchadnezzar, king of Babylon, conquered Jerusalem, destroyed its great temple, and cut from thousands of Jewish prisoners all that the rabbis' circumcision had left behind.

The practice of one man taking another man's privates home as proof of victory was so common in ancient times that it is described in the Bible. David (in 1 Samuel 18:27), to prove he is worthy of becoming Saul's son-in-law, goes off and returns with two hundred foreskins. They are taken from conquered Philistines, men who were not merely circumcised but fully emasculated.

Prisoners were not the only ones to lose their privates. So did their young sons. The best-looking, strongest boys were castrated to serve as sexually nonthreatening eunuchs in royal palaces and as even-tempered scribes in civil service. The Greek historian Herodotus relates that the Persians had an almost unquenchable passion for collecting phalli and castrating children. Persian generals, in bitter campaigns against the Greeks, no sooner won possession of a town when, wrote Herodotus, "they chose out all the best favored boys and made them eunuchs."

Socially, a eunuch in Persia could rise high. Bagoas, fully castrated as a boy captive, rose to become confidential minister of Artaxerxes III, the fourth-century B.C. king of Persia's Achaemenid Empire. (*Bagoas* was Greek for the Persian "eunuch.") Commander in chief of the Persian forces that conquered Egypt in 343 B.C., he became the real master of the Achaemenids, the king doing nothing without his eunuch's advice. Bagoas was alleged also to exert an amorous influence over the king, a rumor that might contain truth, since as "the Persian boy" he was the lover of Alexander the Great.

In the end, Bagoas gave a bad name to eunuchs in high places. He murdered the aged king, then poisoned all of the king's sons except Arses, whom he placed on the throne as co-ruler with Darius III. Two years later he poisoned Arses for attempting to have a mind of his own. And when Darius, then sole king, attempted to assert his independence, Bagoas laced the royal wine with poison. In the midst of such machinations it was not hard to be suspicious, and Darius was: He forced his chief eunuch to drink the libation, proving the suspicion and putting an end to the tyranny. One could say, so much for eunuchs being docile and nonaggressive, but it is easier to imagine Bagoas as temperamental, spoiled, and willful. He never was violent.

Historians record that the Persians were the world's first great political castrators. Walls of Persian palaces predating 1000 B.C. depict beardless, voluptuously curved men posed in sharp contrast beside muscular, lean, hirsute counterparts. The full-figured males appear in the paintings and stone reliefs as bread bakers, cooks, musicians, chaperons of women, guardians of children, and high civil servants.

Interestingly, the Greeks were the only ancient culture that did not go in for castration to subdue prisoners or to produce a class of men not fully male. Such was the high esteem in which the Greeks held manhood. The eunuchs who lived in Greek territories were attributed to the work of the Phoenicians. They were often brought to Greece by the aristocracy as instructors for their children, but they were despised by the lower classes and subjected to ridicule. Legally, castration was employed in Greece for only one offense: rape. (Though there are accounts of husbands demanding, and getting, the castration of a man caught flagrante delicto with his wife.)

Castration as Punishment: 4000 B.C., Egypt

In an eye-for-an-eye kind of justice, the Egyptians, six thousand years ago, were the first people to punish sex crimes with castration. A man convicted of rape suffered complete ablation of his genitals, whereas a woman guilty of adultery forfeited her nose. The male's loss rendered him incapable of intercourse, and the female's unattractiveness diminished her chance of finding subsequent lovers. She was visibly stigmatized, hence ostracized; his punishment, though severe, could at least be concealed.

A greater inequity was initiated a century later by the Asiatic Huns who punished a male rapist or adulterer with castration, whereas a female adulteress was cut in half.

The punishment of castration was not meted only to the crime of rape. In ancient China, a man involuntarily became a eunuch for killing his father; thus the loss of one male was matched by the forfeiture of another's maleness.

During the twelfth-century reign of England's Henry II, castration was reserved for refractory priests who refused to side with the king against his counsel-turned-critic, Thomas à Becket. Scottish philosopher David Hume, in his *History of England,* recounts how the king "ordered a whole of them [priests] to be castrated, and caused all their testicles to be brought to him on a platter." The empiricist philosopher viewed the loss as insignificant: "Of the pain and danger they, the monks, might justly complain, yet since they had vowed chastity, he deprived them of a superfluous treasure."

But throughout history castration was usually reserved for rapists. For first offenders, the ancient Romans crushed a man's gonads between stones, making him a *thlibio* rather than a *spandone* ("no testicles") or a *castrato* (then meaning "no genitals"). The ancient Greeks, as mentioned, used castration only to punish rapists, and the offender was called a *spao,* meaning "to draw out" or "drag," a description of how the testes were removed from the scrotum. Despised in Greek society and denied employment, such men are said to have masqueraded as women—the origin of the slang expression "drag" for a man in woman's attire.

Some punishments were more gruesome than others. The Greek historian Herodotus tells of a unique treatment of a rapist or adulterer devised by the Samaritans, fifth-century B.C. nomads. A sturdy rope would be drawn tightly around the man's genitals, then he would be hanged from a tree, one hand bound behind his back, a sharp knife placed in his other hand. If he chose, he could free himself by self-castration.

In France, castration as punishment was finally abolished by Napoleon who, instead, instituted a scale of fines for sex offenses: thirty-five francs for a man guilty of lifting a woman's skirt to the knee; seventy francs if he lifted it to the thigh; two hundred francs if he had his way with her. The modest fine for adultery versus the privation of castration is a chasm bridged by reason.

Chemical Emasculation.   Castration as punishment continued in other parts of the world into this century, and this is true not only in the Middle East. According the contemporary *Almanac on Crime,* "During the 20th century it [castration] has been used several hundred times in California and less frequently in some other states."

As recently as 1975, two California criminals convicted of child molestation—Paul de lay Haye and Joseph Kenner—requested they be castrated instead of risking a likely life sentence. The judge agreed. Arrangements were made to have the men hospitalized, anesthetized, and surgically castrated. But the operations were canceled when the urologist scheduled to perform the surgery was advised by his colleagues at San Diego's University Hospital that he was risking a lawsuit for assault and battery that probably would not be covered by his malpractice insurance. When the county urological society proffered the same opinion, the surgeon backed out. The two men were sent to prison, genitalia intact.

According to reports in the British press, a sophisticated technique called "chemical castration" continues to be practiced in certain Communist countries, particularly East Germany. The imprisoned rapist is surgically given a subdermal implant of a dime-size disc that contains synthetic female hormones. The time-released drugs trickle into his bloodstream, gradually altering his secondary sexual characteristics. Beard growth slows, fatty deposits accumulate in his breasts and buttocks, and sexual drive is greatly diminished, if not destroyed. When one drug disc is emptied, it is replaced.

The time-released treatment is supposedly replacing earlier chemical castration that was done by injection. British articles have reported that a large one-time infusion of female hormones excessively feminized a man, giving him larger breasts and a rounded rump that other male prisoners viewed as irresistible. Such feminized rapists were often themselves raped by inmates, making them victims of their own crime. Two men's breasts grew so pendulous that the victims, distressed by their popularity, voluntarily underwent mastectomies. The therapy has not been tried in western European countries or in America, at least not openly.

Medical Castration: 5th Century B.C., Greece

The most abusive form of testicular castration in history occurred in the name of medical therapy, as treatment for such problems as hernia, epilepsy, and mental illness. It began with the ancient Greeks and Romans, on the mistaken observation that eunuchs never seemed to suffer from hernias, and the practice continued well into the nineteenth century. Once a treatment, it became a panacea and a preventative.

Tens of thousands of male children, and even more adult sufferers of mental disorders, forfeited their gonads as doctors groped for therapies to prevent or cure disease. In France, where abuses were severest, certain towns had female castrators, the paramedical equivalent of a midwife, who, as a disease preventative, removed a boy's testicles as soon as they descended into the scrotum. It was supposed to ward off a host of adult ailments; it must have significantly limited population.

Thucydides, the fifth-century B.C. Athenian historian, first commented on testicular castration as a last-ditch effort to cure victims of a plague, characterized by skin lesions. When the disease descended "to those parts of their anatomy," he wrote, the physician amputated the gonads—as was routinely done in cases of elephantiasis. The latter disease, caused by obstruction of the lymphatic vessels, often due to infestation by filarial worms, results in gross enlargements of body parts, especially the legs and genitals. Early physicians reasoned that diseased parts were swollen with a reflux of fluid from the testes and removed the malfunctioning organs. It never cured the disease, but doctors felt compelled to do something, so the surgery continued.

The Roman use of testicular castration to cure and prevent hernias was even less grounded in physiology. Perhaps no eunuch was known to suffer from a hernia simply for statistical reasons: The population sample was small. Nonetheless, in parts of Europe the surgery eventually became the standard treatment for the complaint.

Ambroise Paré, one of the most notable surgeons of the Renaissance and the Father of Modern Surgery, was the first doctor to condemn the practice, offering the unarguable maxim that a husband must have gonads, for *"cequi fait la paix du ménage"* ("this makes peace in the home"). Paré was already renowned when he made the plea. He had replaced the use of a searingly hot iron to seal a hemorrhage with the tying off of a large artery; he introduced the implantation of teeth, artificial limbs, and artificial eyes made of inert metals like gold and silver; and for a hernia he introduced the simple solution of a truss.

Paré's advice—and his truss—were largely ignored, particularly in France. Barber-surgeons and female castrators, as well as many leading physicians, continued the radical and useless treatment of castration. Parents were assured that castration of a boy at puberty was a guarantee of a long and healthy life. And parents, with the advice of clergy, sacrificed their heirs in quantity. The bishop of one French diocese was responsible for the castration of five hundred pubescent boys—though of only one testicle each, for he thought removal of two excessive.

The timid and diffident Louis XIII (psychically castrated in his youth by his mother, Marie de' Medici, and in later years by his chief administrators, Richelieu and Mazarin) forbade the all-purpose preventative during his reign (1610–43) by any but the most "reputable" surgeons, putting the female castrators out of business—for a time. In the eighteenth century, Pierre Dronis, surgeon to Maria Theresa, the mother of Marie Antoinette and wife of Emperor Francis I, wrote of one French female castrator whose adolescent clients were so numerous that she was able to use their testicles as her dog's sole source of food.

Finally the French Royal Society of Medicine took steps to stop the abuses—not primarily because the operation was ineffective, but because too many young men were butchered to a degree that left them unfit for military service. Mental defectives, already unfit for the military, were still castrated to "cure" their derangements. The madness, though, was the physicians'.

Social Misfits.   As Roman doctors had mistakenly observed that eunuchs never suffered from hernias (certainly not from the gonadal type), during the Victorian era British physicians decided that epileptics were onanists, or masturbators, in a state of perpetual sexual arousal. Their fits and limb flailings were erotic releases. Thus the obvious cure was genital castration. This clearly put an end to masturbation, but it did nothing to stop electrical brain seizures.

Other physicians, in England and the United States, began to recommend castration of criminals, homosexuals, cretans, alcoholics, Jews, and other "social misfits." In February 1888, a major paper presented before the Cincinnati Academy of Medicine, by a Dr. P. Everts, detailed how castration (read, eugenics) could constitute the most significant factor in social reform in history. The idea was incorporated into the statutes of most states. The recommended method of castration was severing of the spermatic cord. Connecticut, Indiana, Iowa, Kansas, Michigan, New York, and North Dakota adopted the technique as long as it "shall be performed in a safe and humane manner."

In Nevada and Washington the surgery was punishment for any sexual crime with a female under the age of ten. In California the law allowed surgeons to cut the seminal ducts not only of rapists, but also of convicted adulterers. In New Jersey and Wisconsin the law allowing the castration of epileptics remained on the books well into this century. Zoologist and sex researcher Alfred Kinsey summarized the state of affairs in the 1950s:

In more recent decades, both in Europe and this country, castrations have been rationalized as attempts to modify some aspects of the individual's sexual behavior: to stop masturbation, to transform homosexual into heterosexual patterns of behavior, to control exhibitionism and, in particular, to control adults who sexually molest children. Castrations have been used in both Europe and in this country to prevent feeble-minded, criminal or irresponsible individuals from becoming parents.

Today, in our litigious society, involuntary medical castration (or sterilization) has become extremely rare, confined to cases of severe feeble-mindedness, for even with parental consent the surgeon risks a lawsuit from groups representing the victim.

Eunuchs for Pleasure: Pre–Christian Era, Rome

Like capons (Latin *capo,* "to cut"), like geldings (Middle English *geldr,* "barren"), and like oxen (German *ochse,* "bull"), eunuchs (Greek *eunouchos,* "guardian of the bed") have had their special uses. And in decadent Imperial Rome the principal use of eunuchs, testicular and total, was for the sexual pleasures of the nobility.

Fittingly called a *voluptas,* for the soft, rounded, feminine distribution of body fat, eunuchs became the main attraction in the orgies staged by the emperors Octavius (27 B.C.-A.D. 14), Tiberius (14–37), and Caligula (37–41).

Octavius, as Augustus Caesar, made no secret of his fondness for castrated men, and his indulgences with them led to him being referred to as effeminate and emasculated himself. Once, when he was attending a play, an actor spoke a line about a favorite fey eunuch beating a tambourine—*"Videsne ut Cinaedus orbem digito temperet?"* ("Do you see how this queen's finger beats the orb?") ("beats the orb" meaning "governs the world")—and the knowledgeable audience immediately glanced toward the royal box and burst into wild applause, to which Octavius bowed.

Tiberius, even more licentious, introduced at his orgies of testicular eu-

Emperors Augustus (right) and Tiberius favored testicular eunuchs.

nuchs the *spintriae,* or "daisy chain," which Suetonius, the first-century biographer, relates as "men joined front to back in sexual union."

Caligula, among the most debauched of Rome's Imperial emperors, enjoyed public copulation with a favorite eunuch priest and was eventually slain by Chaerea, his military guard and frequent bed partner, for embarrassing the soldier in front of his peers. (Chaerea, by all accounts, was not a eunuch.)

A Lady's Man.   In Roman times, it was the testicular eunuchs (and not the nobility, who made liberal use of them) who were blamed for the decline in morals. One reason offered was the obvious: Roman noblewomen could engage in sex willy-nilly without fear of pregnancy. Martial, the first-century Roman epigrammatist, wrote: "The Roman woman wants the flower of marriage and not the fruit." His contemporary, the satirical poet Juvenal, explained that, "Some women always delight in soft eunuchs and tender kisses, and in the absence of a beard, and the fact that the use of abortives is unnecessary."

As the pill in modern times is said to have sexually liberated women, two thousand years ago the pill's equivalent was the gonadless *spandone* (aka *voluptas*). These safe men became an essential part of a lady's retinue, accompanying their mistresses to the opulent Roman baths, lounging with them on their silk-draped litters, and pleasuring them on command. In Imperial Rome the elegance of a woman was measured by the number of eunuchs in attendance.

A Man's Man.   The emasculated young man was even more popular among men. Lucian, the second-century Greek satirist, writing about the *"vice grec"* or "Greek vice" (homosexuality), argues that eunuchs corrupted Roman morals because of their temptingly androgynous appearance to heterosexual men in high places. Looking both male *(andros)* and female *(gyne),* they provided an easy rationalization for borderline bisexuals to crisscross the border. Being plump, soft, smooth-skinned, and hairless, says Lucian, "with breasts even firmer than a woman's," eunuchs tempted everyone from emperors to generals.

The most flagrant emperor to flaunt his exploits with *spandones* was Nero, who ruled from A.D. 54 to 68. He is said to have indulged in orgies of up to sixty eunuchs at a time, and his favorite, Sporus, dressed as a woman, he married in public with much pomp. Nero claimed that he took Sporus as a bride because the castrated youth bore a resemblance (which not everyone saw) to his deceased pregnant wife Poppaea—whom, as legend has it, he murdered with a kick to her stomach. Nero was, as Juvenal observed, "not afraid to appear on the Via Flaminia [Street of Offices] with this castrated spouse whom he publicly caressed."

Eunuchs, as we're about to see, became the easy scapegoats for a general decline in Roman morals. Whereas it is true that emasculated men were used by nobles of both sexes, it is equally true that eunuchs were the ones truly being *used*—by adults, who could judge right from wrong, and who demanded boys be surgically castrated for purposes of pleasure.

Sex and the Fall of Rome: 3rd Century
to 5th Century

In Imperial Rome, the penchant for sex with eunuchs was responsible, claimed Livy, in his monumental first-century history, *Ab urbe condita libri,* for the tidal wave of "pederasty" that swept across the empire, into every class, corrupting and weakening society.

Today we think of pederasty exclusively as sex between a man and a young boy, and indeed the word's roots mean that literally: *paidos,* "boy"; *eran,* "to love." But the coupling Livy referred to included the adult eunuch, who in his androgyny was boylike, and who if testically castrated early enough underwent arrested penile development, leaving him even more like a boy.

Historians agree that the period of Roman licentiousness and the popularity of eunuchs strongly coincided. In Rome, an entire street, the Via de Toscani, the red-light district, became the province of prostitutes, perverts, eunuchs, and their assorted clients. By slur the sellers were called *pathici* ("the suffering"), but they were undeniably popular, especially the emasculated men who were forceably castrated as boys, or who, on their own, could have the job done by the street's *tonsores* ("barbers").

By the beginning of the reign of Caracalla in A.D. 211, Rome had so many castrati and *spandones,* as young as seven years of age, that they could be bought for a talent, a small silver coin. Age seven was the lower limit only because the emperor Domitian, around A.D. 84, ordered that no boy should be prostituted or emasculated prior to his seventh birthday.

When did the abuses end?

In a sense they didn't; the empire fell first.

The Christian emperor Constantine I, early in the fourth century, made a dent in the number of eunuchs when he ordered capital punishment for castrators. In the same century, the firebrand St. Jerome railed against patrician matrons who surrendered to libidinous pleasures because of the certainty of nonconception. When Constantine moved his court east to Byzantium, many of Rome's emasculated men were relegated to monasteries throughout the countryside. One in the Taurus mountains, called Topos, was reserved exclusively for castrati and *spandones.*

But whereas Constantine I embraced Christianity, his sons and their successors embraced concupiscence. Eunuchs quickly returned as a centerpiece of the Roman court. When Constantine died in 337, his three sons—Constantine II, Constans I, and Constantius II—each adopted the title of augustus and divided the empire among themselves. Constantine became ruler of Britain, Gaul, and Spain, and he soon claimed Italy and Africa from Constans. He granted high office to the eunuch Eusebis, who proceeded to fill the palace and its many administrative positions with co-castrates.

Castration became a prerequisite, at the top of one's résumé, to achieve choice civil service jobs. For eunuchs, without their own families, could and did devote full loyalties to the emperor. "Even the noblest parents," wrote a later historian, "were not above mutilating their sons to help their advancement, nor was there any disgrace in it."

Eunuchs wielded such power and influence that eighteenth-century English historian Edward Gibbon, in his *History of the Decline and Fall of the Roman Empire,* summed up the decades after Constantine the Great's rule: "They multiplied in the palaces of his [Constantine's] degenerate sons, and insensibly acquired the knowledge, and at length the direction of the secret councils."

Gibbon concluded, in a sweeping and questionable generalization, that "if we examine the general history of Persia, India, and China, we shall find that the power of the eunuch has uniformly marked the decline and fall of every dynasty." He maintained that eunuchs were mentally inferior to "whole men" and consequently mishandled matters of government.

But the case for diminished capability is unsupported by fact. On the other hand, if hedonism played a part in the fall of the empire (one of numerous standard arguments), eunuchs, at court and in the red-light district, were perhaps minor players if not pawns in the larger game of moral corruption that weakened the weave of Roman society.

The Last Eunuch: 1951, China

It is ironic that Byzantium, which under Constantine the Great was to have no eunuchs, became in time the world's leading center for castrating men.

In the seventh century, the caliph Muawiyah, founder of the Umayyad dynasty, initiated the practice of using eunuchs to guard harems. (Early sultans, little more than nomad chieftains, were unacquainted with the concepts of eunuchs and harems.)

During the so-called seraglio period of the Byzantine Empire, a corps of well over a thousand castrates not only protected the royal harem, but ran the academy that trained men for government service and headed the branch that decided which boys, from which families, would be honored with emasculation and its fringe benefits. Islamic historians claim that the practice of having eunuchs guard women was unknown among the Ottoman Turks until they took over the Byzantine Empire in the fifteenth century.

Palace eunuchs remained a reality in China until the middle of this century. In the 1930s, the American diplomat to Peking, Vincent Starrett, interviewed and photographed the final thirty-three surviving eunuchs of the imperial palace. They ranged in age from sixty to eighty, and Starrett reported to the Western world that the emasculated elders were "thin, hairless, fat-lipped and bejowled old men with shrill voices and hair which hung down to their necks." Relieved of servile duties, they were "fellows of a certain spirit . . . one still wearing the velvet pants of the days of former splendor, whereas most of the others were dressed in coolie cloth."

In an abandoned garden overgrown with weeds, Starrett walked among the tombstones of more than one thousand seven hundred eunuchs from past dynasties. Most prominent was the grave of Kang Ping Tieh, patron saint of Chinese eunuchs and known as the Iron Duke. Five centuries earlier, Kang,

Abduction into a seraglio was a beauty's fate. Harem eunuchs survived into the present century.

with his genitalia intact, was general to Emperor Yung Lo. As the story goes, one day the emperor went hunting and left Kang to oversee Peking's Forbidden City, whose most forbidden inhabitants (to anyone but the emperor) were the bevy of imperial concubines.

The honor was great, as was the temptation; previous generals had been executed for allegations of sexual dalliances in the emperor's absence. Kang, certain that palace rivals who wanted him out of the way would level similar charges against him, despite his intended chastity, took into his own hand his genitalia and amputated them the night before the emperor's departure. He secreted the severed organs deep in the emperor's saddlebag, and, a little light-headed from loss of blood, assumed his duties as guardian of the Forbidden City.

No sooner had the emperor returned than Kang was called to account for how he had spent his nights. To the charge that he had frolicked among the seventy-three royal ladies, Kang ordered, "Bring in the Emperor's saddle." He requested that the emperor himself reach into a remote pocket of the bag.

The extracted organs, black, pungent, and shriveled, were nonetheless recognizable for what they once had been. The emperor, overwhelmed by the selfless gesture, promoted the general to chief eunuch, lavished him with gifts, and proclaimed him holy.

By coincidence, the last of the Chinese eunuchs died in 1951, the same year the world was titillated by news that doctors in Denmark had surgically emasculated an American ex-GI named George Jorgensen. Jorgensen, of course, did not remain a eunuch for long; he became Christine and launched the phenomenon of transsexual surgery. Within months, the Danish medical team had received more than five hundred letters from people around the world, all pleading for the same operation. The centuries-old phenomenon of the eunuch as a castrato or a *spandone* had ended, replaced by a medical procedure which, with scalpel and hormones, transformed a man briefly into a eunuch and then permanently into a woman. One wonders what the ancients would have said.

Singing Castrati: 3rd Century, Rome, to 1922

At puberty a male's vocal cords thicken, a response to large spurts of testosterone from the gonads, and the voice deepens. By analogy, imagine moving across the neck of a guitar from the thinnest string to the thickest. Remove the gonads early enough, say between the ages of seven and ten, and the boy, if he sang in a high soprano, never descends to the depth of a baritone or bass.

But—and this is crucial—the boy still grows in size to a man. His lung capacity expands, his diaphragm muscles strengthen, and his weak soprano blossoms into a booming soprano, one that no woman ever produced, or could.

It is an unnatural voice, a she-he sound, and one we will never hear firsthand. But the practice of castrating young choirboys with the best voices to keep their vocal cords thin ended only late in the last century. So late that one castrato was able to make gramophone recordings.

We saw in previous sections that testicular castration was practiced by early man for a variety of reasons: political, medical, and hedonistic. But at what point in history did male children begin to be castrated specifically for the beauty of their voices?

The first historical reference to a castrato appears in the eighty-volume *Romaika,* by the third-century Roman statesman Dio Cassius. His immense history of the empire, which begins with the landing of Aeneas in Italy and ends in the reign of Alexander Severus (222–235), seems to place the origin of the practice during the time of Emperor Septimius Severus (193–211). Dio Cassius says little of testicular castration in the service of singing, but in the decades straddling the year 200, castration of children had reached fad proportions. At some point, a youth with a lovely voice must have been castrated to produce a voice which, as he aged, grew more powerful but no deeper.

Thus the singing castrato (invariably with penis intact, as the word will be used in this section) appears to have been a serendipitous discovery made around the year 200. We know with certainty that it was the flowering of Christianity that created the musical milieu in which the practice flourished.

St. Paul, in fact, unintentionally paved the way for singing castrati. As the apostle of Christianity to the Gentiles in the first century, he wrote emphatically that women were forbidden to sing in church (an interdiction that ended only in the seventeenth century). A composer who scored a piece requiring a high voice had two options in singers: a prepubescent boy or a man straining in a falsetto.

Each had its drawbacks. A boy could be mischievous, unable to maintain concentration throughout a long church service, and just when he mastered the soprano repertoire his voice could deepen. The falsetto, on the other hand, possessed a peculiar and harshly unpleasant vocal quality as well as a range more limited than a soprano's. For many years these less-than-ideal vocalists comprised church choirs. Then someone discovered the castrato, and the church had a third option.

For the next seventeen hundred years church fathers would openly deplore castration of boy sopranos but eagerly accept the singers into cathedrals and the Vatican chapel. Cardinals collected castrati for their private choirs and boasted of their possessions. Though poor families castrated singing sons for a fee from a bishop or cardinal, the standard explanation offered by church fathers was that the unfortunate lad was accidentally emasculated by a charging boar. "The pig did it" theory fooled no one, but it kept the practice thriving for centuries.

It would be misleading to blame the castrati phenomenon solely on the church's need for sopranos. The practice of castrating boys would reach its peak centuries later, due to two other vocal events: the development in the fifteenth century of an a cappella singing style that required a wider range of voices and a greater degree of virtuosity than a boy or a falsetto could muster, and, more significantly, the creation of opera at the end of that century.

Opera turned castrati into superstars. In fact, the phenomenon of a superstar in the field of entertainment, with a crazed and devoted following, originated with these emasculated men whose temperament and talent kept an audience worshipful.

First Superstars: Early 17th Century, Italy

Our word "opera" is an abbreviation of the Italian phrase *opera in musica* ("work in music") and today represents a form of theater consisting of a dramatic text or libretto ("little book") combined with singing and instrumental accompaniment. Though works in antiquity had combined poetic drama and music, thus prefiguring operatic development, the first true opera, composed by Jacopo Peri, was staged in Florence in 1597.

In 1599, Pope Clement VIII launched the castrati phenomenon with his pronouncement of the voice's "sweetness and flexibility."

Peri's *Dafne* did not feature castrati, but two years later, and a short distance away, the first male sopranos dazzled audiences in Rome. The castrati, two Italian men who as boys were supposedly goaded by pigs, were Pietro Paolo Folignato and Girolamo Rossini. That year, 1599, Pope Clement VIII heard each man sing at the Vatican and was much impressed with the "sweetness and flexibility" of their voices. Vatican records show that the pope, a lawyer-turned-priest who sharpened the severity of the Inquisition, immediately preferred the castrato voice to the "shrill and acidulous tones of the soprano falsettists" who were then singing in the Vatican chapel.

Clement was a popular and influential pope. Although as a cardinal he had been charged with nepotism (for making three favorite nephews cardinals, one age fourteen), as pope he won wide support for his strict orthodoxy and his banning of Jewish books. Thus when the highest authority in Christendom sanctioned emasculated men as singers, the phenomenon became vogue. The falsettos were out, and within twenty-five years all adult singers in the Vatican choir and most singers in major Italian cathedrals were castrati.

That is rapid progress, considering it takes several years for a castrated seven-year-old to mature into an adult soprano. Clement's favorable review clearly had sent knives aflailing throughout the countryside.

Meanwhile, opera's popularity had spread throughout Europe. Composers were writing for high and higher voices. For the first time in history a kind of international star-system arose. The stars were *divi* (Latin for male "gods"), emasculated men, whom audiences discussed, compared, and criticized in fashionable drawing rooms from Portugal to Russia.

Baldassare Ferri. The first star castrato was born in Perugia, Italy, in 1610. A tall, handsome young boy, Ferri possessed an extraordinary natural voice much appreciated by a wealthy, dilettantish cardinal named Crescenzi. At some time before the age of eleven, Ferri's parents consented to having him castrated. The details are unknown, but Cardinal Crescenzi appears to have convinced the family that the boy's future would be brightest as a soprano.

By all outward measures, it was. At eleven, Ferri moved in with Crescenzi

Caricature of a castrato singing at Naples's Sant' Onofrio Conservatory.

and lived lavishly on the cardinal's estate until he was fifteen, when he launched an enormously successful stage career. Women found his androgynous handsomeness irresistible, and he was feted in every city he sang in. On his way to Florence to appear in an opera of Monteverdi, the young Ferri, already a celebrity, was met three miles from the city gates by an adoring coterie of the town's most eminent men and women who escorted him to his lodgings.

The world had never heard a voice like Ferri's, and word of mouth spread rapidly.

Virtually every king or queen of a European or Asian capital begged the singer to give a royal performance. He sang for King Sigismund III of Poland, then Queen Christina of Sweden invited Ferri to Stockholm, though her country and Poland were at war. He consented, and an armistice was declared so that the singer could travel safely between lines of opposing armies, escorted by opposing troops. He arrived in Stockholm, war resumed, and Ferri sang nightly for two weeks. At age forty-five, he performed at the court of Vienna and was persuaded to stay there twenty years, amassing a fortune in fees and gifts.

Opera's first star castrato died in 1680, age seventy, worth the equivalent today of three million dollars, which he left to charity.

What did Ferri (or any good castrato) sound like?

An early critic wrote: "Their timbre is as clear and piercing as that of choirboys and much more powerful; they appear to sing an octave above the natural voice of women. Their voices . . . are brilliant, light, full of sparkle, very loud, and astound with a very wide range." In Italy, the center of opera, women were banned from the stage until the late eighteenth century and all female parts were taken by male sopranos (or occasionally by a woman *en transvesti,* though their popularity never equaled that of the castrati).

200-Year Fad. By the late 1600s, indigent parents were selling their most gifted young sons outright to church cardinals, singing teachers, and music schools. The slightest aptitude for singing could result in genital mutilation.

Thousands of Italian boys lost their gonads but never acquired the compensating fame and wealth of a star castrato. For there was no way to forecast which youthful voice would mature into a spectacular instrument. Yet parents eagerly sold a son into musical slavery as an investment, in the hope that he would return a profit as the most affluent singer of his generation. So that they could spend their dotage in comfort, if not extravagance.

The operation became standardized. Even humane. Too many promising choirboys had been lost to bungled testicular castration. By the late 1600s the surgery had been modified to minimize bleeding and infection. Drugged heavily with opium, the boy was immersed for a half-hour in a hot bath. When he was nearly insensate, his scrotum sufficiently slackened, a physician or barber would cut open the sack, tug down the testes, and sever the sperm-carrying ducts. It was a vasectomy, and being performed on a prepubescent boy, his small incompletely formed testicles soon shriveled and vanished.

Such a boy usually ended up in Naples, the training center for castrati. The most famous of the city's four conservatories was Sant' Onofrio, which began the practice of dressing student castrati in black, like priests. So many young boys were being castrated (or butchered and killed by poor surgery) that the Italian government and the church were forced by public opinion to take a stand. They condemned the practice, of course. The government made castration illegal, but often turned its back on practitioners; the church made castration punishable by excommunication, but welcomed its most talented mutilates with open arms.

The operations went underground, performed clandestinely, in even greater numbers, and more and more pigs were blamed for having run amok. A physician known to have castrated a youth typically claimed the boy's testes were diseased and removal saved his life.

By the middle of the eighteenth century, as many as two thousand boys in Italy alone were castrated annually. Seventy percent of all Italian singers were supposedly without testicles. Philosophers played apologist for the operation, coining a sophistic syllogism: Man was distinguished from animals by his voice; voice must be a faculty more precious than virility; therefore, if to embellish the voice required suppression of virility, it could be done without fear of impiety.

The operation remained illegal. A writer of the period attempted to learn the city in Italy that was turning out the most castrati. As he traveled from province to province, he met with frustration: "The operation is against law in all of these places," he wrote, "as well as against nature; and all Italians are so much ashamed of it, that in every province they transfer it to some other."

The castration capital of the country was Bologna. Though now it is known for its cuisine, in the eighteenth century it was the medical center of Italy. If parents wanted to entrust their prized child to the best surgeons, they traveled to Bologna's famous medical school. Doctors there became so adept at the operation, achieving such low mortality rates, that their services were in demand throughout Europe, rather like contemporary horse gelders.

With his seminal ducts severed, a boy typically studied at a conservatory until the age of eighteen, when he attempted a debut. Most failed to establish a career, for the opera-going public was already merciless in its expectations. The failures could not become fathers, so marriage was usually not an option. Even if a castrato found a willing woman (and most vocal castrati were heterosexual), the church forbade a nonprocreative marriage. Vatican records are replete with petitions from failed and famous castrati alike for dispensations to marry, but no request was granted. In addition, the Vatican would not accept a mutilated man into the priesthood (only into its choir).

Thus the church, which became the principal full-time employer of vocal castrati, also became their greatest adversary.

Swan Song.   What put an end to the phenomenon of the singing castrati was neither the illegality of the operation nor the church's ostensible opposition to testicular mutilation. Musical historians attribute the castrati's downfall to an abuse of the power they came to wield over composers.

At their pinnacle in the eighteenth century, castrati could make or break a new opera by either appearing in, or refusing to appear in, its debut. In addition to the control this gave them over composers, the singers also demanded flashy, audience-pleasing arias, and altered and embellished a score to suit their whims. It was as if today a popular actor forced a playwright to revamp his or her masterwork merely to be a better vehicle for the star. By the beginning of the nineteenth century, composers were simply tired of the tampering and the temperamental demands. And perhaps not a little jealous of a singer outshining a song.

Italian composer Gioacchino Rossini is said to have sung the burial service over the castrati in opera. In 1813 he composed *Aureliano in Palmira* for Giovanni Velluti, the greatest castrato of the day. Though the florid work was already tailored to show off its star, Velluti, claimed Rossini, vulgarized the music with endlessly tasteless vocal pyrotechnics. Rossini, also popular with audiences, swore never to allow another singer to depart from his written notes. Velluti threw a public tantrum and promised never to sing another Rossini score (though he did, for he was unable to resist the composer's music).

Rossini's contemporary, Giacomo Meyerbeer (the last composer to write for the male soprano voice), also took a firm stand on singers adhering to the written score. He composed *Il Crociato in Egitto* for Velluti but kept the castrato reined.

At the time, Wagner and Verdi were rapidly achieving fame, and they, even more than other composers, refused to tolerate musical tampering. Wagner was impressed with the force of the castrato voice and contemplated enticing one singer from Rome to play the part of Klingsor, willing to transpose the role, but he eventually abandoned the idea.

Also, female sopranos had gained greatly in popularity, relegating the male soprano to something of a freak. A new generation of opera goers came to view the male mutilated for the sake of art as a pathetic figure to be pitied, not praised. Thus after two centuries of adoration the castrati became an endangered species on the brink of extinction.

Castrati's downfall at the hands of Wagner (left), Verdi (center), and the rise of female superstars like soprano Jenny Lind.

Last Great Castrato: Giovanni Velluti, d. 1861, age 80

When the French invaded Italy in 1796, Giovanni Battista Velluti was a boy of
fifteen, already in possession of a glorious and celebrated voice. Napoleon heard
the young Velluti sing and exclaimed, "One must be only half a man to sing like
that!"

The general was more right than wrong for the singer had already lost his
testicles—not from a charging pig but from a surgeon's knife in a case that
today would be one of monumental malpractice.

Giovanni Velluti Senior of Montolmo (now Pausula), Italy, wanted a son. In
1780 when Giovanni Junior was born, the proud father forecast the child would
grow up to be a military hero. Though the boy's mother had had her heart set
on a girl, shortly after the birth she confided to a friend: "You ask whether I
would have been happier at the birth of a girl baby. Oh, yes! But in that case,
how could my husband have made her the valiant captain of whom he dreams?"
The family name, Velluti, is from *velluto,* Italian for "velvet," and the mother's
letter concluded with: "Just think that the other day, while admiring him, his
father exclaimed, 'This will be the first iron velvet!' "—meaning first military
member in the family.

How did a boy who was to embody his father's most manly aspirations end
up castrated? By mistake, conclude musical historians.

Around the age of eight the young Giovanni came down with a cough and
high, persistent fever. His exact ailment remains unknown, but the boy's health
was entrusted to a local physician, who, to better attend to the youth, had him
moved into his own home. At the time, castration was regarded as a cure for
hernia, mumps, and a broad grab bag of complaints. The Vellutis allowed the
doctor to treat their son at his own best medical discretion. Days later the lad
was carried home on a stretcher, his groin bandaged. The fever was gone and
so were his gonads. The shattered father made the best of a deplorable situation
and started the boy, who had already displayed a natural voice, with musical
training.

As a teenage castrato making his debut, Velluti sang a cantata and greatly
impressed Cardinal Luigi Chiaramonte, soon to become Pius VII (the pope who
would excommunicate Napoleon). The cardinal and the castrato became great
friends. The older man's praises and financial support propelled the boy's
career, and Velluti made his operatic debut at Forlì in 1800, the year his sponsor
was invested at Rome.

The two men remained on friendly terms, though sexuality was a thorny
issue between them. The pope was chaste; Velluti was anything but, his wild
escapades with women admirers publicized throughout Italy. The tall, handsome, nonimpregnating *spandone,* traveling through France, Italy, Germany,
and Russia, became the lover of countless women, including an Italian baroness
and a grand duchess, a relative of the czar. It was said that many husbands, not
understanding that the castrato still had functional genitalia, disbelieved that
their wives were involved in sexual affairs with the singer.

In 1849, the sixty-eight-year-old Velluti was retired and living in Venice when Austrian troops besieged the city. On his way to visit a local doctor for melancholia, the singer was arrested and imprisoned. In his cell, Velluti occupied himself singing an aria, which happened to be a favorite of the arresting officer, an opera lover. The officer boasted to the singer that his father had heard the great Velluti perform that piece, to which the singer announced, "I am the great Velluti." The two men talked opera into the night, and in the morning the prisoner was given a military escort back to his villa.

Velluti lived his remaining twelve years as such a recluse that his death in 1861 came as a shock to the public, who already thought he was dead, a legend from the distant past. Several Italian newspapers commented that Velluti was the last of the castrati. Last of the *great* castrati, but not the end of the breed.

Papal Holdouts.   Emasculated men continued singing for more than a half-century in only one place in the world: the Vatican chapel. This was an astonishing irony since in 1851 Pius IX (the epileptic pope who originated the doctrine of papal infallibility) promulgated a bull condemning the castration of young boys to turn them into sopranos. At the time, most of the Vatican choir consisted of castrati, and director of papal music was the celebrated castrato Domenico Mustafa. As long as the Vatican continued to employ the singers, freshly mutilated young men continued to appear and apply for openings. The Vatican condemned the castrations but ensconced the castrated.

The practice continued until the first decade of this century, when Pius X put a stop to the active recruitment of castrati for the Sistine Chapel. The Vatican continued to use the ones already employed, even claiming that several of them were not true castrati but falsettos with an unusually high range.

Public ridicule of existing castrati, and outrage at the idea of fresh mutilations, led many of the men to deny that they were without testicles. To fortify such claims, the church allowed many male sopranos to marry, providing them with medical certificates alleging intact genitalia. When Vatican kapellmeister Mustafa died in 1912, one male soprano remained: Allessandro Moreschi.

There is discussion to this day whether or not Moreschi was a castrato or an exceptionally gifted falsetto. Though the Vatican is skimpy on Moreschi's biographical material, he was as a youth regarded as a true castrato by the public and by his own admission, and testes are not regenerative organs. Papal authorities do not deny that Moreschi might have been castrated in the 1860s, before his teen years; they simply claim to this day that no one ever peeked under his cassock and examined him for the record.

Was Allessandro Moreschi a castrato? Probably. First, few men, and perhaps especially Italian men, boast of not having testes when indeed they do. More significantly, the majority of music historians are convinced that Moreschi was a castrato.

Not the greatest of his kind in terms of vocal strength and purity, Moreschi performed at the funerals of two of Italy's kings, Victor Emmanuel II and Umberto I, and retired from the stage in 1913 at age fifty-five. Between 1902 and 1903, he made ten gramophone records, on which he was given the title

"Soprano della Cappella Sistina." The poor recording quality of that day only
further diminishes whatever vocal brilliance he may have possessed at the time.
But his ten records are the only relic of a breed of man that is not likely to
reemerge.

Reassigned by the church as a possible falsetto, he lived at the Vatican,
singing and serving as director of papal music until his death in 1922 at the age
of sixty-four. (Suspiciously, his autopsy never explored that part of his anatomy
that could have cleared up the castrato-falsetto debate.) An era in music ended.

A final tribute to the art of the castrati, as well as an excellent description
of that unique voice, is provided by the nineteenth-century music critic Enrico
Panzacchi. Late in the 1800s, after listening enraptured to several of the Vatican's surviving male sopranos, Panzacchi wrote:

> What singing! Imagine a voice that combines the sweetness of the flute, and the
> animated suavity of the human larynx—a voice that leaps and leaps, lightly and
> spontaneously, like a lark that flies through the air and is intoxicated with its
> own flight; and when it seems that the voice has reached the loftiest peaks of
> altitude, it starts off again, leaping and leaping still with equal lightness and equal
> spontaneity, without the slightest sign of forcing or the faintest indication of
> artifice or effort; in a word, a voice that gives the immediate idea of sentiment
> transmuted into sound, and of the ascension of a soul into the infinite on the
> wings of that sentiment. What more can I say?

What more indeed.

Ritual Circumcision: Antiquity, Near and Middle East

A five-minute operation of dubious benefit, done within days of a child's birth
and without his consent, marks a male for life.

For doctors, circumcision is a highly profitable operation—it is America's
most common surgical procedure. For parents, to circumcise or not is a vexing
question, since medical evidence suggests that removal of the foreskin of the
penis has no clearcut health benefits. While the operation itself holds the
inherent risks of genital mutilation or castration.

The centuries-old ritual seems headed for extinction.

Today the American Academy of Pediatrics and the American College of
Obstetricians and Gynecologists state that routine circumcision is medically
unjustified. Parents apparently feel the same way. In 1979, sixty-eight percent
of newborn American boys were circumcised, but by 1985 (the most recent
year for which statistics are available), the figure was down to fifty-nine percent, with clear signs it would continue to drop.

The end to routine circumcision might well occur in this century. Our
uncircumcised grandsons may one day justifiably wonder why any loving parent
would ever have subjected a newborn to the pain and trauma of unanesthetized
surgery. In the previous chapter we looked at many bygone practices—all of

them useless and dangerous—that once were advocated medical procedures. There exists the real possibility that one day circumcision will go the way of those antiquated beliefs, performed only as a religious ritual, its original function in the first place.

How did a religious ritual confined to one part of the world become a routine medical procedure in many other regions?

Semitic Rite.   The word "circumcision" comes from the Latin for "cutting around," and the once exclusively Semitic ritual, though ancient, was not routine until recent times. In fact, a non-Jewish male born in the United States or Europe prior to 1900 would definitely *not* have been circumcised. It simply wasn't done.

Routine circumcision was adopted gradually, and as a result of two factors: the Victorian era's strictures against masturbation and the medical community's belief that that odious form of "self-pollution" could be restrained by removal of the foreskin. Nineteenth-century doctors convinced parents and preachers that the presence of a tight, gripping foreskin put a male in a state of almost perpetual arousal. The issue of cleanliness initially played no role in the matter.

The man who popularized the practice among non-Jews was the nineteenth-century British surgeon and pathologist, Sir Jonathan Hutchinson. A pioneer in the study of congenital syphilis, Hutchinson was an authority on eye and skin diseases, especially leprosy. Outside his specialty, he maintained masturbation to be a detriment to spiritual and mental health. Almost two decades before he was knighted in 1908, he published "On Circumcision as Preventative of Masturbation," which is generally accepted as the first position paper for routine modern infant circumcision. Thus the fundamental reason behind the practice in this century was not so much medical as religious. Circumcision arose in modern America and Europe as a deterrent to sin; only later did we affix to the surgery a health rationale.

Ironically, ancient peoples circumcised males to rejoice in their sexuality, not to shun it.

Early man believed that nothing good in life was free; a god or goddess had

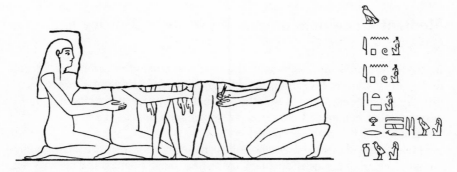

Circumcision began as a youth's fertility rite, the foreskin offered to the gods.

always to be paid for beneficence, present and future. A man's sexual prowess was viewed as a gift from the god of fertility, and to maintain virility he felt compelled to sacrifice a small part of the instrument of propagation, the smallest part possible. The excess skin at the tip of the penis seemed a fair payment.

Hence, ritual circumcision originated as a symbolic offering of the entire male member. Among all ancient societies that practiced the surgery, the excised foreskin was dedicated to the fertility deity and sacrificially burned. Egyptian writings and drawings from 5000 B.C. attest to this custom, as do primitive tribal practices in which boys were circumcised not at birth when they were sexually immature, but at the onset of puberty, or just prior to first intercourse. In Hebrew and Arabic the term for bridegroom, *chatan,* derived from the ancient expression "one who is circumcised." For centuries the practice belonged to the sacred initiation rites of manhood and marriage. Circumcision was the fee a man paid up front (so to speak) for lifelong reproductive license.

Why, then, circumcise a newborn? Who pushed the puberty rite back to infancy?

In addition to a coming-of-age ceremony, circumcision also served as a man's tribal mark of distinction. The cut of circumcision was a visible band that announced the loyalty of a man, identified him for life with his group, and for the Hebrews it became a covenant between man and God. It was such loyalty connotations that in time pushed the practice back to infancy. Semitic peoples began to label a newborn a member of their tribe and to forge his covenant with God soon after birth.

In Genesis (17:9–14), circumcision is established as a sacred obligation for Abraham and his descendants: "a token of the covenant betwixt me and you." To this day Jews refer to the circumcision initiation of a newborn into Judaism on the eighth day after his birth as *b'rith,* meaning "pact."

The lack of a foreskin became the indelible "signature" to a contract imprinted into the genital of every male. And circumcision also became a sign of divine protection by the Lord. Even among the ancient Hebrews, circumcision initially had nothing to do with health considerations. The uncircumcised penis was not thought of as a repository of diseases waiting to spread.

Medical Circumcision and Myth: 5th Century B.C., Greece

Myths, in time, began to surround the religious ritual of circumcision. In the first century, Philo of Alexandria taught that circumcision facilitated conception: "By the penis being circumcised, the seminal fluid proceeded in its path more easily, neither being at all scattered, nor flowing on its passage into what may be called the bags of the prepuce."

Philo asserted that peoples who enforced the practice were the most prolific on the face of the earth, destined to be the most populous. This was an understandably appealing doctrine for any group that wanted to rise up in station. In effect, Philo said, the circumcised will rule the world. Needless to say, Philo was himself circumcised, being a Greek-speaking Jew, the first philosopher to distinguish between the knowability of God's existence and the unknowability of his essence, issues foreshadowing Christian theology.

But not all Jews in Philo's time were proud of their penile signature. When Hellenistic Jews shared the gymnasia with their uncircumcised Greek friends, exercising in the nude, unavoidably flaunting their mark of distinction, they often became the butt of ridicule, flouted for being "de-manned." Still worse was the charge that they seemed to have constant semierections, the result of a tight circumcision.

Many Jews underwent the unpleasantness of reconstruction therapy to restore genital foreskin. The procedure was known as "stretching," in which the residue of foreskin was forcibly pulled up over the glans penis and tied. The treatment was repeated until there was sufficient stretched skin to conceal the "seal of Abraham."

Health considerations, though, had already entered the picture. Herodotus, the fifth-century B.C. Greek historian, wrote that circumcision could prevent penile infections and supplant the need for regular washings. By the time of Christ's birth, the practice was suggested for both religious and hygienic reasons. Christ, being a Jew, was circumcised on the eighth day after his birth, which for the church later became the January first Feast of the Circumcision. For centuries a dried ring of skin alleged to be Christ's "holy prepuce" was venerated as a sacred relic in at least a dozen churches throughout Europe. Pastors used their relic (no one questioned the authenticity of so much foreskin from one infant) to bestow fertility on barren parishioners and to lessen the pain of childbirth.

Circumcision Threatens the Spread of Christianity. In its early days, Christianity was forced to abandon circumcision (or at least make it optional), and for purely practical reasons. The new religion was eager to convert the pagan world. The majority of pagan men shuddered at the thought of painful foreskin surgery as a prerequisite to becoming a Christian. To non-Semitic peoples, the practice was foreign and repugnant, as well as agonizing and dangerous; as it was, particularly for an adult in an age that lacked anesthetics and antiseptics. In short, the required religious ritual was holding back the spread of the new religion.

It was St. Paul who realized the magnitude of the problem and proposed a solution. After his dramatic conversion to Christianity, he began a series of missionary journeys throughout Asia Minor and Greece. He witnessed first-hand grown men's fear of circumcision and realized a compromise had to be struck. By letter, he maintained contact with the major Christian churches, and in his Epistle to the Romans (2:28–29) he finally lifted the need for converts to be circumcised. All that was required, he wrote, was a circumcision "of the heart, in the spirit, and not in the letter." In A.D. 50 the Apostolic Council ruled that Gentile proselytes could retain their foreskins.

With circumcision out, baptism achieved new cachet. Several early church fathers argued that baptism for Christians was the precise equivalent covenant with God as circumcision was for Jews. Thus for almost two thousand years Christian men throughout the Western world were routinely baptized but not routinely circumcised, if cut at all.

It was Victorian doctors, as mentioned, who reinstituted the neonatal ritual. But even before publication of Sir Jonathan Hutchinson's 1891 seminal paper on the subject, more and more foreskins were being cut each year. Whereas British doctors in the reign of Queen Victoria performed the surgery to thwart masturbation, their counterparts under Elizabeth I had strongly recommended it to parents for another mistaken reason. The medical profession in the sixteenth and seventeenth centuries believed that a loss of semen weakened a man's mind and body.

The life-creating fluid was to be withheld as much as possible, to be reabsorbed into the body as a rejuvenating agent. Moderate copulation in marriage was permissible in that it perpetuated life through offspring. Masturbation was more self-destructive than alcohol intemperance. In a nutshell: Each ejaculate brought a man one step closer to senility and death. A physician of the period, commenting on two patients who found the practice impossible to break, reported to professional colleagues: "One of the two men who indulged in excessive masturbation became insane; the other dried out his brain so prodigiously that it could be heard rattling in his skull."

The same physician then laid down the full spectrum of physical evils of self-abuse: "The effects range from impotence to epilepsy, and include consumption, blindness, imbecility, insanity, rheumatism, gonorrhea, priapism (painful continuous erection due to disease), tumors, constipation, hemorrhoids, female homosexuality, and finally the shameful habit leads to death." That prognosis fit neatly with the morality of America's founding fathers.

Circumcision in America: 17th Century to Present

That American Indians were not circumcised, and were viewed as savages, was one impetus for the early Puritans favoring the ritual. It made them different, civilized, European. But dread of sexual self-abuse played an even larger role.

A wit once described puritanism as "the haunting fear that someone, somewhere might be having a good time." The Puritans of the seventeenth century were not the unmitigated prudes historians once thought them to be, but they did harbor an obsessive fear of masturbation, rooted in part in European medical misconceptions. Barbaric methods were often employed to stop a boy's self-abuse. A commentator of the time wrote, "Some doctors recommend covering the penis with plaster of Paris, or leather, or making the lad wear a chastity belt or spiked rings."

Consequently, when seventeenth-century doctors began to suggest that circumcision "lessened erotic self-stimulation," parents offered up newborn males without guilt. After Hutchinson's paper was printed in America, parents begged physicians to circumcise their infant sons. There are many accounts from the 1890s of adult males willingly submitting to the surgery in the hope of breaking themselves of the habit of masturbation. And there are testimonials to the effectiveness of the operation.

Indeed, the foreskin itself came to be seen as a direct health threat. A standard American medical textbook of the early 1900s claimed that the ring of skin leads to "nocturnal incontinence, hysteria, epilepsy, and feeble-mindedness."

Enlightenment did not come quickly. In the 1940 edition of another standard text on pediatrics, Holt's *Diseases of Infancy and Childhood,* masturbation is presented as "medically harmful" and the preventative is "circumcision in boys." The editors did, however, expunge the recommendation in an earlier edition of "mechanical restraint and corporal punishment in the very young." The same text goes so far as to "advocate female circumcision, cauterization of the clitoris, and even blistering of the vulva and prepuce for recalcitrant female masturbators." This is what American pediatricians were learning as recently as World War II.

The practice of routine male circumcision went hand in hand with another twentieth-century phenomenon: hospitalization for childbirth. In 1900 less than five percent of American women delivered in hospitals; by 1920 the figure stood at forty percent, and a decade later it was up to seventy-five percent. For the first time in history, the majority of infants were not being born at home. With the new mother recovering from delivery at one end of a hospital and the father isolated in the waiting room, parents often had little say about and even less awareness of what was being done to their newborn son. The infant was given to the mother already cut, and she assumed that that was standard procedure, surgery performed in the best interest of her baby. Few questions were asked in an era when doctors were revered without reserve.

It is no coincidence that the circumcision of male infants became routine and widespread during the period when nearly all births took place in hospitals. Whether the fact that doctors charged for the surgery (which now runs about $125) influenced their belief in its benefits is always open to debate and may never be thoroughly discredited.

Today circumcision is an elective procedure. A recent study concluded that uncircumcised infants and adult males run a slightly higher risk of urinary-tract infections if the area under the foreskin is not cleaned regularly. A 1988 report suggested the spread of AIDS among heterosexuals in Africa might be due to penile skin lesions beneath foreskins. But proper hygiene seems to place cut and uncut males in the same risk categories for all infections and sexually transmitted diseases.

If the operation is abandoned by the medical profession, only Jewish males will be circumcised. And the reason for the surgery will be an ancient one: the religious belief that circumcision marks a man and serves as a "signature" to the covenant between that man and his God. Circumcision would revert to being purely a religious ritual, its original intent more than two thousand years ago.

CHAPTER 13

Past Sex Practices—Hers

Sacred Prostitution to Chastity Belt

Female Circumcision: 2000 B.C., Near East

Most people are unaware that a female can be circumcised. The butchery exists and is called a clitoridectomy—for the excision of the clitoris, and often the labia minora. It is far more mutilating to the genitals than male circumcision, and mitigating to orgasm. In fact, they are two reasons for its use.

The origins of female circumcision are less clearly understood than those of the counterpart male surgery. One theory holds that it arose to disfigure the genitalia of a wife to diminish her appeal to other men; another maintains that the excised tissue was a fertility offering to ensure a bounty of offspring, the original purpose of male circumcision.

As a religious ritual it was performed by many ancient peoples, including the Egyptians, Malayans, Peruvian Indians, and virtually all Semitic peoples.

Evidence for the practice in the Near East dates from about four thousand years ago. Abraham, first of the Hebrew patriarchs—father of Judaism, Christianity, and Islam—played an early role in the custom. One Muslim tradition holds that God commanded Abraham, living in the Mesopotamian city of Ur, to cut out the clitoris of his barren wife, Sarah, at the time he lost his own prepuce. As the prototypical faithful servant, whose "seed" was to inherit the land, Abraham obeyed the Lord and at age one hundred successfully fertilized his wife, who bore him Isaac.

Another Arab legend alleges that it was Sarah who introduced female circumcision in a fit of pique. During her barren years, she was jealous of her

South Pacific virgins circumcised as puberty fertility rite.

husband's affair with her maidservant and rival, Hagar. When the concubine bore Abraham a son, Ishmael, Sarah, in a rage, is said to have grotesquely disfigured the girl's genitals. She cut out the clitoris and removed the outer labia majora, as well as the mucous membranes of the inner labia minora. The same mutilation was then supposedly forced on Egyptian women at puberty to lessen their appeal to the opposite sex and to eliminate a primary source of arousal, for even ancient peoples recognized the clitoris as a center of sexual excitation.

Apart from such legends, historians maintain that the practice of cutting away some part of the female genitalia and burning it evolved as an imitation of the male rite and a symbol that a girl had sexually come of age.

In most practicing cultures, a girl was circumcised in preparation for her first coitus, with the surgery part of a general defloration that included the rupturing of the hymen. The skin and collected blood were then offered to the tribe's fertility deity. Depending on the peoples, the surgery was carried out by a priest, a male relative, or, most often, an elder woman. The adolescent girl, held down by men, screamed and struggled frantically, making the outcome of the operation often haphazard and not infrequently fatal.

The husband could benefit from the surgery. Cutting of the labia minora at the entrance of the vagina formed scar tissue on healing, which constricted the opening and enhanced his sexual pleasure. But the same scar tissue presented a problem at the time of childbirth. The wife underwent a second operation to make the vagina large enough for delivery. Then after the birth she had further surgery to retighten the opening—all this with no anesthetics or antiseptics. This brutal succession of procedures was routine among tribes in Peru, Australia, and throughout parts of Africa.

In Arab countries, prostitutes also had their vaginas periodically tightened by surgical mutilation to increase their value on the market as "fresh women." This, after the clitoris had been removed to diminish sexual arousal.

Modern Clitoridectomy: Pre–19th Century, Middle East and England

In the Middle East, female circumcision has had the longest and most bizarre tradition.

The male-prescribed operation was a necessary part of a woman's social status, a prerequisite for marital intercourse and a simple duty for female decency. No Arab man would wed a woman unless she had been "purified and made ready" by vaginal surgery. And among the greatest insults a boy or girl could receive was to be called "child of an uncircumcised mother." A woman not cut at puberty was shunned as unclean and unfit to marry. Attempts by Western physicians in the nineteenth century to stop the mutilation met with failure, since uncircumcised women could not find husbands. The operation continued into the early years of this century; it continues to this day in North Africa.

In the Islamic world, where a woman could be put to death for adultery, radical circumcision served another purpose. The surgery, performed early in a girl's life, consisted of a clitoridectomy (to suppress arousal) and an infibulation (from the Latin *fibula,* "safety pin"), which partially closed the vaginal entrance, forming what was called "a chastity belt forged by her own flesh." Physically unable to engage in intercourse—her virginity thus assured—the girl was "opened" at the time of marriage to receive her husband. The operation became a necessity for a woman's own protection; an "opened" girl had only her word to offer against a sexual allegation. Girls most tightly closed in the years prior to marriage were most highly sought for their guarantee of purity.

The clitoridectomy was one of the passing fads of Victorian gynecology, a supposed cure for nymphomaniacs and overly responsive wives.

An even more dangerous procedure was the ovariectomy, or removal of the ovaries, which persisted into the late 1800s. Many Victorian doctors considered the ovaries the seat of the feminine personality and prescribed their removal as treatment for everything from irritability to insanity, including, as one text stated, "simple cussedness" and "eating like a plowman."

The American pioneer of the ovariectomy in the 1870s was Dr. Robert Battey, an ambitious surgeon from Rome, Georgia. Battey and his colleagues excised more than 2,000 sets of ovaries and displayed them at medical society meetings. Battey guaranteed husbands that they would find their postoperative wives "tractable, orderly, industrious, and cleanly." By 1906 an estimated 150,000 American women had had their ovaries needlessly removed.

Ignorance of Female Sexuality. As recently as the 1950s, in America and England, there were attempts to institute a modified form of female circumcision. Arguments for removal of the prepuce, or hood of the clitoris, ranged from alleged health and hygiene benefits to even more dubious sexual considerations. A 1936 article in a leading medical journal suggested that women more passionate than their husbands undergo circumcision to reduce sex drive. A respectable wife was not supposed to enjoy intercourse, and if she were honest enough (or foolish enough) to admit she did, mild mutilation was the solution.

Until recently, most doctors were male and conflicting medical opinion on female circumcision showed men's ignorance of women's sexuality. In 1958 one journal article advocated the removal of the prepuce to *decrease* arousal and stop masturbation, whereas another paper suggested the same procedure for nonorgasmic wives to *increase* arousal and guarantee a sexual climax.

During the same decade a gynecologist recommended a woman undergo circumcision to expose the glans clitoris if her husband is "awkward or difficult to educate," since "the clitoris is quite small and difficult to contact" and surgery would "make it easier for the loving husband to find."

In the historical literature of sexuality, there is scant explanation why female circumcision was never practiced as universally as the male surgery. Two reasons are most frequently offered: Among many peoples women were too unimportant to warrant a special ritual, and in societies where the ritual was practiced, too many women died because the highly vascular nature of female genitalia tissue, as compared with the male foreskin, resulted in fatal hemorrhaging and infection.

One reads through the history of female sexuality with the uncomfortable certainty that the male authors most often wrote out of ignorance, wishful thinking, and dread of psychological emasculation. Women's liberation and women doctors have done much to clear up confusion and do away with dubious surgical procedures.

Marriage-Bed Virginity: Antiquity to Present

Virginity sounds like a straightforward, unambiguous term; you are a virgin or you aren't. But linguistically and ethnographically the word is fraught with confusion.

In many cultures, an unmarried woman remains a virgin even if she is a prostitute; only through marriage does she forfeit her virginity. In other parts of the world, a married woman without children is a virgin; loss of virginity arrives with her first birth. Among some peoples who superstitiously fear the "blood of the first night," a man will marry a woman only after her hymen is ruptured through intercourse with a stranger, her virginity then even "purer."

In the West we have none of these latitudes. But if the above definitions of virginity sound amusing or absurd to us, our own restricted use of the word might draw a wry smile or disapproving frown from people in other cultures. Technically, a woman in Western society remains a virgin until she has vaginal intercourse; any number of oral or anal encounters, with any number of men, does not deflower her, though it can spoil her image.

By all measures, the virgin is an endangered species, and in some high schools extinct. According to recent statistics, fifty-six percent of American high school girls admit to being sexually active (the figure is substantially higher for boys). In an era when bumper stickers and lapel buttons display the prurient legend "Virginity Is Curable" and couples live together before exchanging vows, one must wonder if the centuries-old concept of marriage-bed virginity is not nearing its end. A poll in a leading women's magazine showed that even today's faithful wife, who never bedded a man other than her husband, was most likely not a virgin on her wedding day. Once virginity was lost *in* marriage.

Virgin Power.   The concept of virginity is ancient. It is integral to history, war, myth, and legend, and often in the most unsuspecting ways. The sun-bleached bones of virgins, for instance, were indispensable in Europe's medieval building trades, as desirable as bricks and cement. A virgin's thighbone or elbow mixed with mortar when erecting a fortress supposedly protected it from falling into the hands of enemies. And if a fortified castle fell, it meant the bones had not belonged to a virgin.

This superstition is the origin of the nursery rhyme about London Bridge. When the first version of the bridge was constructed late in the twelfth century, the skeletal remains of a child virgin ("my fair lady" of the rhyme) were incorporated into the pilings. The superstition then was that water gods did not take kindly to humans spanning and trampling across their domain and had to be appeased with the bones of a virgin—and one who did not die a violent death. The rumor that London Bridge was falling got started when it became known that the virgin had not died the natural death her parents alleged, but that she plummeted from a turret window of her family's weekend castle, pushed by unseen hands.

Virginity in a child, of course, is expected. The first time in history that we read of a mystique attached to an adult female with an intact hymen is in ancient mythology. Though the virgin goddess of different legends goes by countless names, her story is essentially the same: Suppressed sexuality imbues her with magical powers that can win wars, protect forts, fertilize crops, and fructify marriages.

The Egyptians and Greeks believed that a young virgin could rejuvenate an aging man, and not in the way we might imagine today. In ancient times, the

Superstition: Sleeping beside a virgin rejuvenates a man; a virgin's bones protect a bridge from collapse.

young girl and elderly man bedded down for the night, not for intercourse but for a "spiritual transference" of youth that occurred through stillness, proximity, and sleep. The couple was warned to avoid intercourse, which supposedly had an enervating effect. The biblical King David took this prescription to regain vanished strength; he was provided with "a young virgin" who could "cherish him" so "that my lord the king may get heat" (1 Kings 1:2). If indeed in the morning an old man arose with newfound vigor after a sexless night near a cherishing virgin, it was more likely a display of pent-up frustration that kept him active for days.

Virginity was also thought to serve as a potent satanic repellent. It was needed in abundance at a wedding, when demonic powers most forcefully threatened a bride. The unmarried bridesmaids and procession of child flower girls existed not to toss petals and pick up a train, but so that their combined virginity would keep the devil from the service. Thus the bride's court was originally a supernatural defense against evil.

Virgin Travails. The alleged special powers of virgins also caused them much suffering, as when sacrificed as the best offering man could make to a god.

In the Americas, this was done most frequently by the Indians of the Yucatán at the Sacred Well of Sacrifice at Chichén Itzá. Following a solemn ceremony, scores of beautiful teenage virgins were cast into the well. They gratefully accepted their fate, regarding the act a high honor, since at the bottom of the well resided the rain god and his magnificent palace, where they would dwell forever.

The virgins' responsibility for the wealth and well-being of their people was burdensome. They were sacrificed to ward off catastrophe, and if disaster struck, they were slain in greater numbers for the miscalculation.

In Rome, six of the twenty virgins who served at the Temple of Vesta were custodians of the building's sacred fire. Virginity was believed to be the force that kept alive the fire, and for a sexual indiscretion an ex-virgin was severely punished.

Plutarch, the first-century historian, gives a detailed account of the treatment of a vestal virgin who broke her vow of chastity and jeopardized the eternal flame: "No spectacle was more horrible, nor any day which Rome spends in deeper gloom." Arms and legs bound, the guilty vestal was placed in a litter that was securely wrapped "so that not a sound could be heard from within." Carried through the Forum amid throngs of spectators, she arrived at the site of her live entombment, an ominous swell in the earth known as the agger.

The actual tomb was as an underground chamber reached by a ladder. It was furnished with a bed, a burning oil lamp, a knife, and a provision of food and water. Sealed in, she contemplated a quick blood death, or a slow but equally inevitable end. Her punishment was not so much in dying, but in the agonizing choice of the means and time.

Dread of venereal disease also put a premium on virgin brides, though not for the obvious, medically valid reason. A medieval superstition maintained that any of a man's genital diseases (lumped together then as the "pox") could be cured by intercourse with a chaste girl, and without infecting her. This was virginity as therapy, which cured no one and contaminated every girl involved.

Bloodied Sheets. Public proof of a bride's virginity was routinely demanded in earlier times. Elder women of the tribe poked and probed to examine a girl internally. And the morning after the consummation of marriage, the blood-stained bed sheet was hung out for relatives and neighbors to witness.

The variations on this bygone practice are numerous and suspiciously voyeuristic. In some cultures wedding guests lingered while the couple copulated in a nearby bed, then they inspected the sheets as well as the bridal garments. Elsewhere, to eliminate the fraud of a sheet deliberately stained with animal blood, relatives insisted on witnessing the act of defloration. Fraudulent chastity was severely punished. In Deuteronomy, biblical law ordained that a bride who deceived her husband was to be stoned to death.

Surrogate Defloration: 600 B.C., Greece, to 19th Century

Today a bride might arrive at the altar deflowered—by her husband-to-be, by a past boyfriend, or as the result of a one-night stand. But there was a time when a prospective bridegroom requested that a stranger undertake that task, for the "blood of the first night" was surrounded by superstition.

In many parts of Africa, especially among tribes in Uganda, a king would be insulted if offered a virgin as a bride whose hymen was not ruptured. She was, by law, deflowered by proxy. Technically this did not sully her virginity; it made it even purer.

In ancient Greece, the proxy was not always a man; a statue of a male with an erection sufficed. A young Greek girl of marrying age and belonging to the aristocratic class ceremonially had her hymen pierced by the stone penis of the god Priapus, the embodiment of male procreative power. The deflowered virgin was then fit for marriage and guaranteed progeny since her first "lover" was Priapus himself.

In an era when phallic worship was commonplace, when statues and effigies sported erect members, it is not surprising to find numerous ceremonies in which virgins and childless women employed dildos (from the Latin *dilatare*, "to open wide") for sacred reasons.

In Rome, the wooden penis of the fertility deity Liber deflowered brides-to-be. On March 17, his feast day, a six-foot-high wooden phallus was mounted on a wagon and drawn through city streets as part of the Liberalia celebration. Crowds followed the phallus, and a virgin, selected by high priests, crowned the effigy with a wreath. St. Augustine witnessed one such procession of "this disgraceful effigy" but could not dissuade the Romans from a form of worship he viewed as immoral and depraved.

A deflowered Roman virgin might enhance her fertility before marriage by eating certain phallic foods. These were not oysters or olives, but breads called *coliphila* and *siligone* and shaped in the form of female and male genitalia.

In Germany, there existed equivalent fertility foods for brides-to-be and for barren wives. The *mandelcher* was an almond cookie topped with two blanched nuts to represent testicles. The *liebesknochen* ("bone of love") was a cream-filled eclair of unmistakable symbolism, while the *vielliebchen* ("much-little-love") was a cake made of two almonds resting on an elongated pastry shell. These were not ribald novelties, but earnest folk remedies for fertility.

In southern France, phallic worship by betrothed girls and barren wives took place at the shrine of St. Foutin, the first bishop of Lyons at Embrun. Centuries later, in 1585, when Protestants captured the town and destroyed the local church, they discovered several statues of the genitally tumescent saint. The tips of the penises were colored red, which generated much debate as to how they became stained. The official church explanation holds that the worshiping women poured red wine over the erect organs, then drank it to promote fertility. The other likelihood, of course, is that the statues were employed as Greek girls had once used the organs of Priapus.

Today no tourist to the Greek isle of Delos can miss the row of erect stone penises and accompanying testes at the entrance to what was once a sacred temple to phallus worship. Though many have their tips broken off, others are intact and measure up to four feet in length.

Hymen as Hymn.   Deflowering a virgin meant rupturing the hymen; a word cloaked in mystery, a flap of skin of questionable function.

The membrane has been compared with the appendix as a vestigial organ that over time lost its usefulness. It's believed that at an earlier stage of evolution rudimentary intercourse may have been practiced in childhood, much the way a juvenile animal mimics later adult copulatory behavior. If so, the hymen, or maidenhead, partially closing the vaginal orifice, may have served as a functioning tissue to grip the boy's small, immature organ.

The origin of the word "hymen" is less speculative. Hymen was the Greek god of marriage, and the word spelled with a lowercase *h* meant "membrane" to Greek physicians. Etymologists suspect that our prayerful word "hymn" might circuitously derive from a Greek custom in which a man on his wedding day sang hymeneal songs to the marriage god. And the new husband, on first entering his bride, invoked the god's assistance and blessing with the wedding cry, "Hymen, O Hymenaeus!" Other authorities suggest that "hymen" might derive from a Sanskrit word for "suture."

The practice of artificial defloration before marriage continued longest among African tribes. This "first step" toward marriage was fraught with peril, since hymenal blood was viewed as an evil discharge. The task of rupturing the membrane with a phalliclike artifact (or the real thing) was relegated to the most pious person in the tribe, or, at the other extreme, to a stranger who was paid for his services. The fact that the deflowering person was either religious or disinterested (in a social sense, that is) made him invulnerable to contamination and demonic possession. The artificial phalluses were made of metal, stone, or ivory and frequently decorated with the fertility god's image.

This kind of defloration, as mentioned, did not rob a girl of her prized virginity, but made it an even purer offering to her husband. But what began as a superstitious rite evolved into a much abused practice that came to be known to medieval feudal lords in Europe, and white plantation owners in the American South, as the "right of the first night."

Right of the First Night: 3000 B.C., Sumer, to 19th Century

The privilege, always a male prerogative, went by several names: *jus primae noctis* to the Romans of antiquity; *droit de seigneur* for the French in feudal Europe; and "the master's obligation," the euphemism used by a Southern white plantation owner who explained that it was his duty to sleep with a young black bride on the night of her wedding. Though the right of the first night may seem like a transparent scrim for lust (as it later clearly was), its roots predate the Romans and are entangled in religious superstition of the Sumerians.

The Sumerian people inhabited the fertile valley between the Tigris and Euphrates rivers about five thousand years ago. Civilization's first true innovators, they gave humankind cuneiform writing; the concepts of grammar school and high school, along with teachers, principals, and a head disciplinarian called "man with whip"; the first pharmacopoeia; the first farmer's almanac; the first bicameral congress; and history's first literary epic, *Tales of Gilgamesh*. It is in this epic, a five-cycle tale about the Mesopotamian King Gilgamesh, half human and half divine, who searches for immortality, that we find mention of the right of the first night.

It is already a controversial practice.

The epic refers to the annoyance of the people of Uruk that their king clings

Right of the first night: Bridegroom pays to have his new wife deflowered by feudal lord.

stubbornly to the ancient custom that he sleep with every new bride in the realm. Husbands in Uruk express silent outrage but submit to the king's divine right. It is in the expression divine right that historians find the origin of the unpopular custom, which was not always scorned.

The Sumerian people also gave the Western world the concept of kingship and divine right. In 3000 B.C., religion was at the hub of Sumerian life and priests wielded supreme authority over the city-state. As God's avatar on earth, a priest embodied divine power over harvests and human fertility; for a bride to spend the first night of her married life in the arms of the earthly incarnation of the fertility god guaranteed her copious offspring.

But when invaders began regularly to attack Sumer, priests could offer no defense, and the position of king was created, a man to oversee armies and wars. In time, kings usurped much of the authority of priests, including earthly divinity and the accompanying right of the first night. In short: Priests became celibate, kings promiscuous, and by the time of the writing of the Gilgamesh epic bridegrooms wanted to deflower their own brides.

Kings, though, don't give paybacks, certainly not to commoners, and the custom of the right of the first night transferred from the Sumerians to the Babylonians, who adapted *Tales of Gilgamesh* to their own prose style.

Ritual to Rape. If Mesopotamian kings had a good thing going for them, ancient Roman chieftains had it still better. They argued, disingenuously, that *jus primae noctis* was in no way an abuse of their despotic power, nor was it pleasurable. To deflower virgin after virgin, night after night, was an exhausting task they were willing to perform to ensure communal fertility. With further effrontery, to prove they did not enjoy the mandatory sex, they charged every new bridegroom a fee for deflowering his bride. And a man who could not afford the price was forbidden to marry. (More than a thousand years later Buddhist priests would adopt the same deflowering practices.)

As the population of Rome expanded, not even a priapic ruler could personally fulfill *jus primae noctis*. Thus arose the use of artificial phalluses. Prior to consummating marriage with her husband, a bride ceremoniously straddled a stone statue of a fertility god, lowering herself onto his effigy.

This was not a private ritual, but part of the public wedding ceremony, so that all guests could witness the bloodied evidence of virginity as well as the girl's avowal to be fruitful and multiply. Using the real penis of a king or the stone member of a statue, the right of the first night was also practiced by the Chinese, Kurds, and Muslims.

The practice continued in Europe, on and off, up until feudal times when it became an egregious case of sexual abuse. Lord only by title, possessing no traditional divine right, the feudal nobleman instituted the practice on his estate with little pretense that he was fructifying the race or ensuring a good harvest. He called *droit de seigneur* a duty, but reserved the right to waive in some cases this "lordly privilege" (they were no doubt considered unattractive by the lord), leaving the task to the women's husbands. The rejected brides-to-be may well have been relieved, while any bride invited into the master's bed could not decline.

Even less pretense surrounded the right of the first night in the American South. Plantation lords owned slaves as property. And the comely black daughter of a slave family could end up in the master's bed on the first night, second night, or any night or day he fancied her. As coercion without the cloak of tradition or ritual, the plantation practice does not qualify as a true example of the right of the first night, a practice that really ended centuries ago when a high priest no longer could claim divinity and direct descent from a fertility god. Since then, all else under the guise of the right of the first night has been rape.

Sacred Prostitution: Antiquity to Christian Era, East and West

Even in countries where prostitution is legal today, its practitioners are not considered sacred or holy. Yet such women were once personages of high station—priestesses who ran religions, not razed them through scandal.

How did the woman of yore go from a sacred prostitute to a street whore?

Sex is not what it used to be: When prostitutes were sacred, brothels were in temples; sex was a sacrament and intercourse was holy communion with the gods. Prostitutes were married to divinity (as nuns are now), and paid-for coitus was a pious act that put a man *in* a state of grace, not out of it. Then a prostitute's nightly fees were turned over to a priest, not a pimp, used for the maintenance of the temple-cum-brothel and to provided for her well-being.

Sacred prostitution was widespread and popular, as one might imagine. And it was profitable, indulged in throughout the Middle East, Near East, and in Greece and Rome. Greek soldiers returning from battle would scale the scraggy bluffs outside of Corinth to reach the summit temple-brothel of Aphrodite. The beleaguered men would stay several days and pay the sacred women in gold and gems, the spoils of war. Ostensibly they sought spiritual rejuvenation after months on a battlefield.

The cynical among us (or the envious) might be inclined to view all this as a flimsy ruse, a male's rationalization for sexual license. And maybe it was, to a degree. But in ancient times religion was ineluctably entwined with every aspect of life; all actions had sacred underpinnings. Early states were theocracies.

Also: A major concern throughout the ancient world was fertility. It was an obsession. Today we are overpopulated, straining the earth's resources; machine power has usurped manpower. But at the time civilization began, communities were small, laborers few, extinction a low birth rate away. When we today abort babies and pop pills to prevent conception, it is hard to imagine a time when fecundity was an issue of survival of the species. Little wonder that all early societies were preoccupied with fertility rites, mother goddesses, and bacchanalia that paired teenage men and women by lottery. Religion not only encouraged sex, sex cults were religions.

Four thousand years ago the Sumerians and Babylonians honored their harlots. In the second millennium B.C. of Hammurabi, women from the best families sought positions as temple prostitutes. In *Sex in History,* popular historian Reay Tannahill concludes that sacred prostitution "had its origin in fertility rituals" and that "the sacred prostitutes' earnings accounted for a substantial part of the temples' income." In other words, sex supported religion.

The Babylonians classified sacred prostitutes into three groups. The *qadishtu* was a full-time temple harlot; the *ishtaritu* was a servant of the goddess Ishtar and cohabited only with nobility; and the *harimtu* (the word is related to "harem") was the semisecular prostitute who, once married, could no longer work at her profession. A girl's parents usually determined her future as wife or prostitute.

The Bible records how the Canaanites and their neighboring tribes worshiped idols through sacred prostitution. For at least two thousand years the people of Canaan engaged in sacred prostitution, which the first Semites to the region, the Amorites, found irresistible. Even the later Israelite conquerors were strongly attracted by the holy prostitute system of worship and, against their own leaders' vehement opposition, converted to the ancient sex cult.

"It is significant to note," writes a contemporary biblical scholar, "that the Bible's protest against prostitution proscribed its practice not so much for its immorality as for its idolatry." He concludes: "Prostitution persisted among the Hebrews for many generations and it was occasionally even pursued in the Temple itself. . . . Only the most stringent measures eventually abolished the cult." Not surprisingly, the ancient Hebrew biblical word for prostitute (derived from the Babylonian), *k'deshah,* relates to "holiness" and "consecration."

Decline of the Sacred Harlot.   Time corrupts custom. A thousand years after Hammurabi, the Greeks had turned sacred prostitution into a one-time chore for a housewife. "Every woman who is a native of the country," wrote historian Herodotus, "must once in her life go and sit in the temple and there give herself to a strange man. . . . She is not allowed to go home until a man has thrown a silver coin into her lap and taken her outside to lie with him."

A Greek woman could not select her one-time mate: "She must go with the first man who throws her the money. When she has lain with him, her duty to the goddess is discharged and she may go home."

This was token prostitution, at a pedestrian level, and it could be cruel. "Tall, handsome women quickly manage to get home," says Herodotus. "But the ugly ones stay a long time before they can fulfill the condition which the law demands, some of them, indeed, as much as three or four years."

Sacred prostitution was strongly weakened by the compilers of the Old Testament, and done in by the later rise of Christianity.

The biblical language that condemns prostitution is at times racy, and the Book of Ezekiel uses harlotry as a synonym for the sins of Jerusalem. Damned women are pictured "lying in wait at every corner," they solicit a man by "capturing him with their eyelids," then hold him in their beds "until the morning." She "doted upon her paramours," men "whose members [penises] were like those of asses, and whose issue [ejaculate] was like that of horses," and the Lord assures that her "harlotry shall be uncovered" and that she will suffer in hatred.

And so, after two thousand years, the sacred prostitute was pushed out of the temple and onto the street. Communion with her no longer linked a man directly with divinity, though an ecstasy still went with the experience. She kept her money for herself, and churches made up the deficit by selling other things, like indulgences. She became a despised woman of low, disreputable standing, socially ostracized, though not entirely unpopular. In time she became a professional. And in many countries her profession became legal.

Though one can safely write that sacred prostitution has ended, no writer will probably ever record the end of prostitution itself. The end is certainly not coming in an era when top politicians and major television ministers pay women for sexual favors. Indeed, at times it seems that it would be easier, and politically safer, if the prostitute were sacred, her profession holy, her fees taxed, and her house of operation if not a temple then not a motel either.

Women as Second-Class Human Beings: Antiquity to Women's Liberation

Women never had it easy at the hands of philosophers and theologians. Although the view of them as temptresses, sinners, necessary evils, and second-class citizens is ancient in some cultures, it reached a frightening peak—misogyny—in the early years of Christianity, with repercussions into modern times.

In the centuries following Christ's death, Christians genuinely believed the world was about to end; the Day of Judgment was expected with the next sunrise. Faced with earthly annihilation and heavenly rebirth, procreation became unimportant, salvation of the soul paramount. This meant refraining from sin, especially sexual sin, and the major church fathers exhorted unmarried men to remain celibate and married men to avow chastity.

Indeed, celibacy was deemed a higher human calling than marriage. Woman, once indispensable as wife and mother, lost her raison d'être in society and came to be viewed as man's greatest obstacle to salvation.

To state the case succinctly, if harshly by a hair: When men swear off women, women are bound to be devalued and debased. And they were. It is a chapter in history that the church would like to expunge but cannot since it was written in large part by the greatest Latin doctors of the faith.

To set the stage: The Hellenic philosophers had relegated women to an inferior status in most things, and the Jews characterized Eve and her descendants as temptresses. The Essenes, a Jewish sect that greatly influenced the creation of Christian teaching (as has been confirmed by the Dead Sea Scrolls), were not exactly woman-haters but they portrayed females as "unclean" and "polluting" and viewed intercourse as a risk to be performed at one's spiritual peril. The doctrine of celibacy that rose in the years following Christ's death fit in frighteningly well with the atmosphere of the day.

Here is what the Latin doctors of the church taught about women that relegated them for centuries to the status of second-class human beings.

St. Paul: "Better to marry than to burn."

In the first century, Paul, himself a sinner before becoming a saint, was the leading proponent of celibacy. A trained rabbi, having sworn off women, he expressed the wish that all Christians would emulate him. He held that man (literally the male of the species) was created in God's image and that woman was of an inferior nature. This was supposedly why Eve, not Adam, was the human responsible for introducing sin into the world.

In a concession to human concupiscence, he taught that it was "better to marry than to burn." That is, if one cannot be abstemious, wed, but be aware: At the time of the Last Judgment heaven's upper echelon would be reserved for virgins. In fact, preached Paul, lifelong virgins would be the first to be saved, followed by convert celibates like himself; last would be folk who succumbed to the temptation to marriage. Hell was reserved for those who had sex outside of marriage.

Paul's chaste theories were warmly received by first-century Christians. Mostly from the lower socioeconomic classes, they detested (or envied) the blatant hedonism of Rome's rich. Thus with the spread of Christian idealism, celibacy became a superior state and women were repeatedly redefined: Tertullian, the second-century church father from Carthage, labeled woman "a temple built over a sewer." Himself a sworn celibate who continually fought sexual temptation, he wrote: "Woman! You are the devil's doorway! You lead astray one whom the devil would not dare attack directly."

As several women writers of today have pointed out, a man battling sexual temptation too easily turns his anger on the object of his lust. He is not weak; she is evil incarnate.

When the monk Jovinian, himself chaste, dared to argue that celibacy was not necessarily holier than marriage, he drew down the wrath of Saints Jerome, Ambrose, and Augustine—all celibates. It was now the early fourth century (the world still had not ended) and women were excluded from active participation in the church—not truly for doctrinal reasons, but because they had become synonymous with "temptation" and "man's fall": "Woman is the origin of all sin and it is through her that we all die," as Ecclesiasticus put it.

St. Ambrose: "I consider chastity higher than marriage."

As bishop of Milan, Ambrose advocated austere asceticism and glorified virginity. Borrowing from Stoic philosophy the notion that reason must overtake passion, particularly sexual passion, he preached that the wisest course for any woman was that of lifelong chastity; only by remaining a virgin could she redeem the sin her parents committed in conceiving her.

The impact of that single thought on the minds of impressionable young girls is incalcuable. As we'll see, it helped give rise to the cult of virginity and a slew of adolescent suicides in the name of salvation. In a concession to the continuance of the species, Ambrose wrote: "Naturally I do not condemn marriage, only I consider chastity higher. The former is permissible, the latter I admire."

St. Jerome: "Virginity is natural."

On the whole, the fourth century was disastrous for women. Calls for male celibacy came from every corner, even from the desert where St. Jerome had gone to be among the "wild beasts and scorpions" to cool his overheated fantasies. The monk and scholar wrote candidly of his battle with temptation: "My face was pale and my frame chilled from fasting, yet my mind was burning with the cravings of desire, and the fires of lust flamed up from my flesh that was that of a corpse."

Jerome decreed all sex dirty, marriage an unholy state, and a husband and wife were unfit for prayer and communion for an interval after intercourse. Three centuries later this doctrine would appear as dogma in a manual for priests, the *Penitential:* "Those joined together in matrimony should abstain from cohabitation three nights before receiving communion."

Jerome's retort to Jovinian on the superiority of the celibate life was: "Virginity is natural and marriage came after the fall." However, the loudest call for chastity and celibacy—the one that would echo the longest in the church—was about to be heard, voiced by Jerome and Ambrose's young contemporary, Augustine.

St. Augustine: Passionless Procreation.

The bishop of Hippo (modern Annaba, Algeria), Augustine is regarded as the greatest thinker of Christian antiquity, having fused the religion of the New Testament with the Platonic tradition of Greek philosophy, which he studied as a nineteen-year-old student at Carthage.

He came to Christianity late in life, after a period of dissolute pagan living chronicled in his *Confessions*. Before his conversion, he was a member of the Manichean church, whose elect were celibate monks, though Augustine chose to be "unelected" since he refused to give up a young concubine: "Lord, give me chastity and continency, but do not give them yet." The pellucid hypocrisy in the much quoted phrase, tossed off today with a bemused smile, is too often missed or overlooked.

Though his mother, Monica, was a devout Christian, Augustine was not baptized until age thirty-three, when he met Bishop Ambrose in Rome, who performed the service in 387. Stories of the heroic actions of ascetic Christians had fired Augustine's self-contempt, and he wrote that his release from the clutches of women came when a child's voice told him "take up and read." By chance the book beside him fell open to St. Paul's warning to the Romans: "Make no provisions for the flesh, to fulfill the lust."

So imperative an event was this to the guilt-ridden Augustine that he converted to Christianity that day, vowing celibacy. Sworn off sin and women, he returned to his native Africa and was ordained a priest in 391, five years later becoming bishop of Hippo at age forty-two. He lived a long life, till age seventy-six, and wrote voluminously—not infrequently about the obsession of his younger days. His masterwork, *De Civitate Dei* ("The City of God"), contains chapter headings such as, "Were Adam and Eve troubled by passion before they ate of the tree of knowledge?"

His extraordinary views on human sexuality influenced not only his own time, but the centuries that followed.

Augustine maintained that pure, "innocent" conception occurred between Adam and Eve in Eden: "In Paradise, then, generative seed would have been sown by the husband, and the wife would have conceived . . . by deliberate and not by uncontrollable lust." That is, sex without arousal. "Human organs, without the excitement of lust, could have obeyed the human will for all the purposes of parenthood."

How can an organ such as the penis work without excitation?

Augustine gives several examples of human voluntary actions that must have been cogent in their day: "Some people can make their ears move, either one at a time or both together." Or: "There are individuals who can make musical notes issue from the rear of their anatomy, so that you would think they were singing." Thus Adam and Eve mated to produce Cain and Abel with willful concentration, without arousal or passion.

He concludes his discussion of Adam and Eve's conception of children with: "At a time when there was no unruly lust to excite the organs of generation . . . the seminal flow [of Adam] could have reached the womb [of Eve] with as little rupture of the hymen and by the same vaginal ducts as is at present the case, in reverse, with the menstrual flux. . . . Perhaps these matters are somewhat too delicate for further discussion."

Augustine became a pathological opponent of sexual intercourse—in and out of marriage. He urged all men who could not refrain from wedlock to turn to God for assistance in sexual self-denial. With the greatest zeal he defended the already established dogma that humankind was corrupted by the sexual sin of Adam (caused by Eve), and he repeatedly pointed out that God created man without resorting to sex, just as God asexually formed Jesus Christ in the womb of a virgin. He employed these arguments not only to condemn the act of sexual intercourse, but also to label it unnatural.

As Princeton University religion professor Elaine Pagels wrote in her 1988 book, *Adam, Eve, and the Serpent:* "Augustine's pessimistic views of sexuality, politics, and human nature would become the dominant influence on western Christianity and color all Western culture, Christian or not, ever since."

Celibacy became *the* state to aspire to, and women were (to borrow an expression Thomas Aquinas would coin eight centuries later) *vir occasionatus* ("unsuccessful men")—unfit for political life, ecclesiastical office, functioning best as full-time, lifelong virgins.

When the apocalypse did not arrive, the church was in a doctrinal bind; its dim view of intercourse could not only condemn the race but also the religion. So it reached a simple, if sophistic, compromise between the ideal of celibacy and the necessity of marriage: passionless procreation. St. Augustine, through analogies, "proved" it was possible.

Another church father, Clement of Alexandria (also a celibate), made it doctrine: When a couple must copulate, do so, but don't enjoy it. Thus the attitude arose—and persists—that sex is acceptable but desire is not, a philosophy whose inherent contradiction has caused incalculable heartache. As Pagels concludes, passionless procreation "virtually ensures that anyone who takes it seriously will judge himself or herself to be deficient." No wonder there arose a cult of virginity, a clamor for martyrdom.

Virgin Cults: Christian Era, Europe

To be sure, there were many women in the early centuries of Christianity who were genuine martyrs who chose death rather than compromise their virtue. Other women, though—and their numbers are not small—martyred themselves at a young age for the guarantee of dying as a virgin, fearful of forfeiting chastity even to a husband. To women, the church's clarion message was: Copulate and be like Eve, a fallen woman; abstain and be like Mary.

Scores of fanatical young women chose the latter. Today, by the church's own admission, it is often hard to separate the humble saint from the hysterical teenage suicide—this, because of the accretion of myth surrounding members of the Cult of the Virgin Martyr. Cynical as it sounds, the myth was often official early-church public relations, a kind of manufactured romantic fiction Hollywood-style, meant to inspire, to instill virtue, and to imitate.

As the 1980 book *Saints* portrays the typical virgin martyr, living in an age of poverty and illiteracy: "She was always beautiful, intelligent and good. Innocently provoking lust in her persecutor, she is ultimately martyred by torture and eventual death." Part real, fictional, she was a heroine, and the reason for the tale's hortatory hype was straightforward enough: A new religious movement was under way and it needed role models to help it build up steam. Apparently, from church documents, the legend of the virgin martyr began as a fiction.

St. Catherine. The first virgin martyr to the early Christians, St. Catherine of Alexandria most likely never existed. Veneration of Catherine began in the early years of Christianity, and the legend, acknowledges *The Penguin Dictionary of Saints,* "is one of the most famous and most preposterous of its kind."

As the story goes: Catherine's attributes of noble birth, regal beauty, and learned mind attracted the attention of the Roman emperor, Maxentius, but her refusal to worship idols incensed him. Maxentius proposed marriage, Catherine spurned him. To humiliate her, he set her up against the realm's fifty brightest philosophers in a theological debate; she demolished their arguments one by one. For the men's failure to successfully rebut her, Maxentius had all fifty losers burned alive. Again he proffered marriage, but she cherished her virginity above life itself.

Catherine was imprisoned, stripped, beaten, and starved (though secretly fed by a luminous dove). When tied to a spiked wheel and stretched, she prayed and the contraption miraculously shattered, splinters piercing pagan bystanders like lethal arrows. This prompted the conversion of two hundred of the emperor's soldiers, who were straightaway beheaded. When Catherine herself

Mary's virginity prompted the fictitious legend of St. Catherine (top). Ursuline nuns, whence the name Virgin Islands.

was beheaded, milk, not blood, gushed from her wound. Angels bore the body to Mount Sinai, site of a later monastery and shrine that exist in her honor.

The fantastical tale is significant because there is no evidence for such a historical personage in civil or ecclesiastical records. Yet Catherine spawned an immense cult in the East and West that led countless teenage women to nip blossoming sexuality with suicide, to preserve a virginity unthreatened. Butler's classic *Lives of the Saints* suggests that Christianity's first virgin martyr most likely existed only in the "mind of some Greek writer who composed what he intended to be simply an edifying romance," a paradigm of early Christian zeal.

The fictitious heroine became a role model, spawning extremist cults and also genuine church worship, and in the Middle Ages Catherine was revered as a mystical bride of Christ, married through martyred virginity. A virgin's death came to symbolize a sacred marriage of the highest order (like Mary's to God the Father), a concept that prompted nuns to start wearing wedding rings on their right hands. Catherine is only the first in a long line of such legends. (See "St. Rose," page 338 and "St. Marina," page 339.)

Virgin Islands.   It was the bloody legend of another virgin martyr, Ursula, fourth-century British princess of Cornwall, that prompted Christopher Columbus to christen an archipelago in the West Indies after her. Ursula's husband-to-be, a Scottish nobleman, requested his betrothed find eleven virgins as brides for his chief soldiers. The twelve women set sail for their rendezvous but were driven off course by a storm. They eventually docked at Cologne, on the Rhine, only to be greeted by a horde of Huns whose intentions were obvious. To defend their virtue, Ursula chose martyrdom, stabbing herself in the heart as an example to her companions.

In this case, Ursula was a real person. And a church built at Cologne bears stone inscriptions attesting to the martyrdom of several virgins, perhaps a dozen. But in the twelfth century the legend was multiplied a thousand-fold. Imaginative visionaries misinterpreted a large public burial ground in Cologne as the resting place of St. Ursula and her *eleven thousand* virgin followers. False relics were hawked, forged epitaphs from nonexistent tombstones published.

Columbus was smitten with the romantic legend in its hyperbolic form. When, after a long and stormy voyage to unknown territory (like Ursula's), he landed in the West Indies, greeted (not by Huns) but by dark-skinned natives, he proposed calling the isles *Las Once Mil Virgines.* Today St. Ursula is the patron saint of young girls and their instructresses, while the Virgin Islands are a resort popular with virgins and nonvirgins alike.

Polygamy: Pre–Christian Era, Europe and Asia

The term "polygamy" (from the Greek *polys gamos,* "many marriages") is routinely misused. We conversationally employ it to signify a man having several wives, though it equally applies to a woman having several husbands— historically a rarer phenomenon.

The precise term for the union of one man with more than one wife is polygyny (*gyne,* "woman"), which goes back itself to a root word meaning "bearer of children." (The word for the converse union is polyandry, *andros* being Greek for "man.") For the sake of convention and clarity in discussing the past sex practice of polygyny, the term polygamy is used throughout.

The Bible takes polygamy for granted, not criticizing the custom of earlier centuries. Jacob was the husband of Leah and Rachel. David, before settling in Jerusalem, had eight wives. Solomon is said to have enjoyed several hundred— though at some point the concept became more a symbol of a man's virility, wealth, and power than a sexual accomplishment.

Neither does the New Testament condemn polygamy; nor does the Muslim Koran, though it sensibly limits a man to four wives.

Polygamy is thought to have begun for purely practical reasons. Wars claimed the lives of countless men, and a warrior who died in battle, leaving many widows impregnated, replenished a tribe's ranks. Manpower was also needed for farming and building, and a community's worth was directly related to the size of its population. Children counted as free labor, and a family's prosperity depended on the number of its offspring.

But there was a sexual reason, too, for polygamy. Menstrual blood was superstitiously dreaded, and sex with a menstruating wife was taboo. Many tribes further made wives off-limits throughout pregnancy and the months, or years (up to three), of breast feeding. Thus when one or more wives was proscribed, a polygamist had other wives for the purposes of propagation and pleasure.

In time, for a man to own and be able to provide for several wives became a matter of prestige. And a woman was proud to be the legal mate of such a wealthy and powerful husband.

However, as any man (or woman) who has ever attempted to divide sexual favors among two or more lovers soon learns, the situation is fraught with jealousies. The jockeying for position in both the house and the bed is made clear in the Bible when Rachel and Leah dispute who should sleep with Jacob "this night."

A stab at orderliness arose through the law of "seniority." The first bride became "chief wife," all others concubines (from the Latin *concumbere,* "to lie down with"). This peacemaking distinction is found in history's oldest promulgation of laws, the Code of Hammurabi. These second-millennium B.C. edicts compiled under the rule of Babylonia's sixth ruler acknowledge polygamy's economic benefits to a community. The text labels the first bride the "proper wife" while others are "lesser wives."

Babylonian laws and customs were copied by many societies, and polygamy codes influenced the early Hebrews, accounting for the references and leniencies in the Old Testament. Historians claim that the fundamental reality of polygamy is that it was practiced where and when it worked for the betterment of society. And it ended in those societies when economic factors, particularly population density and size of the labor force, no longer made immense families necessary or desirable.

The one exception—and it's a major one—is in the Middle East, where Arab sultans maintained large harems for purposes of pleasure and as a visible statement of wealth, power, and virility. In 1909, Sultan Abdül Hamid II admitted to having a harem of 370 concubines (and 127 eunuchs to watch over them and to settle quarrels and internal intrigues). Harems were outlawed in Turkey in 1926, when Kemal Atatürk banned the practice of polygamy.

Though polygamy is a dying practice, it is not yet dead. Ended throughout most of the world, it exists among many fringe Mormon groups in the United States. Today there are as many as thirty thousand practicing polygamists in the state of Utah, most of them adherents to the polygamous philosophy of Joseph Smith.

Polygamy in America: 1830 to 1890

Joseph Smith, founder of the Church of Jesus Christ of Latter-Day Saints (commonly known as Mormons), instituted plural marriages for men in the 1830s as a divinely sanctioned way of life. With a nod toward the Bible, Smith dubbed the pleasure "Jacob's blessing." He once confessed, "Whenever I see a pretty woman, I have to pray for grace." He later resolved that temptation by taking as many as fifty wives.

It has been suggested (perhaps unfairly, maybe not) that Smith got tired praying for grace and simply sanctioned polygamy. Whereas Smith liked to describe himself as an unschooled, pious youth who grew up at a time of intense religious revivalism, his neighbors in Palmyra, New York, remembered him as a hot-blooded teenager, a self-styled ladies' man who, second to romantic dalliances, enjoyed searching for buried treasure.

Smith knew from the start that polygamy would be a controversial issue, and that if the practice became known to the outside world, it might sink his religion. For a time, plural marriages were kept secret. Polygamy for men, preached Smith, was the ultimate solution to adultery and prostitution. Certainly if a man must account for his time to a dozen or more wives, his chances for cheating are diminished, if not his desire to do so.

A man with fifty wives can remain a secret for only so long. News that Joseph Smith had married Emma and Eliza and Susan and Nancy . . . and that his Mormon *Doctrine and Covenants* allowed a man to marry any number of virgins roused enormous public outrage. In February of 1844, when the thirty-nine-year-old Smith announced his candidacy for the U.S. presidency, his rivals made polygamy a campaign issue. This made for one of the most unusual platforms in the history of American politics.

The consequences were predictable. Outbreaks of violence ensued and Smith was eventually arrested, charged with treason, and imprisoned in Illinois's Carthage city jail. Despite promises of protection from the state's governor, Thomas Ford, on June 27 a mob of armed men with blackened faces, brandishing clubs and guns, stormed the jail and murdered Smith. He thus became a martyr of the Mormon Church.

Throughout his life, Joseph Smith had governed his followers by announcing periodic revelations, often on widely divergent matters. These continued to come to church elders after Smith's murder. On September 14, 1852, eight years after Joseph Smith's death, the Mormon Church announced its founder's "final revelation" on plural marriage. The practice was to be official doctrine: "if any man aspouse a virgin, and desire to aspouse another, and the first give her consent, and if he aspoused the second, and they are virgins, and have vowed to no other man, then he is justified; he cannot commit adultery . . . and if he have ten virgins given unto him by this law, he cannot commit adultery, for they belong to him."

Privilege Canceled.   America, though, would not stand for even pockets of polygamy in the country. The Republican presidential platform of 1856 called for the elimination of "the twin relics of babarism," slavery and polygamy, stating it "both the right and imperative duty of Congress" to take immediate action. Laws were enacted mandating heavy fines and long prison terms for convicted polygamists. Between 1885 and 1900 more than one thousand Mormon men were caught and convicted.

The Mormon Church, though, refused to conform to these laws and declared the legislation an unconstitutional infringement of religious liberty. But when the Supreme Court upheld the government ruling in 1890, the Mormons had no choice except to end the practice.

The head of the church at that time, Wilford Woodruff, promulgated a new law outlawing the practice of multiple wives, presenting it as a newly received "divine command"—which coincidentally arrived around the time of the court's decision. Since then, certain fundamentalist Mormon sects, officially excommunicated, have continued the custom in isolated parts of Utah and Arizona.

Polygamy is a chapter in Mormon history that the religion's devout followers would like to close and forget, much the way the Roman Catholic Church wold like to expunge the era of hysterical virgin suicides and castrated male sopranos. Or, to show no favoritism, the way Christian fundamentalists would like to forget the sexual indiscretions of Jim Bakker and Jimmy Swaggart. Or . . . The point is, religion exists only because men and women are fallible and often do the stupidest of things.

Perhaps it should be expected that the most sinful acts are of a sexual nature, sexuality being a primary aspect of human nature. After all, humankind's first sin, committed in the Garden of Eden, was sexual; the knowledge forbidden to Adam and Eve was assumed to be carnal knowledge even before St. Augustine's time. In a story about a naked man, a naked woman, a tempting snake, and taboo knowledge, it is hard *not* to see the sexual overtones.

Chastity Belt, Pre–Christian Era to 19th Century

Nothing speaks worse of a husband's lack of trust in his wife (or of his own paranoia) than the chastity belt, also known as the "girdle of purity." The lockable device, which for centuries came in two strategic designs, fitted around a woman's genital zone. It reached peak popularity during medieval times, when crusaders and other peripatetic knights were away from the marital bed for months at a time.

The belts existed in quantity at one time, the handiwork of blacksmiths. Many can be observed today, mounted on mannequins or suspended by wires at museums such as the Cluny in Paris.

A husband during the Middle Ages, about to embark on a journey, could lock his wife into a "partial pudenda" whose metal plate covered only the region of the vagina. The pudenda (from the Latin *pudere*, "to be ashamed," the origin

Wife in a chastity belt filches keys from her husband for her lover.

of "prudishness") contained a narrow vertical slit through which she could urinate with no special accuracy. The aperture was usually fitted with outwardly pointing metal teeth (sometimes spring-loaded) to discourage a suitor's exploration with as much as a fingertip.

On the other hand, a husband who suspected his wife might indulge in kinkier pleasures could resort to a "full pudenda." This covered both anterior and posterior regions of a woman's anatomy and made cleanliness even more difficult. In addition to the front slit, the full pudenda had a larger rear aperture to permit defecation, but the orifice could not be too large since it had to prevent anal intercourse, which was also discouraged by another set of metal teeth. Physicians of the period claimed that a woman could wear a full or partial chastity belt for months at a time without ill effects so long as she bathed frequently.

There are anecdotes of horror and humor associated with chastity belts: The village blacksmith, commissioned by a soon-to-crusade knight to forge a pudenda for his wife, who makes an extra key for himself. The faithful wife who learns she is carrying her husband's child only after he has gone and she's locked into the belt. The saintly maiden who puts herself beyond the temptation of self-abuse and the violation of rape by donning a full pudenda and throwing away the key.

While most individual stories are probably apocryphal, together they represent a general picture of reality in an era when women were belted in to keep out admirers. Among pudenda lore it is not always easy to separate fact from ribald fiction, or a true chastity belt from a noveltylike hoax. Indeed, in the 1950s the Cluny Museum stopped displaying all but one of its belts under the suspicion that the artifacts were a latter-day blacksmith's joke. But there are authentic cases, such as that of two Christian saints.

St. Rose.   Born Isabel de Flores y del Oliva in Lima in 1586, Rose became the first person in the Americas to be canonized a saint by the church (though her holy status has since been questioned). She supported her aged and indigent parents by selling flowers and handmade embroidery. Extraordinarily devout, at an early age she underwent an agonizing surgical procedure (its nature unknown) that awoke in her an appetite for suffering. Her self-inflicted tortures, which the church has since come to view as pathological rather than pious, are chilling: To deface her beauty, and thus preserve her virtue, she cut her cheeks and rubbed pepper into the wounds.

At age twenty, Rose shunned a marriage proposal to become a Dominican nun. She donned a chastity belt, threw away the key, and her self-inflicted penances became increasingly cruel. There were daily scourgings, the continual chewing of bitter herbs, submerging her hands in caustic lime, and fasting until anorexic. Throughout all of this, she wore a hair shirt and a silver circlet studded on the inside with thorns. Whenever she had to walk more than a few feet, she dragged a heavy wooden cross over her shoulder.

Family, friends, and fellow nuns criticized her actions. Rose claimed that the pain induced mystical experiences. An ecclesiastical inquiry concluded that she was visited regularly by the devil and the tortures were necessary to keep him at bay.

Perhaps unkindly, she has been called the founder of the School of Aggressive Chastity. Nonetheless, after her death, the church in Peru identified a spate of miracles in her name and petitioned Rome to have her canonized.

Today Rome honors Rose for her many charitable works among Lima's poor; her saintliness is a touchy issue. *The Penguin Dictionary of Saints* states that Rose's "penitential practices were so extravagant as to savour of morbid fanaticism." She was, the book hedges, "simply seeking to follow Christ in his sufferings, but the means were not always prudently chosen . . . such saints pose delicate questions of religion and psychology."

St. Rose's feast day is August 30 and her sanctuary in Lima is a place of annual pilgrimage. Its greatest treasure, pictured on postcards and photographed by devout visitors, is the deep well into which the young Rose threw the key to her chastity belt.

St. Marina.   Like Rose, Marina de Jesus Paredes y Flores, the seventeenth-century Lily of Ecuador, also wore an iron girdle. There are additional similarities between the two young women, as F. P. Keyes makes clear in his dual biography, *The Rose and the Lily*. At age eight, Marina was already punishing herself by wearing crowns and belts of thorns. At puberty, swearing lifelong virginity, she strapped herself into a chastity belt and embellished the garment with rows of thistle spikes and iron teeth.

For the duration of her reclusive life, Marina ate only one slice of bread a day, slept for no more than three hours a night, and kept as her sole companion an effigy in a coffin as a continual reminder of death. Every Friday, the day of Christ's crucifixion, she would remove the effigy, climb into the coffin, fold her arms across her chest, and sleep her three hours there. During two South American catastrophes—an earthquake and an epidemic—Marina offered her life in expiation of mankind's sins but the offer was not immediately accepted. Venerated as a holy virgin, she was canonized in 1950. Her feast day is May 26.

First Chastity Belt.   In various forms, mechanically imposed chastity has been forced on women since ancient times. Homer's *Odyssey* describes how Aphrodite betrays her husband, Hephaistos, and to prevent further infidelities he forges a "girdle" for her privates. The Greeks, though, never adopted the device. It is thought that twelfth-century crusaders learned about chastity belts during their travels in the East, where they also encountered the practice of female infibulation, in which the lips of the vagina are temporarily fastened closed with rings or wires.

The Bible, some scholars claim, records the existence of a chastity belt in antiquity. It does so in connection with the building of the Tabernacle during the Israelites' wandering through the desert from Egypt to the Holy Land. Moses requested that the people donate possessions to raise funds for the construction of the Tent of Meeting, and women brought forth bracelets, earrings, signet rings, "all jewels of gold." Among the objects is a *koomaz* (today the word is translated to mean "plate"). Rabbi Rashi, the renowned eleventh-century biblical scholar, claimed that the word originally described "a golden vessel fixed on a woman's private part." In support of this interpretation he offered quotations from the Talmud, collected writings of Jewish civil and religious law, in which the authors assert that *koomaz* is an abbreviation of the phrase "here is the place of shameful deeds."

Florentine Girdle.   The use of chastity belts did not flourish until the twelfth century. The first models were produced in Italy, called Florentine girdles. As they were adopted throughout a Europe engaged in the holy Crusades, the contraptions acquired names such as "girdle of Venus," "padlock of purity," and "drawers of iron." The earliest extant description of a Florentine belt is found in a military encyclopedia, *Bellifortis,* published in 1405.

The oldest model in existence once belonged to the infamous despot Novello Carrara, who in 1388 upon his father's abdication as ruler of Padua, Italy, became Francesco II. The medieval Carrara family dominated Padua in the fourteenth century, serving as patrons of the arts. The noble family's most ignoble member was the sadistic Novello, Tyrant of Padua, who personally designed an array of torture devices that are displayed today in the armory collection of Venice's Doges' Palace.

Novello preferred a full pudenda for his wife to wear in his absence, which for her comfort he internally padded with leather. Her frontal chastity was fortified by thirty-six steel porcupinelike spikes, while the small anal orifice discouraged entry with fifteen razor-sharp teeth. When at home, the sexually adventurous Novello liked to hazard intercourse by violating his wife through the girdle.

Imprisoned following a political battle between Padua and Venice, Novello was strangled by his Venetian captors in 1406. His wife's pudenda remains in prefect condition today, prominently displayed among medieval armory.

A chastity belt from the same period was discovered in 1889 during an exhumation of corpses from an Austrian churchyard. The woman had been buried in her locked belt, which four hundred years later encircled her fleshless skeleton.

A husband's insistence that a wife wear a pudenda in his absence was not considered harsh treatment. For centuries a woman's body was the exclusive property of her mate (more than it was her own); he could do with it what he wished. In a perverse way, to be locked into a chastity belt was a compliment; it showed a husband cared. The devices were still being advertised in the late nineteenth century, but then to prevent young girls from masturbating.

Male Chastity Belt.   During the Victorian era, a male version of the chastity belt was introduced, though more accurately it was a form of male infibulation. An adolescent boy's foreskin was pulled down over the tip of the penis, gathered together, and four holes were punched around the skin, then laced through with two opposing lock-and-key rings. The Victorian device not only prevented masturbation, it also made tumescence so agonizing that pain nipped nascent sexual thoughts.

A professor of surgery at the University of Halle, Germany, Karl August Weinhold replaced the rings with tight loops of wire topped off with sealing wax. A parent could periodically check to see if a son had broken the seal and was masturbating. During the Victorian years when self-abuse was among the most dangerous of vices, physically and spiritually, Weinhold suggested that all indigent bachelors between the ages of fourteen and thirty who had dim prospects for marriage be rounded up and infibulated with a wire that was then soldered closed.

The plan was never carried out, but in hospitals and mental institutions masturbators (those caught, at least) were routinely infibulated. A colleague of Weinhold instituted the procedure at one asylum and reported in 1876: "The sensation among the patients was extraordinary. I was struck by the conscience-stricken way in which they submitted to the operation on their penises. I mean to try it on a large scale, and go on wiring all masturbators."

Today, though infibulation rings and the metal chastity belt are gone as serious items, they exist as playthings, their original purpose perverted to provide pleasure, not prevent it. Purchased through sexually oriented catalogues and novelty shops, the modern equivalent of the infibulation ring is a small brass spike or ring that fits through a pierced foreskin, like an earring loops through a pierced ear. The Pleasure Chest, a New York–based chain of erotic appliance stores, marketed a "male chastity device" that consisted of a metal tube that slipped over the penis and fastened round the testicles with a chain and combination lock; the incentive was for the lover to find the right combination.

The modern female chastity belt is of leather, and the thrill it supposedly provides is as a temporary impediment to the inevitable act, the way intricate wrapping and ribbon elevate expectation in opening a gift. It's been estimated that more chastity belts are manufactured today than during the height of the Crusades. They no longer ensure chastity, but invite its violation.

PART IV

Thanatographies

CHAPTER 14

Last Agonies
of Historic Figures
Buddha to Casanova

THE CONCLUDING FOUR CHAPTERS of this book deal with last words, final hours, farewells, modes of dying, and places of rest of people rich, renowned, famous, and infamous. The subject matter does not fall easily under the rubric biography, a writing *(graphia)* of a life *(bios)*. Nor does it come under the heading obituary, a death notice.

More accurately, it is a writing of a death *(thanatos)* in all its aspects—a "thanatography."

Thanatographies approximate what Joyce Carol Oates has defined as a "pathography": "dysfunction and disaster, illness and pratfalls, failed marriages and failed careers, alcoholism and breakdowns and outrageous conduct." This is because the ending of a life does not always occur compactly in a final few hours before death. Rather, the end is often signaled years or decades in advance by just such misfortunes as dysfunctions, failures, and breakdowns. However, the goal of a thanatography is not merely to highlight for its own sake life's pathos or suffering, but to show how such hardships hasten a life to its end.

Here, then, are the thanatographies of many of history's most colorful figures.

The Buddha Gautama: d. 483 B.C., age 80

> **Cause of death:** Intestinal hemorrhaging from acute indigestion following a large, spicy meal

Mode of burial: Cremation

Last words: *"Never forget it: decay is inherent in all things."*

For Prince Siddhartha Gautama, the buddha (a title like the messiah), his last supper was as fateful as Jesus Christ's. Each died following a banquet, the buddha, though, from the food itself.

Born in 563 B.C. a prince—"I was delicately nurtured, exceedingly delicately nurtured, delicately nurtured beyond measure"—Gautama experienced a religious conversion and call to celibacy at age thirty, ten years after he had married. Abandoning a wife, son, and the life of the idle rich for a homeless asceticism, he donned beggar's clothes and moved into a cave in India's wilderness. "The world is built on pain and its foundations are laid in agony," he perceived, developing the religious philosophy that bears his name.

Diet was a problem from the start. To achieve enlightenment, or *bodhi,* he ate only mosses, roots, grains, and an occasional wild fruit. Growing emaciated—"Because of so little nourishment, all my limbs became like some withered creepers with knotted joints"—he permanently damaged his health.

The buddha graphically described his appearance and was proud of it: "My buttocks was like a buffalo's hoof, my ribs like rafters of a dilapidated shed, the pupils of my eyes appeared sunk deep in their sockets as water appears shining at the bottom of a deep well." He frequently fainted, keeled over, and was taken for dead by his disciples. "My scalp became shrivelled and shrunk; when I stroked my limbs with my hand, hairs rotted at the roots fell away from my body."

Enlightenment did not come with starvation, he learned. Returning to the traditional Indian diet, he put on weight, a gut that would become a hallmark, and experienced intense stomach and intestinal burning—most likely from ulcers. He ate the food that is thought to have caused his death in 483 B.C. after preaching a sermon in a mango grove at the village of Pava.

The Buddha Gautama's last supper.

There were several fetes that day thrown by the town's wealthiest folk. Food and drink were varied and abundant. A prosperous blacksmith named Cunda hosted the most lavish banquet, honoring the buddha with meats, flavored rices, bamboo sprouts trodden by pigs, milk sweets, and a spicy pork dish called *sukara-maddava.*

Gautama, bloated, seized with stomach cramps and burning, did not finish the meal. A modern analysis holds that "a sizable artery, lying in or contiguous to a duodenal ulcer, ruptured and loosed a large quantity of blood into the intestinal tract." Stoically Gautama attempted to conceal the extent of his symptoms, until profuse rectal bleeding alarmed his disciples.

Determined to preach at his next stop, Kusinara, he left Pava on foot, supported by friends. He did not get far. Seized with a rapacious thirst from dehydration, he lay on the roadside and begged for water from a nearby stream. The water may have quenched his thirst, but it is also likely that it aggravated his intestinal symptoms, for the stream flowed past a village and was probably unfit for drinking.

Bleeding, vomiting, and torpidly weak, the philosopher continued to the outskirts of Kusinara where lethargy felled him. His disciples claimed that the buddha died without noticeable suffering, lapsing into longer and longer spells of unconsciousness. During a lucid moment, he delivered his final words on the inevitability of the decay of living things and exhorted his companions, "Try to accomplish your aim with diligence."

Today, physicians studying the Indian Pali texts, the oldest record of the Buddha Gautama's life, conclude that an acute attack of indigestion killed off one of the East's greatest philosophers. In addition to stomach ulcers, there is evidence he also suffered from cancer of the colon. With severe fluid loss from rectal bleeding and vomiting, he would have experienced oxygen deficiency and in the end cardiac arrest.

Gautama's body was cremated and a dispute arose over which of eight groups of followers should preserve the ashes. Conceding to the inanity of fighting over the relics of a man who preached peace, the groups' leaders sifted the ashes into eight equal portions. Eight golden urns were sent to the rulers of the eight Indian kingdoms, and altars were erected over the relics, each a site of worship. The belly of the buddha, his most prominent feature in subsequent statuary, stands as a reminder of the nature of his death.

Socrates: d. 399 B.C., age 70

Cause of death: Hemlock poisoning

Place of rest: Grave site unknown

Last words: As paralysis crept throughout his body, he requested of a friend: *"I owe a cock to Asclepius; will you repay him?"*

Socrates's ending was most likely given a latter-day Hollywood-like treatment by his chronicler Plato. For death by coniine, a poisonous alkaloid of the hemlock plant, is marked not only by ascending motor paralysis, as Plato recorded, but also by intense nausea, vomiting, and limb-flailing convulsions—unpleasantries that are found nowhere in Plato's noble end to the life of his friend and teacher, "the wisest and justest and best."

Socrates, first of the great trio (along with Plato and Aristotle) of ancient Greek philosophers, wrote down nothing of his thoughts. What we know of his personality, doctrines, and death comes chiefly from Plato's dialogues. The picture is of a stout, broad-nosed, homely philosopher whose moral preaching pricked the consciences of his fellow Greeks to the point where he became intolerable. Though he had a wife and three sons, he seems to have spent all his time in the streets, marketplaces, and gymnasiums of Athens, lecturing to young men of promise on politics, poetry, and his own brand of self-analysis captured in his famous admonition, "Know thyself."

It was his teaching that in 399 B.C. that got him into a fatal conflict with Greek authorities. Specifically, he was indicted for "impiety" on two counts: "corruption of the young" and "neglect of the gods whom the city worships and the practice of religious novelties." (That is, he introduced new divinities.)

The charge against Socrates of corrupting Athenian youths carried no sexual overtones. The corruption was that Socrates taught teenage boys to question the wisdom of their parents and the leaders of Athenian society, which was far worse. And when the Delphic oracle announced that "no man is wiser than Socrates," leading Athenians cringed with resentment and envy. The city's politicians wanted the philosopher banished from the country (as did many parents), but no one wished for his death, which would (and did) make him a martyr to his devoted followers. The wise Socrates, however, knew how to stage a memorable exit.

His trial took place before 501 jurors, who also served as judges (the odd number precluded a tied verdict). The seventy-year-old philosopher—who abhorred hypocrisy, loathed opportunism, and embraced a virtuous life lived in accordance with the laws of nature—was found guilty and offered banishment or death. He viewed banishment as a disgrace. He had preached the importance of law, and now that the law pronounced him guilty—rightly or wrongly—he argued that the only honorable course of action was death. Not to end his life, he said, was a crime against the state.

His last day was spent at home, answering philosophical questions posed by friends. Around sunset he bathed, to avoid "giving the women the trouble of washing me when I am dead." His wife, Xanthippe, and sons were admitted to his room to bid him farewell, then he returned to conversation with his male followers on the fate of the human soul, a fitting subject given the circumstances. He attempted to cheer them with the argument that death was a good, not an evil. When the court-appointed executioners arrived as witnesses, Socrates ordered, "Let the poison be brought if it is already mixed, if not, let the man mix it."

One executioner presented the hemlock. "Well, my friend," said Socrates, "I must ask you, since you have had experience in these matters, what I ought to do."

"Nothing," replied the man, "but walk about after drinking until you feel a heaviness in your legs, and then, if you lie down, the poison will take effect of itself."

With a prayer to the gods, recounted Plato in his *Phaedo,* Socrates tossed down the libation. His companions burst into tears, and their leader was amazed: "What are you doing, you strange people? My chief reason for sending away the women was that we might be spared such discordance as this; for I have heard that a man ought to die in solemn stillness. So pray be composed, and restrain yourselves."

Socrates began to pace around the room. Soon, sensing the muscle paralysis advancing up his legs and throughout his body, he lay down and covered his face with a sheet. He was not dead; and the gesture, perhaps a fictive nicety employed by Plato, served symbolically at least to conceal the nausea, vomiting, and convulsions of hemlock poisoning.

Periodically one executioner pinched his limbs, and Socrates claimed he felt no sensation. When his friend Crito asked how the dying philosopher wanted to be buried, Socrates answered, "In whatever way you wish in accordance with our customs. But remember, Crito, it shall not be me that you bury, only my body. I shall be gone."

He did not go just yet. When paralysis reached his groin, he peeked out from under the sheet and said to Crito, "I owe a cock to Asclepius; will you repay him?" Asclepius was the Greek god of healing and medicine, and it's thought that Socrates was making a gesture of thanks for being cured of life itself.

Crito replied, "It shall be done," then asked if the philosopher had a final insight to express. He received no answer. The description of a calm and painless death that must have been neither tranquil nor without discomfort was most certainly Plato's final tribute to his dear friend.

Archimedes: d. 212 B.C., age 75

Cause of death: Homicide

Place of rest: Syracuse, Sicily, near the Agrigentine Gate

Last words: Absorbed in a geometrical computation, he admonished his assailant: *"Stand away, fellow, from my diagram!"*

Archimedes, born around 287 B.C. in the Greek city-state of Syracuse, Sicily, literally died a practicing scientist, slain while making a mathematical computation. In accordance with his last wish, his tombstone was etched with a diagram familiar to centuries of later geometry students: a sphere inscribed in a cylinder. It symbolized his discovery of the relationship between the volumes of the two objects (the former being two-thirds that of the latter), and it was the achievement Archimedes was proudest of, though he had many impressive accomplishments.

He is supposed to have invented contraptions for warfare—such as an array of glass mirrors that reflected the sun's heat and set ablaze the sails of advanc-

Archimedes discovering buoyancy, master of military contrivances.

ing Roman ships. He certainly invented the water screw, a device for raising fluids that is still used in Egypt to irrigate fields. To Archimedes, the mechanical contrivances that made him famous in his day were diversions from serious ruminations on theoretical mathematics.

The most famous story about his life typifies the concentration—and absentmindedness—that surrounded his death.

He was asked by King Hieron II if a newly minted crown, purportedly of pure gold, was not devalued by traces of silver. Perplexed for days, Archimedes was stepping into a bath when he realized that his bulk displaced a certain quantity of water. Could buoyancy, he wondered, be used to answer the king's question? Gold weighs more than silver. Thus a crown of pure gold would displace more water than one of a gold-silver alloy. Preoccupied with the buoyancy concept (which would be named Archimedes's principle), he leaped from the bath and raced naked to the palace, shouting, "Eureka! Eureka!" ("I have found it! I have found it!"). Years later, another conceptual preoccupation led to his death.

In 212 B.C., Archimedes's hometown of Syracuse was captured by the Romans. Under General Marcellus, Roman forces attacked by land and sea. Greek soldiers used many of Archimedes's mechanical weapons to launch arrows and catapult stones at the invaders, driving them into retreat.

The brilliant Marcellus, realizing his weapons were no match against Archimedes's, waited patiently, and, as he had hoped, the citizens of Syracuse became complacent in their apparent victory. One night after the Greeks had thrown a celebratory feast inside the city wall, the Romans scaled the wall and easily overtook a citizenry sleeping off a hangover.

Hundreds of Greeks were slaughtered. But Marcellus ordered that the famous Archimedes be taken alive. The seventy-five-year-old mathematician, oblivious to the plundering, was found in his house, seated on the ground, contemplating a diagram drawn in the sand. For some time he did not realize that soldiers had entered the room. When a Roman advanced to arrest Archimedes, the scientist extended his arm ordering, "Stand away, fellow, from my diagram!" He did not see the sword of the soldier that pierced through his back.

Archimedes was dead. And soon after, so was his assailant, executed for disobeying orders. In the midst of the military triumph, Marcellus mourned the scientist's death. The general realized the worth of the inventor of warfare gadgets and he directed that the body of Archimedes be given an honorable Greek burial. Marcellus even befriended Archimedes's relatives, those who survived the bloody siege of the city. It was Marcellus who, learning of Archimedes's last wish, had the diagram of the sphere and cylinder etched into his tombstone.

Cleopatra: d. 30 B.C., age 39

Cause of death: Suicide by poison

Place of rest: Beside her lover, Mark Antony, in a tomb beneath the modern city of Alexandria

Last words: As the venomous asp was brought to her: *"So here it is!"*

Cleopatra's suicide, to avoid the humiliation of being paraded through the streets of Rome as a captive, marked two endings: the end of her life and the end of the Macedonian dynasty that ruled Egypt from the death of Alexander the Great in 323 B.C. until Egypt's annexation by Rome in 31 B.C.

Egypt's last queen—a Macedonian Greek who had no Egyptian blood—was much maligned in her time and after it. Called the Harlot Queen, she came to

Cartouche of Cleopatra's name from the Rosetta stone: snakebite may be fiction.

represent, as did no other woman in antiquity, the femme fatale—and much more: Depicted as the personification of lust, obsessed with the act of fellatio, she was dubbed *Meriochane* ("She who gapes wide for ten thousand men").

Was she that bad?

There is no doubt that the woman born Thea Phiopater (Greek for "goddess loving her father") used feminine wiles to survive and compete in the male-dominated politics of her day. It's now believed that her lascivious reputation owes much to Roman male rumor. For her chief rivals, male rulers and generals, were galled by her statesmanship, irate at her success in keeping Egypt independent, and envious of her wealth. What better male weapon against a powerful woman than to slander her virtue?

The slander, interestingly, altered history's image of the Egyptian queen. Cleopatra was not beautiful. Coin portraits of her day show a countenance dynamic rather than comely, with large lips, a firm but small chin, a broad forehead, and a prominent hooked nose. Yet later images portray her as exotically beautiful. It's believed that her real image was romanticized by later male artists to fit more appropriately with the reputation of a femme fatale, that is, to fit a male notion of how a seductress should look.

Whatever her mirror knew and her morals lacked, we know for certain that the queen was twenty-seven years old when, in the autumn of 43 B.C., she met the "ruggedly handsome, muscular" Mark Antony. Within a little more than a decade, they'd both be suicides.

Antony at the time was the powerful Roman ally Cleopatra needed to guarantee Egypt's independence, and she cleverly exploited his raffish and unstable character. They may have married, though he had a wife, Fulvia, whom he never divorced. For twelve years he was Cleopatra's devoted "husband," father of her three children, co-ruler of Egypt, and joint founder of the society of "inimitable livers," a club whose members enjoyed a life of debauchery and folly.

The decline leading to their suicides began with the Battle of Actium. As general, Mark Antony argued that the best way to defeat the advancing Roman army of Octavian was on land; the influential Cleopatra insisted on a sea battle, a disastrous miscalculation. When it was clear that Egyptian forces were about to be defeated, the two lovers ceased styling themselves "inimitable livers" and swore to be "diers together."

But the suicide pact may have been merely Cleopatra's plan to rid herself of Mark Antony, soon to be political deadweight.

Egypt fell to Rome, we know. The rest is arguable. Cleopatra retreated to her mausoleum. Then, it's thought, she sent a messenger to Mark Antony reporting that she had killed herself. Or he heard through rumor she was dead. Whatever, he "fell upon his sword" and, fatally wounded, asked to be carried to her mausoleum.

History records that he found her alive, but makes no mention of whether he felt relief or betrayal. Supposedly his last words to her were: *"You must not pity me in this last turn of fate. You should rather be happy in the remembrance*

of our love and in the recollection that of all men I was once the most powerful."
Those are not words of resentment.

Mark Antony's life ended, but not Cleopatra's. Some historians believe that the ambitious, wily queen attempted to captivate her conqueror, Octavian. They argue that the thirty-nine-year-old woman, accustomed to getting her way, would not end her life except as a desperate act, only after all attempts at survival and return to power had failed.

Octavian, though, was interested in the fallen queen for only one thing: to parade her triumphantly through Rome and her beloved Egypt as his captive, a humiliation the proud Cleopatra would not brook. Learning of his plans, she prepared to end her life.

On August 30, 30 B.C., she bathed, perfumed her body, and donned royal robes of purple, then reclined on a golden couch to eat her last meal. By messenger she sent a request to Octavian that she be buried beside her dead husband. Then she is supposed to have taken a venomous asp from a basket of figs and applied its fangs to the flesh of her arm.

Octavian, correctly seeing in the message her suicide, sent guards to the palace. "The messengers came at full speed," recounted Plutarch, the first-century biographer, "and on opening the doors they saw her stone dead, lying upon a bed of gold." One of her handmaidens, Iras, lay lifeless not far from the queen. A guard demanded of another handmaiden, Charmian, herself near death, "Was this well done by your lady?"

"Exceedingly well," the faithful servant replied, "as became a descendant of a long line of kings."

Cleopatra died of poison. But was it from a snakebite or lethally spiked wine?

Plutarch favored a snake, though in one account of her death he has the asp concealed in a basket of figs and in another the viper is hidden in a vase. And "asp" itself is vague, since it can refer to any of several small, poisonous snakes of Africa and Europe, such as the horned viper, the common European viper, or the Egyptian cobra. Another theory, and one that better accounts for the deaths of the queen *and* her servants, maintains that they drank wine laced with poison.

Octavian promoted the snakebite theory. He believed there were faint puncture marks on Cleopatra's arm and ordered a statue carried into Rome depicting the queen with a common European viper wrapped around her upper arm, an act that established the legend.

Octavian granted Cleopatra's last wish. She was buried beside Mark Antony. The grave has never been found, but it's believed to adjoin the Temple of Isis, itself near the royal palace of Alexandria, now beneath the modern city of that name.

William the Conqueror: d. 1087, age 59

Cause of death: Festering internal abscess from being injured on his horse

Place of rest: St. Stephen's Church, Caen; grave later desecrated,
   bones scattered

On his way to a reducing spa, the obese king of England was injured on his
horse. He acquired an internal abscess that festered, killed him, and at his
funeral caused him to explode, the stench of rotted innards driving worshipers
from the church in haste. That sounds like a Monty Python routine, but it's
actually part of British history, the manner in which William the Bastard, duke
of Normandy, met his inglorious end.

As a boy, William was big-boned and stocky. As a young man, who would
win the Battle of Hastings in 1066, William was corpulent. By middle age,
having alienated the pope (by refusing to pay him homage, then organizing the
church as a dependency of the Crown), William was, by all accounts, obese. He
may have suffered from a genetic or metabolic obesity, since writers of the
period stress the king was abstemious in food and drink. He was also an active
outdoors man, a hunter and a soldier. Yet as he aged, he packed on pounds,
and weight, directly and indirectly, played a role in the accident that led to his
painful death.

Three years before invading England, William suffered some severe illness
that almost ended in death. Though the nature of the trouble is unknown, its
onset appears to have been sudden and agonizing. "So sore was he," wrote a
chronicler of the time, "he was laid on the ground as one about to die."

He recovered sufficiently to defeat Harold II in the Battle of Hastings and
to be crowned king of England in Westminster Abbey on Christmas Day.
Around this time, William and his entire army were stricken with an epidemic
of dysentery that "had the army on its haunches" and left the king incapacitated
for several weeks. Though none the thinner. Behind his back, he was ridiculed
as "fat man" and said to be "lying in," a euphemism for being pregnant.
(Perhaps he was used to slurs; born to his father's mistress, Arlette, daughter
of a commoner, he had to endure being called a bastard.)

Advised by court physicians to lose weight, William journeyed to Rouen,
France, in the summer of 1087. There he planned to undergo a regimen of
dieting, herbs, and medications alleged to shed fat. Philip of France, told of
William's plans, publicly mocked the British monarch's obesity. Defiantly William announced he would march into Paris and "light a thousand candles": The
custom of lighting a candle was then a practice followed by a woman after
childbirth; for William, it would symbolize the loss of the paunch he was to shed
at Rouen.

But the well-intentioned corpulent king never lit a candle, or shed a pound.

The final business before beginning his weight-loss program was retaliation
against an invading French garrison at the border town of Mantes. The king
and his army captured, sacked, and burned the town. But while the obese victor
was riding his horse among smoldering ruins, the animal stepped on a fiery
ember and jostled its rider violently against the saddle's iron pommel. The
internal injury was severe, rupturing the intestines, allowing waste matter to
poison the abdomen. Peritonitis set in and spread quickly.

William was carried to a suburb of Rouen, where he lay for five weeks in agonizing pain. The discomfort was aggravated by an intense July heat, humidity, "flies, and the innumerable noises of the city." For company he had his bishops, doctors, half-brother Robert (who would soon become king of Normandy and Maine), and younger sons, Henry and William Rufus (who would rule the British part of the kingdom). When the summer heat became life threatening, William was moved to a cool, shaded priory on a hill west of the town. But from rampant peritonitis he deteriorated rapidly. On the morning of September 9, surrounded by a group of noblemen, the king folded his hands in prayer and lapsed into a coma.

The noblemen, fearful of the anarchy that would follow the announcement of William's death, fled from the priory to protect their estates. The king's body was entrusted to local attendants, but by the time clergy arrived to administer last rites, the corpse had been stripped of valuables and the room plundered, the king's personal possessions nowhere to be found.

William's funeral service was held on a blisteringly hot day. When the body was lifted from the bier and transferred to an expressly made sarcophagus, it was discovered that the fit was considerably on the snug side. From postmortem decay the abscess had turgidly putrified, bloating the corpse and expanding its girth. A group of bishops applied pressure on the king's abdomen to force the body downward, but it moved only inches; the lid still would not shut. Again they pushed, and the abdominal wall, already under intense internal pressure, burst. Pus and putrifaction drenched the king's death garb and seeped throughout the coffin. The stench so overpowered chapel mourners that, hands to noses, many raced for the doors. The bishops, able only partially to close the coffin's lid, conducted a hasty service and turned the corpse over for quick interment.

The king was buried in St. Stephen's Church, which he had built at Caen. His bones were allowed to molder peacefully until the year 1562, when the Huguenots, in an act of futile spite, dug them up and strewed them about the courtyard.

Joan of Arc: d. 1431, age 19

> **Cause of death:** Burning at the stake
>
> **Place of rest:** Remains thrown into the Seine
>
> **Last words:** As flames ignited her robe: *"I have great fear you are going to suffer by my death . . . Jesus! Jesus!"*

It is difficult to separate Joan of Arc's life and brutal death from what George Bernard Shaw called "the whitewash which disfigures her beyond recognition." Her ending, though—involving a sensational trial and public execution—is at least more extensively documented than her early years.

Jeanne D'Arc, Jeannette to her family, was the youngest of five children, born of well-to-do peasant parents at Domrémy in the French duchy of Bar. She received no formal education, could neither read nor write, and worked as a housemaid and a shepherdess. Intensely pious and patriotic, she was disturbed

Joan of Arc: visions accompanied by vomiting and vertigo.

by the ongoing Hundred Years War between her homeland and England.

At age thirteen, something miraculous—or at least medically significant—happened to the religious teenager. She heard voices and saw visions of St. Michael, dressed as a knight, attended by St. Margaret and St. Catherine. For three years the numina whispered in her ear.

In 1428, when Joan was sixteen, the voices bade her go to the dauphin, Charles VII, and reveal she had a divine mission: to drive the English and Burgundians from his country, to dedicate the cleansed kingdom to the service of God, and to see the dauphin's coronation (which had occurred eleven years earlier) finally consecrated (something that had been impossible since the traditional consecration site, Rheims, was deep within English-held territory). The dauphin liked what he heard. He entrusted the fervent teenager with his troops.

By this time, Joan had dramatically altered her appearance. Her long dark hair was cropped to above the ears and her stocky muscular figure was swathed in masculine garb. In the name of God, Joan rallied French forces, and her victory at Orléans was read by the dauphin and his men as a miracle, proof of her divine mission. Two months later, the king was consecrated at Rheims.

It was both Joan's victory and her voices that led to her end. On May 22, 1430, the eighteen-year-old Joan was captured and imprisoned by the English she helped defeat. Twelve serious charges were brought against her, including the "abomination" of wearing men's clothing, the shedding of British blood, and refusal to disavow her saintly voices.

Were the voices real or imaginary?

Centuries ago, a young girl reporting voices and visions was thought to be in touch with a saint or a demon. Today she would be placed in a mental institution for observation. Many medical historians have, in effect, placed Joan of Arc under their care and come up with diagnoses.

First the facts.

At her trial in 1431, Joan gave the court several intriguing specifics about the voices. She first heard them only when she was afraid. She could not decipher their sotto voce messages until the third visitation, when the saints first materialized visually. And she could never interpret the voices if there were noises in the house or yard. The apparitions, she said, were accompanied by a "pleasant odor," and the fear they instilled (which she later experienced as awe) brought her to her knees.

From a modern perspective, she confessed a most telling fact: "I heard the voice on the right hand side . . . and rarely do I hear it without a brightness . . . [that] comes from the same side. It is usually a great light."

Joan's jailers, who observed her over many weeks, claimed that occasionally her rapturous attacks were accompanied by fits of vomiting.

Now the modern medical opinion.

It is most likely that from the age of puberty Joan suffered from intermittent attacks of severe tinnitus, the annoying singing or ringing in the ears that many sufferers translate into speech. The tinnitus was unilateral, on the right side, and accompanied by visual disturbances in the form of bright lights, not an uncommon phenomenon. In acute cases, the flashing lights often bring on disorientation, nausea, and vomiting—all symptoms Joan experienced. The tinnitus probably also affected the ear's semicircular canals that control balance, for the sounds and images often caused her to sit down or fall down. Today this condition of imbalance is called Ménière's disease.

An alternate medical opinion is that Joan of Arc suffered from a particular type of brain tumor, a tuberculoma. Occurring in the temporo-sphenoidal region of the brain, the growth can produce symptoms of voices and visions. Whatever the diagnosis, today Joan would be hospitalized.

Her inquisitors ordered: "Death, by burning at the stake." The nineteen-year-old Joan was terrified to burn, yet she would not denounce the saintly nature of her apparitions.

At 9:00 A.M. on May 30, 1431, Joan stepped into the prison cart and was drawn to the marketplace at Rouen. The square was packed with soldiers, church dignitaries, nobles, and townsfolk. As she was being dragged to the stake, Joan pleaded that a crucifix be brought from the church so she might fix her gaze on it until the end. This was done. She was tied to the stake, and the miter of the Inquisition—a headband bearing the familiar slogan, "Heretic, Relapse, Apostate, Idolatress"—was slipped over her hair.

Executioners lighted cordwood at strategic locations and flames flickered up and around her feet. A monk held the cross she had requested high in the air, forcing her to stare upward, away from the mounting flames. From the smoke, she coughed, and, licked by the first flames, she screamed. The rambunctious crowd froze. From that moment, a deathly silence hung over the square, broken only by the crackling of timber. As her clothes were engulfed, Joan glanced heavenward, and half imploring, half screaming, cried: *"Jesus! Jesus!"*

When her clothing was entirely seared off—but her flesh not yet consumed—the burning wood was yanked away so spectators could view that the sentence had been carried out. "They saw her quite naked," said one account, "revealing all the secrets of a woman, and when this vision had lasted long enough, the executioners rekindled the fire high around the poor corpse." The executioners knew how to give a crowd its money's worth.

Her remains were thrown into the Seine.

Terrible Mistake.   A quarter-century after her death, the church that had condemned Joan posthumously retried her. It concluded that Joan of Arc was in fact a good Catholic, privy to saintly apparitions, and had been unjustly punished by hasty but well-intentioned clerics. There were political reasons for this new verdict: Exonerating Joan removed the shadow that hung over the dauphin's holy consecration as king at Joan's behest; and, too, a growing mass of Catholics were beginning to view Joan's death as martyrdom.

But for centuries the issue remained a delicate one for the church. Finally, in 1909, the Vatican officially declared Joan "blessed," and in 1920 Pope Benedict XV canonized her a saint. With an important proviso: Joan of Arc is not a martyred saint of the Catholic Church, because her death was brought about by a properly constituted court of that church. That court had simply made a mistake. Technically, the church can err and execute, but it cannot martyr. It can recognize a martyr, appreciate a martyr, but a martyr can be made only by someone other than the church.

Christopher Columbus: d. 1506, age 55

> **Cause of death:** Rheumatic heart disease
>
> **Place of rest:** Columbus monument, Cathedral of Santo Domingo
>
> **Last words:** *"Into Thy hands, O Lord, I commend my spirit."*

Pain, gout, poor vision, arthritis, delusions, and delirium plagued Christopher Columbus at the end of his life. In a sense, they were brought on or aggravated by his four arduous voyages to a new land that would ultimately be named not for him but for another explorer. When he landed in Spain at the end of his last ocean crossing, he could barely walk unaided. Each trip had brought the tall, freckled, red-headed discoverer of the New World one step closer to death.

The eldest of five children of the Colón family (perhaps of Spanish-Jewish ancestry) residing in Genoa when Christopher was born, Columbus went to sea at age fourteen. He was healthy—a condition he would enjoy until about forty-five—when, on Friday, August 3, 1492, he sailed westward from Palos de la Prontera, Spain, inaugurating an epoch of maritime discovery.

His first health complaint was minor. Gone from Europe for 225 days, he recorded in his journal only "sore eyes," or "ophthalmia" as an early biographer called it. The condition, today known as trachoma, is brought on by long exposure to the glare of bright sunlight, and Columbus is known to have spent countless hours gazing toward the western horizon. Minor though it was, the ailment plagued him for the rest of his life.

On his second voyage, in 1494, Columbus became severely ill. His symp-

Christopher Columbus; woodcut from his report on discovery of the Antilles.

toms were a high fever and delirium, most likely from typhus. He recorded (in third person) that the ailment "cast him into a dangerous disease between a pestilential fever and lethargy, which deprived him of sense and memory." Lying stuporous, he thought himself near death.

Yet he believed life could not end before completion of his "divinely ordained" mission to find a westward passage to the east coast of Asia. As he later wrote of his New World landing to King Ferdinand and Queen Isabella: "neither reason nor mathematics nor maps were any use to me: fully accomplished were the words of Isaiah." (The reference is to Isaiah 11:10–12, which he believed forecast the discovery.)

Within two weeks, the fever and delirum passed. But for the next five months, spent largely in the West Indies, febrile attacks came and went with irregular frequency. During that time, many of his men came down with syphilis, and perhaps Columbus himself. Whether the admiral and his sailors gave it to the American natives or vice versa is a medical issue still unsettled. (See "Syphilis," page 236.)

His third trip to the New World, begun on May 30, 1498, brought more serious health complaints. Throughout June and into August, his joints ached and swelled and he battled a high fever. He wrote (when he could, and now in first person): "The ailment . . . [that] afflicts me is so bad. . . . My illness prevents me writing except at night. In the daytime my hands have no strength." Though early biographers attributed the condition to gout, later ones narrowed it more precisely to rheumatoid arthritis, a disease that was taking a fatal toll on his heart.

"Ambassador of God."   It was also during this third voyage that serious evidence of mental derangement and auditory hallucinations occurred (which have prompted speculations of syphilis). On Christmas Day, 1499, Columbus recorded that he heard a heavenly voice: "Take courage. Be not afraid, nor fear. I will provide for all." The voice would speak to him at length on his fourth, and last, trip, by which time Columbus was referring to himself as the Ambassador of God.

This is an interesting reference, for though he never identified himself with Christ, Columbus's final words—*"In manus tuas, Domine, commendo spiritum meum"*—are Christ's dying words on the cross.

Despite acute disablement from rheumatoid arthritis and mental confusion (or because of the latter), Columbus set off in May of 1502 on an unsuccessful voyage to the New World. He was ill, confined to his cabin most of the journey. His plight was aggravated by inadequate food supplies, storm, shipwreck, mutiny, and being marooned for a year in Jamaica. In addition, he was bitter because other explorers were now sailing westward in "his seas" and landing on "his islands," depriving him of future finds.

He confided sarcastically to his journal: "They all made fun of my plan then; now even tailors wish to discover."

When he returned to Spain for the last time in 1504, he had to be carried ashore.

His body was severely swollen, especially from the chest down, which led early physicians posthumously to diagnose "cardiac dropsy" due to syphilis-damaged heart valves. Bedridden, with a grossly distended belly and stiff limbs, Columbus lingered until May 20, 1506. A priest was finally summoned, a Mass said, and in the presence of friends and relatives the great explorer, called the modern Aristotle, received the last rites. His heart simply stopped beating—a heart that, contemporary physicians say, was most likely damaged by rheumatic fever rather than syphilis.

With fitting irony, Columbus's corpse traveled almost as far as the navigator had himself. First buried at the Church of San Francisco in Valladolid, his body was moved in 1513 by order of his son Diego to a chapel in the monastery of Santa Maria de las Cuevas, Seville. Then in 1542, his bones, along with his son's, were taken in lead caskets to Santo Domingo and interred before the high altar of the cathedral. When Santo Domingo was ceded to the French in 1795, Columbus's remains were moved to Havana. When Cuba won its independence, Columbus was taken to Spain and placed in a modern monument in Seville Cathedral.

But in 1877, when the presbytery of the Cathedral of Santo Domingo was enlarged, a small lead casket was discovered bearing at both ends the letters "CCA," probably standing for *Cristóbal Colón Almirante.* Had Columbus never been moved to Havana and Spain? Historians today feel certain that the authentic remains of Christopher Columbus are under his monument in the Cathedral of Santo Domingo.

John Paul Jones: d. 1792, age 45

Cause of death: Chronic kidney inflammation and bronchial pneumonia

Place of rest: U.S. Naval Academy, Annapolis, Maryland

Most memorable words: *"I have not yet begun to fight!"*

The most traumatizing event in the life of John Paul Jones, naval hero of the American War of Independence, was not a military defeat but the charge of rape of a ten-year-old girl. Once asked if he had ever been wounded, the embittered seaman alluded to the alleged pedophilia: "Never on the sea, but on the land I have been bled by arrows never launched by the English." The besmirching charge hounded the notorious ladies' man up until his early death at age forty-five.

Born to the Paul family of Scotland, John left home at age thirteen to become an apprentice seaman. In 1773, while in port in Tobago in the West Indies, the crew of the ship under his command mutinied and he killed their leader. Convinced he could not get a fair trial on the island, he fled to Fredericksburg, Virginia, assuming the name John Jones. By the time of the Revolutionary War, he felt safe in calling himself John Paul Jones. It was in a fierce sea battle with the British, which Jones's forces were losing, that he shouted the memorable "I have not yet begun to fight!," which turned out to be stunningly true.

His weakness lay in women, particularly young women, as young as thirteen. This was no secret to his male intimates. On a trip to Paris in the spring of 1780, Jones took to heart Ben Franklin's advice that the fastest way to learn French was to find oneself "a sleeping dictionary." "The men of France I esteem," Jones penned in his journal. "But the women of France! What words can I find to express my homage, my worship, my devotion!"

But it was a Russian—a ten-year-old girl—who inflicted an emotional wound

John Paul Jones: a penchant for young girls.

from which the naval hero never recovered. At the time she alleged rape, Jones was an appointed rear admiral in the Russian navy, having been enlisted by Empress Catherine II to assist her country in fighting the Turks. Jones maintained that the child had "lent herself to do all that a man would want of her," but that he had honorably marshaled restraint and not "deflowered" her. The enticement, he insisted, was actually an entrapment, a ruse plotted by rival Russian naval officers to sully his honor.

Not surprisingly, his legendary philandering worked against him, and under the stress of nationwide Russian disbelief his health began to deteriorate. Before Jones left Russia, Catherine the Great cleared him of the charge, though insiders believed the empress herself, jealous of an affair between Jones and her lady-in-waiting (who supposedly bore Jones a son), had entrapped the American seaman.

Jones settled in France, an embittered and broken man. Although he was only forty-three, his hair was gray, his face deeply creased, his posture stooped, and he coughed and wheezed incessantly. French doctors diagnosed pulmonary tuberculosis. He would live less than two years.

In 1792, near the end of his life, parts of his body filled with fluid and the flesh discolored; his physician diagnosed dropsy of the breast and jaundice. That summer the swelling traveled upward, bloating the lower abdomen. He was visited by friends on the afternoon of July 18 and last seen alive sitting in his favorite armchair. Some time during that night, with the cannons of the French Revolution breaking around his apartment, John Paul Jones must have attempted to make it into bed. His body was discovered the next day lying facedown on the mattress, with his feet dangling to the floor.

Placed in a lead coffin, he was ceremoniously buried in the St. Louis Protestant Cemetery, a plot of French ground reserved for foreigners. The naval hero was forgotten. The cemetery, subsumed under the sprawling expansion of the city of Paris, was itself buried and lost.

In 1899, the United States ambassador to France, Horace Porter, learned that a slum-clearance project had uncovered a field of toppled tombstones. At his own expense, Porter began a search for the hero's grave. Shafts were sunk, with tunnels dug laterally. By 1905, five lead coffins had been retrieved. Three bore other nameplates; one contained the skeleton of a man taller than Jones had been. The remaining body, autopsied by a dozen physicians, was determined to be that of the seaman.

The corpse, though not internally embalmed, had been sealed in the lead coffin and drenched in an alcohol bath. It was in remarkably good condition; John Paul Jones had been pickled. The kidneys indicated that he had suffered for years from chronic interstitial nephritis, a kidney inflammation. But the immediate cause of death was most likely bronchial pneumonia, perhaps contracted during his hardships and ill health in Russia. The initial diagnosis of "dropsy of the breast" to account for the distended limbs and abdomen was revised to "a decompensated heart which had resulted from the high blood pressure incidental to chronic glomerular nephritis." Clinically, as occurs in cases of fatal pneumonia, the patient actually dies of cardiac arrest.

In July of 1905, under orders from President Theodore Roosevelt, the

U.S.S. *Brooklyn,* escorted by a squadron of seven American warships, brought the body of John Paul Jones back to the United States. Commemorative services were held at the U.S. Naval Academy at Annapolis the following April, and the corpse was sealed in a specially designed tomb below the academy chapel, which today is a national monument.

Giovanni Casanova: d. 1798, age 73

Cause of death: Kidney infection caused by acute prostatitis and toxic venereal disease treatment

Place of rest: St. Barbara Chapel Cemetery, Duchcov, Czechoslovakia

Last words: On receiving extreme unction: *"Bear witness that I have lived as a philosopher and die as a Christian."*

It is perhaps fitting that history's best-known seducer—who said, "A woman is like a book which, be it good or bad, must begin to please with its title page"—met his end through venereal disease infections and their accompanying toxic treatments. Before the age of forty, Casanova was treated for no fewer than eleven bouts of syphilis and gonorrhea; in time his kidneys failed and his prostate became acutely inflamed. The last thirteen years of his life were chaste, his only pleasure eating, of which a biographer noted: "Since he could no longer be a god in the gardens, he became a wolf at the table."

History's great lover, who fathered an uncountable number of bastards, was himself illegitimate, born in Venice on April 5, 1725, to a promiscuous Italian actress, Zanetta Farussi, and one of her many lovers—which one is uncertain, perhaps Michele Grimani, of a patrician theatrical family. Casanova himself was never able to unravel his parentage; he believed that his brother, Francesco, was sired by the Prince of Wales while Zanetta was performing in England.

Casanova: satyr to impotent librarian.

Sex brought about his downfall, and the dalliances—heterosexual and homosexual—began at an early age. At eleven, he claimed, the stroking of a woman bathing him woke him to sexuality. Not long afterward, he lost his virginity—to two women at once. As a young man he entered the seminary of St. Cyprian to become a priest, but was soon expelled for a homosexual intrigue with a priest.

In 1789, when he was sixty-four and sexually spent, he decided to alleviate boredom by committing to paper recollections of a lifetime of amorous encounters. The vivid autobiography, *Histoire de ma vie* ("The Story of My Life"), runs 4,545 pages and covers his sex life only up to the summer of 1774, when he was forty-nine.

From an unexpurgated English version of the memoir, published in twelve volumes between 1966 and 1971, and from a detailed 1969 biography, we know about the diseases that led to his death. In addition to the eleven bouts of venereal disease—which did not render him even temporarily chaste, but only compelled him to wear an "overcoat," a euphemism of the day for a waxed cloth prophylactic—he is believed to have suffered and survived smallpox, pleurisy, pneumonia, and two attacks of malaria. It is remarkable that he lived to age seventy-three—and died, as he claimed, "a Christian."

Casanova was more than a full-time lover. He was also a part-time humorist, writer, occultist, compulsive gambler, and served briefly as the organizer of the French state lottery. He considered marriage a "tomb of love," preferring instead the "inexpressible charm of stolen pleasures," which he stole indiscriminately: from his daughter, Leonilda; from a Russian lieutenant, Lunin; from an Italian nun, whom he referred to as "Mother Mary M."

Modern physicians believe that Casanova's venereal infections, and the harsh and largely ineffective mercuric treatments of the era, permanently weakened his urogenital tract, leading to a fatal septic infection of prostatitis.

When the ailment struck full force, he was librarian to Count Waldstein in the chateau at Dux, Bohemia (modern Duchcov, Czechoslovakia). He had published verse, criticism, a translation of the *Iliad,* satirical pamphlets on the Venetian patriciate, and in 1788, a year before his death, a fantastic futuristic tale called *Icosameron* that anticipates science fiction.

But he was a quarrelsome, garrulous curmudgeon, bored, impotent, and in agonizing pain from an inflamed prostate. Doctors could do nothing for him; friends nursed him. His penultimate words show he remained in character to nearly the end: "Life is a wench that one loves, to whom we allow any condition in the world, so long as she does not leave us." When a priest arrived, the great lover confessed enough transgressions to conclude, "I die as a Christian." He passed away that morning of June 4, 1798, in Dux. Anyone who has read through Casanova's immense autobiography will have noticed that the obsession with women diminished as his craving for fame and intellectual accomplishments increased.

He was buried behind the Saint Barbara Chapel in the town cemetery in Dux. In 1922, a stone bearing his name and the date 1799 was discovered, but no trace was found of his remains. A memorial tablet erected in recent years reads "Jakob Casanova/Venedig 1725/Dux 1798."

CHAPTER 15

Final Farewells of Artists and Writers

Pepys to Poe

Samuel Pepys: d. 1703, age 70

Cause of death: Degenerative heart disease and arteriosclerosis, plus uremic poisoning

Place of rest: St. Olave's Church, London

Last diary entry: On the belief he was going blind: "It is almost as much as to see myself go into my grave . . . the good God prepare me!"

Samuel Pepys, England's first secretary of the Admiralty—better remembered for the 1,250,000-word diary he kept from 1660 to 1669, between his 27th and 36th years—made two significant farewells to life: his death, of course, and the abandonment of his extraordinary diary under the belief that he faced blindness. He remained sighted, but Pepys never resumed the tell-all journal that spared no personage of the time, including the sexually insatiable Pepys himself. Among other weaknesses, he confessed to an obsession for kissing and fondling the breasts of women, particularly women of the lower classes. The lower the better. He did this frequently, and was caught often.

The diary, written in a secret shorthand, fills six volumes. Far more than a talented writer's dirty thoughts and deeds, it is a work of art, vividly depicting England during the reign of Charles II, including London's devastating plague and great fire. With an artist's gift for detail, Pepys brought to life not only

Samuel Pepys: a fondness for fondling breasts.

historical events, but people's infidelities, foibles, and vanity.

So explicit was the diary that he kept it under lock and key. Passages detailing his erotic affairs were disguised beyond the shorthand by the strategic use of words in Spanish, French, Dutch, Greek, Italian, and Latin. Although the diary was first published in 1825, over a hundred passages that dealt too explicitly with sex and defecation were not made public until the 1970s.

There is evidence today that eyestrain from writing the diary, coupled with astigmatism, caused Pepys to believe he was going blind. But when he abandoned the work at age thirty-six, he was already a man living on borrowed time.

At twenty-two, he was "cut for the stone," that is, he underwent major bladder stone surgery—two hundred years before physicians used anesthetics or antiseptics. The survival rate from the operation was less than five percent. A patient submitted to the surgeon's unsterilized knife and unwashed hands only when desperate and nearly mad from unrelenting pain. Pepys's surgeon removed a stone the size of a tennis ball, weighing two ounces.

The operation brought Pepys great relief, but it led to a lifetime of urinary tract disorders, as well as to kidney failure and uremic poisoning that helped end his life. Pepys preserved the stone in a bottle and toasted it every March 26, the anniversary of his surgery. But he continued to pass many minor stones and gravel, and later endured the agony of a kidney stone that could not be surgically removed. A physician prescribed daily doses of turpentine, which cured nothing and irritated his urogenital track and poisoned his kidneys.

Pepys enjoyed an unexpected benefit from the bladder stone surgery: a slip of the knife accidentally left him sterile. He and his wife led an active sex life, especially, he confessed, after she would catch him fondling a servant girl's breasts. And when she found him with his head under a girl's skirt, Pepys wrote that he and his wife made love "more times since this falling-out than in, I believe, twelve months before. And with more pleasure to her than, I think, in all the time of our marriage before."

When his wife, Elizabeth, died in a typhoid epidemic that struck London in 1669, Pepys became even more sexually active, despite continual kidney pain. As he aged, the stones and urinary tract disorders worsened, and a rich meal washed down with wine, which he enjoyed almost as much as women, brought on acute indigestion and fire in his bladder. Yet he never gave up wine or women, convinced his death would come from bleeding hemorrhoids, a topic given much exposure in the diary.

Pepys spent the last fourteen years of his life in retirement from his military career. Much of his time was devoted to collecting material for a comprehensive history of the British navy, a masterwork he never completed. After his death on May 26, 1703, an autopsy authenticated numerous bladder and kidney stones, as well as severe arteriosclerosis. It is impossible to say whether hardening of the arteries or suppressed kidney function and its subsequent uremic poisoning did him in. His doctors and friends marveled that he remained so productive and promiscuous up until nearly the end.

Samuel Johnson: d. 1784, age 75

Cause of death: High blood pressure and renal disease

Place of rest: Westminster Abbey, London

Last words: To a sickbed visitor: *"God bless you, my dear . . . I am dying now."*

A brilliant mind can function and even thrive in a diseased body, as was the case with Samuel Johnson. He met his end at age seventy-five, after as many years of ill health. In fact, his problems started *before* birth.

Poet, essayist, critic, journalist, lexicographer, and, chiefly, conversationalist, Johnson is regarded as one of the outstanding men of letters of the eighteenth century. After Shakespeare, he is possibly the best-known figure and the most frequently quoted in the whole of English literature. But the disparity between the vigor of Johnson's mind and body was vast. His mind was one of the most brilliant of the age, whether he was writing on Shakespeare or compiling his forty-thousand-word *Dictionary,* long the greatest of the English language. His body, however, had to be one of the time's most troubled, with aches and ailments that could fill a medical dictionary.

Born in 1709, when his mother was forty years old, Johnson was initially thought to be a stillbirth. Fortunately, he was not abandoned; after strenuous shakes and forceful slaps, he unleashed life's cry. Then, unwittingly, he was fed infected cow's milk that carried tuberculosis bacteria. The infant developed scrofula, or the "king's evil," a glandular infection of the neck. The cure was thought to be a touch by royalty, and the young Johnson, age three, was taken to see Queen Anne, the last British sovereign to perform this ceremony. On the way, he caught a severe cold that nearly killed him.

The royal touch did no good, though throughout his infirm life he treasured the gold amulet the queen had hung around his neck. Eventually the infected glands were surgically incised, after the disease had destroyed sight in his left eye and hearing in his left ear; the surgery itself almost killed him. "My health," Johnson later wrote, "seldom afforded me a single day of ease."

An abridged dictionary of his complaints:

- Asthma. For the most severe attacks, he was bled, often with more than thirty-six ounces taken over three days of treatment.
- Aphasia, the temporary loss of speech. Johnson suffered only one attack, during which time he mentally translated prayers into Latin to comfort himself that he was not going insane. The attack is thought today to have been due to a minor cerebral hemorrhage.
- Bronchitis, a condition he suffered chronically.
- Corneal ulcerations, which resulted in blindness in the left eye.
- Deafness. He had a peculiar form of hearing loss called paracusis. It is characterized by the ability to hear better in a noisy environment than a quiet one. (The disease was first described in the seventeenth century by Dr. Thomas Willis, and in a woman who could hear her husband only when a drum was beaten.) Today it's thought that intense vibrations shake an otherwise rigid inner ear mechanism to help it transmit ordinary sound.
- Dropsy, an early term for edema, the excessive accumulation of fluids in body tissues. Johnson frequently experienced severe swelling of the thighs and calves and was bled in those areas. Once, when no doctor was available, he used a household scissors to puncture both calves, draining off ten ounces.
- Emphysema, which, when compounded by Johnson's asthma and bronchitis, terrified him that he'd suffocate to death.
- Flatulence. Johnson's gas, by his own admission, was excessive and embarrassing; "My nights are flatulent and unquiet. . . . I was last night almost convulsed with flatulence." Intolerant of the trait in others, he once castigated a friend: "Do not be like the spider, man, and spin conversation incessantly out of thine own bowels."
- Gallstones. At autopsy, one was found to be "the size of a common gooseberry." His gallstones and his persistent indigestion where thought to have contributed to his flatulence.
- Gout, which he called "rheumatism."
- Hydrocele, a collection of body fluid in the scrotum, for which Johnson had to be drained.
- Tics of the face and limbs. A friend described him as often having "convulsive starts and odd gesticulations which tended to one's surprise and ridicule." Another acquaintance spotted Johnson "shaking his head and rolling himself about in a strange ridiculous manner" like "an idiot."

Manic Depression.   The ailment that most incapacitated the great conversationalist throughout his lifetime was melancholia. Today it's believed that Samuel Johnson suffered from a hereditary form of manic depressive psychosis, perhaps inherited from his father, whom he described as "robust in body . . . but addicted to a vile melancholy." Bouts of depression were so severe in Johnson's twenties that he took walks of up to thirty miles in the hope of relief through fatigue. Depression was accompanied by fear of approaching insanity: "I would consent to have a limb amputated to recover my spirits."

Interestingly, the trait for which Samuel Johnson is most remembered—his spirited conversation—was by his own admission a means of escaping from depression. He talked incessantly, compulsively, to drown out inner dark moods. His biographer, Boswell, said Johnson believed "the great business of life was to escape from himself." Solitude was a horror. And when Johnson could not overpower depression with conversation, he turned to brandy "to get rid of myself; to send myself away."

Depression plagued him up until the end, as did his dread of solitude. As an old man, with many friends deceased, he formed clubs to provide him with the conversation he loved and needed desperately. A year before his death, and gravely ill, he formed a club near his home. Friends described him as "hungry for conversation," particularly late in the evening when his listeners thinned out, retiring to bed.

In December of 1784, when it was clear that the end was near, Johnson welcomed death. The bronchitis and edema were imminently life-threatening. Bled by doctors, he pleaded they cut deeper and take more. When they would not, he bled himself. Though in great pain, he refused drugs so "that I may render up my soul to God unclouded." His diseased bladder left him incontinent. As Boswell wrote of Johnson's end: "The Doctor, from the time that he was certain his death was near, appeared to be perfectly resigned, was seldom or never fretful or out of temper."

On his last day, December 13, he was visited by a lady friend, a Miss Morris. But the great conversationalist, who charmed listeners and could never have a large enough audience, managed only a few words: "God bless you, my dear . . . I am dying now." By nightfall the end was near. "His difficulty of breathing increased till about seven o'clock in the evening," recorded Boswell, "when Mr. Barber and Mrs. Desmoulins, who were sitting in the room, observing that the noise he made breathing had ceased, went to the bed, and found he was dead."

Jane Austen: d. 1817, age 41

> **Cause of death:** Addison's disease
>
> **Place of rest:** Winchester Cathedral, Winchester, England
>
> **Last words:** Asked what might relieve her suffering: *"I want nothing but death."*

The illness that killed English novelist Jane Austen on July 18, 1817, is the same that afflicted President John F. Kennedy.

Addison's disease, an insidious and progressive atrophy of the adrenal cortex, causes weakness, weight loss, and dangerously low blood pressure. If untreated (by corticosteroids) it darkens the skin of the face, sometimes to black, and can be fatal. Jane Austen's ailment was not diagnosed correctly until 1964, when Dr. Zachary Cope, writing in the *British Medical Journal,* concluded that her symptoms, recorded in detail by the novelist, most closely fit Addison's disease. Prior to that time she was thought to have died of tuberculosis of the adrenals.

Addison's disease was unknown in Jane Austen's day. It was first described by Dr. Thomas Addison, the Father of Endocrinology, in 1849, thirty-two years after her death.

Up until the onset of the painful ailment in the summer of 1816, Jane Austen was a healthy, highly productive woman. The disease that brought her to an early death at age forty-one greatly altered her life and her work.

Born on December 16, 1775, in the Hampshire village of Steventon where her father was rector, Jane was the second daughter and seventh child in a family of eight: six boys and two girls. Her closest companion throughout life was her elder sister, Cassandra, who, like Jane, never married. Her first novel, *Sense and Sensibility,* was begun in 1795, when she was twenty. And through a series of books, including *Pride and Prejudice* (1813) and *Persuasion* (published posthumously the year of her death), she gave the English novel its distinctly modern character through her detailed treatment of ordinary people going about everyday life.

Fortunately she recorded with equal accuracy the aches and ailments of her own everyday life. Unlike her novels, her life was no comedy of manners. The disease struck suddenly, when she was in her intellectual prime. In a year she would be dead.

A few months after her fortieth birthday she was overcome with feelings of weakness and chronic fatigue. A sharp ache developed in her back muscles. By July of that year, 1816, the backache was acute and unending, forcing her to turn down several dinner invitations. Despite the pain and her inability to sit up for long periods of time, she finished *Persuasion* and resumed work on

Jane Austen: concerned about the discoloration of her skin.

an earlier manuscript that would become *Northanger Abbey*. She admitted that she was pushing herself, and the effort probably exacerbated her symptoms: Addison's disease reaches crisis proportions under periods of maximum stress.

A further symptom of the disease is severe gastrointestinal irritation. It's accompanied by persistent nausea and sometimes vomiting. By New Year's Day of 1817, Jane Austen was battling all of these ailments, though unaware of the seriousness of her condition. The theory of "ill humors" (see page 260) then clouded medical reasoning, and Austen felt her symptoms were due to rank bile: "I am more and more convinced that *bile* is at the bottom of all I have suffered." She continued treating herself.

That same month, though languid and feverish, she plunged into work on another novel. It would be her last book, *Sanditon,* and in less than eight weeks she wrote and polished more than twenty-four thousand words. But the effort, she realized, was a race against time. By March her skin was discoloring and her sleep fitful. Forced to put aside the novel because of "fever at times and indifferent nights," she wrapped warm flannel around her knees, which creaked and throbbed.

What troubled her most, though, was her face.

Addison's disease causes an overproduction of melanin, the skin-darkening pigment. The browning is not uniform, as a suntan can be, but blotchy. Jane Austen stared frequently into a mirror and recorded her complexion as "black and white and every wrong colour." She thought the rancorous "bile" was backing up into her bloodstream. Profoundly weak, her hands now shaky, she wrote very little, spending her days confined to a couch, checking her complexion—a fair barometer of the illness's advance.

As her novels had been wry comedies, she recorded her own dire symptoms with humor and not a trace of self-pity. In March she experienced one final burst of energy, and that was channeled into *Sanditon,* which, coincidently, was a scathing satire on nineteenth-century health resorts, medicine, and invalidism.

In April, convinced the end was near, she wrote her will. Cassandra would be the guardian of Jane's privacy and her writings; after Jane's death Cassandra took it upon herself to destroy many of Jane's notes, letters, and to irretrievably censor much of her correspondence.

In May, Austen was taken from her home in Chawton to Winchester, seventeen miles away, to be under the continual care of an expert physician and surgeon, who, unfortunately, was unable to do anything useful for her. In her new lodgings she wrote, "I live chiefly on the sofa, but am allowed to walk from one room to another."

With the censorious Cassandra at her side, Jane Austen died at 4:30 A.M. on July 18, 1817. Six days later she was buried in Winchester Cathedral.

Only with the end of her life could her fame begin (though not immediately, since her sharp comedies of Regency society would for a time be enjoyed as "merely domestic" novels). Jane Austen had written anonymously and had taken pains to conceal her identity. She was the "nameless author." Now, after her death, her favorite brother, Henry, who greatly encouraged her writing and helped to get her novels published, announced her authorship to the world. In a "Biographical Notice of the author," Henry paid tribute to his sister's keen qualities of mind and noble character. And it was Henry who recorded Jane Austen's last words, uttered with characteristic decorum and economy: "I want nothing but death."

Unfortunately, it was also Henry who might have unknowingly contributed to the onset of his sister's Addison's disease. Emotional crises can trigger the ailment. And in 1815, Henry, who had been healthy and highly prosperous, fell seriously ill. Jane nursed him back to health, but in 1816 he went bankrupt. Both his illness and financial problems were shocks to Jane, and she began to record her own symptoms during the time of his crises.

Jane Austen did more than write timeless novels; through her detailed personal notes she also was the first person to describe the syndrome that became Addison's disease.

Francisco de Goya: d. 1828, age 82

> **Cause of death:** Stroke, after suffering a bizarre viral disorder, or severe lead poisoning
>
> **Place of rest:** Interred in a single coffin along with the remains of a friend, though only one head is present; Church of San Antonio de la Florida, Madrid

When Francisco Goya was forty-six years old—a skilled, successful, thoroughly conventional painter—he suffered an agonizing and mysterious illness. It almost ended his life. It definitely altered his personality and his art—and it seems to have thrust greatness upon him.

His paintings had been skilled, charming, some cloyingly picturesque. But the Goya who emerged from the illness, deaf and partially blind, was a tormented soul with a new perspective: His works were now filled nightmarishly with despair, vice, and cruelty—all depicted with originality and genius. The illness, whose nature has confounded biographers, marked the end of the conventional painter and the emergence of a revolutionary one.

There are clues to what caused this first major ending in Goya's life.

Goya's home outside Madrid; a victim of lead poisoning.

The onset of his illness was sudden, striking late in 1792. He was terrified by the bizarre spectrum of symptoms: dizziness, giddiness, nausea, impaired balance, mental confusion, hallucinations, convulsions, paralysis of the right side, impaired hearing and speech, relentless ringing in his ears, and, most frightening to an artist, partial blindness. Today it is clear that some agent assaulted his central nervous system. But what?

All Goya's biographers have played the guessing role of biohistorian. Syphilis acquired in youth might account for some of the symptoms, but not his almost miraculous recovery.

One recent and likely guess, made in 1962 by British virologist Dr. Terence Cawthorne, is a rare viral infection, Vogt-Koyanagi, named after the two physicians who identified it in 1906, A. Vogt and V. Koyanagi. Cawthorne himself had treated five people with symptoms like Goya's. He learned that the ailment typically begins with a temporary inflammation of the uveal tract of the eye, and progresses to deafness, paroxysms of giddiness, and often blindness. Some symptoms subside; others are permanent.

But an even more recent theory was advanced in 1972. In "Goya's Illness," published in the *New York State Journal of Medicine,* Dr. William Niederland argued that the artist suffered from extreme lead (and possibly mercury) poisoning, which damages the brain. From studying unpublished archival material about Goya's work habits and use of certain paint pigments, Niederland uncovered that the artist used cinnabar (a mercury compound) and most of his paintings were done over primings of homemade lead white. "Grinding this poisonous compound into paint is particularly hazardous," writes Niederland, "since it facilitates inhalation or ingestion by manual handling."

Niederland wondered why Goya should have suffered so acutely from lead poisoning when many other painters of his day did not. The answer lay in further details about Goya's artistic techniques.

First, Goya used lead white massively, more than any other hue, to achieve his famous mother-of-pearl luminosity. Second, Goya was amazingly prolific and probably the fastest great portraitist in history, sometimes finishing a painting in one or two sittings. Niederland calculated that when lead is ingested, less than ten percent is absorbed by the intestines and enters the bloodstream; the rest is excreted through the bowels. But lead inhaled as dust—as might occur with a painter grinding his own pigments—is far more dangerous: As much as sixty percent is retained by the body. Through inhalation alone, discounting skin and lip contact, Goya, because of his heavy reliance on white paint, probably absorbed three times as much lead as most painters who have suffered mild symptoms of lead poisoning.

Niederland also showed that Goya suffered a whole series of attacks that temporarily disabled him, the first at age thirty-two, the worst at age forty-six, and the last about two years before his death. Most interestingly, each bout kept Goya from painting, that is, away from toxic lead, allowing his body's level of the metal to drop slightly. Goya was always healthier after a respite from painting, and invariably some combination of symptoms returned after he resumed grinding pigments and painting feverishly.

Some biographers claim that Goya fathered nineteen stillborn and miscarried children, a medically significant clue if true. Chronic lead poisoning, or plumbism, deforms sperm and could account for the string of deaths.

As for the abrupt change in Goya's painting style—from conventional and gentle to embittered and cruel—dating from his life-threatening attack at age forty-six, the residual deafness, partial blindness, and chronic depression could easily account for the dark shift in personality and artistic perspective.

Despite bouts of illness, Goya thrived as the Spanish court painter. Even his sensual "Maja" paintings escaped the wrath of the Inquisition, though charges of obscenity were lodged against him. When in 1824 the autocratic Ferdinand VII initiated a political crackdown on liberals that threatened Goya's security, the elderly painter took refuge in Bordeaux, France, where he lived and worked in self-imposed exile.

On April, 16, 1828, he died of a stroke and was buried in the Cemetery of the Chartreuse in Bordeaux. In 1899, when the grave was opened to relocate the corpse to its permanent resting place in Madrid, Goya's remains were found to be jumbled together with those of a friend, Martin Goscoechea, whose tomb he shared. The box contained two skeletons but only one skull. Uncertain exactly which bones belonged to the painter, authorities transferred the full contents of the box to Madrid.

Today the confusion of relics lie side by side in a single sarcophagus in the Church of San Antonio de la Florida, below a dome decorated with magnificent frescoes by the man in the box who was Goya—and the transformed Goya at that. In terms of artistic greatness, had the painter's career ended prior to his major 1792 ailment, it would have survived with only passing mention, the work of a gifted artist, popular in his day, who missed greatness by a wide margin.

John Keats: d. 1821, age 26

> **Cause of death:** Tuberculosis
>
> **Place of rest:** The Protestant Cemetery, Rome
>
> **Last words:** Asked of a friend to facilitate breathing: *"Lift me up for I am dying. I shall die easy. Don't be frightened. Thank God it has come."*

Remembered as a poet, John Keats was also a licensed physician and he correctly diagnosed the consumption that tragically claimed his life at the age of twenty-six. He had prior personal experience with the ailment, the scourge of his century.

The eldest of four children born to a London livery stable manager, Keats, at age fifteen, watched his mother die a protracted tubercular death. Her consumption affected him profoundly, and he studied medicine at the renowned Guy's Hospital, London, being licensed in 1816.

Ironically, one of his first patients was his brother Tom, whose fatal ailment was also tuberculosis. Helpless to prevent a second family death, Keats abandoned medicine, devoting himself to writing poetry, an enjoyment begun in his youth. Medicine had been a detour, a mistake, but also a frightening eye-opener, for he had learned of tuberculosis's contagiousness and its penchant for running in families.

In the summer of 1818, Keats was vacationing on the island of Mull in the Hebrides, Scotland, when he caught a cold that refused to clear up. Aware of the ominousness of a persistent sore throat and fever—particularly in an otherwise healthy young male twice exposed to tuberculosis—Keats poured his energies into poetry, to forget and to produce as much as he could in the years remaining him, which would be three.

The following summer he vacationed on the Isle of Wight, another scenic but dank landmass surrounded by misty seas; the doctor was not taking his own best advice. Keats composed verse by daylight and at night wrote letters to friends, confiding in one correspondence: "I find my body too weak to support me to the height." If he rested and slept soundly, his throat did not bother him, but "on exertion or cold," he recorded, the soreness "continually threatens me."

The death knell symptom he had been dreading for two years arrived on the evening of February 3, 1820.

Following a coach ride through London, he returned to his lodgings, sweating from a high fever and with a hacking cough. No sooner had his close friend Charles Brown helped the poet into bed, when Keats, in a convulsion of coughing, spit blood-stained phlegm into a handkerchief. "Bring me a candle, Brown, let me see this blood." Brown fetched not only a candle but also a tall glass of whiskey. The twenty-five-year-old poet studied the stained cloth: "It is arterial blood! I cannot be deceived in that color. That drop of blood is my death warrant. I must die."

From that night onward, Keats's health sharply declined, but for a number of reasons. Chiefly because of his tuberculosis, but also from the severe depression he suffered in response to criticism of his published poetry. Additional stress came in the shapely form of his fiancée, Fanny Brawne. Keats was possessive of the young beauty, and her refusal to sleep with him because of

Keats (left) to companion Joseph Severn: "How long is this posthumous life of mine to last?"

his illness drove him into jealous rages. He was convinced there was another man.

Between sessions in which he was bled by his physician, Keats revised several of his poems. And he composed alternately passionate and poisonous letters to his fiancée. In June, he began to experience intermittent delusions of persecution, first blaming the illness on his literary critics and the torment they caused him, then on Fanny Brawne, whose infrequent visits seemed to him proof of her infidelity.

In August, he suffered a severe lung hemorrhage. The quantity of blood coughed up, and its puce color, encouraged him to contemplate suicide. He did not wish to die the agonizing death of his mother and brother. Advised to spend time in the relative warmth and dryness of Italy, Keats, accompanied by a friend, painter Joseph Severn, set sail on September 13.

The voyage to the land that was supposed to be his salvation turned out to be a nightmare. On the chilly seas, Keats became feverish, continually coughing up blood. Then near Naples the ship was quarantined for a hellish ten days due to rumors of typhoid. Ranting from fever, drenched in perspiration, Keats hovered between life and death. More than once he begged Severn to allow him to take his own life.

In Rome, the two men took lodgings in the Piazza di Spagna, the Spanish Steps, in what is now the Keats-Shelley Memorial house. His lungs hemorrhaged daily, and Severn had to hide knives and toxic drugs, for Keats was bent on suicide. He wrote of himself in the grave: "The flowers prowing over me," and frequently called to his friend, "How long is this posthumous life of mine to last?"

In February of 1821, a calm came over Keats. He accepted death and the torment leading up to it, and he began to cherish the devotion of Joseph Severn, even comforting the painter about the suffering ahead: "Now you must be firm, for it will not last long." On the 23rd, at 11:00 P.M., he asked Severn to elevate his upper body to facilitate breathing from his fluid-filled lungs. When his friend held him close, Keats begged, "Don't breathe on me—it comes like ice." Severn pulled his face away and Keats spoke his last words: "Thank God it has come."

It was a miracle that Keats lived as long as he did. The autopsy revealed that his lungs contained virtually no healthy tissue. Every inch was diseased, black with blood.

He was buried on February 26 in the Protestant Cemetery in Rome. A few days before his death, he had requested that his gravestone be nameless, and, convinced of the impermanence of his work, composed his epitaph: "Here lies one whose name was writ in water."

Percy Bysshe Shelley: d. 1822, age 29

> **Cause of death:** Accidental drowning at sea
>
> **Place of rest:** Cremated on the beach at Viareggio; buried in the Protestant Cemetery, Rome

Last seen: Reclining on the deck of his boat, *Don Juan,* reading a copy of Keats's latest poems

A violent freak storm off the coast of Italy, lasting no more than twenty minutes, ended the life of Percy Bysshe Shelley, son of a baronet, who in his short career became one of the most controversial of English Romantic thinkers and poets. He died a year after his friend Keats, swept overboard from his small yacht, *Don Juan,* and when his body washed ashore, a copy of Keats's last poems was found in Shelley's breast pocket.

Born on his family's estate in Sussex on August 4, 1792, he grew into a slender, attractive, rather feminine-looking boy with bright blue eyes and long curling hair, the era's quintessential picture of a budding poet.

He was a rebel from an early age. Entering Eton College at twelve, he launched his first rebellion against the establishment when he ran afoul of the school's "fag system" by which younger boys were made to perform menial tasks for older boys. And he was expelled from Oxford at age nineteen for publishing a pamphlet defending atheism, a belief that would later lead to his being branded an "unfit parent," costing him custody of two children from an early marriage.

His end came in Italy, but not before a succession of tragedies.

In delicate health, Shelley was advised that the Italian climate would rejuvenate him. He set out for the country with his second wife, Mary Wollstonecraft Godwin, a woman of intellectual stature, who in 1818 would publish her masterpiece, *Frankenstein.* But no sooner had the couple settled into their new home than their infant, Clara, died of a high fever. The following year their two-year-old son William fell ill and succumbed after an agonizing bedside vigil by his father.

Despite sorrow, and perhaps partly because of it, Shelley wrote much of his best poetry in Italy, including *The Cenci,* "Ode to Liberty," and *Prometheus Unbound.* And one of his greatest verses followed the next tragedy.

In the winter of 1821, he received news that Keats had died in Rome. Deeply moved, in poor health himself, Shelley plunged into a poetic tribute, "Adonais," a pastoral elegy that he regarded as his perfect poem. He hoped the work would please the public, who found much of his writing harshly political and socially distasteful. Good reviews, though, proved as elusive as ever, and bitterly disappointed, Shelley withdrew from writing; he was already living the summer that would be his last.

In precarious health, he contemplated suicide, procuring poison that he concealed in his room. To this day his ailment has never been satisfactorily diagnosed; it's known that he experienced nightmares and hallucinations, as when he saw Byron's dead daughter, Allegra, rise up from the sea and beckon him to join her—a vision that was to be prophetic.

Hoping to alleviate depression and reawaken interest in life, he set sail in July with a companion, Edward Williams. The *Don Juan* headed toward Leghorn, Italy, where the poet spent a week visiting with Byron and sightseeing in Pisa. He was in improved health and better spirits when the yacht pulled out of Leghorn harbor at two in the afternoon for its return trip. Williams handled the boat while Shelley reclined on the tiny quarterdeck reading Keats's latest volume of poetry.

Minutes later a wind suddenly arose. The sky darkened and a soupy mist scudded in from the sea. Many small fishing craft came back to port, and an experienced sea adventurer, Trelawny, who had befriended Shelley and greatly admired his works, waved frantically to the *Don Juan* to return, aware of the freakishness that was brewing. Trelawny watched helplessly as the *Don Juan* exited the mouth of the harbor.

The storm struck violently and destructively. In less than a half-hour the sea was again calm, the sky clear. Trelawny, pacing the dock, asked the captain of every vessel pulling into port if he had seen the small yacht.

For a few days Mary Shelley clung to the hope that her husband's boat might have been blown to Elba or Corsica. But Trelawny, reconnoitering the coast, learned that two bodies had washed ashore. Both were young males, and both had been partly eaten by fish. Nonetheless, Trelawny identified Shelley's body without difficulty.

To satisfy Tuscan quarantine requirements on washed-up corpses, the bodies had to be cremated on the spot. On August 14, on the beach at Viareggio in a portable iron furnace, the corpse of Edward Williams was cremated. The next night, in the presence of few friends and a group of curious villagers, Shelley's body was reduced to ash. At Mary Shelley's request, the remains were sent to Rome for burial beside those of their son William.

Legend has it that Shelley's heart refused to burn and that Trelawny thrust his hand into the flames and plucked out the organ. It is probably closer to the truth that before the heart had completely burned, Trelawny, whose admiration of the poet bordered on worship, used iron tongs to remove it from the fire. Mary Shelley kept her husband's heart in a bottle in her desk; in 1889 it was buried in the grave of the couple's last son.

Several weeks after the burial, Trelawny visited the grave and, dissatisfied with the site and the stone, purchased a lusher plot against an ancient Roman wall. Despite meager finances, he built two handsome tombs, had Shelley's remains interred in one of them, then encircled the plots with cypresses and laurels. He wrote a full account of his unsolicited actions to Mary Shelley, and, in what can only be regarded as extraordinary hubris and idol worship, he informed her that the grave adjacent to her husband's was not for her; it was for himself. Years later Trelawny's ashes were buried alongside Shelley's. The sea captain had known the poet only during the last six months of his life.

Keats had died in 1821. Shelley in 1822. And two summers later Mary Shelley found herself at the grave side of another poet and friend, Byron. She wrote in her journal: "What should I have said to a Cassandra who three years ago should have prophesied that I . . . should watch the funeral procession of Lord Byron up Highgate Hill?"

Lord Byron: d. 1824, age 36

Cause of death: Complications from malaria

Place of rest: The family's ancestral vault, Hucknall Torkard Church, Nottingham, England

Last words: *"The damned doctors have drenched me so that I can scarcely stand. I want to sleep now."*

A fortune-teller told Byron's mother that her infant son would die at age thirty-seven, a prediction off by only one year. The augury made no mention that the death would be surrounded by such sensational sexual scandal that Byron's body would be denied burial in Westminster Abbey.

The incarnate symbol of romanticism, George Gordon Noel Byron created through his poetry the "Byronic hero": typically a mysterious, gifted, lonely young man, defiantly hiding some unspeakable sin. Byron had no shortage of unspeakable offenses, including a penchant for pubescent boys (the thought of sex with adult males repelled him), the procuring of female prostitutes (two hundred by his own count), and transgressing the ultimate sexual taboo, incest, by seducing his married half-sister, Augusta Leigh, fathering a daughter, Medora. To mention a few.

Throughout his life, the stocky, 5-foot-8-inch-tall Byron fought a continual battle against obesity. At age 17, he entered Cambridge University weighing 212 pounds, the heaviest boy in his class. To maintain his weight at a reasonable level in adult life, he fasted frequently, downed narcotic drugs to reduce, and kept to a bland diet of hard biscuits and rice washed down with soda water or diluted wine.

The great poet and lover had two "deformities," the best known being a right clubfoot, which he sought to conceal with a specially designed shoe. The foot was so grotesque (at least in Byron's mind) that he once begged a doctor to amputate it. The other deformity, revealed publicly at autopsy, was a "sexual organ of quite abnormal [read, large] development."

Byron's sexual excesses almost killed him. During three years at Trinity College he fell in love with choirboy John Edleston, simultaneously maintained two mistresses, cavorted nightly with female prostitutes (later estimating that half his annual funds went to purchase sex), and nearly destroyed his health with the hallucinogenic drug laudanum, a tincture of opium. He measured genuine love (with a nineteen-year-old Italian countess) by a bizarre yardstick: "I have not had a whore in this half year."

The real path to his end began in the autumn of 1823 with a bout of malaria. In Greece to aid Greek patriots in their rebellion against the Turks, Byron came down with a chill and fever, and, while visiting a historic monastery, "suddenly went berserk . . . raving and cursing, [he] chased everybody from the room, barred the doors, and then fell to the floor writhing with abdominal cramps." Byron himself diagnosed "rheumatic temperament." His physicians, unable to agree on a malady, bled him by applying lancets (leeches) to his temples.

Modern doctors suggest the ailment was malaria.

Byron's health never completely returned. On April 9 of the following year, he caught another chill while horseback riding during a storm. Hot drinks and warm clothing could not warm him. To reduce his fever and relieve his "rheumatic pain," doctors prescribed castor oil and, unwittingly, nearly poisoned him with a quaff of antimony, a toxic metal and long a bogus cure-all.

By April 13 his condition was critical. Doctors arrived with several jars of lancets, but this time Byron protested: "Have you no other remedy? There are more deaths by the lancet than lance." Thwarted, the doctors attempted to reduce his high fever by inducing diarrhea with a purgative and vomiting with an emetic. The dehydrated patient, though, showed no improvement.

On the morning of April 16, realizing his condition was hopelessly deteriorating, Byron allowed the doctors to open a vein of his arm and draw off a pint of blood. An hour later, when he had not rallied, they bled him again.

The next morning he seemed a modicum improved. The physicians took this as a sign that their treatment was working and bled him of ten more ounces. He relapsed, which one doctor attributed to having taken too little blood, so the unconscious patient, unable to protest, had leeches applied to his temples. His respiration became jerky and he moaned with each exhalation. When he was sensate enough to swallow, they forced him to drink a solution of laudanum.

The doctors reported that Byron then "slept," but it was a sleep from which he could not be roused the next morning. His respiration grew fainter throughout the day, and he died at 6:15 P.M.

A postmortem was inconclusive. But a modern reading of the findings suggests Byron died of complications from a relapse of malaria. An eminent British physician who studied the case in 1924 suggested that the poet might have been saved if his doctors had administered quinine, a malarial treacle then available, and concluded that his death was hastened by "remorseless bleeding."

His body was returned to his native England, which he had left under several clouds of scandal. He had been charged with forcefully sodomizing his wife in the final month of her pregnancy; he had attempted to rape a thirteen-year-old girl, the daughter of Lady Oxford; and he had conducted an affair with the aging Lady Melbourne, mother-in-law of one of his former mistresses, Lady Caroline Lamb, who once confided to her journal that the handsome Byron was "mad, bad, and dangerous to know."

When Westminster Abbey refused the body of the famous poet, his family interred him in their ancestral vault in Hucknall Torkard Church, five miles northwest of Nottingham. Byron's heart and brain, removed at autopsy, were placed in a large urn beside the coffin. In the summer of 1938, the vault was opened and the poet's body found to be well preserved, his features easily recognizable. Only the arms and lower legs were reduced to bone.

A modern analysis of the skeleton casts light on the deformity that caused Byron to walk with a peculiarly sliding gate. Doctors conclude that his calf was grotesquely thin, the muscles so tight as to bend his small, narrow foot slightly inward. He probably had very little movement at the ankle.

Ludwig van Beethoven: d. 1827, age 57

Cause of death: Cirrhosis of the liver, with chronic pancreatitis and irritable bowel syndrome

Place of rest: Central Cemetery, Vienna

Last words: When wine he requested was slow in coming: *"Pity, pity—too late!"*

The first great ending in the life of Ludwig van Beethoven was his tragic loss of hearing, perhaps the worst fate that can befall a composer. His deafness, along with the liver failure that killed him, was long attributed to syphilis. But a modern evaluation of medical evidence reveals another cause for the impairment that sunk one of the world's greatest composers into maddening silence.

Born in 1770 into a musical family of Flemish descent, Beethoven became the first important composer to make a living from his music, that is, the first composer unshackled from court and church subsidies, the first to receive a salary with no strings, enabling him to compose whatever he liked.

Beethoven began composing—with full and acute hearing—at age eleven, the pupil in Vienna of both Mozart and Haydn. The first reference to his deafness is contained in a letter dated June 29, 1801, when the composer was thirty-one: "For two years now I avoid all society for I cannot say to people 'I am deaf.' " He was still only hard-of-hearing, for he confesses, "At the theatre I must sit quite near the orchestra in order to follow the actors."

He had already written the Symphony No. 1 in C Major and was working on the Sonata in C-sharp Minor (which would be called the *Moonlight*). For one of the world's greatest figures in the history of Western music, the specter of total silence was alarming. "In another calling such a [disease] might be possible," he wrote to a friend, "but in mine it creates a terrible situation."

To some, the impairment seemed to alter his personality: "They say that I am malevolent, stubborn or misanthropic. How greatly do they wrong me . . . for six years I have been in a hopeless case, made worse by ignorant doctors."

Beethoven: His hearing ailment is curable today.

Encroaching deafness, though, was not Beethoven's only health concern. His deeply pockmarked face and chronically weak constitution were thought to have resulted from a childhood bout of smallpox; today the symptoms are attributed to a systemic autoimmune disease, lupus erythematosus, in which white blood cells mistakenly attack healthy body cells. In addition, he suffered from asthma and feared it as much as his periodic depression, which he called "as great an evil" as his progressive hearing loss. Doctors became Beethoven's least favorite people, yet he needed them.

He was writing sublime music and suffering a medical text of symptoms. During the years 1801 to 1814, when he was composing a prodigious body of work—the *Appassionata* sonata, the Fourth and Fifth *(Emperor)* concerti, the Second through Eighth symphonies, and his only opera, *Fidelio*—he was plagued with migraines and "long-standing intestinal weakness," which included colicky pains, continual diarrhea, and long periods of prostration. Beethoven himself had a theory: He blamed his progressive deafness during this period on all his other physical ailments.

Around 1819, when Beethoven was forty-nine, his deafness became virtually total. He contemplated suicide: "Only Art held me back; for ah, it seemed unthinkable for me to leave the world forever before I had produced all that I felt called upon to produce."

He carried with him "conversation books" in which friends entered questions to which he replied orally. Though he still composed with brilliance, his piano playing, which had been degenerating along with his hearing, came to a halt. "As the leaves of autumn wither and fall, so has my own life become barren." He occasionally appeared in public, but his energies were devoted almost exclusively to composition.

In the summer of 1821, at age fifty-one, he was stricken with jaundice. This marked the prelude to the terminal liver illness that debilitated him in 1826, while working on several string quartets and his Ninth Symphony. That year, his vomiting and diarrhea were so frequent and severe that they in themselves threatened to kill him. "Even that high courage that inspired me in the fair days of summer has now vanished."

His health received a further blow late in the winter of 1826. He had been awarded guardianship in 1815 of his nephew Karl, then a boy of nine and son of Beethoven's recently deceased brother, Caspar Anton Carl. For all the affection Beethoven lavished on the youth, the two quarreled bitterly. Their fighting came to a head in 1826 when, before taking his university examination, Karl attempted suicide. Beethoven rushed the wounded teenager to the home of his surviving brother, Nikolaus Johann, outside of Vienna. He made the return trip in blustery weather in an open cart with inadequate clothing and fell ill shortly before Christmas. During the first two months of the new year, 1827, his last, Beethoven's abdomen swelled painfully with fluids and he had to be "tapped" four times for relief.

He remained bedridden. Pneumonia and cirrhosis of the liver battled as to which disease would slay him. On March 24, he received the last rites and two days later, while a fierce thunderstorm raged over Vienna, rattling windows,

Beethoven requested wine that was slow in coming. "Pity, pity—too late!" he said, and slipped into unconsciousness.

Legend has it that the unconscious, nearly stone-deaf composer did rally once, to a loud clap of thunder. Opening his eyes wide, he lifted his right hand in a clenched fist, shook it at the sky, then fell back, dead.

His liver probably beat his lungs in ending his life. At autopsy, it was found to have atrophied to half the normal size, showing severe cirrhosis. Beethoven's father was an alcoholic, and the composer, though not a steady drinker, indulged in bouts of crapulence.

Also atrophied were his auditory nerves. Today, the diagnosis for his deafness is otosclerosis, the progressive formation of tough, spongy tissue around the tiny stirrup bone of the middle ear, which hinders movement of the tympanic membrane.

Beethoven's funeral, at Wahring on March 29, made clear his status in his own time. The service and procession were attended by twenty thousand people, pallbearers and torchbearers included the famous Hungarian pianist Johann Nepomuk Hummel and Austrian composer Franz Schubert, and the funeral oration was written by Austria's greatest living dramatist, Franz Grillparzer. But three decades later the once impressive grave site was in weedy neglect. The composer's body was exhumed, his ear bones studied, and he was reburied—though only briefly, for in June of 1888 the remains of Beethoven, and his contemporary, Schubert, were transferred to Vienna's Central Cemetery, interred side by side, as they lie today.

In an age that saw the decline of court and church patronage, Beethoven not only supported himself from the sale and publication of his music, but enjoyed the luxury of writing whatever he wanted, melodies that, he claimed, most often came to him on long country walks. "If only I were rid of my affliction," he once wrote, "I would embrace the whole world." Through his music the whole world continues to embrace him.

Elizabeth Barrett Browning: d. 1861, age 55
Robert Browning: d. 1889, age 77

Cause of her death: Acute bronchitis and lung abscess

Cause of his death: Heart attack

Her place of rest: The Protestant Cemetry, Florence

His place of rest: Westminster Abbey, London

Her last words: Quoting from a poem: *"Knowledge by suffering entereth, And life is perfected by death."*

His last words: Informed of a favorable review of a poetry collection: *"How gratifying!"*

Elizabeth Barrett Browning's life closed twice before her death. After falling off her pet pony, the young Elizabeth was a partial invalid from the age of fifteen; she was a complete invalid from the age of thirty-two to forty. Then, in 1846, Robert Browning persuaded her to elope with him. Her health dramatically improved, and the couple, residing mainly in Florence, enjoyed fifteen years of happiness, despite the fact that from taking prescribed medication she was a morphine addict.

In her lifetime, her poetry was more esteemed than her husband's; today the situation is reversed.

As a girl, Elizabeth Barrett was educated at home. She could translate Greek, Latin, Italian, and German, and knew enough Hebrew to read the Old Testament in the original. Following her mother's death, the family moved to London and the two events—an emotional departure and a physical departure—so depressed her that she became confined to her couch.

Her real illness began late in 1837, at age thirty-one. She wrote to a friend, "I caught a cold . . . which has turned into a cough and has kept me to the house ever since and in a very weak state." Her doctor assured her there was no disease, only "an excitability, and irritability of the chest." She was given the heart medication digitalis for "my pulse which keeps pace with the Wild Huntsman."

When the cough persisted, accompanied by "the spitting of blood," which she downplayed to a friend as "very little—almost less than it has been," family and friends rightly feared that Elizabeth had caught the blight of the 1800s, tuberculosis. The main treatment was bed rest; thus began Elizabeth's long imprisonment in her room. Until, that is, her great admirer Robert Browning persuaded her that she had the strength, with him at her side, to escape—not only from the ailment, but also from her repressive, overbearing father. They married: he, thirty-four; she, forty.

A friend visiting Elizabeth in Florence exclaimed, "You are not improved, you are transformed!" The poet herself wrote: "I was buried [in] a morbid and desolate state . . . which I look back now to with a sort of horror."

Almost at once she became pregnant, but at five months miscarried. In 1849, the forty-three-year-old former invalid gave birth to a healthy boy. Two further miscarriages took their toll on her health, causing enormous loss of

The Brownings: as a romantic pictured them.

blood. This probably caused the profound iron deficiency anemia that would account for her years of ghostly pallor and spells of disabling lethargy.

Her addiction to morphine began when the drug was prescribed early in her lung illness. It subdued coughing, allayed apprehension, and helped her sleep. The addiction never interfered with her activities and she was not ashamed of it, except insofar as it troubled her husband. For him, she reduced her dependence on the drug, no easy task, and on her "best days" denied herself it entirely. She was a well-balanced addict, as can be a nicotine or alcohol addict.

On a visit to Rome, Elizabeth caught a cold from which she never recovered. Bronchitis set in, and back in Florence, at their home, Casa Guidi, Robert nursed her. On the morning of June 29, 1861, Robert was feeding her soup when her expression went blank. "Do you know me?" he asked. After a frightening silence, she hugged and kissed him and quoted a line, her final words, from "A Vision of Poets": "Knowledge by suffering entereth,/And life is perfected by death."

The only later word she uttered was "beautiful" when he asked if she was comfortable. She died smiling, in the arms of the man she regarded as her savior. In death her face remained so radiant, "like a girl's," that for several hours Robert Browning could not persuade himself his wife was really gone.

Biohistorians today argue that Elizabeth Barrett Browning suffered a spinal affliction as a teenager, possibly Pott's disease or tuberculosis of the vertebrae. There seems little doubt that she also suffered from a chronic lung ailment—pulmonary tuberculosis, or, less likely, bronchiectasis—which hit acutely in her early thirties. The modern guess is that the ailment was dormant by the time she met and married Robert Browning. And that had Browning not brightened her days and given her hope and reason to live, her life might well have ended years earlier than it did.

Robert Browning. He survived his wife by twenty-eight years. He had written for the stage, though with no success, and his early, emotion-laden poetry received harsh criticism; John Stuart Mill condemned the poet's exposure of raw emotion and the exploitation of his own inner feelings as "intense and morbid self-consciousness."

Though Robert Browning enjoyed excellent health, in November of 1889, walking in a light drizzle on the Lido in Venice, he caught a cold that developed quickly into bronchitis. He was nursed by his son, nicknamed Pen, but the seventy-seven-year-old poet, who still painfully missed his wife, grew weaker.

He had completed a collection of verse, *Asolando,* and on December 12 a telegram arrived from London announcing the book had garnered favorable reviews. His heart had been failing steadily, and he responded to the telegram, "How gratifying!" (Critics and readers had long complained that his cerebral writing, begun after Mill's criticism, was largely incomprehensible.) He smiled, then drifted into sleep. A few hours later, without waking, he suffered a massive heart attack and died.

He had wanted to be buried in Florence's Protestant Cemetery, beside his wife, whose tombstone reads: "Be not afraid; it is I." But by the time of his death, the graveyard was closed. He rests in England's Westminster Abbey.

Walt Whitman: d. 1892, age 73

> **Cause of death:** Cerebral hemorrhage; also present, advanced tuberculosis
>
> **Place of rest:** Harleigh Cemetery, Camden, New Jersey
>
> **Last words:** Voluble throughout life, he boasted on his deathbed: *"Garrulous to the very last."*

Born Walter Whitman, on May 31, 1819, in West Hills, Long Island, the author of *Leaves of Grass* remained a bachelor all his life. He preferred the company of men, addressed men in florid terms of endearment, and, in what has been called "the nudity of his verse," flamed the suspicion he was gay, though latent lifelong. Never was he humble: "I will be your poet, I will be more to you than to any of the rest."

Today it is an accepted belief that Walt Whitman was homosexual. But the evidence marshaled after his death to support that claim says much of the times, and how they've changed. Turn-of-the-century biographers pointed out that Whitman "bathed in eau-de-cologne," that he was "fond of cooking," that he possessed an "infantile configuration" (read, boyish), "delicate skin" (read, feminine), that there was "something womanly in him" (read, sissy), and that he harbored an "attitude and behavior toward sex that could not be considered 'normal' " (read, perverted). One physician asked, with great delicacy, "Could he have been eunuchoid?"

He was actually a tall, thin, healthy boy, who at age eleven left school, beginning a series of undistinguished odd jobs. At eighteen he became a school-teacher, but after two years resigned to edit his own paper, the *Long Islander,* from the town of Huntington. He worked for the presidential campaign of Martin Van Buren in 1840 and adored opera: "But for opera, I could never have written *Leaves of Grass.*"

He lived something of a bohemian life and for a number of years wore an enormous stud of pearls. At age thirty, he submitted to a cranial phrenology examination, a popular fad in which a practitioner, from skull measurements, inferred tendencies for violence, imbicility, criminality, and genius. Whitman's "scientific" confirmation was "genius," which pleased him greatly and perhaps contributed in some way to the expansive role ego played in his verse.

Whitman was even more pleased with the laudatory reviews of his 1855 *Leaves of Grass.* Ralph Waldo Emerson wrote personally to the poet: "I find it the most extraordinary piece of wit and wisdom that America has yet contrib-uted. . . . I greet you at the beginning of a great career." Though no author's name appeared on that first edition, the cover bore a portrait of Whitman for which the author was physically reviewed as "broad shouldered, rouge fleshed, Bacchus-browned, bearded like a satyr."

It was shortly after this success that Whitman began to experience the cerebral strokes that would kill him. A pattern of minor strokes and partial recoveries continued over the next three decades. During much of this time, a biographer wrote, Whitman also "suffered emotional strains related to his sexual ambiguity."

Physically he complained of a "fullness" in his head and of a similar sensation in his chest. Tuberculosis may have existed in his family. His mother, Louisa Van Velsor, of mixed Dutch and Welsh blood, chronically suffered "bad coughing," a "soreness and distress" in her chest, and she is believed to have died of tuberculosis. (Whitman called her death "the great cloud" in his life.) And at least two of the poet's brothers are thought to have suffered from the disease, then still romantically called consumption. At autopsy, Whitman's right lung would be found to show acute tuberculosis, while the left lung had already collapsed under the infection.

As Whitman entered his sixties the frequency and severity of cerebral strokes escalated. The event of 1885 left him unable to climb stairs. The severe stroke of 1888 left him confined to bed, mentally confused, his speech "blurred and indistinct." The poet always recovered to some degree, but in 1891 he was pronounced "the personification of senility." He looked poorly, walked with a cane, and suffered continual indigestion, constipation, bladder irritation, and incontinence.

His long-diseased lungs had attacked the body. Whitman began to spit up mucus, pus, and occasionally blood. He lost all appetite and developed a high fever. Physicians diagnosed "widely diffused broncho-pneumonia." His heart weakened, his lips and fingertips turned bluish, and a rattle developed in his windpipe. By Christmas of 1891, Walt Whitman was mostly stuporous, though by physical effort he could be roused to semialertness and, at times, voluble rambling.

He lingered in this limbo for almost three months. When conscious, he could find no comfort. If he lay on his right side, he broke into a paroxysm of coughing and spitting; on his left side, he experienced suffocation. On March 23, his discomfort was compounded by severe hiccups and increasingly impaired breathing. Three days later he slipped into a coma and died, silently and without a struggle, at his home in Camden, New Jersey.

A postmortem examination revealed not only the extensive lung damage from tuberculosis, but severe cerebral arteriosclerosis, or clogged arteries of the brain. This contributed in no small way to his senility.

Whitman had designed his own granite tomb to resemble a scaled-down version of King Solomon's temple. At the funeral service in Camden's Harleigh Cemetery, a friend eulogized America's arguably greatest poet, saying: "Death is less terrible than it was before. Thousands and millions will walk into the dark valley of the shadow holding Walt Whitman by the hand." Though the poet had no family of his own, he was never alone, not even in death; alongside Whitman rest the bodies of his mother, father, two brothers, a sister, and a sister-in-law.

Guy de Maupassant: d. 1893; age 43

Cause of death: Advanced syphilis

Place of rest: Montparnasse Cemetery, Paris

Most memorable words: *"I don't want to survive myself."*

The celebrated French writer with a prodigious sexual appetite—once called "a foul-mouthed, offensive individual, totally destitute of a sense of decency"— met a tragic end through syphilis. His extended farewell to life encompassed a sixteen-year slide from health launched by a disease he might have picked up from his teenage exploits with prostitutes or that he might innocently have inherited.

Maupassant was scarred by two events in his life. The first was the separation of his parents when he was eleven years old. Raised by his strong, neurotic mother (whom he adored), Maupassant hated his father, despised all husbands, and remained a bachelor.

The other traumatic event, syphilis, he first discovered as a young man of twenty-four. Already sexually promiscuous, he was treated for the disease's skin lesions and mistakenly believed he was cured. Even when the alarming truth became known, he continued to seduce women, hundreds by his reckoning, boasting of his sexual stamina: "I'm as tired after two or three times as I am after twenty. After two or three times you exhausted your stock of semen, so you can go on afterward without further loss."

When fellow writer Gustave Flaubert doubted that endurance, Maupassant had a bookkeeper accompany him to a Paris brothel as a witness; he had "six girls in an hour." Though his first novel, *Une Vie* ("A Life") was called by Leo Tolstoi "the best French novel since *Les Misérables,*" Maupassant was prouder throughout his life of his sexual conquests than of his books. A physician today would probably diagnose sexual addiction.

Wealthy from his writings, owning four homes and two yachts, he lived a high life, but it was syphilis that brought him down hard and young.

The first signs of trouble began in 1878 when he was twenty-seven years old. Fits of melancholia were followed by violent migraines and impaired vision. Refusing to acknowledge the disease, clinging to the illusion he had been cured, he blamed his symptoms on overwork.

By 1884 he had clear evidence of mental derangement. He experienced a "fear of walls, of the furniture, of the familiar objects which seem to me to assume a kind of animal life." Worse still was "the horrible confusion of my thought, of my reason escaping, entangled and scattered by an invisible and mysterious anguish."

He continued to write stories—and to bed women, usually each for only a single encounter under the mistaken belief he might recontaminate himself. With repeat paramours he was decidedly kinky, as with Gisele d'Estoc, who affected close-cropped hair and men's clothes; Maupassant shared her female lovers as well as her hashish.

In 1887, at age thirty-seven, he grudgingly admitted that "some mysterious ailment" had taken over his brain. Insanity was rapidly approaching, as he frighteningly acknowledged in an autobiographical story: "I am lost! Somebody orders all my acts, all my movements, all my thoughts."

For a respite from his overwork (a delusion he continued frequently to entertain), he journeyed to Switzerland in 1891. Out for a stroll, he seduced a young girl and returned to the Hotel Beausejour, proclaiming to friends, "I was brilliant; I am cured!" He was by then certifiably insane.

He spoke endlessly of suicide and wrote, "Between madness and death, there is no question of hesitation." But he could not abandon sex, which obsessed his thoughts to the end of his life, encounters becoming more bizarre. Fearful that he would outlive his insanity, he wrote to a friend, "I don't want to survive myself." He once boasted to an interviewer, "I am a little out of the common sexually, for I can make my instrument stand whenever I please." The newspaperman was disbelieving until Maupassant smiled and said, "Look at my trousers."

A suicide attempt on January 2, 1892, was unsuccessful. Maupassant, found by his valet, François, frantically clawing at the walls of the kitchen, shouted, "I have cut my throat. . . . I am going insane." Five days later, he was committed to a mental sanatorium in Paris.

Attended by his valet, the writer was forbidden female visitors. Sexual deprivation only inflamed his imagination and he acted out past orgies. Finally his insanity reached out to encompass his faithful friend; he accussed François of embezzlement. In his last weeks, he refused to urinate because anything out of his penis, he believed, was priceless as diamonds and should be stored, not flushed away. He licked floors, kicked attendants, and began to sense when a violent fit was coming on and requested he be put into a straitjacket.

Late in June of 1893 he lapsed into a coma from which he never emerged. The master of the short story lived a short life, dying on July 6, at age forty-three. His funeral service was held at the Church of St. Pierre de Chaillot, and fellow French writer Émile Zola read the farewell tribute at the grave side in Paris's Montparnasse Cemetery.

Twenty years after Maupassant's death, the "something" that possessed his brain was first biologically identified under a microscope: *Treponema pallidum,* the spiral-shaped causative agent of syphilis. The discoverer, Rockefeller University bacteriologist Hideyo Noguchi, found it in the brain tissue of another patient whose symptoms had paralleled Maupassant's. How syphilis caused madness through degeneration of neurons was finally understood.

Robert Louis Stevenson: d. 1894, age 44

Cause of death: Cerebral hemorrhage

Place of rest: Vailima, Samoa

Last words: Gripping his temples: *"My head, my head!"*

Robert Louis Stevenson feared that his life would end slowly and torturously from tuberculosis, a disease he suffered. But the end came abruptly and unexpectedly, in the middle of writing the novel that would become his unfinished masterpiece.

The author who entertained generations of youths with *Treasure Island* and *The Strange Case of Dr. Jekyll and Mr. Hyde* was himself a sickly child, afraid of the dark. Held by a nurse, he would gaze out his bedroom window, imagining, as he later wrote, "there might be sick little boys and their nurses waiting like us for the morning."

He was born in Edinburgh, Scotland, on November 13, 1850, a robust, healthy infant, but he enjoyed good health for barely eighteen months. From his mother, he caught pulmonary tuberculosis and would sum up his childhood saying, "I lay awake troubled continually with a hacking exhausting cough and praying for sleep or morning from the bottom of my shaken little body."

Like his mother, the adult Stevenson traveled far and wide in search of the perfect climate for the tubercular sufferer. The south of France he found favorable; dank England, positively life-threatening; sunny California, nearly ideal—though once settled in the United States lack of money and poor nutrition brought him close to death.

In California in 1880, at age thirty, the yet-to-be-famous author married Fanny Osbourne, an American divorcée. Together they embarked on a relentless search for a still more perfect climate, trying Switzerland, the French Mediterranean, the New York Adirondacks, and finally, in 1890, the South Pacific, where they made their permanent home on the island of Upolu, Samoa. There Stevenson enjoyed the best health he had known—excellent for him, dismal by the norm. He made this clear in a letter he wrote from Samoa in 1893, the year before his death.

As a sickly child Robert Louis Stevenson enjoyed few restful nights.

I have not had a day's real health. I have wakened sick and gone to bed weary and I have done my work unflinchingly. I have written in bed and written out of it, written in hemorrhages, written in sickness, written torn by coughing, written when my head swam for weakness, and for so long, it seems to me, I have won my wager and recovered my glove. I am better now; have been, rightly speaking, since first I came to the Pacific; and still few are the days when I am not in some physical distress. And the battle goes on—ill or well is a trifle—so it goes.

The young tubercular author was now famous. He'd published *Kidnapped* and *A Child's Garden of Verses,* poems that from an adult perspective vividly capture the emotions and sensations of childhood. His own boyhood memories of sickness and fear of the dark gave Stevenson a special sensibility, and the poems are regarded as unique in all of English literature.

His early and unexpected death came on December 3, 1894.

Stevenson spent the morning at his hilltop Samoan house, Vailima, dictating to his step-daughter, Bell Strong, the ninth chapter of his unfinished *Weir of Hermiston.* Untroubled that day by coughing, a rare event, he exuberantly outlined the book's conclusion and his own plans for the future.

In the afternoon, having finished his correspondence, he went downstairs to find his wife troubled by a powerful presentiment. Something dreadful was about to happen, she insisted, but despite her husband's prodding she was unable to articulate the vague foreboding. Her concern was so palpable that Stevenson himself became uncomfortable and several times attempted to change the subject. He went to the cellar for a bottle of Burgundy, then returned to the veranda to help Fanny prepare a salad of pineapple, guava, papaya, and other local fruits. He was mixing a homemade mayonnaise, his specialty, when suddenly his hands shot up to his temples and he shouted, "What's that?" Both Fanny and his step-daughter were puzzled. He asked them, curiously, "Do I look strange?" then collapsed to his knees, shouting, "My head, my head!"

He never regained consciousness, and died at 8:10 P.M. that evening, at the age of forty-four.

With no facilities for embalming on the island, and given its baking heat, burial had to be quick. Samoan natives, who had revered Stevenson as their *Tusitala* ("teller of tales"), rubbed his body with coconut oil, while others constructed a hardwood coffin. Throughout the night, natives hacked a path through lush vines and vegetation to Stevenson's chosen burial site, the summit of the island's twelve-hundred-foot Mt. Vaea.

With daylight, they formed a relay team, passing the coffin up the slopes to the grave. Even when the corpse was lowered into the ground late that afternoon, Fanny could not believe her husband was dead. The sudden death on the tropical paradise seemed a cruel irony. Having traveled the globe in search of a natural sanatorium for the tuberculosis that was supposed to kill Stevenson, they had found the spot and he had begun to improve, only to have been felled by a stroke.

Edgar Allan Poe: d. 1849, age 40

Cause of death: After suffering from diabetes and alcoholism, he died of cerebral edema following a drinking binge

Place of rest: Westminster Presbyterian Cemetery, Baltimore, Maryland

Last words: *"Lord, help my poor soul."*

Master of macabre tales and originator of modern American detective fiction, Edgar Allan Poe fought a long battle with the alcoholism that would finally end his life. Biohistorians have recently argued, however, that Poe actually suffered a great intolerance for alcohol, such that a single drink could produce violent, disruptive behavior.

Specifically, given what is known of Poe's drinking and health, it's suspected that he suffered from genetic hypersensitivity to a body chemical called cAMP. Found in all humans, and essential for metabolic function, the substance in alcoholics is altered by ethanol, going through pendulumlike extremes that produce profound inebriation and shaking withdrawals. If genetic alcoholism was Poe's curse, the author of "The Fall of the House of Usher" and "The Murders of the Rue Morgue" compounded the problem with heavy binge drinking, lasting up to a week at a time.

What lead Poe to drink?

Fear is one popular hypothesis, though not the macabre dreads that Poe used so effectively to terrify his readers. Rather, fear of sex. Chaste himself, he married late, at age twenty-seven, and the bride was his thirteen-year-old virginal cousin, Virginia Clemm. Their relationship is thought to have been entirely platonic. She was a frail, sickly, innocent girl, and friends of the couple claimed that his role was really that of foster father.

Poe professed great devotion for his wife, and her slow and torturous death from tuberculosis did not help his drinking problem. Of how her illness affected him he wrote: "I became insane, with long intervals of horrible sanity. . . . I drank; God knows how often or how much."

Poe's drinking companions were often amazed that a single shot of alcohol could transform a courtly gentleman with erect, aristocratic bearing into a boisterous, pugnacious drunk. Despite the drinking—his excesses and his sensitivity—he was prolific. In the period between 1844 and 1846 he wrote his greatest poem, "The Raven," and such classic horror stories as "The Pit and the Pendulum" and "The Premature Burial." His life and work support the contention that genius is sometimes a species of insanity.

Poe's final days began on October 3, 1849, when the virtually penniless forty-year-old writer was found in a gutter semiconscious. He was in Baltimore, where he may have been on a five-day binge; his exact activities during that period have never been determined. His prone body, in a tattered, cheap suit, was recognized by a newspaperman with the Baltimore *Sun;* it was later determined that the suit was not his own.

Poe ranted and raved at the end; a raven is on his tombstone.

At Baltimore's Washington Hospital, Poe's doctor recorded that the author was delirious, constantly prattling, having "vacant converse with spectral and imaginary objects on the walls," as if inhabiting one of his own horror tales. The doctor's wife, a religious woman, attempted to soothe Poe's troubled mind by reading aloud passages from the Bible. But the author, mesmerized by his own demons, shouted her down, and in a burst of lucidity exclaimed, "The best thing my friend could do would be to blow out my brains with a pistol."

Over the next three days he became increasingly delirious and violent. He replied incoherently and bizarrely to questions, and nurses often had to tie his flailing arms and legs to the bed. Friends thought Poe was possessed. Interestingly, abrupt changes in the blood's level of cAMP caused by ethanol withdrawal in hypersensitive individuals can produce violent behavior and incongruous patterns of thought.

On the night of October 6, Poe began mysteriously to shout, "Reynolds! Oh, Reynolds!" The refrain was incessant and resounded throughout hospital halls well into Sunday morning. It is now assumed that the reference might have been to Jeremiah Reynolds, author of sea adventures Poe is known to have admired as a youth.

Around 3:00 P.M. that day, October 7, he began again to thrash violently about in bed and had to be restrained. His doctor wrote: "The patient became quiet and seemed to rest for a short time; then gently moving his head he said: 'Lord, help my poor soul,' and expired."

Poe died penniless. His attending physician, Dr. J. J. Moran, donated money for a mahogany coffin, and the funeral of the great writer was attended by only the undertaker and four people, all unidentified. He was buried in the same Baltimore graveyard that in life he wandered through for "atmosphere" and inspiration. And his death contained another twist, seemingly out of one of his tales: In 1875, when Poe's body was exhumed to be relocated to another section of the cemetery, the sturdy mahogany coffin, which should have endured decades unaltered, was found split down the top. Poe's skeleton was exposed. Hair still clung to his skull and his pearly white teeth stared up at the gravediggers.

His epitaph, etched in a stone marker and bearing a raven in relief, is "Quoth The Raven, Nevermore."

CHAPTER 16

Death Styles
of the Rich and Renowned

Darwin to Duncan

Charles Darwin: d. 1882, age 73

> **Cause of death:** Heart attack following a life plagued by chronic illness
>
> **Place of rest:** Westminster Abbey, London
>
> **Last words:** *"I am not the least afraid to die."*

Today we know that stress, by undermining the body's immune system, can precipitate real and serious illness. Among scientists, Charles Darwin is probably the classic example of a man made sick by the originality and unorthodoxy of his own discoveries. For fifty of Darwin's seventy-three years, the pioneering British biologist lived with heart palpitations, vomiting, lassitude, migraines, eczema, boils, chills, tics, trembling, painful flatulence, and hellish insomnia. He suffered from what might be called "the shock of the new"—evolution and natural selection of species, which were then blasphemy.

After Darwin's death in 1882, many physicians and biographers suggested causes for his protracted illnesses. The spectrum was broad: parasitic Chagas' disease (or South American trypanosomiasis), which weakens the heart; arsenic poisoning; allergic reaction to his beloved pigeons; "simple hypochondria" (which is never simple); and emotional distress—the latter for decades regarded as the *least* likely possibility. But that has changed given the current evidence of the stress-health connection.

Charles Darwin: endured jokes about his simian brow.

There were two aspects of Darwin's life-work that caused him such suffering.

Murder.   With his theory of evolution through survival of the fittest, Darwin provided a plausible explanation for the origin of species. Though only a theory, with no proof, it offered an escape from the necessity of having God create each individual flower, insect, bird, and mammal. It was the theological implications of the theory in Darwin's day—that science would oust God as the demiurge of nature—that gnawed at the great naturalist, making him sick much of his life. He wrote that to discover that species are not immutable, as claimed in the Bible, but evolve through mutation, "is like confessing to a murder." And he lived for fifty years with a murderer's guilt and society's corresponding disdain.

Throwaway Nature.   Another aspect of evolutionary theory equally troubled Darwin: the brutality and wastefulness inherent in a survival-of-the-fittest struggle for existence. The strongest survive often by directly or indirectly killing off the weakest of their kind. It is less emotionally stressful to assume that massacre of any kind is an inexplicable part of God's master plan than to argue that it's a mere game of numbers in which living things are deliberately overproduced so the less hearty can be discarded—sort of a throwaway nature. That view, thought Darwin, diminishes the nobility of life, adds to life a large dollop of the absurd, and harshly calls into question God's ability to come up with a more efficient plan.

Even the concept of predator and prey troubled the biologist as being unnecessarily cruel: Some animals exist specifically as a meal for others. He wrote to a botanist friend, Joseph Hooker, "What a book a Devil's Chaplain might write on the clumsy, wasteful, blundering, low and horribly cruel works of nature!"

Columbia University psychiatrist Dr. Ralph Colp, who has published extensively on Darwin's lifelong stress-induced illnesses, summed up Darwin's dilemma as "two of his most painful feelings: his horror about the War of Nature and his apprehension that his ideas will be considered immoral and irreligious."

Darwin did experience healthful, symptomless periods and, tellingly, they correlated with his being away from his studies of evolution and natural selection. Before the publication in 1859 of his canonical work, *The Origin of Species,* he made a correct self-diagnosis: "I have been extra bad of late, with the old severe vomiting rather often and much distressing swimming of the head. My abstract [book] is the cause, I believe, of the main part of the ills to which my flesh is heir to."

How deeply the ideas in the book troubled him is also evident in that he fretted for a quarter of a century delaying its publication.

We know that Darwin had formulated his main ideas as early as 1832, when he was twenty-three years old. He made a draft of those ideas in 1844 and confided them to only a few intimate friends. Many were scandalized by the notion that species evolved from less advanced to more advanced states, that a shrew started the mammalian lineage that led to chimps and man. It seemed like a bad joke and in the worst taste, telling a society lady she had simian ancestors.

Darwin's friends feared that if the theory were true it would revamp man's outlook on the living world and threaten all established religions. He withheld publication of *Origin* as long as he emotionally and scientifically could; and its hostile reception in 1859 by religious-minded critics, plus its advantageous use by confirmed agnostics and atheists, only reinforced his fears and intensified his mental and physical anguish. His later *The Descent of Man,* which fully drew *Homo sapiens* into the evolutionary fray—and all humankind's mental and moral precepts, to boot—brought him more burdensome fame.

Darwin lived more than two decades beyond the hostile reception of his revolutionary ideas. He may well have suffered from parasitic Chagas' disease picked up in his travels. But from emotional stress he went prematurely from a tall, erect gentleman to a stoop-shouldered man with a furrowed brow, which looked both impressively intellectual and risibly simian—a combination which, during the height of the evolution controversy that engulfed him, caricaturists penned to the hilt. In their hands, Darwin became his unorthodoxy.

At age seventy-two and still intellectually vigorous, Darwin suffered a mild heart attack while out walking near his home at Down, Kent, England. A second and more severe attack a few months later confined him to bed. He was nursed by his wife, Emma Wedgwood (daughter of potter Josiah Wedgwood), whose staunch religious beliefs allowed no room for her husband's evolutionary theories, providing stress on the homefront.

Heart pain continued to trouble Darwin. Shortly before midnight on April 18, 1882, he suffered a severe attack from which he never really rallied. He died the next day, surrounded by his family, offering *them* comfort: "I am not the least afraid to die." Friends who recognized his genius petitioned that he be buried in Westminster Abbey, for however revolutionary his ideas, they argued, the views represented how life was, is, and will be.

Oscar Wilde: d. 1900, age 46

Cause of death: Cerebral meningitis following an ear infection, and/or syphilis

Place of rest: Père-Lachaise Cemetery, Paris

Last words: Penniless, sipping champagne: *"I am dying as I've lived: beyond my means."* Glancing around the room: *"This wallpaper is killing me; one of us has got to go."*

Oscar Fingall O'Flahertie Wills Wilde was born in Dublin, Ireland, in 1854, to an eccentric Irish mother who had wanted a girl and in some ways must have thought she had one: For years she attired Oscar in dresses. At Oxford University, the twenty-year-old undergraduate announced his heady ambitions: "I'll be a poet, a writer, a dramatist. . . . I'll be famous, and if not famous, notorious." He became both and lived by a line from one of his plays: "Nothing succeeds like excess."

Fame came quickly to Wilde. His wit gained him entry into London's literary and political salons. His conversation was considered brilliant and peerless and his comedies played to large and enthusiastic audiences. Reinforcing his image as a dandy, he favored lilac shirts and heliotrope neckties, knee breeches and outlandish overcoats that shimmered under lights. Preaching art for art's sake, he achieved the most glittering renown of his era, as well as the most abject humiliation. As he had flown higher than his contemporaries, he fell farther.

His decline and fall came even faster than his fame.

Though married and with two sons, he began a promiscuously homosexual life at age thirty-two with his "first boy," seventeen-year-old Robert Ross. Ross, like Wilde, was witty and cultivated, and when Wilde woke one morning saying, "I dreamed I supped with the dead," Ross answered, "My dear, you must have been the soul of the party." They made a pair, and Ross would remain a devoted friend throughout the trial and jail term that brought Wilde's career—and his life—to an end.

At thirty-seven Wilde met in one person the love and bane of his existence: the twenty-one-year-old Lord Alfred Douglas, called Bosie. A poet of questionable promise from a prominent family, Douglas was exceedingly handsome, and with a passion for purchasing street boys, he introduced his mentor to London's seamier streets, backroom bars, and male brothels. Wilde found it an element to wallow in.

Ironically, Wilde's fall began during the period of his greatest success. On February 14, 1895, *The Importance of Being Earnest* opened at London's St. James's Theatre. Four days later, Douglas's eccentric and erratic father, the marquess of Queensberry, delivered a card for the playwright. It read: "To Oscar Wilde posing as a somdomite [*sic*]." The marquess, a short, coarse, avid sportsman—he laid down the Queensberry rules for boxing—was humiliated by the affair his son and the dandyish Wilde conducted largely in public.

Wilde sued Queensberry for criminal libel. Queensberry then charged that

Oscar Wilde. His accuser, the marquess of Queensberry, strikes his son, Wilde's lover.

the playwright was committing acts of gross indecency with numerous young boys. Wilde was arrested, and all of London became a spectator to the most entertaining trial of the century.

Wilde's fame and wit drew enormous audiences to the proceedings. An effusively affectionate letter he had written to Douglas was presented as evidence, and the prosecution asked Wilde:

Q: Have you often written letters in the same style as this?
A: I don't repeat myself in style.

Wilde argued that all the letters he wrote to Douglas were "innocent" and "ordinary." The prosecution then produced a passionate and more damaging paper.

Q: Is that an ordinary letter?
A: Everything I write is extraordinary. I do not pose as being ordinary, great heavens!

Wilde was winning the case when his wit served to trap him. When asked if he ever kissed a male servant of Lord Alfred Douglas, he answered carelessly and flippantly: "Oh, dear no. He was a peculiarly plain boy. He was, unfortunately, extremely ugly."

So he had not kissed the boy only because of his ugliness. That was the rope the prosecution used to trip Wilde to defeat.

"Why, sir, did you mention his ugliness?"

Wilde was speechless.

"Why? Why? Why did you add that?" the prosecution persisted.

Wilde mumbled; he began several answers, all inarticulate and incomplete.

At last the humiliated and wounded Wilde answered, "You sting me and insult me and at times one says things flippantly." From there on the trial went against the playwright.

A street boy testified: "I was asked by Wilde to imagine that I was a woman and that he was my lover. . . . I used to sit on his knees and he used to play with my privates as a man might amuse himself with a girl. . . . He suggested two or three times that I would permit him to insert 'it' in my mouth, but I never allowed that."

The jury was out less than three hours before returning with a verdict of guilty. The world-renowned man of letters, who once referred to his sexuality as "the Love that dare not speak its name," was given the maximum sentence: two years' imprisonment and hard labor.

Venereal Disease. It was while in the Reading Gaol that Wilde fell, struck his head on the stone floor, and incurred the ear injury that would later most likely contribute to his death.

After two agonizing years in prison, the professionally destroyed, penurious playwright spent two declining years shambling about the Continent, cadging drinks and bearing old friends pass him on the boulevards without acknowledgment.

Toward the end of September 1900, while living on credit in two small rooms in Paris, Wilde was struck by a recurrence of the ear infection and confined to bed.

On October 10 he was operated on. The precise nature of the surgery is unknown, though it was probably for his painful and persistent ear ailment. The operation was not successful and may, indeed, have hastened his decline by aggravating the infection and causing it to spread from the middle ear to the tissue lining of the brain, the meninges.

Robert Ross, his "first boy," kept the ill and defeated writer company. He described Wilde as being in "very good spirits, though he assured me his sufferings were dreadful." Uninterested in food and realizing the end was near, Wilde drank whenever a guest was kind enough to bring a bottle. To a friend's suggestion that Wilde's alcoholism was self-destructive, the writer replied, "You are qualifying for a doctor. When you can refuse bread to the hungry, and drink to the thirsty, you may apply for your Diploma."

By late November his ear was extremely painful and he drifted in and out of consciousness. The busy furnishings of the rented room had always offended Wilde, and once when he opened his eyes he was heard to murmur, "This wallpaper is killing me; one of us has got to go." Another biographer claims Wilde's last words were in reference to sipping champagne: "I am dying as I've lived: beyond my means."

Wilde had expressed interest in being baptized into the Roman Catholic faith and a priest was summoned. The playwright, unable to speak, signaled assent with a wave of his hand and received the sacrament. He died at 1:50 P.M. on November 30, 1900.

Shortly after his death, his body, riddled with infection, exploded with pent-up pus. That evidence has convinced some biohistorians that Oscar Wilde's cause of death was actually neurosyphilis, contracted from the female prostitutes he frequented as a university student. He seemed to have had some form of venereal disease. Before proposing to his future wife, Constance Lloyd, in 1884, Wilde consulted a doctor, who assured him that mercury treatments had cured him of a sexual infection. A few years later, Wilde claimed to have discovered new chancres on himself and thus gave up sex with Constance; this could have been a convenient ruse, for at the same time he began his affairs with boys.

Other biohistorians maintain Wilde's life was ended by cerebral meningitis caused by the suppurative disease of the middle ear. It leads first to mastoiditis, then to meningitis. This theory holds that Wilde's botched operation punctured the roof of the middle ear, introducing the infection to the meninges of the brain and possibly to the temporal lobe. Wilde's death certificate cites cerebral meningitis; since then only the cause of the brain infection has been at issue. Whether it was syphilis or suppurative otitis media will probably never be known.

Florence Nightingale: d. 1910, age 90

> **Cause of death:** Heart failure after fifty-four years as an invalid
>
> **Place of rest:** East Wellow Church Cemetery, Hampshire, England
>
> **Near the end:** *"I am becoming quite a tame beast."*

Most people are familiar with the story of Florence Nightingale: the high-born lady who carried the lamp of hospital reform; the nurse whose selfless devotion brought comfort, and often life, to thousands of sick and wounded British soldiers in the Crimean War; the tireless woman who single-handedly transformed nursing from a lowly thankless chore to a skilled and respected profession. That is the stuff of upbeat biography.

But her decline, and the events that led to her death, is another story entirely, in a way a longer one since it involves the last fifty-four years of her ninety-year life.

After returning to England from heroic service in the 1854–56 Crimean War, the 36-year-old dean of nursing was never quite the same woman. For reasons seemingly mysterious, Nightingale became an invalid. She was at war for 632 days and came home with an extraordinary reputation that would last her all her life, yet she chose to spend that life—all 54 years of it—in bed. From her bed, she issued a steady stream of orders that were carried out by devoted followers.

It is true that off her feet Florence Nightingale accomplished more than most of us do fully ambulatory. But was she really physically sick? Perhaps not.

Her sickbed accomplishments were considerable. From the comfortable couch in her home in Mayfair she organized the Army Medical Department, sanitated portions of India, and founded her nurses' training school. She also

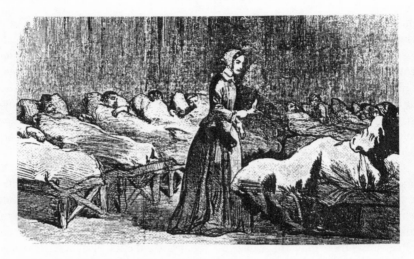

Florence Nightingale: the Lady with the Lamp enjoying a brief period of good health.

wrote *Notes on Nursing,* consulted on the best saucepans for hospital kitchens, the best books of hospital libraries, and the best color for hospital walls (pale pink, today considered the color that most speeds recovery). She also published *A Treatise on Sinks* (hospital sinks, that is), and promulgated her maxim: "The very first requirement in a Hospital is that it should do the sick no harm." In addition, cabinet ministers, generals, viceroys, and doctors entered her bedroom beseeching her for advice on matters administrative, political, and antiseptic.

The mystery, of course, is what made this woman, intellectually vigorous and vital into her late eighties, a bedridden invalid for more than half a century?

In her day, people kindly said that her exhaustive two years treating the war wounded left her drained. Less kindly it was pointed out that she did have fifty-four years to recover. The medical diagnosis in her time was "dilatation of the heart and neurasthenia." That is, according to a turn-of-the-century medical book, "A condition of weakness or exhaustion of the nervous system, giving rise to mental and bodily inefficiency." This despite the evidence that she worked for fifty years with great mental acumen and remarkable energy and efficiency.

Productive Hypochondria.   Today it's thought that Florence Nightingale's problems were, to put it bluntly, located conveniently in her head. Modern psychiatrists claim that the dean of nursing suffered from profound psychoneurosis, a stratagem as much as a symptom in which the mind tricks the body to manifest ailments when, and for the exact duration, they best serve the person's interests. Florence Nightingale is perhaps the best textbook case of the phenomenon.

Her "convenient" symptoms were alarming attacks of breathlessness, palpitation, giddiness, and acute anxiety—all induced by an event or person she did not wish to deal with. Her "illness" (real to her), allowed her to accomplish prodigious amounts of work from her bed, by excluding all visitors she wished not to see and by playing on the illness to win sympathy for herself and, thus, for her most cherished causes.

Dr. George Pickering, in *Creative Malady,* proffers a single cause for Florence Nightingale's psychoneurosis: "The unresolved conflict between what she wanted to do, namely to help the less fortunate, and the circumstances preventing her from doing so, chiefly her mother and sister."

Her mother most of all. When, at the age of twenty-four, Nightingale had announced her nursing ambitions to her rich and fashionable parents, they were horror-struck. A nurse then was lower socially than the maid who emptied her family's chamber pots. Her mother did everything possible to frustrate Nightingale's desire.

Previously, Nightingale had been strong and healthy; now her illnesses began. Each family argument—and they were numerous—initiated another attack of breathlessness, palpitation, and anxiety. And her family's fury over her rejection of two highly desirable marriage proposals drove her to bed for weeks.

Nightingale left home in 1853 at age thirty-three. She pursued her dream of nursing and almost overnight her symptoms ceased. She was healthier still during the two-year labor of love of ministering to the sick during the Crimean War, despite the real physical diseases she contracted: "I have now had," she wrote, "all that this climate can give, Crimean fever [typhoid or typhus], Dysentery, Rheumatism and believe myself thoroughly acclimatised and ready to stand out the war with any man."

Her healthy, symptomless period ceased almost to the day that the war ended and she returned to England. She was a national hero; she needed to be a nurse to dying soldiers. And in the wartime military hospital she had been a veritable dictator; at home, bureaucratic channels clogged to frustrate her every move at revolutionizing England's hospital system.

Her mother and sister made matters worse. Their Florence was a celebrity; shouldn't she make the most of that socially? There were parties in her honor, award banquets, and Britain's most desirable suitors to be selected from. Her mother and sister simply could not understand why Florence shunned the glories, preferring to devote her life to sanitation. Just the word!

Reclusive Years. To survive, to achieve her dream, Florence Nightingale subconsciously conspired ingenious debility. She also became unbearably short-tempered and tyrannical. Anyone wishing to serve the wartime nurse had to take wartime commands unquestioningly. One such unfortunate "servant," her faithful Aunt Mai, fell from Nightingale's favor for twenty years. The aunt's sin: She acceded to her family's request to leave Nightingale for several weeks and return home to prepare for her daughter's wedding. For the next two decades Nightingale refused to speak to the woman for having "abandoned her post." Little wonder that Florence Nightingale accomplished so much.

Her productivity did drop considerably around age fifty. Several possible causes have been suggested: genuine exhaustion; a difficult and protracted menopause; an addiction to opium, which she took not infrequently for a chronic, though undiagnosed, pain. And, too, the major conflict that had caused her psychoneurosis had become less intense: She was back on good terms with her mother and sister.

However, she continued to live the life of an invalid until the end. Perhaps out of habit. Perhaps because illness had served her so well for so many years. Also, the indomitable-spirit-rising-above-physical-debility was by now part of her legend. The Lady of the Lamp was a more romantic figure in the form of an elderly invalid recluse whose influence was known to be immense.

Dr. Pickering concludes his analysis of Florence Nightingale's psychoneurosis with this: "Of one thing I am quite sure, I should not have liked to be the doctor who tried to explain to Miss Nightingale the nature of her illness."

She became so reclusive in her eighties that most of the world believed she had died. When, in 1907, she became the first woman to have the Order of Merit conferred upon her, many newspapers pointedly remarked that this was *not* a posthumous honor.

On August 13, 1910, about noon, the ninety-year-old queen of nursing simply closed her eyes and passed quietly and quickly away. She died as she had lived, with efficiency and dignity.

Her last will and testament was characteristically explicit. She ordered that her body "be carried to the nearest convenient burial ground," that "no more than two persons" accompany the coffin, and that the service be "without trappings."

On her deathbed she had turned down the offer of a national funeral and burial in Westminster Abbey. English officials begged to ceremoniously honor the memory of Florence Nightingale, but her family—out of respect or conditioned by fear—followed her will more or less to the letter. Her corpse was carried to the nearest convenient churchyard, East Wellow, and buried without trappings, though many more than two mourners dared to accompany the coffin.

Rudolph Valentino: d. 1926, age 31

Cause of death: Perforated gastric ulcer and peritonitis from a ruptured appendix

Place of rest: Hollywood Cemetery, California

Last words: *"Don't pull down the blinds! I want the sun to greet me."*

The screen idol and "great lover" of the 1920s was struck down at the height of his career. His final farewell and funeral were every bit as dramatic, flamboyant, and exaggerated as his brief life had been.

Valentino was born on May 6, 1895, in the small Italian town of Castellaneta, and with a name that would never fit on a marquee: Rodolfo Alfonzo Raffaelo Pierre Filibert Gugliemi di Valentina D'Antonguolla. An agricultural student in Italy, then a lover of the night life in France, the young Valentino went by the name Rodolfo Guglielmi. At age eighteen he arrived in New York City friendless, penniless, and unable to speak English; his single asset was his suave European charm, which by all accounts was considerable and put to immediate use—primarily as a dancing partner for unescorted ladies at Manhattan cabarets.

His big break came in 1921 when (working as a chorus boy) he landed a role in *The Four Horsemen of the Apocalypse.* He was twenty-six. By the time of his death at thirty-one, the seductive "sheik" that H. L. Mencken dubbed as "catnip to women" would complete fourteen films and be adored worldwide; it was a meteoric rise even by Hollywood standards.

The events that would take his life began on Saturday, August 14, 1926, when the screen idol was resting in his suite at New York's Hotel Ambassador.

Valentino felt a sharp and sudden pain in his lower abdomen. Gripping his stomach, he fell to the floor in agony. He refused to go to a hospital, passing the night feverish and fitful. When his temperature soared the next day, he was rushed to Polyclinic Hospital and operated on for a perforated gastric ulcer. Surprised surgeons also discovered that Valentino's appendix had ruptured and infection was spreading rapidly throughout his peritoneum.

Word that Valentino was hospitalized caused nationwide concern. Later word that he was on the critical list and might not recover produced mass hysteria. Women—teenagers and adults—wept openly; hundreds promised to kill themselves if Valentino died. The hospital issued press releases hourly, as might be done for a president. For eight days suspense built as the public fed on a stream of medical bulletins alternating between hope and gloom. For sheer melodrama, press stories outdid any of the scripts Hollywood had tailored for the silent-screen star.

His ex-wives and fiancée were interviewed and attempted to upstage each other. Actress Jean Acker, wife number one, visited Valentino and told the press, "The shock of seeing him lying there was terrible. That white face. His labored breathing." She claimed that the dying star confessed that he loved her best.

Wife number two, Natacha Rambova (born Winifred Shaunessy), spoke with Valentino and days later announced that he loved her so much that he spoke with her again *after* his death: "He was quite put out at the holiday spirit with which many viewed his remains," she reported. "It was difficult for Rudy to reconcile himself to his departure."

Pola Negri, the actress who was to have been wife number three, addressed Valentino only in her prayers, for as she explained to a reporter in Hollywood, "I would like to hasten to his bedside, but I am in the middle of a picture."

One newspaper faked a front-page photograph of Valentino on the operating table. The next day, August 23, the *Daily News,* swept up in the high drama, led off its edition with the cliff-hanger: "The Great Director today stood ready to call Rudolph Valentino off the screen of life."

And that very day, the great director did call—at ten minutes after noon. One paper, abandoning any attempt at realism, ran a drawing of Valentino entering the kingdom of heaven, greeted not by God but by someone who sold more papers: fellow deceased Italian Enrico Caruso.

Receiving word that the grim reaper had struck, Pola Negri held a press conference at which she fainted, was revived, fainted again, then announced she was stopping work on her picture to hole up in Valentino's mountaintop hideaway, Falcon's Lair, atop Beverly Hills. Louella Parsons, mother confessor to the movie colony, reported that for Pola Negri, the love nest of the "sheik" was "the one place that offered her a solitary grain of comfort in her bitter anguish."

If Valentino's illness had generated drama, his death brought hysteria and more deaths. A British actress, clutching a batch of love poetry she had written about Valentino, took a lethal dose of poison. A New York housewife fatally shot herself with one hand while the other cradled her collection of Valentino photos. The press reported that in Japan two lovelorn fans, unable to live in a world without the screen lover, leaped into a volcano. And it was reported in Italy that Il Duce himself appealed to Italian women to pray for the great idol but not to attempt to join him.

What were Valentino's last words?

The phrase printed above is only one possibility. The press claimed that hospital visitors had heard him murmur faintly in his native Italian, "Don't pull down the shades. I want the sunlight to greet me." United Artists, with a box office stake in Valentino's newly released *Son of the Sheik,* issued something that sounded suspiciously tailor-made: "Let the tent be struck!" Pola Negri, who had not been present, claimed through hearsay that Valentino breathed, "Tell Pola I have been thinking of her."

Wife number two, claiming still to be conversing with the dead film star, announced that even to mention last words was nonsense; Valentino was as voluble as ever: "Rudy is really quite happy 'over there.' He spends his time listening to Caruso sing, and he is going to theatres and lectures, too." Asked if he would act again, she said, "Yes, but only on stage," since, she clarified, movie equipment was absent on the astral plane.

Funerary Furor.   Valentino's public viewing, held on August 24 at New York City's Frank Campbell's Funeral Chapel, caused pandemonium. The crowd, mostly screaming, crying women, young and old, numbered thirty thousand and stretched up Broadway. *The New York Times* reported that "the rioting was without precedent." Fearing souvenir hunters might strip the corpse of clothes and jewelry, the funeral director ordered the bronze casket sealed closed. Foiled, the crowd stripped the funeral home.

For the second day of viewing, the casket was moved from the now bare Gold Room to a room that was essentially bare. Despite rain, the street crowd numbered fifty thousand. People were pushed and trampled by fans—and by police, who lost control and charged their horses through the worshipers. Shop windows were smashed, cars overturned; ambulances took away fainting women, while police rounded up hundreds of abandoned children. At the funeral home, a wreath arrived labeled "From Benito Mussolini," and people believed it was.

On September 2, Valentino's body left New York by rail, bound for California on the Lakeshore Limited. For protection, the corpse was sealed in *two* coffins, the inner one silver and bronze, the outer one gold and bronze. And the doors of the railroad compartment were padlocked. At a stop in Chicago, scores of women were injured trying to break into the train. In Los Angeles, the body was removed at a small suburban station, fooling throngs of fans waiting at the main depot.

The funeral service, held in Beverly Hills and covered by worldwide media, was attended by a galaxy of stars: Douglas Fairbanks, Mary Pickford, Gloria Swanson, and Marilyn Miller, as well as Pola Negri and Jean Acker. The press reported that most mourners carried their own smelling salts. Movie studios ceased filming for the hour duration of the service.

Valentino, the world's "great lover," received a Catholic burial in a private mausoleum of imported Italian marble in Hollywood Cemetery. How could a womanizer and a man twice divorced receive a church-sanctioned Roman Catholic burial?

The answer was tricky, to be sure, and was explained officially by an editorial in the *Catholic News of New York*. The headline read, "Was Valentino Ever Validly Married?" and the explanation began with, "In the eyes of God and the church, no." In short, Valentino had never been married by a priest, therefore he was never married. What about his numerous highly publicized affairs? The editorial made it clear that, "The pastor of St. Malachi's Church . . . was called to the bedside of Valentino" and the "public sinner" confessed all. Thus the church claimed that *it* was privy to the screen star's actual last words, which it would keep as secret as the Virgin's Fatima message. "Since Valentino died a Catholic," the editorial reasoned, "he was entitled to a Catholic burial. The church gave him what she gives all her children, simply this and nothing more."

For many years after Valentino's death a mysterious "lady in black"— sometimes many more than one—arrived at his burial crypt on the anniversary of his death. She (they) always bore a red rose.

Thomas Edison: d. 1931, age 84

> **Cause of death:** Uremic poisoning
>
> **Place of rest:** Glenmont, West Orange, New Jersey
>
> **Last words:** Coming out of a coma: *"It is very beautiful over there."*

Edison's death emphasized the importance of his greatest inventions, the light bulb and the power plant, in a way that would surely have delighted him. Suggestions were made that on the day of his funeral, October 20, 1931, electric power across the United States be turned off for a few solemn minutes. But

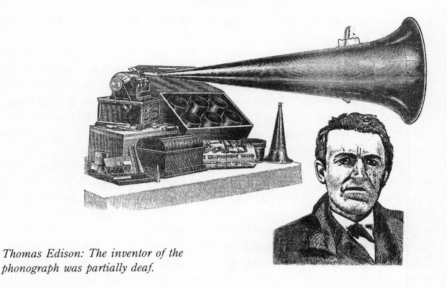

*Thomas Edison: The inventor of the
phonograph was partially deaf.*

Congress determined that the loss of electricity on so large a scale, even briefly, could precipitate a national disaster and pose a security risk. Thomas Edison, in a little more than four decades, had made a nation, indeed a world, totally dependent on one of his brightest ideas.

There was a great irony in Edison's life. Whereas it is well known that history's greatest composer, Beethoven, was deaf, few people realize that the man who invented the phonograph and made practical the telephone—ushering in the audio age—was himself increasingly deaf after the age of seven. In fact, as a boy, Edison was expelled from school for being retarded, when his real problem was a growing inability to hear his teachers.

Edison liked to blame his partial deafness on a physical injury incurred at the age of twelve when an adult, in a reprimand, boxed his ears: "I felt something snap inside my head, and the deafness started from that time and has progressed ever since."

But there is ample evidence that Edison was already partially deaf at age seven. More likely his deafness was the result of a juvenile bout of scarlet fever that left him with recurrent middle-ear infections. His impaired hearing disposed him to enjoy solitude, which, in turn, provided an ideal environment for his creativity to flourish. "I'm long on ideas but short on time," he said in midlife, "I only expect to live to be about one hundred." He almost made the century mark.

In his long and productive life, deafness was not his only bane; he suffered from diabetes and gastric ulcers. The latter ailment led him to a diet largely of milk, two cups every two hours, preferably obtained from a particular brown cow kept in a pasture in Parsippany, New Jersey, near his laboratory. The sparse diet eventually led to malnutrition, but that did not diminish his productivity. He patented 1,093 inventions, almost sticking to his youthful boast that he'd turn out a minor brainstorm "every ten days" and a "big trick" every six months. Though extremely self-assured, Edison had no highfalutin pretension about inventing, even advertising that he would produce "inventions to order." He has since been dubbed "the man who made a business of invention."

He became a national treasure and his last few months provoked a national death watch. A press room was set up in his home, with frequent medical bulletins going out to newspapers and to Herbert Hoover's Oval Office.

For years Edison had suffered from chronic Bright's disease, a kidney malfunction. Also known as glomerulonephritis, the disease causes a buildup of fluids and waste in the body, producing swelling, increased blood pressure, and severe back pain. Red blood cells attempting to pass through the inflamed kidneys are damaged, which leads to anemia, and the accumulation of urea can poison the body.

For Edison, the ailment reached a critical stage in October of 1929. Age eighty-two, he was Henry Ford's honorary guest at a dinner in Dearborn, Michigan, to celebrate the fiftieth anniversary of the birth of the electric light. President Hoover had just finished his own tribute to Edison when the inventor collapsed from acute renal failure. Back home at his mansion, Glenmont, in West Orange, New Jersey, Edison grew steadily weaker from uremic poisoning.

Though he was seen by many doctors, Edison largely treated himself. He measured out and administered his own medication. He interpreted his clinical charts, updated by nurses. And he took his own blood specimens and scrutinized them under a microscope. All of this did nothing to cure him, and nothing known to medicine at that time could have.

In August of 1931, weak and unable to take nourishment for several days, he collapsed in his living room. In the days that followed, Edison's mind, once rigorously lucid, began to cloud, and President Hoover was told that the nation would shortly lose the man who had helped usher America into the technological age.

On October 15, Edison lapsed into a coma. He lay near death for two days. Reporters waited on the lawn for a sign, which came at 3:24 A.M., on October 18: All the lights in his bedroom were turned *on.* The day before, he had opened his eyes, and, glancing at his wife, Mina, uttered his last words: "It is very beautiful over there."

Much, perhaps too much, has been made of the utterance. After his death, many people interpreted the phrase as a clear reference to the afterlife. Edison, a man of undeniable foresight, had seen still farther and was reporting on the Lord's own great invention, heaven. In the 1970s, when there was a popularity for so-called near-death encounters—tales from people resuscitated from clinical death—the Edison quote was offered as yet another confirmation that a dying person can, through an altered state of consciousness, glimpse the next realm.

However, when the eighty-four-year-old dying Thomas Edison surfaced briefly from a coma and spoke, he was, at that moment, glancing straight out his bedroom window across the valley beside his home. It was a view he loved, often contemplated, and even complimented for its natural beauty. His wife believed that Edison's last utterance was simply another compliment on the earthly landscape: "It is very beautiful over there."

Many people who have since looked out the window agree that the view is beautiful but find the sentiment too mundane for a dying genius. Whether Thomas Edison meant more . . . well, we will decide for ourselves, sooner or later.

Sigmund Freud: d. 1939, age 83

> **Cause of death:** Cancer of the jaw, palate, throat, and tongue
>
> **Place of rest:** Following cremation, his ashes were placed in his favorite Grecian urn
>
> **Last words:** To his doctor on his planned euthanasia: *"You promised me you would help me when I could no longer carry on."* Then of his daughter: *"Tell Anna about our talk."*

The Father of Psychoanalysis, who established new directions for understanding and treating mental illness, died a long and agonizing death. Sigmund Freud's final years—sixteen of them—were a nightmare: of spreading disease, of brutal surgery (under local anesthesia), and of suffering excruciating pain, for which the stoical patient consented to take—but only in his last months—aspirin.

Freud's views on sexuality can be summed succinctly: Whereas other psychiatrists observed that the penis is attached to the man, Freud discovered that the man is attached to the penis. His terms "penis envy," "Oedpius complex," "libido," "death wish," "repression," "neurosis," and others entered everyday speech and suspicion. He justified the tobacco habit that would kill him with the romantic observation that "smoking is indispensable if one has nothing to kiss."

Sigmund Freud: In agony he requested death.

Then, perhaps in a subconscious reference to his own possible bisexuality, declared that cigars were a substitute for masturbation.

Freud was a brilliant student at the University of Vienna. Though he wished to be a politician, that career was limited for a Jew in the nineteenth century so he pursued medicine. At age thirty, he married Martha Bernays, a slim, attractive twenty-one-year-old from a traditional Jewish family. Within nine years the couple had six children, and the great sexual theorizer lost interest in practicing the subject he preached.

He plunged himself into work. And into his own analysis under a Berlin friend, Dr. Wilhelm Fliess. The two men developed a strong attachment, and Freud once wrote, "I am looking forward to our congress as to a slaking of hunger and thirst. . . . I live gloomily . . . until you come and then I pour out all my grumbles to you, kindle my flickering light at your steady flame and feel well again."

Was there anything homosexual about the friendship?

Perhaps latently. Freud himself confessed, "There is some piece of unruly homosexual feeling at the root of the matter." Fliess and Freud went on to develop the theory of a universal bisexual impulse, in which every infant is born innately bisexual, and Freud went so far as to state that by adulthood, "Every sexual act is one between four individuals."

Wilhelm Fliess tried desperately to get his friend and patient to stop smoking twenty cigars a day. Even though Freud viewed smoking (as well as gambling and drug abuse) as a substitute for that "primal addiction," masturbation, he could not kick the habit. The pleasure smoking afforded him could in no measure compensate for the pain and death the nicotine addiction would bring.

His terminal illness first signaled itself in 1917 when Freud was sixty-one years old. He noticed an ominous and painful swelling on the right side of his palate, but chose to ignore it, convinced he would die of a heart attack. But by 1923 the tumor, pronounced malignant, had invaded the right jaw and had to be excised.

The out-patient surgery, ineptly performed in a local clinic, nearly killed the psychiatrist. Profusely bleeding, Freud had to be hastily put up on a cot overnight, where further hemorrhaging almost choked him to death. The surgeon had neglected to take the necessary steps to guard against shrinkage of the operational scar, and the result was that Freud's mouth permanently contracted, which was to cause him untold hardship and suffering for the rest of his life.

That same year the cancer reappeared. The second operation was more radical. Freud's lip and cheek had to be split wide open and the entire jaw and palate on the right side removed, along with part of his tongue—all done under local anesthetic. Fed through a nasal tube and unable to talk for a week, Freud wrote one morning of dressing himself: "What is left of me, put into clothes."

With so much of his inner face missing, he needed a prosthetic. Its necessarily tight fit against the palate caused him constant irritation and excruciating pain. Yet removal of the piece for more than a few hours invariably resulted in shrinkage of the surrounding tissue, which necessitated painful stretching procedures.

For Freud, who had always taken great pleasure in food, eating became an agony and an embarrassment. From this time onward he rarely ate in the presence of others. When talking, he frequently had to hold the prosthesis in place with his thumb. His speech became increasingly thick and nasal, and his hearing, also impaired by the surgery, would in time leave him deaf in the right ear.

Freud was now sixty-seven. Yet with all the suffering—and with thirty-one operations still ahead of him, an average of one every six months for the rest of his life—the ground-breaking psychiatrist continued to write, deliver conference papers, and psychoanalyze four to six patients a day.

Despite continual pain, he refused all palliating drugs because they would dull his intellect. And, he discovered to his horror, this was the same reason he could not renounce the "sweet habit," smoking: Nicotine kept him alert; its absence, for even a half-day, muddled his thoughts. So he continued puffing on twenty cigars daily, though to get one into his mouth required that he force open his bite with the aid of a clothespin.

Mercy Killing.   In 1926, at age seventy, Freud developed his long-feared heart trouble: angina pectoris. But while recuperating in a sanatorium, the jaw malignancy surfaced with new ferocity. More operations followed, with more jaw and palate cut away and more grotesque prostheses forced into place. Freud, still working a full schedule, now needed daily medical supervision and a young internist, Max Schur, became his steady companion.

"I can stand a great deal of pain," Freud confided to Schur, then added meaningfully, "I trust you will not let me suffer unnecessarily."

During these painful years, Freud's international reputation was growing enormously. He wrote abundantly and delivered as many conference papers as could be fitted between his responsibilities to private patients. Accounting for his stoical endurance, he stated, "I see no use quarrelling with fate." He actually viewed himself as fortunate: "I regard it as a triumph to retain a clear judgment in all circumstances. . . . To grow so old; to find so much warm love in family and friends."

The year 1930 brought five new operations to contain the cancer and refit prostheses. Regular radiation therapy started.

But in the summer of 1936, Freud's doctors admitted to him that the malignancy was spreading so rapidly and tenaciously they could only electrically burn away new blotches as they appeared. The disease, on a rampage throughout his mouth, was uncontainable. During one burning session, Freud, normally unflinching, cried, "I can't go on any longer!" Postoperative drugs, when offered, were still refused: "I prefer to think in torment, than not to be able to think clearly."

In 1938, the eighty-two-year-old Freud had no sooner fled Nazi-occupied Austria for England when his cancer again necessitated major surgery. In order to get at the deep-seated tumor, Freud's trademark beard was shaved and his entire cheek split open. The radical operation left him utterly spent; he never recovered from its effects.

At Christmastime, a new and highly invasive malignancy appeared inside his right cheek. Though the tumor grew insidiously, no more of his jaw or palate could be removed; eating already was a virtual impossibility and Freud was skeletally thin. His doctors told him they could only use X rays and radium perhaps to slow the inevitable advance of the disease. That summer Freud wrote that the radiation treatment was itself causing pain and tissue destruction: "The radium has once more begun to eat in, with pain and toxic effects." He described his world as "a little island of pain floating on a sea of indifference."

In July of that year, 1939, the cancer, which had been confined to the inside of Freud's mouth, ruptured through to the cheek's surface. The festering ulceration was excruciatingly painful and for the first time the eighty-three-year-old psychiatrist consented to take a painkiller—aspirin. Nothing stronger, and not frequently, only when needed, for he was still psychoanalyzing four patients a day and needed his "wits."

In August he had to terminate his practice. The fetid odor that emanated from the ulcerated cheek offended patients and friends; even Freud's faithful dog shied away from him. He spent his days in his room, gazing out the window at summer flowers.

Unable to chew, devoid of appetite, Freud consumed practically nothing throughout August and September. On September 21, he bravely confronted his personal physician: "My dear Schur, you remember our first talk. You promised me you would assist me when I could no longer carry on. It is strictly torture now. It no longer makes any sense." Then, thinking of his devoted daughter who had remained unmarried and nursed him ever since his first operation in 1923, he added, "Tell Anna about our talk."

Dr. Schur complied with Freud's last wish and injected his world-famous friend and patient with a third of a grain of morphine. Even such a small amount had the desired effect on Freud's wasted and weakened body. The father of modern psychiatry drifted into a profound sleep from which he never awakened. Two days later, on September 23, 1939, the eighty-three-year-old Freud died.

On September 26, at a ceremony in Golders Green, London, attended by some of the world's greatest scientists and artists, Sigmund Freud's body was cremated. At his request, his ashes were placed in a Grecian urn he was especially fond of.

Yukio Mishima: d. 1970, age 45

Cause of death: Suicide by disembowelment and decapitation

Mode of burial: Cremation

Last words: To an assembled crowd: *"Long live the emperor!"* Turning to a companion: *"I don't think they even heard me."*

Japan's flamboyant and prolific writer was obsessed with blood, death, and suicide. He was also torn between ancient and modern values: old Japan's militaristic samurai tradition and the country's contemporary Westernization. For Mishima, the resolution of the conflict of cultures and the apotheosis of his obsession with death was a public ritual suicide at the height of his fame.

The endings of few people are as clearly prefigured in their life and work as was Yukio Mishima's final act. He had fantasized suicide as a child, written about it as an adult, and enacted ritual seppuku on film. No ending of a famous figure was more predictable or rehearsed.

His end was, in a way, seeded in his beginning. Born on November 14, 1925, to a father who deeply admired Hitler and Nazism, Kimitake Hiraoka later took the pseudonym Yukio Mishima, which he scripted in Japanese so that the characters also read "mysterious devil bewitched with death." As he liked to tell friends, "It's eerie, but that's the way to write my name."

He was raised by his paternal grandmother, an ailing, embittered invalid who kept Mishima in her darkened sickroom until he was twelve. She nurtured the boy, frail and introspective, on legends of medieval Japan. It was a story-book world of violence, pageantry, and nobly inspired suicides that the lonely Yukio hungrily absorbed, finding it infinitely more colorful and compelling than the real world around him.

For amusement he drew pictures of handsome knights dying of battle wounds. And he was appalled to learn that a martyr whose picture he mooned over was not a man, as he had thought and eroticized about, but a boyish-looking French girl named Joan. From that revelation onward, Mishima hated the sight of women in mannish attire and forbade his wife to wear slacks.

Sex and death were bizarrely fused in his mind by age twelve. He then had his first orgasm, fantasizing on a picture of St. Sebastian bound and pierced by arrows, an incident he featured in his first novel, *Confessions of a Mask,* published in 1949 when he was twenty-four. Partly autobiographical, it served as Mishima's homosexual coming-out, and once out publicly, the now famous young writer became notoriously promiscuous.

Nonetheless, he married and fathered two children, though his wife, Yoko Sugiyama, was locked in a continual battle with Mishima's jealous and posses-sive mother, Shizue, who regarded the writer more as a lover than a son. The wife and mother were in a minority: Japanese women found Mishima physically unattractive to repulsive, and in a magazine poll, fifty percent of the female readers admitted that they'd rather kill themselves than be his mistress.

Mishima's ritualistic death is eerily prefigured in his 1966 short story "Patri-otism." And when it was made into the film *Yukoku,* Mishima directed and played the lead, literally living out his fate of four years later. Mishima wrote of the character, a lieutenant, who has just ripped open his gut with a knife:

> The five or six inches of naked point vanished completely into his flesh. . . .
> He returned to consciousness. The blade had certainly pierced the wall of his stomach, he thought. It was difficult to breathe, his chest pounded, and in some deep distant region which he could hardly believe was part of himself, a

fearful excruciating pain came welling up as if the ground had opened to disgorge a boiling stream of molten lava. . . .

So this was *seppuku!*

The proximate events that lead to Mishima's real act of seppuku, Japan's form of ritual suicide, began in 1970.

Although he maintained an essentially Western life-style and possessed a vast knowledge of Western culture, he raged against Japan's imitation of the West. He had diligently developed the age-old Japanese arts of karate and swordsmanship and built a controversial private army, the *Tatenokai* ("Shield Society"). Its purpose was to preserve Japanese martial spirit and to assist the regular armed forces in case of an uprising from the left or a Communist attack (though the press derided it as Mishima's "toy army").

On November 25, 1970, with four Shield Society followers, Mishima seized control of the commanding general's office at the military headquarters near downtown Tokyo. He gave a ten-minute harangue from a balcony to a thousand assembled servicemen in which he attacked the weakness of Japan's post–World War II constitution, which forbids war and Japanese rearmament. His hope was to invade the diet, Japan's parliament, and compel it to revise the constitution. And he would take a hostage.

If he failed in this effort (and from the start Mishima was virtually certain of that outcome), he would commit seppuku, which in Mishima's twisted mind was not only an honorable means of death, but the spilling of gut was, as he said, "the ultimate form of masturbation." Once disemboweled, he was to be beheaded by his twenty-five-year-old second-in-command, Masakatsu Morita, whom friends of the writer called Mishima's "fiancé." Morita was then to experience *morte* himself, by seppuku, with the third-in-command, Furu-Koga, doing the beheading.

Plans went wrong from the start.

With a hostage, General Masuda, secured inside the building, Mishima mounted the balcony and addressed the crowd. From the first word he uttered his voice was drowned out by the spectators' angry shouts. The din of circling police helicopters further muffled his message, which was supposed to last for a half-hour but ended after seven chaotic minutes.

Mishima and Morita shouted in unison, "Long live the emperor!" then retreated into the building, Mishima uttering his last words: "I don't think they even heard me."

With eerie calm, Mishima knelt and with both hands drove a short sword into his left side. As he had amply rehearsed—in print, on film, and in his mind—he dragged the blade horizontally to the right, cutting open the inner wall of the abdomen. He experienced what the lieutenant had in "Patriotism": "By the time the lieutenant had at last drawn the sword across the right side of his stomach the blade was already cutting shallow and had revealed its naked tip, slippery with blood and fat."

But Mishima had not expected the pain to be unendurable. Next to him on the floor was a sheet of paper and a watercolor brush. He had intended to paint the Japanese character for "sword" in his own blood. But when he slumped forward in agony, Morita immediately brought down the large sword to decapitate his commander. Again reality refused to mimic fantasy. The first blow, forceful as it was, did not do the job. Nor did the second. Furu-Koga grabbed the sword from Morita and finally severed Mishima's head.

Morita then knelt beside his hero, commander, and probably his lover. With equal calm and resolve, he disemboweled himself, drawing the short blade left to right. Extracting the knife, he commanded Furu-Koga, "Now!" and his head fell too. Furu-Koga and two fellow cadets then freed their hostage and surrendered to police. They were led crying from the building.

For the funeral, as Mishima had requested, his body was dressed in the military uniform of his own army. And for the viewing, attended by family and friends, his head was returned to his rightful place, the gash concealed by a scarf. Before the casket was closed for cremation, Mishima's wife—who had heard news of his death while attending a luncheon—laid beside him his favorite fountain pen and a manuscript he had been working on.

Isadora Duncan: d. 1927, age 49

Cause of death: Accidental strangulation

Place of rest: Père-Lachaise Cemetery, Paris

Last words: Moments before her fatal accident: *"Adieu, my friends. I go off to glory!"*

Fourteen years before her life ended tragically in a freak car accident, Isadora Duncan endured the painful loss of her two young children—Deirdre, five, and Patrick, three—who also died in a car accident. The children drowned, trapped in a car that rolled into the Seine. Duncan would be strangled when her shawl, draped twice around her neck, caught and wound in the spokes of a sports car wheel. The day before her death, she spotted a girl on the street who reminded her of Deirdre and confided to a friend: "I cannot continue to live in a world where there are beautiful blue-eyed, golden-haired children. I cannot!"

Born in San Francisco on September 14, 1878, the young Isadora startled a theatrical producer she was to audition for, saying, "I have discovered the art which had been lost for two thousands years. I bring you the idea that is going to revolutionize our entire epoch."

Though she did not discover interpretive dancing, she was the first to raise ancient Greek principles of freestyle movement to the status of creative art in her age. Eschewing the rigid formalism of ballet, she based her dancing on the calisthenics systems of François Delsarte, which advocated emotionalism, spontaneity, and coordination of voice with body gestures.

In December of 1904, at age twenty-six, she began a torrid love affair with a theatrical designer, Gordon Craig, which produced her daughter, Deirdre. Then in 1906, she became the mistress of Paris Singer, one of the twenty-three children of sewing-machine magnate Isaac Singer. The playboy millionaire gave

Carefree in dance, Isadora Duncan was surrounded by tragedy.

her seven years of lavish living, and her second love child, Patrick. After her art, the children were the center of her life.

It was in 1913, while living in Paris, that the first automobile accident occurred. Duncan lunched with her two children then returned to her rehearsal hall. The car hired to drive the children home stalled on an embankment overlooking the Seine. The chauffeur got out to crank the motor and discovered to his horror that he had accidentally left the gear in reverse. Before he could stop the rolling vehicle, it had backed off the embankment, plummeting into the river at a spot where the water was exceptionally deep. By the time the police located and raised the car, Deirdre and Patrick were dead.

More tragedy was in store for the dancer.

In 1922, when she was forty-four and world famous, Duncan set aside her aversion to marriage to become the wife of the Russian Revolution's poet laureate, Sergei Esenin, seventeen years her junior. The marriage was brief and disastrous. Esenin, half mad and an alcoholic, committed a horrible suicide on the last day of 1925. Like his life and his marriage, his death was characteristically violent and dramatic. In a hotel room, he burned his manuscripts, cut open his wrist, penned a farewell poem with his own blood, then hanged himself.

A shocked Duncan contemplated taking her own life: "I am so unhappy," she wrote to a friend. "I often think of following his example, but in a different way. I would prefer the sea."

This was two years before her own death, and she was virtually penniless, living in Nice. Desperate for money and on the verge of being evicted from her hotel for unpaid bills, she accepted a meager advance from an American publisher for her autobiography. Duncan wanted to write about her art; her Manhattan publisher was more interested in her illustrious romances. From Nice she submitted a sample of the material and received a cable from New York: "Enough of your hifalutin ideas . . . Send love chapters . . . Make it spicy."

Duncan continued to write about art, and after completing several chapters without a word of an affair, she joked defiantly to a friend, "Twenty thousand words and I am still a virgin."

Never penny-wise, she admired a red Bugatti in a showroom and contemplated buying it. She had always loved fast cars and now she walked past the Italian racing car almost daily. On Tuesday, September 13, 1927, she entered the showroom and asked for a test drive. The proprietor, Benoit Falchetto, agreed that he himself would call on the famous dancer the following night for a trial drive. It was that day, walking home, that Duncan spotted a young girl who reminded her of her dead Deirdre.

The next evening, the handsome young Falchetto pulled up in front of her hotel in the sports car. The night was cool, and Duncan shivered. A friend, Mary Desti, offered Duncan her own cloth cape. The dancer declined. Falchetto then offered his leather jacket, but instead Duncan tossed a long, silk-fringed red shawl over her shoulders and twice around her neck. Climbing into the car, she waved and called, "Adieu, mes amis. Je vais a la gloire!"

As Falchetto started to pull away, the loose end of the shawl dragged the ground. Mary Desti shouted to Duncan to pull it in. But within moments the shawl's heavy fringe caught in the spokes of the rear wheel. The car was accelerating and the shawl, as if yanked by some huge invisible hand, whipped back and snapped Duncan's neck. By the time her head struck the side of the door—a blow that smashed her nose—the dancer was dead.

Falchetto slammed on the brakes and Duncan's friends raced toward the car, still uncertain of what had happened. But Falchetto was now shouting frantically in Italian, "Madonna mia! I've killed the lady!" The shawl was so tightly bound—to Duncan's neck and the car's wheel—that it could not be disentangled and had to be cut.

Three days later, on September 19, in a drizzling rain, a hearse bearing Isadora Duncan's coffin, draped in her purple cape, solemnly wound through the side streets of Paris. The procession was to have passed through the Champs Élysées, but on the day of the funeral the famous thoroughfare belonged to the marching American Legion parade. Thousands of the dancer's fans gathered outside the Père-Lachaise crematorium, and after a brief service, her ashes were interred alongside those of her children, Deirdre and Patrick.

CHAPTER 17

Last Stands
of Wild West Legends

Calamity Jane to Buffalo Bill

Calamity Jane: d. 1903, age 51

Cause of death: Pneumonia following a bout of heavy drinking

Place of rest: Mt. Moriah Cemetery, Deadwood, South Dakota

Last words: Of her hero and self-proclaimed lover, Wild Bill
Hickok: *"It's the 27th anniversary of Bill's death. Bury me next to
Bill."*

Calamity Jane endeared herself more to folklore than to any folk who ever knew
her. She brought misfortune into the lives of those she touched, earning her
moniker, and her own life contained at least as much travail. But the ending of
this colorful legend of the American West—who wore men's clothing, packed
a man's gun, drank a man-size drink, and burned life's candle at both ends and
along the middle—is more celebratory than tragic. In death the West's most
eccentric, nineteenth-century bag lady (a nomad who lived out of a duffel bag)
was mythologized into a true American heroine. The mythic Jane became a
fierce Indian fighter, intrepid scout, and the beautiful, buckskin-clad tamer of
frontier anarchy.

She was born Martha Jane Canary, on May 1, 1852, in Princeton, Missouri.
In her teens, she accompanied her parents on a trip west, settling, upon their
deaths, in Deadwood, South Dakota, a town teeming with miners, Civil War
veterans, gamblers, outlaws, pimps, whores, and mule skinners. Without re-

sources, Jane supported herself by turning to prostitution, and during a small-pox epidemic she nursed men back to health using drugs bought with her own hard-earned funds.

Her legend began in Deadwood and spread across the nation mostly through dime-store novels of the 1870s and 1880s.

She was depicted as a "natural beauty," the "sweetheart" of Wild Bill Hickok, "the finest demonstration of firearms of her time." Never mentioned to the Eastern public were her lawlessness, drunkenness, or stints of prostitution at the notorious Coffey's "Hog Farm" near Fort Laramie. In the nineteenth century, the comfortably settled Easterner viewed the hardships of settling the West as romantic and nobly adventurous, and published fact and fiction reinforced the illusion.

Jane adored her accreting legend and added to it—particularly with her fanciful seven-page autobiography, which she hawked to gold miners for from fifty cents to twenty dollars, depending on the dryness of her throat and destitution of her finances. The high point in her autobiography takes place when she was twenty-four and Wild Bill Hickok, already a Western hero, rode into Deadwood and into her life. For a brief period she was, factually, part of his gang and shined in his reflected glory, but there is no evidence he paid her much attention, let alone torridly romanced her, as she and other writers fictionalized.

A trustworthy contemporary biography describes the real Calamity Jane: "There is little doubt she should have been a man. She had a marvelous constitution which withstood years of her horrible debauches. She was completely at ease in the roughest saloons with the most desperate of men. They accepted her as one of their own kind." A Western newspaper in Jane's day claimed the coarseness of her cursing "awed hard-drinking railroad workers and mule skinners" (her objective, no doubt). However, none of these colorful negatives traveled east, where Jane remained to readers heroic and unsullied.

Calamity Jane's ending can be chronicled from May 1900 when, age forty-eight, she was discovered by novelist Josephine Winifred Blake destitute in "a negro house of ill repute, sick and half dead from a long debauch."

Blake helped Jane live another three years. She persuaded the authentic sharpshooter to accompany her east to become a featured attraction of wild West shows and the 1901 Pan-American Exposition. Jane made her appearances in a scout's costume, whipping a six-horse team and wagon recklessly around a ring, shooting and shouting. Easterners loved it. Jane, though, was miserable on parade, longing, if not for the debauches of Deadwood, at least for its reality.

She returned west "a woman," a newspaper noted, that is, dressed in "a ragged black dress, battered flower hat, worn heeled-boots, and a grin framing two yellow teeth." She looked better, and was happier, as a man. Her final days are charted in newspaper clippings in which she "shot up a saloon," was "drunk and disorderly in public," and was "found sleeping in the street." She cadged drinks by offering bartenders dog-eared copies of her autobiography.

Her death came in the summer of 1903.

One July afternoon she appeared in the doorway of the Calloway Hotel outside of Deadwood. To support herself, she clutched the doorjamb, whispering into the bar, "I'm ailing." The owner carried her to a room. "I guess I'm ready to cash in," Jane told the maid who undressed her and put her to bed. A doctor diagnosed bronchitis, which was actually pneumonia. Former friends from Deadwood who rode out to the hotel found that the hard-living years had left Jane a grotesque shadow of her former spunky self. Though age fifty-one, she was said to look at least seventy.

Around four o'clock, August 2, her breathing became labored. In a hoarse whisper she asked a bedside visitor the date, then observed, "It's the 27th anniversary of Bill's death. Bury me next to Bill." She closed her eyes, slept, and an hour later a friend noticed Jane's body shudder and then come to rest.

She had died destitute but not without friends. The women of Deadwood washed and dressed the corpse in a pressed, long black dress. A pine coffin was donated by a local undertaker, and her funeral was the largest in the town's history. Many mourners came to express sympathy, others pointed to the wizened corpse as a reminder of the wages of sin. The Methodist minister who preached the service, Dr. C. B. Clark, tactfully omitted mention of Jane's debaucheries and concentrated on the smallpox plague of 1878 in which Jane had selflessly played the role of nurse. And as if a writer had scripted Jane's departure, the man who lowered the coffin into the grave at Mt. Moriah Cemetery was C. H. Robinson, church rector, who, as a boy in 1878, was nursed through smallpox by Jane. Honoring her last wish, she was buried beside Wild Bill Hickok.

Wild Bill Hickok: d. 1876, age 39

Cause of death: Homicide: shot through the back of the brain while playing poker

Place of rest: Mt. Moriah Cemetery, Deadwood, South Dakota

Last act: Mulling over a poker hand, now known as a deadman's hand

One of General Custer's bravest scouts and a part-time frontier marshal of the West, James Butler Hickok had two uncanny presentiments about his death, both within days of the event. A week before his cold-blooded murder, he remarked to a friend: "I feel my days are numbered. Somebody is going to kill me. I don't know who, or why."

The other premonition is contained in a letter to his wife, written twenty-four hours before he was shot through the back of the head: "Darling, if such should be we never meet again, while firing my last shot I will gently breathe the name of my wife—Agnes—and with wishes even for my enemies I will make the plunge and try to swim to the other shore."

The plunge-and-swim metaphor was a poetic vogue of the day, and its use was not uncharacteristic of a simple, hard-living man who first learned that he

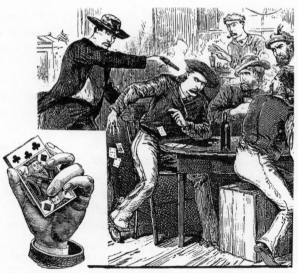

*The murder of Wild Bill
Hickok. A deadman's hand.*

was a "glamorous gunfighter, defender of the helpless, and scourge of evil" when he read an article about himself in the February 1867 issue of *Harper's New Monthly Magazine.*

Hickok was thirty at the time. And he could not recall enjoying a past nearly so illustrious as the dime-store fiction before his eyes. Yet he liked what he read. *Harper's Monthly,* distributed widely in the East, actually launched the legend of Wild Bill Hickok. (The author was Colonel George Ward Nicholas, a former soldier under General Sherman who became the magazine's West correspondent.)

Born in Troy Grove, Illinois, in 1837, James Butler Hickok was originally called, and bullied, by the nickname Duck Bill. It made pointed reference to his long nose and protuberant upper lip (which as an adult he concealed under a mustache). Once he demonstrated his skill and speed with a gun, the jibe Duck Bill gave way to the praise Wild Bill and his life was forever changed.

Tall and sturdy, Hickok fought bravely under General Custer. He did, as history records, save thirty-four men in an Indian siege in the Colorado Territory by riding through the attackers' ranks to get help. He did not, as the Eastern press romanticized, knock off fifty Confederate soldiers with fifty consecutive bullets.

The major event, though, that served as the cornerstone of his fame, was another one-man-wipeout tale: It alleged that in 1861 the twenty-four-year-old sharpshooter terminated the so-called McCanles gang of nine "desperadoes, horse-thieves, murderers and regular cutthroats" in "the greatest one-man gunfight in history." This is the story that *Harper's Monthly* later picked up, embellished, and popularized.

But there never was a McCanles gang. Just a single Dave McCanles, an honest rancher who was owed money by a freight company that employed Hickok. McCanles, unarmed, went to collect his due. An argument ensued with the company manager, and Hickok, hiding behind a calico curtain, shot the rancher dead. The gang fantasy stemmed from the fact that company officials then shot the two unarmed friends who had accompanied McCanles to town. Hickok was charged with murder but never convicted. Not the stuff of legend.

Except in the hands of an imaginative writer of fiction, the same hands that a few years later turned an honorable face-to-face shoot-out between boyhood friends—Hickok and a man named Dave Tutt—over a girl's reputation into a standoff in which the heroic Wild Bill gunned down a savage outlaw. The legend was growing.

In the years prior to his death, Hickok served as sheriff in two Western towns. Hired by the city of Abilene, Kansas, the thirty-four-year-old marshal had a mandate to clean up corruption and lawlessness. In truth, Hickok did little by way of reform; he found it more gratifying to take protection money from gamblers and pimps than to interfere with their lucrative ventures. His afternoons were spent at the card table, his evenings in different rooms of the town's red-light district. After a few months at the job, town citizens fired him for accidentally and recklessly killing his own deputy, Mike Williams, who had come to his aid in a gunfight.

As a Hickok biographer writes of the durability of legend: "Although his record in Abilene actually was a sorry one, it is still cited today as one of the greatest reigns by a lawman in the history of the West."

From Abilene, Hickok found his life going steadily downhill. He performed briefly in Buffalo Bill Cody's Wild West Show, but found the effort exhausting and degrading. He tried his hand at prospecting, then professional gambling, but was arrested several times as, a newspaper reported, "a vagrant, having no visible means of support."

Murder in Deadwood. In June 1876, when he turned up in Deadwood, South Dakota, and met Calamity Jane, his eyesight was failing, a dire handicap for a gunman. At Nuttall & Mann's Saloon, 10 Main Street, he played poker almost daily. Until the game on August 2, in which he was fatally shot.

That day the saloon in the gold-boom town was crowded. Hickok was playing cards with three old friends: Carl Mann, Nuttall's owner; Captain William Massie, a former Missouri River pilot; and Charles Rich, gambler and gunman. They were enjoying the house specialty, beans and whiskey. And Hickok, who always insisted on sitting with his back to a wall, had violated his own precaution. He picked up a hand as a twenty-five-year-old drifter named Jack McCall, with a known ambition to become a famous gunfighter, entered the room.

McCall suspected that Hickok had gunned down his brother. Later, at his trial, when asked why he hadn't confronted Hickok face-to-face, he would shrug and say, "I didn't want to commit suicide." A shot through the back of the head killed Wild Bill Hickok instantly. His body ricocheted backward and his cards fell to the floor: ace of spades, ace of clubs, eight of spades, eight of clubs, jack of diamonds—from that day on known as a deadman's hand.

McCall's Ending. The following day, outside of Deadwood, Jack McCall was tried for murder by a miners' court. Despite the eyewitness testimony of many people in the saloon, McCall was acquitted after only minutes of deliberation. The quick verdict had nothing to do with justice, but with a news flash that Indians were advancing toward Deadwood for a raid. Courtroom spectators booed the acquittal, but everyone filed out and hurried home to prepare for the worst. The murder of Wild Bill Hickok had been eclipsed by threat of a massacre.

Hickok was hastily buried in a local graveyard. Three years later his remains were moved to Mt. Moriah Cemetery, where he'd eventually be joined by his one-time follower Calamity Jane. His tombstone was topped with a bust and etched with the inscription: "Custer was lonely without him." A fourteen-inch lock of his shoulder-length hair was cut off and today is in the New York Public Library's Western collection.

Jack McCall got his due. His ambition to be a feared gunfighter prompted him to careless braggadocio of how he killed the legendary Wild Bill Hickok. He was rearrested late in 1876 and retried. The case skirted the issue of double jeopardy, since it was argued that the first trial had been conducted on Indian territory, with vigilante haste, unsanctioned by the U.S. government. Saloon owner Carl Mann was the prosecution's star witness:

> I heard somebody walking on the floor. When I looked up I saw the defendant raise a pistol and fire at Wild Bill's head. It kind of knocked Bill's head forward and then he fell gradually back . . . a bullet came out on his face before he fell. . . . I slipped off to get something to defend myself.

Found guilty, the murderer of Wild Bill Hickok was hanged on March 1, 1877.

Billy the Kid: d. 1881, age 21

Cause of death: Homicide: a bullet above the heart

Place of rest: Fort Sumner Military Cemetery, Fort Sumner, New Mexico

Last words: In Spanish, to his unseen assailant, Sheriff Pat Garrett: *"Who's there? . . . Who's there?"*

The true decline and fall of Billy the Kid is a tale both modern and sadly touching; the legend is false and flashy. The former is actually the better story, though seldom told.

Of all the legends of the old West, that of Billy the Kid is probably the most novelistically romanticized and heroically embellished. Ballads, books, films, and a ballet have been written on his life as a merry-eyed youth, the Robin Hood of the American frontier, whose dead-eyed skill with a six-shooter protected oppressed ranchers from evil cattle barons. At twelve, it's told, he murdered a man who insulted his mother (he didn't), and in his brief life of twenty-one years he is supposed to have gunned down twenty-one men (the total is nearer to four, some killed in self-defense).

Much of the legend, historians believe, has to do with the fact that Billy died a kid.

The real Billy—five foot seven, pale blue eyes, light brown hair, slender, with two buckteeth—was neither a hero nor a pathological killer. He was a disturbed, lonely young man, honest, loyal to his friends, dedicated to his beliefs, and, most of all, devoted to his mother, Catherine.

Born Henry McCarty, in a Manhattan slum tenement on November 23, 1859, "Billy" became a drifter early in life. His father had moved the family from their delapidated city apartment to a home in Coffeyville, Kansas, but soon died, leaving three-year-old Billy and his mother to fend for themselves. With a knack for business, she supported the family by dealing in real estate, then by operating hotels, boardinghouses, and laundries—services much needed in the frontier communities. By all accounts, Billy was a happy youth, dutifully attending school and working diligently in one of his mother's laundries.

Life changed forever when he turned twelve.

His mother developed tuberculosis, a death warrant in those days. For more than two years she suffered worsening fits of coughing and spitting up blood. Billy dropped out of school to be at her side. For her last four months of life, spent confined to bed, he seldom left the sickroom, feeding her and cradling her head when she was convulsed with suffocating coughs. Watching helplessly as his mother died an agonizing death permanently altered Billy. Despondent, the fifteen-year-old boy lost himself in alcohol, gambling, and the prankish lawlessness of unsavory friends. His life to this point sounds almost clichéd, tragically so.

It was around this critical juncture, in 1875, that the teenage Henry McCarty began to call himself Billy Bonney.

The reason is unclear. The standard explanation is noble, and if true, fittingly characteristic of Billy: Sheriff Whitehall, the first frontier lawman to arrest the now rambunctious Billy, already with the reputation of a hoodlum, claimed the teenager made the change "in order to keep the stigma of disgrace" from his mother's name. Friends who knew the McCarty family said that Henry never referred to himself as Billy until after his mother's death and his subsequent hooliganism.

Others named him "the Kid" for his youth, clumsiness, and eager desire to please and impress. By the time he arrived in Grant City at age eighteen—an incongruous, somewhat comical figure in businessmen's shoes (not boots) and with a six-shooter stuck in his belt (not a holster)—Billy had already acquired the youthful sobriquet. In fact, he so resembled a kid that the town's rough-hewn miners and hectoring cowboys treated him as one, mercilessly so, which is what led to his first killing.

Billy murdered his first man in a Grant City saloon on August 17, 1877. The man was a blacksmith named Windy, a brusque, bullying individual, who, according to an eyewitness account in the *Arizona Daily Citizen,* "would throw

Billy on the floor, ruffle his hair, slap his face and humiliate him before the men in the saloon." The paper graphically pictured the opponents: Windy was "a large man with a gruff voice and blustering mane"; eighteen-year-old Billy was "rather slender . . . dressed like a 'country jake' with store pants on and shoes instead of boots."

As customers in the saloon laughed at the hazing, Billy reached for his .45. The next morning the *Daily Citizen* reported: "The blacksmith felt the gun in his side. There was a deafening roar. Windy slumped to one side and the Kid squirmed free and ran to the door and vaulted into the saddle." Murdering a bully and escaping in fear—of the law and probably of his own impromptu action—is not the fodder of legend, but that incident began the myth of Billy the Kid, "teen killer."

Wanted for Murder.   Billy drifted among the cow camps that dotted the New Mexico–Arizona border. He gambled, drank, worked odd jobs, and mastered the crime of his era: cattle rustling. His rowdy, roving life briefly took an inspiring turn when he met a sophisticated English rancher named John Tunstall. Refined, educated, and humane, Tunstall appealed to the boy who was, at heart, sensitive. Billy worked for the gentleman rancher, idolized him, and once remarked that Tunstall "was the only man that ever treated me like I was free-born and white." And Tunstall complimented: "That's the finest lad I ever met. He's a revelation to me every day and would do anything on earth to please me. I'm going to make a man of that boy yet."

Tunstall never got the chance. Billy was about to make his last stand—and in defense of Tunstall.

Cattle rustlers threatened Tunstall, demanding half his herd. When they fatally shot the unarmed Englishman, Billy mentally snapped. He'd lost his father, then his mother, and now the man who had become his surrogate father. He swore vengeance on everyone involved in the murder, including a local sheriff, Jim Brady, who was paid off to overlook the crime. Days later, on April 1, 1878, Billy ambushed and killed Brady. He was again on the run.

For two years he hid out successfully.

But in 1880 he was arrested by, paradoxically, Sheriff Pat Garrett, himself a former cattle rustler who once raided herds with Billy as his novice sidekick. Garrett was not so much reformed as now cleverly working both sides of the law. When Billy escaped jail on April 28, 1881, killing two guards, Garrett swore to recapture his former friend.

On July 15, Garrett found Billy hiding at the ranch in Fort Sumner, New Mexico. Concealing himself in a darkened room, he waited for Billy to enter the house. Billy sensed a shadowy figure seated on the bed directly across from the doorway, but believed it was a Mexican acquaintance playing a joke. He called in Spanish, "Who's there?" Squinting, he tentatively crossed the dark room, touched the edge of the mattress with his left hand, and demanded, "Who's there!"

Garrett had come to arrest Billy, but instead, at close range, he fired twice. The first bullet slammed into Billy's chest, the other struck the wall. In the blackness of the room, Garrett wasn't certain he'd even killed the right man.

He struck a match, lit a candle, and drew it near the body.

Later Garrett testified that the bullet "struck [Billy] just above the heart and cut through the ventricles." A coroner's jury deemed the homicide "justifiable . . . inflicted by the said Garrett in the discharge of his official duty as sheriff."

Billy's Mexican friends fashioned a simple pine coffin and surrounded the corpse with lighted candles. A girlfriend dressed Billy in borrowed pants and shirt said to be "five sizes too big," such that Billy in death looked as gawky as he had in life. They buried him the next day, July 15, in an old military cemetery at Fort Sumner. He had lived twenty-one years, seven months, and twenty-two days.

No sooner had dirt hit the coffin than the legend makers went to work. The speed is amazing even by today's standards.

The first "biography" that fictionalized Billy's life appeared three weeks after his death, upping the number of men he had killed. Several books followed, one written by Sheriff Pat Garrett, which, predictably, vilified the subject and glorified the author. Billy's "corpse" became a money-making curiosity and many traveling showmen and swindlers claimed to have robbed his grave and be in possession of his bones. People paid to view this body and that body, even though Sheriff Garrett maintained that, "The Kid's body lies undisturbed in the grave, and I speak of what I know."

Later at the grave site a tombstone was etched with an epitaph in sympathy with the escalating legend: "Truth and History. 21 men. The Boy Bandit King—He Died As He Lived." Its hyperbole eclipses the heartfelt farewell posted by the girlfriend who had clothed and helped bury Billy: "Sleep well, beloved."

Garrett's Ending.   As Billy the Kid achieved notoriety, his killer, Sheriff Pat Garrett, who continued to straddle the law, achieved celebrity. There had been a five-hundred-dollar reward for Billy's capture, and Garrett, though a paid lawman, attempted to collect it. It proved to be an uphill fight, but one that Garrett finally won. Today it's thought that he bribed friends in the New Mexico legislature, for the state passed a special act that enabled him to collect the reward on top of his salary. In 1908, he was shot to death by a ranch hand, a disgruntled employee working the Garrett stead.

Tecumseh: d. 1813, age 45

> **Cause of death:** Slain in a battle with the U.S. Cavalry: a bullet through the heart and the skull crushed with a gun butt
>
> **Place of rest:** The Tecumseh Cairn, Walpole Island Indian Reservation, Ontario, Canada
>
> **Last words:** Entering into a hopeless battle: *"May the Great Spirit welcome us all, for at least we can stand honorably tomorrow while we are destroyed."*

Tecumseh, Indian for "panther passing across," was born in 1768, at a time when a shooting star, the Panther, soared above the Shawnee tribal camp in an area near present-day Springfield, Ohio. Chief of all North American Shawnees, he became a gifted orator who urged "Americanized" Indians to restore the integrity of their culture by freeing themselves from the white man's ways of life.

In short, Tecumseh attempted to save for his people their ancient lands, which at the time were being either seized with impunity by white settlers or, worse, bartered by Indian chiefs for bangle-and-bead annuities to cushion their old age.

Tecumseh failed, obviously. Civilization (white man's) advanced inexorably. The slim, muscular Indian chief with copper skin and hazel eyes made his valiant last stand at the age of forty-five, and his death was more than just his own end. More significantly, it marked the end of Indian resistance throughout the Midwest and South and the subsequent domination of land east of the Mississippi by European whites.

In battle, Tecumseh was fierce. In conversation, he was suave and urbane. In dress, he shunned the garments of the whites, preferring unadorned buckskin with a tomahawk and silver-hilted hunting knife thrust through his belt.

He hated whites from the age of six, when they cold-bloodedly murdered his father; but he also harshly rebuked fellow Shawnees for the cruelties they themselves practiced against white settlers. At fifteen he had watched horrified as a white prisoner was staked, skinned, and burned. He inveighed his savage tribesmen with such abuse that they never again tortured a prisoner in his presence. He had discovered that words could be as powerful as weapons.

Like most Indians, Tecumseh viewed the whites' concept of private ownership of land as inherently wrong. Gods owned land, men merely lived off it. Land, he and other Indians argued, was like air and water, a shared possession of humans, animals, and plants. His impassioned oratory—often on the doctrine

Tecumseh: Every peace treaty he negotiated white men violated.

of communal ownership of land—was compared, by white men, with that of the young Henry Clay.

Yet his efforts were continually frustrated. He negotiated peace treaties only to have the whites violate their own promises. He beseeched the whites not to give whiskey to Indians—which, through drunkenness, was destroying entire tribes—but they continued to give all kinds of alcohol, often without charge, precisely for its desocializing effects. At the same time, the floodtide of settlers pushed game from Indian hunting grounds; Indian economies broke down, tribes starved.

Little wonder that in the War of 1812 between the Americans and British, Tecumseh fought for the British. In fact, he brought together perhaps the most formidable force ever commanded by a North American Indian, an accomplishment that was a decisive factor in the capture of Detroit and of twenty-five hundred U.S. soldiers in 1812.

But Tecumseh was nearing his final days.

Fired with the promise of triumph after the fall of Detroit, Tecumseh departed on a long campaign to rouse other tribes to other victories. Indians joined the British for the invasion of Ohio, but after a fierce battle they were forced to retreat up the Thames River into present-day southern Ontario. There, on October 5, 1813, the British and the Indians were routed by American forces. Demoralized and without reserve ammunition, Tecumseh and a group of about six hundred Indians made a resolute last stand. Wounded again and again, with blood pouring from his mouth, he continued to reload his rifle and fire on the U.S. Cavalry. When the ammunition was exhausted, Tecumseh and his followers fought with tomahawks.

Indian legend has it that when the battle calmed down, several survivors searched the field for their chief's body. A bullet had passed through his heart and the butt of a rifle had been used to bash in his skull. Otherwise the body was not mutilated (mutilation of a corpse being a racial humiliation practiced by both Indians and whites). They lifted the corpse and carried it over rough terrain for about five miles and buried it in an unmarked grave.

Who killed one of the greatest Indian chiefs?

Perhaps a U.S. vice president.

It was initially believed that Tecumseh was shot by Colonel William Whitley, seconds before Whitley himself was fatally killed by a Shawnee brave.

But more credence is now given to the hypothesis that the shot came from the gun of Kentucky Colonel Richard Johnson who, twenty-four years later, served as the country's ninth vice president (1837–41) in the Democratic administration of Martin Van Buren. At the time of the battle, Johnson was a member of the House of Representatives. In addition to the dubious distinction of having killed Tecumseh, Johnson, due to intense unpopularity during his first term in office, prompted the Democratic national convention of 1840 to adopt an action unprecedented in American history: They refused to nominate *anyone* for the office of vice president.

Many years after the 1813 battle, a group of Shawnees attempted to exhume Tecumseh's body for a more fitting burial at one of their Oklahoma reservations. Indian legend claims that the effort failed because a creek near the originàl grave site had overflowed, obliterating evidence of the spot. Nonetheless, in September 1941, bones believed to belong to Tecumseh were disinterred and moved to a burial site on the bank of the St. Clair River on Ontario's Walpole Island Indian Reserve. The spot is clearly marked today by a cairn.

With Tecumseh's death came the end of the great dream of an independent Indian nation. At the Treaty of Ghent negotiations, which in 1814 closed the war between England and the United States, the British attempted to create an Indian state that would act as a buffer zone between Canada and the United States—something Tecumseh had favored. But the Americans refused to relinquish any territory they had won. As Tecumseh had foreseen, with the Indians pushed beyond the Mississippi, a new people *owned* the East, a nation that would not rest until it sprawled, conquered, and expanded to the Pacific.

George Armstrong Custer: d. 1876, age 36

Cause of death: Possibly suicide: a bullet through the left temple

Place of rest: United States Military Academy, West Point, New York

Last seen: In battle, wearing buckskins and a flannel shirt, crawling on hands and knees, blood issuing from his mouth

The last stand of George Armstrong Custer, who graduated lowest in his West Point class of 1861, involves one of the most controversial battles in U.S. military history.

The picayune points are these: Unlike in the famous 1878 Steinegger painting of Custer's last stand, Custer was not long-haired at the time of his death (his much admired locks had been sheared for battle), nor was he wearing his major general's Civil War uniform (but plain functional buckskins and a flannel shirt); and in the fateful battle at Little Bighorn, Custer was not a major general (but a lieutenant colonel). Nor did he, or any of his men, brandish a saber; the swords had been left behind.

The major controversies surrounding Custer's last stand do not stack up so neatly. To backtrack.

Born on December 5, 1839, in New Rumley, Ohio, George Custer first distinguished himself nationally in the Civil War. His relentless pursuit of Confederate commander in chief General Robert E. Lee helped to hasten Lee's surrender at Appomattox, Virginia, on April 9, 1865. But during his entire military career, the dashing and daring fighter had continual disciplinary problems with the U.S. Army. He was, for instance, court-martialed and suspended without pay two years after the Appomattox victory for being absent without leave; he'd left his post to visit his wife, Elizabeth.

Custer then spent five leisurely years writing his autobiography, *My Life on the Plains*. The year it was published—1874, when he was thirty-four and two years away from death—he led a gold rush expedition into the Black Hills of South Dakota, a fateful and foolish adventure that ultimately led to the battle at Little Bighorn. First, his participation lent credibility to rumors of gold and precipitated a rush. Second, serious trouble was inevitable, since a treaty recognized the region as the sacred hunting ground of the Sioux and Cheyenne tribes.

The whites wanted gold, and the U.S. government, quite audaciously, defined Indians living in the richly ored hills as "hostile" and ordered their relocation to a distant reservation where they would be redefined as "harmless." The gold rush was on, as was the great Sioux War.

Historians believe that numerous Indian tribes, in their remote and scattered winter camps, were unaware of efforts to relocate them and thus remained in the region. Other tribes simply were not going to be moved. In the spring of that year, 1876, all tribes assembled for action at the encampment of Chief Sitting Bull on the Little Bighorn River in Montana Territory.

Last Stand. Custer, in command of one of two columns of a projected two-pronged attack, arrived near the Little Bighorn on the night of June 24. The other column, lead by General Alfred Terry, was to join him in two days. Instead of waiting for Terry, Custer decided to attack, possibly, it's thought, because he suspected his presence was known to the Indians.

On the morning of June 25, after a brutally fatiguing forty-mile march, Custer's six hundred or so exhausted troopers neared the huge Sioux-Cheyenne village on the Little Bighorn River. He ignored the advice of his scout, Bloody Knife, who said that an attack would be tantamount to suicide, since thousands of Indians watched and waited under the command of Sitting Bull and Crazy Horse.

To Custer's question as to the outcome of the battle, his scout replied with one word: "Death."

Revamping his strategy, Custer split his own command into three battalions. Two—the Benteen and Reno battalions—were to prevent Sitting Bull's escape, while the third, consisting of 267 men, Custer would lead himself to make the central attack.

The 120 men of the Benteen battalion headed south on a scouting mission, under the crusty Captain Frederick Benteen, a man who detested Custer's flamboyant style.

The 112 men of the Reno battalion moved toward the Indian village across the Little Bighorn River, under Major Marcus Reno, a capable Civil War officer but a man who lacked experience fighting Indians—and who would become a convenient scapegoat for Custer's defeat.

Custer took his own men also toward the Indian village.

A hurricane of Indians first drove Reno and Benteen into retreat. Then Custer himself attempted to escape, but hordes of Sioux and Cheyennes forced him and his men higher into the hills from which the only exit was extinction. Around four o'clock in the afternoon, Custer faced up to the dire predicament and ordered his men to stop running, dismount, and fight to the death. Within

Custer's final stand: He saved the last bullet for himself.

a half-hour the band had been reduced to fifty men, and Indians continued to close in.

As a last-ditch effort, Custer ordered his men to shoot their horses and stack the carcasses into a protective wall. The summer day was hot; the stench was overpowering and it grew worse as a hail of bullets and arrows ripped apart the animals that offered no shield at all. By 5:00 P.M. all the white men were dead or downed and bleeding to death. Custer, called "Yellowhair" by the Indians, was last seen crawling for cover; he'd been shot through the side and the bullet must have pierced his lungs or esophagus for blood flowed from his mouth.

After the battle, Indian squaws stripped the cavalrymen of their uniforms. Indian children found that many uniform pockets were stuffed with rolls of green and white paper, which they used to decorate their toys.

It's thought that Custer's Indian "wife," Meyotzi, and their six-year-old son, Yellow Bird, discovered his body, since when whites first saw it, it was naked and washed free of blood. And unlike other soldiers' bodies, Custer's was not mutilated. This last fact, along with the bullet wound in his left temple, has led historians to suspect that the fighter saved his final bullet for himself, aware than an Indian would never touch, let alone mutilate, the body of a suicide.

The lone survivor of the battle was a horse, Comanche, that had belonged to Captain Myles Keogh and for years thereafter served as the mascot of the Seventh Cavalry, appearing in parades, riderless.

At West Point, on October 10, 1877, Custer received a military funeral. The massacre at Little Bighorn jolted and sobered a nation then celebrating its first hundred years of independence. To the public, and to many military officers, Custer had been the most dashing Indian fighter in the West. His death had to be avenged. That meant, in part, capturing and punishing Sitting Bull.

Sitting Bull: d. 1890, age 59

Cause of death: Shot in the back, left side, bullet exiting between the tenth and eleventh ribs

Place of rest: Standing Rock Indian Reservation, Mobridge, South Dakota

Last words: Resisting arrest: *"Do with me what you like, I'm not going."* Then to his supporters: *"Take action! Let's go!"*

The arrest and death of Sitting Bull, chief of the Sioux tribes of the Great Plains, was a setup, a police stratagem of the sort, "get the suspect to overreact, then kill him for being violent."

Two white military men with firsthand knowledge of the death realized this. "I am positive that no trouble need be apprehended from Sitting Bull and his followers, unless they are forced to defend themselves," advised one agent just prior to the fatal incident. After the event another agent wrote: "The attempt to arrest Sitting Bull was so managed as to place the responsibility for the fight that ensued upon Sitting Bull's band which began the firing."

Sitting Bull died not because of his victory over General Custer at Little Bighorn fourteen years earlier (though he was hated for that), but because of the white man's hysteria over an Indian ritual, the ghost dance.

Born in 1831, the proud and haughty Sitting Bull is remembered today for his lifelong distrust of the whites, who he thought made treaties just to break them. He never signed a treaty with the U.S. government, nor would he accept the tawdry presents in the form of bribes that many chiefs cherished.

His first major confrontation with the whites came when he was ordered by the U.S. government to relocate his entire village some 240 miles over rough

The ghost dance led to the frame-up and death of Sitting Bull.

terrain in the bitter cold because gold was discovered on his land—the incident, related previously, that led to the massacre of Custer and his men at the battle of Little Bighorn.

Strong public reaction to the battle and to Custer's death caused the U.S. Cavalry to aggressively pursue Sitting Bull and his followers. But it was famine, from the steady loss of Indian hunting grounds, that finally forced Sitting Bull and his remnant to surrender to the U.S. military on July 19, 1881. Though promised amnesty, Sitting Bull was imprisoned for two years, which did little to win his trust of white men.

In May of 1883, the great Indian chief was allowed to rejoin his people, who had been relocated to the small reservation at Standing Rock, South Dakota. The white agent in charge of the Indian group, Major James McLaughlin, encouraged Sitting Bull to join Buffalo Bill's Wild West Show in the summer of 1885, in which he traveled, gaining international fame as the archetype of an American Indian chief. He found the experience degrading and eagerly returned to the reservation, where he was living quietly until the ghost dance debacle.

The ghost dance cult originated in 1889. It was an Indian ritual symbolizing the extremes of hope and despair. By that time most Sioux land was owned by white settlers. Along with the Indians' reduced land holdings, that year also brought a shrinking allotment of food, clothing, and other supplies, all at the parsimonious hands of whites running the reservations. The Indians, stripped of land and near starvation, turned to religion. The ghost dance cult maintained that an Indian who adhered to certain precepts and performed the proper ritual dance—called the ghost dance by whites because of its association with resurrection of the dead—would glimpse the afterlife into which he would soon be reborn for eternity. The dance was, in essence, a last-ditch effort at psychological survival.

Sioux followers of the ghost dance wore special "ghost shirts." These were painted with magical symbols alleged to repel white men's bullets. White Indian agents and army officers grew increasingly suspicious of the innocent dance. If the ritual was so peaceful, they asked, why did its adherents need "bulletproof" garments?

Also, missionaries to the Indians complained that the ghost dance, a "pagan" ritual, posed a direct threat to the government's joint program of assimilation and Christianization. How could Indians become good Christians if they believed that a frenzied dance would give them a glimpse of their spiritual rebirth? The irony is that the messianic cult had distinctly Christian aspects, the notion of bodily death and glorious spiritual resurrection.

Hysteria. By midautumn of 1890, many of the Sioux were half starved and sick. They turned even more fervently to their religious cult, and the ghost dance was performed with abandon. Indians spurned daily tasks and spent days and nights dancing and chanting, their equivalent to round-the-clock prayer at a time when they were on the brink of mass death. White officials looked on this delirium with emotions ranging from tight-lipped disapproval to alarming discomfort.

Indian agent James McLaughlin, head of the Standing Rock Agency, wrote: "A more pernicious system of religion could not have been offered to a people who stood on the threshold of civilization." Threshold of extinction would have been closer to the truth.

From another white agent came a panicky appeal to the government: "Indians are dancing in the snow and are wild and crazy. . . . We need protection and we need it now!"

Only one man, former Indian agent Valentine McGillycuddy, viewed the ghost dance as harmless. He wrote to the U.S. government, which was considering sending in armed troops, "If the Seventh-Day Adventists prepare their ascension robes for the second coming of the Savior, the United States Army is not put in motion to prevent them. Why should not the Indians have the same privilege?" Unfortunately, no one listened to McGillycuddy's reasoned appeal.

Rumors grew of an impending Indian uprising, possibly to be led by the still influential Sitting Bull.

In truth, Sitting Bull saw the ghost dance precisely for what it was: a desperate effort of a dying people to conceive a better life in the hereafter. He did not perform it himself but he declined to interfere with its performance, as agents beseeched him to do. Agent McLaughlin contended, despite evidence to the contrary, that the religious frenzy had been set off by Sitting Bull and urged he be arrested as "an agitator."

On the morning of December 15, McLaughlin's Sioux Indian police arrived at Sitting Bull's cabin to take him into custody. He was awakened and dragged naked from bed. The police harassed him as he dressed, and at one point Sitting Bull sat on the bed, indignant, and refused to leave the room. The elderly chief was forced outside, and, in front of other Sioux, roughed up, taunted, and repeatedly kicked.

"Do with me what you want," he shouted. "I'm not going." Then he attempted to rally his supporters: "Take action! Let's go!"

That was the excuse they had been waiting for. The police shot Sitting Bull in the back, on the left side between the tenth and eleventh ribs. One Indian brave called, "You've been trying to do it, now you have," and the melee turned bloodier. Several Indians were killed, many others wounded. Soon after the incident, about 350 fearful Indians sneaked off the reservation and headed south though the Dakota Badlands, settling at a place named Wounded Knee Creek. They were, of course, to become another historical atrocity, another ending.

Genocide. The battle at Wounded Knee occurred on December 29, 1890. The Seventh Cavalry, including some members of Custer's old command, found and circled the renegades. When the Indians refused to surrender, soldiers opened fire, cutting down men, women, and children until winter's snow was crimson with blood. So grisly was the scene that one member of the burial party recalled: "It was a thing to melt the heart of a man, if it was of stone, to see those little children, with their bodies shot to pieces, thrown naked into the pit."

Many historians refer to the battle at Wounded Knee as the Indians' last bid for freedom.

But that freedom had already been irretrievably lost. A way of life—and a people—ended. The federal government had imposed its will on most aspects of Indians' lives through legislation that dispensed with the concept of tribes as sovereign entities, making them legal wards of the state. In effect, the legislation classed Indians as children, with the U.S. government cast in the role of the stern, and often unjust, parent, urging its impetuous charges summarily to adopt a new culture, new civilization, and new religion.

And, of course, with Indians as wards of the state, treaties were no longer necessary, nor did the government feel obliged to honor past annuities. What Congress appropriated for the surviving tribes in food, clothing, and implements one year, it could deny the next—and often did.

The situation got deplorably worse. Public outcries over the cost of maintaining the Indians, even at subsistence level, soon pressured Congress to reduce aid to them, an action that even the reformers sometimes applauded as necessary to prod the "lazy red men" into becoming farmers, when their centuries-old tradition was as free hunters on sacred land.

The end of Sitting Bull, and the subsequent battle at Wounded Knee, capped off the virtual extermination of a people, a genocide that we hear too little about only because there were so few survivors and their descendants to speak loudly and incessantly, as is required of a crime too uncomfortable to remember.

Belle Starr: d. 1889, age 41

> **Cause of death:** Ambushed and shot twice by her son and sometime lover
>
> **Place of rest:** Youngers Bend, Eufaula, Oklahoma
>
> **Last words:** Wounded, whispering to her daughter: *"Baby, your brother Eddie shot me. I turned and seen him cross the fence, after he cracked down on me the second time."*

To the Eastern reader in the late 1800s, Belle Starr was "the Bandit Queen," a daring and noble woman, possessed of "dazzling beauty," charm, wit, and the heart of a female Robin Hood. Dressed in a velvet gown, draped with double six-shooters at the hip, she rode a mare, Venus, and, unlike other old West legends, Starr was said to be educated. To boot, she was a pianist so accomplished that her playing seduced horse thieves and outlaws and drew around her hearth homesteaders and squatters.

Not long after her life ended—at the hands of her abused son and sometime lover—her romanticized legend ended too. It had all been hype, fabricated by dime novelists to thrill Eastern readers. Such fiction was, as we've seen with the legend of Calamity Jane, the type of fantasy that a few decades later would be turned out by Hollywood studios about stars who were nothing like their public images either.

To extend the analogy: Belle Starr was something of the "Mommy Dearest" of her day.

Belle Starr: shot by her son and sometime lover.

The "dazzling beauty" (reassessed by a contemporary biographer as "hatchet-faced") was a cruel and abusive mother, a free-living horse thief and frequent whore who enjoyed beating her horse and sexually molesting her son. As for her mesmerizing virtuosity at the keyboard, one modern biographer challenges, "It would be impossible to squeeze a piano through the door of the one-room cabin in which Belle slept."

The real Belle Starr was born Myra Belle Shirley in a log cabin near Carthage, Missouri, on February 5, 1848. Her father, John, was neither the "judge" nor "Southern aristocrat" Starr portrayed him as. At eight, she attended the Carthage Female Academy, a grammar school, where a classmate later described the young Belle as a "bright, intelligent girl, but of a fierce nature," who "would fight anyone, boy or girl."

When her brother, Edward, began to ride with outlaws, Belle made her first unsavory friends; his murder is thought to be the trauma that launched her bandit career.

Her thievery was confined mostly to cattle rustling and horse stealing; she never robbed trains and stagecoaches as a "female Jesse James"—though for a while she lived with a member of the James gang, Cole Younger, and by him had her first illegitimate child, a daughter, Pearl.

By her second paramour, badman Jim Reed, she bore the son, Eddie, who would kill her. By the time of Eddie's birth, Starr was the undisputed leader of a band of cattle and horse thieves headquartered in the Indian-held sections of Oklahoma. She viewed outlaws as "jolly lads," taking many as lovers. One, a Cherokee named Sam Starr, she claimed to have married, but there is more paper documentation for a prison term they served together than for a marriage.

Throughout her amorous and thieving adventures, her embellished legend back East was flowering; when released from prison she found herself a celebrity. The popular, pink-paper *Police Gazette* (which contained more tall tales than truth) had immortalized her as the "Petticoat Terror," part "female Robin Hood," part "Jesse James." Such was her fame that she signed on with a wild West show, playing the part of an outlaw who held up a stagecoach, among whose passengers was the judge who sentenced her to jail. A nice touch that always brought down the house.

Her ending came unexpectedly.

On the morning of February 2, 1889, the forty-one-year-old Starr rode with her latest lover, a "wanted" Indian named Jim July. They were headed to Fort Smith, Oklahoma, where July was going to surrender to a United States marshal on a charge of larceny. Starr had persuaded July—described by the *Dallas News* as a "tall, well formed Creek Indian, with long black hair falling down over his shoulders"—to give himself up. They stayed overnight in a farmhouse, and the next morning, a Sunday, July set off alone.

Starr, also alone, began the ride back home.

Around sunset, Starr's daughter Pearl was alarmed to see her mother's horse, still saddled, galloping up to the house without a rider.

Pearl later testified that she searched the road and found her mother, who "was shot in back with buckshot, and in the left side of the face with fine shot. The shot came out on the right side of her neck." She also claimed that Starr was ambushed from about twenty feet and in her last breath identified the assailant: "Baby, your brother Eddie shot me. I turned and seen him cross the fence, after he cracked down on me the second time."

Jim July did not believe that story. At the funeral, as the coffin was lowered into the ground, July drew his gun and accused a neighbor, Edgar Watson, of having murdered Starr. Watson was arrested, but due to lack of evidence charges were dropped.

Today, historians believe that Belle Starr's murderer was indeed her eighteen-year-old son, Eddie Reed. She was known to have alternately attacked him with a bullwhip and forced him into an incestuous relationship. Eddie, a silent and sullen youth who ran away from home after one particularly severe whipping, had numerous times threatened to take his mother's life. There is evidence that after one such threat his mother had him arrested. For many years people believed that Belle Starr's murderer was one of the many lovers she had discarded, but it seems he may well have been the one lover who never wanted a relationship with her in the first place.

Pearl, though, never believed her brother was capable of the murder. And a few months after their mother's death, Pearl and Eddie hired a stone cutter to prepare a monument for Starr's grave. At the top of the stone was a carved image of Starr's favorite mare, Venus (which she also beat periodically). The children chose this epitaph:

> Shed not for her the bitter tear,
> Nor give the heart to vain regret,
> 'Tis but the casket that lies here,
> The gem that fills it sparkles yet.

Kit Carson: d. 1868, age 58

Cause of death: Ruptured aneurysm hemorrhaging into the lungs

Place of rest: Kit Carson Memorial Park, Taos, New Mexico

Last words: Spitting out bloodied saliva: *"Doctor, I'm goin'."*
Gripping a friend's hand: *"Adiós, compadre."*

The last agonizing days in the life of Kit Carson—frontiersman, trapper, soldier, and Indian agent—were played out in authentic mountain fashion. Fatally ill, he shunned a bed, preferring to be nursed on the floor atop his thick buffalo robe and covered with a blanket.

An expanding aneurysm pressed on the pneumogastric nerve, causing bronchial spasms and intense chest pain. Smoking was prohibited, but he puffed heartily on his clay pipe. Swallowing solid food was nearly impossible, yet for his last meal he ate an immense buffalo steak washed down with black coffee. Throughout the dreadful final hours, before the aneurysm burst and blood gushed into his lungs, he inhaled the new invention of chloroform to lessen his suffering as well as his fear of suffocating to death.

America's genuine folk hero, who helped the states expand westward, had lost the will to live. A month earlier his beloved wife, Josefa, had died from complications following childbirth. Though he'd been sick for some time, her ending hastened his own.

Christopher Carson, born December 24, 1809, in Madison County, Kentucky, was an experienced fur trapper and trader by the age of eighteen. His life would have been largely uneventful had he not met by chance at age thirty-three the great explorer and mapper of the West, John Charles Frémont.

Frémont—who would run unsuccessfully as the country's first Republican presidential candidate in 1856—inspired the fur trapper to join the exploration westward, which would eventually extend the boundaries of the continental United States to its present size (excluding Alaska). As a guide, Carson helped federal troops claim California for the United States. For his bravery and loyalty, he won friends in high office, and though handicapped by illiteracy, he admirably held the appointment of superintendent of Indian affairs for the Colorado Territory until the time of his death. He dictated his memoirs in 1856, at the age of forty-seven.

By the time Carson assumed the position of Indian agent, it was evident he suffered from a serious health problem.

Persistently aware of a knotlike presence in his chest, he experienced frightening spasms and intense attacks of dyspepsia (indigestion) and dyspnea (painful breathing). While traveling on government business, he consulted medical specialists in New York, Philadelphia, and Boston. Though the diagnoses were different, they all implicated a weak heart with a prognosis that was terminal.

In April of the year he would die, 1868, Carson put himself under the care of a surgeon at Fort Lyon, Colorado, a Dr. Tilton. Tilton made a correct diagnosis and later wrote: "I explained to him the probable mode of termination of the disease. That he might die from suffocation or more probably the aneurysm would burst and cause death by hemorrhage. He expressed a decided preference for the latter mode."

On April 13, Josefa gave birth to a daughter, Josefita, the couple's seventh child. Ten days later, Mrs. Carson was dead from a raging fever and uterine infection. The shock and grief Carson felt were immediately apparent in the toll they took on his own frail health. Breathing was an agony; solid food passed the ballooning aneurysm as if it were glass shards. "I was compelled," wrote Tilton, "to give chloroform to relieve him, at considerable risk of hastening a fatal result."

Carson begged for more of the numbing gas, and Tilton complied: "If I killed him by chloroform while attempting relief, it would be much better than death by suffocation."

Carson dictated his will. It consisted of ten clauses, all bequests to his seven motherless children: "my seven yoke of steers . . . my four horses and one carriage . . . my house and lot," plus cash, furnishing, and landholdings. In the last letter he dictated in early May, three weeks before his death, he made his final request to a friend, Aloys Scheurich: "to have my own body . . . and that of my wife's sent together to Taos, to be buried in the church."

On the night of May 22, he first coughed up blood. The aneurysm had burst and Tilton told him the end was near. For whatever complexity of reasons, he slept that night the soundest he had in years. And the next day he heartily polished off a rare buffalo steak, much black coffee, then smoked his favorite clay pipe. He was still smoking late in the afternoon when suddenly blood began to trickle from between his lips, progressing quickly to a gush.

"Doctor, I'm goin'," he told Tilton. Then he gripped the hand of Aloys Scheurich and whispered, "Adiós, compadre." The two men tilted Carson forward over the floor so he could spit out blood; Scheurich later wrote, "I supported his forehead on my hand while death speedily closed the scene."

He died at 4:25 P.M., May 23, 1868. At Fort Lyon, the flag was lowered to half-mast. A homemade coffin was hammered together and lined with the only fabric at the fort that seemed fittingly formal: the wedding dress of the wife of a fort soldier. Fresh flowers were unavailable, so women of the fort stripped paper and cloth bouquets from their bonnets and best gowns to produce a floral arrangement.

Although Kit Carson had asked to be buried in Taos, New Mexico, it was more than a year before his body and that of his wife were taken there. Once the relocations did occur, the new graves went neglected until 1908, when a group of Masons, to honor Carson who had been a Master Mason, erected marble headstones. His short epitaph sums up in four simple words his adventurous years expanding the boundaries of the United States: "He led the way."

Jesse James: d. 1882, age 34

Cause of death: Homicide: a bullet through the back of the skull

Place of rest: Mt. Olivet Cemetery, Kearney, Missouri

Last words: To the friend who'd momentarily surprise him with gunfire: *"It's awfully hot today."*

Jesse James, the most notorious bandit of the West, was a mama's boy: He ran back home to his mother after violent crimes; he married a woman with the same name as his mother—Zerelda (not a common name even in the 1800s); his slain corpse was buried in his mother's backyard; and his mother dictated his tombstone inscription: "In loving memory of my Beloved Son, Murdered by a Traitor and Coward whose name is not worthy to appear here."

She did not see her Jesse as violent, callous, or even bad. And in fact, for a long time many people's image of Jesse James confirmed hers.

"Jesse W. James," wrote Theodore Roosevelt, "is America's Robin Hood." That beneficent picture of the country's most famous bank robber persisted for decades. James—five foot eleven, blue eyes, light brown hair, muscular build, and missing the tip of a finger shot off while cleaning a pistol—was depicted as the good-hearted holdup man who ripped off the wicked banker about to foreclose on a homestead and gave the loot to the impoverished widow to meet mortgage arrears.

However, the real Jesse James believed that charity begins at home, and every penny he stole he kept for himself. He was, as a contemporary biographer puts it, "a callous killer" who thought nothing of shooting an unarmed victim or citizens caught on the street during a robbery—"a strange man with a dark streak of violence."

There is ample evidence that young James was deeply scarred by the Civil War that split his state of Missouri, and that his relationship with his mother was loving but pathologically so. On one visit home, with a bounty on his head, James was hiding out when his pursuers tossed a bomb through a window. Jesse was spared, but the blast killed his nine-year-old half-brother, and, worse by James's reasoning, it tore off his mother's right arm. The incident drew him even closer to her.

He was born on September 5, 1847, in Kearney, Clay County, Missouri, son of a preacher who died when the boy was three. He received little education and at the age of seventeen hooked up with a band of Confederate guerrillas and brutally murdered a Union officer, his first killing. Many followed. By nineteen he had his own gang, and soon Missouri lawmen were claiming that every bank robbery in the state from 1866 to 1869 was carried out by Jesse James and his men.

However, Jesse James and his gang were much loved.

What made the "James boys" popular throughout much of Missouri—and helped start his Robin Hood myth—was their relentless harassment of railroad executives, ogres of the era. With a mandate to lay more and more track, the officials were allowed to seize private land under condemnation orders, with reimbursement a pittance. Jesse James was unarguably a villain, but he robbed the bankers who financed the railroads, and in Missourians' eyes, they were the greater evil.

Ironically, Jesse James's death came not at the hands of the law, but a greedy member of his own gang, Bob Ford. The ambitious Ford, a recent recruit, sought the ten-thousand-dollar reward for killing America's most wanted bank robber; as much, he wanted the celebrity that would accompany the deed.

Last Minutes.   On the morning of April 3, 1882, the thirty-four-year-old James was at his Lafayette Street home in St. Joseph, Missouri. In an image that belied his violence, James was standing on a chair, holding a feather duster and cleaning off a framed picture of a racehorse named Skyrocket. His wife Zerelda and their two young children were in the kitchen. It was a domestic scene about to turn bloody.

When the doorbell rang, James was not at all surprised to see two of his newest gang members, Bob Ford and his older brother, Charlie.

As Bob Ford would later tell the press in an interview he clearly savored, James had boasted to them while he dusted of his plan to rob the Platte City Bank, which he called, said Ford, "a fine scheme," bragging that "our exploits . . . would be published all over the United States" as one more "daring robbery."

What James did not know was that the Ford brothers, though his own gang members, were temporary lawmen. Before calling at the James home, they had traveled to Kansas City, Missouri, to be "deputized" by the governor, Thomas Crittenden, specifically to assassinate Jesse James. And they had struck a favorable deal with the governor: the five-thousand-dollar rewards on each of their own heads would be combined as their bounty for the killing. No longer would they be wanted men.

The Ford brothers waited for the opportunity to take the quick-draw Jesse James by surprise, that is, by their own admission, to shoot him from behind. They got the chance when James returned to dusting, his back to Bob Ford. He was standing near a window, in intense sunlight, when he spoke his last words: "It's awfully hot today."

Bob Ford drew his concealed revolver and cocked it. The sound alerted James, but before he could turn Ford fired a shot from about three feet away that struck James in the back of the head. He was on the floor, the Ford brothers standing over him, when Zerelda raced in, followed by the children.

She accused Bob Ford, still holding a .44-caliber Colt, "You did this!" But he swore straight-faced, "It went off accidentally." Zerelda held a cloth to her husband's head to stop the bleeding, though he was already dead.

When the police arrived, an astonished officer asked, "My God, do you mean to tell us this is Jesse James?"

"Yes, this is Jesse James," beamed Bob Ford. Then he admitted gleefully, "We have killed him and don't deny it. We feel proud that we have killed a man who is known all over the world as the most notorious outlaw who ever lived."

At least that is how the dialogue—conversationally stilted as it is—was reported in the morning edition of the *St. Joseph Western News.* The writer had interviewed the Fords and Zerelda James, who were no longer on speaking terms. As for the trajectory of the fatal bullet, Ford told the press, "The ball struck him just behind the ear and he fell like a log, dead."

While the inquest was being held the following afternoon, souvenir hunters, reading of James's murder and the time of the courtroom meeting, took the opportunity to ransack his house. Everything was taken. Thus the man who made a career of robbery was himself posthumously robbed.

James's body was taken to his mother's farm at Kearney, Missouri. She chose a favorite corner in the backyard and he was interred seven feet down. The grave marker reads in full: "Jesse W. James, Died April 3, 1882. Aged 34 years, six months, 28 days . . . In loving memory of my Beloved Son, Murdered by a Traitor and Coward whose name is not worthy to appear here." Then James's mother led family members in a chorus of "We Will Wait Until Jesus Comes."

Years later, after Jesse's criminal brother Frank "went straight," he earned money by taking tourists through their mother's backyard to view his brother's grave. And he pocketed a little more by selling them stones from a small conical death cairn (which, suspiciously, never got smaller).

This fraud and desecration, as well as the irreverent traipsing through the backyard, enraged the mother, who ordered that her beloved son, her favorite, be reburied in Mount Olivet Cemetery. As the rotted pine coffin was lifted, it fell into pieces and the skull, no longer attached by skin, rolled out. Behind the right ear was the hole made by the bullet, about the size of a quarter.

The Ford brothers learned not to trust promises made even by governors. Of the ten-thousand-dollar reward they expected to collect, they got only about twelve hundred dollars. As formerly wanted, self-confessed criminals, they had little bargaining power, and less resolve to right the injustice.

Buffalo Bill Cody: d. 1917, age 70

Cause of death: Uremic poisoning

Place of rest: Buffalo Bill Grave and Museum, Lookout Mountain Park, Golden, Colorado

Last words: Told the end was near: *"Let's forget about it and play high five."* Of his adopted son: *"I wish Johnny would come."*

There are three prominent endings associated with Buffalo Bill Cody: his death, with its grand funeral, called "Denver's gaudiest"; the termination of his world-famous Wild West Show; and the end of an era in the nation's history.

Born on February 26, 1846, in Scott County, Iowa, William Cody was a Pony Express rider, Indian scout, and Civil War soldier before the age of twenty. He earned the nickname Buffalo Bill during an 18-month period starting in 1867 in

Buffalo Bill: the end of the old West.

which he shot 4,280 buffalo hunting for food contractors who supplied meat to the men building America's railroads.

At the age of thirty-seven, he organized his first wild West exhibition, a spectacular featuring sharpshooting; a buffalo hunt; capture of the famous Deadwood, South Dakota, stagecoach; a Pony Express ride; rowdy cowboys and refractory Indians; and old West celebrities such as Sitting Bull and Annie Oakley. A publicity flier advertised: "Grand, realistic battle scene depicting the capture, torture and death of a scout by the savages."

The show was a smash hit. It toured America and Europe for nearly three decades, reinforcing the growing myth of the American frontier West. Interestingly, Cody's inclusion of live buffalo in the show helped draw attention to the fact that the American buffalo, outrageously overhunted to feed railroad crews (not least of all by Cody), was in danger of extinction.

The Wild West Show made Cody millions, every penny of which he lost in unwise investments. According to his star attraction, Annie Oakley: "He was totally unable to resist any claim for assistance . . . or refuse any mortal in distress . . . and until his dying day he was the easiest mark . . . for every kind of sneak and gold-brick vendor that was mean enough to take advantage of him."

In 1913, his Wild West Show burdened by debts, Cody literally took down the tent. In better days, he had given a command performance for Queen Victoria and been toasted across Europe. Poor, and with an ailing heart and failing kidneys, Cody might have passed away sooner had it not been for World War I and his eagerness to make a patriotic statement. President Woodrow Wilson made "preparedness" the nation's wartime watchword, and Cody resurrected his show as a nationalistic "pageant of Preparedness" to raise Americans' morale.

Though Cody legally failed to get a share in the show's ownership, he made a windfall. In addition to his $100-a-day salary, he collected one-third of all profits over $2,750 daily, and in one good week (and there were many) pocketed $4,161.35. The "Military Pageant," presented "by Buffalo Bill himself," featured batteries of field guns and charging cavalry, high-jumping horses, and "Real Wild West" acts.

Cody made his last public appearance at Portsmouth, Virginia, on November 11, 1916, two months before his death from uremic poisoning.

He had planned to complete a series of autobiographical articles for the Hearst newspapers. But his heart, lungs, and kidneys were rapidly failing him. He could not stop smoking, despite his doctor's orders, and on January 3, he attempted to improve his health by soaking in the "health waters" at Glenwood Springs, Colorado. Instead, he collapsed. Returned to his home in Denver, he shocked friends with his request to be baptized into the Roman Catholic Church—an act, historians believe, prompted by his wife.

Cody was a Catholic for less than a day, dying at noon on January 10, 1917.

President Wilson was among the first people to send sympathies, and he accepted the office of vice president of the Buffalo Bill Memorial Association. Former president Theodore Roosevelt eulogized Cody as "an American of Americans. . . . He embodied those traits of courage, strength, and self-reliant hardihood which are vital to the well-being of the nation."

His funeral was something of a circus, and intentionally so. Cody's body lay in state in the rotunda of Denver's capitol, and a "master of ceremonies" with a high silk hat and cane shooed along a crowd of twenty-five thousand in single file, belting, "Step lively, please. Big crowd behind. Step along. Hurry up, folks." The state infantry and a regimental band preceded the hearse, which was followed by Cody's famous white horse (actually the last of several) named McKinley, which was saddled and riderless.

Cody's last request presented a problem. He wanted to be buried atop Lookout Mountain, near Denver, but in winter's cold the ground was frozen solid. So his coffin was taken to a mortuary and kept in a crypt until the first spring thawing.

The intervening months allowed for further mourning and celebrating. Schoolchildren contributed money for a monument, which was carved by Gertrude Vanderbilt Whitney, and when Cody was buried, five months after his death, it was in a granite grave filled with cement to thwart entrepreneurs from featuring him posthumously in a show. Something the real Cody might not have been averse to.

End of the Old West.   The passing of Buffalo Bill Cody put the final stamp on the end of an era. The frontier West had already changed forever. An invention as simple as barbed-wire fencing, patented in the 1870s, had helped usher in the demise. It not only kept herds from straying and being rustled, it enabled big ranchers to control vital waterholes and streams, in effect partitioning the country's great plains.

And an invention as vital as the railroad had transformed dangerous wild stretches into tourists' sightseeing vistas. The country's great beef bonanza of the late 1800s, under the natural stresses of drought and the worst snows of the century, had also come to an end.

From his cattle ranch in the Dakota Badlands, Teddy Roosevelt viewed the future with foreboding and assayed the recent past with nostalgia. In a remarkably accurate bit of prognostication, he wrote of the end of the old West:

> The free, open-air life of the ranchman, the pleasantest and healthiest life in America, is from its very nature ephemeral. The broad and boundless prairies have already been bounded and will soon be made narrow. It is scarcely a figure of speech to say that the tide of white settlement . . . has risen . . . like a flood; and the cattlemen are but the spray from the crest of the wave, thrown far in advance, but soon to be overtaken. . . . The great fenceless ranches . . . will be . . . divided into corn land, or else into small grazing farms where a few hundred head of stock are closely watched and taken care of.

When Roosevelt wrote those words, Buffalo Bill Cody was already an anachronism, a parading relic of the country's unique past. While the Wild West Show was an undeniable thrill for its liveliness, it was also an ineffably sad threnody for its entombment of heroes and legends of the old West into a living, traveling museum for an era that had come to an end.

References

IN A WORK SUCH AS THIS, in which the curious fact and colorful anecdote are culled from a complex of journals, trade books, encyclopedias, and little-known specialty volumes, it would be impractical to cite a reference for each and every entry. I feel that the reader would be better served by a list of the most relevant sources I was able to turn up on each topic covered in this book.

To ensure accuracy, I have attempted to employ at least two sources for the story behind each ending—the ending of a custom, practice, or a person's life. Biographies of famous people served as a major source for what I've termed "thanatographies," death sketches of a person's final weeks or hours.

Curiously, I discovered that "older" biographies (say, prior to 1970) detail a subject's life but often are scant on facts about that person's exit from this world. More recent biographies, however, seem to spend more time, and furnish more details, on death. Perhaps because the topic is no longer as taboo as it once was. And perhaps, too, because a famous person's death can contain as much gossip and high drama as all the previous years of that life.

Each major reference below is accompanied by comments on what further information a reader will find in that particular book, journal, or article.

1   Death, The Ultimate Ending

The opening discussion, relating death and sex, is based on arguments presented by the renowned biologist Dr. George Wald. A 1967 recipient of the Nobel prize in medicine for research on the presence of vitamin A in the retina, Wald contributed an essay on the origin of bodily death for *The End of Life,* edited by J. D. Roslansky, 1973, North-Holland Publishing Co., London. The article delves in detail into the relationship between bodily death and sexual reproduction.

On funerals and death rituals: An excellent source, beginning with ancient funeral customs, is *Death and Dying,* by R. Benton, 1978, Van Nostrand. The author draws parallels between human burial practices and those engaged in by animals, such as the elephant (an animal not known for its digging ability), which thoughtfully kicks a light blanket of sand over the deceased's head and tusks. Benton also considers species of birds and primates that, like humans, grieve and display other emotional reactions to the loss of a family member.

The degree to which humans are set apart in the elaborateness of their mourning is detailed in: *Acute Grief and the Funeral,* edited by V. R. Pine, 1976, Charles C. Thomas; *The Golden Bough,* by J. G. Frazer, 1958, Macmillan; *Suicide in Victorian and Edwardian England,* by Olive Anderson, 1987, Oxford University Press; and *Strange Facts About Death,* by Webb Garrison, 1978, Abingdon. For the browser addicted to curious facts, this last volume (out of print, but available at libraries) is hard to beat.

On modern cremation and burial practices: *Funerals: Consumers' Last Rights,* by the editors of Consumer Reports, 1977, Norton. The chapters I found most valuable: "To Embalm or Not to Embalm," "Cemeteries," and "Cremation."

2   Cemeteries, Our Last Address

Anyone fascinated by burial sites can find no more comprehensive a book than *Famous and Curious Cemeteries,* by John Francis Marion, 1977, Crown. This is a pictorial, historical, and anecdotal overview of American and European graveyards and the famous and infamous people interred there. Marion takes the reader on a tour of fifteen of the notable grounds in Europe, thirty-six in the United States, and twenty-three military cemeteries on both sides of the Atlantic.

A much abbreviated browser's companion to cemeteries is *Permanent Addresses: A Guide to the Resting Places of Famous Americans,* by J. Arbeiter and L. Cirino, 1973, Evans. This "veritable *Guide Michelin*" to graveyards is organized both geographically and by profession of the deceased, and is, as its jacket touts, "a treasure trove for the weekend traveler or the armchair morbidity buff." If you wish to know where a dead American lies, this is a major reference. Another is *Final Placement: A Guide to the Deaths, Funerals, and Burials of Notable Americans,* by Robert Dickerson, 1982, Reference Publications, Algonac, Mich. This slender volume is a trove of details of famous people's final hours and funerals. Dickerson, more than any author familiar to me, covers such specifics as the hymns sung at notable funerals, routes taken by the cortege, and clothes worn by mourners. My one caution about this book is that it contains several incorrect dates.

An encyclopedic reference in this area is *Project Remember: 5,000 Names and Final Places,* by Arthur Koykka, 1986, also from Reference Publications.

On the romanticization of death and the Garden Cemetery Movement: Although Marion, above, covers these topics, a richer and more detailed account is found in *Death in America,* edited by David E. Stannard, 1975, University of Pennsylvania Press. The book's essays, written by cultural historians, anthropologists, and art historians, take the reader into Puritan and Victorian New England, rural Mexico, and pioneer settlements in the nineteenth-century Midwest. The changing relationships between death and childhood, death and religion, and death and social class are only a few of the topics covered. I found particularly fascinating "The Cemetery as Cultural Institution," by Stanley French, "Death and the Puritan Child," by David Stannard, and "The Reversal of Death: Changes in Attitudes Toward Death in Western Societies," by Philippe Ariès.

Also helpful in assembling this chapter: *The Obituary Book,* by Alden Whitman, 1971, Stein and Day; and *The Way We Die,* by David Dempsey, 1975, Macmillan, which surveys death rites and customs.

3 Wills, Our Last Wishes

Three books are highly recommended; they provide an excellent source for the wills of famous people: *Wills: A Dead Giveaway,* by Millie Considine and Ruth Pool, 1974, Doubleday. This thoroughly entertaining volume highlights the last wills and testaments of such people as W. C. Fields, Benjamin Franklin, William Shakespeare, Harry Houdini, and Adolf Hitler.

Equally fascinating to browse is *Last Will and Testament: Wills, Ancient and Modern,* by Frank Thomas, 1972, St. Martin's Press. Thomas covers such notables as Napoleon and William the Conqueror, and ends with a breakdown of the amounts of money left by famous people. Chapters group the deceased into "Royalty," "Literary Wills," "Great Men," and the like.

Equally entertaining is *The Last Caprice,* by Robert Menchin, 1963, Simon and Schuster. The wills of John B. Kelly and Charles Millar are among the hundreds of documents Menchin presents in brief or in detail.

Augmenting information found in the above three references, I used:

The Medical Casebook of Adolf Hitler, by L. Heston and R. Heston, 1980, Stein and Day. This is a mesmerizing volume by a physician and his wife, a nurse, on the major and minor, physical and mental, ailments Hitler suffered. The authors construct a "medical workup" on the "patient," as well as provide "hospital charts" and consider the possible historical consequences of Hitler's illnesses. Also: "Adolf Hitler: His Life and Illness," by P. J. Stolk, *Psychiatr. Neurol. Neurochi.,* volume 71, 1968.

Kahlil Gibran: His Life and World, by J. Gibran and K. Gibran, 1974, New York Graphic Society, Boston.

On Napoleon: "General Napoleon and General Typhus," in *Disease and History,* by Frederick Cartwright, 1972, Crowell. "The Illness and Death of Napoleon," in *Tenements of Clay,* edited by Arnold Sorsby, 1974, Scribner's. "Napoleon Bonaparte," in *Medical Biographies,* by P. M. Dale, 1952, University of Oklahoma Press, Norman.

On Benjamin Franklin: *Franklin in Philadelphia,* by E. Wright, 1986, Harvard University Press. *Benjamin Franklin,* by Ronald Clark, 1983, Random House.

On George Bernard Shaw: *Bernard Shaw,* by St. John Ervine, 1956, Morrow.

On Dickens: *Charles Dickens,* by J. B. Priestly, 1961, Viking.

On Peter the Great: "Peter the Great," in *Medical Biographies. Peter The Great,* by Michael Gibson, 1975, Wayland Publishing, London.

On John Donne: *John Donne, A Life,* by R. C. Bald, 1970, Oxford University Press.

On Henry VIII: "Henry VIII," in *Medical Biographies.* "The Medical Problems of Henry VIII," by Ove Brinch, in *Tenements of Clay.* "Henry VIII," in *Idols and Invalids,* by James Kemble, 1936, Doubleday.

On Shakespeare: "Shakespeare's Skull and Brain: An Anthropological Study," by A. Keith, in *Tenements of Clay.* "The Evidence of Disease in Shakespeare's Handwriting," by Ralph Leftwich, in *Tenements of Clay.*

4 & 5   Bequests & Behests
of Dying Presidents

This chapter owes a great debt to *Wills of the U.S. Presidents,* by Herbert Collins and David Weaver, 1976, Trusts & Estates Magazine, a division of Communications Channels. Collins, associate curator of political history at the Smithsonian Institution, and Weaver, professor of law at George Washington University, have collected in one place all the wills and codicils of America's deceased presidents. The interested reader can read the actual documents, Weaver's "notes" explaining legal fine points from many testaments, and Collins's biographical sketches of the presidents. This book is certainly the single best source on presidential wills.

Augmenting the above reference, I have ransacked scores of presidential biographies and "trivia" books. Of particular help were:

Medical Biographies, the chapters on Andrew Jackson, George Washington, William McKinley, Grover Cleveland, and James Garfield.

Tenements of Clay, Harold Schwartz's essay, "Abraham Lincoln's Marfan Syndrome."

Our Assassinated Presidents: The True Medical Stories, by S. M. Brooks, 1985, Bell Publishing. Highly recommended.

The Presidents: Tidbits and Trivia, by Sid Frank and Arden Melick, 1984, Greenwich House. A fact-filled bonanza for browsing. Always entertaining.

Equally appealing is *Presidential Anecdotes,* by Paul Boller, 1981, Oxford University Press.

A recent book that deserves more recognition than it has received is *Medical Cover-Ups in the White House,* by Edward MacMahon and Leonard Curry, 1987, Farragut. This is a hair-raising volume detailing information the American public was told—and not told—about the ailments of presidents Wilson, Harding, F.D.R., Eisenhower, J.F.K., Cleveland, and Garfield. Fascinating from cover to cover.

"The Precarious Role of the President's Physician," by Bill McAllister, *The Washington Post,* February 3, 1988.

6   Capital Endings

On death by lethal injection: "Execution by Injection," *Science News,* October 3, 1981, provides a technical overview of the chemicals used and their actions on the body and brain. "A New Executioner: The Needle," *Time,* September 14, 1981. "Execution by Injection," by Marcia Cohen, *Us,* February 14, 1983, details the death of Charles Brooks, the first man executed by lethal injection.

There are many sources on the guillotine, but a particularly entertaining one on Dr. Guillotin himself is "The Dying Art," in *Great Medical Disasters,* by Richard Gordon, 1976, Dorset.

Death is a Noun, by John Langone, 1972, Little, Brown, gives an excellent history of capital punishment. Even more detailed is *The History of Capital Punishment,* by John Laurence, 1960, Citadel Press, Secaucus, N.J. Beautifully illustrated, it is a reprint of an earlier work, with a foreword by Clarence Darrow. Chapter on beheading, hanging, electrocution, the guillotine, etc. This work also covers famous executioners and places of execution.

A History of the Guillotine, by Alister Kershaw, 1958, London.

A comprehensive and always entertaining volume is *Almanac of World Crime,* Jay Robert Nash, 1986, Bonanza. It offers not only a history of capital punishment, but scores of cases told in grisly detail.

7   Engineered Endings

The life-spans of articles of clothing and household products are routinely calculated by and available from: American Society of Appraisers, P.O. Box 17265, Washington, D.C. 20041; Appraisers Association of America, 60 East 42 Street, New York, N.Y. 10165; National Association of Independent Insurance Adjusters, 222 West Adams Street, Chicago, Ill. 60606; National Association of Public Insurance Adjusters, 300 Walter Street, Suite 400, Baltimore, Md. 21202.

An excellent book on the life expectancy of appliances, furnishings, and clothing is *How To Double and Triple the Useful Life of Everything You Own,* by H. Holtje and J. Stockwell, 1977, Prentice-Hall.

A book that goes into the subject of obsolescence and considers the various kinds of obsolescence is *How Things Don't Work,* by Victor Papanek and James Hennessey, 1977, Pantheon. The authors consider in some detail the stratagems used by manufacturers to bring about a product's unexpected and early demise.

On human life-spans: *The Longevity of Athletes,* edited by A. P. Poledank, 1979, Charles Thomas. *Longevity,* by Ken Pelletier, 1981, Delacorte. *American Averages,* by Michael Feinsilber and William B. Mead, 1980, Doubleday, is a browser's delight for lovers of statistics.

"Why Do Women Live Longer Than Men?," *Science,* volume 238, October 9, 1987.

The Longevity Factor, by W. McQuade and A. Aikman, 1979, Simon and Schuster. Everything you ever wanted to know about life expectancy.

An enjoyable book covering a broad spectrum of subjects is *Lifespans: Or How Long Things Last,* by F. Kendig and R. Hutton, 1979, Holt.

Animal and Plant Life Spans, by Alice Hopf, 1978, Holiday House.

On biological time: "Our Allotted Lifetimes" in *The Panda's Thumb,* by Stephen Jay Gould, 1980, Norton.

A fascinating book (for anyone not afraid of growing old) is *How a Man Ages,* by Curtis Pesmen and the editors of *Esquire* magazine, 1984, Ballantine. The authors detail the deterioration of the body, organ by organ. Also on this topic: "Life's Peaks," by Charles Panati, *Family Circle,* May 31, 1977 (research facts were updated for inclusion in this book).

"Are You a Spendaholic?" by J. E. Frook, *Family Circle,* November 10, 1987.

8 & 9   Ancient and Modern Extinctions

Only in this century has it become clear that humanity is seriously damaging the chances for future survival by forcing living species into extinction. *Extinction: The Causes and Consequences of the Disappearances of Species,* by Paul and Anne Ehrlich, 1981, Random House, examines the results of humankind's "never-ending quest for progress." While over the several billion years of life on earth species have been disappearing, until very recently they were also being replaced. The Ehrlichs dramatically demonstrate that this is no longer the case. The book is excellent in presentation, encompassing in scope.

As for specific endangered animals: *Last Survivors: 48 Animals in Danger of Extinction,* edited by Noel Simon, 1970, World. This detailed, thorough volume discusses extinctions by continent and examines the accomplishments of conservationists.

Also excellent is *These are the Endangered,* by Charles Cadieux, 1981, Stone Wall Press, Washington, D.C. Cadieux uses case histories drawn from a lifetime of wildlife research in all of America's states and he defines how a species qualifies for the status of "endangered" or "extinct." Detailed, thorough, highly readable.

The Endangered Ones, by James Cox, 1975, Crown. A superbly illustrated work with stories of over three hundred endangered mammals, birds, reptiles, and fishes. This work is based on the *Red Date Book,* the most authoritative report on endangered species, maintained by the International Union for Conservation of Nature and Natural Resources.

An excellent, highly recommended book is *The Endangered Species Handbook,* by Greta Nilsson, published by The Animal Welfare Institute, P.O. Box 3650, Washington, D.C. 20007. It is comprehensive—examining extinct species from 1600 to the present—and available by mail for $5.00. Illustrated and with charts.

Also providing an excellent overview: *The Last Extinction,* edited by L. Kaufman and K. Mallory, 1986, M.I.T. Press.

On the destruction of rain forests: "Scientists See Mass Extinction As Rain

Forests are Cleared," *The Washington Post,* September 29, 1986. "The Quiet Apocalypse," *Time,* October 13, 1986.

Additional references on dinosaurs and prehistoric life: *The Prehistoric Age,* edited by H. W. Ball, 1983, Sterling. *The Riddle of the Dinosaur,* by John Noble Wilford, 1986, Knopf, a detailed, highly readable work. *The Field Guide to Prehistoric Life,* by David Lambert et al., 1985, Facts on File.

"A Mass Extinction without Asteroids," *Science,* volume 234, October 3, 1986.

"Fragmentary Theory of Dinosaur Extinctions," *New Scientist,* February 11, 1988.

"Was There a Prelude to the Dinosaurs' Demise?" *Science,* February 12, 1988.

"Abrupt extinctions at end of Triassic," *Science News,* September 5, 1987.

The Auk, the Dodo, and the Oryx: Vanished and Vanishing Creatures, by Robert Silverberg, 1967, Crowell. This is a delightful book that tells extinction stories in vivid detail. Silverberg covers not only the dodo, passenger pigeon, great auk, and heath hen, but also the rukh, the giant ground sloth, and many others. Unfortunately, the book is out of print, but it is available at libraries.

10 Decimating Disease

There are several excellent books that cover the history of plagues that have decimated populations. One of the most ambitious is *Epidemics,* by Geoffery Marks and William Beatty, 1976, Scribner's. This fascinating volume is laid out chronologically, beginning with the scourges of ancient and classical times— what is known as well as what can be inferred from written accounts for the existence of such diseases as smallpox, polio, and the bubonic plague. The plague of Justinian, the Black Death, syphilis, diseases of filth, polio, and the influenza epidemic of 1918 are some of the illnesses covered. The book contains an extensive bibliography for further investigations.

Also comprehensive is *Plagues and People,* by William McNeill, 1976, Doubleday. McNeill is primarily interested in uncovering the historical impact of disease on the rise and fall of civilizations. He reveals infectious disease as an unseen combatant in many decisive rivalries and battles that changed the course of history.

Also excellent in this regard is *Disease and History,* by Frederick Cartwright, 1972, Crowell. A physician and medical historian, Cartwright considers the role of disease in the weakening of the Roman Empire, the anarchy of the Middle Ages, the triumphs of Napoleon, the conquering of the New World, and the exploration of Africa.

On the Black Death: *The Black Death and Peasant Revolt,* by Leonard Cowie, 1986, Wayland, London, provides an excellent overview of what it was like to live through one of history's worst scourges. The tremendous toll of the disease is clearly pictured in *The Black Death,* by Philip Ziegler, 1971, Harper.

"The Terrifying Normalcy of Plague," by Stephen Jay Gould, *The New York*

Times magazine, April 19, 1987, places the current AIDS epidemic in the context of past infectious diseases.

On Smallpox: *The Invisible Fire,* by Joel Shurkin, 1978, Putnam, presents a complete account of the disease from ancient times and mankind's triumph over it. As for the modern-day debate over whether to destroy the laboratory samples of smallpox virus in Atlanta and Moscow, an overview is provided by "Last Samples of Smallpox Pose a Quandary," by H. M. Schmeck, *The New York Times,* November 3, 1987.

On tuberculosis and its resurgence: "TB Troubles: Tuberculosis is on the rise," by R. Weiss, *Science News,* volume 133, February 6, 1988. "The Return of Tuberculosis," *Newsweek,* February 22, 1988.

On the 1918 influenza: *Epidemic and Peace, 1918,* by Alfred Crosby, 1976, Greenwood Press, Westport, Conn. *Influenza: The Last Great Plague,* by W. Beveridge, 1977, Prodist. Both works are thorough, highly recommended, and make for hair-raising reading.

An excellent reference on the history and devastation of viruses is *Virus Hunters,* by Greer Williams, 1959, Knopf. In writing of the quest to develop vaccines, Williams provides a sweeping background on viral diseases. Also: "The 10 Most Hunted Viruses," by K. Osterholm, *American Health,* January/February 1988.

11   Bygone Beliefs

Any reader already frightened of doctors is advised to avoid *Modern Medical Mistakes,* by Edward Lambert, 1978, Indiana University Press. Lambert's observations of what can go awry in twentieth-century medical treatment makes for riveting reading. Autointoxication is just one of the abuses covered.

In a similar vein but more popularly written is *Great Medical Disasters,* by Richard Gordon, 1976, Dorset, which covers such figures as Typhoid Mary, Florence Nightingale, Sir William Arbuthnot Lane, and King Charles II.

Pagans and Christians, by Robin Lane Fox, 1987, Knopf, examines religious life and daily practices from the second to the fourth century, when, as the book's jacket reads, "The Gods of Olympus lost their Dominion and Christianity, with the Conversion of Constantine, Triumphed in the Mediterranean World." This work served as an excellent general reference for Chapters 11, 12, and 13.

Magic, Myth, and Medicine, by John Camp, 1973, Taplinger, gives a fascinating historical perspective on such topics as abortion, fertility myths, and birth superstitions.

12 & 13   Past Sex Practices

Circumcision, male and female, is extensively covered in *Circumcision: The Painful Dilemma,* by Rosemary Romberg, 1985, Bergin & Garvey, South Hadley, Mass. Highly recommended for any parent with questions about the practice.

Also: "Circumcision: Parents Think Twice," *U.S. News and World Report,* May 30, 1988, provides figures on how the surgery is steadily declining in popularity. As does: "Circumcision Under Criticism As Unnecessary to New-born," by Robert Lindsey, *The New York Times,* February 1, 1988.

Of special interest: "African Study Finds AIDS Risk to be Higher in Uncir-cumcised Men," by Lawrence Altman, *The New York Times,* August 4, 1988.

On the church's historical views on marriage, celibacy, and sex, a superb source is *Adam, Eve, and the Serpent,* by Elaine Pagels, 1988, Random House. Also excellent is *The Eunuch and The Virgin,* by Peter Tompkins, 1962, Clarkson Potter.

All you have ever wanted to know about virgins is delightfully presented in *Virgins: Reluctant, Dubious and Avowed,* by Muriel Segal, 1977, Macmillan. This is a history of the virgin in society as she was worshiped, segregated, protected, sacrificed, ravished, eaten, and scorned. A fun read.

More serious in tone—and in subject matter—is *The Curse,* by J. Delaney, M. Lupton, and E. Toth, 1976, Clarke-Irwin, Canada/N.Y. This definitive work examines sex customs, myths, and taboos throughout the ages that have sur-rounded menstruation. It demonstrates how men's superstitions and fears have inflicted untold suffering on women.

The Sex Life of the Animals, by H. Wendt, 1965, Simon and Schuster, provides a wonderful discussion of such bygone beliefs as spontaneous genera-tion and a host of mistaken theories of human sexuality and fertilization.

Also: *Hen's Teeth and Horse's Toes,* by Stephen Jay Gould, 1983, Norton, covers a variety of animal and human sex myths.

Perhaps the best single source on singing castrati is *The Castrati in Opera,* by Angus Heriot, 1974, De Capo. This work examines the rise and fall of the phenomenon, as well as presenting fascinating minibiographies on most of the famous singers.

A delightful overview of myriad sex practices and taboos from the time of Adam and Eve is found in *How Did Sex Begin?* by R. Brasch, 1973, David McKay.

On sexual tolerance (or lack of it) throughout the ages: *Christianity, Social Tolerance, and Homosexuality,* by John Boswell, 1981, University of Chicago Press, a thoroughly original work. *Sexual Variance in Society and History,* by V. Bullough, 1976, University of Chicago Press. *Sex in History,* Reay Tannahill, 1982, Stein and Day.

On virgin cults: *Saints,* by Caroline Williams, 1980, St. Martin's Press.

On Christian saints: *The Penguin Dictionary of Saints,* by D. Attwater, 1965, Penguin (republished in 1981 by Avenel/Crown).

On St. Paul and his views toward marriage and celibacy, an iconoclastic work is *The Myth-Maker: Paul and the Invention of Christianity,* by Hyam Maccoby, 1986, Harper. A more traditional overview is found in *The Early Church,* by Henry Chadwick, 1986, Dorset.

On modern-day polygamy: "A Hand from the Grave: The Polygamy Mur-ders," *Newsweek,* December 21, 1987. "Return of the Patriarch: A Clan of Messianic Polygamists," *Time,* February 1, 1988.

A wonderful source on the papacy is *The Oxford Dictionary of Popes,* by J. Kelly, 1986, Oxford University Press. Fascinating for its scandal (and history) is *The Bad Popes,* by E. Chamberlin, 1969, Dorset.

14, 15, & 16   Thanatographies

Aside from individual biographies (the most significant of which are presented below), I found invaluable in assembling death sketches:

Last Words of Distinguished Men and Women, by F. Marvin, 1970, Gale. *Last Words of Famous Men,* by A. Bega, 1973, Folcroft, Darby, Pa. *Last Words of Saints and Sinners,* by Herbert Lockyner, 1975, Kregel, Grand Rapids, Mich. Excellent in this category is *Famous Last Words,* by B. Conrad, 1961, Doubleday.

Analyses of diseases of famous people are covered by several thorough sources to which I am indebted:

If there is a standard, it is *Medical Biographies: The Ailments of Thirty-three Famous Persons,* by P. M. Dale, 1952, University of Oklahoma Press. (The bibliography is also of great use to a researcher.) Of particular interest were the chapters on Buddha, William the Conqueror, Columbus, Henry VIII, Samuel Pepys, Peter the Great, George Washington, John Paul Jones, Andrew Jackson, Napoleon Bonaparte, Lord Byron, John Keats, Edgar Allan Poe, Charles Darwin, Walt Whitman, James Garfield, Grover Cleveland, William McKinley, Guy de Maupassant, and Robert Louis Stevenson. I have updated Dr. Dale's medical opinions with information published since his book first appeared. One such work is:

Napoleon's Glands, and other Ventures in Biohistory, by Arno Karlen, 1984, Little, Brown. Karlen also undertakes studies of Goya and Poe, and examines Edison's deafness, Franklin Roosevelt's polio, and more. Highly recommended to anyone interested in biohistory.

Another standard venture into biohistory is *Tenements of Clay,* edited by Arnold Sorsby, 1974, Scribner's. This is a collection of essays taken from medical literature on such topics as Henry VIII's syphilis, Shakespeare's possible ailments, Jane Austen's Addison's disease, Beethoven's deafness, Napoleon's poisoning, Darwin's psychosomatic complaints, and Abraham Lincoln's Marfan syndrome. Highly recommended.

In a similar vein is *Creative Malady,* by George Pickering, 1974, Oxford University Press. A physician, Pickering argues that psychoneurosis plays an important role in the creative process; he examines the illnesses of Charles Darwin, Florence Nightingale, Sigmund Freud, and Elizabeth Barrett Browning. A fascinating work.

An excellent book for browsing is *How Did They Die?,* by Norman and Betty Donaldson, 1980, Greenwich House/Crown. With great accuracy and brevity this volume presents the last days, words, afflictions, and resting places of over three hundred notables throughout history.

A somewhat similar book, though much sketchier in detail, is *Exits,* by Scott

Slater and Alex Solomita, 1980, Dutton. In short paragraphs this work presents "stories of dying moments and parting words."

Quite the opposite for its detail is *Endings: Death Glorious and Otherwise. As Faced by Ten Outstanding Figures of our Time,* by Leon Prochnik, 1980, Crown. In considerable depth the author covers the deaths of Freud, Houdini, Duncan, and Mishima, to mention only the chapters I have borrowed from. Highly readable and recommended.

Also of use in assembling thanatographies was *The New York Times Obituaries Index: 1858 to 1968.*

Freud: A Life for Our Times, by Peter Gay, 1988, Norton. Comprehensive, consistently informative, and entertaining.

Oscar Wilde, by Richard Ellmann, 1988, Knopf. Brings Wilde vividly to life.

"Cleopatra: Love and Eugenics" in *Idols and Invalids,* by James Kemble, 1936, Doubleday.

Christopher Columbus, by Gianni Granzotto, 1985, Doubleday. Also the chapter on Columbus in *Idols and Invalids.*

Byron and Greek Love: Homophobia in 19th Century England, Louis Crompton, 1985, University of California Press.

A Pictorial History of the World's Greatest Trials, From Socrates to Jean Harris, by B. Aymar and E. Sagarin, 1985, Bonanza. An excellent source on the criminal trials of Socrates, Joan of Arc, Andrew Johnson, and Oscar Wilde, to mention only the chapters I used.

17 Last Stands of Wild West Legends

To assemble the material for the thanatographies in this chapter I used several of the general sources cited above, plus specific biographies:

They Called Him Wild Bill, by J. Rosa, 1982, University of Oklahoma Press.

Alias Billy the Kid, by Donald Cline, 1986, Sunstone Press, Santa Fe, New Mexico.

Tecumseh: Destiny's Warrior, by David Cooke, 1974, Messner.

Great Indian Chiefs, by Albert Roland, 1966, Collier. Contains material on Tecumseh and Sitting Bull.

Belle Starr, by Glenn Shirley, 1982, University of Oklahoma Press.

The Lives and Legends of Buffalo Bill, by Don Russell, 1973, University of Oklahoma Press.

Kit Carson, by M. Estergreen, 1979, University of Oklahoma Press.

Outlaws of the Wild West, by James Horan, 1977, Crown. A superb book covering Jesse James and many others.

Gunfighters of the Wild West, by James Horan, 1976, Crown. Also highly recommended; includes Billy the Kid.

Desperate Women, by James Horan, 1952, Putnam. Fascinating; includes Calamity Jane.

A History of the Indians of the U.S., by Angie Debo, 1970, University of Oklahoma Press.

Phoenix: The Decline and Rebirth of the Indian People, by William Coffer, 1979, Van Nostrand.

Famous Characters of the Wild West, by R. Garrett, 1977, St. Martin's.

On revisionist views on American history: *America Revised,* by Frances FitzGerald, 1979, Little, Brown. *Historians' Fallacies,* by David Hackett Fischer, 1970, Harper. From these books one comes away with quite a different picture from the standard schoolroom view of American history.

On myth: *The Mythic West,* by Robert Athearn, 1986, University Press of Kansas.

Additional material was gleaned from:

The Encyclopedia of American Crime, by C. Sifakis, 1982, Facts on File. Highly recommended for browsing.

And two fascinating books by Jay Robert Nash: *Almanac of World Crime,* 1986, Bonanza, and *Bloodletters and Badmen,* 1973, Evans.

Index